The Bilingualism Reader

From review.   eaition:
'A volume that would serve well as a textbook in an introductory course on bilingual-ism and will also prove extremely valuable to students and researchers alike.'

Language

'This book is clearly a bargain, and it is difficult to see how it could fail to become a core textbook for courses in bilingualism.'

System

'The bringing together of different fields of specialisation is enriching, yet it also brings home to the reader the great diversity of interests, opinions and agendas that exist . . . an excellent compilation and an invaluable companion.'

Language Awareness

'This outstanding collection of the key articles in the field is an essential guide for incoming students and a wonderful resource for bilingualism scholars.'

Annotated Bibliography of English Studies

The Bilingualism Reader is the definitive reader for the study of bilingualism. Designed as an integrated and structured student resource it provides invaluable editorial material that guides the reader through different sections and covers:

- definitions and typology of bilingualism
- language choice and bilingual interaction
- bilingualism, identity and ideology
- grammar of code-switching and bilingual acquisition
- bilingual production and perception
- the bilingual brain
- methodological issues in the study of bilingualism.

The second edition of this best-selling volume includes nine new readings and post-scripts written by the authors of the original articles, which evaluate them in the light of recent research. Critical discussion of research methods, revised graded study questions and activities, a comprehensive glossary, and an up-to-date resource list make *The Bilingualism Reader* an essential introductory text for students of linguistics, psychology and education.

Contributors: Jubin Abutalebi, Peter Auer, Jan-Petter Blom, Kees de Bot, Stefano F. Cappa, Charles A. Ferguson, Joshua A. Fishman, Fred Genesee, David W. Green, Annette M.B. de Groot, François Grosjean, John J. Gumperz, Monica Heller, Janice L. Jake, Judith F. Kroll, Li Wei, Jürgen M. Meisel, Lesley Milroy, Pieter Muysken, Carol Myers-Scotton, Loraine K. Obler, Michel Paradis, Daniela Perani, Shana Poplack, Ben Rampton, Traute Taeschner, Jyotsna Vaid, Virginia Volterra and Robert J. Zatorre.

Li Wei is Professor of Applied Linguistics at Birkbeck, University of London, UK. He is Editor of the *International Journal of Bilingualism*.

The Bilingualism Reader
Second Edition

Edited by Li Wei

Routledge
Taylor & Francis Group

LONDON AND NEW YORK

First published 2000
by Routledge
Reprinted 2001, 2004, 2005, 2006

Second edition published 2007
by Routledge
2 Park Square, Milton Park, Abingdon, Oxon OX14 4RN

Simultaneously published in the USA and Canada
by Routledge
270 Madison Ave, New York, NY 10006

Routledge is an imprint of the Taylor & Francis Group, an informa business

Typeset in Perpetua and Bell Gothic by
RefineCatch Limited, Bungay, Suffolk
Printed and bound in Great Britain by
The Cromwell Press, Trowbridge, Wiltshire

British Library Cataloguing in Publication Data
A catalogue record for this book is available from the British Library

Library of Congress Cataloging in Publication Data
The bilingualism reader/edited by Li Wei.—2nd ed.
p. cm.
Includes bibliographical references and index.
ISBN 0–415–35555–9 (pbk.) — ISBN 0–415–35554–0 (hardback)
1. Bilingualism. I. Wei, Li
P115.B553 2006
404'.2—dc22
2006018917

ISBN 10: 0–415–35555–9 (pbk)
ISBN 10: 0–415–35554–0 (hbk)

ISBN 13: 978–0–415–35555–1 (pbk)
ISBN 13: 978–0–415–35554–4 (hbk)

CONTENTS

CONCLUSION

PREFACE

ONE INCIDENT DURING my years as a PhD student changed my views on academic research considerably: I was drafting a joint paper with my supervisor, Lesley Milroy, and in it I cited a textbook writer's comments on William Labov's work which included a quote from Labov. Lesley, who knows Labov's work well, asked me, 'Have you read Labov's original paper?', and pointed out that the comments by the textbook writer were in fact misguided and misguiding. Rather sheepishly I had to admit that I had not read that particular paper of Labov's. When I did read the paper, I was astonished to find what Labov meant in the original paper was very different from what the textbook writer suggested in his comments. Since then, I have been rather suspicious of authors' interpretations and comments, especially the sharply worded ones, on other people's work. I have learnt the benefit of reading the originals.

I am often amazed to see many of our otherwise quite brilliant students readily base their arguments on 'second-hand' interpretation and remarks. I understand that, once on that 'degree assembly line', students do not have much choice but to turn out essays and reports very quickly. They do not normally have the time to delve into the wide array of publications, ranging from history and anthropology to neurology and artificial intelligence, in which research papers on bilingualism typically appear. I am nevertheless concerned that a new generation of 'scholars' might be emerging out of a 'hearsay' tradition.

I have also learnt from my visits to Central America, and East and Southeast Asia, that many of the books and journals which we use routinely in our teaching and learning and which we take for granted are not always readily available in those places, because of inadequate library facilities. I have become concerned that research on bilingualism which deals with linguistic and cultural diversity is in fact inaccessible to the very people we wish to represent.

It is with these concerns that I decided to compile *The Bilingualism Reader*. The main objective of the Reader is to make available in a single, affordable volume a selection of the most important research papers on bilingualism. I have focused primarily on the 'classics' in bilingualism research — papers that every newcomer to the field must read and the more established researchers frequently cite. I have deliberately excluded papers on bilingual education, language planning, language maintenance and language shift, and language attitude. A good reader on policy and practice in bilingual education already exists (Garcia and Baker, 1995), and the sociolinguistics readers edited by Coupland and Jaworski (1997), Trudgill and Cheshire (1997) and Paulston and Tucker (2003) all contain key articles on language planning, language maintenance and language shift, and language attitude. Consequently, most of the papers in the present Reader focus on the micro aspects of bilingualism, especially on the language behaviour of bilingual individuals.

The success of the first edition of the Reader has enabled the publisher to be more generous in allowing me to include a few more important papers in the second edition. There is now a new section on code-switching and ethnicity and ideology, as well as additional chapters on psycholinguistic models of the bilingual lexicon and neuroimagining research on the bilingual brain.

All the chosen papers are journal articles or book chapters. Extracts from single authored monographs are not included, as a decontextualised digest is deemed inappropriate for student use. Some of the more recent papers published in easily accessible journals and books are also excluded. They, and the important single authored monographs, are listed under Further Reading at the end of each section of the Reader.

An important new feature of the second edition is the addition of postscripts written by the original authors specially for this Reader. Some of the authors took the opportunity to reflect on the changes both in their own thinking and in the field generally since the publication of the original piece, while others elaborated on some key points. Where appropriate, contact details of the authors are also given so that readers can approach the authors directly if they wish.

Recently, handbooks have become a popular commodity. They are usually compilations of specially commissioned survey-type articles. There is no doubt that they provide a handy resource for students and lecturers. However, handbooks do not address the concerns I have specified above. In fact, handbook users may be more at risk of believing that they know the subject without actually consulting, let alone understanding, the original formulation of ideas. I therefore declined the suggestion that was put to me to compile a handbook of bilingualism and chose instead to edit a reader of classic articles. Some of the recent state-of-the-art collections are listed in the Resource List.

In theory, a reader represents a diversity of voices rather than a single authorial one as is normally the case with a textbook. But I am fully aware of the fact that I, as the editor, imprint my views via selection of the papers and the leading comments in the introductory remarks and even in the suggested study activities and Further Reading. Nevertheless I believe that all these papers are essential reading for anyone interested in bilingualism and hope the Reader as a whole gives a good representation of the various dimensions of bilingualism research.

ACKNOWLEDGEMENTS

The editor and publisher were enormously encouraged by the very positive reviews of the first edition of the Reader. The second edition has benefited from the comments received by the publisher through a huge number of feedback questionnaires. The editor is especially grateful to all the authors for their cooperation. Special thanks go to Brigid O'Connor, who proofread a considerable amount of the material very quickly and efficiently. As always, Zhu Hua has been the most important source of inspiration and understanding without which this Reader would not have been possible.

The editor and publisher would like to acknowledge the copyright holders for permission to reprint the following material:

Abutalebi, Jubin, Cappa, S.F. and Perani, D. (2001) The bilingual brain as revealed by functional imaging. *Bilingualism: Language and Cognition* 4: 179–90. Copyright © 2001 Cambridge University Press, reproduced with permission of the authors and publisher.

Auer, P. (1995) The pragmatics of code-switching: a sequential approach. In L. Milroy and P. Muysken (eds) *One Speaker Two Languages*, Cambridge: Cambridge University Press, pp. 115–35. Copyright © 1995 Cambridge University Press, reproduced with permission of the author and publisher.

Blom, J.-P. and Gumperz, J.J. (1972) Social meaning in linguistic structure: code-switching in Norway. In J.J. Gumperz and D. Hymes (eds) *Directions in Socio-linguistics*, New York: Holt, Rinehart and Winston, pp. 407–34, by permission of the authors.

de Bot, K. (1992) A bilingual production model: Levelt's 'speaking' model adapted. *Applied Linguistics* 13: 1–24, by permission of the author and Oxford University Press.

Ferguson, C.A. (1959) Diglossia. *Word* 15: 325–40, by permission of Shirley Brice Heath, executrix of Charles Ferguson's estates and the International Linguistics Association.

Fishman, J.A. (1965) Who speaks what language to whom and when? *La Linguistique* 2: 67–88. Reproduced with permission of the author and Blackwell Publishing.

Fishman, J.A. (1967) Bilingualism with and without diglossia; diglossia with and without bilingualism. *Journal of Social Issues* 23(2): 29–38, by permission of the author and Blackwell Publishing.

Genesee, F. (1989) Early bilingual language development: one language or two? *Journal of Child Language* 16: 161–79. Copyright © Cambridge University Press, reproduced with permission of the author and publisher.

Green, D.W. (1986) Control, activation, and resource. *Brain and Language* 27: 210–23. Copyright © 1986 with permission of the author and Elsevier.

Grosjean, F. (2001) The bilingual's language modes. In Janet Nicol (ed.) *One Mind Two Languages*, Oxford: Blackwell, pp. 1–22. Reproduced with permission of the author and Blackwell Publishing.

Heller, Monica (1995) Code-switching and the politics of language. In L. Milroy and P. Muysken (eds) *One Speaker Two Languages*, Cambridge: Cambridge University Press, pp. 158–74. Copyright © 1995 Cambridge University Press, reproduced with permission of the author and publisher.

Kroll, Judith and de Groot, Annette (1997) Lexical and conceptual memory in the bilingual: mapping form to meaning in two languages. In Annette de Groot and Judith Kroll (eds) *Tutorials in Bilingualism: Psycholinguistic perspectives*, Mahwah, NJ: Lawrence Erlbaum, pp. 169–200, by permission of the authors and Lawrence Erlbaum Associates.

Li Wei, Milroy, L. and Pong, S.C. (1992) A two-step sociolinguistic analysis of code-switching and language choice. *International Journal of Applied Linguistics* 2(1): 63–86. Reproduced with permission of the authors and Blackwell Publishing.

Meisel, J.M. (1994) Code-switching in young bilingual children: the acquisition of grammatical constraints. *Studies in Second Language Acquisition* 16: 413–41. Copyright © 1994 Cambridge University Press, reproduced with permission of the author and publisher.

Muysken, Pieter (1995) Code-switching and grammatical theory. In L. Milroy and P. Muysken (eds) *One Speaker Two Languages*, Cambridge: Cambridge University Press, pp. 177–98. Copyright © 1995 Cambridge University Press, reproduced with permission of the author and publisher.

Myers-Scotton, C. (1988) Code-switching as indexical of social negotiations. In M. Heller (ed.) *Codeswitching*, Berlin: Mouton de Gruyter, pp. 151–86. Reproduced by permission of the author and Mouton de Gruyter. (This paper was originally published under the name C.M. Scotton.)

Myers-Scotton, C. and Jake, J. (1995) Matching lemmas in a bilingual competence and production model. *Linguistics* 33: 981–1024. Reproduced by permission of the authors and Mouton de Gruyter.

Obler, L.K., Zatorre, R.J., Galloway, L. and Vaid, J. (1982) Cerebral lateralization in bilinguals. *Brain and Language* 15: 40–54. Copyright © 1982 with permission of the authors and Elsevier.

Paradis, M. (1990) Language lateralization in bilinguals. Reproduced from *Brain and Language* 39: 570–86. Copyright © 1990 with permission of the author and Elsevier.

Poplack, S. (1980) Sometimes I'll start a sentence in Spanish *y termino en español*. *Linguistics* 18: 581–618, by permission of Mouton de Gruyter.

Rampton, B. (1995) Language crossing and the problematisation of ethnicity and socialisation. *Pragmatics* 5(4): 485–513. Reproduced by permission of the author and the International Pragmatics Association.

Volterra, V. and Taeschner, T. (1978) The acquisition and development of language by bilingual children. *Journal of Child Language*, 5: 311–26. Copyright © 1978 Cambridge University Press, reproduced with permission of the author and publisher.

Every effort has been made to obtain permission to reproduce copyright material. If any proper acknowledgement has not been made, or permission not received, we would invite copyright holders to inform the editor and publishers of that oversight. The copyright of the postscripts belongs to the named authors.

All the original papers and chapters are reproduced as faithfully as possible. The authors' original writing styles and conventions, whether in British or North American norms, have been kept. This policy results, in some cases, in maintaining the sexist-pronoun usage. Given the inevitable restrictions of space and the need to produce a coherent and readable collection, the editor has changed or omitted references to other papers in the same original collection (e.g. 'see Chapter 6 in this volume' has been changed to 'see XXX, date'), and put all the bibliographical details of the original papers at the end of the Reader. Where a work exists in different editions which have been variably cited by the original authors, the different dates are all listed with the later ones given in parenthesis. Other minor textual changes and omissions are indicated by the insertion of [. . .] in the text.

HOW TO USE THE READER

The Reader is intended for use as a teaching text, either on its own or as a secondary source-book, on a variety of courses. All the papers are selected from journals and collected volumes. No extracts from single authored monographs are included here. The papers are grouped into different parts, each having a brief introduction highlighting its theme. They are further divided into sections within the main parts, according to topics. Within each section, the papers are arranged, as far as possible, in a chronological order.

The general Introduction and Conclusion, which I have written, aim to provide links between the sections. The Introduction aims to place the other papers in this Reader in a wider context, and thus should be read first. Users can then choose to read the papers in different parts and sections which interest them most, although I have organised the papers in such a way that the focus of discussion moves from the macro-external (social and sociolinguistic) to the micro-internal (linguistic and psychological) aspects of bilingualism. The editorial material I have added, in the form of introductions to the parts, points out the differences and similarities in the theoretical and method-ological stances of individual papers. I have followed the model of other successful readers and provided a set of Study Questions and Study Activities at the end of each section. The Study Questions are intended for reviewing some of the essential themes and concepts in the individual papers and can be used on beginners' level courses or for self-study. The Study Activities aim to extend reading by generalisation to the user's own locality or experience. Some of the activities require research, and may be used as topics for essays or dissertation projects. These are particularly suitable for use at an intermediate level. There is also a short list of Further Reading which suggests additional sources of material for those who are interested in following up particular issues and ideas. The Conclusion chapter highlights some of the methodological issues in bilingualism research. Although it is placed at the end of the volume, it can (and perhaps should) be read before reading the individual papers.

The second edition of the Reader has two added features: contact details of the authors and postscripts specially written by the original authors for the Reader. Some of the postscripts comment on developments since the publication of the original articles; others elaborate on key points in the original papers. The Resource List contains key reference books and textbooks, and important journals and book series, as well as key websites and electronic mailing lists. The Glossary contains the key terms in bilingualism research. A full Bibliography, listing all the references for the individual chapters and postscripts in this Reader, is provided at the end.

Introduction

Dimensions of bilingualism

LI WEI

Languages in contact

Estimates vary as to how many languages are spoken in the world today. Most reference books give a figure of around 6,000 (e.g. Crystal, 1987). This is in fact a conservative estimate, as many parts of the world have been insufficiently studied from a linguistic point of view. We simply do not know exactly what languages are spoken in some places. What we do know, however, is that there are fewer than 200 countries – that politico-geographic unit to which most of us belong – in the world. It is inevitable perhaps that an enormous amount of 'language contact' takes place.

There is a popular metaphor in linguistics that language is a living organism, which is born, grows and dies. However, language is a human faculty: it co-evolves with us, *Homo sapiens*; and it is we who give language its life, change it and, if so desired, abandon it. When we speak of 'language contact', we are therefore talking about people speaking different languages coming into contact with one another.

There are many reasons for speakers of different languages to come into contact. Some do so out of their own choosing, while others are forced by circumstances. Key external factors contributing to language contact include (for further discussion, see Crystal, 1987; Baker and Prys Jones, 1998):

- *Politics:* Political or military acts such as colonisation, annexation, resettlement and federation can have immediate linguistic effects. People may become refugees, either in a new place or in their homeland, and have to learn the language of their new environment. After a successful military invasion, the indigenous population may have to learn the invader's language in order to prosper. Colonisation is exemplified by the former British, French, Spanish, Portuguese and Dutch colonies in Africa, Asia and South America, most of which achieved independence in the nineteenth century. A modern example of annexation can be found in the absorption of the Baltic republics – Lithuania, Latvia and Estonia – into the Soviet Union after the Second World War. In the latter part of the twentieth century, military conflicts in Central Africa and the former Yugoslavia saw the resettlement of people of different ethnic back-grounds. Examples of federation where diverse ethnic groups or nationalities are united under the political control of one state include Switzerland, Belgium and Cameroon.

- *Natural disaster:* Famine, floods, volcanic eruptions and other such events can be the cause of major movements of population. New language contact situations then emerge as people are resettled. Some of the Irish and Chinese resettlements in North America were the result of natural disasters.
- *Religion:* People may wish to live in a country because of its religious sig-nificance, or to leave a country because of its religious oppression. In either case, a new language may have to be learnt. The Russian speakers in Israel are a case in point.
- *Culture:* A desire to identify with a particular ethnic, cultural or social group usually means learning the language of that group. Minority ethnic and cultural groups may wish to maintain their own languages, which are different from the languages promoted by the governing state or institution. Nationalistic factors are particularly important.
- *Economy:* Very large numbers of people across the world have migrated to find work and to improve their standard of living. This factor accounts for most of the linguistic diversity of the US and an increasing proportion of the bilingualism in present-day Europe.
- *Education:* Learning another language may be the only means of obtaining access to knowledge. This factor led to the universal use of Latin in the Middle Ages, and today motivates the international use of English.
- *Technology:* The availability of information and communication technologies (ICT), such as the internet, has led to a further expansion of the use of English across the world. The vast majority of ICT users are non-native speakers of English.

From the above list we can see that one does not have to move to a different place to come into contact with people speaking a different language. There are plenty of opportunities for language contact in the same country, the same community, the same neighbourhood or even the same family. The usual consequence of language contact is bilingualism, or even multilingualism, which is most commonly found in an individual speaker.

Who is a bilingual?

People who are brought up in a society where monolingualism and uniculturalism are promoted as the normal way of life often think that bilingualism is only for a few 'special' people. In fact, one in three of the world's population routinely uses two or more languages for work, family life and leisure. There are even more people who make irregular use of languages other than their native one; for example, many people have learnt foreign languages at school and only occasionally use them for specific purposes. If we count these people as bilinguals then monolingual speakers will be a tiny minority in the world today.

The question of who is and who is not a bilingual is more difficult to answer than it first appears. Table 0.1 is a list of terms which have been used to describe bilingual speakers (for further discussions, see Baetens Beardsmore, 1982: Chapter 1).

The key variables to be considered in defining a bilingual person include:

- age and manner of acquisition;
- proficiency level in specific languages;
- domains of language use;
- self-identification and attitude.

Age and manner of acquisition help to distinguish those people who are exposed to two or more languages from birth from the ones who acquire a second language later in life, and those who have acquired languages in a naturalistic context (e.g. born to bilingual/multilingual parents or living in a bilingual/multilingual community) from the ones who have learnt languages through formal instruction. Such distinctions are useful in designing research projects and in interpreting and comparing research findings. For example, Weinreich's (1953) famous typology of bilinguals – coordinative, subordinative and compound – was based on assumptions of the effects of differences in age and manner of acquisition on the cognitive organisation and representation of bilingual knowledge. Later research on psycholinguistic modelling of the bilingual lexicon tried to account for the differences in age and manner of acquisition (see Chapter 18).

Contrary to popular assumptions, age and manner of acquisition have little bearing on the proficiency level of the individual in specific languages. There is plenty of evidence that late acquisition in an unstructured context can still result in a very high level of proficiency in the target language, while early acquisition of languages without continued use and support often leads to a low proficiency level, incomplete acquisition or attrition. Assessing the bilingual's language proficiency is a very complex issue. All four modalities – listening, speaking, reading and writing – should be considered. Inadequate measuring can result in misclassification of bilingual speakers and misinterpretation of research findings.

Many people believe that, to be described as bilingual, the person has to have equal proficiency in both languages. The fact is, however, that balanced bilinguals of this kind are a rarity. The two languages in a bilingual's linguistic repertoire are in constant contact and competition with each other. Bilinguals use their languages differently for different purposes in different domains. In some cases, the domains of language use do not overlap, resulting in different manifestations of the bilingual's knowledge e.g. one may use Spanish at home with family and friends and English at work with colleagues and other contacts. In other cases, the bilingual uses both languages all the time in all contexts, resulting in a large amount of code-switching. There are also many cases of bilinguals who understand and even speak two or more languages perfectly well but can read or write in only one of them.

An important factor that is often neglected in defining the bilingual is attitude.

Table 0.1   A variety of bilinguals

---

achieved bilingual   same as *late bilingual*.

additive bilingual   *someone* whose two languages combine in a complementary and enriching fashion.

ambilingual   same as *balanced bilingual*.

ascendant bilingual   someone whose ability to function in a second language is developing due to increased use.

ascribed bilingual   same as *early bilingual*.

asymmetrical bilingual   see *receptive bilingual*.

balanced bilingual   someone whose mastery of two languages is roughly equivalent.

compound bilingual   someone whose two languages are learnt at the same time, often in the same context.

consecutive bilingual   same as *successive bilingual*.

coordinate bilingual   someone whose two languages are learnt in distinctively separate contexts.

covert bilingual   someone who conceals his or her knowledge of a given language due to an attitudinal disposition.

diagonal bilingual   someone who is bilingual in a non-standard language or a dialect and an unrelated standard language.

dominant bilingual   someone with greater proficiency in one of his or her languages and uses it significantly more than the other language(s).

dormant bilingual   someone who has emigrated to a foreign country for a considerable period of time and has little opportunity to keep the first language actively in use.

early bilingual   someone who has acquired two languages early in childhood.

equilingual   same as *balanced bilingual*.

functional bilingual   someone who can operate in two languages with or without full fluency for the task in hand.

horizontal bilingual   someone who is bilingual in two distinct languages which have a similar or equal status.

incipient bilingual   someone at the early stages of bilingualism where one language is not fully developed.

late bilingual   someone who has become a bilingual later than childhood.

maximal bilingual   someone with near native control of two or more languages.

minimal bilingual   someone with only a few words and phrases in a second language.

natural bilingual   someone who has not undergone any specific training and who is often not in a position to translate or interpret with facility between two languages.

passive bilingual   same as *receptive bilingual*.

primary bilingual   same as *natural bilingual*.

productive bilingual   someone who not only understands but also speaks and possibly writes in two or more languages.

receptive bilingual   someone who understands a second language, in either its spoken or its written form, or both, but does not necessarily speak or write it.

recessive bilingual someone who begins to feel some difficulty in either understanding or expressing him or herself with ease, due to lack of use.

secondary bilingual someone whose second language has been added to a first language via instruction.

semibilingual same as *receptive bilingual*.

semilingual someone with insufficient knowledge of either language.

simultaneous bilingual someone whose two languages are present from the onset of speech.

subordinate bilingual someone who exhibits interference in his or her language usage by reducing the patterns of the second language to those of the first.

subtractive bilingual someone whose second language is acquired at the expense of the aptitudes already acquired in the first language.

successive bilingual someone whose second language is added at some stage after the first has begun to develop.

symmetrical bilingual same as *balanced bilingual*.

vertical bilingual someone who is bilingual in a standard language and a distinct but related language or dialect.

Not all bilinguals want to be described as bilinguals. Some bilinguals may find themselves in a socially disadvantaged position and would prefer to conceal their true bilingual identity; others may have a particular view of what constitutes bilingualism and would not self-identify as bilinguals. Back in 1962, William Mackey remarked: 'Bilingualism is not a phenomenon of language; it is a characteristic of its use. It is not a feature of the code but of the message. It does not belong to the domain of "language" but of "parole".' We can add to this that bilingualism is not simply a person's cognitive capacity but their attitude.

The term 'bilingual' primarily describes someone with the possession of two languages. There are, of course, many people in the world who have varying degrees of proficiency in and interchangeably use three, four or even more languages. In many countries of Africa and Asia, several languages co-exist and large sections of the population speak three or more languages. Individual multilingualism in these countries is a fact of life. Many people speak one or more local or ethnic languages, as well as another indigenous language which has become the medium of communication between different ethnic groups or speech communities. Such individuals may also speak a foreign language – such as English, French or Spanish – which has been introduced into the community during the process of colonisation. This latter language is often the language of education, bureaucracy and privilege.

Multilingualism can also be the possession of individuals who do not live within a multilingual country or speech community. Families can be trilingual when the husband and wife each speak a different language as well as the common language of the place of residence. People with sufficient social and educational advantages can learn a second, third or fourth language at school or university, at work or in leisure time. In many continental European countries, children learn two languages at school – such as English, German or French – as well as being fluent in their home language –

such as Danish, Dutch or Luxembourgish. Some researchers use 'bilingualism' as a general term to include multilingualism as well, while others prefer to maintain a distinction between the two. More research is needed to understand how bilingualism and multilingualism differ from each other.

What's in a language?

The above discussion of the causes of language contact and types of bilingual or multilingual people presupposes a definition of language. But what exactly is a language? This question has troubled linguists for decades.

One way of thinking about language is as a systematic combination of smaller units into larger units to create meaning. For example, we combine the sounds of our language (*phonemes*) to form meaningful words (*lexical items*) and we do so according to the rules of the language we speak. Those lexical items can be combined to make meaningful structures (*sentences*) according to the syntactic rules of our language. Language is hence a rule-governed system. Many linguists have devoted their lives to the scientific study of the rules that govern our language.

However, this kind of approach only works in a general, abstract way. As soon as we focus on a specific language of a specific speech community, we find that many other factors, mostly non-linguistic, have to be considered. For instance, when we want to work out the rules of English, we need to have some kind of agreement as to what 'English' refers to. The *Concise Oxford Dictionary* defines 'English' as 'the language of England'. What then is the language spoken by a large number of people in Australia, Canada, South Africa and the USA? What is the language spoken by people from Adelaide, Houston or Liverpool? Questions such as these have led some linguists to suggest that the notion of 'language' is essentially a social one in the sense that it is defined in terms of the people who speak it, and that as people vary in terms of their social characteristics – such as age, gender, place of origin and ethnicity – the language they speak will have various manifestations.

Traditionally, linguists make a distinction between 'language' and 'dialect', based on two criteria: *size* and *prestige* (for a more detailed discussion, see Hudson, 1996 (1980): Chapter 2). A language is believed to be larger than a dialect. That is, a variety called a language would contain more items than one called a dialect. In this sense we may refer to English as a language, containing the sum total of all the terms in all its dialects, such as Texan English and Yorkshire English. A language is also thought to have prestige which a dialect lacks. English as a language, for example, is supported institutionally through schools and the mass media; Appalachian and Geordie are not, and are hence often classified as dialects.

However, the two criteria of size and prestige sometimes contradict each other in distinguishing language and dialect. For example, the so-called 'standard English' must be a dialect if we consider its size only, as it does not contain items from many other varieties of English. Yet standard English has far more prestige than other English dialects because its use is encouraged in formal contexts. It should therefore be regarded not as a dialect but as a language. In fact, standard English, or any standard language, is a result of a direct and deliberate, and in some cases prolonged, intervention by society. This intervention – known as 'standardisation' – produces a standard language where before there were just dialects.

There are many counter-examples for the language and dialect distinction based on size and prestige. For instance, Luxembourgish is a language according to the constitution of Luxembourg, but linguistically it is a Rhenish dialect. Philipino is a language in the process of corpus building, but it is unclear whether it is bigger than Tagalog or Ilocano or any other Philippine languages/dialects. There are some very prestigious 'dialects', which may also be supported institutionally. For example, the European Charter of Minority Languages of the Council of Europe gives institutional support to a number of what used to be called dialects across the European Union.

One obvious candidate for an extra criterion for distinguishing language and dialect is that of *mutual intelligibility*. If the speakers of two linguistic varieties can understand each other, then the varieties concerned are dialects of the same language; otherwise they are separate languages. This is a widely used criterion. However, it cannot be taken seriously because there are a number of problems with its application.

First, even popular usage does not correspond consistently to this criterion. There are varieties which we as lay people call different languages but which are mutually intelligible – such as Danish, Norwegian and Swedish – and varieties which we call dialects of the same language but which may not be mutually intelligible, for example the so-called dialects of Chinese (see Figure 0.1 for an illustration). Popular usage tends to reflect a prestige-based definition of language. If two varieties are both standard languages, or are subordinate to different standards, they must be different languages and, conversely, if they are both subordinate to the same standard they are considered as the same language.

Second, mutual intelligibility is a matter of degree, ranging from total intelligibility down to total unintelligibility. How high up on the intelligibility scale do two varieties need to be in order to count as members of the same language? Unfortunately the answer to this question must be arbitrary.

Third, mutual intelligibility is not really a relationship between linguistic varieties, but between people, since it is they, and not the linguistic varieties, that understand one another. This being so, the degree of mutual intelligibility depends not just on the amount of overlap between the linguistic items in the two varieties, but also on the perceptions of the people concerned. For instance, how much does speaker X want to understand speaker Y? How much experience have they had of the variety to which they are listening? And how strongly do they want to identify themselves as speakers of the same language?

Another popular way of delimiting languages is by the names they have. All the 'major' languages of the world have a single name which translates neatly into other languages, such as Arabic, English, French, German, Russian and Spanish. If we want to refer to a particular variety of these languages, we can simply attach a place name, for instance Moroccan Arabic, Australian English and Puerto Rican Spanish. Dialects, on the other hand, tend not to have a proper name or at least tend not to have one that is easily translatable into other languages. For example, many communities in Africa have no specific names for their languages. The names they use are the same as a common word or phrase in the language, such as the word for 'our language' or

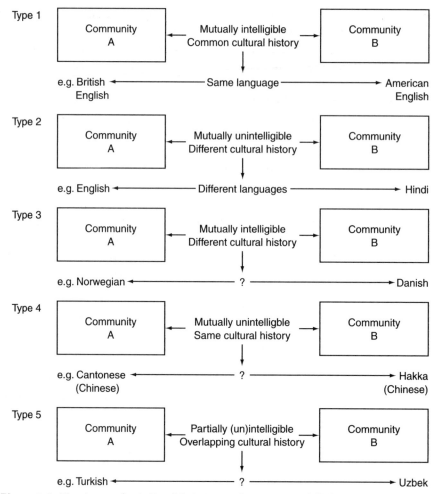

Figure 0.1 Five types of relationship between language and dialect
Source: adapted from Crystal, 1997 (1987): 289.

'our people'. The various English names for the Chinese dialects – such as Mandarin and Cantonese – are virtually unknown to native speakers of these varieties, and the London dialect, Cockney, would be known as the 'dialect of London' to speakers of French, German, Chinese and Japanese, rather than by its name. It is also as common to find a community whose language has numerous names as it is to have the same name applied to two different languages. Sometimes speakers from different backgrounds disagree as to which language they are speaking or if the varieties they are speaking are related at all.

To complicate the matter even further, there are what have been called 'mixed languages', whose sources are diverse and sometimes unknown (e.g. Bakker and Mous, 1994). 'Mixed languages' are just one of the many outcomes of language contact. Others include code-switching, the borrowing of lexical and other linguistic items and features, language shift, substratal influence, pidginisation and creolisation. However, 'mixed languages', as the linguists who study them point out, are not pidgins or creoles, or relexified languages. While a large amount of borrowing and mixing can be traced in them, they do not fit into any of the models of bilingual speech. They do not have names until linguists provide them. They are a product of contacts between people and a symbol of an emerging social identity.

So there is no simple answer to the question 'What is a language?' There is no pure linguistic definition of a language, nor is there a real distinction to be drawn between language and dialect. Language is a social notion; it cannot be defined without reference to its speakers and the context of its use. Language boundaries are boundaries between groups of people, as language contacts are contacts between people. Thus, language is not simply a system of sounds, words and sentences. Language also has a social function, both as a means of communication and as a way of identifying social groups.

Language as a socio-political issue

In many countries of the world a lot of the social identification is accomplished through language choice. By choosing one or other of the two or more languages in one's linguistic repertoire, a speaker reveals and defines his or her social relationships with other people. At a societal level, whole groups of people and, in fact, entire nations can be identified by the language or languages they use. Language, together with culture, religion and history, becomes a major component of national identity.

Multilingual countries are often thought to have certain problems which monolingual states do not (see Fasold, 1984: Chapter 1; Edwards, 1994). On the practical level, difficulties in communication within a country can act as an impediment to commerce and industry. More seriously, however, multilingualism is a problem for government. The process of governing requires communication both within the governing institutions and between the government and the people. This means that a language, or languages, must be selected as the language for use in governing. However, the selection of the 'official language' is not always easy, as it is not simply a pragmatic issue. For example, on pragmatic grounds, the best immediate choice for the language of government in a newly independent colony might be the old colonial language, since the colonial governing institutions and records are already in place in that language, and those nationals with the most government experience already know it. The old colonial language will not, however, be a good choice on nationalist grounds. For a people which has just acquired its own geographical territory, the language of the state which had denied it territorial control would not be a desirable candidate for a national symbol. Ireland has adopted a strategy whereby both the national language, Irish, and the language of the deposed power, English, are declared as official; the colonial language is used for immediate, practical purposes while the national language is promoted and developed. However, in many other multilingual countries which do not have a colonial past, such as China, deciding which language should be selected as the national language can sometimes lead to internal, ethnic conflicts.

Similarly, selecting a language for education in a multilingual country is often problematic. In some respects, the best strategy for language in education is to use the various ethnic languages. After all, these are the languages the children already speak, and school instruction can begin immediately without waiting until the children learn the official language. Some would argue, however, that this strategy could be damaging for nation-building efforts and disadvantage children by limiting their access to the wider world.

It should be pointed out that there is no scientific evidence to show that multilingual countries are particularly disadvantaged, in socio-economic terms, compared to monolingual ones. In fact, all the research that was carried out in the 1960s and 1970s on the relationship between the linguistic diversity and economic well-being of a nation came to the conclusion that a country can have any degree of language uniformity or fragmentation and still be underdeveloped; and a country whose entire population speaks the same language can be anywhere from very rich to very poor. It might be true that linguistic uniformity and economic development reinforce each other; in other words, economic well-being promotes the reduction of linguistic diversity. It would, however, be too one-sided, to say the least, to view multilingualism as the cause of the socio-economic problems of a nation (Coulmas, 1992).

Multilingualism is an important resource at both the societal and the personal level. For a linguistically diverse country, maintaining the ethnic-group languages alongside the national or official language(s) can prove to be an effective way to motivate individuals while unifying the nation. Additionally, a multi-ethnic society is arguably a richer, more exciting and more stimulating place to live in than a community with only one dominant ethnic group.

For the multilingual speaker, the availability of various languages in the community repertoire serves as a useful interactional resource. Typically, multilingual societies tend to assign different roles to different languages; one language may be used in informal contexts with family and friends, while another is used for the more formal situations of work, education and government. Imagine two friends who are both bilingual in the same 'home' and 'official' languages. Suppose that one of them also works for the local government and that her friend has some official business with her. Suppose further that the government employee has two pieces of advice to give to her friend: one based on her official status as a government representative, and one based on their mutual friendship. If the official advice is given in the 'government' language and the friendly advice in the 'home' language, there is little chance that there will be any misunderstanding about which advice is which. The friend will not take the advice given in the 'home' language as official (for specific examples, see Chapter 4).

There is a frequent debate in countries where various languages co-exist concerning which languages are a resource. The favoured languages tend to be those that are both international and particularly valuable in international trade. A lower place is given in the status ranking to minority languages which are small, regional and of less perceived value in the international marketplace. For example, French has traditionally been the number one modern language in the British school curriculum, followed by German and Spanish, and then a choice between Italian, Modern Greek and Portuguese. One may notice that all of these are European languages. Despite large numbers of mother-tongue Bengali, Cantonese, Gujarati, Hakka, Hindi, Punjabi, Turkish and Urdu speakers, these languages occupy a very low position in the school curriculum. In the British National Curriculum, the languages Arabic, Bengali, Chinese (Cantonese or Mandarin), Gujarati, Modern Hebrew, Hindi, Japanese, Punjabi, Russian, Turkish and Urdu are initially only allowed in secondary schools (for 11- to 18-year-olds) if a major European language such as French is taught first (Milroy and Milroy, 1985).

Clearly, multilingualism as a national and personal resource requires careful planning, as would any other kind of resource. However, language planning has something that other kinds of economic planning do not usually have: language has its own unique cultural symbolic value. As has been discussed earlier, language is a major component of the identity of a nation and an individual. Often, strong emotions are evoked when talking about a certain language. Language planning is not simply a matter of standardising or modernising a corpus of linguistic materials, nor is it a reassignment of functions and status. It is also about power and influence. The dominance of some languages and the dominated status of other languages are partly understandable if we examine which people are in positions of power and influence, which belong to elite groups that are in control of decision-making, and which are in subordinate groups upon whom decisions are implemented. It is more often than not the case that a given arrangement of languages benefits only those who have influence and privileges (Kaplan and Baldauf, 1997).

For the multilingual speaker, language choice is not only an effective means of communication but also an act of identity (Le Page and Tabouret-Keller, 1985). Every time we say something in one language when we might just as easily have said it in another, we are reconnecting with people, situations and power configurations from our history of past interactions and imprinting on that history our attitudes towards the people and languages concerned. Through language choice, we maintain and change ethnic-group boundaries and personal relationships, and construct and define 'self' and 'other' within a broader political economy and historical context (see Chapters 8 and 9).

What does it mean to be a bilingual?

A frequently asked question is whether a bilingual speaker's brain functions differently from that of a monolingual's brain. A more technical way of asking the question is whether language is differently organised and processed in the brain of a bilingual compared with that of the monolingual. In the majority of right-handed adults, the left hemisphere of the brain is dominant for language processing. There is some evidence to suggest that second language acquisition, especially adult second language acquisition, involves the right hemisphere more than first language acquisition in language processing. As proficiency in a second language grows, right hemisphere involvement decreases and left hemisphere involvement increases. However, quantitative analyses of the existing data often show that the left hemisphere strongly dominates language processing for both monolinguals and bilinguals, and that differences between them are the exception rather than the rule. Bilinguals do not seem to vary from monolinguals in neurological processes; the lateralisation of language in the brains of the two groups of speakers is similar (see Chapters 20, 21 and 22).

A related issue concerns the mental representation of a bilingual's two languages and the processing emanating from such representation. Evidence exists for both separate storage and shared storage of the two languages in the bilingual's brain, resulting in the suggestion that bilinguals have a language store for each of their two languages and a more general conceptual store. There are strong, direct interconnecting channels between each of these three separate stores. The interconnections between the two languages consist of association and translation systems, and common images in the conceptual store act as mediators. Furthermore, speakers of different proficiency levels or at different acquisitional stages vary in the strength and directness of the interconnections between the separate stores in language processing; for instance, those who are highly proficient in two languages may go directly from a concept to the target language, while those whose second language is weaker than their first tend to use the first language to mediate (see Chapters 16, 17, 18 and 19).

Although the more general definitions of 'bilingualism' would include people who understand a second language – in either spoken or written form or both – but do not necessarily speak or write it, a more common usage of the term refers to someone who can function in both languages in conversational interaction. We have already mentioned that bilingual speakers choose to use their different languages depending on a variety of factors, including the type of person addressed (e.g. members of the family, school-mates, colleagues, superiors, friends, shop-keepers, officials, transport personnel, neighbours), subject matter of the conversation (e.g. family concerns, schoolwork, politics, entertainment), location or social setting (e.g. at home, in the street, in church, in the office, having lunch, attending a lecture, negotiating business deals) and relationship with the addressee (e.g. kin, neighbours, colleagues, superior–inferior, strangers). However, even more complex are the many cases when a bilingual talks to another bilingual with the same linguistic background and changes from one language to another in the course of conversation. This is what is known as code-switching. Figure 0.2 illustrates a decision-making process of the bilingual speaker in language choice and code-switching.

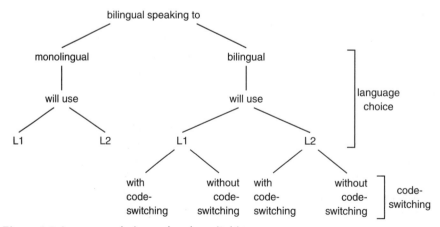

Figure 0.2 Language choice and code-switching
Source: adapted from Grosjean, 1982: 129.

There is a widespread impression that bilingual speakers code-switch because they cannot express themselves adequately in one language. This may be true to some extent when a bilingual is momentarily lost for words in one of his or her languages. However, code-switching is an extremely common practice among bilinguals and takes many forms. A long narrative may be divided into different parts which are expressed in different languages; sentences may begin in one language and finish in another; words and phrases from different languages may succeed each other. Linguists have devoted much attention to the study of code-switching. It has been demonstrated that code-switching involves skilled manipulation of overlapping sections of two (or more) grammars, and that there is virtually no instance of ungrammatical combination of two languages in code-switching, regardless of the bilingual ability of the speaker.

One important feature of bilingual code-switching is that the two languages involved do not play the same role in sentence making. Typically one language sets the grammatical framework, with the other providing certain items to fit into the framework. Code-switching therefore is not a simple combination of two sets of grammatical rules but grammatical integration of one language in another. Bilingual speakers of different proficiency levels in their two languages or speaking two typologically different languages can engage in code-switching and indeed vary it according to their needs (see Chapters 6, 10, 11 and 12).

Code-switching provides strong evidence for what some researchers have termed 'bilingual competence' – the capacity to coordinate two or more languages in accordance with the grammatical constraints of both or all languages – and calls into question the traditional view of the bilingual as two monolinguals in one person (for further discussion, see Grosjean, 1985). One consequence of the 'two-in-one' perspective is that bilingual speakers are often compared to monolinguals in terms of their language proficiency. For example, some researchers have suggested that bilingual children have smaller vocabularies and less developed grammars than their monolingual peers, while their ability to exploit the similarities and differences in two sets of grammatical rules to accomplish rule-governed code-switching was not considered relevant. In some experimental psycholinguistic studies, tests are given without taking into account that bilingual speakers may have learnt their two languages under different conditions for different purposes, and only use them in different situations with different people. It is important to emphasise that bilingual speakers have a unique linguistic and psychological profile; their two languages are constantly in different states of activation; they are able to call upon their linguistic knowledge and resources according to the context and adapt their behaviour to the task in hand.

In addition to the social use of code-switching, some bilinguals regularly change their speech production from one language to another in their professional life. Interpreters and translators, for example, switch between languages as a routine part of their job. They typically do so by reiterating in one language a message which was originally in a different language, either in the oral or in the written mode. They also tend to operate at the sentence level, rather than mixing two languages within sentences. Often we think of professional interpreters and translators as special people with highly developed language skills in each of their languages. In fact, even they are rarely perfectly balanced in two languages. More often than not, interpreters use one language actively and with greater ease than the other which they understand perfectly but in which their production is weaker. They are trained to translate from the 'passive' to the 'active' language. They are also trained to think rapidly of appropriate wording of ideas and produce words from a restricted area of meaning.

Another group of bilinguals engage themselves in cross-modality language production. This is the case with speech-sign bilinguals who, in addition to the oral modality, use the manual–visual modality in everyday communication. They are special in one aspect, i.e. the two different modalities allow for the simultaneous production of the two languages. In other words, one can speak and sign at the same time. Research has shown that such simultaneous bi-modal production is typically exemplified by the use of lexical items from both languages but only one set of grammatical rules, which is usually from the spoken language. Our current knowledge about how the two linguistic systems interact in the language production and processing of speech-sign bilinguals is still limited (for a review of existing studies of sign bilingualism, see Dufour, 1997). Indeed, much more work needs to be undertaken before we can fully appreciate the complexity of the language behaviour of bilinguals generally.

Changes in attitudes towards bilingualism

From the early nineteenth century to about the 1960s, there was a widespread belief that bilingualism has a detrimental effect on a human being's intellectual and spiritual growth. Stories of children who persisted in speaking two languages in school having had their mouths washed with soap and water or being beaten with a cane were not uncommon. The following is a quote from a professor at Cambridge University which illustrates the dominant belief of the time, even among academics and intellectuals:

> If it were possible for a child to live in two languages at once equally well, so much the worse. His intellectual and spiritual growth would not thereby be doubled, but halved. Unity of mind and character would have great difficulty in asserting itself in such circumstances.
>
> (Laurie, 1890: 15)

This view of Professor Laurie represented a commonly held belief through the twentieth century that bilingualism disadvantages rather than advantages one's intellectual development. The early research on bilingualism and cognition tended to confirm this negative viewpoint, finding that monolinguals were superior to bilinguals on intelligence tests. One of the most widely cited studies was done by Saer (1923), who studied 1,400 Welsh–English bilingual children between the ages of seven and 14 in five rural and two urban areas of Wales. A 10-point difference in IQ was found between the bilinguals and the monolingual English speakers from rural backgrounds. From this Saer concluded that bilinguals were mentally confused and at a disadvantage in intelligence compared with monolinguals. It was further suggested, with a follow-up study of university students, that 'the difference in mental ability as revealed by intelligence tests is of a permanent nature since it persists in students throughout their university career' (1924: 53).

Controversies regarding the early versions of IQ tests and the definition and measurement of intelligence aside, there were a number of problems with Saer's study and its conclusions. First, it appeared to be only in the rural areas that the correlation between bilingualism and lower IQ held. In urban areas monolinguals and bilinguals were virtually the same; in fact the average IQ for urban Welsh–English bilingual children in Saer's study was 100, whereas for monolingual English-speaking children it was 99. The urban bilingual children had more contact with English both before beginning school and outside school hours than did the rural bilinguals. Thus the depressed scores of the rural population were probably more a reflection of lack of opportunity and contexts to use English and were not necessarily indicative of any socio-psychological problems.

More important, however, is the issue of statistical inference in this and other studies of a similar type. Correlations do not allow us to infer cause-and-effect relationships, particularly when other variables – such as rural versus urban differences – may be mediating factors. Another major factor is the language in which such tests were administered, particularly tests of verbal intelligence. Many such studies measured bilinguals only in the second or non-dominant language.

At around the same time as Saer conducted studies on bilinguals' intelligence, some well-known linguists expressed their doubts about bilingual speakers' linguistic competence. The following is Bloomfield's characterisation of a Menomini Indian man in the US whom he believed to have 'deficient' knowledge of Menomini and English:

> White Thunder, a man around 40, speaks less English than Menomini, and that is a strong indictment, for his Menomini is atrocious. His vocabulary is small, his inflections are often barbarous, he constructs sentences of a few threadbare models. He may be said to speak no language tolerably.
>
> (Bloomfield, 1927: 395)

This is one of the early statements of a view which became fashionable in educational circles, namely that it was possible for bilinguals not to acquire full competence in any of the languages they spoke. Such individuals were said to be 'semilingual'. They were believed to have linguistic deficits in six areas of language (see Hansegard, 1975; Skutnabb-Kangas, 1981):

1   size of vocabulary;
2   correctness of language;
3   unconscious processing of language;
4   language creation;
5   mastery of the functions of language;
6   meanings and imagery.

It is significant that the term 'semilingualism' emerged in connection with the study of language skills of people belonging to ethnic minority groups. Research which provided evidence in support of the notion of 'semilingualism' was conducted in Scandinavia and North America and was concerned with accounting for the educational outcomes of submersion programmes where minority children were taught through the medium of the majority language. However, these studies, like the ones conducted by Saer, had serious methodological flaws and the conclusions reached by the researchers were misguided.

- First, the educational tests which were used to measure language proficiencies and to differentiate between people were insensitive to the qualitative aspects of languages and to the great range of language competences. Language may be specific to a context; a person may be competent in some contexts but not in others.

- Second, bilingual children are still in the process of developing their languages. It is unfair to compare them to some idealised adults. Their language skills change over time.

- Third, the comparison with monolinguals is also unfair. It is important to distinguish if bilinguals are 'naturally' qualitatively and quantitatively different from monolinguals in their use of the two languages, i.e. as a function of being bilingual.

- Fourth, if languages are relatively underdeveloped, the origins may not be in bilingualism per se, but in the economic, political and social conditions that evoke underdevelopment.

The disparaging and belittling overtone of the term 'semilingualism' itself invokes expectations of underachievement in the bilingual speaker. Thus, rather than highlighting the apparent 'deficits' of bilingual speakers, the more positive approach is to emphasise that, when suitable conditions are provided, languages are easily capable of development beyond the 'semi' state (for a critical analysis of the notion of semilingualism, see Martin-Jones and Romaine, 1986).

One of the specific issues Bloomfield raised in his comments on the language behaviour of members of the Menomini Indians in North America was the frequent mixing of their own language and English. It has been described as 'verbal salad', not particularly appealing but nevertheless harmless, or 'garbage', which is definitively worthless and vulgar. Unfortunately, although switching and mixing of languages occurs in practically all bilingual communities and all bilingual speakers' speech, it is stigmatised as an illegitimate mode of communication, even sometimes by the bilingual speakers themselves. Haugen (1977: 97), for example, reports that a visitor from Norway made the following comment on the speech of the Norwegians in the United States: 'Strictly speaking, it is no language whatever, but a gruesome mixture of Norwegian and English, and often one does not know whether to take it humorously or seriously.' Gumperz (1982: 62–3) reports that some bilingual speakers who mixed languages regularly still believed such behaviour was 'bad manners' or a sign of 'lack of education or improper control of language'. One of the Punjabi–English bilinguals Romaine interviewed said:

I'm guilty as well in the sense that we speak English more and more and
then what happens is that when you speak your own language you get two
or three English words in each sentence . . . but I think that's wrong.

(Romaine, 1995 (1989): 294)

Attitudes do not, of course, remain constant over time. At a personal level,
changes in attitudes may occur when there is some personal reward involved. Speakers
of minority languages will be more motivated to maintain and use their languages if
the languages prove to be useful in increasing their employability or social mobility.
In some cases, certain jobs are reserved for bilingual speakers only. At the societal
level, attitudes towards bilingualism change when the political ideology changes. In
California and elsewhere in the south-western United States, for instance, *pocho* and
calo used to serve as pejorative terms for the Spanish of local Chicanos. With a rise in
ethnic consciousness, however, these speech styles have become symbolic of Chicano
ethnicity and are now increasingly used in contemporary Chicano literature.

Since the 1960s, there has been a political movement, particularly in the US,
advocating language rights. In the US, questions about language rights are widely
discussed, not only in college classrooms and language communities but also in
government and federal legislatures. Language rights have a history of being tested in
US courtrooms. From the early 1920s to the present, there has been a continuous
debate in US courts of law regarding the legal status of language minority rights. To
gain short-term protection and a medium-term guarantee for minority languages,
legal challenges have become an important part of the language rights movement. The
legal battles concerned not just minority language vs. majority language contests, but
also children vs. schools, parents vs. school boards, state vs. the federal authorities,
etc. Whereas minority language activists among the Basques in Spain and the Welsh
in Britain have been taken to court by the central government for their actions, US
minority language activists have taken the central and regional government to court.

The language rights movement has received some support from organisations
such as the United Nations, UNESCO, the Council of Europe and the European Union.
Each of these four organisations has declared that minority language groups have the
right to maintain their languages. In the European Union, a directive (77/486/EEC)
stated that member states should promote the teaching of the mother tongue and the
culture of the country of origin in the education of migrant workers' children. The kind
of rights, apart from language rights, that minority groups may claim include: protection, membership of their ethnic group and separate existence, non-discrimination
and equal treatment, education and information in their ethnic language, freedom to
worship, freedom of belief, freedom of movement, employment, peaceful assembly and
association, political representation and involvement, and administrative autonomy.

However, real changes in attitudes towards bilingualism will not happen until
people recognise, or better still experience, the advantages of being bilingual. Current
research suggests that there are at least eight overlapping and interacting benefits for
a bilingual person, encompassing communicative, cognitive and cultural advantages
(adapted from Baker and Prys Jones, 1998: 6–8):

Communicative advantages

1   *Relationships with parents:* Where parents have differing first languages, the advantage of children becoming bilingual is that they will be able to communicate in each parent's preferred language. This may enable a subtler, finer texture of relationship with the parent. Alternatively they will be able to communicate with parents in one language and with their friends and within the community in a different language.

2   *Extended family relationships:* Being a bilingual allows someone to bridge the generations. When grandparents, uncles, aunts and other relatives in another region speak a language that is different from the local language, the monolingual may be unable to communicate with them. The bilingual has the chance to bridge that generation gap, build closer relationships with relatives and feel a sense of belonging and rootedness within the extended family.

3   *Community relationships:* A bilingual has the chance to communicate with a wider variety of people than a monolingual. Bilingual children will be able to communicate in the wider community and with school and neighbourhood friends in different languages when necessary.

4   *Transnational communication:* One barrier between nations and ethnic groups tends to be language. Language is sometimes a barrier to communication and to creating friendly relationships of mutual respect. Bilinguals in the home, in the community and in society have the potential for lowering such barriers. Bilinguals can act as bridges within the nuclear and extended family, within the community and across societies.

5   *Language sensitivity:* Being able to move between two languages may lead to more sensitivity in communication. Because bilinguals are constantly monitoring which language to use in different situations, they may be more attuned to the communicative needs of those with whom they talk. Research suggests that bilinguals may be more empathic towards listeners' needs in communication. When meeting those who do not speak their language particularly well, bilinguals may be more patient listeners than monolinguals.

Cultural advantages

6   Another advantage of being a bilingual is having two or more worlds of experience. Bilingualism provides the opportunity to experience two or more cultures. The monolingual may experience a variety of cultures, for example from different neighbours and communities that use the same language but have different ways of life. The monolingual can also travel to neighbouring countries and experience other cultures as a passive onlooker. However, to penetrate different cultures requires the language of that culture. To participate and become involved in the core of a culture requires a knowledge of the language of that culture.

7   There are also potential economic advantages to being bilingual. A person with two languages may have a wider portfolio of jobs available. As economic trade barriers fall, as international relationships become closer, as unions and partner-

ships across nations become more widespread, an increasing number of jobs are likely to require a person to be bilingual or multilingual. Jobs in multinational companies, jobs selling and exporting, and employment prospects generated by transnational contact make the future of employment more versatile for bilinguals than monolinguals.

Cognitive advantages

8   More recent research has shown that bilinguals may have some advantages in thinking, ranging from creative thinking to faster progress in early cognitive development and greater sensitivity in communication. For example, bilinguals may have two or more words for each object and idea; sometimes corresponding words in different languages have different connotations. Bilinguals are able to extend the range of meanings, associations and images, and to think more flexibly and creatively. Therefore, a bilingual has the possibility of more aware-ness of language and more fluency, flexibility and elaboration in thinking than a monolingual.

It would be misleading to suggest that there is no disadvantage to bilingualism. Some problems, both social and individual, may be falsely attributed to bilingualism. For instance, when bilingual children exhibit language or personality problems, bilingualism is sometimes blamed. Problems of social unrest may unfairly be attributed to the presence of two or more languages in a community. However, the real possible disadvantages of bilingualism tend to be temporary. For example, bilingual families may be spending significantly more of their time and making much greater efforts to maintain two languages and bring up children bilingually. Some bilingual children may find it difficult to cope with the school curriculum in either language for a short period of time. However, these are challenges that bilingual people have to face. The individual, cognitive, social, cultural, intellectual and economic advantages bilingualism brings to a person make all the efforts worthwhile.

A more complex problem associated with bilingualism is the question of the identity of a bilingual. If a child has both a French and an English parent and speaks each language fluently, is he or she French, English or Anglo-French? If a child speaks English and a minority language such as Welsh, is he or she Welsh, English, British, European or what? It has to be said that, for many bilingual people, identity is not a problem. While speaking two languages, they are resolutely identified with one ethnic or cultural group. For example, many bilinguals in Wales see themselves as Welsh first, possibly British next but not English. Others, however, find identity a real, problematic issue. Some immigrants, for instance, desperately want to lose the identity of their native country and become assimilated and identified with the new home country, while some others want to develop a new identity and feel more comfortable with being culturally hyphenated, such as Chinese-American, Italian-Australian, Swedish-Finn or Anglo-French. Yet identity crises and conflicts are never static. Identities change and evolve over time, with varying experiences, interactions and collaborations within and outside a language group.

Bilingualism is not a static and unitary phenomenon. It is shaped in different ways, and it changes depending on a variety of historical, cultural, political, economic, environmental, linguistic, psychological and other factors. People's attitudes towards bilingualism will also change as the society progresses and as our understanding of bilingual speakers' knowledge and skills grows. However, one thing is certain: more and more people in the world will become bilinguals, and bilingualism will stay as long as humankind walks the earth.

Notes for students and instructors

Study questions

1   Of the names and labels of bilingual speakers listed in the Introduction, which describes yourself and your bilingual friends most appropriately, and why?

2   In your view, how useful are the terms 'balanced bilingual' and 'semilingual'? Can you see any problems when you apply them to anyone you know?

3   Why is it important to distinguish language 'proficiency' and language 'use' in defining a bilingual? How important is it to consider bilingual ability across the four language skills: listening, speaking, reading and writing?

Study activities

1   Select five individuals each of whom you would describe as bilingual. Ask each of them whether he or she would consider himself or herself to be bilingual and why. Compare your definition with theirs, and make a table or diagram to illustrate the important factors that need to be taken into account in defining bilingual speakers.

2   Investigate the history of language contact and attitudes towards bilingualism in a community or region of your choice. You may need to consult historical documents and design a short questionnaire on language attitudes. Pay particular attention to how politico-economic changes have affected people's attitudes towards bilingualism.

3   Using a local school (this could be state or private), find out what languages are spoken by the children, their parents and the teachers. What tests or assessment, if any, does the school use to measure the language ability of the children whose 'home' language is different from the 'school' language? If it is a bilingual school, how are the different languages being used (e.g. is one language confined to one setting/subject)?

Further reading

There is a range of introductory texts on bilingualism. S. Romaine, 1995, *Bilingualism* (2nd edn), Blackwell, is probably the most comprehensive, covering all aspects of bilingualism ranging from the bilingual brain and code-switching to bilingual education and attitudes towards bilingualism. An earlier introductory text written from a bilingual speaker's point of view and in a highly readable style is F. Grosjean, 1982, *Life with Two Languages*, Harvard University Press. A more recent textbook is C. Myers-Scotton, 2005, *Multiple Voices: An introduction to bilingualism*, Blackwell. Other textbooks include J. Hamers and M. Blanc, 2000, *Bilinguality and Bilingualism* (2nd edn), Cambridge University Press.

An introductory text, focusing on bilingual education, is C. Baker, 2006, *Foundations of Bilingual Education and Bilingualism* (4th edn), Multilingual Matters. It has a companion reader: O. Garcia and C. Baker (eds), 1995, *Policy and Practice in Bilingual Education*, Multilingual Matters. An introduction to social aspects of language contact is J. Edwards, 1994, *Multilingualism*, Routledge. Chapter 1 of R. Fasold, 1984, *The Sociolinguistics of Society*, Blackwell discusses how multilingual nations develop.

Sociolinguistic dimensions of bilingualism

Introduction to Part One

LI WEI

The articles reprinted in Part One of this Reader serve to illustrate what may be called the sociolinguistic approach to bilingualism. There are nine articles altogether; three are grouped under 'Language choice', four under 'Bilingual interaction' and two under 'Identity and ideology'.

Language choice

Researchers of bilingualism generally agree that language choice is an 'orderly' social behaviour, rather than a random matter of momentary inclination. Where perspectives differ is in the conceptualisation of the nature of achievement and management of that orderliness. Charles A. Ferguson's article on diglossia (Chapter 1) is a true classic in that it not only defines a concept but also develops an approach to bilingualism which has been extremely influential. It originates from the fact that the co-existing languages of a community are likely to have different functions and to be used in different contexts. The notion of diglossia describes the functional differentiation of languages in bilingual and multilingual communities. A distinction is made between High (H) and Low (L) language varieties, and Ferguson noted nine areas in which H and L could differ. One important implication of Ferguson's conception of diglossia is that bilingual speakers' language choice is seen to reflect a set of society-wide norms.

The concept of diglossia can be usefully examined alongside the notion of bilingualism, as Joshua A. Fishman does in Chapter 2. Bilingualism, argues Fishman, is a subject matter for linguists and psychologists and refers to an individual's ability to use more than one language; diglossia, on the other hand, is a concept for sociologists and sociolinguists to study. He describes four language situations where bilingualism and diglossia may exist with or without each other. In doing so, Fishman has incorporated the factor of change in language use. According to Fishman, relative stability can be maintained as long as societal compartmentalisation of language lasts. When two languages compete for use in the same situations, as in the case of bilingualism without diglossia, language shift – a process in which a speech community collectively gives up a language in favour of some other – may occur.

The second article by Fishman (Chapter 3) asks the now famous question 'Who speaks what language to whom and when?', a question which set the agenda not only for bilingualism research but also for the study of language in society in general. The way in which Fishman proposes to answer this question is through what he calls *domain analysis*. Domain refers to a cluster of characteristic situations around a prototypical theme which structures both the speakers' perception of the situation and their social behaviour, including language choice. Extending Weinreich's (1953) earlier work, Fishman tries to link the analysis of societal norms and expectations with language use in face-to-face encounters, using the concept of *domain* as a pivot. His analysis concentrates on stable systems of choice, or 'proper' usage as he calls it, and relates specific language choices to general institutions and spheres of activity, both in one society and between societies comparatively.

Bilingual interaction

The second section of Part One focuses more specifically on the microinteractional aspects of language choice. The article by Jan-Petter Blom and John J. Gumperz (Chapter 4) is one of the most frequently cited articles on bilingualism. It introduces the now widely used dichotomy of 'situational' versus 'metaphorical' code-switching. On the basis of extensive participant observation in a bi-dialectal community in Hemnesberget, Norway, Blom and Gumperz identify two types of linguistic practice which they argue have different social meanings:

1   changes of language choice corresponding to changes in the situation, par-
     ticularly participant, setting and activity type, i.e. situational code-switching;
     and
2   changes in language choice in order to achieve special communicative effects
     while participant and setting remain the same, i.e. metaphorical code-switching.

They regard metaphorical code-switching as symbolic of alternative interpersonal relationships; in other words, choices of language are seen as a 'metaphor' for the relationship being enacted. This study of the meaning of language choice exemplifies what is meant by an integrated sociolinguistic approach. Both ethnography and linguistics are drawn upon. The outcome is an understanding of social constraints and linguistic rules as parts of a single communicative system.

The idea that language choice and code-switching are symbolic of the social relationships between individuals is further developed in Carol M. Scotton's (later as Myers-Scotton) paper (Chapter 5). She proposes the notion of *markedness* as a basis for understanding the effectiveness of code-switching in defining social rights and obligations. She shows how certain sets of rights and obligations are convention-ally associated with certain social situations, and how language use in those situations is unmarked. She goes on to discuss two ways in which situation and language use co-vary: externally motivated language choice signals changes in situation and, therefore, change in unmarked language choice. However, within single encounters participants can deviate from conventional verbal behaviour and, through such marked switches, redefine role relations and, consequently, situations.

The article by Peter Auer (Chapter 6) approaches the meaning of language choice and code-switching from a different perspective. Auer uses a framework derived from *conversation analysis* (CA) to account for the ways in which speakers use code-switching either to manage social relations or to accomplish discourse objectives. He argues that the primary function of language alternation – a general term that Auer uses to cover various types of code-switching and transfer – is to establish various kinds of *footing* (in Goffman's terms: Goffman, 1979), which provide the basis for the conversation to be interpretable by participants. This analysis of bilingual conversation offers a useful alternative to the macro-sociolinguistic studies of language choice and code-switching. It provides the basis for a pragmatic theory of code-switching.

The article by Li Wei, Lesley Milroy and Pong Sin Ching (Chapter 7) proposes a two-step analysis which integrates language choice at the macrocommunity level with code-switching at the micro-interactional level. Utilising the analytic concept of *social network* and framework provided by *conversation analysis* (similar to Auer's analysis), they demonstrate, via an analysis of the sociolinguistic patterns of a Chinese community in Britain, that bilingual speakers use code-switching as an organisational procedure for conversational interaction and that the different code-switching practices displayed by speakers of different generations may be described as inter-actional reflexes of the network-specific language choice preferences. They further argue that, while network interacts with a number of other variables, it is capable of accounting more generally for patterns of language choice than variables such as generation, sex of speaker, duration of stay and occupation with which it interacts. It can also deal in a principled way with differences within a single generational group. In their view, therefore, social network analysis can form an important component in an integrated social theory of language choice: it links with the interactional level in focusing on the everyday behaviour of social actors, and with the economic and socio-political level in that networks may be seen as forming in response to social and economic pressures.

Identity and ideology

The last section of Part One contains two articles. Like Blom and Gumperz and Myers-Scotton, Heller (Chapter 8) regards code-switching as an important communicative resource on which bilingual speakers can draw for their social interaction. However, instead of focusing on the interactional details of bilingual conversation, Heller argues for code-switching to be studied in its historical and ideological context. In particular, the distribution of code-switching practices, which is often uneven and unstable, needs to be understood from a political economy perspective. Through analysis of code-switching patterns, Heller demonstrates how bilingualism can be, and should be, investigated concomitantly as a matter of ideology, communicative practice and social process.

The final chapter in Part One (Chapter 9) is by Ben Rampton in which he looks at a specific linguistic phenomenon which he calls 'language crossing'. It involves code-switching into language varieties that are not generally thought to belong to the speaker. Like Heller, Rampton places language crossing in a broader socio-political context and proposes a way of investigating the phenomenon as part of a wider socialisation process. But the specific issue that Rampton is concerned with in his analysis is the concept of ethnicity. He contrasts ethnicity-as-communicative-inheritance with ethnicity-as-discursive-construct, and argues that 'language crossing' plays an important role in the emergence of 'new ethnicities'.

Language choice

Chapter 1

Diglossia

CHARLES A. FERGUSON

IN MANY SPEECH COMMUNITIES two or more varieties of the same language are used by some speakers under different conditions. Perhaps the most familiar example is the standard language and regional dialect as used, say, in Italian or Persian, where many speakers speak their local dialect at home or among family or friends of the same dialect area but use the standard language in communicating with speakers of other dialects or on public occasions. There are, however, quite different examples of the use of two varieties of a language in the same speech community. In Baghdad the Christian Arabs speak a 'Christian Arabic' dialect when talking among themselves but speak the general Baghdad dialect, 'Muslim Arabic', when talking in a mixed group. In recent years there has been a renewed interest in studying the development and characteristics of standardized languages (see especially Kloss, 1952, with its valuable introduction on standardization in general), and it is in following this line of interest that the present study seeks to examine carefully one particular kind of standardization where two varieties of a language exist side by side throughout the community, with each having a definite role to play. The term 'diglossia' is introduced here, modeled on the French *diglossie*, which has been applied to this situation, since there seems to be no word in regular use for this in English; other languages of Europe generally use the word for 'bilingualism' in this special sense as well. (The terms 'language', 'dialect', and 'variety' are used here without precise definition. It is hoped that they occur sufficiently in accordance with established usage to be unambiguous for the present purpose. The term 'superposed variety' is also used here without definition; it means that the variety in question is not the primary, 'native' variety for the speakers in question but may be learned in addition to this. Finally, no attempt is made in this paper to examine the analogous situation where two distinct (related or unrelated) languages are used side by side throughout a speech community, each with a clearly defined role.)

It is likely that this particular situation in speech communities is very widespread, although it is rarely mentioned, let alone satisfactorily described. A full explanation of it can be of considerable help in dealing with problems in linguistic description, in historical linguistics, and in language typology. The present study should be regarded as preliminary in that much more assembling of descriptive and historical data is required;

[handwritten margin note: Arabic group]

its purpose is to characterize diglossia by picking out four speech communities and their languages (hereafter called the defining languages) which clearly belong in this category, and describing features shared by them which seem relevant to the classification. The defining languages selected are Arabic, Modern Greek, Swiss German, and Haitian Creole. (See the references at the end of this chapter.)

Before proceeding to the description it must be pointed out that diglossia is not assumed to be a stage which occurs always and only at a certain point in some kind of evolution, e.g. in the standardization process. Diglossia may develop from various origins and eventuate in different language situations. Of the four defining languages, Arabic diglossia seems to reach as far back as our knowledge of Arabic goes, and the superposed 'Classical' language has remained relatively stable, while Greek diglossia has roots going back many centuries, but it became fully developed only at the beginning of the nineteenth century with the renaissance of Greek literature and the creation of a literary language based in large part on previous forms of literary Greek. Swiss German diglossia developed as a result of long religious and political isolation from the centers of German linguistic standardization, while Haitian Creole arose from a creolization of a pidgin French, with standard French later coming to play the role of the superposed variety. Some speculation on the possibilities of development will, however, be given at the end of the chapter.

For convenience of reference the superposed variety in diglossias will be called the H ('high') variety or simply H, and the regional dialects will be called L ('low') varieties or, collectively, simply L. All the defining languages have names for H and L, and these are listed in Table 1.1.

It is instructive to note the problems involved in citing words of these languages in a consistent and accurate manner. First, should the words be listed in their H form or in their L form, or in both? Second, if words are cited in their L form, what kind of L should be chosen? In Greek and in Haitian Creole, it seems clear that the ordinary conversational language of the educated people of Athens and Port-au-Prince respectively should be selected. For Arabic and for Swiss German the choice must be arbitrary,

Table 1.1   Terms for H and L in the defining languages

Language	Term for H	Term for L
Arabic		
Classical (=H)	*'al-fuṣḥā*	*'al-'āmmiyyah, 'ad-darij*
Egyptian (=L)	*'il-faṣīḥ, 'in-nahawi*	*'il-'ammiyya*
Swiss / German		
Standard German (=H)	*Schriftsprache*	*(Schweizer) Dialekt, Schweizerhdeutsch*
Swiss (=L)	*Hoochtüütsch*	*Schwyzertüütsch*
Haitian Creole		
French (=H)	*français*	*créole*
Greek		
H and L	*katharévusa*	*dhimotikí*

and the ordinary conversational language of educated people of Cairo and of Zürich are used here. Third, what kind of spelling should be used to represent L? Since there is in no case a generally accepted orthography for L, some kind of phonemic or quasi-phonemic transcription would seem appropriate. The following choices were made. For Haitian Creole, the McConnell–Laubach spelling was selected, since it is approximately phonemic and is typographically simple. For Greek, the transcription was adopted from the manual *Spoken Greek* (Kahane *et al.*, 1945), since this is intended to be phonemic; a transliteration of the Greek spelling seems less satisfactory not only because the spelling is variable but also because it is highly etymologizing in nature and quite unphonemic. For Swiss German, the spelling backed by Dieth (1938), which, though it fails to indicate all the phonemic contrasts and in some cases may indicate allophones, is fairly consistent and seems to be a sensible systematization, without serious modification, of the spelling conventions most generally used in writing Swiss German dialect material. Arabic, like Greek, uses a non-Roman alphabet, but transliteration is even less feasible than for Greek, partly again because of the variability of the spelling, but even more because in writing Egyptian colloquial Arabic many vowels are not indicated at all and others are often indicated ambiguously; the transcription chosen here sticks closely to the traditional systems of Semitists, being a modification for Egyptian of the scheme used by Al-Toma (1957).

The fourth problem is how to represent H. For Swiss German and Haitian Creole standard German and French orthography respectively can be used even though this hides certain resemblances between the sounds of H and L in both cases. For Greek either the usual spelling in Greek letters could be used or a transliteration, but since a knowledge of Modern Greek pronunciation is less widespread than a knowledge of German and French pronunciation, the masking effect of the orthography is more serious in the Greek case, and we use the phonemic transcription instead. Arabic is the most serious problem. The two most obvious choices are (1) a transliteration of Arabic spelling (with the unwritten vowels supplied by the transcriber) or (2) a phonemic transcription of the Arabic as it would be read by a speaker of Cairo Arabic. Solution (1) has been adopted, again in accordance with Al-Toma's procedure.

Characteristic features

Function

One of the most important features of diglossia is the specialization of function for H and L. In one set of situations only H is appropriate and in another only L, with the two sets overlapping only very slightly. As an illustration, a sample listing of possible situations is given, with indication of the variety normally used:

	H	L
Sermon in church or mosque	X	
Instructions to servants, waiters, workmen, clerks		X
Personal letter	X	
Speech in parliament, political speech	X	
University lecture	X	
Conversation with family, friends, colleagues		X

	H	L
Newsbroadcast	X	
Radio 'soap opera'		X
Newspaper editorial, news story, caption on picture	X	
Caption on political cartoon		X
Poetry	X	
Folk literature		X

The social importance of using the right variety in the right situation can hardly be overestimated. An outsider who learns to speak fluent, accurate L and then uses it in a formal speech is an object of ridicule. A member of the speech community who uses H in a purely conversational situation or in an informal activity like shopping is equally an object of ridicule. In all the defining languages it is typical behavior to have someone read aloud from a newspaper written in H and then proceed to discuss the contents in L. In all the defining languages it is typical behavior to listen to a formal speech in H and then discuss it, often with the speaker himself, in L.

(The situation in formal education is often more complicated than is indicated here. In the Arab world, for example, formal university lectures are given in H, but drills, explanation, and section meetings may be in large part conducted in L, especially in the natural sciences as opposed to the humanities. Although the teachers' use of L in secondary schools is forbidden by law in some Arab countries, often a considerable part of the teachers' time is taken up with explaining in L the meaning of material in H which has been presented in books or lectures.)

The last two situations on the list call for comment. In all the defining languages some poetry is composed in L, and a small handful of poets compose in both, but the status of the two kinds of poetry is very different, and for the speech community as a whole it is only the poetry in H that is felt to be 'real' poetry. (Modern Greek does not quite fit this description. Poetry in L is the major production and H verse is generally felt to be artificial.) On the other hand, in every one of the defining languages certain proverbs, politeness formulas, and the like are in H even when cited in ordinary conversation by illiterates. It has been estimated that as much as one-fifth of the proverbs in the active repertory of Arab villagers are in H.

Prestige

In all the defining languages the speakers regard H as superior to L in a number of respects. Sometimes the feeling is so strong that H alone is regarded as real and L is reported 'not to exist'. Speakers of Arabic, for example, may say (in L) that so-and-so doesn't know Arabic. This normally means he doesn't know H, although he may be a fluent, effective speaker of L. If a non-speaker of Arabic asks an educated Arab for help in learning to speak Arabic, the Arab will normally try to teach him H forms, insisting that these are the only ones to use. Very often, educated Arabs will maintain that they never use L at all, in spite of the fact that direct observation shows that they use it constantly in all ordinary conversation. Similarly, educated speakers of Haitian Creole frequently deny its existence, insisting that they always speak French. This attitude cannot be called a deliberate attempt to deceive the questioner, but seems almost a self-deception. When the speaker in question is replying in good faith, it is often possible to break through these attitudes by asking such questions as what kind of language he uses in speaking to his children, to servants, or to his mother. The very revealing reply is usually something like: 'Oh, but they wouldn't understand [the H form, whatever it is called].'

Even where the feeling of the reality and superiority of H is not so strong, there is usually a belief that H is somehow more beautilul, more logical, better able to express important thoughts, and the like. And this belief is held also by speakers whose command of H is quite limited. To those Americans who would like to evaluate speech in terms of effectiveness of communication it comes as a shock to discover that many speakers of a language involved in diglossia characteristically prefer to hear a political speech or an expository lecture or a recitation of poetry in H even though it may be less intelligible to them than it would be in L.

In some cases the superiority of H is connected with religion. In Greek the language of the New Testament is felt to be essentially the same as the *katharévusa*, and the appearance of a translation of the New Testament in *dhimotiki* was the occasion for serious rioting in Greece in 1903. Speakers of Haitian Creole are generally accustomed to a French version of the Bible, and even when the Church uses Creole for catechisms and the like, it resorts to a highly Gallicized spelling. For Arabic, H is the language of the Qur'an and as such is widely believed to constitute the actual words of God and even to be outside the limits of space and time, i.e. to have existed 'before' time began, with the creation of the world.

Literary heritage

In every one of the defining languages there is a sizable body of written literature in H which is held in high esteem by the speech community, and contemporary literary production in H by members of the community is felt to be part of this otherwise existing literature. The body of literature may either have been produced long ago in the past history of the community or be in continuous production in another speech community in which H serves as the standard variety of the language. When the body of literature represents a long time span (as in Arabic or Greek) contemporary writers – and readers – tend to regard it as a legitimate practice to utilize words, phrases, or constructions which may have been current only at one period of the literary history and are not in widespread use at the present time. Thus it may be good journalistic usage in writing editorials, or good literary taste in composing poetry, to employ a complicated Classical Greek participial construction or a rare twelfth-century Arabic expression which it can be assumed the average educated reader will not understand without research on his part. One effect of such usage is appreciation on the part of some readers: 'So-and-so really knows his Greek [or Arabic]', or 'So-and-so's editorial today, or latest poem, is very good Greek [or Arabic].'

Acquisition

Among speakers of the four defining languages, adults use L in speaking to children and children use L in speaking to one another. As a result, L is learned by children in what may be regarded as the 'normal' way of learning one's mother tongue. H may be heard by children from time to time, but the actual learning of H is chiefly accomplished by the means of formal education, whether this be traditional Qur'anic schools, modern government schools, or private tutors.

This difference in method of acquisition is very important. The speaker is at home in L to a degree he almost never achieves in H. The grammatical structure of L is learned without explicit discussion of grammatical concepts; the grammar of H is learned in terms of 'rules' and norms to be imitated.

It seems unlikely that any change toward full utilization of H could take place without a radical change in this pattern of acquisition. For example, those Arabs who ardently desire to have L replaced by H for all functions can hardly expect this to happen if they are unwilling to speak H to their children. (It has been very plausibly suggested that there are psychological implications following from this linguistic duality. This certainly deserves careful experimental investigation. On this point, see the highly controversial article which seems to me to contain some important kernels of truth along with much which cannot be supported; Shouby, 1951.)

Standardization

In all the defining languages there is a strong tradition of grammatical study of the H form of the language. There are grammars, dictionaries, treatises on pronunciation, style, and so on. There is an established norm for pronunciation, grammar, and vocabulary which allows variation only within certain limits. The orthography is well established and has little variation. By contrast, descriptive and normative studies of the L form are either non-existent or relatively recent and slight in quantity. Often they have been carried out first or chiefly by scholars OUTSIDE the speech community and are written in other languages. There is no settled orthography and there is wide variation in pronunciation, grammar, and vocabulary.

In the case of relatively small speech communities with a single important center of communication (e.g. Greece, Haiti) a kind of standard L may arise which speakers of other dialects imitate and which tends to spread like any standard variety except that it remains limited to the functions for which L is appropriate.

In speech communities which have no single most important center of communication a number of regional L's may arise. In the Arabic speech community, for example, there is no standard L corresponding to educated Athenian *dhimotikí*, but regional standards exist in various areas. The Arabic of Cairo, for example, serves as a standard L for Egypt, and educated individuals from Upper Egypt must learn not only H but also, for conversational purposes, an approximation to Cairo L. In the Swiss German speech community there is no single standard, and even the term 'regional standard' seems inappropriate, but in several cases the L of a city or town has a strong effect on the surrounding rural L.

Stability

It might be supposed that diglossia is highly unstable, tending to change into a more stable language situation. However, this is not so. Diglossia typically persists for at least several centuries, and evidence in some cases seems to show that it can last well over a thousand years. The communicative tensions which arise in the diglossia situation may be resolved by the use of relatively uncodified, unstable, intermediate forms of the language (Greek *mikti*, Arabic *al-lugah al-wusṭā*, Haitian *créole de salon*) and repeated borrowing of vocabulary items from H to L.

In Arabic, for example, a kind of spoken Arabic much used in certain semiformal or cross-dialectal situations has a highly classical vocabulary with few or no inflectional endings, with certain features of classical syntax, but with a fundamentally colloquial base in morphology and syntax, and a generous admixture of colloquial vocabulary. In Greek a kind of mixed language has become appropriate for a large part of the press.

The borrowing of lexical items from H to L is clearly analogous (or for the periods when actual diglossia was in effect in these languages, identical) with the learned borrowings from Latin to Romance languages or the Sanskrit *tatsamas* in Middle and New Indo-Aryan. (The exact nature of this borrowing process deserves careful investigation, especially for the important 'filter effect' of the pronunciation and grammar of H occurring in those forms of middle language which often serve as the connecting link by which the loans are introduced into the 'pure' L.)

Grammar

One of the most striking differences between H and L in the defining languages is in the grammatical structure: H has grammatical categories not present in L and has an inflectional system of nouns and verbs which is much reduced or totally absent in L. For example, Classical Arabic has three cases in the noun, marked by endings; colloquial dialects have none. Standard German has four cases in the noun and two non-periphrastic indicative tenses in the verb; Swiss German has three cases in the noun and only one simple indicative tense. *Kotharévusa* has four cases, *dhimotiki* three. French has gender and number in the noun, Creole has neither. Also, in every one of the defining languages there seem to be several striking differences of word order as well as a thorough-going set of differences in the use of introductory and connective particles. It is certainly safe to say that in diglossia *there are always extensive differences between the grammatical structures of H and L.* This is true not only for the four defining languages, but also for every other case of diglossia examined by the author.

For the defining languages it may be possible to make a further statement about grammatical differences. It is always risky to hazard generalizations about grammatical complexity, but it may be worthwhile to attempt to formulate a statement applicable to the four defining languages even if it should turn out to be invalid for other instances of diglossia (cf. Greenberg, 1954).

There is probably fairly wide agreement among linguists that the grammatical structure of language A is 'simpler' than that of B if, other things being equal:

1   The morphophonemics of A is simpler, i.e. morphemes have fewer alternants, alternation is more regular, automatic (e.g. Turkish *-lar ~ -ler* is simpler than the English plural markers).
2   There are fewer obligatory categories marked by morphemes or concord (e.g. Persian with no gender distinctions in the pronoun is simpler than Egyptian Arabic with masculine–feminine distinction in the second and third persons singular).
3   Paradigms are more symmetrical (e.g. a language with all declensions having the same number of case distinctions is simpler than one in which there is variation).

4   Concord and government are stricter (e.g. prepositions all take the same case rather than different cases).

If this understanding of grammatical simplicity is accepted, then we may note that in at least three of the defining languages, the grammatical structure of any given L variety is simpler than that of its corresponding H. This seems incontrovertibly true for Arabic, Greek, and Haitian Creole; a full analysis of standard German and Swiss German might show this not to be true in that diglossic situation in view of the extensive morphophonemics of Swiss.

Lexicon

Generally speaking, the bulk of the vocabulary of H and L is shared, of course with variations in form and with differences of use and meaning. It is hardly surprising, however, that H should include in its total lexicon technical terms and learned expressions which have no regular L equivalents, since the subjects involved are rarely if ever discussed in pure L. Also, it is not surprising that the L varieties should include in their total lexicons popular expressions and the names of very homely objects or objects of very localized distribution which have no regular H equivalents, since the subjects involved are rarely if ever discussed in pure H. But *a striking feature of diglossia is the existence of many paired items – one H, one L – referring to fairly common concepts frequently used in both H and L, where the range of meaning of the two items is roughly the same, and the use of one or the other immediately stamps the utterance or written sequence as H or L.*

For example, in Arabic the H word for 'see' is *ra'ā*, the L word is *šāf*. The word *ra'ā* never occurs in ordinary conversation and *šāf* is not used in normal written Arabic. If for some reason a remark in which *šāf* was used is quoted in the press, it is replaced by *ra'ā* in the written quotation. In Greek the H word for 'wine' is *ínos*, the L word is *krasí*. The menu will have *ínos* written on it, but the diner will ask the waiter for *krasí*. The nearest American English parallels are such cases as *illuminatian* ~ *light*, *purchase* ~ *buy*, or *children* ~ *kids*, but in these cases both words may be written and both may be used in ordinary conversation: the gap is not so great as for the corresponding doublets in diglossia. Also, the formal–informal dimension in languages like English is a continuum in which the boundary between the two items in different pairs may not come at the same point, e.g. *illumination*, *purchase*, and *children* are not fully parallel in their formal–informal range of usage.

A dozen or so examples of lexical doublets from three of the sample languages are given in Table 1.2. For each language two nouns, a verb, and two particles are given.

It would be possible to present such a list of doublets for Swiss German (e.g. *nachdem* ≅ *no* 'after', *jemand* ≅ *öpper* 'someone', etc.), but this would give a false picture. In Swiss German the phonological differences between H and L are very great and the normal form of lexical pairing is regular cognation (*kiefli* ≅ *chly* 'small', etc.).

Phonology

It may seem difficult to offer any generalization on the relationships between the phonology of H and L in diglossia in view of the diversity of data. H and L phonologies may be quite close, as in Greek; moderately different, as in Arabic or Haitian Creole; or

Table 1.2   Lexical doublets

Greek		
H		L
íkos	house	*spíti*
ídhor	water	*neró*
éteke	gave birth	*eyénise*
alá	but	*má*

Arabic		
H		L
ḥiδā'un	shoe	*gazma*
'anfun	nose	*manaxīr*
δahaba	went	*rāh*
mā	what	*'ēh*
'al'āna	now	*dilwa'ti*

Creole		
H		L
homme, gens	person, people	*moun* (not connected with *monde*)
âne	donkey	*bourik*
donner	give	*bay*
beaucoup	much, a lot	*âpil*
maintenant	now	*kou-n-yé-a*

strikingly divergent, as in Swiss German. Closer examination, however, shows two statements to be justified. (Perhaps these will turn out to be unnecessary when the preceding features are stated so precisely that the statements about phonology can be deduced directly from them.)

1   *The sound systems of H and L constitute a single phonological structure of which the L phonology is the basic system and the divergent features of H phonology are either a subsystem or a parasystem.*

   Given the mixed forms mentioned above and the corresponding difficulty of identifying a given word in a given utterance as being definitely H or definitely L, it seems necessary to assume that the speaker has a single inventory of distinctive oppositions for the whole H–L complex and that there is extensive interference in both directions in terms of the distribution of phonemes in specific lexical items. (For details on certain aspects of this phonological interference in Arabic, cf. Ferguson, 1957.)

2   *If 'pure' H items have phonemes not found in 'pure' L items, L phonemes frequently substitute for these in oral use of H and regularly replace them in* tatsamas.

   For example, French has a high front rounded vowel phoneme /ü/; 'pure' Haitian Creole has no such phoneme. Educated speakers of Creole use this vowel in *tatsamas* such as *Luk* (/lük/ for the Gospel of St Luke), while they, like uneducated speakers, may sometimes use /i/ for it when speaking French. On the other hand /i/ is the regular vowel in such *tatsamas* in Creole as *linèt* 'glasses'.

In cases where H represents in large part an earlier stage of L, it is possible that a three-way correspondence will appear. For example, Syrian and Egyptian Arabic frequently use /s/ for /q/ in oral use of Classical Arabic, and have /s/ in *tatsamas*, but have /t/ in words regularly descended from earlier Arabic not borrowed from the Classical (see Ferguson, 1957).

Now that the characteristic features of diglossia have been outlined it is feasible to attempt a fuller definition: DIGLOSSIA *is a relatively stable language situation in which, in addition to the primary dialects of the language (which may include a standard or regional standards), there is a very divergent, highly codified (often grammatically more complex) superposed variety, the vehicle of a large and respected body of written literature, either of an earlier period or in another speech community, which is learned largely by formal education and is used for most written and formal spoken purposes but is not used by any sector of the community for ordinary conversation.*

With the characterization of diglossia completed we may turn to a brief consideration of three additional questions: How does diglossia differ from the familiar situation of a standard language with regional dialects? How widespread is the phenomenon of diglossia in space, time, and linguistic families? Under what circumstances does diglossia come into being and into what language situations is it likely to develop?

The precise role of the standard variety (or varieties) of a language *vis-à-vis* regional or social dialects differs from one speech community to another, and some instances of this relation may be close to diglossia or perhaps even better considered as diglossia. As characterized here, diglossia differs from the more widespread standard-with-dialects in that no segment of the speech community in diglossia regularly uses H as a medium of ordinary conversation, and any attempt to do so is felt to be either pedantic and artificial (Arabic, Greek) or else in some sense disloyal to the community (Swiss German, Creole). In the more usual standard-with-dialects situation the standard is often similar to the variety of a certain region or social group (e.g. Tehran Persian, Calcutta Bengali) which is used in ordinary conversation more or less naturally by members of the group and as a superposed variety by others.

Diglossia is apparently not limited to any geographical region or language family. (All clearly documented instances known to me are in literate communities, but it seems at least possible that a somewhat similar situation could exist in a non-literate community where a body of oral literature could play the same role as the body of written literature in the examples cited.) Three examples of diglossia from other times and places may be cited as illustrations of the utility of the concept. First, consider Tamil. As used by the millions of members of the Tamil speech community in India today, it fits the definition exactly. There is a literary Tamil as H used for writing and certain kinds of formal speaking, and a standard colloquial as L (as well as local L dialects) used in ordinary conversation. There is a body of literature in H going back many centuries which is highly regarded by Tamil speakers today. H has prestige, L does not. H is always superposed, L is learned naturally, whether as primary or as a superposed standard colloquial. There are striking grammatical differences and some phonological differences between the two varieties. (There is apparently no good description available of the precise relations of the two varieties of Tamil; an account of some of the structural differences is given by Pillai (1960). Incidentally, it may be noted that Tamil diglossia seems to go back many centuries, since the language of early literature contrasts sharply with the language of early inscriptions, which probably reflect the spoken language of the time.) The situation is only slightly complicated by the presence of Sanskrit and English for certain functions of H; the same kind of complication exists in parts of the Arab world where French, English, or a liturgical language such as Syriac or Coptic has certain H-like functions.

Second, we may mention Latin and the emergent Romance languages during a period of some centuries in various parts of Europe. The vernacular was used in ordinary conversation but Latin for writing or certain kinds of formal speech. Latin was the language of the Church and its literature, Latin had the prestige, there were striking grammatical differences between the two varieties in each area, etc.

Third, Chinese should be cited because it probably represents diglossia on the largest scale of any attested instance. (An excellent, brief description of the complex Chinese situation is available in the introduction to Chao (1947: 1–17).) The *weu-li* corresponds to H, while Mandarin colloquial is a standard L; there are also regional L varieties so different as to deserve the label 'separate languages' even more than the Arabic dialects, and at least as much as the emergent Romance languages in the Latin example. Chinese, however, like modern Greek, seems to be developing away from diglossia toward a standard-with-dialects, in that the standard L or a mixed variety is coming to be used in writing for more and more purposes, i.e. it is becoming a true standard.

Diglossia is likely to come into being when the following three conditions hold in a given speech community:

1   There is a sizable body of literature in a language closely related to (or even identical with) the natural language of the community, and this literature embodies, whether as source (e.g. divine revelation) or reinforcement, some of the fundamental values of the community.
2   Literacy in the community is limited to a small elite.
3   A suitable period of time, of the order of several centuries, passes from the establishment of (1) and (2).

It can probably be shown that this combination of circumstances has occurred hundreds of times in the past and has generally resulted in diglossia. Dozens of examples exist today, and it is likely that examples will occur in the future.

Diglossia seems to be accepted and not regarded as a 'problem' by the community in which it is in force, until certain trends appear in the community. These include trends toward:

1   more widespread literacy (whether for economic, ideological, or other reasons);
2   broader communication among different regional and social segments of the community (e.g. for economic, administrative, military, or ideological reasons);
3   desire for a full-fledged standard 'national' language as an attribute of autonomy or of sovereignty.

When these trends appear, leaders in the community begin to call for unification of the language, and for that matter, actual trends toward unification begin to take place.

These individuals tend to support either the adoption of H or of one form of L as the standard; less often the adoption of a modified H or L, a 'mixed' variety of some kind. The arguments explicitly advanced seem remarkably the same from one instance of diglossia to another.

The proponents of H argue that H must be adopted because it connects the community with its 'glorious past' or with the world community and because it is a naturally unifying factor as opposed to the divisive nature of the L dialects. In addition to these two fundamentally sound arguments there are usually pleas based on the beliefs of the community in the superiority of H: that it is more beautiful, more expressive, more logical; that it has divine sanction, or whatever the community's specific beliefs may be. When these latter arguments are examined objectively their validity is often quite limited, but their importance is still considerable because they reflect widely held attitudes within the community.

The proponents of L argue that some variety of L must be adopted because it is closer to the real thinking and feeling of the people; it eases the educational problem since people have already acquired a basic knowledge of it in early childhood; and it is a more effective instrument of communication at all levels. In addition to these fundamentally sound arguments there is often great emphasis given to points of lesser importance such as the vividness of metaphor in the colloquial, the fact that other 'modern nations' write very much as they speak, and so on.

The proponents of both sides or even of the mixed language seem to show the conviction – although this may not be explicitly stated – that a standard language can simply be legislated into place in a community. Often the trends which will be decisive in the development of a standard language are already at work and have little to do with the argumentation of the spokespeople for the various viewpoints.

A brief and superficial glance at the outcome of diglossia in the past and a consideration of present trends suggests that there are only a few general kinds of development likely to take place. First, we must remind ourselves that the situation may remain stable for long periods of time. But if the trends mentioned above do appear and become strong, change may take place. Second, H can succeed in establishing itself as a standard only if it is already serving as a standard language in some other community and the diglossia community – for reasons linguistic and non-linguistic – tends to merge with the other community. Otherwise H fades away and becomes a learned or liturgical language studied only by scholars or specialists and not used actively in the community. Some form of L or a mixed variety becomes standard.

Third, if there is a single communication center in the whole speech community – or if there are several such centers all in one dialect area – the L variety of the center(s) will be the basis of the new standard, whether relatively pure L or considerably mixed with H. If there are several such centers in different dialect areas with no one center paramount, then it is likely that several L varieties will become standard as separate languages.

A tentative prognosis for the four defining languages over the next two centuries (i.e. to about AD 2150) may be hazarded:

- Swiss German: relative stability;
- Arabic: slow development toward several standard languages, each based on an L variety with heavy admixture of H vocabulary; three seem likely:

- • Maghrebi (based on Rabat or Tunis?);
- • Egyptian (based on Cairo);
- • Eastern (based on Baghdad?);
- • unexpected politico-economic developments might add Syrian (based on Damascus?);
- • Sudanese (based on Omdurman-Khartoum), or others;
- • Haitian Creole: slow development toward unified standard based on L of Port-au-Prince;
- • Greek: full development to unified standard based on L of Athens plus heavy admixture of H vocabulary.

This paper concludes with an appeal for further study of this phenomenon and related ones. Descriptive linguists in their understandable zeal to describe the internal structure of the language they are studying often fail to provide even the most elementary data about the socio-cultural setting in which the language functions. Also, descriptivists usually prefer detailed descriptions of 'pure' dialects or standard languages rather than the careful study of the mixed, intermediate forms often in wider use. Study of such matters as diglossia is of clear value in understanding processes of linguistic change and presents interesting challenges to some of the assumptions of synchronic linguistics. Outside linguistics proper it promises material of great interest to social scientists in general, especially if a general frame of reference can be worked out for analysis of the use of one or more varieties of language within a speech community. Perhaps the collection of data and more profound study will drastically modify the impressionistic remarks of this paper, but if this is so the paper will have had the virtue of stimulating investigation and thought.

References on the four defining languages

The judgements of this chapter are based primarily on the author's personal experience, but documentation for the four defining languages is available, and the following references may be consulted for further details (see the Bibliography at the end of the book for full details). Most of the studies listed here take a strong stand in favor of greater use of the more colloquial variety since it is generally writers of this opinion who want to describe the facts. This bias can, however, be ignored by the reader who simply wants to discover the basic facts of the situation.

Modern Greek

Hatzidakis, 1905 (*Die Sprachfrage in Griechenland*)
Kahane *et al.*, 1945 (*Spoken Greek*)
Krumbacher, 1902 (*Das Problem der modernen griechischen Schriftsprache*)
Pernot, 1898 (*Grammaire Grecque Moderne*)
Psichari, 1928 (*Un Pays qui ne veut pas sa langue*)
Steinmetz, 1936 (*Schrift und Volksprache in Griechenland*)

Swiss German

Dieth, 1938 (*Schwyzertütsch Dialäkschrift*)
von Greyerz, 1933 (*Vom Wert und Wesen unserer Mundart*)
Kloss, 1952 (*Die Entwicklung neuer germanischer Kultursprachen von 1800 bis 1950*)
Schmid, 1936 (*Für unser Schweizerdeutsch*)
Senn, 1935 (*Das Verhältnis von Mundart und Schriftsprache in der deutschen Schweiz*)

Arabic

Al-Toma, 1957 (*The teaching of Classical Arabic to speakers of the colloquial in Iraq*)
Chejne, 1958 (*The role of Arabic in present-day Arab society*)
Lecerf, 1932 (*Littérature Dialectale et renaissance arabe moderne*)
Marçais, 1930–31 (*Three articles*)
Comhaire-Sylvain, 1936 (*Le Créole haitien*)
Hall, 1953 (*Haitian Creole*)
McConnell and Swan, 1945 (*You Can Learn Creole*)

Other references

Chao, 1947 (*Cantonese Primer*)
Ferguson, 1957 (*Two problems in Arabic phonology*)
Greenberg, 1954 (*A quantitative approach to the morphological typology of language*)
Pillai, 1960 (*Tamil: literary and colloquial*)
Shouby, 1951 (*The influence of the Arabic language on the psychology of the Arabs*)

Source: Ferguson, C.A. (1959) Diglossia. *Word* 15: 325–40, by permission of Shirley Brice Heath, executrix of Charles Ferguson's estates and the International Linguistics Association.

Charles A. Ferguson, PhD (1921–1998), was Professor of Linguistics at Stanford University, USA.

Chapter 2

Bilingualism with and without diglossia; diglossia with and without bilingualism

JOSHUA A. FISHMAN

Until the 1950s the psychological literature on bilingualism was so much more extensive than its sociological counterpart that workers in the former field have often failed to establish contact with those in the latter. Since the 1960s a very respectable sociological (or sociologically oriented) literature has developed dealing with bilingual societies. It is the purpose of this chapter to relate these two research traditions to each other by tracing the interaction between their two major constructs: bilingualism (on the part of psychologists) and diglossia (on the part of sociologists).

Diglossia

In the few years that have elapsed since Ferguson (1959) first advanced it, the term diglossia has not only become widely accepted by sociolinguists and sociologists of language, but it has been further extended and refined. Initially it was used in connection with a society that used two (or more) languages for internal (intra-society) communication. The use of several separate codes within a single society (and their stable maintenance rather than the displacement of one by the other over time) was found to be dependent on each code's serving functions distinct from those considered appropriate for the other. Whereas one set of behaviors, attitudes and values supported – and was expressed in – one language, another set of behaviors, attitudes and values supported and was expressed in the other. Both sets of behaviors, attitudes and values were fully accepted as culturally legitimate and complementary (i.e., nonconflictual) and indeed, little if any conflict between them was possible in view of the functional separation between them. This separation was most often along the lines of a High (H) language, on the one hand utilized in conjunction with religion, education and other aspects of high culture, and a Low (L) language, on the other hand, utilized in conjunction with everyday pursuits of hearth, home and work. Ferguson spoke of H and L as superposed languages.

To this original edifice others have added several significant considerations. Gumperz (1961; 1962; 1964; 1964a; 1966) is primarily responsible for our current awareness that diglossia exists not only in multilingual societies which officially recognize several "languages" but, also, in societies which are multilingual in the sense that they employ separate dialects, registers or functionally differentiated language varieties of whatever kind. He has also done the lion's share of the work in providing the conceptual apparatus by means of which investigators of multilingual speech communities seek to discern the societal patterns that govern the use of one variety rather than another, particularly at the level of small group interaction. On the other hand, I have attempted to trace the maintenance of diglossia as well as its disruption at the national level (Fishman, 1964; 1965a; 1965c; 1965d; 1965e; 1966b; 1966c), and in addition have attempted to relate diglossia to psychologically pertinent considerations such as compound and co-ordinate bilingualism (1965). The present chapter represents an extension and integration of these several previous attempts.

For purposes of simplicity it seems best to represent the possible relationships between bilingualism and diglossia by means of a four-fold table such as that shown in Figure 2.1.

Speech communities characterized by both diglossia and bilingualism

The first quadrant of Figure 2.1 refers to those speech communities in which both diglossia and bilingualism occur. At times such communities comprise an entire nation, but of course this requires very widespread (if not all-pervasive) bilingualism. An example of this type of nation is Paraguay, where almost the entire population speaks both Spanish and Guarani (Rubin, 1962; 1968). The formerly monolingual rural population has added Spanish to its linguistic repertoire in order to talk and write about education, religion, government, high culture and social distance or, more generally, the status stressing spheres; whereas the majority of city dwellers (being relatively new from the country) maintain Guarani for matters of intimacy and primary group solidarity even in the midst of Spanish urbanity. A further example is the Swiss-German cantons in which the entire population of school age and older alternates between High German (H) and Swiss German (L), each with its own firmly established and highly valued functions (Weinreich, 1951; 1953; Ferguson, 1959).

Below the level of nationwide functioning there are many more examples of stable diglossia co-occurring with widespread bilingualism. Traditional (pre-First World War) Eastern European Jewish males communicated in Hebrew (H) and Yiddish (L). In more

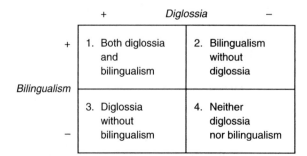

Figure 2.1 The relationship between bilingualism and diglossia

recent days their descendents have continued to do so, adding to their repertoire a Western language (notably English) for *intragroup* communication as well as in domains of *intergroup* contact (Weinreich, 1951; 1953; 1962; Fishman, 1965d).[2] A similar example is that of upper and upper middle-class males throughout the Arabic world who use classical (koranic) and vernacular (Egyptian, Syrian, Lebanese, Iraqui, etc.) Arabic and, not infrequently, also a Western language (French or English, most usually) for purposes of *intragroup* scientific or technological communication (Ferguson, 1959; Nader, 1962; Blanc, 1964).

All of the foregoing examples have in common the existence of a fairly large and complex speech community in which the members have available to them both a range of *compartmentalized* roles as well as ready *access* to these roles. If the *role repertoires* of these speech communities were of lesser range, then their *linguistic repertoires* would, also be, or become, more restricted in range, with the result that separate languages or varieties would be, or become, superfluous. In addition, were the roles not compartmentalized, i.e., were they not *kept separate* by dint of association with quite separate (though complementary) values, domains of activity and everyday situations,[3] one language (or variety) would displace the other as role and value distinctions merged and became blurred. Finally, were widespread access not available to the variety of compartmentalized roles (and compartmentalized languages or varieties), then the bilingual population would be a small, privileged caste or class (as it is or was throughout most of traditional India or China) rather than a broadly based population segment.

These observations lead to the conclusion that many modern speech communities that are normally thought of as monolingual are, rather, marked by both diglossia and bilingualism if their several registers (speech varieties related to functional specificity; Halliday, 1964) are viewed as separate varieties or languages in the same sense as the examples listed above. Wherever speech communities exist whose speakers engage in a considerable range of roles (and this is coming to be the case for all but the extremely upper and lower levels of complex societies); wherever access to several roles is encouraged or facilitated by powerful social institutions and processes; and finally, wherever the roles are clearly differentiated (in terms of when, where and with whom they are felt to be appropriate), both diglossia and bilingualism may be said to exist. The benefit of this approach to the topic at hand is that it provides a single theoretical framework for viewing bilingual speech communities and speech communities whose linguistic diversity is realized through varieties not (yet) recognized as constituting separate "languages." Thus, it becomes possible for us to note that while nations characterized by diglossia and widespread bilingualism (the latter term being understood in its usual sense of referring to separate languages) have become fewer in modern times, those characterized by diglossia and diversified linguistic repertoires have increased greatly as a consequence of modernization and growing social complexity. The single theory outlined above enabling us to understand, predict and interrelate both of these phenomena is an instance of enviable parsimony in the behavioral sciences.[4]

Diglossia without bilingualism

There are situations in which diglossia obtains whereas bilingualism is generally absent (quadrant 3). Here, two or more speech communities are united religiously, politically or economically into a single functioning unit notwithstanding the socio-cultural cleavages that separate them. At the level of this larger (but not always voluntary) unity, two or more languages or varieties are recognized as obtaining. However, one (or both) of the speech communities involved is (are) marked by relatively impermeable group boundaries such that for "outsiders" (and this may well mean all those not born into the speech community, i.e., an emphasis on ascribed rather than on achieved status) role access and linguistic access are severely restricted. At the same time, linguistic repertoires in one or both groups are limited due to role specialization.

Examples of such situations are not hard to find (see, e.g., the many instances listed by Kloss, 1966). Pre-First World War European elites often stood in this relationship with their countrymen, the elites speaking French or some other fashionable H tongue for their *intragroup* purposes (at various times and in various places: Danish, Salish, Provençal, Russian, etc.) and the masses speaking another, not necessarily linguistically related, language for their intragroup purposes. Since the majority of elites and the majority of the masses never interacted with one another *they did not form a single speech community* (i.e., their linguistic repertoires were discontinuous) and their inter-communications were via translators or interpretors (a certain sign of *intragroup* mono-lingualism). Since the majority of the elites and the majority of the masses led lives characterized by extremely narrow role repertoires their linguistic repertoires too were too narrow to permit widespread societal bilingualism to develop. Nevertheless, the body politic in all of its economic and national manifestations tied these two groups together into a "unity" that revealed an upper and a lower class, each with a language appropriate to its own restricted concerns.

Thus, the existence of national diglossia does *not* imply widespread bilingualism amongst rural or recently urbanized African groups (as distinguished from Westernized elites in those settings); nor amongst most lower caste Hindus, as distinguished from their more fortunate compatriots the Brahmins, nor amongst most lower class French-Canadians, as distinguished from their upper and upper middle-class city cousins, etc. In general, this pattern is characteristic of polities that are economically underdeveloped and unmobilized, combining groups that are locked into opposite extremes of the social spectrum and, therefore, groups that operate within extremely restricted and dis-continuous linguistic repertoires. Obviously, such polities are bound to experience language problems as their social patterns alter in the direction of industrialization, widespread literacy and education, democratization, and modernization more generally. Since such polities rarely developed out of initial socio-cultural consensus or unity, the educational, political and economic development of the lower classes is likely to lead to secessionism or to demands for equality for submerged language(s). The linguistic states of Eastern Europe and India, and the language problems of Wales, Canada and Belgium stem from origins such as these.[5] This is the pattern of development that may yet convulse modern African nations if their de-ethnicized Westernized elites and diglossic language policies continue to fail to create bilingual speech communities, incorporating the masses, within their ethnically arbitrary political boundaries.

Bilingualism without diglossia

We turn next to those situations in which bilingualism obtains whereas diglossia is generally absent (quadrant 2 in Figure 2.1). Here we see even more clearly than before that bilingualism is essentially a characterization of individual linguistic behavior whereas diglossia is a characterization of linguistic organization at the socio-cultural level. Under what circumstances do bilinguals of similar cultural extraction nevertheless function without the benefit of a well-understood and widely accepted social consensus as to which language is to be used between which interlocutors, for communication concerning what topics or for what purposes? Under what circumstances do the varieties or languages involved lack well-defined or protected separate functions? Briefly put, these are circumstances of rapid social change, of great social unrest, of widespread abandonment of prior norms before the consolidation of new ones.

Many studies of bilingualism and intelligence or of bilingualism and school achievement have been conducted within the context of bilingualism without diglossia, often without sufficient understanding on the part of investigators that this was but one of several possible contexts for the study of bilingualism. As a result many of the purported "disadvantages" of bilingualism have been falsely generalized to the phenomenon at large rather than related to the absence or presence of social patterns which reach substantially beyond bilingualism (Fishman, 1965c; 1968).

The history of industrialization in the Western world (as well as in those parts of Africa and Asia which have experienced industrialization under Western "auspices") is such that the means (capital, plant, organization) of production were often derived from one speech community while the productive manpower was drawn from another. Initially both speech communities may have maintained their separate diglossia-with-bilingualism patterns or, alternatively, that of an over-arching diglossia without bilingualism. In either case, the needs as well as the consequences of rapid and massive industrialization and urbanization were frequently such that members of the speech community providing a productive workforce rapidly abandoned their traditional socio-cultural patterns and learned (or were taught) the language of the means of production much earlier than their absorption into the socio-cultural patterns and privileges to which that language pertained. In response to this imbalance some react (or reacted) by further stressing the advantages of the newly gained language of education and industry while others react (or reacted) by seeking to replace the latter by an elaborated version of their own largely pre-industrial, pre-urban, pre-mobilization tongue.

Under circumstances such as these no well-established, socially recognized and protected functional differentiation of languages obtains in many speech communities of the lower and lower middle classes. Dislocated immigrants and their children (for whom a separate "political solution" is seldom possible) are particularly inclined to use their mother tongue and other tongue for intragroup communication in seemingly random fashion (Nahirny and Fishman, 1965; Fishman, 1965c). Since the formerly separate roles of the home domain, the school domain and the work domain are all disturbed by the massive dislocation of values and norms that result from simultaneous immigration and industrialization, the language of work (and of the school) comes to be used at home (just as in cases of more radical and better organized social change the language of the home comes to be established in school and at work). As role compartmentalization and value complementarity decrease under the impact of foreign models and massive change the linguistic repertoire also becomes less compartmentalized. Languages and varieties formerly kept apart come to influence each other phonetically, lexically, semantically and even grammatically much more than before. Instead of two (or more) carefully separated languages each under the eye of caretaker groups of teachers, preachers and writers, several intervening varieties may obtain, differing in degree of interpenetration.

Such fused varieties may, within time, become the mother tongue and only tongue of a new generation. Thus, bilingualism without diglossia tends to be transitional[6] both in terms of the linguistic repertoires of speech communities as well as in terms of the speech varieties involved per se. Without separate though complementary norms and values to establish and maintain functional separation of the speech varieties, that language or variety which is fortunate enough to be associated with the predominant drift of social forces tends to displace the other(s). Furthermore, pidginization is likely to set in when members of the workforce are so dislocated as not to be able to maintain or develop significantly compartmentalized, limited access roles (in which they might be able to safeguard a stable mother-tongue variety) and, furthermore, cannot interact sufficiently with those members of the "power class" who might serve as standard other-tongue models.

Neither diglossia nor bilingualism

Only very small, isolated and undifferentiated speech communities may be said to reveal neither diglossia nor bilingualism (Gumperz, 1962; Fishman, 1965e). Given little role differentiation or compartmentalization and frequent face-to-face interaction between all members of the speech community no fully differentiated registers or varieties may establish themselves. Given self-sufficiency no regular or significant contacts with other speech communities may be maintained. Nevertheless, such groups – be they bands or clans – are easier to hypothesize than to find. All communities seem to have certain ceremonies or pursuits to which access is limited, if only on an age basis. Thus, all linguistic repertoires contain certain terms that are unknown to certain members of the speech community, and certain terms that are used differently by different subsets of speakers. In addition, metaphorical switching (Blom and Gumperz, 1972) for purposes of emphasis, humor, satire or criticism must be available in some form even in relatively undifferentiated communities. Finally, such factors as exogamy, warfare, expansion of population, economic growth and contact with others all lead to internal diversification and, consequently, to repertoire diversification. Such diversification is the beginning of bilingualism. Its societal normification is the hallmark of diglossia. Quadrant 4 of Figure 2.1 tends to be self liquidating.

Many efforts are now underway to bring to pass a rapprochement between psychological, linguistic and sociological work on bilingualism. The student of bilingualism – most particularly the student of bilingualism in the context of social issues and social change – may benefit from an awareness of the various possible relationships between individual bilingualism and societal diglossia illustrated in this paper. Since all bilingualism occurs in a social context, and since this context is likely to influence both the manifestations and the concomitants of bilingualism, it is incumbent on the student of bilingualism to differentiate accurately between the particular and the more general phenomena that pertain to his field of study.

Notes

1   Note that Guarani is not an official language (i.e., recognized and utilized for purposes of government, formal education, the courts, etc.) in Paraguay. It is not uncommon for the H variety alone to have such recognition in diglossic settings without this fact threatening

the acceptance or the stability of the L variety within the speech community. However, the existence of a single "official" language should not divert the investigator from recognizing the fact of widespread and stable bilingualism at the levels of societal and interpersonal functioning.

2   This development differs significantly from the traditional Eastern European Jewish pattern in which males whose occupational activities brought them into regular contact with various strata of the non-Jewish coterritorial population utilized one or more coterritorial languages (usually involving H and L varieties of their own, such as Russian, German or Polish on the one hand, and Ukrainian, Byelorussian or "Baltic" varieties (e.g. Estonian, Latvian and Lithuanian), on the other), but did so for *intergroup* purposes almost exclusively.

3   The compartmentalization of roles (and of domains and situations as well) requires the redefinition of roles, domains and situations in any encounter in which a seemingly inappropriate topic must be discussed between individuals who normally stand in a given role relationship to each other. Under such circumstances one or other factor is altered (the roles are redefined, the topic is redefined) so as to preserve the cultural norms for appropriateness (grammaticality) of behavior between interlocutors.

4   A theory which tends to minimize the distinction between languages and varieties is desirable for several reasons. It implies that *social* consensus (rather than inherently linguistic desiderata) differentiates between the two and that separate varieties can become (and have become) separate languages given certain social encouragement to do so, just as purportedly separate languages have been fused into one, on the ground that they were merely different varieties of the same language.

5   Switzerland as a whole is not a case in point since it is not an example of discontinuous and hierarchically stratified speech communities under a common political regime. Switzerland consists of geographically stratified speech communities under a common regime. Except for the Swiss-German case there is hardly any societally patterned bilingualism in Switzerland. Only the Jura region, the Romansch area and a very few other small areas have (had) a recent history of diglossia without bilingualism.

6   At an individual level this need not be the case since translation bilingualism can be maintained for intragroup communication purposes and for individual vocational purposes without the formation of natural bilingual speech communities.

Source: Fishman, J.A. (1967) Bilingualism with and without diglossia; diglossia with and without bilingualism. *Journal of Social Issues* 23(2): 29–38, by permission of the author and Blackwell Publishing.

Postscript

This framework for empirical research and theoretical elaboration is still very much alive and in use, particularly at the macrolevel for which it was originally intended. It has been extensively referred to and is the major theoretical and empirical organizational paradigm in use. Ausbau and abstand discussions have most recently been enriched by a new dimension, labeled "einbau," and if this proves to be a useful contribution, particularly at the level of "policy" development, the overall nature of ausbau/abstand distinctions will probably increasingly develop in the direction of viewing both of them as continua (e.g. in terms of "degree of ausbauization") rather than as the dichotomies that they are now conceived of.

Joshua A. Fishman, PhD, is Distinguished University Research Professor Emeritus of Social Sciences of Yeshiva University, USA.
JoshuaAFishman@aol.com

Chapter 3

Who speaks what language to whom and when?

JOSHUA A. FISHMAN

The analysis of multilingual settings

Multilingual settings differ from each other in so many ways that every student of multilingualism must grapple with the problem of how best to systematize or organize the manifold differences that are readily recognizable. This chapter is primarily limited to a formal consideration of several descriptive and analytic variables which may contribute to an understanding of *who* speaks *what* language *to whom* and *when* in those settings that are characterized by widespread and relatively stable multilingualism. It deals primarily with "within-group (or intragroup) multilingualism" rather than with "between-group (or intergroup) multilingualism," that is with those multilingual settings in which a single population makes use of two (or more) separate codes for internal communicative purposes. As a result of this limitation, general knowledge of mother tongue and other tongue may be ruled out as an operative variable since most individuals *could* communicate with each other quite easily in *either* of the available languages. It seems clear, however, that habitual language choice is far from being a random matter of momentary inclination, even under those circumstances when it could very well function as such from a purely probabilistic point of view. "Proper" usage, or common usage, or both, dictate that only *one* of the theoretically co-available languages *will* be chosen by particular classes of *interlocutors* on particular *occasions*.

How can these choice-patterns be described? Our basic conceptual problem in this connection is to provide for the variety of patterns that exist in stable within-group multi-lingual settings throughout the world in such a way as to attain factual accuracy, theoretical parsimony and stimulation of future research. Once we have mastered the problem of how to describe language choice on the level of individual face-to-face encounters, we can then approach the problem of the broader, underlying choice determinants on the level of larger group or cultural settings (Fishman, 1964). Once we have mastered the problem of how to describe language choice in stable within-group bilingual settings (where the limits of language mastery do not intrude), we can then approach the problem of choice determinants in less stable settings such as those characterizing immigrant– host relationships and between-group multilingual settings more generally.

Group, situation, topic

(a) One of the first controlling factors in language choice is *group membership*. This factor must be viewed not only in a purportedly objective sense, i.e., in terms of physiological, sociological criteria (e.g., age, sex, race, religion, etc.), but also, and primarily, in the subjective socio-psychological sense of *reference group membership*. A government functionary in Brussels arrives home after stopping off at his club for a drink. He generally speaks standard French in his office, standard Dutch at his club and a distinctly local variant of Flemish at home.[1] In each instance he identifies himself with a different group to which he belongs, wants to belong, and from which he seeks acceptance. Nevertheless, it is not difficult to find occasions at the office in which he speaks or is spoken to in one or another variety of Flemish. There are also occasions at the club when he speaks or is addressed in French; finally, there are occasions at home when he communicates in standard Dutch or even French. It would be too much to claim that a shift in reference group occurs on *each* of these supposedly atypical occasions. In addition, the very existence of certain reference groups (e.g., club member) seems to depend largely on location, setting or other environmental factors (which, we will see, may deserve recognition in their own right rather than need to remain hidden under a vague "group" rubric), rather than on group-consciousness or group-experience as such. Finally, even were this not to be the case, it seems unnecessarily difficult to analyze language choice within large, complex, literate societies in terms of the enormous repertoire of shifting reference groups which these provide. Thus, while we may admit that the concept of reference group membership enables us to recognize *some* invariables of habitual language choice in stable multilingual settings (e.g., that our hypothetical functionary *is* Flemish and would probably know no Dutch Flemish at all were this not the case), it does so only at a considerable risk, while leaving many exceptional cases in the dark. Obviously, additional clarificatory concepts are needed.

(b) A further regulating factor is recognized via the concept of *situation*.[2] This term has been used to designate a large (and, at times, confusing) variety of considerations. Indeed, it has been used to designate various *separate* considerations as well as their *co-occurrence*. Thus, Ervin (1964) observes that various situations (settings) may be restricted with respect to the *participants* who may be present, the *physical setting*, the *topics* and *functions* of discourse and the *style* employed (my italics). Each of these aspects of "situation" may shed light on certain regularities in language choice on particular social occasions. However, the possible *co-occurrence* of so many variables must also make it exceedingly difficult to use the concept "situation," when so characterized, for analytic purposes. Let us, therefore, limit our use of this term to considerations of "style" alone, and attempt to cope with the other itemized features in other ways and in their own right. Situational styles, following Joos (1962), Labov (1963), Gumperz and Naim (1960) and others, pertain to considerations of intimacy–distance, formality–informality, solidarity–non-solidarity, status (or power) equality–inequality, etc. Thus, certain styles within every language (and, in multilingual settings, certain languages in contrast to others) are considered by particular interlocutors to be indicators of greater intimacy, informality, equality, etc. Not only do multilinguals frequently consider one of their languages more dialectal, more regional, more sub-standard, more vernacular-like, more argot-like than the others, but, in addition, they more frequently associate one of their languages with informality, equality, solidarity than the other. As a result, one is more likely to be reserved for certain situations than the other. Our hypothetical government functionary is most likely to give and get Flemish at the office when he bumps into another functionary who hails from the very same Flemish-speaking town. The two of them grew up together and went to school together. Their respective sets of parents strike them as being similarly "kind-but-old-fashioned." In short, they share many common experiences and points of view (or think they do, or pretend they do) and therefore they tend to speak to each other in the language which represents for them the intimacy that they share. The two do not cease being government functionaries when they speak Flemish to each other; they simply prefer to treat each other as intimates rather than as functionaries. However, the careful observer will also note that the two do not speak Flemish to each other invariably. When they speak about work affairs, or the worlds of art and literature, not to mention the world of government, they tend to switch into French (or to reveal far greater interference in their Flemish), even though (for the sake of our didactic argument) the mood of intimacy and familiarity remains clearly evident throughout. Thus, neither reference group membership nor situational style, alone or in concert, fully explain(s) the variations that can be noted in habitual language choice in multilingual settings. It must also be observed that situational styles, however carefully delineated, may still not provide us with much substantive or procedural insight into the socio-cultural organization of any particular multilingual setting.

(c) The fact that two individuals who obviously prefer to speak to each other in X nevertheless switch to Y (or vacillate more noticeably between X and Y) when discussing certain topics leads us to consider topic per se as a regulator of language use in multilingual settings. It is obviously possible to talk about the national economy (topic) in a thoroughly informal way (situational style) while relating oneself to one's family (reference group). Under such circumstances – even when reference group and situation agree in requiring a particular language – it is not uncommon to find that topic succeeds in bringing another language to the fore.[3]

The implication of topical regulation of language choice is that certain topics are somehow handled better in one language than in another in particular multilingual contexts. This situation may be brought about by several different but mutually reinforcing factors. Thus, some multilingual speakers may "acquire the habit" of speaking about topic x in language X partially because that is the language in which they were *trained* to deal with this topic (e.g., they received their university training in economics in French), partially because *they (and their interlocutors) may lack the specialized terms* for a satisfying discussion of x in language Y, partially because *language Y itself may currently lack as exact or as many terms for handling* topic x as those currently possessed by language X, and partially because *it is considered strange* or inappropriate to discuss x in language Y. The very multiplicity of sources of topical regulation suggests that *topic* may not in itself be a convenient analytic variable when language choice is considered from the point of view of the social structure and the cultural norms of a multilingual setting. It tells us little about either the process or the structure of social behavior. However, topics usually exhibit patterns which follow those of the major spheres of activity in the society under consideration. We may be able to discover the latter if we enquire why a significant number of people in a particular multilingual setting at a particular time have received certain kinds of training in one language rather than in another; or *what it reveals* about a particular multilingual setting if language X *is* actually less capable of coping with topic *x* than is language Y. Does it not reveal more than merely a topic–language relationship at the level of face-to-face encounters? Does it not reveal that certain socio-culturally *recognized spheres of activity* are, at least temporarily, under the sway of one language (and, therefore, perhaps of one sub-population) rather than another? Thus, while topic is doubtlessly a crucial consideration in understanding language choice variance in our two hypothetical government functionaries, we must seek a means of examining and relating their individual, momentary choices to relatively stable patterns of choice that exist in their multilingual setting as a whole.

Domains of language behavior

(a) The concept of domains of language behavior seems to have received its first partial elaboration from students of language maintenance and language shift among *Auslands-deutsche* in pre-Second World War multilingual settings.[4] German settlers were in contact with many different non-German speaking populations in various types of contact settings and were exposed to various kinds of socio-cultural change processes. In attempting to chart and compare the fortunes of the German language under such varying circumstances Schmidt-Rohr (1963) seems to have been the first to suggest that *dominance configurations* (to be discussed below) needed to be established to reveal the overall status of language choice in various domains of behavior. The domains recommended by Schmidt-Rohr were the following nine: the family, the playground and street, the school (subdivided into language of instruction, subject of instruction, and language of recess and entertainment), the church, literature, the press, the military, the courts, and the governmental administration. Subsequently, other investigators either added additional domains (e.g., Mak, 1935, who nevertheless followed Schmidt-Rohr in overlooking the work-sphere as a domain), or found that fewer domains were sufficient in particular multilingual settings (e.g., Frey, 1945, who required only home, school and church in his analysis of Amish "triple talk"). However, what is more interesting is that Schmidt-Rohr's domains bear a striking similarity to those "generally termed" spheres of activity which have more recently been independently advanced by some anthropologists (Dohrenwend and Smith, 1962), sociologists (Kloss, 1929), social psychologists (Jones and Lambert, 1959) and linguists (Mackey, 1962) for the study of acculturation, intergroup relations, and bilingualism. The latter are defined, regardless of their number,[5] in terms of *institutional contexts* or *socio-ecological co-occurrences*. They attempt to designate the *major clusters of interaction situations that occur in particular multilingual settings*. Domains such as these help us understand that *language choice* and *topic*, appropriate though they may be for analyses of individual behavior at the level of face-to-face verbal encounters, are, as we suggested above, related to widespread socio-cultural norms and expectations. Language choices, cumulated over many individuals and many choice instances, become transformed into the processes of *language mainten-ance* or *language shift*. Furthermore, if many individuals (or sub-groups) tend to handle topic *x* in language X, this may well be because this topic pertains to a *domain* in which that language is "dominant" for their society or for their sub-group as a whole. Certainly it is a far different social interaction when topic *x* is discussed in language Y *although it pertains to a domain in which language X is dominant*, than when the same topic is discussed by the same interlocutors in the language most commonly employed in that domain. By recognizing the existence of domains it becomes possible to contrast the language of topics for individuals or particular sub-populations with the language of domains for larger parts, if not the whole, of the population.

(b) The appropriate designation and definition of domains of language behavior obviously calls for considerable insight into the socio-cultural dynamics of particular multilingual settings at particular periods in their history. Schmidt-Rohr's domains reflect not only multilingual settings in which a large number of spheres of activity, even those that pertain to governmental functions, are theoretically open to both or all of the languages present, but also those multilingual settings in which such permissiveness is at least sought by a sizable number of interested parties. Quite different domains might be appropriate if one were to study habitual language use among children in these very same settings. Certainly, immigrant-host contexts, in which only the language of the host society is recognized for governmental functions, would require other and perhaps fewer domains, particularly if younger generations constantly leave the immigrant society and enter the host society. Finally, the domains of language behavior may differ from setting to setting not only in terms of number and designation but also in terms of level. Thus, in studying acculturating populations in Arizona, Barker (who studied bilingual Spanish Americans; 1947) and Barber (who studied trilingual Yaqui Indians; 1952) formulated *domains at the level of socio-psychological analysis*: intimate, informal, formal and intergroup. Interestingly enough, the domains defined in this fashion were then identified with domains at the *societal-institutional level* mentioned above. The "formal" domain, e.g., was found to coincide with religious-ceremonial activities; the "inter-group" domain consisted of economic and recreational activities as well as of interactions with govern- mental-legal authority, etc. The inter-relationship between domains of language behavior defined at a societal-institutional level and domains defined at a socio-psychological level (the latter being somewhat similar to situational analyses discussed earlier) may enable us to study language choice in multilingual settings in newer and more fruitful ways. We will present one approach to the study of just such inter-relationships in our discussion of the *dominance configuration*, below.

(c) The "governmental administration" domain is a social nexus which brings people together *primarily* for a certain *cluster of purposes*. Furthermore, it brings them together *primarily* for a certain set of role-relations (discussed below) and in a delimited environment. Although it is possible for them to communicate about many things, given these purposes and contexts, the topical variety is actually quite small in certain media (e.g., written communication) and in certain situations (e.g., formal communication), and is noticeably skewed in the direction of *domain purpose* in most domains. Thus, domain is a socio-cultural construct abstracted from topics of communication, relation-ships between communicators, and locales of communication, in accord with the institu-tions of a society and the spheres of activity of a culture, in such a way that *individual behavior and social patterns can be distinguished from each other and yet related to each other.*[6] The domain is a higher order of abstraction or summarization which is arrived at from a consideration of the socio-cultural patterning which surrounds language choices. Of the many factors contributing to and subsumed under the domain concept some are more important and more accessible to careful measurement than others. One of these, topic, has already been discussed. Another, role-relations, remains to be discussed. Role-relations may be of value to us in accounting for the fact that our two hypothetical governmental functionaries, who usually speak an informal variant of Flemish to each other at the office, except when they talk about technical, professional or sophisticated "cultural" matters, are themselves not entirely alike in this respect. One of the two tends to slip into French more frequently than the other, even when reference group, situational style, topic and several other aspects of communication are controlled. It would not be surprising to discover that his role is different, that he is the supervisor of the other for example.

Domains and role-relations

In many studies of multilingual behavior the family domain has proved to be a very crucial one. Multilingualism often begins in the family and depends upon it for encouragement if not for protection. In other cases, multilingualism withdraws into the family domain after it has been displaced from other domains in which it was previously encountered. Little wonder then that many investigators, beginning with Braunshausen (1928), have differentiated *within* the family domain in terms of "speakers." However, two different approaches have been followed in connection with such differentiation. Braunshausen (and also Mackey, 1962) have merely specified family "members": father, mother, child, domestic, governess and tutor, etc. Gross (1951), on the other hand, has specified *dyads* within the family: grandfather to grandmother, grandmother to grandfather, grandfather to father, grandmother to father, grandfather to mother, grandmother to mother, grandfather to child, grandmother to child, father to mother, mother to father, etc. The difference between these two approaches is quite considerable. Not only does the second approach recognize that interacting members of a family (as well as the participants in most other domains of language behavior) are *hearers* as well as *speakers* (i.e., that there may be a distinction between multilingual *comprehension* and multilingual *production*), but it also recognizes that their language behavior may be more than merely a matter of individual preference or facility but also a matter of *role-relations*. In certain societies particular behaviors (including language behaviors) are *expected* (if not required) of *particular individuals vis-à-vis each other*. Whether role-relations are fully reducible to situational styles for the purpose of describing habitual language choice in particular multilingual settings is a matter for future empirical research.

The family domain is hardly unique with respect to its differentiability into role-relations. Each domain can be differentiated into role-relations that are specifically crucial or typical of it in particular societies at particular times. The religious domain (in those societies where religion can be differentiated from folkways more generally) may reveal such role relations as cleric–cleric, cleric–parishioner, parishioner–cleric, and parishioner–parishioner. Similarly, pupil–teacher, buyer–seller, employer–employee, judge–petitioner, all refer to specific role-relations in other domains. It would certainly seem desirable to describe and analyze language use or language choice in a particular multilingual setting in terms of the crucial role-relations within the specific domains considered to be most revealing for that setting. The distinction between one-group-interlocutor and other-group-interlocutor may also be provided for in this way.[7]

Domains and other sources of variance in language behavior

Our discussion thus far has probably succeeded in making at least one thing clear, namely that any simultaneous attempt to cope with *all of the theoretically possible* sources of variance in language behavior in multilingual settings is likely to be exceedingly complex. It is even more complex than indicated thus far, for we have not yet attended to the questions of what *kind of language data to recognize* in a study of multilingualism or of language maintenance and language shift. Should we follow the linguist's dominant tradition of testing for phonetic, lexical and grammatical interference (not to mention semantic interference) in the several interacting languages? Should we follow the psychologist in testing for relative speed or automaticity of translation or response? Should we follow the educator in testing for relative global proficiency? Certainly, each of these traditional approaches is legitimate and important. However, each of them has been set aside in the discussion below, in favor of the sociologist's grosser concern with *relative frequency of use*, a perspective on multilingualism which seems to be particularly appropriate for the study of language maintenance or language shift (Fishman, 1964). However, even when we limit ourselves in this fashion we can barely begin to approximate data collection and analysis in accord with all possible interactions between the many sources of variance and domains of language use mentioned thus far. Any study of multilingualism can select only an appropriate sub-cluster of variables for simultaneous study. Hopefully, all other variables can remain, temporarily, at the level of unexplained error variance until they too can be subjected to study.

For the purpose of illuminating patterns of language choice in multilingual settings, it would seem appropriate to distinguish at least between the following sources of variance:

1   *Media variance: writing, reading and speaking*: Degree of mother tongue maintenance or displacement may be quite different in each of these very different media.[8] Where literacy has been attained *prior* to interaction with an "other tongue" reading and writing use of the mother tongue may resist displacement longer than speaking usage. Where literacy is attained subsequent to (or as a result of) such interaction the reverse more frequently obtains (Fishman, 1964).

2   *Role[9] variance*: Degree of maintenance or shift may be quite different in conjunction with *inner speech* (the language of thought, of talking to one's self, the language of dreams, in short, all of those cases in which ego is both source and target), *comprehension* (decoding, in which ego is the target), and *production* (encoding, in which ego is the source). There is some evidence from individual as well as from group data that where language shift is resisted by multilinguals, inner speech remains most resistant to interference, switching and disuse of the mother tongue. Where language shift is desired the reverse frequently obtains (Fishman, 1964).

3   *Situational variance*: Degree of maintenance or shift may be quite different in conjunction with *more formal, less formal* and *intimate* communication (Fishman, 1965a). Where language shift is resisted more intimate situations seem to be most resistant to interference, switching or disuse of the mother tongue. The reverse obtains where language shift is desired.

4   *Domain variance*: Degree of maintenance or shift may be quite different in each of several distinguishable domains of language behavior. Such differences may reflect differences between interacting populations and their socio-cultural systems with respect to autonomy, power, influence, domain centrality, etc. Domains require sub-analysis in terms of the role-relations that are crucial to them, as well as sub-analysis in terms of topical variance.

A description and analysis of the *simultaneous, cumulative effect* of all of the above-mentioned sources of variance in language choice provides a dominance configuration (Weinrich, 1953). Dominance configurations summarize data on the language choice behavior of many individuals who constitute a defined sub-population. Repeated dominance configurations for the same population, studied over time, may be used to represent the evolution of language maintenance and language shift in a particular multilingual setting. Contrasted dominance configurations may be used to study the relative impact of *various* socio-cultural processes (urbanization, secularization, revitalization, etc.) on the *same* mother tongue group in different contact settings, or the relative impact of a *single* socio-cultural process on *different* mother tongue groups in similar contact settings (Fishman, 1964).

The dominance configuration

Table 3.1 is primarily intended as a summary derived from an attempt to estimate the relationships obtaining between *domains* of language behavior and the particular *sources of variance* in language behavior specified earlier. The resulting dominance configuration reveals several general characteristics of this mode of analysis:

1   A complete cross-tabulation of all theoretically possible sources and domains of variance in language behavior does not actually obtain. Certain co-occurrences appear to be logically impossible. Other co-occurrences, while logically possible, are either necessarily rare or so rare for the particular population under study that it may not be necessary to provide for them in the dominance configuration.

2   Each cell in the dominance configuration summarizes detailed process data pertaining to the particular role-relations most pertinent to it and the topical range encountered.

3   The domains of language behavior that figure in a particular dominance configuration are selected for their demonstrated utility (or for their theoretical promise) in analyzing language choice in a particular multilingual setting at a particular time.

4   An exhaustive analysis of the data of dominance configurations may well require sophisticated pattern analyses or other mathematical techniques which do not necessarily assume equal weight and simple additivity for each entry in each cell.[10]

5   The integrative summary-nature of the dominance configuration should enable investigators to avoid the reporting of atomized findings although the configuration as such must be based upon refined details. In addition, the dominance configuration does not preclude the combining of domains or other sources

of variance in language choice whenever simpler patterns are recognizable (e.g., public vs. private spheres or formal vs. informal encounters). In general, the dominance configuration may best be limited to those aspects of *degree of bilingualism* and *location of bilingualism* which empirical analysis will ultimately reveal to be of greatest *independent importance*.

6　A much more refined presentation of language maintenance or language shift becomes possible than that which is provided by means of traditional mother tongue census statistics (Fishman, 1965c).

Although the dominance configuration still requires much further refinement, it seems to merit the time and effort that such refinement might necessitate.

Some empirical and conceptual contributions of domain analysis

The domain concept has facilitated a number of worthwhile contributions to the understanding of bilingualism and language choice. It has helped organize and clarify the previously unstructured awareness that language maintenance and language shift proceed quite unevenly across the several sources and domains of variance in habitual language choice. Certain domains appear to be more resistant to displacement than others (e.g., the family domain in comparison to the occupational domain) across all multilingual settings characterized by urbanization and economic development, regardless of whether between-group or within-group comparisons are involved (Fishman, 1964). Under the impact of these same socio-cultural processes other domains (e.g., religion) seem to be very strongly maintenance oriented during earlier stages of interaction and strongly shift oriented once a decision is reached that their organizational base can be better secured via shift (Fishman, 1965c). The simultaneous, concomitant effect of certain domains and other sources of variance seems to be protective of recessive languages, even when language shift has advanced so far that a given domain as such has been engulfed.[11] On the other hand if a strict domain separation becomes institutionalized, such that each language is associated with a number of important but distinct domains, bilingualism can become both universal and stabilized even though an entire population consists of bilinguals interacting with other bilinguals (Rubin, 1963). The domain concept has also helped refine the distinction between coordinate bilingualism and compound bilingualism (Ervin and Osgood, 1954) by stressing that not only does a continuum (rather than a dichotomy) obtain, but by indicating how one stage along this continuum may shade into another. Thus, as indicated by Figure 3.1, most late nineteenth- and early twentieth-century immigrants to America from eastern and southern Europe began as compound bilinguals with each language assigned to separate and minimally overlapping domains. With the passage of time (involving increased interaction with English-speaking Americans, social mobility, and acculturation with respect to other-than-language behaviors as well) their bilingualism became characterized, first, by far greater domain overlap (and by far greater interference) and then by progressively greater coordinate functioning. Finally, language displacement advanced so far that the mother tongue remained only in a few restricted and non-overlapping domains. Indeed, in some

Table 3.1   Yiddish–English maintenance and shift in the United States: 1940–60

Sources of variance			Domains of language behavior					
Media	Role	Situational	Family	Friends	Acquaintances	Mass media	Jewish organizations	Occupations
	Inner*	Formal	X	X	X	X	X	X
		Informal	Y, E	Y, E	Y, E	E, E	Y, E	E, E
		Intimate	Y, E	Y, E	Y, E	E, E	Y, E	E, E
Speaking	Comp.	Formal	X	X	E, E	E, E	Y, E	E, E
		Informal	E, E	E, E	E, E	E, E	Y, E	E, E
		Intimate	Y, E	Y, E	X	X	X	X
	Prod.	Formal	X	X	E, E	X	Y, E	E, E
		Informal	E, E	E, E	E, E	X	Y, E	E, E
		Intimate	Y, E	Y, E	E, E	X	X	X

Reading	Comp.	Formal	Y, E	X	X	X	Y, E	X
		Informal	Y, E	X	X	X	Y, E	X
		Intimate	E, E	X	X	X	X	X
	Prod.**	Formal	Y, E	X	X	Y, E	Y, E	X
		Informal	Y, E	X	X	Y, E	Y, E	X
		Intimate	E, E	X	X	E, E	X	X
Writing	Prod.	Formal	X	X	X	X	Y, E	X
		Informal	E, E	E, E	X	X	Y, E	X
		Intimate	E, E	E, E	X	X	X	X

Notes: Comparisons for immigrant generation "secularists" arriving prior to the First World War (first language shown is most frequently used; second language shown is increasing in use; X indicates no data for this particular population or not applicable).

* For "speaking-inner" combinations the domains imply topics as well as contexts. In all other instances they imply contexts alone.
** For "reading-production" combinations the distinction between "family" and "mass media" domains is also a distinction between reading to others and reading to oneself.

Source: Fishman, 1965a

Bilingual functioning type	Domain overlap type	
	Overlapping domains	Non-overlapping domains
Compound (interdependent or fused)	2. *Second Stage:* More immigrants know more English and therefore can speak to each other either in mother tongue or in English (still ←— mediated by the mother tongue) in several domains of behavior. Increased interference. ↓	1. *Initial Stage:* The immigrant learns English via his mother tongue. English is used only in those few domains (work sphere, governmental sphere) in which mother tongue cannot be used. Minimal interference. Only a few immigrants knew a little English.
Coordinate (independent or discrete)	3. *Third Stage:* The languages function independently of each other. The number of bilinguals is at its maximum. Domain overlap is at its maximum. The →— second generation during childhood. Stabilized interference.	4. *Final Stage:* English has displaced the mother tongue from all but the most private or restricted domains. Interference declines. In most cases both languages function independently; in others the mother tongue is mediated by English (reversal of Stage 1, but same type).

Figure 3.1   Type of bilingual functioning and domain overlap during successive stages of immigrant acculturation

cases, compound bilingualism once more became the rule, except that the ethnic mother tongue came to be utilized via English (rather than vice-versa as was the case in the early immigrant days). Thus, the domain concept may help place the compound–coordinate distinction in greater socio-cultural perspective, in much the same way as it may serve the entire area of language choice. More generally, we are helped to realize that the initial pattern of acquisition of bilingualism and subsequent patterns of bilingual functioning need not be in agreement (Figure 3.2). Indeed, a bilingual may vary with respect to the compound vs. coordinate nature of his functioning in each of the sources and domains of variance in language choice that we have discussed. If this is the case then several different models of interference may be needed to correspond to various stages of bilingualism and to various co-occurrences of influence on language choice.

Bilingual acquisition type	Domain overlap type	
	Overlapping domains	Non-overlapping domains
Compound (interdependent or fused)	Transitional bilingualism: the older second generation. The "high school French" tourist who remains abroad somewhat longer than he expected.	"Cultural bilingualism": the bilingualism of the "indirect method" classroom, whereby one language is learned through another but retained in separate domains.
Coordinate (independent or discrete)	Widespread bilingualism without social cleavage: the purported goal of "responsible" French-Canadians. The "direct method" classroom.	"One-sided bilingualism" or bilingualism with marked and stable social distinctions, such that only one group in a contact situation is bilingual or such that only particular domains are open or appropriate to particular languages.

Figure 3.2   Initial type of bilingual acquisition and subsequent domain overlap type

Source: Fishman, 1964

Some remaining problems and challenges for domain analysis

Nevertheless, as is the case with most new integrative concepts, the major problems and the major promises of domain analysis still lie ahead. There are several methodological problems of data collection and data analysis, which cannot be enumerated here, but which do not seem to be in any way unprecedented. The substantive challenges pertaining to domain analysis are more varied, for they will depend on the interests of particular investigators. Domain analysis and the dominance configuration merely seek to provide a systematic approach to descriptive parameters. Some will wish to utilize these parameters in connection with *other formal features of communication than code-variety*. Thus, the study of "sociolinguistic variants" (i.e., of those linguistic alternations regarded as "free" or "optional" variants *within* a code) may gain somewhat from the greater socio-cultural context provided by domain analysis. Other investigators may seek to establish cross-cultural and diachronic language and culture files in order to investigate the relationship between changes in language behavior (including changes in language choice) and other processes of socio-cultural change. In this connection, domain analysis may facilitate language use comparisons between settings (or between historical periods) of roughly similar domain structure. Still other investigators, more centrally concerned with multilingualism and with language maintenance or language shift, may well become interested in refining the typologies and stages that are currently on record: e.g., Vildomec's (1963) "local" vs. "cultural" multilingualism,[12] Kloss's

(1929) much earlier five-fold classification of patterns of stabilized multilingualism, Carman's (1962) recent ten-stage analysis of language shift among immigrants settling in Kansas, and many others. Domain analysis (within the context of a dominance configuration) may enable us to see unexpected relationships *between* these several formulations and to improve upon them both on theoretical and empirical grounds.

Conclusions

The concept of "domains of language choice" represents an attempt to provide socio-cultural organization and socio-cultural context for considerations of variance in language choice in multilingual settings. When systematically interrelated with other sources of variance in language behavior (media variance, role variance, situational variance) and when based upon underlying analyses of the role-relations and topics most crucial to them, domains of language behavior may contribute importantly to the establishment of dominance configuration summaries. Domain analysis may be a promising conceptual and methodological tool for future studies of language behavior in multilingual settings and for socio-linguistic studies more generally. Ultimately, a relatively uniform but flexible analytic scheme such as that described here may enable us to arrive at valid generalizations concerning (1) the kinds of multilingual settings in which one or another configuration of variance in language choice obtains and (2) the language maintenance or language shift consequences of particular configurations of dominance or variance.

Notes

1   This example may be replaced by any one of a number of others: Standard German, Schwytzertüsch and Romansch (in parts of Switzerland); Hebrew, English and Yiddish in Israel; Riksmaal, Landsmaal and more local dialectal variants of the latter in Norway; Standard German, Plattdeutsch and Danish in Schleswig, etc.

2   *Situation* and *setting* are frequently used interchangeably in the socio-linguistic literature. In this paper *setting* is intended to be the broader and more multifaceted concept. (Thus, a complete consideration of "the multilingual setting" requires attention to language choice data, socio-cultural process data, historical perspective on the particular intergroup context, data on attitudinal, emotional, cognitive and overt behaviors toward language (Fishman, 1964), etc.) *Situation* is reserved for use in characterizing certain circumstances of communication at the time of communication.

3   This effect has been noted even in normally monolingual settings, such as those obtaining among American intellectuals, many of whom feel obliged to use French or German words in conjunction with particular professional topics. The frequency of lexical interference in the language of immigrants in the United States has also often been explained on topical grounds. The importance of topical determinants is discussed by Haugen, 1953; 1956; Weinreich, 1953; Gumperz, 1962; and Ervin, 1964. It is implied as a "pressure" exerted upon "contacts" in Mackey's (1962) description of bilingualism.

4   The study of language maintenance and language shift is concerned with the relationship between change or stability in habitual language use, on the one hand, and ongoing psychological, social or cultural processes of change and stability, on the other hand, in multilingual settings (Fishman, 1964).

5   We can safely reject the implication encountered in certain discussions of domains that there must be an invariant set of domains applicable to all multilingual settings. If language behavior is related to socio-cultural organization, as is now widely accepted, then different kinds of multilingual settings should benefit from analyses in terms of different domains of language use, whether defined intuitively, theoretically, or empirically.

6   For a discussion of the differences and similarities between "functions of language behavior" and "domains of language behavior" see Fishman, 1964. "Functions" stand closer to socio-psychological analysis, for they abstract their constituents in terms of individual motivation rather than in terms of group purpose.

7   These remarks are not intended to imply that *all* role-relation differences are necessarily related to language-choice differences. This almost certainly is *not* the case. Just which role-relation differences *are* related to language-choice differences (and under what circumstances) is a matter for empirical determination within each multilingual setting as well as at different points in time within the same setting.

8   Writing and reading are differentiated as separate media not only because they may be pursued in different languages but because each is capable of independent productive and receptive use. In general, the formal dimensions presented here make use of more distinctions than may be necessary in all multilingual settings. Both empirical and theoretical considerations must ultimately be involved in selecting the dimensions appropriate for the analysis of particular settings.

9   Unfortunately, the term *role* is currently employed in several somewhat different ways, e.g., "role in society" (*mayor, untouchable, bank president*), "role relation" vis-à-vis particular others (*husband–wife, father–child, teacher–pupil*), "occasional role" (*chairman, host, spokesman*), and "momentary role" (*initiator of a communication, respondent, listener*). It is in this last sense that the term "role" will be used in connection with "role variance" above, while it is in the sense of "role-relation" that the term "role" has been used previously in our discussion of differentiations within the domains of language behavior.

10   Disregarding this stricture an inspection of Table 3.1 reveals:

    1   there is no cell in which the use of Yiddish is currently increasing in the studied population;

    2   reading is the most retentive area of media variance;

    3   inner speech is the most retentive area of role variance;

    4   formal usage is the most retentive area of situational variance;

    5   the organizational context is the most retentive area of domain variance whereas the occupational context is the least retentive.

All in all, this dominance configuration leaves one with the impression of greatest retention of Yiddish in those circumstances that are either most private and subject to personal control or most structured and generationally restricted (Fishman, 1965a).

11   Note, for example, the mass media interaction with either reading-production-formality or with reading-production-informality in Table 3.1.

12   This seems to be the latest in a long tradition of attempts to reduce multilingualism to a dichotomy. For many earlier attempts along such lines see Weinreich, 1953: 9–10, 35, 81–2; Fishman, 1964.

Source: Fishman, J.A. (1965) Who speaks what language to whom and when? *La Linguistique* 2: 67–88. Reproduced by permission of the author and Blackwell Publishing.

Postscript

Current thinking and publishing are much more ethnographic than they were when this paper was originally authored and, therefore, its macroscopic focus is probably considered to be better suited for presenting areal-summaries based on many individual or local neighborhood records. It is more a useful guide to midlevel research or to midlevel comparative conclusions derived from questionnaires or focused interviews.

Joshua A. Fishman, PhD, is Distinguished University Research Professor Emeritus of Social Sciences of Yeshiva University, USA. JoshuaAFishman@aol.com

Notes for students and instructors

Study questions

1 Give two examples from the language contact situations that you know of which may be described in terms of Fishman's model of the four relationships between diglossia and bilingualism.

2 Central to the concept of domain is the notion of congruence on two levels: (a) congruence among domain components (e.g. participant, topic and setting); (b) congruence of domain with specific language or language variety. Give an example from the community you are familiar with and demonstrate how language choice varies across domains.

Study activities

1 Carry out a 'domain analysis' of the language choice patterns of a bilingual family or a small group of bilingual speakers, using a questionnaire or through interview. Summarise your findings in a table or graphical format.

2 Find a three-generation family from an ethnic minority background (if you live in a multilingual area, find a three-generation multilingual family) and ask one person from each generation about his/her language preference and language use in key domains. Ask them to list ten of their most important and regular contacts who are not members of the family, including the age, sex, occupation and language background of each of the contacts. Can you see any relationship between the three speakers' language preference and language choice patterns and the social characteristics of their key contacts?

Further reading

General introductions to the study of bilingual language choice can be found in Chapter 4 of R. Wardhaugh, 2005, *An Introduction to Sociolinguistics* (5th edn),

Blackwell, and Chapter 7 of R. Fasold, 1984, *The Sociolinguistics of Society*, Blackwell.

On the notion of 'diglossia', see R.A. Hudson, 1992, Diglossia: A bibliographic review, *Language in Society*, 21: 611–74, and M. Fernandez, 1994, *Diglossia: A comprehensive bibliography 1960–1990 and supplements*, John Benjamins.

For Fishman's contributions, see *Language in Sociocultural Change: Essays by J.A. Fishman*, selected by A.S. Dil, 1972, Stanford University Press; *The Rise and Fall of the Ethnic Revival: Perspectives on language and ethnicity*, 1985, Mouton; and *Reversing Language Shift*, 1991, Multilingual Matters. Two recent collections introduce Fishman's work to a new generation of students: O. Garcia and H. Schiffman (eds), 2006, *Language Loyalty, Continuity and Change: Fishman's contributions to international sociolinguistics*, and N. Hornberger and M. Putz (eds), 2006, *Language Loyalty, Language Planning and Language Revitalization: Recent writings and reflections from Joshua Fishman*, both published by Multilingual Matters.

For classic examples of earlier studies of bilingualism and language contact, see U. Weinreich, 1953, *Languages in Contact: Findings and problems*, Linguistic Circle of New York, and E. Haugen, 1953, *The Norwegian Language in America*, Pennsylvania University Press.

Examples of community-based studies of language choice include: S. Gal, 1979, *Language Shift: Social determinants of linguistic change in bilingual Austria*, Academic Press; N. Dorian, 1981, *Language Death: The life cycle of a Scottish Gaelic dialect*, Pennsylvania University Press; V. Edwards, 1986, *Language in a Black Community*, Multilingual Matters; Li Wei, 1994, *Three Generations Two Languages One Family: Language choice and language shift in a Chinese community in Britain*, Multilingual Matters; and M. Sebba, 1993, *London Jamaican: Language systems in interaction*, Longman.

For an anthropological perspective on language choice, see J.H. Hill and K.C. Hill, 1986, *Speaking Mexicano: Dynamics of syncretic language in Central Mexico*, University of Arizona Press, and D. Kulick, 1992, *Language Shift and Cultural Reproduction: Socialisation, self and syncretism in a Papua New Guinean village*, Cambridge University Press.

Bilingual interaction

Chapter 4

Social meaning in linguistic structure: code-switching in Norway

JAN-PETTER BLOM AND
JOHN J. GUMPERZ

I N HIS DISCUSSIONS OF the problem of language and society, Bernstein (1961; 1964) explores the hypothesis that social relationships act as intervening variables between linguistic structures and their realization in speech. His formulation suggests that the anthropologists' analysis of social constraints governing interpersonal relationships may be utilized in the interpretation of verbal performances. This chapter attempts to clarify the social and linguistic factors involved in the communication process and to test Bernstein's hypothesis by showing that speakers' selection among semantically, grammatically, and phonologically permissible alternates occurring in conversation sequences recorded in natural groups is both patterned and predictable on the basis of certain features of the local social system. In other words, given a particular aggregate of people engaged in regular face-to-face interaction, and given some knowledge of the speakers' linguistic repertoire (Gumperz, 1964), we wish to relate the structure of that repertoire to the verbal behavior of members of the community in particular situations.

Data on verbal interaction derive from approximately two months' field work in Hemnesberget, a small commercial and industrial town of about 1,300 inhabitants in the center of the Rana Fjord, close to the Arctic circle in northern Norway. The settlement owes its existence to the growth of local trade and industry following the abolition of government-sanctioned trade monopolies covering most of northern Norway in 1858. Since the Middle Ages, these monopolies had kept the area's economy dependent upon a small elite of merchant and landholding families with connections to southern Norway, separated by great differences in wealth, culture, and education from the tenant farmers, fishermen, estate laborers, and servants who formed the bulk of the populace. Apart from a few shop owners and government officials, present-day Hemnesberget residents are mostly descendants of these latter groups. They have been attracted to the town from the surroundings by new economic opportunities there, while around one hundred years of relatively free economic development have splintered the old ruling circles. Many of this former elite have moved away, and the remainder no longer form a visible social group in the region.

Present inhabitants of Hemnesberget earn their livelihood mainly as craftsmen in family workshops or in the somewhat larger boat-building and lumber-processing plants, all of which are locally owned. The area serves as a major source of wood products and fishing equipment for the northernmost part of Norway. A significant group of merchant middlemen deal in locally produced boats and other products, which they ship north for resale, and maintain sales agencies for motors and other appliances and manufactured goods from the south.

While at the beginning of the twentieth century Hemnesberget was the most important communications and commercial center in the area, it was eclipsed in the 1960s by government-sponsored economic development which turned the town of Mo i Rana, at the mouth of Rana Fjord, into Norway's major iron- and steel-producing center. The region of Mo grew from about 1,000 inhabitants in 1920 to almost 9,000 in 1960, largely through immigration from the region of Trøndelag and southern Norway. It now boasts several modern department stores, hotels, restaurants, and cinemas. The railroad from Trondheim in the south through Mo and on north to Bodø was completed shortly after the Second World War, and the road system has steadily improved. All these new communication arteries, however, bypass Hemnesberget, which has all but lost its importance as a communication link for both land and sea traffic.

Although the immediate ecological environment has changed greatly, Hemnesberget remains an island of tradition in a sea of change. There is a regular once-a-day boat service to Mo, buses leave for the railroad station twice a day, and a few people commute to Mo by private automobile or motorcycle. However, the bulk of the residents spend most of their working and leisure time in and around Hemnesberget. Those who can afford it build vacation cabins in the unsettled areas across the fjord a few miles away. Our interviews uniformly show that social events in Mo i Rana are only of marginal interest to local inhabitants.

The community linguistic repertoire

Most residents of Hemnesberget are native speakers of Ranamål (R), one of a series of dialects which segment northern Norway into linguistic regions roughly corresponding to other cultural and ecological divisions (Christiansen, 1962). As elsewhere in Norway, where local independence and distinctness of folk culture are highly valued, the dialect enjoys great prestige. A person's native speech is regarded as an integral part of his family background, a sign of his local identity. By identifying himself as a dialect speaker both at home and abroad, a member symbolizes pride in his community and in the distinctness of its contribution to society at large.

Formal education, however, is always carried on in the standard language, the language of official transactions, religion, and the mass media. Norwegian law sanctions two standard languages: Bokmål (formally called Riksmål) and Nynorsk (formerly Landsmål), of which only Bokmål (B) is current in northern Norway.

Education is universal and, allowing for certain individual differences in fluency, all speakers of Ranamål also control the standard. Both Bokmål and Ranamål, therefore, form part of what we may call the community linguistic repertoire (Gumperz, 1964), the totality of linguistic resources which speakers may employ in significant social interaction. In their everyday interaction, they select among the two as the situation demands. Members view this alternation as a shift between two distinct entities, which are never mixed. A person speaks either one or the other.

The fact that the two varieties are perceived as distinct, however, does not necessarily mean that their separateness is marked by significant linguistic differences. Pairs such as Hindi and Urdu, Serbian and Croatian, Thai and Laotian, and many others which are regarded as separate languages by their speakers are known to be grammatically almost identical. The native's view of language distinctions must thus be validated by empirical linguistic investigation.

We began our analysis by employing standard linguistic elicitation procedures. A series of informants selected for their fluency in the dialect were interviewed in our office and were asked to produce single words, sentences, and short texts, first in the dialect and then in the standard, for taping or phonetic recording by the linguist. These elicitation sessions yielded a series of dialect features which are essentially identical to those described by Norwegian dialectologists (Christiansen, 1962).

The vowel system distinguishes 10 vowels in three tongue heights:

- high: front unrounded i, front rounded y, central rounded u, back rounded o;
- mid: front unrounded e, front rounded ö, back rounded å;
- low: front unrounded æ, front rounded ø, back a.

Consonants occur either singly or as geminates. Vowels are phonetically short before geminates, consonant clusters, and palatalized consonants. There are two series of consonants: unmarked and palatalized. Unmarked consonants include stops p, b, t, d, k, g; spirants f, v, s, ʃ, j, ç; nasals m, n, ŋ; trill r, lateral l, and retroflex flap ḷ. The palatal series contains tj, dj, nj, and lj. On the phonetic level, a set of cacuminal or retroflex allophones occur for the sequences rs [ʃ], rd [d], rt [t], and rn [ɳ].

The local pronunciation of the standard differs from the "pure" dialect as follows: Bokmål does not have the phonemic distinction between the palatalized and non-palatalized series of consonants. Only nonpalatalized consonants occur. In addition, it does not distinguish between mid front rounded /ö/ and low front rounded /ø/; only the former occurs. On the purely phonetic level, dialect allophones of the phonemes /æ/ and /a/ are considerably lower and more retracted than their standard equivalents. The dialect furthermore has a dark allophone [ł] of /l/ where the standard has clear [l]. The cacuminal or retroflex allophones of /s/, /d/, /t/, and /n/, and the flap /ḷ/, however, which are commonly regarded as dialect features, are used in both varieties, although they tend to disappear in highly formal Bokmål.

Morphological peculiarities of the dialect include the masculine plural indefinite suffix -æ and the definite suffix -an, e.g., (R) hæstæ (horses), hæstan (the horses), contrasting with (B) hester and hestene. In verb inflection the dialect lacks the infinitive suffix -e and the present suffix -er of regular verbs. Further differences in past tense and past participle markers and in the assignment of individual words to strong or weak inflectional classes serve to set off almost every dialect verb from its standard Norwegian equivalent. Some examples of common regular and irregular verbs and their standard equivalents are shown in Table 4.1.

Other important dialect features appear in pronouns, common adverbs of time, place, and manner, conjunctions, and other grammatically significant function words. Some of the most common distinctive forms of personal pronouns and possessive pronouns are shown in Table 4.2. Table 4.3 shows interrogatives, relatives, and indefinites, while Table 4.4 shows adverbs and conjunctions.

Table 4.1   Examples of common regular and irregular verbs and their standard equivalents

Infinitive		Present		Past		Past participle		
Ranamål	Bokmål	Ranamål	Bokmål	Ranamål	Bokmål	Ranamål	Bokmål	English
finj	finne	finj	finner	fanj	fant	fønje	funnet	(find)
vara or va	være	e	ær	va	var	vøre	vært	(be)
få	få	får	får	fekk	fikk	fått	fått	(get)
stanj	stå	står	står	sto	sto	stie	stått	(stand)
jær	jøre	jær	jør	jol	jøre	jort	jort	(do)
læs	lese	læs	leser	læst	leste	læst	lest	(read)
ta	ta	tek	tar	tok	tokk	tatt or tiçe	tatt	(take)

Table 4.2   Examples of personal pronouns and possessive pronouns

Bokmål	Ranamål	English	Bokmål	Ranamål	English
jæjj	og	(I)	hunn	ho	(she)
mæjj	meg	(me)	hanns	hanjs	(his)
dæjj	deg	(you)	hennes	hinjers	(hers)
hann	hanj	(he)	dere	dåkk	(you) (plural)
			di	dæmm*	(theirs)

Note:
* Sometimes also *di* and *deres*.

Table 4.3   Examples of interrogatives, relatives, and indefinites

Bokmål	Ranamål	English
såmm	så	[who, which (relative)]
va	ke	[what (interrogative)]
vemm	kem	(who)
noe	nåkka	(something)
vorfårr	kefør	(what for)
vilket	kefør nokka	[which (thing)]
vilken	kefør nann	[which (person)]
vær	kvar	(every)
en	ein	(one)

Table 4.4   Examples of adverbs and conjunctions

Bokmål	Ranamål	English
till	tell	(to, toward)
menn	mænn	(but)
hær	her	(here)
fra	ifra	(from)
mellam	imeljæ	(in between)
vordan	kelesn	(how)
viss	vess	(if)

These data constitute empirical evidence to support the view of the dialect as a distinct linguistic entity. By comparing information collected in this manner with local speech forms elsewhere in northern Norway, dialectologists interested in historical reconstruction identify Ranamål as one of a series of northern Norwegian dialects set off from others by the fact that it shows influences of eastern Norwegian forms of speech (Christiansen, 1962). In this discussion however, we are concerned with social interaction and not with history, and this leads us to raise somewhat different problems.

The elicitation sessions which provide the source data for dialect grammars are conducted in the linguist's, and not in the informant's, frame of reference. Although by asking speakers to speak in the dialect, the linguist may be interested in purely descriptive or historical information, the native speaker, mindful of the association between dialect, local culture, and local identity, is, of course, anxious to present his locality in the best possible light. Consistency of performance in linguistic interview sessions might well be the result of the interviewer's presence; it need not reflect everyday interaction. Furthermore, when comparisons with other forms of speech are made, it is the linguist's analysis which serves as the basis for these comparisons, not the speaker's performance.

Ranamål and Bokmål as codes in a repertoire

In order to understand how natives may perceive the dialect standard language differences, some further discussion of the way in which distinctions between what are ordinarily treated as separate linguistic systems may be manifested in everyday speech is necessary. Thus if we compare a bilingual's pronunciation of the Norwegian sentence *Vill du ha egg og beiken till frokast?* with the same speaker's pronunciation of the English equivalent "Will you have bacon and eggs for breakfast?" the two utterances will show phonetic distinctions in every segment. The Norwegian voiced spirant [v] has much less spirantal noise than its English equivalent, the [i] is tense as compared to the lax English [i], the Norwegian [l] may be clear or dark but it is phonetically different from English [l]. The Norwegian central rounded [u] in *du* has no direct English equivalent. In *egg* the Norwegian has a tense [e] and the [g] has an aspirate release, whereas in English the vowel is lax and [g] has a voiced release. Similarly, the Norwegian has a stressed vowel in *beiken* [æi] whereas the English has [ey]. Bilinguals whose entire articulation shifts in this way can be said to have two distinct articulation ranges in addition to two sets of grammatical rules.

Analysis of recordings of Hemnesberget speakers' switching from the dialect to the standard reveals a different situation. In a sentence pair like *hanj bor på nilsen's paɲʃonat* and its Bokmål equivalent *hann bor pa nilsen's paɲsonat* "He lives in Nilsen's pensionat," only the realizations of /a/, /ł/, and /nj/ which appear in our list of dialect character-istics differ. In other relevant respects the two utterances are identical. Furthermore, even in the case of these dialect characteristics, speakers do not alternate between two clearly distinguishable articulation points; rather, the shift takes the form of a displace-ment along a scale in which palatalized consonants show at least three degrees of palatalization, strong [nj], weak [nʲ], and zero [n] and /a/ and /æ/ each show three degrees of retraction and lowering.

While the switch from Norwegian to English implies a shift between two distinct structural wholes, the Bokmål–Ranamål alternation, in phonology at least, seems more similar to conditions described by Labov (1966) for New York speech. A speaker's standard and dialect performance can be accounted for by a single phonetic system. The bulk of the constituent phones within this system are marked by relatively stable, easily identifiable points of articulation. The palatalized consonants and the vowels listed here differ in that they vary within a much greater articulation range. They are instances of what Labov has called variables (1964). It is the position of such variables along the scale of possible articulations which, when evaluated along with morphological information, signals dialect vs. standard speech.

Not all items identified in our elicitation sessions as Ranamål features, function as variables, however. The contrast between /ø/ and /ö/ was never produced spon-taneously. In normal discourse only [ö] occurs. Furthermore, as stated previously, the flap allophone /ł/ and the retroflex stop allophones which find a prominent place in dialect grammars are also used in local Bokmål as well as in eastern varieties of standard Norwegian; thus their status as dialect markers is doubtful.

Our texts also reveal some individual differences in the pronunciation of the palatal-ized consonant and vowel variables. While the normal dialect speech of most residents shows strong palatalization of these consonants and extreme vowel retraction, some of the more highly educated younger residents normally have medium palatalization and medium vowel retraction. Regardless, however, the direction of variation is the same for all individuals.

In the realm of morphology–syntax it is also possible to set up a single set of grammatical categories to account for what on the surface seem like striking differences between the two varieties. All nouns, e.g., appear in an indefinite form consisting of the noun stem and in an indefinite form made up of stem plus suffixed article, both of which are inflected for singular and plural. There are three subcategories of noun gender: masculine, feminine, and neuter, and the case categories are shared. Verbs appear in imperative, infinitive, present, past, and past participle forms. Basic function word categories, including pronouns, conjunctions, and adverbs, are shared, etc.

Ranamål shows a few peculiarities in the order of pronouns and verbs in sentences such as (R) *ke du e ifrå*, (B) *vor ær du fra* "Where are you from?" But even without detailed analysis, it is obvious that these differences correspond to relatively low-order syntactic rules. The majority of the distinctions between the dialect and the standard thus do not affect the basic grammar but only what we may call the morphophonemic realization of shared grammatical categories.

Even at the morphophonemic level, variation is not without pattern. Examination of such alternates as the following suggests a general process of lowering of front vowels in the dialect:

- (B) *till*, (R) *tell* "to";
- (B) *fikk*, (R) *fekk* "received";
- (B) *hest*, (R) *hæst* "horse"; and
- (B) *menn*, (R) *mænn* "but."

This lowering process is also found elsewhere in Norway, although it may occur in different linguistic forms. Similarly, other sets of alternates such as *icce/ikke* "not," *dæmm/di* "they," and *ifra/frå* "from" are common in other Norwegian regions.

Leaving aside historical considerations, it is almost as if all dialect variation within Norway were generated by selection of different forms from a common reservoir of alternates. Ranamål differs from other dialects not so much because it contains entirely different features, but because of the way in which it combines features already found elsewhere. Furthermore, Hemnesberget pairs such as (B) *lærer*, (R) *lerar*, and (B) *hær*, (R) *her*, which conflict with the lowering process just mentioned, suggest that here as elsewhere selection may at times be motivated by social pressures favoring maintenance of distinctions (Ramanujan, 1967). No matter what the actual historical facts are, however, the narrow range of variation we find lends support to our view of dialect features as variables within a single grammatical system.

The effect of structural similarities on speakers' perception of speech differences is somewhat counterbalanced by the fact that choice among these variables is always restricted by sociolinguistic selection constraints such that if, for instance, a person selects a standard morphological variant in one part of an utterance, this first choice also implies selection of pronunciation variables tending toward the standard end of the scale. A speaker wishing to ask for another's place of residence may, e.g., start his sentence either with (R) *ke* "where" or (B) *vor*. In the first case, the rest of the sentence will be *hanj e ifrå* "is he from?" In the second case, it will be *ær hann fra*; *vor* and *hanj* do not co-occur. Similarly, selection of *e* "is" requires dialect pronunciation; the form *ær* "is" would sound odd if it appeared in the same sentence with *hanj*.

It is the nature of these selection constraints and the manner in which they cut across the usual boundaries of phonology and morphology to generate co-occurrences among phonetic and allomorphic and lexical variables, which lends the Ranamål–Bokmål variation its peculiar stamp, and sets it off, e.g., from the phonologically similar situation in New York. Sociolinguistic selection rules also account to some extent for the speaker's view of the two varieties as separate entities.

Since the dialect and the standard are almost isomorphic in syntax and phonetics and vary chiefly in morphophonemics, and since most speakers control the entire range of variables, it would be unreasonable to assume, as is frequently done wherever two distinct dialects are spoken, that selection patterns affecting the above selection rules are motivated by considerations of intelligibility. The most reasonable assumption is that the linguistic separateness between the dialect and the standard, i.e. the maintenance of distinct alternates for common inflectional morphemes and function, is conditioned by social factors.

Some idea of how this came about can be obtained by considering the conditions under which the two varieties are learned. The dialect is acquired in most homes and in the sphere of domestic and friendship relations. As a result, it has acquired the flavor of these locally based relationships. However, dialect speakers learn the standard in school and in church, at a time when they are also introduced to national Norwegian values. It has therefore become associated with such pan-Norwegian activity systems.

Since the adult population has equal access to both sets of variants, however, the developmental argument does not provide sufficient explanation for the maintenance of distinctness. Immigrants to urban centers around the world, e.g., frequently give up their languages after a generation if social conditions are favorable to language shift. The hypothesis suggests itself, therefore, that given the initial acquisition patterns, the dialect and the standard remain separate because of the cultural identities they communicate and the social values implied therein. It is this aspect of the problem that we intend to explore in the remaining sections of the chapter. Before we proceed, however, something more needs to be said about the process of social symbolization.

Students of communication usually distinguish between semantics proper, or reference, and pragmatics (Ervin-Tripp, 1964). Reference indicates verbal categorization of objects' actions and experience in terms of their objective properties; pragmatics deals with the effect of symbols of various kinds on speakers and listeners, i.e. with the significance of what is communicated for the actors involved. Most discussions of pragmatics ordinarily do not distinguish between individual intent and interpersonal significance of usage patterns, although it is evident that without such a distinction it would be impossible to explain the fact that the same message may indicate praise in some instances and disapproval in others. Effective communication requires that speakers and audiences agree both on the meaning of words and on the social import or values attached to choice of expression. Our discussions will be confined to the latter. We use the term *social significance*, or *social meaning*, to refer to the social value implied when an utterance is used in a certain context.

In general, the assignment of value to particular objects or acts is as arbitrary as the referential naming of objects. Just as a particular term may refer to a round object in one group and a square object in another, so also the value of actions or utterances may vary. Thus the same term may indicate geographical distinctions in one community and symbolize social stratification elsewhere. Social meanings differ from referential meanings in the way in which they are coded. Whereas reference is coded largely through words, social meaning can attach not only to acoustic signs but also to settings, to items of background knowledge, as well as to particular word sequences. In Hemnes, e.g., values attached to a person's family background or to his reputation as a fisherman are important in understanding what he says and influence the selection of responses to his actions.

It must also be pointed out that referential meanings are at least to some extent recoverable through the study of individual words. They are, to use Pike's (1967) term, segmental, while social meanings are not. A sentence like *ke du e ifrå* "Where are you from?" can be divided into units of reference like *ke* "where," *du* "you," *e* "are," and *ifrå* "from." Social significance attaches to the utterance as a whole; it is not segmentable into smaller component stretches. Sociolinguistic co-occurrence patterns along with intonation contours enable the speaker to group language into larger pragmatic wholes and to interpret them in relation to signs transmitted by other communicative media.

Local organization and values

Social life in Hemnesberget shows a fluidity of class structure quite similar to that described for southern Norway by Barnes (1954). Extremes of poverty and wealth are absent. Expressions of solidarity such as "We all know each other here in Hemnes," and "We are all friends here" recur in our interviews. The majority of those who claim local descent show a strong sense of local identification. To be a *hæmnesværing* "Hemnes resident" in their view is like belonging to a team characterized by commonalty of descent. Members of this reference group act like kin, friends, and neighbors, co-operating in the pursuit of community ideals. In everyday behavior they symbolize this quality of their ties through greetings, exchanges of personal information, and general informality of posture toward fellow members. The dialect is an important marker of their common culture. Residents of neighboring settlements, of Mo i Rana, as well as other Norwegians, stand apart from this local community. They are potential competitors who must at least initially be treated with reserve. Their dialects are said to be different. The linguist interested in structural significance may wish to disregard such variation as minor. Nevertheless, they have important social meanings for inter-community communication within the Rana region. They are constantly commented upon and joked about and seem to play an important role in the maintenance of local identity.

Despite the intense sense of local identification, perceptions of closeness within this local group are not everywhere the same among Hemnes residents. More detailed interviews and observations of visiting and recreational patterns and of the exchange of assistance suggest a clear distinction between personal relations and the more general local relations. The range of effective personal relations for any single individual tends to be fairly small and stable over time. For most people it includes only certain near kin, in-laws, neighbors, or fellow workers. The community can thus be described as segmented into small nuclei of personal interaction. Since these groups are not marked linguistically, however, the behavioral signs of friendliness and equality constitute a communicative idiom which applies to both these nuclei and to other relations or shared local identification.

The meaning attached to local descent and dialect use – to being part of the "local team" – is clearly seen when we consider those members of the community who dissociate themselves from this "team." Traditionally, in northern Norway the local community of equals was separated from the landowning commercial and administrative elite by a wide gulf of social and judicial inequality. Since the latter were the introducers and users of standard Norwegian, the standard form was – and to some extent still is – associated with this inequality of status. Many of the functions of the former elite have now been incorporated into the local social system. Individuals who fill these functions, however, continue to be largely of nonlocal descent. Although they may pay lip service to locally accepted rules of etiquette and use the dialect on occasion, their experience elsewhere in Norway – where differences in education, influence, and prestige are much more pronounced – leads them to associate the dialect with lack of education and sophistication. Therefore, they show a clear preference for the standard.

Such attitudes are unacceptable to locals, who view lack of respect for and refusal to speak the dialect as an expression of social distance and contempt for the "local team" and its community spirit. It is not surprising, therefore, that their loyalty to the dialect is thereby reaffirmed. For a local resident to employ (B) forms with other local residents is in their view to *snakk fint* or to *snakk jalat* "to put on airs."

Since the different social meanings which attach to the dialect are regular and persistent, they must in some way be reinforced by the pattern of social ties. This relationship can best be described if we consider the socio-ecological system which sustains the community. There is a correlation between a person's regional background, his reference group, and the niche he occupies in this system (Barth, 1964). This information enables us to segment the local population into three distinct categories:

1   artisans;
2   wholesale–retail merchants and plant managers; and
3   service personnel.

Members of the first two categories are the basic producers of wealth.

The more than 50 percent of the population which falls into the first category includes draftsmen who may or may not own their own shops, as well as workmen employed in the larger plants and their dependents. Most of them are locally born or have been drawn to Hemnes from the surrounding farms by the demand for their skills. Since they live and work among their relatives and among others of the same social background, they tend to choose their friends and spouses from within their own reference group and thus become strong supporters of local values.

Wholesale–retail merchants buy lumber products and finished boats from producers in the Rana area, furnishing them with supplies and gear and appliances in exchange. They sell boats, lumber products, and fishing supplies to customers all the way up to the northernmost tip of Norway. Relationships between merchants and their customers most commonly take the form of long-term credit arrangements based on personal trust in which credit is given to artisans against their future production. Also part of the second category are the managers of large local enterprises who achieve their position partly because of their special commercial and managerial skills and partly through their ability to get along with and keep the confidence of owners, workers, and foremen.

Like artisans, members of category 2 are largely of local descent. Although they tend to be in the higher income brackets, they maintain kin and conjugal relationships among craftsmen and fishermen-farmers. The fact that their livelihood depends to a great extent on their standing within the system of locally based relations leads them to associate more closely with the local values. The circumstances of their commercial enterprises, however, also take them outside this local network. They must be able to act within the urban commercial ethic, and they must also maintain personal ties with their customers in the north and elsewhere. The range of their social connections includes both local and supralocal ties, involving different and sometimes conflicting standards of behavior. The result is that while they maintain strong loyalty to general local values, they tend to avoid close personal ties with their kin in the first category and confine their friendships to others who are in similar circumstances.

The third category is a composite one, consisting of individuals whose position depends on the productivity of others. It includes persons engaged in purely local services – private and administrative – of all kinds such as salesmen, clerks, repairmen, shopkeepers, professionals, and those who are employed in repair shops and in transportation. The socio-cultural background of these people varies. Those who perform manual labor tend to be of local descent and are culturally indistinguishable from members of the first category. The same is true for the lower echelons of employees in stores and in administrative offices. Among the owners of retail businesses – clothing, shoe, pastry, and stationery shops – many belong to families who have moved to Hemnesberget from other urban or semi-urban centers in northern Norway. Their kin and friendship relations tend to be dispersed among these communities, and this leads them to identify with the differentiated nonlocal middle-class value system. Shopowners of local background also aspire to these standards, at the same time trying to maintain their position in the "local team" by showing loyalty to its values. Professionals are similarly drawn to Hemnes from the outside because of their technical expertise. The more stable core of this group, the schoolteachers, tend to be of north Norwegian background. Doctors, veterinarians, dentists, and priests frequently come from the south. Invariably their values are those of the pan-Norwegian elite.

Economic conditions in Hemnes leave little room for the academically trained and those with technical skills outside local niches. Consequently, young people from all categories who aspire to higher education must spend most of their student years away from Hemnes and will eventually have to seek employment somewhere else. While they remain students, however, they are partly dependent on their families. They tend to return home during the summer vacation and seek local employment.

Contextual constraints

Previous sections have dealt with the linguistic repertoire, internal cultural differences, and relevant features of social organization. We have suggested that linguistic alternates within the repertoire serve to symbolize the differing social identities which members may assume. It is, however, evident from our discussion that there is by no means a simple one-to-one relationship between specific speech varieties and specific social identities. Apart from the fact that values attached to language usage vary with social background, the same individual need not be absolutely consistent in all his actions. He may wish to appear as a member of the local team on some occasions, while identifying with middle-class values on others. In order to determine the social significance of any one utterance, we need additional information about the contextual clues by which natives arrive at correct interpretations of social meaning.

Recent linguistic writings have devoted considerable attention to speech events as the starting point for the analysis of verbal communication. It has been shown that aside from purely linguistic and stylistic rules, the form of a verbal message in any speech event is directly affected by:

1   the participants, i.e. speakers, addressees, and audiences;
2   the ecological surroundings; and
3   the topic or range of topics (Hymes, 1964; Ervin-Tripp, 1964).

In visualizing the relationship between social and linguistic factors in speech events, it seems reasonable to assume that the former restrict the selection of linguistic variables in somewhat the same way that syntactic environments serve to narrow the broader dictionary meanings of words. For the purpose of our analysis, we can thus visualize verbal communication as a two-step process. In step 1, speakers take in clues from the outside and translate them into appropriate behavioral strategies. This step parallels the perceptual process by which referential meanings are converted into sentences. In step 2, these behavioral strategies are in turn translated into appropriate verbal symbols. The determinants of this communicative process are the speaker's knowledge of the linguistic repertoire, culture, and social structure, and his ability to relate these kinds of knowledge to contextual constraints. For Hemnesberget, it seems useful to describe these constraints in terms of three concepts representing successively more complex levels of information processing.

We will use the term *setting* to indicate the way in which natives classify their ecological environment into distinct locales. This enables us to relate the opportunities for action to constraints upon action provided by the socially significant features of the environment. First, and most important among local settings in Hemnesberget, is the home. Homes form the center for all domestic activities and act as meeting places for children's peer groups. Houses are well built and provide ample space for all. Also, friends and kin prefer the privacy of meetings at home to restaurants or other more public places.

Workshops and plants where productive activity is carried on are separated for the most part from residential areas, although some families continue to live next to their workshops along the shore of the fjord. The workforce normally consists of male members of the group of owners, whether managed by a single nuclear family or by a group of families connected by filial, sibling, or in-law ties. Employees in the larger plants frequently also include groups of kin who work together as work teams. In view of the homogeneity of workers, it is not surprising that the place of work frequently forms the center for informal gathering among males. In offices, shops, and merchant establishments, however, where the expertise requirements favor socially more differentiated personnel, work relations tend to be less colored by pre-existent social ties.

A second group of settings lacks the specific restrictions on personnel which mark those just mentioned. These include the public dock, where visiting boats and the steamer are moored, as well as a few of the larger stores, e.g., the co-operative society store located near the central square, the square itself, and the community park. Here all local residents may meet somewhat more freely without commitments, subject, of course, to the constraints imposed by lack of privacy. The primary school, the junior high school, the church, and community meeting hall all form somewhat more restricted meeting grounds for more formal gatherings, such as classroom sessions, religious services, political meetings, meetings of various voluntary associations, and occasional movies. The church is used only for church services.

The socio-ecological restrictions on personnel and activities still allow for a wide range of socially distinct happenings The school, e.g., is used for class sessions during the day and for meetings of voluntary associations during the evening. Similarly, in the town square, men gather for discussions of public affairs, women shoppers stop to chat with acquaintances, adolescent peer groups play their various games, etc. A closer specification of social constraints is possible if we concentrate on activities carried on by particular constellations of personnel, gathered in particular settings during a particular span of time. We will use the term *social situation* to refer to these. Social situations form the background for the enactment of a limited range of social relationships within the framework of specific status sets, i.e. systems of complementary distributions of rights and duties (Barth, 1966).

Thus alternative social definitions of the situation may occur within the same setting, depending on the opportunities and constraints on interaction offered by a shift in personnel and/or object of the interaction. Such definitions always manifest themselves in what we would prefer to call a *social event*. Events center around one or at the most a limited range of topics and are distinguishable because of their sequential structure. They are marked by stereotyped and thus recognizable opening and closing routines. The distinction between situation and event can be clarified if we consider the behavior of Hemnes residents who are sometimes seen in the community office, first transacting their business in an officially correct manner, and then turning to one of the clerks and asking him to step aside for a private chat. The norms which apply to the two kinds of interaction differ; the break between the two is clearly marked. Therefore, they constitute two distinct social events, although the personnel and the locale remain the same.

The terms setting, social situation, and social event as used here can be considered three successively more complex stages in the speaker's processing of contextual information. Each stage subsumes the previous one in such a way that the preceding one is part of the input affecting the selection rules of the next stage. Thus, a speaker cannot identify the social situation without first having made some decision as to the nature of the setting. To demonstrate how these factors influence language usage in Hemnesberget, we turn now to some examples drawn from participant observation.

The fact that the dialect reflects local values suggests that it symbolizes relationships based on shared identities with local culture. Casual observations and recording of free speech among locals in homes, workshops, and the various public meeting places where such relationships are assumed do indeed show that only the dialect is used there. However, statuses defined with respect to the superimposed national Norwegian system elicit the standard. Examples of these are church services, presentation of text material in school, reports, and announcements – but not necessarily informal public appeals or political speeches – at public meetings. Similarly, meetings with tourists or other strangers elicit the standard at least until the participants' identity becomes more clearly known.

Situational and metaphorical switching

When within the same setting the participants' definition of the social event changes, this change may be signaled among others by linguistic clues. On one occasion, when we, as outsiders, stepped up to a group of locals engaged in conversation, our arrival caused a significant alteration in the casual posture of the group. They took their hands out of their pockets and their expressions changed. Predictably, our remarks elicited a code-switch marked simultaneously by a change in channel cues (i.e. sentence speed, rhythm, more hesitation pauses, etc.) and by a shift from (R) to (B) grammar. Similarly, teachers report that while formal lectures – where interruptions are not encouraged – are delivered in (B), the speakers will shift to (R) when they want to encourage open and free discussion among students. Each of these examples involves clear changes in the participants' definition of each other's rights and obligations. We use the term *situational switching* to refer to this kind of a language shift.

The notion of situational switching assumes a direct relationship between language and the social situation. The linguistic forms employed are critical features of the event in the sense that any violation of selection rules changes members' perception of the event. A person who uses the standard where only the dialect is appropriate violates commonly accepted norms. His action may terminate the conversation or bring about other social sanctions. To be sure, language choice is never completely fixed; sociolinguistic variables must be investigated empirically. Furthermore, situations differ in the amount of freedom of choice allowed to speakers. Ritual events, like the well-known Vedic ceremonies of South Asia, constitute extreme examples of determination, where every care is taken to avoid even the slightest change in pronunciation or rhythm lest the effectiveness of the ceremony be destroyed. The greetings, petitions, and similar routines described by Albert (1972) similarly seem strictly determined.

In Hemnesberget, as our example below shows, speakers are given relatively wide choice in vocabulary and some choice in syntax. Selection rules affect mainly the variables discussed previously. Values of these variables are sociolinguistically determined in the sense that when, on the one hand, we speak of someone giving a classroom lecture or performing a Lutheran church service or talking to a tourist, we can safely assume that he is using (B) grammatical forms. On the other hand, two locals having a heart-to-heart talk will presumably speak in (R). If instead they are found speaking in (B), we conclude either that they do not identify with the values of the local team or that they are not having a heart-to-heart talk.

In contrast with those instances where choice of variables is narrowly constrained by social norms, there are others in which participants are given considerably more latitude. Thus, official community affairs are largely defined as nonlocal and hence the standard is appropriate. But since many individuals who carry out the relevant activities all know each other as fellow locals, they often interject casual statements in the dialect into their formal discussions. In the course of a morning spent at the community administration office, we noticed that clerks used both standard and dialect phrases, depending on whether they were talking about official affairs or not. Likewise, when residents step up to a clerk's desk, greeting and inquiries about family affairs tend to be exchanged in the dialect, while the business part of the transaction is carried on in the standard.

In neither of these cases is there any significant change in definition of participants' mutual rights and obligations. The posture of speakers and channel clues of their speech remain the same. The language switch here relates to particular kinds of topics or subject matter rather than to change in social situation. Characteristically, the situations in question allow for the enactment of two or more different relationships among the same set of individuals. The choice of either (R) or (B) alludes to these relationships and thus generates meanings which are quite similar to those conveyed by the alternation between *ty* or *vy* in the examples from Russian literature cited by Friedrich (1972). We will use the term *metaphorical switching* for this phenomenon.

The semantic effect of metaphorical switching depends on the existence of regular relationships between variables and social situations of the type just discussed. The context in which one of a set of alternates is regularly used becomes part of its meaning, so that when this form is then employed in a context where it is not normal, it brings in some of the flavor of this original setting. Thus, a phrase like "April is the cruelest month" is regarded as poetic because of its association with T.S. Eliot's poetry. When used in natural conversation, it gives that conversation some of the flavor of this poetry. Similarly, when (R) phrases are inserted metaphorically into a (B) conversation, this may, depending on the circumstances, add a special social meaning of confidentiality or privateness to the conversation.

The case of the local who, after finishing his business in the community office, turns to a clerk and asks him to step aside for a private chat further illustrates the contrast between metaphorical and role switching. By their constant alternation between the standard and the dialect during their business transaction, they alluded to the dual relationship which exists between them. The event was terminated when the local asked the clerk in the dialect whether he had time to step aside to talk about private affairs, suggesting in effect that they shift to a purely personal, local relationship. The clerk looked around and said, "Yes, we are not too busy." The two then stepped aside, although remaining in the same room, and their subsequent private discussion was appropriately carried on entirely in the dialect.

The experiment

Our discussion of verbal behavior so far has relied largely on deductive reasoning supported by unstructured ethnographic observation. Additional tests of our hypothesis are based on controlled text elicitation. We have stated that gatherings among friends and kin implying shared local identities must be carried on in the dialect. If we are correct in our hypothesis, then individuals involved in such friendly gatherings should not change speech variety regardless of whether they talk about local, national, or official matters.

In order to test this, we asked local acquaintances whom we knew to be part of the network of local relationships to arrange a friendly gathering at which refreshments were to be served and to allow us to record the proceedings as samples of dialect speech. Two such gatherings were recorded, one in the living room of our local hosts, and the other in the home of an acquaintance. The fact that arrangements for the meeting were made by local people means that the groups were self-recruited. Participants in the first group included two sisters and a brother and their respective spouses. One of the men was a shopkeeper, one of the few in this category who claims local descent; his brothers-in-law were employed as craftsmen. All three men are quite literate compared to workmen elsewhere in the world and well read in public affairs. They are active in local politics and experienced in formal committee work. The second group included three craftsmen, friends and neighbors who worked in the same plant, and their wives. One of these had served as a sailor on a Norwegian merchant vessel for several years and spoke English. Participants were all quite familiar with standard Norwegian, and our recorded conversations contain several passages where the standard was used in quoting nonlocal speech or in statements directed at us.

Methodologically, self-recruitment of groups is important for two reasons. It ensures that groups are defined by locally recognized relationships and enables the investigator to predict the norms relevant to their interaction. Furthermore, the fact that participants have pre-existing obligations toward each other means that, given the situation, they are likely to respond to such obligations in spite of the presence of strangers. Our tape recording and our visual observations give clear evidence that this in fact was what occurred.

Our strategy was to introduce discussion likely to mobilize obligations internal to the group, thus engaging members in discussion among themselves. This proved to be relatively easy to do. When a point had been discussed for some time, we would attempt to change the subject by injecting new questions or comments. In doing this we did not, of course, expect that our own interjections would predictably affect the speakers' choice of codes. Participants were always free to reinterpret our comments in any way they wished. Nevertheless, the greater the range of topics covered, the greater was the likelihood of language shift.

As a rule, our comments were followed by a few introductory exchanges directed at us. These were marked by relatively slow sentence speeds, many hesitation pauses, and visual clues indicating that people were addressing us. Linguistically, we noted some switching to the standard in such exchanges. After a brief period of this, if the topic was interesting, internal discussion began and arguments that referred to persons, places, and events we could not possibly be expected to have any knowledge about developed. The transition to internal discussion was marked by an increase in sentence speed and lack of hesitation pauses and similar clues. The tape recorder was run continuously during the gatherings, and after some time participants became quite oblivious to its presence.

Only those passages which were clearly recognizable as internal discussion were used in the analysis; all others were eliminated. The texts obtained in this way consist of stretches of free discussion on diverse topics. The following passages show that our hypothesis about the lack of connection between code-switching and change in topic was confirmed.

Group I   Topic: Chit-chat about local events
Gunnar: *ja de va ein så kåmm idag – ein så kåmm me mælka – så så hanj de va så varmt inj på mo i går – ja, sa eg, de va no iççe vent anjæ dåkk må no ha meir enn di anjrann bestanjdi.*
(Yes, there was one who came today – one who came with milk – so he said it was so warm in Mo yesterday. Yes, I said, there is nothing else to be expected, you people must always have more than anybody else.)

Topic: Industrial planning
Alf: *her kunj ha vore eit par sånn mellomstore bedreftæ på ein førtifæmti manu so ha beſæftigæ denna fålke detta så ha gådd ledi amm vinjtærn.*
(There might have been here some medium-size plants employing forty to fifty men which then could offer work to those who have nothing to do in winter.)

Topic: Governmental affairs
Oscar: *vi jekk inj før denn forste injstiljingæ ifrå Seikommitenn.*
(We supported the first proposal made by the Schei Committee.)

The first item in Group I deals with a local topic in a somewhat humorous way; the second and third items concern planning and formal governmental affairs. All these passages are clearly in the dialect. Of the phonological variables, [nj] and [lj] show the highest degree of palatalization and [a] and [æ] the highest degree of retraction throughout. Morphophonemic dialect markers are (R) *ein* "one," *så* "who," *içe* "not," *dåkk* "you," *meir* "more," *her* "here," *jekk* "went," *ifrå* "from." Even lexical borrowings from the standard such as *injstiljing* "proposal" and *bedreftæ* "plants" are clearly in dialect phonology and morphology. We find one single instance of what seems to be a standard form: (B) *mellom* / (R) *imelja* "middle." But this only occurs as part of the borrowed compound *mellomstore* "medium-size." In several hours of conversation with both groups, marked by many changes in topic, we have found a number of lexical borrowings but not a clear instance of phonological or grammatical switching, in spite of the fact that all informants clearly know standard grammar.

While our hypothesis suggests that switching is constrained in those situations which allow only local relationships to be enacted, it also leads us to predict that whenever local and nonlocal relationships are relevant to the same situation, topical variation may elicit code-switching. To test this, we selected members of a formerly quite active local peer group. For the last few years these individuals had all been at universities in Oslo, Bergen, and Trondheim. They returned home in the summer either for vacation or to take up local employment. In conventional interview sessions, all participants claimed to be pure dialect speakers and professed local attitudes about dialect use. They thus regarded themselves as members of the local "team." As fellow students, however, they also shared statuses that are identified with pan-Norwegian values and associated with the standard. Our assumption, then, is that if topical stimuli are introduced which elicit these values, switching may result.

Three gatherings were arranged in the home of one of our informants. Refreshments were again served. Elicitation strategies were similar to those employed with the first two groups, and similar ranges of topics were covered. The examples cited here show that our hypothesis was again confirmed.

> *Group II* Topic: Chit-chat about drinking habits
> *Berit*: *ja, ja, mæn vi bjynjt anjer veien du — vi bjynjt i barnelofen — så vi har de*
> *unjajort.*
> (Yes, yes, we started the other way, we started in the children's anti-alcoholic league. So we have finished all that.)
>
> Topic: Industrial development
> *Berit*: *jo da viss di bare fikk de te lønn seg — så e i værtfall prisnivåe hær i Rana*
> *skrudd høger enn de e vanligvis anner stann i lanne.*
> (Yes, if they could only manage to make it profitable — so in any case the prices tend to be higher here in Rana than is common in other places in the country.)
>
> Topic: Informal statement about university regulations
> *Ola*: *mænn no ha dæmm læmpæ pa de.*
> (But now they have relaxed that.)
>
> Topic: Authoritative statement about university regulations
> *Ola*: *de voel du mellom en faemm saeks.*
> (You choose that from among five or six.)

Comparison of Berit's and Ola's first statement with their second statements shows considerable shifting in each case. Thus, Berit's second utterance has such unpalatalized forms as *anner* (vs. *anjer*), and raised and less retracted [a] in *da*. She also uses standard variables (B) *fikk* / (R) *fekk*, (B) *viss* / (R) *vess*, (B) *værtfall* / (R) *kvartfall*, (B) *hær* / (R) *her*, etc. Ola's second statement is characterized by (B) *mellon* / (R) *imelja* and (B) *en* / (R) *ein*. Similarly, his [æ] in *fæm* and *sæks* is raised and fronted. In neither case is the shift to the standard complete; after all the situation never lost its informality. Berit's statement still contains dialect words like (R) *lønn* / (B) *lønne* "to be profitable," (R) *stan* / (B) *steder* "places," and Ola has (R) *væl* / (B) *velger* "to choose." What we see then is a breakdown of co-occurrence rules, an erosion of the linguistic boundary between Ranamål and Bokmål. The tendency is to switch toward standard phonology while preserving some morphophonemic and lexical dialect features of (R). Features retained in this manner are largely those which also occur in other local dialects and to some extent also in standard Norwegian. They have thus gained some acceptance as proper dialect forms. Those characteristics which locals refer to as broad speech – i.e. those that are known as local peculiarities – tend to be eliminated.

It must also be noted that Berit and Ola also differ in their pronunciation of the phonological variables. Ola's normal pronunciation shows the strong palatalization of consonant and extreme vowel retraction characteristic of most residents. Berit's normal pronunciation has medium palatalization and medium retraction. Both, however, switch in the same direction, in response to similar situational and topical clues, and this agreement on the rules of stylistic manipulation is clearly more important in this case than the mere articulatory difference in Berit's and Ola's speech.

The social character of the style switch was clearly revealed when the tape-recorded conversations were played back to other Hemnes residents. One person who had been working with us as a linguistic informant at first refused to believe that the conversations were recorded locally. When he recognized the voices of the participants, he showed clear signs of disapproval. Apparently, he viewed the violation of co-occurrence rules as a sign of what is derogatorily called *knot* "artificial speech" in colloquial Norwegian. Some of the participants showed similar reactions when they heard themselves on tape. They promised to refrain from switching during future discussion sessions. Our analysis of these later sessions, however, revealed that when an argument required that the speaker validate his status as an intellectual, he would again tend to use standard forms in the manner shown by Berit and Ola. Code selection rules thus seem to be akin to grammatical rules. Both operate below the level of consciousness and may be independent of the speaker's overt intentions.

Additional information about usage patterns was provided through an accident. One of our sessions with this group was interrupted by a somewhat mentally retarded young person, who has the habit of appearing in people's homes to solicit assistance for his various schemes. Here are some examples of remarks addressed to him by Berit and Solveig. Of all the members of the group, Solveig was the most prone to use standard forms. Her normal pronunciation shows the least amount of consonant palatalization. She is socially more marginal to Hemnes than other members of the group.

> *Group III*   Topic: Talking to a retarded local youth
> Berit: *e de du så vikarier førr hanj no.*
>   (Are you a stand-in for him now?)
> Solveig: *hanj kanj jo jett gåte, haj kanj no va me.*
>   (He is good at word games, he should participate.)

Both Berit and Solveig's pronunciation in these examples become identical with the ordinary speech of Ola and of the members of Group I. The extreme palatalization of [nj] and the lowering of [a] is not normal for them; they are clearly talking down in this case. Their stylistic range, as well as their facility in switching, seem to be greater than those of the others.

In comparing the behavior of the first two groups with that of Group III, we find two different kinds of language-usage patterns. All three groups speak both the dialect and the standard. Groups I and II, however, show only situational switching. When members talk to each other, differences of formality or informality to topic are reflected only in the lexicon. Pronunciation and morphology do not change. Those groups shift to (B) phonology and grammar only when remarks are addressed directly to us who count as outsiders or in indirect quotes on such matters as government rules, on officials' statements, etc. In such instances of situation switching, therefore, Ranamål and Bokmål are kept separate throughout by strict co-occurrence restrictions. In Group III, however, deviation from the dialect results both from metaphorical and situation switching. Metaphorical switching, furthermore, involves a breakdown of the co-occurrence restrictions characteristic of situational shifts.

The dialect usage of locals, on the one hand, corresponds to their view that the two varieties are distinct, and to their insistence on maintaining the strict separation of local and nonlocal values. For the students, on the other hand, the distinction between dialect and standard is not so sharp. Although they display the same general attitudes about the dialect as the team of locals, their behavior shows a range of variation rather than an alternation between distinct systems. It reflects a de facto recognition of their own nonlocal identification.

A fourth conversational group further illustrates the internal speech diversity in the community. The principal speakers here were two men (A and B) and a woman (C), married to A. All came from families who tended to dissociate themselves from the egalitarian value system of the local team. Their normal style of speech was Bokmål for remarks directed at us, as well as for in-group speech. Only in a few instances when A began telling local anecdotes did he lapse into Ranamål. (R) forms were introduced as metaphorical switches into what were basically (B) utterances to provide local color, indicate humor, etc., in somewhat the same way that speakers in Group III had used (B) forms in (R) utterances.

In the course of the evening A and C's teenage daughter joined the conversation. She expressed attitudes toward the dialect which are quite similar to those of the students in Group III and thus are somewhat different from those of her parents. The few samples we have of her speech show (R) phonology similar to that of Berit and Solveig in Group III.

Although the picture of language usage derived from the four groups seems at first highly complex, it becomes less so when viewed in relation to speakers' attitudes, interactional norms, and local values. All Hemnes residents have the same repertoire. Their linguistic competence includes control of both (R) and (B) rules. They vary in the way in which they use these rules. Expressed attitudes toward (R) and (B) do not provide an explanation for these differences in speech behavior. The most reasonable explanation of the ways in which these groups differ seems to be that the dual system of local values, differences in individual background, and the various social situations in which members find themselves operate to affect their interpretation of the social meaning of the variables they employ.

Conclusion

Our analysis in this chapter is based on the assumption that regularities in behavior can be analyzed as generated from a series of individual choices made under specifiable constraints and incentives (Barth, 1966). This position implies an important break with previous approaches to social structure and to language and society. Behavioral regularities are no longer regarded as reflections of independently measurable social norms; on the contrary, these norms are themselves seen as communicative behavior. They are reflected in what Goffman (1959) calls the rules of impression management or, in our terms, in the social meanings which constrain the actor's adoption of behavioral strategies in particular situations.

In interactional sociolinguistics, therefore, we can no longer base our analyses on the assumption that language and society constitute different kinds of reality, subject to correlational studies. Social and linguistic information is comparable only when studied within the same general analytical framework. Moving from statements of social constraints to grammatical rules thus represents a transformation from one level of abstraction to another within a single communicative system.

As Bernstein (1961) has pointed out, verbal communication is a process in which actors select from a limited range of alternates within a repertoire of speech forms determined by previous learning. Although ultimately this selection is a matter of individual choice, this chapter shows that the rules of codification by which the deep structure of interpersonal relations is transformed into speech performances are independent of expressed attitudes and similar in nature to the grammatical rules operating on the level of intelligibility. They form part of what Hymes (1972b) has called the speaker's communicative competence. Sociolinguistic constraints on the selection of variables seem to be of central importance in this codification process. We argued that they determine the speaker's perception of the utterances as a unit of social meaning. By accepting the native's view of what is and what is not properly part of a dialect or language, linguists have tended to assume these co-occurrences rather than investigate them empirically. We have attempted to develop descriptive procedures suitable for the empirical investigation of these rules by combining various ethnographic field techniques with conventional linguistic elicitation methods.

In Hemnes, where Ranamål and Bokmål communicate the same objective information, we were led to ask how the apparent separateness of the dialect and the standard can exist and be maintained. Ethnographic investigation suggests the hypothesis that Ranamål has social value as a signal of distinctness and of a speaker's identification with others of local descent. This social significance of the dialect can only be understood by contrast with the meanings which locals assign to the standard, the language of nonlocal activities. The standard is associated with education and power on the national scene and carries connotations of differences in rank which are unacceptable in the realm of informal local relations. When used casually among Hemnes residents, therefore, it communicates dissociation from the "local team."

Since most Hemnes natives live, marry, and earn their livelihood among others of their own kind, their values are rarely challenged. Their personal relations have all the characteristics of network closure (Barnes, 1954). On the other hand, those with nonlocal background and who maintain significant ties in other communities tend to seek their friends among those in similar circumstances, even though they may have resided in Hemnes for more than a generation. Their contacts with members of the "local team" remain largely nonpersonal, focusing around single tasks, and are thus similar in kind to nonlocal contacts. This lack of personal ties between individuals of dissimilar backgrounds and cultural identification reinforces the general social meanings ascribed to the dialect by those who share local background and identity, and thus contributes to maintaining the separateness of dialect and standard.

While this information provides the background for our study, it does not explain the fact that all residents frequently switch between the dialect and the standard. This can only be explained through the analysis of particular speech events. The concepts of setting, social situation, and social event represent an attempt to explain the natives' conception of their behavioral environment in terms of an ordered set of constraints which operate to transform alternative lines of behavior into particular social meanings. Our distinction between metaphoric and role switching shows how constraints at different levels of inclusiveness produce appropriate changes in the way speech performances are interpreted.

Although locals show an overt preference for the dialect, they tolerate and use the standard in situations where it conveys meanings of officiality, expertise, and politeness toward strangers who are clearly segregated from their personal life. In private gatherings where people meet as natives and equals, a speaker's use of standard variables suggests social dissociation, an attitude which is felt to be out of place. Although the students in our experimental sessions meet as locals and friends, they differ from other members of the local team because they share the additional status of intellectuals. This fact modifies the social meaning of standard forms when they are used among the students. To refrain from using standard forms for these topics which elicit participants' shared experience as intellectuals would constitute an unnatural limitation on their freedom of expression. Group IV demonstrates the effect of intracommunity differences in value systems on language-usage patterns. Because of this identification with the urban middle classes, the adult members of this group use (B) as their normal form of speech while employing (R) only for special effect. Such usage distinctions, however, are not necessarily very stable. The teenage daughter of the adult members seems to follow local usage, thus symbolizing her identification with her peer group rather than with her family.

Our experiments, and the analysis presented in this chapter, demonstrate the importance of social or nonreferential meaning for the study of language in society. Mere naturalistic observation of speech behavior is not enough. In order to interpret what he hears, the investigator must have some background knowledge of the local culture and of the processes which generate social meaning. Without this it is impossible to generalize about the social implication of dialect differences. The processes studied here are specific to particular small communities. Predictions of language maintenance or language shift in larger societies will, of course, have to depend on statistical generalizations. More studies along the lines suggested here, however, should materially improve the validity of such generalizations. For Hemnesberget, the fate of the dialect seems assured as long as local identification maintains its importance, and the socio-ecological system continues to prevent any significant accumulation of individuals who, like the students, fail to maintain the situational barrier between the dialects and the standard.

Source: Blom, J.-P. and Gumperz, J.J. (1972) Social meaning in linguistic structure: code-switching in Norway. In J.J. Gumperz and D. Hymes (eds) *Directions in Sociolinguistics*, New York: Holt, Rinehart and Winston, pp. 407–34, by permission of the authors.

Jan-Petter Blom, PhD, is Professor Emeritus of Social Anthropology at the University of Bergen, Norway. jan.blom@sosantr.uib.no

John J. Gumperz, PhD, is Professor Emeritus of Anthropology at the University of California, Berkeley, USA. gumperz@education.ucsb.edu

Chapter 5

Code-switching as indexical of social negotiations

CAROL MYERS-SCOTTON

T HIS CHAPTER PROVIDES AN overall explanation of code-switching, using primarily an East African data base. A number of previous studies have dealt with code-switching in East African contexts. Their emphasis, however, has been different (Abdulaziz-Mkilifi, 1972; Whiteley, 1974; Abdulaziz, 1982; Scotton, 1982), or their explanations have not been comprehensive (Parkin, 1974; Scotton, 1976; Scotton and Ury, 1977). Some of these studies are mentioned in the synthesis given here.

The model developed here focuses on social consequences as motivating linguistic code choices and how speakers use conversational implicatures to arrive at the intended consequences. In this sense, it extends the markedness model of Scotton (1983), proposed to explain code choice in general, but its focus is more specific. The premise of Scotton (1983) is that in addition to relying on a cooperative principle, its associated maxims, and the conversational implicatures which they generate in understanding the content of what is said (Grice, 1975), speakers use a complementary negotiation principle to arrive at the relational import of a conversation. The negotiation principle directs the speaker to 'choose the form of your conversational contribution such that it symbolizes the set of rights and obligations which you wish to be in force between speaker and addressee for the current exchange' (Scotton, 1983: 116). A set of maxims referring to the choice of one linguistic variety rather than another relates to this principle, and the speaker's following or flouting the maxims generates implicatures about proposed interpersonal relationships.

While conveying referential information is often the overt purpose of conversation, all talk is also always a negotiation of rights and obligations between speaker and addressee. Referential content – what the conversation is about – obviously contributes to the social relationships of participants, but with content kept constant, different relational outcomes may result. This is because the particular linguistic variety used in an exchange carries social meaning. This model assumes that all linguistic code choices are indexical of a set of rights and obligations holding between participants in the conversational exchange. That is, any code choice points to a particular interpersonal balance, and it is partly because of their indexical qualities that different languages, dialects, and styles are maintained in a community.

Speakers have tacit knowledge of this indexicality as part of their communicative competence (Hymes, 1972). They have a natural theory of markedness. The result is that all speakers have mental representations of a matching between code choices and rights and obligations sets. That is, they know that for a particular conventionalized exchange, a certain code choice will be the unmarked realization of an expected rights and obligations set between participants. They also know that other possible choices are more or less marked because they are indexical of other than the expected rights and obligations set. Their reference to other sets depends on their association with other conventionalized exchanges for which they are unmarked choices. While the theory is universal, actual associations are speech community specific, with speakers knowing what code choice is unmarked and which others are marked for exchanges conventional-ized in the community.

A conventionalized exchange is any interaction for which speech community members have a sense of 'script'. They have this sense because such exchanges are frequent in the community to the extent that at least their medium is routinized. That is, the variety used or even specific phonological or syntactic patterns or lexical items employed are predictable. In many speech communities, service exchanges, peer-to-peer informal talks, doctor–patient visits, or job interviews are examples of conventionalized exchanges.

Exchanges themselves are realized as speech events consisting of specific partici-pants, a code choice and a rights and obligations balance between the participants. The rights and obligations balance for a speech event is derived from whatever situational features are salient to the exchange, such as status of participants, topic, etc. The salient features will not be the same across all types of exchanges; they are, however, relatively constant across speech events under a single type of exchange. The following example shows a change in feature salience as the exchange type changes from an interaction between strangers to an interaction as ethnic brethren. Initial interactions with security guards at places of business in Nairobi constitute a conventionalized exchange in the speech community. The most salient feature in this exchange is the visitor's appearance of being a Kenyan African or not. If the visitor is apparently a local African, the unmarked choice is Swahili, a relatively ethnically neutral lingua franca widely used across the Kenyan populace. (Observations at a number of Nairobi places of business showed that Swahili is, indeed, the unmarked choice across a number of different speech events realizing this type of exchange.) However, if the conversation develops so that shared ethnic group membership is recognized, then the interaction is perceived as a speech event under a different conventionalized exchange type. It is not an exchange between strangers who are Africans, but an exchange between strangers who share ethnic identity. In this case the most salient of their social features is the shared ethnicity and the unmarked choice for such an exchange is the shared mother tongue. The following example illustrates changes in the salience of the social features of the situ-ation. It also shows that the same uninterrupted sequence of conversational turns can constitute more than one exchange type.

> (*Entrance to the IBM Nairobi head office. The visitor, who is a school principal in the Luyia area of Western Kenya, approaches. He speaks English and Swahili fluently in addition to his first language, a Luyia variety.*)

Security Guard (Swahili): Unataka kumwona nani?
(Whom do you want to see?)
Visitor (Swahili): Napenda kumwona Solomon Inyama.
(I want to see Solomon Inyama.)
Guard (Swahili): Unamjua kweli? Tunaye Solomon Amuhaya – nadhani ndio yule.
(Do you really know him? We have a Solomon Amuhaya – I think that's the one you mean.)
Visitor (Swahili): Yule anayetoka Tiriki – yaani Mluyia.
(The one who comes from Tiriki – that is, a Luyia person.)
Guard (smiles) (switches to Luyia): Solomon mwenuyu wakhumanya vulahi?
(Does Solomon know you?)
Visitor (Luyia): Yivi mulole umovolere ndi Shem Lusimba yenyanga khukhulola.
(You see him and tell him that Shem Lusimba wants to see you.)
Guard (Luyia): Yikhala yalia ulindi.
(Sit here and wait.)
(At this point another visitor comes in.)
Visitor 2 (Swahili): Bwana Kamidi yuko hapa?
(Is Mr. Kamidi here?)
Guard (Swahili): Ndio yuko – anafanya kazi saa hii. Hawezi kuiacha mpaka iwe imekwisha. Kwa hivyo utaketi hapa mpaka aje. Utangoja kwa dakika kama kumi tano hivi.
(Yes, he's here – he is doing something right now. He can't leave until he finishes. Therefore you will wait here until he comes. You will wait about five or ten minutes.)
(Then Guard goes to look for Solomon Amuhaya.)

Speech events among white-collar office personnel constitute another type of conventionalized exchange in Nairobi. In this case, educational attainment is a more salient feature than simply being a Kenyan African or not. English is a frequent unmarked choice in such speech events, as extensive observation indicated. An example follows:

(The conversation takes place in a downtown office building. Herman, a young man who has finished secondary school and who comes from Western Kenya, is visiting a relative of his. They first converse alone in their shared mother tongue. Then, the relative switches to English as he shows him around within earshot of fellow workers.)

Relative (to Herman): And, you, are you looking for employment or have you got a job already? You look very smart as someone who is working.
Herman: I haven't got a job yet. I'm still looking for one.
Fellow worker of relative: So you have visitors. I can see you're showing someone around.
Relative: Yes, these are my visitors.

While I speak of an unmarked choice, the singular is used only as a convenience. The model calls for a markedness continuum: speakers operate with degrees of markedness, not categorical distinctions. They perceive one or more choices are more unmarked than others; and among marked choices some are more marked than others. Further, the same choice is not necessarily unmarked for all participants in the same exchange. For example, structured observations in many Nairobi offices showed that English and Swahili are both unmarked choices for conversation among fellow workers, although each one seems more unmarked under different conditions (see Scotton, 1982a).

Of course far from all exchanges are conventionalized. Very often, situations arise for which norms of behaviour are not established, or conflicting norms apply, and an unmarked choice is not clear. In such cases, community members have no communal sense of how individual participants are expected to carry out such an exchange, no sense of 'script'. Non-conventionalized exchanges typically include such situations as lengthy conversations with strangers (if their social identities remain unknown), interactions as the superior of a former peer, or conversation as a peer with someone of a much older generation. In such cases, both speaker and addressee recognize that any linguistic choice is exploratory, intended as a candidate to become the index of a mutually acceptable relationship, i.e. to become the unmarked choice.

Speaking of choices as marked or not assumes that they take place in a normative framework. Yet, norms do not determine choices. Rather, norms determine the relative markedness of a linguistic code for a particular exchange, given the association of the code with a specific rights and obligations set. What the norms do, then, is give all speakers a grammar of consequences. Speakers are free to make any choices, but how their choices will be interpreted is not free. The mental representations of the 'histories' of possible choices (and their associated rights and obligations sets) is the backdrop against which the choosing of one linguistic variety rather than another is played out. (This sets up a three-way association between the speaker, the addressee, and the speech event.)

The choices themselves are negotiations in the sense that, given the normative framework, speakers make their choices as goal-oriented actors. They weigh the relative costs and rewards of their choices in seeking a good outcome (Thibaut and Kelley, 1959; Brown and Levinson, 1978). In this way, choices are creative and 'localize' the construction of a speech event.

Three main types of choices are possible. Making the unmarked choice in a conventionalized exchange is a negotiation to recognize the status quo as the basis for the present speech event, since it is indexical of the rights and obligations balance which is expected, given the salient situational factors. But speakers also can make marked choices in conventionalized exchanges. Such a choice is a dis-identification with the expected. It is a call for some balance other than the expected one since it indexes a rights and obligations set which is unexpected, given the salient situational factors. Finally, far from all exchanges are conventionalized and choices in such cases are seen as the nominating of some rights and obligations set as, in effect, for the present exchange, i.e. as the unmarked basis pro temp.

It can be seen, then, that there is an interplay between societal factors and more dynamic, individual considerations in the choice of linguistic varieties as media for conversational exchanges. The mentally represented normative framework is the primary source of the consequences of choices. It makes speakers aware of the relative markedness of choices for a given exchange and likely outcomes. Speakers, however, are free to assert their individual motivations since, whatever their markedness, all choices are open to them. Finally, another dynamic aspect is that all choices, unmarked or not, are basically negotiations, requiring reciprocity from the addressee, making the construction of any speech event an ultimately cooperative enterprise.

Specifically in reference to code-switching, this markedness model has some of the same concerns as Scotton and Ury (1977). That is, both models stress switching as simultaneously a tool and an index. For the speaker, switching is a tool, a means of doing something (by affecting the rights and obligations balance). For the listener, switching is an index, a symbol of the speaker's intentions. Switching, therefore, is both a means and a message. The model developed in Scotton and Ury (1977), however, treated all switching as a strategy to change social relationships. Within the terms of the markedness model, attempting to change relationships involves making a marked choice, but it is only one possible motivation for switching. The markedness model predicts switching as a realization of one of three negotiations: in conventionalized exchanges, switching may be an unmarked choice between bilingual peers, or with any participants it may be a marked choice; in non-conventionalized exchanges, switching is an exploratory choice presenting multiple identities.

The psychological reality of switching as encoding such negotiations has been demonstrated empirically in two studies of reactions of local speech community members to switching in contexts familiar to them (Scotton and Ury, 1977; Scotton, 1982). In both studies, facsimile audio recordings of actual conversations were played to subjects. Local persons served as amateur actors, with the identities of the original participants masked. Subjects were told they would hear possible conversations taking place in Western Kenya, their home area. They were told they would be asked questions 'about the relationships' of the people in the conversation, but their attention was not drawn to the code-switching, or even language usage in general.

Results were consistent with the explanations proposed here and were significant, according to certain statistical tests.[1] Also of interest is that subjects regularly attributed to speakers socio-psychological motivations with interpersonal consequences, based on their language use. That is, first of all, they regularly mentioned code choices and, second, they did not link switching to folk explanations taking account only of the speaker (rather than the interaction), such as 'he switches because he can't think of the right word' or 'he is just used to speaking different languages'.

Code-switching is defined as the use of two or more linguistic varieties in the same conversation, without prominent phonological assimilation of one variety to the other. Most studies have dealt with switching between two or more distinctive languages, but the same motivations account for switching between dialects (see Chapter 5 of this volume) or styles of the same language (Gumperz, 1978; Scotton, 1985); switching may be either intrasentential or intersentential and often (but not necessarily) involves stretches of more than one word. East African data, at least, show that the free morpheme constraint on switching proposed by Sankoff and Poplack (1979/81) does not apply.[2] In Scotton (1982a) numerous switches between a first language (L1) bound morpheme and a second language (L2) morpheme which is not integrated into L1 are shown. For example:

(Swahili) Ni nani alispoil kamba yetu?
(Who spoiled our rope?)

a-	-li-	-i-	-spoil
SUBJECT	PAST TENSE	OBJECT	VERB STEM

Such hybrid forms occur especially where an international language is used daily as a second language *and* is expanding into settings in which an indigenous language had been the dominant or exclusive unmarked choice. Among educated bilinguals in various African capitals, for example, or in other parts of the Third World, something approaching a melange of two varieties (an international language which either has official status locally or is the unmarked medium of international contacts and an indigenous mother tongue) is common, especially for informal interactions. (The discussion below on overall code-switching as an unmarked choice relates to such usage.)

Agreeing on labels for these innovating varieties is a problem, with the use of 'code-mixing' alongside 'code-switching' as somewhat unfortunate. This is so for two reasons. First, some writers use 'mixing' for what is referred to here as 'switching'; but others use mixing for intrasentential shifts only, reserving 'switching' for intersentential switches. The overlap of reference results in confusion. Second, others use 'mix' for what they see as a development beyond switching, with more integration of the two varieties than under switching (Kachru, 1978: 108). The problem is that the term 'mix' implies unprincipled chaos.

The fusion may be such that the two components form something distinct from either donor system. Gibbons speaks of the combination of English and Cantonese, used by some in Hong Kong in these terms, as 'an autonomous system' (1979: 116). (Within the model developed here, such a fused variety could develop from an overall pattern of switching as an unmarked choice, especially if it remains in place with frequent use over a period of time. However, this is not a necessary development, nor does it follow that the use of the innovating variety need convey the same social meaning as overall switching does. This is discussed below.)

In some (or in many?) cases, such amalgamating varieties may be ephemeral, associated with age grading in a way analogous to teenage slang. For example, such a variety called 'Sheng' is current today in Nairobi among the young. While it combines elements of Swahili and English (its name coming from the 's' and 'h' from Swahili and 'eng' from English), the results diverges from both. Sheng does seem to follow many of the syntactic rules of Swahili (but not all); but it has a new lexicon, including some Swahili morphemes (especially the inflectional ones), many English ones (but typically with new meanings), and also some entirely novel morphemes.[3]

Distinguishing code-switching from borrowing presents another problem.[4] Trying to resolve this problem on a structural basis, considering degree of assimilation, yields no useful results. First, assimilation is a gradient, not a categorical, concept, and can provide us only with a continuum as a metric for evaluation. Second, while an expected hypothesis is that borrowed morphemes are more assimilated phonologically into Ll than switched morphemes, what about the many clearly established borrowings which show little assimilation? (For example, *town* [taun] 'city center' shows next to no assimilation as a common loan into diverse Kenyan African languages spoken in Nairobi.) Third, what about the relative weight of phonological assimilation vs.

morphological assimilation? One may or may not be accompanied by the other. Thus, an educated Tanzanian who knows both English and Swahili may say:

> *u-si-ni-misundastand.*
> (second person singular subject prefix-NEGATIVE prefix-first person singular object prefix-MISUNDERSTAND)
> ('Don't misunderstand me.')

As a verb stem *misundastand* shows little phonological assimilation (since Swahili does not permit closed syllables or consonant clusters such as *-st-*, but it shows deep morphological assimilation (i.e. it accepts Swahili verbal inflections). The fact the same person also might say *ni-ta-cheki mambo hayo* 'I will check on those matters', with *cheki* showing both types of integration does not make it easy to claim that categorical structural criteria identifying borrowings exist.

As I hope will become clear below, however, the problem of distinguishing borrowing and switching is solved if it is approached in terms of social content, not structure. Just as, for example, all phonological or syntactic features in a social dialect are not distinctive and therefore are not crucial defining features of the dialect (they are not all socially diagnostic of social group membership), all incorporations of L2 into L1 are not diagnostic of interpersonal negotiations. Those which carry social significance (as a negotiation) constitute code-switching while those which do not are borrowings. (The only complication is that a borrowing can appear as a code-switch when it is part of style-switching. But this development is entirely consistent with the model: any style (and its components) becomes socially meaningful when it is used in a marked way. For example, a speaker may switch in an informal discussion to a style interlarded with learned loan words. This is a marked choice, possibly to negotiate a position of erudition.)

Code-switching as an unmarked choice

As noted above, the markedness model most crucially consists of a negotiation principle and a set of maxims which participants in conversation use to calculate conversational implicatures about the balance of rights and obligations which the speaker proposes for the present speech event. The unmarked choice maxim is the keystone of these maxims, directing speakers to 'make the unmarked code choice when you wish to establish or affirm the unmarked rights and obligations set associated with a particular conventionalized exchange'. Making the unmarked choice, then, gives rise to the implicature that the speaker is negotiating a normative position, the status quo (Scotton, 1983: 120).

Sequential unmarked choices

What Blom and Gumperz (see Chapter 5 of this volume) refer to as situational switching is seen within this model as a movement from one unmarked choice to another. Such sequences occur in a chain of conventionalized exchanges when participants wish to engage in normative behaviour and acknowledge that the change from one type of exchange to another has altered the expected rights and obligations balance, and therefore the relevancy of the indexical quality of one code vs. another. The example above of the security guard and visitor who first interact in Swahili and then, when their shared ethnic membership is known, in Luyia, shows sequential unmarked choices. New information (about ethnic identity) brought about a re-definition of the exchange. Another example makes even clearer how external factors are involved in changing the unmarked choice. Two East Africans from the same ethnic group will chat about personal affairs in their shared mother tongue if they are making the unmarked choice for such an exchange. But if they are joined by a friend from another ethnic group, the exchange is no longer the same. They will switch to a neutral lingua franca now if they are making the unmarked choice.

Because what stimulates the change in code is external to the participants themselves (situational features or their relative saliency are what change), calling this type of code choice situational switching clearly has its motivations. But within the model developed here, situations do not determine choices. Rather, speaker motivations do. Speakers make decisions within a framework of predictable consequences, with situations figuring only indirectly in that they alert speakers (they 'situate' them) to consequences since markedness of choices is determined by situational features. Characterizing such choices as sequential unmarked choices highlights speakers as actors and the element of predictability. While part of what happens is that the situation changes, what counts more is the change in the appropriateness of the present choice to encode the unmarked relationship between speakers, and then their decision (conscious or not) to recognize this new relationship.

Overall switching as the unmarked choice

When participants are bilingual peers, the unmarked choice may be switching with no changes at all in the situation. That is, the pattern of using two varieties for the same conventionalized exchange is itself unmarked. For example, many educated persons from the same Kenyan or Zimbabwean ethnic group alternate between their own first language and English in many conversations with peers.

The motivation for such switching is the same as that for choosing a single linguistic variety which is an unmarked choice: any variety is indexical of the speaker's position in the rights and obligations balance. When the speaker wishes more than one social identity to be salient in the current exchange, and each identity is encoded in the particular speech community by a different linguistic variety, then those two or more codes constitute the unmarked choice. In most parts of Africa, for example, speech communities are multilingual, with each language having particular associations. Ethnic identity is signaled by use of mother tongue. In addition, ability to speak the official language fluently is associated with membership in a multi-ethnic elite. Other associations are also possible. For example, speaking an indigenous lingua franca well, such as Swahili in East Africa, signals participation in a travel syndrome, usually involving experience in urban multi-ethnic areas. Knowing the language of another ethnic group is also indicative of a special social identity.

The unmarked choice for many speakers having two such identities, when talking with persons similar to themselves, is a pattern of switching between the two varieties indexical of the rights and obligations sets which the speakers wish to be in force for the speech event. The two varieties are both indexical of positively valued identities, but from different arenas, such as ethnic group membership and being part of an educated and/or urban elite.

Each switch need have no special significance; rather it is the overall pattern of using two varieties which carries social meaning (the negotiation of two different rights and obligations balances as simultaneously salient). Note that this feature distinguishes over-all switching as an unmarked choice from all other forms of code-switching since, for them, each switch signals a new negotiation.

The following example (Scotton, 1982) shows switching as an unmarked choice.

(1) *Setting: Veranda of a restaurant in Western Kenya. All participants are native speakers of Lwidakho, a Luyia variety. A staffing officer in the ministry of education, a local school teacher and his wife, who is also a school teacher, greet a secondary school headmaster who has just driven up.*

Staffing office (English): It's nice that we've met. I haven't seen you for long.

Headmaster (English): Yes, it's really long – and this is because I'm far
   from this way.

Staffing officer (Lwidakho): Yikhala yaha khulole nuva nuvula haraka.
   (Sit down if you're not in a hurry. [Note: *haraka* is Swahili loan for
   'hurry'])

Headmaster (English; Lwidakho): I'm not very much in a hurry. Nuva noveye
   na khasoda khambe.
   (Lwidakho: If you have to offer some soda, let me have it.)

Male teacher (English): Tell us about X place. How are the people there
   treating you?

Headmaster (English; Lwidakho): X is fine, the people are OK, but as you
   know, they are very tribalistic. Nuwatsa kwanalani navo ni miima jiavo.
   (Lwidakho: But now I am used to their behavior.)

Female teacher (Lwidakho): Kwahulda vakukuyagaku, gall ndi?
   (Lwidakho: We heard they attacked you and beat you up. How was
   this?)

Headmaster (Lwidakho; English): Gali madinyu. (Lwidakho: It was very
   serious.) I've seen a place where men can beat up a headmaster.
   But now they can't tell me personally. Kalunu ku tsiharambe tsya
   khohola lwayumbaha. (Lwidakho: Due to harambee spirit, we've put
   up a modern dining hall to cater for all students at once) . . .
   Ndevahe, Peter – Kekokeka Kalmosi yiki? (Lwidakho: May ask, Peter
   – what's happening at Kaimosi?)

A fragment of a conversation between two University of Nairobi students shows a conventionalized exchange for which switching between Swahili and English is an unmarked choice for bilingual peers. This is the case even though the participants share the same first language (Luo) since the setting is a university dining room, with students from other ethnic groups also participating.

(2) *Onyango (Luo; Swahili; English)*: Omera,   umesoma   katika   papers
   kwamba government imekuwa frozen.

(Luo: I say. Swahili: Have you read in the papers that the government is frozen? Meaning: there is a freeze on employment.)

Owino (Swahili): Kitambo sana.

(Swahili: Long ago.)

Onyango (Swahili; English): Na huoni kuna need ya kujaza zile forms za TSC badala ya kungojea zile za PSC?

(Swahili: And don't you think there's a need to fill in the forms of the Teacher Service Commission rather than wait for those of the Public Service Commission?)

Owino (English; Swahili): Yea, you have a point there. Singejali kuwa part-time cheater.

(Swahili: I wouldn't mind being a part-time teacher. [Note: cheater = 'teacher' in student word play.])

Onyango (Swahili; English): Hutaki kuwa full-time cheater.

(Swahili: You don't want to be a full-time teacher.)

Owino (English): No way.

Other writers in Heller (1988) – McConvell (1988) on switching among Gurindji Aborigines in Australia and Poplack (1988) on Spanish-English switching among Puerto Ricans in New York – recognize a type of switching matching these examples and the above characterization of overall switching as an unmarked choice. They do not, however, fit such switching into a model of code choice as a principled type, as is proposed here. When McConvell (1988) mentions this type of switching, though, it is in making a theoretical point which is – within my model – an important motivation for overall switching as an unmarked choice. His point is that the possibility of defining an interaction as belonging to more than one exchange type simultaneously (a 'nesting' of arenas in his terms) should be accommodated in any model. And Poplack's (1988) comment about some of the switching in New York, that 'it could be said to function as a mode of interaction similar to monolingual language use' (p. 217) is reminiscent of my claim that this type of switching is analogous to using a single code which is the unmarked choice for an exchange, the only difference being that using two codes in a switching pattern happens to be what is unmarked. Once more, her comments that this type of switching shows transitions between varieties and apparent unawareness of participants of the particular alternations between languages would apply to the type of prosody and lack of self-consciousness which would be expected when speakers are simply making the unmarked choice. Further, her description of this type of switching among Puerto Ricans in New York fits the examples from Kenya just cited. She notes that 'in the course of a single utterance the language of the discourse oscillated from English to Spanish and back to English; and during each stretch in one language there are switches of smaller constituents to the other'.

As for the function of such switches, Poplack's observation that 'individual switches cannot be attributed to stylistic or discourse functions' seems to support an important distinction this chapter makes above: that overall switching as an unmarked choice differs from other types of switching in that each switching is not socially meaningful on its own. (Rather, only the overall pattern has a discourse function.)

As noted above, overall switching as an unmarked choice seems to be the first step to what has been called the development of a semi-autonomous 'mix'. Overall switching, for example, seems to include more alternations at the bound morpheme level ('deep switching') than other types of switching, although this claim needs to be supported empirically. But typical examples are the following, taken from natural conversations of bilingual East and Central African university students:[5]

> *One student to another at the University of Nairobi:*
> Alikuwa amesit papa hapu tu . . .
> (A-li-ku-wa a-me-sit = he/she-PAST-BE-VERBAL SUFFIX he/she-PERFECT-sit)
> (Swahili/English: He/she had been sitting just right here . . .)
> [Note that SIT is used with Swahili inflectional morphemes, not English -*ing*, to convey the progressive meaning 'sitting'.]

> *One student to another at the University of Zimbabwe:*
> Huana kuda ku-mbo-react-a zvokuda ku-mu-kis-a here kana kuti?
> (Ku-mbo-react-a = INFINITIVE PREFIX-NEGATIVE INTENSIFIER 'sometimes'-react-VERBAL SUFFIX; ku-mu-kis-a = INFINITIVE PREFIX-THIRD PERSON SINGULAR OBJECT PREFIX-kiss-VERBAL SUFFIX)
> (Karanga dialect of Shona/English: Didn't you react by wanting to kiss her or to . . .)

Does overall switching as an unmarked choice occur in all bilingual communities? The answer seems to be 'no'. Elsewhere (Scotton, 1986), I suggest that overall switching as an unmarked choice would be hypothesized as unlikely in a narrow diglossic community where there is strict allocation of the two varieties involved. But not only is the degree of normative compartmentalization of the varieties important, what must be considered is the evaluation of the varieties (as vehicles of the identities they encode), as is discussed more fully below.

Let us first consider some data. Poplack (1988) notes that this type of switching (she refers to it at times as 'skilled' switching but elsewhere as 'true' switching) occurs only infrequently in an Ottawa–Hull study of French–English switching. She says this is the case 'despite the fact that the participant constellation, mode of interaction and bilingual situation appear to be similar to those in the Puerto Rican study' (p. 230). (Most of the switching she reports among the French Canadians would be classified as making marked choices in terms of this model.)

A similar lack of switching as an overall pattern for informal interactions was reported for instructors of English at the University of Panama in the 1980s (Alnouri, personal communication). Staff room interactions were almost all entirely in Spanish for these native speakers of Spanish who taught English. One possible reason for not switching to English was that such usage would provide invidious comparisons among persons whose livelihood depended on their English competence. But another reason may have been that there was hostility toward the United States at the time over the Panama Canal. Therefore, a persona as an English speaker was not valued for informal interactions with Panamanian peers.

These examples support the hypothesis that overall switching as an unmarked choice between bilingual peers is only frequent when both varieties are indexical of identities which are positively evaluated for the specific exchange type. For example, this means the point is not that English is never associated with positive values by French

Canadians, or that they do not see themselves as bilinguals. Rather, this hypothesis would predict that an overall pattern of switching is infrequent because an identity encoded by English is not valued specifically for informal exchanges with French Canadian peers. Obviously, data from other communities, including attitudinal studies, would be necessary to support this hypothesis in any meaningful way. But the overall insight that the specific type of switching possible will depend on evaluations of the varieties involved (and that evaluations are not of one fabric, but are exchange specific) seems valid.[6]

Code-switching as a marked choice

Switching away from the unmarked choice in a conventionalized exchange signals that the speaker is trying to negotiate a different rights and obligations balance as salient in place of the unmarked one, given the situational features. Such switching constitutes a marked choice, a flouting of the unmarked choice maxim.

Because a marked choice is a violation, it is always disruptive, although it can be so in a positive or negative sense. That is, a marked choice can be positive by narrowing social distance if it is indexical of a relationship of solidarity, given the normative matrix of associations between varieties and social meanings in the community. Or, it can be negative in that it increases social distance because it encodes anger or the desire to make a power differential salient (when it would not be salient ordinarily). As noted above, marked choices are interpreted by matching them with the exchanges in which they would be unmarked choices. Thus, in the following speech event a passenger begins speaking to the bus conductor in the passenger's own native language, not in the unmarked choice for this event, Swahili. Everyone present laughs (including the passenger, who seemed to intend his use of his language as a joke). How is the choice of his own language to be interpreted? By reference to those exchanges in which it would be the unmarked choice. And those are largely exchanges in which solidarity is salient. Thus, as a marked choice, using his native language is a negotiation for solidarity with the bus conductor, if only facetiously. While the conductor rejects the bid for solidarity as such, he does give the passenger a discount, indicating the bid to alter the unmarked rights and obligations balance has worked.

> Setting: A bus in Nairobi, with Swahili as the unmarked choice for the conven-
> tionalized exchange of passenger to conductor. A Luyia man who has just got on the
> bus speaks to conductor.

> Passenger (Lwidakho) (Speaking in a loud and joking voice): Mwana weru,
>   vugula khasimoni khonyene.
>   (Dear brother, take only fifty cents.) (Laughter from conductor and
>   other passengers)
> Passenger (Lwidakho): Shuli mwana wera mbaa?
>   (Aren't you my brother?)
> Conductor (Swahili): Apana. Mimi Si ndugu wako, kama ungekuwa ndugu
>   wangu ningekujua kwa jina. Lakini sasa sikujui wala sikufahamu.
>   (No, I am not your brother. If you were my brother, I would know
>   you by name. But, now I don't know you or understand you.)

> *Passenger (Swahili)*: Nisaidie, tu, bwana. Maisha ya Nairobi imenishinda kwa
> sababu bei ya kila kitu imeongezwa. Mimi ninaketi Kariobang'i, pahali
> ninapolipa pesa nyingi sana kwa nauli ya basi.
> (Just help me, mister. The life of Nairobi has defeated me because the
> price of everything has gone up. I live at Kariobang'i, a place to which
> I pay much money for the bus fare.)
>
> *Conductor*: Nimechukua peni nane pekee yake.
> (I have taken 80 cents alone.)
>
> *Passenger (English; Swahili)*: Thank you very much. Nimeshukuru sana kwa
> huruma ya huyu ndugu wango.
> (I am very thankful for the pity of this one, my brother.)

Scotton and Ury (1977: 16–17) cite another example showing a marked choice in a conversation on a bus in Nairobi. But in this case, the passenger's marked choice is to encode authority and educational status, not solidarity. The conductor counters by matching the passenger's marked choice, showing that he too can compete in any power game (involving here ability to speak English):

> *Setting: A conductor on a Nairobi bus has just asked a passenger where he is going in order to determine the fare (in Swahili).*
>
> *Passenger (Swahili)*: Nataka kwenda posta.
> (I want to go to the post office.)
>
> *Conductor (Swahili)*: Kutoka hapa mpaka posta nauli ni senti hamsini.
> (From here to the post office, the fare is 50 cents.)
> *(Passenger gives conductor a shilling from which there should be 50 cents in change.)*
>
> *Conductor (Swahili)*: Ngojea change yako.
> (Wait for your change.)
> *(Passenger says nothing until a few minutes have passed and the bus nears the post office where the passenger will get off.)*
>
> *Passenger (Swahili)*: Nataka change yangu.
> (I want my change.)
>
> *Conductor (Swahili)*: Change utapata, Bwana.
> (You'll get your change, mister.)
>
> *Passenger (English)*: I am nearing my destination.
>
> *Conductor (English)*: Do you think I could run away with your change?

Another example shows how a marked choice is used to narrow social distance. Even though the speech event in this case is discontinuous, its parts constitute a single scenario and therefore show switching in a broad sense.

> *Setting: A young, well-educated Luyia woman is driving her car into a Nairobi athletic club where she is a member. She has stopped her car and wants the gatekeeper to open the club gate. A middle-aged man, the gatekeeper also turns out to be a Luyia, although that is not obvious until later. An ethnically neutral lingua franca, Swahili, is the unmarked choice for this speech event no matter whether speakers share*

ethnicity or not. This is probably so because, in the face of the substantial status differential between the gatekeeper (as an unskilled, little educated worker) and the upper middle-class club members, ethnicity has little or no salience as a factor in affecting the rights and obligations balance.

Gatekeeper (to young woman stopped in the middle of the gate) (Swahili): Ingla kwa
   mlango mmoja tu. (Enter by using only one gate.)
Young woman (looks behind her and sees another car pulled up so that she cannot move easily) (Swahili): Fungua miwili. Siwezi kwenda revas! Kuna magari mengine nyuma.
   (Open both. I can't reverse! There are other cars behind me.)
   (Seeing the situation, the gatekeeper very grudgingly opens both gates.)
Young woman (driving by the gatekeeper, she says to him) (Swahili): Mbona wewe mbaya sana leo?
   (Why are you so difficult today?)
   (She says to her companions in the car – in English – 'The man is a Luyia.' She determines this by his pronunciation.) (Several hours later, she drives through the gate as she leaves.)
Young woman (to gatekeeper) (Maragoli, a Luyia variety): Undindiyange vutwa.
   (You were being unkind to me.)
Gatekeeper (Swahili; Maragoli): Pole, simbere nikhumany ta.
   (Sorry. I didn't know it was you.)

The young woman's use of Luyia for the final part of this interaction was a conscious effort to establish co-ethnic identity, she reported.[7] After all, she expected to have to deal with the gatekeeper again and did not want the next encounter to be as irritating as this one had started out to be. By switching from the unmarked choice of Swahili, encoding the neutral relationship of club member: club employee, to a Luyia variety, she is asserting common ethnicity and negotiating a different relationship. The gatekeeper's reply, 'I didn't know it was you,' was interpreted by the young woman as meaning 'I didn't know you were of my ethnic group' (since he definitely did not know her personally). Both his switch from Swahili to Luyia and the content of this utterance encode a movement away from the unmarked relationship for this exchange.

   There are many variants of switching as a marked choice, with many of them relatively brief in duration – only a word or two. Yet, the same motivation characterizes such momentary switches as longer ones: a bid to dis-identify with the unmarked rights and obligations balance for the exchange. It is as if the switch is made to remind other participants that the speaker is a multi-faceted personality, as if the speaker were saying 'not only am I X, but I am also Y'. This ploy, in and of itself, is a powerful strategy because the speaker 'enlarges' himself or herself through marked choices in a mainly unmarked discourse, asserting a *range* of identities (Scotton, 1985: 113). In addition, of course, the specific associations of the variety making up the marked choice are also part of the attempted negotiation.

   A very common type of momentary marked switching is change in code for emphasis.[8] Such switching often involves repetition (in the marked code) of exactly the same referential meaning conveyed in the unmarked code. The fact there is this repetition makes it very clear that the new information is the change in code and therefore its social associations. The following examples, both involving a refusal to give money, show this. In both, the marked choice is a negotiation to increase the social distance between the speaker and his supplicant, since the switch is to a variety symbolizing authority and also unmarked for formal interactions. Such a choice reinforces the speaker's denial.

> *Setting: A farmer in rural Western Kenya is asking money of a salaried worker who is in his home area on leave. The conversation takes place in a bar where all speak the same mother tongue, Lwidakho, the unmarked choice for this exchange* (Scotton, 1983: 128).

> *Farmer (finishing an oblique request for money) (Lwidakho)*: . . . inzala ya mapesa, kambuli.
>   (Hunger for money. I don't have any.)
> *Worker (who had been speaking only Lwidakho before the request)*
>   *(English)*: You have got a land.
> *(Swahili)*: Una shamba.
>   (You have a farm/land.)
> *(Lwidakho)*: Uli mulimi.
>   (You have land.)

> *Setting: A Zimbabwean university student is refusing to give a fellow student money. He has already refused once in their shared mother tongue, the Ndau dialect of Shona; but the petitioner persists. The student switches to English.*

> *Student (English; Ndau)*: I said, 'Andidi'. I don't want!

'Permissible' marked choices

Marked choices under certain circumstances in conventionalized exchanges are allowable. These choices are marked because they do not encode the unmarked rights and obligations expected for the overall exchange. But at the same time, they are almost unmarked 'in context' because they signal what becomes a conventionalized suspension of the current rights and obligations balance. Two types seem universal: those which encode deference and those which take account of lack of ability to speak the unmarked choice.

Choices encoding deference

These choices are made when the speaker wishes special consideration from the addressee, or when the speaker wants to perform a 'face-threatening act' (Brown and Levinson, 1978) but also wants to maintain a good relationship with the addressee. Scotton (1983: 123) refers to such choices as following a *deference maxim* which, in a revised form, is 'Show deference in your code choice to those from whom you desire something or to mitigate a face threatening act.'

A major way of expressing deference is to accommodate to the addressee by switching to the variety used in his or her turn, or to a variety otherwise associated with the addressee (e.g. his or her mother tongue). Many of the subtle shifts in phonological features which Giles and his associates refer to under their accommodation hypothesis would be included here (e.g. Giles and Powesland, 1975; Thackerar *et al.*, 1982). Another way of showing deference is to switch to a variety (or sub-variety) whose unmarked use is to express respect. For example, the use of an elaborate directive form – which is in a marked style for the expected rights and obligations balance – when performing a face-threatening act illustrates this (e.g. Professor to student: 'If it is not out of your way, I would appreciate it if you would please check on whether the library received my reserve list.').

The use of a term of respect, which is part of a style, dialect or language whose use is not called for by the unmarked rights and obligations balance, is also an instance of following the deference maxim. Scotton and Zhu (1984) report that many customers in Beijing service encounters call unskilled personal *shi fu*, a term whose meaning is now changing, but generally it means either 'elder craftsman' or at the very least 'skilled worker'. Scotton and Zhu refer to such switching as 'calculated respect' since the choice elevates the addressee so that the speaker can gain some advantage.

Choices taking account of lack of ability to speak the unmarked choice

A conversation starting out in the unmarked choice may shift into a marked choice because of limits on speaking abilities. Scotton (1983: 125) accounts for such choices as following the *virtuosity maxim*: 'Make an otherwise marked choice whenever the linguistic ability of either speaker or addressee makes the unmarked choice for the unmarked rights and obligations set in a conventionalized exchange infelicitous.'

Many times the switching away from the unmarked choice because of lack of fluency is overtly acknowledged by the speaker, who says, 'I'm sorry, but I can't speak X very well' meaning – in the terms of this model – 'I know the unmarked relationship calls for the use of X.' (Note that it seems to be a marked choice for the other participant – the one who *is* fluent in the unmarked choice – to initiate a switch under the virtuosity maxim. That is, the speaker following the virtuosity maxim must self-select. For another speaker to take the initiative often elicits a negative affective response.)

The following conversation (Parkin, 1974: 194–5) illustrates the use of a marked choice to show deference, as well as a switch to the unmarked choice because of lack of virtuosity. A Kikuyu market seller in Nairobi greets a Luo customer in his own language, clearly a move designed to flatter the Luo by acknowledging his personal distinctiveness. The customer accepts this accommodation, but it soon becomes apparent that the seller cannot speak much Luo. The customer switches to the unmarked choice of Swahili, jocularly accusing the seller of attempting flattery. Thus, the deference negotiation fails, showing that, as the model claims, code choices are made with normative expectations of consequences, but at the same time are negotiations whose success depends on the dynamics of the individual speech event.

Setting: A Kikuyu woman stallholder greets a Luo male customer in a Nairobi market.
(Dashes indicate switching.)

Seller (Luo): Omera, nadi!
 (How are you, brother?)
Customer (Luo): Maber.
 (Fine.)
Seller (Kikuyu; Swahili): Ati-nini?
 (What-what?)
Customer (Swahili): Ya nini kusema lugha ambao huelewi, mama?
 (Why (try) to speak a language you don't know, madam?)
Seller (English): I know Kijaluo very well!
 (English with Swahilized form, Kijaluo).
Customer (Swahili; English; Swahili): Wapi! – You do not know it at all –
 Wacha haya, nipe mayai mbili.
 (Go on! You do not know it at all – Let's leave the matter; give me
 two eggs.)
Seller (Swahili; Luo; Swahili): Unataka mayai – anyo, omera – haya ni –
 tongolo – tatu.
 (You want two eggs, brother. OK, that's thirty cents. Note: 'two',
 'brother', and 'thirty' are Luo.)

In his analysis of such conversational exchanges, Parkin uses games as an analogy, emphasizing the to-and-fro movement of turn taking and the influence of turns on each other. The dynamic nature of conversation and the possibility for a variety of choices are also important aspects of the markedness model presented here. This model, however, depicts more a 'grammar of consequence' than a 'grammar of choice'. While the speech event itself may be likened to a competition, with speakers making choices to accumulate points, the scoring is only incidentally dependent on the choice in a previous turn or someone else's choice, according to my model. Rather, the specific choices which are made and the outcome depends more on the indexicality of choices and, accordingly, their expected consequences. This is what makes it a grammar of consequences.

A marked choice or a sequence of unmarked choices?

One problem for the overall model is to distinguish a marked choice following or embedded in an unmarked choice from a sequence of two unmarked choices. They can be distinguished in two ways. First, as noted above, there is always some change in factors external to the ongoing speech event when there is a shift from one unmarked choice to another; the topic changes, or new participants are introduced, or new information about the identity of participants which is salient in the exchange becomes available, etc. Second, a sequence of unmarked choices is expected, given the change in factors. In contrast, a marked choice is unexpected. Furthermore, it evokes an affective response, as noted above.

The claim that the distinction between unmarked and marked choices has psychological reality can be empirically tested, although I know of no existing studies. Such expectations and affect are amenable to measurement. Significant differences between marked and unmarked choices would be predicted, although they would be gradient, not categorical.

Ervin-Tripp's discussion of expected vs. unexpected directive forms is relevant here (1976: 61–2). She notes, 'In normal circumstances, when an expected form occurs, *listeners need make no affective interpretation at all*' [italics in original]. She goes on to contrast this reaction with that of an unexpected directive:

> If social features are clear, but the form is unexpected by his own coding rule, the hearer assumes that the speaker is imputing different social features than he thinks he has, and reacts to the imputation as deference, sarcasm, arrogance, coldness, undifferentiated annoyance, or a joke. *These inferences appear to be relatively systematic to the point of being like marking rules* [italics added].

Switching to exclude? Permissible marked choices or not?

In many multilingual societies, switching to a language not known by all participants is a common means of exclusion, often conscious. At the least, it withholds information from those not knowing the language of switching. It may also contain negative comments about those excluded. Such switching is predicted to be most frequent when there is a sharp power differential between those participants who switch to the new code and those who are excluded; for example, parents vs. children. The switching itself conveys that the speakers share an identity others do not have and narrows the social distance between them while increasing that between speakers and those left out. Because of the relatively greater power of the speakers, others may not like this marked choice, but they must permit it.

When the power differential is less great, such switching may not be condoned, but considered rude. Among other things, the speakers are overtly accused of 'back-biting' and, of course, they are figuratively speaking behind the non-participants' backs. Given the unmarked rights and obligations balance, such switching is clearly a marked choice. Is it though? The markedness of exclusive switching in many parts of Africa, for example, seems very unresolved. Exclusive switching there is normally to an ethnic language. Those who accept such switching may do so because ethnic identity and giving priority in social relations to affinity with ethnic brethren are facts of life in many parts of Africa. Switching which is indexical of these facts simply seems unmarked to many. But not all agree. And, not surprisingly, it seems to be members of the larger, more powerful groups who do more exclusive switching.

This state of affairs indicates that there is not necessarily a categorical consensus including all speech community members on the relative markedness of varieties available. In this case, for example, an interethnic conversation may still be considered a conventionalized exchange by all concerned, but they may not agree on the markedness of a non-neutral ethnic language. (It remains a conventionalized exchange because participants do recognize unmarked choices; that is, they do recognize 'scripts' for the exchange. It is just that they do not recognize the same scripts. If the views about markedness become very fragmented, such exchanges may become unconventionalized. This seems to be what happened in Montreal in the late 1970s when the relative unmarkedness of French vs. English became a political issue, especially for exchanges in public institutions; Heller, 1982a: 116–17.[9])

A typical example of switching to exclude in a multi-ethnic conversation in Nairobi follows.

Setting: Four young Kenyan men who have completed secondary school and who work in the same government ministry in Nairobi are chatting. Two are native speakers of Kikuyu, one of Kisii and one of a Kalenjin language. Swahili and/or Swahili/ English are unmarked choices.

Kiikuyu 1 (Swahili): Sasa mumesema nini juu ya hiyo plan yetu? Naona kama siku kama siku zinaendelea kwisha.
(Now, what do you all say about the plan of ours? I think time is getting short.)

Kikuyu 2 (Swahili; English): Mlisema tu collect money, lakini hakuna mtu hata mmoja ambaye amenipatia pesa.
(You said collect money, but there isn't even one person who has got money for me.)

Kalenjin (Swahili): Makosa ni yako kama mweka hazina. Tulisema uwe ukitembelea watu mara kwa mara lakini hufanyi hivyo. Watu wengi hawawezi kufanya kitu bila kuwa harassed.
(The fault is yours as treasurer. We said you should visit people (us) from time to time but you don't do that. Many people can't do a thing unless they are harassed.)

Kikuyu 1 (Swahili; English): Mjue ni vibaya for the treasurer akimaliza wakati wake akiona watu ambao hawawezi kupeana pesa.
(You should know it's bad for the treasurer to waste his time if he sees people who can't give money.)

Kisii (Swahili): Mweka hazina hana makosa hata kidogo. Mtu anatakiwa lipe pesa bila kuulizwa.
(The treasurer hasn't made any mistakes. Each person is required to pay without being asked.)

Kikuyu 2 (Kikuyu): Andu amwe nimendaga kwaria maundu maria matari na ma namo.
(Some people like talking about what they're not sure of.)

Kikuyu 1 (Kikuyu): Wira wa muigi wa kigina ni kuiga mbeca. No tigucaria mbeca.
(The work of the treasurer is only to keep money. Not to hunt for money.)

Kisii (Swahili; English): Ubaya wenu ya Kikuyu ni kuassume kila mtu anaelewa Kikuyu.
(The bad thing about Kikuyus is to assume that everyone understands Kikuyu.)

Kalenjin (Swahili; English): Si mtumie lugha ambayo kila mtu hapa atasikia? We are supposed to solve this issue.
(Shouldn't you use a language which every person here understands? We are supposed to solve this issue.)

Kikuyu 2 (Swahili; English): Tunaomba msameha. Sio kupenda kwetu. Ni kawaida kwa most people kupendelea lugha yao.

(We are sorry. It isn't that we favor our side. It's normal for most people to prefer their own language.)

Code-switching as a strategy of multiple identities

In uncertain situations (non-conventionalized exchanges) when an unmarked choice is not apparent, speakers nominate an exploratory choice as the basis for the exchange. The nominated variety is recognized as indexical of a certain rights and obligations balance existing in the conventionalized exchange for which it is unmarked. By analogy, it is proposed that the 'new' exchange be treated as an instance of the 'old'.[10]

Many times, however, at the outset of a conversation a speaker is not sure that any one balance would be preferable to another, even as a candidate, for the exchange. In such cases, a speaker may open an exchange with one choice, but be prepared to switch to another choice, depending on the addressee's own code choice in his or her response. If the speaker changes in his or her second turn to the addressee's choice (first turn), this is a form of showing deference, or accommodation. By using two codes in two different turns, however, the speaker has also been able to encode two identities – and the breadth of experience associated with them. For this reason, participants may find it socially useful to treat certain speech events as non-conventionalized exchanges, if it is at all possible. (Scotton and Zhu (1983) discuss some other social advantages of maintaining various ambiguities in linguistic systems.)

Initial contacts with strangers in situations other than service encounters typically are treated as non-conventionalized exchanges. In the following example, a young man switches from Swahili to English, apparently in an effort to please the young woman with whom he wants to dance.

> Setting: A dance at a Nairobi hotel. A young man (his native language is Kikuyu) asks a young woman to dance.

> He (Swahili):   Nisaidie na dance, tafadhali.
>   (Please give me a dance.)
> She (Swahili): Nimechoka. Pengine nyimbo ifuatayo.
>   (I'm tired. Maybe a following song.)
> He (Swahili):   Hii ndio nyimbo ninayopenda.
>   (This is the song which I like.)
> She (Swahili): Nimechoka!
>   (I'm tired!)
> He (Swahili):   Tafadhali –
>   (Please.)
> She (interrupting) (English): Ah, stop bugging me.
> He (English):   I'm sorry. I didn't mean to bug you, but I can't help it if I like this song.
> She (English): OK, then, in that case, we can dance.

Conclusion

An explanation for code-switching has been proposed which emphasizes linguistic choices as negotiations of personal rights and obligations relative to those of other participants in a talk exchange. This explanation follows from a markedness model of code choice which claims that speakers make choices and others interpret them by considering their probable consequences. This process involves a consensus concerning the relative markedness of any choice for a specific exchange and a view of all choices as indexical of a negotiation of rights and obligations between participants. Because all community members have this theory of markedness, they are able to use conversational implicatures to arrive at the intended consequences of any code-switching. (As has been noted, this explanation is not merely speculative but is based on studies of the social interpretation of switching by subjects in their own communities (Scotton and Ury, 1977; Scotton, 1982). However, as has also been mentioned, not all claims of the markedness model have been empirically tested, although the fact that they can be tested seems clear.)

The principle guiding some earlier explanations of code-switching in East Africa was the need to detail situational factors. For example, while Whiteley (1974) explicitly recognizes the failures of certain situational factors to account for switching in rural Kenya, his solution is only a more thorough study of the situation. Thus, he writes, 'It does not seem possible to correlate the choice of any particular language with a shift along the scale of formality', but then offers as a solution that 'much more needs to be known about the total social situation than can be gleaned from the language diaries' (1974: 331).

The point of view taken here is, of course, quite different. Situational factors *are* paramount in determining the unmarked choice in a conventionalized exchange: the unmarked rights and obligations set is derived from the salient configuration of social features for the exchange, and the unmarked linguistic choice as indexical of that set. But because not all exchanges are conventionalized and because the relevant features and their hierarchy will differ from exchange to exchange, it is impossible to provide any set of features as universally crucial independent variables. The features themselves even may be dependent variables in the sense that their saliency is context sensitive. In addition, feature salience is dynamically related to a specific exchange in that it may co-vary with content and linguistic choices in progressive turns by participants (for example, the example above involving the security guard and visitor, or Genesee and Bourhis, 1982).

Some other more general explanations do acknowledge personal motivations (as does Parkin (1974) for East Africa, mentioned above), although not exactly along the lines of the markedness model. For example, Blom and Gumperz (see Chapter 4 of this volume) recognize that non-situationally motivated switching occurs, referring to it generally as metaphorical switching. Their primary emphasis, however, remains on the concepts of setting, social situation, and social event to explain choice. In Gumperz' later work, however, switching is recognized much more as a strategy which the speaker employs at will to generate conversational inferences. He writes, 'Code-switching signals contextual information equivalent to what in monolingual settings is conveyed through prosody or other syntactic or lexical processes. It generates presuppositions in terms of which the content of what is said is decoded.' Specifically in relation to what he terms metaphorical usage, he writes:

This partial violation of co-occurrence expectations then gives rise to the inference that some aspects of the connotations, which elsewhere apply to the activity as a whole, are here to be treated as affecting only the illocutionary force and quality of the speech act in question.

(Gumperz 1982: 98)

While some aspects of the treatment here are reminiscent of such statements, more of an attempt is made in the markedness model to provide a comprehensive and principled treatment, explicitly assigning roles to a normative framework in implicating consequences and to individual, interactive choices as tools of specific negotiations.

Much more psychologically centered is the accommodation hypothesis and related hypotheses of Giles and his associates (mentioned above) which seek to explain switching and specifically subjective reactions to the process. The accommodation model handles very well switching motivated by a desire to narrow the social distance between the addressee or not, such as those choices encoding deference. However, it seems limited because it seeks to explain all choices in terms of either accommodation or non-accommodation to the addressee. It is argued here that choices have a broader range of motivations. Most important, many are much more speaker-centered (such as choices encoding authority or education). Further, a framework of markedness seems essential in order to deal with the consequences of choices.

In conclusion, this paper has argued that the guiding research question for studies of switching should not be so much, what social factors or interactional features determine code choice? But rather, what is the relation between linguistic choices and their social consequences, and how do speakers know this? From this, more specific questions follow: is there an unmarked choice for a specific exchange? Given that the unmarked choice will have dominant frequency, for what effect do speakers employ switching away from this choice? If there is not an unmarked choice, how do speakers make sense out of choices made?

The several hypotheses and the overall markedness model suggested here respond to these questions. First, it is claimed that choice is not so much a reflection of situation as a negotiation of position, given the situation. People make the choices they do because of personal motivations. Second, it is proposed that these motivations can be characterized and all switching explained parsimoniously in the framework of unmarked, marked, and exploratory choices outlined here. Finally and in general, it has been argued that expected consequence structures code choices. Speakers are restrained only by the possibility and attractiveness of alternative outcomes. This involves, of course, their own linguistic abilities and, more important, their framework of expectations.

Notes

1   In Scotton and Ury (1977), 70 subjects were asked open-ended questions about four audio-recorded conversations. In Scotton (1982), 35 subjects were played audio recordings of six conversations and then asked to select one of five possible answers from a fixed list. In both cases, it was stressed there were no 'right' or 'wrong' answers.

Three of the four test conversations in the 1977 study illustrated switching as a marked choice. The majority of the subjects provided responses about 'what happened in the conversation' entirely consistent with the claims here about the social negotiation encoded by a marked choice; further, their interpretations were very similar. The fourth conversation showed switching in a non-conventionalized exchange. Perhaps not surprisingly, subjects did not cluster very well in their interpretations; however 69 per cent did mention the different social associations of the three languages involved as a reason for switching (Scotton and Ury, 1977: 14–16).

The six test conversations used in Scotton (1982) were examples of overall switching as an unmarked choice and switching as a marked choice, including one showing deferential switching. In general, over 90% chose the same interpretation and this was the one consistent with the claims of this model (Scotton, 1982: 442–3). More details are available from the author, including statistical test results.

2   This finding is based on more than 100 hours of recordings of natural conversations made in Nairobi and about 20 hours of recordings in Harare in 1983.

3   'Sheng' is discussed in an article in the *Daily Nation* of 14 March 1984. One example cited is *Buda amenijamisha* 'Father has annoyed me' (as a reason for not going home). The origins of *buda* for 'father' are unclear. The verb stem *-jam* comes from the English but means 'feel stuck or annoyed'. It has Swahili inflections, including the causative suffix. Similar examples were found in my 1983 data corpus from recordings of pre-teens in certain areas of the city.

4   Overall switching as an unmarked choice is most difficult to separate from borrowing. For example, a Luo cooking teacher in Nairobi, addressing in Swahili a class of other teachers, peppered her presentation with such utterances as this:

> Wengine wanachemusha (sic), wengine wana*steam*, na mambo mengi mengi.
> Wengine wanakaanga kama mtu ambaye anakaanga nyama.
> (Some boil [bananas], some steam, and a lot of other things. Some fry
> like a person frying meat.)

The use of *steam* is probably motivated by the fact that 'to steam' in Swahili requires a longer expression, *kupika kwa nguvu ya mvuke*. Thus, *steam* seems best described as a loan, since it regularly replaces a longer Swahili expression. The same is true of Shona expressions of number, which have been almost totally replaced by English forms in urban Shona (more or less assimilated phonologically). To express number in Shona requires long phrases. I thank Kumbirai Mkanganwi for this observation.

But what about words such as *fry*? In the passage above, the teacher uses the Swahili verb -kaanga 'fry'. Yet, within five minutes she uses English *fry*:

> Yaondoke kidogo. Kama vile unatake ku*fry*. Ni tamu isipokua (si) ni a bit dry.
> Sisi, hio ndio njia tuna preserve . . .
> (It [water] evaporates a bit. Just as if you want to fry. It is tasty except
> that it is a bit dry. This is the way we preserve . . .)

Is such a usage as *fry* switching or borrowing? Clearly, *fry* is not a replacement loan. Is this a *nonce* borrowing? Or is this passage simply an example of overall switching as an unmarked choice? Because the lesson in question contains many other English words and phrases, this does seem to be a case of switching (given the audience).

5   A Swahili poem by Kineene wa Mutiso (1983) contains a good deal of 'morphemic switching'. The poem is about a conversation between a secretary and someone who has come to her office. Here is one quatrain:

Brother sije ka *sorry*, *Bosie* utam*see*
Kwanza tupiga *story*, ama hauna *say*?
Hata ukiwa me*marry*, kwa nini tusi*enjoy*?
Sema ma*home* ku*how*, na kote kwenye ma*joint*.

(Brother, lest you worry, you'll see the boss
First let's talk, or do you have nothing to say?
Even if you are married, why can't we enjoy?
How are things at home and in all the nightspots?)

6 Nartey (1982) suggests, too, that the socio-cultural environment may impose constraints on the type of switching possible. He, however, refers specifically to whether switching is possible after a bound constituent (providing data showing such switching does occur in the conversations of young, educated Ghanaians).

7 Personal observation and interview on the spot.

8 Another type of momentary switching to a marked choice is to avoid taboo words. For example, a Shona lecturer in Zimbabwe speaking about Shona marriage customs used Shona throughout his lecture to an audience of Shona-speaking university students until he had to mention sexual relations. He switched to English for the two words, *sexual intercourse*, and then went on in Shona. (I thank Caleb Gwasira for this example.) Even within a single language, the use of euphemisms for semi-taboo subjects or objects is a form of marked switching (from one style to a specialized style), with the shift serving to distance the speaker from the taboo item.

9 Heller's comment (1982: 118) emphasizes how, through the use of exploratory choices, a consensus is reached:

> This negotiation [of language] itself serves to redefine the situations in the light of ongoing social and political change. *In the absence of norms, we work at creating new ones* [italics added]. The conventionalization of the negotiating strategies appears to be a way of normalizing relationships, of encoding social information necessary to know how to speak to someone. . .

10 A related strategy, which encodes neutrality more than exploration, is the extended use of two varieties in an uncertain situation so that some entire conversations may be in one variety and some in another. Such a pattern is very similar to overall switching as an unmarked choice because it simultaneously presents two identities while also neutralizing them. Scotton (1976) explains the high incidence of reported use of two languages (rather than either one alone) in urban work situations as such a strategy of neutrality. For example, in Kampala, Uganda many educated persons reported speaking both English (the official language) and Swahili (a widely used lingua franca) with fellow workers of different ethnic groups. Speaking English signals a person is educated and has the necessary expertise for a job, but English is also the language of formality in Uganda, and even pretentiousness. Speaking Swahili there signals an ethically neutral African identity and egalitarianism (since it is known by persons from diverse socio-economic backgrounds); but Swahili also has associations primarily as the lingua franca of the uneducated in Uganda. Which language to use with fellow workers? Results show that a middle choice is preferred: switching or alternating between the two.

Source: Myers-Scotton, C. (1988) Code-switching as indexical of social negotiations. In M. Heller (ed.) *Codeswitching*, Berlin: Mouton de Gruyter, pp. 151–86. Reproduced by permission of the author and Mouton de Gruyter. (This paper was originally published under the name C.M. Scotton.)

Postscript

In looking back over this chapter, which was originally published in 1988, I see little to change, but four points to enlarge upon. First, in more recent publications (e.g. Myers-Scotton and Bolonyai, 2001), the markedness model has been recast more explicitly as a model aligned with the rational choice models found especially in the social sciences of economics, sociology, and political science. This statement from the Norwegian political scientist Jan Elster succinctly characterizes such models: 'When faced with several courses of action, people usually do what they believe is likely to have the best overall outcome. This deceptively simple sentence summarizes the theory of rational choice' (Elster 1989: 22). That is, all actors (and that includes speakers) aim for choices that give them the most rewards and the fewest costs.

But how do they arrive at these choices, which include the switching from one language to another in a single conversation, sometimes within the same conversational turn?

This brings me to the second point that deserves emphasis: Speakers engage in cognitive calculations, which are usually unconscious, to assess in an instant which linguistic variety at their disposal best conveys the impression they wish to make. That is, choices are made in a social setting, but they are cognitively based; this means such choices cannot be simply explained as a response to other speakers' utterances.

As this chapter indicates – and this is elaborated on in Myers-Scotton and Bolonyai (2001) – speakers make use of a 'markedness evaluator' in weighing possible linguistic choices. This evaluator is part of their general cognitive architecture; that is, it is not specific to the linguistic components. I take this opportunity to emphasize the importance of this evaluator: it underlies *the cognitive capacity to evaluate*, and what it evaluates is the markedness of one course of action (selecting one linguistic variety) rather than another.

This component is a mechanism that can operate to give markedness readings based on the input it receives from past experiences (information available in memory and other conceptual sources) from perceptual sources (the senses), the current context, and psychological and sociolinguistic associations that participants connect with the different linguistic varieties available to the speaker in the current context.

Over and above the markedness evaluator, speakers and their listeners rely on a more general innate ability in selecting their speech. They rely on their pragmatic ability to arrive at interpretations of intended meanings. Blakemore (2002) makes this point about pragmatics, writing: 'the fundamental ability in communication is not linguistic encoding and decoding, but the ability to derive inferences which result in assumptions which are entertained as metarepresentations of other people's thoughts, desires and intentions'. That is, the speaker is aware that listeners will make inferences about his/her intended meaning, based not just on the semantic and structural nuts and bolts of the speaker's linguistic utterance, but also on conceptual sources. These pragmatic inferences arise through cognitive calculations.

In making what I call socio-pragmatic inferences, both the speaker and the listener know that the listener is expected to rely a great deal on one conceptual source, the markedness evaluator. Socio-pragmatic inferences are interpretations about how speakers wish to present themselves in relation to various facets of the conversation, but especially in relation to other participants in the conversation. A major idea that the markedness model presents is that code-switching is an important mechanism through which speakers can provide evidence of their intended socially based inferences. The reason this is possible, of course, is that all linguistic varieties available in a given community come with the social and psychological associations mentioned earlier. When a speaker switches from one linguistic variety to another, he/she is switching to the inferential associations that come along with the new variety.

My third point is this: In the current chapter, the assumption that all talk exchanges are negotiations was prominent. This assumption deserves emphasis because it has been overlooked by some readers. Even though the markedness model is speaker-based in the sense that rational choice models are (actors want to achieve maximal rewards), achieving any rewards depends on the speaker's achieving at least some rapport with listeners. Thus, it is important to stress that the markedness model enjoins speakers to take account of their listeners' goals if they, the speakers, expect to achieve their own goals. That is, the most successful choices (i.e. the speaker receives more rewards than costs, however costs and rewards are measured) are achieved by taking into account the addressees' points of view.

Finally, some readers of explications of the markedness model, such as that in Myers-Scotton (1993), have assumed that, because the model is not based on the macro-level factors that are important in the social organization of a community, the model implies that such factors are unimportant in the linguistic choices that speakers make on the micro-level of conversation. This is an incorrect reading of the premises behind the model. The markedness model does emphasize the cognitive calculations that go on in the micro-level arena. It should be clear that where macro-level factors come in is that they are the engines that power the rights and obligations (RO) sets that are indexed by linguistic choices. That is, these RO sets are derived from the weightings that macro-level factors have in specific interaction types in the specific community under analysis. These factors include, of course, ethnic group membership, age, gender, and socio-economic status, among others.

In sum, the markedness model is intended to be seen as a model that has these features: (a) Any linguistic choice a speaker makes is based on cognitive calculations. (b) Speakers make choices as rational actors to achieve optimal outcomes. (c) But they are aware that all choices are only negotiations in which addressees also participate. (d) Readings of markedness rely on the socially relevant indexicality of linguistic choices; that is, no choice is marked or unmarked in a vacuum, but only in terms of a given community and that community's socio-psychological profile and its values.

Carol Myers-Scotton, PhD, is Distinguished Professor Emeritus of Linguistics at the University of South Carolina, USA. carolms@sc.edu

Chapter 6

The pragmatics of code-switching: a sequential approach

PETER AUER

1 Introduction

This paper will deal with code-switching in a specific sense. The perspective I want to take is an important one, but it does not exclude others.

Bilingualism (including multilingualism) is often thought of as multiple linguistic competences, i.e., as a mental disposition which is accessible only indirectly by the usual techniques of psycholinguistic research. In the mentalistic framework of generative grammar, bilingual competence is also accessible via the analysis of well-formed sentences involving two languages which may be treated as a window on the bilingual mind. Yet both the psycholinguist and the generative grammarian treat bilingualism as something which – like competence in general – is basically hidden underneath the skull and therefore invisible; it can be, and must be, made visible by psycholinguistic methods, or the methods of generative grammatical research. Beginning with the discussion of compound vs coordinate bilingualism in its psycholinguistic reformulation, and up to the present generative work on grammatical constraints on code-switching, there is an impressive amount of research which has been gathered from such a perspective.

Contrary to this tradition of research, I will be dealing here with bilingualism from the perspective of the conversationalist. For him or her, it has its foremost reality in the interactive exchanges between the members of a bilingual speech community (as well as between them and monolingual outsiders), by which they display to each other, and ascribe to each other, their bilingualism. According to this perspective, it is the task of the linguist not to discover by tests or other methods something which is basically concealed from the naive language user, but to reconstruct the social processes of displaying and ascribing bilingualism. As a feature of conversational (inter-)action, bilingualism provides specific resources not available to monolingual speakers for the constitution of socially meaningful verbal activities. The relationship between the use of two languages as a form-related property of one or more persons' speech and the conversational meaning of this speech is a relatively indirect and complicated one. It needs some theoretical background in order to be conceived properly, and it is this theoretical background which is the topic of this chapter. I will sketch a theory of conversational code-alternation which should be applicable to a wide range of conversational phenomena subsumed in the literature under such headings as code-switching, language choice, transfer/insertion etc., and to very different bilingual communities and settings. Such a theory of bilingual conversation obviously has to be complemented by another theory which explains who switches in a given community, why and when. The resources available to bilingual conversationalists may be outlined independently, however, from their macro-social embedding. Needless to say, bilingual work on any concrete bilingual community has to refer both to micro and macro theories of code-alternation and to their interdependencies.

By reviewing some of the existing literature, and by referring to empirical work, it will (hopefully) become clear that any theory of conversational code-alternation is bound to fail if it does not take into account that the meaning of code-alternation depends in essential ways on its 'sequential environment'. This is given, in the first place, by the conversational turn immediately preceding it, to which code-alternation may respond in various ways. While the preceding verbal activities provide the contextual frame for a current utterance, the following utterance by a next participant reflects his or her interpretation of that preceding utterance. Therefore, following utterances are important cues for the analyst and for the first speaker as to if and how a first utterance has been understood. The sequentiality of code-alternation in the sense of this paper therefore refers both to preceding and subsequent utterances.

2 Preliminaries on definition and terminology

In view of the lack of a generally accepted terminology, it is necessary to define code-alternation in the specific sense in which the term is employed here, before entering into detailed discussion. *Code-alternation (used here as a cover term, i.e. hyperonym for code-switching and transfer) is defined as a relationship of contiguous juxtaposition of semiotic systems, such that the appropriate recipients of the resulting complex sign are in a position to interpret this juxtaposition as such.*

The criterion of contiguity excludes non-contiguous stretches of talk, for example, one occurring in the beginning, the other at the end of the conversation, or speaker X using language A on one occasion, and language B on another, from being analysed as instances of code-alternation. The criterion of juxtaposition implies that gradual transitions from one code into the other cannot be classified as code-alternation. Thus, a gradual transition from dialect into standard ('style-shifting') may be a very important interactional event, but it works differently from code-alternation and should not be confounded with it. The requirement that semiotic *systems* be juxtaposed excludes the possibility of single parameter changes being analysed as code-alternation. The most important of all the definitional criteria for code-alternation is that of its interpretative reality. It is the users of the signs who decide on their status. When we compare the speech of bilinguals with that of monolinguals in either of their languages, we notice a high number of 'marques transcodiques', 'qui renvoient d'une manière ou d'une autre à la rencontre de deux ou plusieurs systèmes linguistiques' (Lüdi 1987b: 2). Yet inside this very large domain of language-contact phenomena, it is necessary to draw a very basic distinction: that between contact phenomena classified as such by the linguist, and contact phenomena seen and used as such by the bilingual participants themselves. The question 'Do bilingual participants see and use it?' takes us from structural systems continually referring to each other, to the speakers. It implies the shift from a structural towards an interpretative approach to bilingualism.

3 Theories of the pragmatics of code-alternation

It is useful to start the discussion with two somewhat extreme theories of code-alternation which are (for very instructive reasons) bound to fail. The *first theory* of the conversational meaning of code-alternation is based on the assumption that *certain conversational activities prompt the usage of one language or the other qua activity type*. A particular activity type is seen as being linked to language B, such that in the environment of language A, code-alternation occurs. For instance, Fishman (1971a) introduces the chapter on 'Interactional sociolinguistics' in his introductory book with an example which is reproduced here in part as data extract (1), between two Puerto Ricans:

(1) [Boss has been dictating a letter to Mr Bolger to his secretary, Spanish in italics]
    Boss: . . . Sincerely, Louis Gonzalez
    Secretary: Do you have the enclosures for the letter, Mr Gonzalez?
    Boss: Oh yes, here they are.
    Secretary: Okay
    Boss: Ah, this man William Bolger got his organization to con-tribute a lot of money to the Puerto Rican parade. He's very much for it. *¿Tú fuiste a la parada?*
    Secretary: *Sí, yo fui.*
    Boss: *¿Sí?*
    Secretary: *Uh huh.*
    Boss: *¿Y cómo te estuvo?*
    [etc., continues in Spanish] (Fishman 1971: 37ff.)

Fishman recommends finding systematic ('emic') correlations between what he calls speech events and language choice in order to analyse code-switching as in the data extract: 'The first question that presents itself is whether one variety tends to be used (or used more often) in certain kinds of speech acts or events whereas the other tends to be used (or used more often) in others' (p. 41). He does not really apply this research strategy to his example, but it is easy to see that he would expect us to find some correlation between the speech event of an informal chat and Spanish on the one hand, and between a business transaction and English on the other.[1]

Note that in this approach, it is not the switching from one language into another which has meaning, but the association between speech activities and languages. Code-alternation is contingent on the juxtaposition of two activities associated with different languages. Had the 'boss' met his 'secretary' exclusively for the purpose of a chat, the whole interactive episode would have taken place in Spanish, but the usage of this language would have had the same social meaning, i.e., that of indexing a speech activity within the Spanish domain.

The weakness of this approach becomes apparent as soon as language choice is investigated empirically. In modern bilingual societies, the relationship between languages and speech activities is by no means unambiguous. Many speech activities are not tied to one particular language, and even among those which have a tendency to be realised more often in one language than in another, the correlation is never strong enough to predict language choice in more than a probabilistic way. (In Fishman's Puerto Rican case, it is certainly conceivable that the Puerto Rican boss might deal with his secretary in Spanish all the time; and he might well choose to use English even in talk about the Puerto Rican parade.)

Although the idea of Fishman and other scholars that specific speech activities are associated with specific languages receives some support from ritual language usage in 'stable' societies (as has been reported in a number of studies in the ethnography of communication), and although the associations between speech activity and language are not completely free in 'mobile' bilingual societies or speech communities either, this relationship is far more complex than such a simple model would suggest (cf. di Luzio 1984a). Many investigations have shown that the mere fact of juxtaposing two codes can have a signalling value of its own, independent of the direction of code-alternation; in such cases, it is obviously impossible to explain the conversational meaning of code-alternation by any kind of association between languages and speech activities. Striking evidence for such a contrastive signalling value of language alternation comes from one of the reportedly most frequent functions of code-alternation: the setting off of reported speech against its surrounding conversational (often narrative) context. Although one could think that the language of 'quoting is relatively predictable' and that 'all one needs to know to predict the language in which most quotes will be spoken is the language in which the original utterance was spoken' (as is indeed contended by Gal 1979: 109), this is in fact not the case. Instead it is not unusual for code-alternation to occur in cases where the language of reporting and the inferrable language used by the original speaker diverge.[2] As an example, consider the extract from an Italian-German bilingual conversation given in (2), where an Italian student is talking about his quarrels with German classmates:

> (2) [report about German pupils in his class, Italian in italics]
> wenn ä Italiener kommt gell – sofort äh: *guardate*
> Ittakerstinker und so
> [*when Italians come you know – immediately (they say)* look *spaghetti heads*
> *and so on* (Auer 1984: 66)]

It is highly unlikely that the Germans would use an Italian phrase such as *guardate* when insulting their Italian classmates. In such cases, the only function of code-alternation is to provide a contrast between the conversational context of the quote and the reported speech itself. As the speaker is already using German, this can only be done by switching into Italian, at least for the beginning of the quote. Note that the beginning of reported speech is not explicitly marked; more indirect markers such as pausing and code-alternation fulfil this function.

A promising alternative approach to code-alternation might therefore consist of analysing the signalling value of the juxtaposition of languages and deriving the conversational meaning of code-alternation from it. This is quite different from Fishman's approach, since no association between languages and speech activities needs to be presupposed. Obviously, it requires a sequential account of language choice, in which the language chosen for one speech activity must be seen against the background of language choice in the preceding utterance. From this perspective, the question is not what verbal activities are associated with one language or the other, but instead: in which activities do bilinguals tend to switch from one language into the other. In answering this question, researchers on code-alternation have developed elaborate typologies of code-switching. They seem to converge across bilingual communities on certain conversational loci in which switching is particularly frequent, such as:

(i)   *reported speech*
(ii)   *change of participant constellation*, particularly addressee selection – this includes the use of code-switching in order to include/exclude/marginalise co-participants or bystanders
(iii) *parentheses or side-comments*
(iv)   *reiterations*, i.e. quasi-translations into the other language, for example for the purpose of putting emphasis on demands or requests, or for purposes of clarification, or for attracting attention, e.g. in the regulation of turn-taking (also called 'translations', 'repetitions' or 'recycling')
(v)   *change of activity type*, also called 'mode shift' or 'role shift'
(vi)   *topic shift*
(vii) *puns, language play, shift of 'key'*
(viii) *topicalisation, topic/comment structure*.

Although lists such as this one are useful because they demonstrate that some conversational loci are particularly susceptible to code-alternation, the mere listing of such loci is problematic, for a number of reasons.

First, the conversational categories used for the analysis are often ill-defined. Frequently, we get lists of conversational loci for code-alternation and examples, but no sequential analysis is carried out to demonstrate what exactly is meant, for example, by a 'change of activity type', or by 'reiteration'. A more in-depth sequential study of, for example, reiterations would make it clear that this category subsumes a number of very different conversational structures. What is lacking is the proper grounding of the categories employed in a theory of interaction.

Second, so-called typologies of code-alternation often confuse conversational structures, linguistic forms and functions of code-alternation. For instance, 'emphasis' may be a function of code-alternation, whereas 'reiteration' is a (group of) conversational structure(s). Reiteration may or may not serve the function of giving emphasis to a stretch of talk; both categories are on quite different levels. Or, to give another example: interjections and fillers in language A are often observed to be inserted in language B discourse. Yet 'interjection' and 'filler' are names for linguistic structure, their conversational status and their function are another issue. Or, a final example: mitigation and aggravation may be functions of code-alternation, but they are not conversational structures and therefore cannot be dealt with on a par with translations and repetitions (as attempted by Zentella 1981).

Third, lists of conversational loci for code-alternation, or typologies of functions, may give us an initial clue as to what is going on. There is every reason, however, to be sceptical about whether such listing will bring us closer to a theory of code-alternation, i.e., whether it can tell us anything about *why* code-alternation may have a conversational meaning or function. The list itself will hardly ever be a closed one, which shows that code-alternation is used in a creative fashion, and that it can have conversational meaning even if used in a particular conversational environment only once.

Fourth, and most important, the listing of conversational loci for code-alternation implies that code-alternation should have the same conversational status in both directions, i.e. from language A into B or vice versa. Now, although the conversational loci for alternation listed above may in fact be used for switching in both directions in one and the same speech community, the exact conversational meaning of these cases of alternation is often not identical. Consider a very simple example. Zentella (n.d.) lists among the types of code-switching, 'false start repairs' such as in (3):

(3) *you could* – tú puede hacer eso . . .
   (Zentella n.d.)

Obviously, the speaker is correcting his or her language choice here. But why? The following explanations may be proposed: the 'false start repair' could mean that the speaker is accommodating to the recipient's language preference, or complying with the community norms for language choice, or that he or she is distancing him/herself symbolically from the recipient, or from the community norms, by choosing his/her own preferred language. In order to pinpoint the conversational meaning of such a case of code-alternation, we need to know about the 'episode-external' preferences of speakers for one language or the other, or about the community norms for that particular kind of interaction.

The following examples from the literature may show how the direction of conversational code-alternation enters into its interpretation, by virtue of being related to knowledge about the episode-external language preferences involved.

(i) Sebba and Wootton (1984) show on the basis of a careful sequential analysis that:

> participants in a conversation orientate to L[ondon] J[amaican] stretches embedded in a basically L[ondon] E[nglish] turn as having differential status from the adjacent LE material, providing the principal message content. On the other hand, LE stretches embedded within a basically LJ turn correspond to material of secondary importance, such as speakers' comments on thematically more important material, or diversions from the main theme of the turn, for instance those involving speaker-initiated insertion sequences. (p. 3)

Here, sequential analysis of code-alternation warrants an ascription of conversational meanings or functions to the varieties involved (foregrounding/emphasis = London Jamaican; backgrounding = London English); in order to come to an interpretation of an individual instance of alternation, these meanings/functions (i.e., based on a linguistic-stylistic, yet extra-episodic, knowledge) have to be invoked.

(ii) In a study on one particular kind of reiteration, i.e. recycled first pair parts, I have shown (in Auer 1984a) that code-switching may occur on the recycled first pair part if the language chosen by the present speaker is not the 'unmarked' language of interaction between these participants, or if the co-participant is seen to have a preference for the other language. The extra-episodic knowledge necessary in order to interpret correctly the meaning of code-alternation is about language preference in particular speaker dyads.

(iii) In her study on Hungarian-German bilingualism in Oberwart, Austria, Gal (1979: 112ff.) observed that switching from Hungarian into German regularly occurred in a particular sequential position: it was used as a 'topper' in escalating angry arguments. Whenever a speaker switched into German, he or she marked the point of culmination of disagreement and hostility, 'a last word that was not outdone' (p. 117). She concludes from this and other conversational usages of switching into German that, according to the Oberwarters' conception of the languages in their repertoire, German connotes prestige, urban sophistication and authority, but also social distance. These attitudinal values of German are indexed and invoked by switching into this language in turn and contribute to its conversational meaning.

Let me summarise the argument so far. Up to now, two approaches to code-alternation which represent opposite extremes have been sketched and critically evaluated. According to the first, languages are said to be linked to verbal activities such that code-alternation is contingent on switching between two activities associated with different languages. According to the second, it is the juxtaposition of the two languages that constitutes the conversational meaning of code-alternation, but the direction of this alternation is irrelevant. As the discussion has shown, both approaches are empirically inadequate. In the typical bilingual speech community, the correlation between language and activity is not strong enough to make code-alternation predictable, but the direction of switching is nevertheless important for reconstructing its conversational meaning. How can this situation be accounted for?

4 The sequentiality of code-alternation

A framework for analysing code-alternation which is able to handle this kind of situation is available in the theory of contextualisation.[3] If we look upon code-alternation as a contextualisation cue, it is but one of an array of devices such as intonation, rhythm, gesture or posture which are used in the situated production and interpretation of language. Code-alternation works in many ways just like these other cues, a fact that calls for a uniform analysis. Treating code-alternation as a contextualisation cue also explains why the functions of this cue are often taken over by prosodic or gestural cues in monolingual conversation.

It is not possible to outline the theory of contextualisation more than superficially here. In very general terms, contextualisation comprises all those activities by participants which make relevant/maintain/revise/cancel some aspects of context which, in turn, is responsible for the interpretation of an utterance in its particular locus of occurrence. Such an aspect of context may be the larger activity participants are engaged in (the 'speech genre'), the small-scale activity (or 'speech act'), the mood (or 'key') in which this activity is performed, the topic, but also the participants' roles (the participant constellation, comprising 'speaker', 'recipient', 'bystander', etc.), the social relationship between participants, the relationship between a speaker and the information being conveyed via language ('modality'), etc., in short, just those aspects of context that have been found to be related to code-alternation (see above).

Contextualisation cues have the following characteristics.

(i) They do not have referential (decontextualised) meaning of the kind we find in lexical items. Instead, contextualisation cues and the interpretation of the activity are related by a process of *inferencing*, which is itself dependent on the context of its occurrence. The situated meaning of code-alternation therefore cannot be stated unless a sequential analysis is carried out. The same cue may receive a different interpretation on different occasions.

(ii) The way in which inferencing leads to contextual interpretation is twofold: by contrast or by inherent meaning potential. In the first, most simple, case, contextualisation cues establish contrasts and influence interpretation by punctuating the interaction. The mere fact of (usually abruptly) changing one (or more than one) formal characteristic of the interaction may be enough to prompt an inference about why such a thing has happened. In this process of inferencing, it is necessary to rely on information contained in the local context of the cue's occurrence. The only 'meaning' the cue has is (to paraphrase Jakobson's definition of the phoneme) to 'indicate otherness'. The direction of the change is irrelevant.

Yet, many contextualisation cues do more than that. Therefore, we have to distinguish a second case where contextualisation cues establish a contrast and thereby indicate that something new is going to come; but they also and at the same time restrict the number of possible plausible inferences as to what this might be. This is so because cues may have (received) an inherent meaning potential. This may be 'natural', e.g. when we observe a correlation between diminishing fundamental frequency on the one hand, and 'rest' or 'termination' on the other, which is exploited for marking unit closure (e.g. turn termination), or it may be conventionalised (as in the case of code-alternation).

(iii) Contextualisation cues often bundle together, e.g. there is a certain redundancy of coding which has specific interactional advantages. For the analyst, this redundancy provides methodological access to the conversational functions of one cue (e.g., code-alternation), since other cues supporting the same local interpretation can be used as 'external' evidence for the meaning of conversational code-alternation.

Code-alternation can and should be investigated on the conversational level as a contextualisation cue because it shares the above-mentioned features with other contextualisation cues. Yet code-alternation also has some characteristics of its own. For this reason, we need a specification of the contextualisation value of this cue, i.e., a theory of code-alternation.[4] According to my own approach to such a theory (see Auer 1984 and subsequent publications), the situated interpretation of code-alternation as a contextualisation cue is strongly related to sequential patterns of language choice. Four such patterns have to be distinguished.

A first pattern is that usually associated with conversational code-switching of the proto-typical case, such as in Fishman's example (1). In this case, a language-of-interaction (base language, unmarked language), A, has been established; at a certain point, speaker 1 switches to language B; this new language choice is accepted by speaker 2 as the new language-of-interaction so that beyond the switching point, only B is used. Schematically:

Pattern Ia: A1 A2 A1 A2//B1 B2 B1 B2

As a variant of this pattern, language alternation may occur within a single speaker's turn:

Pattern Ib: A1 A2 A1 A2 A1//B1 B2 B1 B2

The interpretation which code-alternation of this structural type usually receives is that of contextualising some feature of the conversation, e.g. a shift in topic, participant constellation, activity type, etc. It contributes to the organisation of discourse in that particular episode; for these types of switches, I use the term 'discourse-related code-switching'.

Another basic pattern looks like this:

Pattern IIa: A1 B2 A1 B2 A1 B2 A1 B2

Here, speaker 1 consistently uses one language but speaker 2 consistently uses another language. While such patterns of language choice have been reported for some bilingual communities (c. Gal 1979; Alvarez 1990), the more usual one is a variant of IIa:

Pattern IIb: A1 B2 A1 B2 A1//A2 A1 A2 A1

After a time of divergent language choice, one participant, 2, accepts the other's language, and the sequence continues with language A as the language-of-interaction. This pattern represents schematically what I call 'language negotiation'. It may occur at the beginning of an interactive episode or after a switching of type I.

Contrary to type I switching, type II tells us first something about speakers' 'preferences' for one language or the other, i.e., instead of redefining the discourse, it permits assessments of/by participants. I have therefore called this type of switching 'preference-related'; here, the term 'preference' must not be understood as a psychological disposition of the speaker, but rather in the more technical, conversation-analytic sense of an interactionally visible structure. The reasons for such a preference are an altogether different issue. By preference-related switching, a speaker may simply want to avoid the language in which he or she feels insecure and speak the one in which he or she has greater competence. Yet preference-related switching may also be due to a deliberate decision based on political considerations. What surfaces in conversation will be the same sequential arrangement of language choices, interpreted differently in different social contexts.[5]

Up to now sequential patterns of language choice have been considered which start from the assumption that a speaker's turn, or at least its final part, is unambiguously in one language or the other; only in such a case is the recipient able to take up the present speaker's language choice. However, it is frequently observed that bilingual speakers keep language choice open by switching between languages within a turn in a way that makes it impossible to decide if language A or B is the 'base language'. The recipient of such a turn may continue in this mode (Pattern IIIa) or choose the language he or she thinks is appropriate or preferred (Pattern IIIb). The turn-internal switches that occur in such an ambiguous turn may have a conversational function, such as in the case of other-language reiterations for emphasis, or topic/comment switching (see below, pp. 135–6); but the fact of keeping the language choice open also provides information about the speaker and his or her conceptualisation of the situation. Therefore, switching of this turn-internal type is often discourse-related and at the same time participant-related.

Pattern IIIa: AB1 AB2 AB1 AB2
Pattern IIIb: AB1//A2 A1 A2

Finally, code-alternation may occur in the middle of a speaker's turn without affecting language choice for the interaction at all. Such momentary lapses into the other language usually occur because a word or another structure in language B is inserted into a language A frame. The insertion has a predictable end; code-alternation defines a unit instead of a momentary departure from the language-of-interaction. Such a type of code-alternation I have called *transfer* (as opposed to code-switching).[6] Schematically, this pattern is represented as IV:

Pattern IV: A1[B1]A1

Transfer may be discourse- or participant-related. In the latter case, it may display a speaker's bilingual competence (for details, see Auer 1981).

The cross-cutting dichotomies of discourse- vs participant-related code-alternation on the one hand, and code-switching vs transfer on the other, provide a theory for the ways in which code-alternation may become meaningful as a contextualisation cue. This theory has been used empirically in a number of studies on Italian–German and Italian–(Canadian) English bilinguals (Auer 1983, 1984, 1991a), but also in partly refined versions in studies by Hannan (1986) and by Panese (1992) on (British) English/ Italian data, by Alfonzetti (1992) on Italian standard/dialect data, and by Li (1994) on (British) English/Chinese data. Examples may be found in these publications and papers and will not be repeated here.

5 Code-alternation and language negotiation

What has been called discourse-related code-switching here (Pattern I) usually runs under the heading of conversational code-switching in the literature, and it has received much attention. On the other hand, matters of language choice for interactive episodes, processes of negotiation of a language-of-interaction between bilinguals, or patterns of language alternation due to a lack of competence (Pattern II, partly Pattern III) are usually not subsumed under conversational code-switching but considered to be either determined by societal macrostructures or by psycholinguistic factors. Thus, while discourse-related switching is analysed within conversational episodes and partly in conversation analytic terms, matters of language choice and language negotiation for an episode are relegated to ethnographic description.

In this section, it will be shown that it is not only discourse-related language alternation that must be given a conversational, sequential analysis, but other types of language alternation as well.[7] As examples, language negotiation and 'code-switching as an unmarked choice' will be discussed.

Why does language negotiation occur at all? The model underlying some approaches to code-alternation (including Blom and Gumperz's distinction between situational and metaphorical code-switching and Fishman's approach mentioned earlier, see above, p. 125) seems to be that language choice is determined by situational parameters such as topic, participant roles or overall speech event. Within the situation defined by these parameters and determining language choice, deviations from the expected or unmarked language may occur for stylistic purposes; but conversational language negotiation has no place in such a conception.

There are at least two empirical problems with this approach (leaving aside theoretical problems concerning the notions of situation and context). First, in many if not all bilingual speech communities situational factors underspecify language choice, i.e. there are at least some situations in which language choice is open; the number of linguistically underspecified situations is particularly high in the 'new' bilingual communities that have come into being in Europe as a consequence of work migration. Here, language choice often ties up with individual histories of interaction in which patterns of language choice may have developed, or is simply a matter of individual preferences, which are, in turn, related to linguistic competences and personal linguistic biographies, as well as to complex matters of bi-cultural identity. The point is that these communities are too young and culturally unstable to have developed shared norms of language choice.

Second, there are many cases in which the situation is simply not defined unambiguously. In such a case, co-participants not only have the task of finding a language; they have to define the situation, among other things, by choosing a language. Carol Myers-Scotton has shown very convincingly for the African context how this can be done and how code-switching can be used in order to 'negotiate interpersonal relationships', instead of being determined by them (e.g., in Myers-Scotton 1991; Scotton 1988).

Due to undefined situations or non-determined language choices, processes of language negotiation occur and are open to conversation analytic treatment. Conversational sequences in which a base-language is negotiated have structural properties of their own. Consider the following examples, one from the Franco-Canadian context (4), the other from Galicia (5):

(4) [at the reception of a hospital]
    01 Clerk: *Central Booking, may I help you?*
    02 Patient: Oui, allô?
    03 Clerk: Bureau de rendez-vous, est-ce que je peux vous aider?
    04   *May I help you?*
    05   (Silence)
    06   Est-ce que je peux vous aider?
    07   (Silence)
    08   Anglais ou français?
    09 Patient: *WHAT?*
    10 Clerk: *MAY I HELP YOU?*
    11   *Oh yes, yes, I'm sorry, I'm just a little deaf*
    (Heller 1982a)

(5) [informal conversation between three Galician men; A, an elementary
    school teacher, has given a lecture on the history of Galicia; R, the
    researcher, is known to study in the USA; he has been introduced to A
    by P, with whom he is acquainted personally]
    [after talk by A in Galician, with P as the primary addressee, A turns to
    R, introducing a new topic; there is a (discourse-related) switching into
    Spanish at this point; Spanish is marked by italics]

```
01  A:  [gazing at R., high] y: qué tal el nivel de la
02      Universidad / es alto no?
03  R:  si:
04  A:  y qué qué haces? filología inglesa? o:
05  R:  nom . . . e:: . . . linguüística . . . pero estou interessado no
06      galego
07  A:  ai, no galego / bueno y fuiste becado, becado para allá? o-
08      o-
09  R:  eh? si, bueno ali estou tamém trabalhando na universidade
10      e:, . . . despois derom-me umha beca pra vir aqui a galiza
11  A:  ai, pra vir a galícia
12  R:  (            ) . . . (e despois) marcho para alá
13  A:  e e a- vas outra vez para alá
14      e [high] quê te- quê anos tes que estar ali
[etc., continues between A and R in Galician]
```

A: *annnd, what about the standards of the universities? They are high aren't they?*

R: yes.

A: *and what what are you studying? English Philology? or* ∴ . . .

R: no, uuh, linguistics, but I'm interested in Galician.

A: oh, in Galician. *So you went there with a scholarship? Or, or-*

R: uh? yes, well, there I'm also working in the university and later they gave me a grant to come here to Galiza.

A: oh, to come to Galicia

R: (   ) (and then) I'm going back there.

A: and and uh- you're going back there. So how many more years will you have to stay there?

[etc.]

(Alvarez 1990: 152f.)

In the first case, the clerk at the reception has the professional duty to accommodate to the client's preferred language, although he or she has to provide the first turn in the interaction. She does so by reformulating her English opening phrase in French after the client's French quasi-response in line 02. In the second case, there is an open clash between A's preference for Spanish and R's preference for Galician. In both cases, political and social considerations go into these preferences. The important point to make here, however, is that the politically, socially, or simply personally motivated preferences for one language or the other are made visible in conversational sequences of language negotiation, and are therefore amenable to sequential analysis. A closer look at such sequences of language negotiation does indeed reveal a number of structural features.

The Canadian example demonstrates one of them: an absence of response after first pair parts such as questions (see, for example, after lines 03, 04, 06) prompts first speakers' inferences, made visible through the repair type carried out by these speakers in order to locate and overcome the recipients' 'problem'. Whereas in monolingual inferences reiterations of first pair parts may lead to reformulations, or to speaking louder, locating 'problems' such as 'misunderstanding', 'not enough detail', or 'too soft', the foremost inference in the bilingual situation analysed by Heller is that of a wrong (inadequate) choice of language.

From the Galician example, we can learn how a language negotiation can be won. A starts to address the visitor from America in Spanish, although the latter has displayed at least passive competence of Galician in the prior discourse. R refuses to take up this language choice, insisting on Galician. There is a conflict over conversational language choice, which is 'won' by R; it is instructive to see how. For this, compare A's and R's language choice in responsive turns. A starts to yield in turns consisting of or containing repetitions, i.e. 07, 11, 13. R, on the contrary, sticks to Galician in his responsive turns (03, 05/6, 09/10). Now, it is a general feature of bilingual language negotiation (c. Auer 1983: 93ff.) that there is more pressure to accommodate to co-participant's language choice for turns or turn components with a high degree of cohesion with previous turns – such as reformulations, repairs and second pair parts – than in initiative turns or turn components, showing little cohesion with previous turn. R wins because he insists on 'his' language even in responsive turns; and he can be said to have won as soon as A uses Galician even for an initiative turn – such as the question in 14.

Language preference and language negotiation are also at play in Pattern III above, i.e., in *code-switching as an unmarked choice*. Scholars of code-switching from Labov (1977: 31) to Heller (1988a) and Scotton (1988) have suggested that frequent conversational code-alternation may be used for creating 'strategic ambiguity' (Heller) or because 'the speaker wishes more than one social identity to be salient in the current exchange' (Scotton). Code-alternation according to this pattern is given a participant-related meaning, indexing globally an ambiguous social situation. This is surely correct. However, it seems from the examples given for this type of alternation that the individual switches, although they are not 'socially meaningful', nevertheless may have individual discourse-related functions. Consider example (6):

(6) [(Non-standard) Swahili-English-Lwidakho code-alternation.] A Luyia man is interviewing a Luyia woman who works in Nairobi as a nurse. They come from the same home area and he is a friend of her husband. As a long-term resident of Nairobi, she now uses Swahili as her main language for informal interaction in Nairobi. [English in italics, Lwidakho underlined]

01	Int.:	unapenda kufanya kazi yako lini? Mchana au usiku?
02	Nurse:	*as I told you, I like my job,*
03		sina ubaguzi wo wote kuhusu wakati ninapofanya kazi.
04		*I enjoy working either during the day*
05		au usiku yote ni sawa kwangu.
06		Hata *family members* w-angu wamezoea mtindo huu.
07		*There is no quarrel at all.*
08		<u>Obubi bubulaho.</u>
09		Saa zengine kazi huwa nyingi sana na.
10		*There are other times when we just have light duty.*
11		<u>Valwale vanji</u>, *more work;*
12		<u>valwale vadi</u>, hazi kidogo.

<table>
<tr><td>01</td><td>Int.:</td><td>When do you like to work? Days or nights?</td></tr>
<tr><td>02</td><td>Nurse:</td><td>*As I told you, I like my job,*</td></tr>
<tr><td>03</td><td></td><td>I have no difficulty at all regarding when I do work.</td></tr>
<tr><td>04</td><td></td><td>*I enjoy working either during the day*</td></tr>
<tr><td>05</td><td></td><td>or at night, all is ok as far as I'm concerned.</td></tr>
<tr><td>06</td><td></td><td>Even my *family members* have gotten used to this plan.</td></tr>
<tr><td>07</td><td></td><td>*There is no quarrel at all.*</td></tr>
<tr><td>08</td><td></td><td><u>There is no badness</u>.</td></tr>
<tr><td>09</td><td></td><td>Sometimes there is a lot of work and</td></tr>
<tr><td>10</td><td></td><td>*there are other times when we just have light duty.*</td></tr>
<tr><td>11</td><td></td><td><u>More patients</u>, more work;</td></tr>
<tr><td>12</td><td></td><td><u>fewer patients</u>, little work.</td></tr>
</table>

(Myers-Scotton 1991)

Surely, the interviewee here wants to leave language choice open; Swahili, English and Lwidakho are used one beside the other. However, the alternation between these three languages is not random. Instead, it seems quite clear that the speaker uses code-switching in order to structure her turn. Among the discourse-related functions of code-switching for this speaker are the following: (a) building up contrasts as in line 04 (English: 'during the day') vs line 05 (Swahili: 'at night'), or in line 09 (Swahili: 'times of hard work') vs line 10 (English: 'times of little work'), or in line 11 (English: 'more work') vs line 12 (Swahili: 'little work'); (b) for grammatically unmarked (asyndetic) 'if/then' structures as in line 11 (protasis: Lwidakho; apodosis: English) and line 12 (protasis: Lwidakho; apodosis; Swahili); (c) for reformulations for the purpose of giving emphasis to a statement, as in lines 07/08 (switching from English into Lwidakho). Leaving the language choice open therefore does not exclude the possibility of using code-alternation for discourse-related purposes.

6 Conclusion

I have tried to argue that between the grammar of code-alternation on the one hand, and its social meaning for the bilingual community at large on the other, there is a third domain that needs to be taken into account: that of the sequential embeddedness of code-alternation in conversation. This domain is relatively independent of the others. Its autonomy is given by the fact that the basic principles by which code-alternation is used in conversation as a meaningful semiotic resource can be stated independently of both the grammar and the macro-social context of code-alternation. Its autonomy is only relative, however, particularly with regard to the social meaning of code-alternation, because in a given bilingual speech community, the conversational patterns of code-alternation and indeed the local meaning given to an instance of code-alternation in a particular context will vary as a function of the status of the codes in the repertoire of the community.

Notes

1   Other researchers have tried to find similar correlations, such as Sapiens (1982) for bilingual classroom interaction.

2   See Gumperz 1982: 82; Auer 1984a: 319ff.; Alvarez 1990: ch. 4; Sebba and Wootton 1984.

3   Cf. Gumperz 1982, 1990, 1992b, etc. For a theoretical summary, c. Auer (1992). Also c. Loke (1991) for an application of Gumperz's theory of contextualisation to code-alternation.

4   Again, I can only give a very short summary here (for details, c.: Auer 1983, 1984, 1984a, 1987; for a summary: Auer 1988).

5   Note that in a sequence of language choices such as IIb, switching recurs from one turn to the next following the dyadic pattern of a two-party conversation. Alternatively, if we focus on one speaker only, the shift of language in this person's speech occurs at the point where he or she 'yields' to the other party's preferred language (the point indicated by double slashes in IIb).

6   Because of this term's unfortunate association with a certain theory of second language acquisition, it may be advisable to speak of 'insertion', rather than 'transfer'.

7   Also c. del Coso-Calame *et al.* 1985; Nussbaum 1990; Auer 1981.

Source: Auer, P., The pragmatics of code-switching: a sequential approach. In L. Milroy and P. Muysken (eds) *One Speaker Two Languages*, Cambridge University Press, pp. 115–35. Copyright © 1995 Cambridge University Press, reproduced with permission of the author and publisher.

Postscript

More than ten years after it was written, 'The pragmatics of code-switching: a sequential approach' still remains valid as a relatively formal outline of the conversational structures involved in the alternating use of two languages in conversation. Although conceived as an overview to the approach first developed in Auer (1984), the paper draws on examples from various other publications, not my own data on Italian/German code alternation. It was written in order to show that the conversational structure of bilingual talk has its own validity which cannot be reduced to the grammar of (sentence-internal) code-switching, or to macro- or micro-social contexts, and transcends the single case description of a particular bilingual community. The structure of bilingual talk was shown to provide an independent level of organisation. The paper draws heavily on two traditions of research: conversation analysis and the theory of contextualisation as developed by John Gumperz. It was an attempt to provide a more technical, sequential basis for contextualisation research, embedding the occurrence of contextualisation cues such as code-switching into the sequential unfolding of talk; at the same time, it enlarged the scope of conversation analysis by conceding that contextualisation cues may have some kind of brought-along meaning 'potential' which enters into the interpretation of their occurrence.

The idea to link code alternation to conversational structure has led to many other studies in which the relationship between preference structure and code-switching has proven to be particularly powerful (cf. Li Wei and Milroy 1995). But 'Pragmatics of code-switching' insists that there are additional types of the meaningful alternation between two languages in addition to this 'discourse-related' type of code-switching. Language negotiation, competence-related switching, and the discourse-related exploitation of insertions should be mentioned here, although they have received less attention in the literature (cf. recently Angermeyer, 2002). Some of the terminology used in the paper I abandoned later on (such as the unhappy term 'transfer' for 'insertions', which I used from 1998 [Introduction to *Code-Switching in Conversation*] onwards to describe those types of code alternation which do not question the language of alternation because they are embedded into a turn which conforms to this language).

But the most important point made in this paper is perhaps one which was often forgotten when reference was made to its sequential formats. It is the definition of code alternation (code-switching in the terminology of Auer 1999) itself: I maintain that code alternation is not simply the alternating use of two or more languages within an interactional encounter, but that it is necessary that 'the appropriate recipients of the resulting complex sign are in a position to interpret this juxtaposition as such' (p. 116 in the original version). As many authors have outlined since, bilingual talk can fail to establish sharp boundaries in which the 'context' of the interaction changes; in fact, as Woolard (1999) and others have pointed out, bilingual talk can be intentionally or unintentionally ambivalent and the borders between one 'code' and the other are often vague. In this case, the juxtaposition cannot become meaningful. Also, what counts as a 'code' is hard to determine on linguistic grounds alone; it is the participants and their interpretative resources who determine this. In fact, many cases of code alternation as an 'unmarked choice' are not suited to build up the contrasts which are necessary for interpreting individual cases of the juxtaposition of one language and another as interactionally meaningful. Such cases of what I call code mixing (Auer 1999) have a totally different semiotic status from the ones discussed in Auer (1984) etc., as pointed out, e.g., by Álvarez-Caccamo (1998), Meeuwis and Blommaert (1998) and Gafaranga (2007).

Peter Auer, PhD, is Professor of Germanic Linguistics at the University of Freiburg, Germany. peter.auer@germanistik.uni-freiburg.de

A two-step sociolinguistic analysis of code-switching and language choice: the example of a bilingual Chinese community in Britain

LI WEI, LESLEY MILROY AND PONG SIN CHING

THE EXTENSIVE LITERATURE ON bilingualism illustrates a range of (sometimes interdisciplinary) approaches to code-switching behaviour, some of which seem rather distant from the primarily social one which we shall present here. However, we would suggest that an adequate account of the social and situational context of code-switching behaviour is an important prerequisite even where the perspective of the researcher is (for example) psycholinguistic rather than social. This article attempts to develop a coherent account of the relationship between code-switching and language choice by individual speakers, and of the relation of both to the broader social, economic and political context. The exposition is presented both in general terms which emphasise its applicability to a range of bilingual situations, and with specific reference to the example of the bilingual Chinese–English-speaking community in Tyneside, north-eastern England.

It is evident from the abundant research literature that a wealth of data and analyses of code-switching behaviour from many very different communities is readily available (for a recent overview of such work, see Heller, 1988). What seems generally to be lacking is a coherent social framework within which to interpret these data and analyses. For example, Heller (1990) remarks that while John Gumperz, an important leader in the field, has always viewed code-switching as constitutive of social reality, he has perhaps been less successful in linking this interactional level with broader questions of social relations and social organisation. While Gumperz himself may not have intended to make this micro–macro link, it is important that those who develop his procedures should attempt to do so. Otherwise, insightful interactional-level analyses of data sets which cannot be compared with each other will continue to proliferate without any corresponding advance in understanding similarities and differences in the code-switching and language choice behaviours of different communities, or in explaining why rapid language shift is likely in one particular community but not in another.

Like Woolard (1985), Gal (1988; 1989) and Heller (1990), we take the starting point for any social or sociolinguistic model to be existing detailed sociolinguistic observations of code-switching behaviour. But such everyday behaviour of social actors and larger scale institutional analysis should be seen as related rather than as dissociated, as tends to be the case in the bilingualism literature (cf. the approaches of Fishman and Gumperz, which are generally considered quite separately). Giddens (1984) has developed a social theory based on the relationships between these two levels, commenting that 'the study of day-to-day life is integral to analysis of the reproduction of institutionalised practices' (1984: 282).

Any attempt to integrate micro and macro levels of analysis entails a consideration of patterns of *language choice* at the *community* (or even national) level, in conjunction with an analysis of *code-switching* at the *interactional* level. Myers-Scotton's (1986) remark that a model of code-choice needs to be in place before one can develop a model of code-switching is particularly relevant here, since it is important before attempting to account for code-switching behaviour to have some idea of how language choice is restricted for some speakers, or affected by social values assigned to community languages. For this reason, we shall have a good deal to say in this chapter about language choice, prior to our remarks on code-switching.

The following sections are structured as follows. First we shall outline relevant aspects of the concept of social network. We then relate the language choice patterns of the community to its informal social structure, considering separately relevant patterns of both inter-generational and intra-generational patterns of variation. We then examine the reflection of these patterns in code-switching behaviour at the interactional level; and, finally, we attempt to relate observations of behaviour at both community level and interactional level to a wider social, political and economic framework.

The network concept

Social network analysis of the kind which is most relevant to sociolinguists was developed in the 1960s and 1970s by a group of mainly British social anthropologists. Personal social networks were generally seen as contextualised within a broader social framework, which was 'bracketed-off' to allow attention to be concentrated on developing less abstract modes of analysis which could account more immediately for the variable behaviour of individuals. However, it is important to remember that such bracketing-off is wholly methodological and does not reflect an ontological reality. While no one claims that personal network structure is independent of the broader social framework which constantly constrains individual behaviour, a fundamental postulate of network analysis is that individuals create personal communities which provide them with a meaningful framework for solving the problems of their day-to-day existence (Mitchell, 1986: 74). This kind of focus has made the social network approach a useful one for sociolinguists investigating relatively clearly definable communities like the Tyneside Chinese, as well as for researchers from other disciplines. For example, Riley *et al.* (1990) describe the application of network analysis in an international project encompassing communities in Sweden, West Germany, the United States and Wales, where the capacities of urban social networks to provide support for families are considered. Many of the methods developed by the research team for investigating and comparing social networks are of relevance to field sociolinguists (see Cochran *et al.*, 1990).

A social network may be seen as a boundless web of ties which reaches out through a whole society, linking people to one another, however remotely. But for practical reasons social networks are generally 'anchored' to individuals, and interest focuses on relatively 'strong' first-order network ties; i.e. those persons with whom ego directly and regularly interacts. This principle of 'anchorage' effectively limits the field of network studies, generally to something between 20 and 50 individuals.

It is, however, useful to distinguish between 'strong' and 'weak' ties of everyday life, using the notions of 'exchange' and 'interactive' networks elaborated by Milardo (1988: 26–36). Exchange networks constitute persons such as kin and close friends with whom ego not only interacts routinely, but also exchanges direct aid, advice, criticism, and support. Interactive networks, on the other hand, consist of persons with whom ego interacts frequently and perhaps over prolonged periods of time, but on whom ego does not rely for personal favours and other material or symbolic resources. An example of an interactive tie would be that between a shop owner and customer. In addition to exchange and interactive ties, we identified a 'passive' type of network tie. Passive ties entail an absence of regular contact, but are valued by ego as a source of influence and moral support. Examples are physically distant relatives or friends, such ties being particularly important to migrant families.

Our basic procedure for comparative analysis of the 'strong tie' exchange network structures of persons in the Chinese community was to compile for each individual a list of 20 others who comprised significant daily contacts. This information was obtained by a mixture of informal interviewing and observation. Once these various 'networks' of 20 had been identified, contrasts between them were examined with respect to the extent of their ethnic and peer orientation. It is their ethnic orientation, expressed by an *ethnic index* to represent the proportion of Chinese ties, which chiefly concerns us here. Ethnic indices were also compiled for interactive and passive networks. For passive networks, the index was based on a figure of 10 ties per individual, and for interactive networks, 20 or 30; the precise figure varied according to the interactional practices of individuals.

These differences in procedure for arriving at the three types of network index are not arbitrary. They reflect the abilities of persons to enumerate individuals with whom they have contracted different types of network tie (in the case of exchange and passive ties), and the capacity of the fieldworker to make reasonably reliable observations (in the case of interactive ties). We have adapted here the approach to network analysis described by Mitchell (1986) with respect to his study of the networks of homeless women in Manchester, Britain. It is quite a different procedure from the one described by Milroy (1987a) in a sociolinguistic study of inner-city Belfast where networks tended to be close-knit and territorially bounded.

Close-knit social networks seem to have a particular capacity to maintain and even enforce local conventions and norms, including linguistic norms. Thus, network analysis offers a basis for understanding the social mechanisms that underlie this process of language maintenance, the converse of language shift. This is true whether we are looking at maintenance in opposition to the publically legitimised code of a stigmatised urban vernacular as in Belfast, or maintenance of an ethnic language. Migrant and other communities are not all equally successful in maintaining their community languages, and they also apparently vary in their intergenerational communication practices; for example the Panjabi and Bengali speakers in Newcastle do not seem to be experiencing such a sharp intergenerational disjunction as the Chinese community (Moffatt and Milroy, 1992). We shall argue that network analysis can illuminate the social dynamics involved in this kind of inter-group difference.

It has sometimes been suggested that close-knit types of community network are nowadays marginal to urban life; for example, since the work of Georg Simnel there has been a large sociological literature on 'the stranger' and the marginal individual who is now often seen as typical of a modern city dweller (Harman, 1988). Wirth, an influential member of the Chicago school of urban sociologists, argued that urban conditions give rise to impersonality and social distance. All this may reflect some kind of truth about urban life, but it does not tell the whole story. Certainly the Italian American 'urban villagers' described by Gans (1962) or the close-knit Yorkshire mining communities described by Dennis et al. (1957) may now seem less salient in American and British cities. But such traditional working-class communities are apparently being replaced, in Europe and elsewhere, by similar types of community created by newer immigrants. Indeed, as Giddens (1989) points out, neighbourhoods involving close kinship and personal ties seem to be actually created by city life. Those who form part of urban ethnic communities, such as the Tyneside Chinese, gravitate to form ties with, and sometimes to live with, others from a similar linguistic or ethnic background. Such ethnic groups seem to use the close-knit network as a means of protecting their interests while the community develops the resources to integrate more fully into urban life. Few of the Tyneside Chinese, for example, want their children to inherit their catering businesses, but prefer them to integrate into British society and train for higher-status employment.

The chief point we wish to emphasise here is that the type of close-knit network structure which seems to help maintain community languages is likely to be a product of modern city life rather than a residue of an earlier type of social organisation. With regard to the associations between this level of social organisation and patterns of face-to-face interaction, we need to remember the role of such close-knit networks in renewing and maintaining local systems of norms and values within which discourse processes of the kind analysed by Gumperz (1982) are understood and enacted. Indeed, as Gumperz' work has suggested, language use is itself an excellent diagnostic of group collectivity.

The Chinese community

We shall examine in this section the relationship between network structure and language choice patterns in the bilingual Chinese community in Tyneside, before relating this analysis to code-switching behaviour at the interpersonal level. The material presented here is derived chiefly from participant observation carried out in the field by Li Wei. Most of the linguistic data was collected during mealtimes, which provided an excellent setting for intergenerational interaction. Code-switching could be observed particularly frequently in such an interactional context.

The Tyneside Chinese number somewhere between 5000 and 7000 persons, most of whom are bilingual in English and one of several Chinese languages for which we shall use the generic label 'Chinese'. Like other researchers who have worked with migrant communities, we are conscious of the need for a model of ongoing social and linguistic change since code-switching and language choice patterns need to be modelled very differently from those in well-established bilingual communities (Boeschoten, 1991). Network analysis can be carried out only after a period of ethnographic observation in the community, in order to discover basic patterns of interaction and informal social organisation. Two initial observations were made at this point, which were critical to a subsequent network analysis:

1   The family is the primary unit of social organisation, having a clear internal authority structure. Like most Chinese migrant communities, the majority of the Tyneside Chinese earn their living from family-based catering businesses which rely almost exclusively on family labour. They thereby avoid high wages, overtime payments and other potential drains on resources. To provide service for the maximum number of potential customers, they do not live in identifiable settlements with a centralised authority structure. In this respect they contrast sharply with other linguistic minority communities in Britain, whose social organisation is less family-based and who cluster in specifiable urban areas. Generally speaking, Chinese caterers keep a low public profile and do not develop close personal ties with non-Chinese people. This dispersed settlement pattern and reliance on kin is important for subsequent network analysis.

2   Three groups were identifiable which are not always exactly isomorphic with the three-generation cohorts of grandparents, parents and children:

(a)   first-generation migrants;

(b)   sponsored immigrants, who are either immediate kin of the first-generation migrants or have personal connections with people already established in Britain;

(c)   the British-born.

Subsequent analysis revealed that these groups contract quite different kinds of interpersonal network ties, which need to be interpreted within the framework of a social organisation which gives primacy to the family and an economic dependence on the catering trade.

Over the years, most first-generation migrants and those sponsored immigrants who are actively involved in the food trade have contracted network ties with *mainly Chinese* non-kin who are associated with their business and professional activities. The rest of the sponsored immigrants, mostly women and the elderly, more or less confine themselves to the household and family. The British-born generation differs from both these groups in having developed extensive network ties outside the family and also often outside the Chinese community. The educational level of this group is much higher than that of the others, and most British-born Chinese seem to want to enter occupations other than the catering trade. Thus, the exchange networks of the economically active group – both men and women who belong mainly to the 'parent' generation cohort – are strongly Chinese-oriented but not restricted to kin; those of the economically less active adults are also Chinese-oriented but largely restricted to kin; and those of the British-born generation are less kin-oriented and less ethnically oriented than either of these groups. It was also clear from this preliminary period of observation that the patterns of language choice in the community corresponded to some extent to these groupings, varying from Chinese monolingualism in the 'grandparent' generation, through various proportions of Chinese–English bilingualism to the English-dominant bilingualism characteristic of the British-born Chinese.

We are now in a position to look at the linguistic consequences of these differing age-related social network types, drawing on analysis of a corpus of 23 hours of spontaneous conversation involving 58 speakers in 10 families. Tables 7.1 and 7.2 implicationally order these speakers (male and female analysed separately) according to customary language choice with different addressees both within and outside the family.

Table 7.1 Implicational scale for observed language choices by male speakers (scalability 98.2%)

A	B	C	a	b	c	Interlocutors											
						1	2	3	4	5	6	7	8	9	10	11	12
25	6GP	73	20	10	10	—	C	C	—	C	C	C	C	C	C	C	C
1	1GP	66	20	10	10	—	C	C	—	C	C	C	C	—	C	C	C
45	9P	53	15	4	10	C	C	C	—	—	C	C	C	—	CE	CE	CE
10	3P	47	18	5	10	C	C	C	—	—	C	C	C	—	CE	CE	CE
5	2P	41	16	0	10	—	C	C	—	—	C	C	C	—	CE	CE	CE
26	6P	56	17	6	10	C	C	C	C	—	C	C	CE	CE	CE	CE	CE
20	5P	37	17	2	10	C	C	C	—	—	C	C	CE	CE	CE	CE	CE
53	10P	44	15	2	10	C	C	CE*	C	—	CE*	C	CE	—	CE	CE	CE
2	1P	35	16	0	10	—	C	C	C	—	C	CE	CE	—	CE	CE	CE
32	7P	49	12	5	10	C	C	C	—	—	CE	CE	CE	CE	CE	CE	CE
51	10GP	68	16	6	10	C	C	C	—	CE	CE	CE	CE	CE	CE	CE	CE
37	8GP	65	14	5	10	C	C	C	—	CE	CE	CE	CE	CE	CE	CE	CE
39	8P	44	14	1	10	C	C	C	CE	—	CE	CE	CE	CE	CE	CE	CE
15	4P	40	2	6	10	C	C	CE	—	—	CE	CE	CE	CE	CE	CE	CE
28	6C	22	1	3	6	—	C	CE	C*	CE	CE	CE	CE	CE	CE	CE	CE
47	9C	24	2	1	7	C	C	CE	—	CE	CE	CE	CE	—	CE	CE	CE
48	9C	22	3	0	9	C	C	CE	—	CE	CE	CE	CE	—	CE	CE	CE
12	3C	21	5	0	8	C	C	CE	—	CE	CE	CE	CE	—	CE	CE	CE
13	3C	19	0	0	8	C	C	CE	—	CE	CE	CE	CE	CE	CE	CE	CE
49	9C	18	0	0	6	C	C	CE	—	CE	CE	CE	CE	—	CE	CE	CE
7	2C	15	2	0	6	—	C	CE	—	CE	CE	CE	CE	—	CE	CE	CE
8	2C	12	0	0	5	—	C	CE	—	CE	CE	CE	CE	—	CE	CE	CE
29	6C	17	0	1	5	—	CE	CE	C*	CE	CE	CE	CE	CE	CE	CE	CE
4	1C	10	0	0	4	—	CE	CE	C*	CE	CE	CE	CE	—	—	CE	E
34	7C	18	0	0	5	C	C	CE	—	CE	CE	CE	CE	CE	CE	CE	E
17	4C	11	1	0	6	C	C	CE	—	CE	CE	CE	CE	CE	—	E	E
43	8C	16	0	0	4	C	C	CE	CE	CE	CE	CE	CE	CE	—	E	E
55	10C	16	0	1	5	C	CE	CE	CE	CE	CE	CE	CE	CE	CE	E	E
35	7C	15	0	0	3	C	CE	CE	—	CE	CE	CE	—	CE	—	E	E
22	5C	14	2	1	3	C	CE	CE	—	CE	CE	CE		CE	—	E	E

Notes: A = speaker number; B = family membership (GP = Grandparent; P = Parent; C = Child; the numbers denote families 1–10) C = age; a = ethnic index of interactive networks (total: 10); b = ethnic index of 'passive' networks (total: 10); Interlocutors: 1 = grandparent, female; 2 = grandparent, male; 3 = grandparent generation, male; 4 = grandparent, male; 5 = parent, male; 6 = parent, female; 7 = parent generation, male; 8 = parent generation, female; 9 = child, female; 10 = child, male; 11 = child generation, male; 12 = child generation, female.

* These cells fail to conform to perfect scalability.

Also included is the ethnic index associated with all three types of network. Tables 7.1 and 7.2 adapt slightly Gal's (1979) application of the implicational scale technique to examine both the social and stylistic dimensions of language choice. In these scales, speakers are ranked on the vertical axis and interlocutors on the horizontal axis. Those who are listed towards the top of the scale are speakers who use Chinese (C) on more occasions (i.e. with more interlocutor types), while those who use more English (E) are listed towards the bottom. Interlocutors are also ranked according to the language choices of the vertically ranked speakers. Those who are spoken to in Chinese by more speakers are listed towards the left, while those spoken to more in English towards the right. Thus, the use of C with any particular interlocutor implies that C will be used with all interlocutors to the left of the scale, while if E is used with any interlocutor, it will be used with all interlocutors to the right. The use of both C and E to the same interlocutor will appear between the use of only C and the use of only E, and these are the situations where code-switching may (but not necessarily) occur. Any choice that does not fit this pattern is considered 'unscalable'. Scalability is calculated as the percentage of cells that fit the scale model, and 85 per cent scalability is normally considered to be a sufficient approximation of perfect scaling (Gal, 1979; Fasold, 1990).

The language choice pattern of any individual speaker can be read across each row, while inter-speaker differences in language choice with particular interlocutors can be read down each column. The relationship between social networks and language choice patterns is indicated by the ethnic indices associated with the three types (exchange; interactive; 'passive'). Information on speaker age and generation cohort is provided in columns B and C.

On the horizontal axis, grandparents are listed at the far left and children at the far right, indicating that Chinese is generally used to grandparents and English to children. This addressee ranking largely corresponds with the speaker ranking on the vertical axis, where grandparents appear towards the top of the scales and children towards the bottom. Broadly speaking, therefore, Chinese tends to be used by grandparents and to grandparents, while English tends to be used by children and to children. Both Chinese and English may be used by parents and to parents.

Gal (1979) suggests that it is through this kind of association between language and interlocutor types that languages acquire their social symbolism. For example, since in the Tyneside community Chinese is associated primarily with the grandparents, it may be described as the 'we code' for that generation and for older speakers generally; English, on the other hand, which is associated chiefly with British-born children, may be regarded as their 'we code'. Note that even this tentative generalisation, which takes some account of intergenerational change in patterns of language use, rejects any assumption that the ethnic language of the community is the 'we code' and the language of the majority the 'they code'.

Closer examination of the implicational scales reveals, however, that the interaction between the social and stylistic dimensions of language choice needs a more sophisticated analysis than this. The first point is that not all speakers of the same generation share the same language choice patterns, and there are cases where speakers are ranked either higher or lower than other members of their generation on the horizontal scale. For instance, speakers 51 and 37 (from families 10 and 8, aged 68 and 65 respectively) are ranked much lower than the other grandparents in Table 7.1 and lower even than

Table 7.2 Implicational scale for observed language choices by female speakers (scalability 99.6%)

A	B	C	a	b	c	Interlocutors											
						1	2	3	4	5	6	7	8	9	10	11	12
44	9GP	72	20	10	10	—	C	C	C	C	C	—	C	—	C	C	C
9	3GP	70	20	10	10	—	C	C	C	C	C	—	C	—	C	C	C
31	7GP	67	20	10	10	—	C	C	C	C	C	—	C	C	C	C	C
14	4GP	65	20	10	10	—	C	C	C	C	C	—	C	C	C	C	C
52	10GP	63	20	10	10	—	C	C	C	C	C	C	C	C	C	C	C
38	8GP	61	20	10	10	—	C	C	C	C	C	C	C	C	C	C	C
19	5GP	58	20	10	10	C	C	C	C	C	C	—	C	C	C	C	C
46	9P	50	18	4	10	C	C	C	—	C	C	—	C	—	CE	CE	CE
11	3P	46	20	5	10	C	C	C	—	C	C	—	C	—	CE	CE	CE
6	2P	38	20	2	10	—	C	C	—	C	C	—	C	—	CE	CE	CE
21	5P	35	20	6	10	C	C	C	—	C	C	—	C	CE	CE	CE	CE
3	1P	32	18	7	10	—	C	C	—	C	C	—	C	—	CE	CE	CE
27	6P	52	17	6	10	—	C	C	—	C	C	C	C	CE	CE	CE	CE
33	7P	42	15	5	10	C	C	C	—	C	C	C	CE	CE	CE	CE	CE
54	10P	45	18	1	10	C	C	C	—	CE	CE	CE	CE	CE	CE	CE	CE
16	4P	37	6	0	10	C	C	C	—	CE	CE	—	CE	CE	CE	CE	CE
40	8P	40	18	5	10	C	C	CE	CE	CE	CE	CE	CE	CE	CE	CE	CE
50	9C	22	2	6	8	C	C	CE	CE	CE	CE	—	CE	—	CE	CE	CE
56	10C	21	3	6	8	C	C	CE	CE	CE	CE	CE	CE	CE	CE	CE	CE
57	10C	18	2	0	5	C	C	CE	CE	CE	CE	CE	CE	CE	CE	CE	CE
41	8C	12	1	0	6	C	C	CE	CE	CE	CE	CE	CE	CE	CE	CE	CE
58	10C	12	1	1	4	C	C	CE	CE	CE	CE	CE	CE	CE	CE	CE	CE
42	8C	8	0	0	4	C	C	CE	CE	CE	CE	CE	CE	CE	CE	CE	CE
30	6C	20	1	1	7	—	CE	CE	CE	CE	CE	C*	CE	—	CE	CE	CE
18	4C	15	0	0	5	C	C	CE	CE	CE	CE	—	CE	—	CE	E	E
24	5C	9	1	0	4	C	C	CE	CE	CE	CE	—	CE	CE	CE	E	E
23	5C	11	0	0	3	C	CE	CE	CE	CE	CE	—	CE	CE	CE	E	E
36	7C	10	2	1	5	C	CE	CE	CE	CE	CE	—	CE	—	CE	E	E

some of the parents, suggesting that they use relatively more English. Furthermore, those who are listed at the extreme bottom of the scales are not always the youngest speakers in the child generation. Because such variations in language choice patterns cannot be accounted for entirely by the variables of age and generation, the social network variable becomes relevant.

Relative to other members of the grandparent generation, speakers 51 and 37 have fewer ethnic ties in their networks, and relative to other members of the child generation those listed at the bottom of the scales have even fewer Chinese contacts. In other words, these 'anomalous' speakers seem to have contracted personal social network ties which are rather different from those characteristic of their generation peers and consequently have developed different behavioural patterns.

Interestingly, however, inter-speaker variations of this kind are closely associated with interlocutor types, in that speakers with different network patterns adopt different language choice patterns with particular interlocutors. For example, while speakers of the parent generation who have relatively more Chinese-oriented networks use Chinese for communication between spouses, those with relatively fewer Chinese ties may use both Chinese and English with this addressee type. And while all children use Chinese with grandparents (especially female grandparents) and both Chinese and English with parents, some (but not all) use only English with their peers. Thus, any attempt to infer the social symbolism of Chinese and English by identifying the generations with which they are associated is too simplistic. Tables 7.1 and 7.2 suggest that particular languages are associated with particular groups of speakers who have contracted similar types of social network, and the variable of social network is plainly associated with the variable of age and generation (and to a lesser extent that of sex). Social networks also vary between individuals, despite these associations. Li Wei (1994) reports the results of an initial statistical analysis (using Analysis of Variance and Rank Order Correlation procedures) which explores more systematically the effects of these interacting variables on patterns of language choice.

Network structure and language choice in the British-born generation

Parallel to Li's observational study of 59 persons from 10 families, some results of which we reported in the previous section, Pong (1991) carried out a questionnaire study of language choice of a further 20 three-generational families, comprising 101 persons. This questionnaire study confirmed the chief findings listed above, revealing the same sharp disjunction between the generations; for example, 24% of the 'children' generation cohort report themselves to be monolingual English speakers, while none were monolingual in Chinese. Although this general pattern of generational difference seems to be common in migrant communities, it is not clear how far details vary between communities; for example, it is less clearly evident in the Tyneside Panjabi-speaking community (see Moffatt and Milroy, 1992). The general social explanation which we are offering is based on the types of network contacts made by the children, which involve non-Chinese people much more than their parents' contacts. While this is not particularly startling in itself, the network variable emphasises the basis of variable language choice patterns in social interaction rather than in duration of residence or in opportunity to use English in any straightforward sense. The social symbolism of the languages and the sense of appropriateness which is felt in choosing a suitable language either for an addressee or an auditor is also involved; some of the children reported embarrassment at using Chinese in the presence of English friends. Following the analysis described above which focused on intergenerational differences, we shall look further at how the network concept can illuminate differences in language choice patterns *within* this British-born generation.

Pong's 20 families consisted of two sets, as follows. Ten of the 20 families had migrated from a group of villages on Ap Chau Island, close to Hong Kong and were associated with the so-called True Jesus Church. The other 10 families were not tied to each other in quite this way, sharing neither pre-migration network ties nor having a centralised institution where they might meet. The chief function of the True Jesus Church seems to be that of maintaining Chinese language and culture, and the activities in which the True Jesus families participate each Sunday do not resemble those of the church-going population of Britain generally. The families are all related to each other either closely or more distantly. They generally eat a meal together and attend one of two relatively short church services; one is conducted entirely in Chinese and one mainly in English with an interpreter (usually a bilingual teenager) translating the sermon. There are also lessons in Chinese language and culture for the children during the afternoon, and the families meet otherwise to celebrate special occasions like Chinese New Year or Christmas. Thus, they have ample opportunity to maintain their pre-existing network ties, which are strongly kin-oriented, and to maintain their knowledge of Chinese language, history and culture.

We might ask what effect this has on the language choice patterns of the True Jesus group. With respect to the older generations, the answer is very little, since there is a strong orientation to Chinese in both of them, a tendency which is related to the strongly Chinese- and kin-oriented network patterns of these groups. This kind of generational contrast has already emerged with respect to the 10 families whose language choice patterns are implicationally scaled in Tables 7.1 and 7.2. But the ability to speak Chinese as self-reported on a three-point scale and arranged implicationally in Table 7.3 shows that the children belonging to the True Jesus group (note *a*) tend to appear towards the top, while non-True Jesus children appear near the bottom. This positional variation reflects a stronger preference for Chinese by the True Jesus group. Interestingly, sex of speaker seems to have very little effect on this pattern, nor do other classic sociolinguistic factors such as difference in length of residence or educational attainment. But we would also want to argue that the formal teaching of Chinese is unlikely to have much effect on the spoken language; this is on the basis of our knowledge of the generally negligible effect of (for example) formal lessons in Urdu on the language competence of Pakistani teenagers, also noted in Tyneside. In short, it is the internal social organisation of the community, the persistence of pre-emigration networks and the strategies evolved by the community for maintaining these networks which seem to be the crucial factors. It seems likely that other communities which are trying to maintain their language and culture in opposition to a state or national language may create similar coalitions, which are effectively networks established for a particular purpose.

In the previous section, we suggested that the network variable could account for generation-specific differences in language choice, while in this section it was used to account for differences within a single generational sub-group. By its very nature, the

Table 7.3   Implicational scale for language choice by children

Speakers	Age	Sex	Chinese-speaking ability	Interlocutors							
				1	2	3	4	5	6	7	8
1[a]	28	M	Very well	C	C	C	C	C	C	CE	CE
2	22	M	Very well	C	C	C	C	C	C	CE	CE
3[a]	21	F	Very well	C	C	C	C	C	CE	CE	CE
4[a]	18	M	Very well	C	C	C	C	C	CE	CE	CE
5[a]	16	M	Very well	C	C	C	C	C	CE	CE	CE
6[a]	16	F	Very well	C	C	C	C	C	CE	CE	CE
7[a]	25	M	Very well	C	C	C	C	C	CE	CE	CE
8[a]	23	F	Very well	C	C	C	C	C	CE	CE	CE
9[a]	20	F	Very well	C	C	C	C	C	CE	CE	CE
10[a]	20	F	Very well	C	C	C	C	C	CE	CE	CE
11[a]	16	M	Very well	C	C	C	C	C	CE	–	CE
12	20	M	Fairly well	C	C	C	C	–	–	CE	CE
13[a]	21	F	Fairly well	C	C	C	C	–	–	CE	CE
14[a]	12	M	Very well	C	C	C	C	C	CE	CE	E
15	18	F	Very well	C	CE[b]	CE[b]	C	C	CE	CE	E
16[a]	10	M	Very well	C	C	C	C	CE	CE	CE	CE
17	18	M	Not well	C	C	C	C	CE	CE	CE	E
18	14	M	Not well	C	C	C	C	–	–	CE	E
19	12	M	Fairly well	C	C	C	C	CE	CE	CE	E
20	10	F	Fairly well	C	C	C	C	C	CE	E	E
21[a]	16	M	Very well	C	C	C	CE	C[b]	CE	CE	E
22[a]	11	M	Very well	C	C	C	CE	C[b]	CE	CE	E
23[a]	9	F	Fairly well	C	C	C	CE	C[b]	CE	CE	E
24	16	F	Very well	C	C	C	CE	CE	CE	–	CE
25[a]	7	M	Fairly well	C	C	C	CE	CE	CE	CE	CE
26[a]	15	F	Very well	C	C	C	CE	CE	CE	E[b]	CE
27	8	F	Not well	C	C	C	CE	CE	E[b]	CE	CE
28	13	F	Not well	C	C	C	CE	CE	E[b]	CE	E
29	10	F	Not well	C	C	C	CE	–	–	E	E
30	6	F	Not well	C	C	C	CE	–	–	E	E
31	13	M	Fairly well	C	C	C	CE	CE	E	E	E
32	9	M	Fairly well	C	C	C	CE	CE	E	E	E
33	11	F	Not well	C	C	C	CE	CE	E	E	E
34[a]	13	F	Fairly well	C	C	CE	CE	CE	CE	CE	E
35	11	M	Fairly well	C	C	E[b]	CE	–	–	E	–
36	15	M	Not well	C	E[b]	E[b]	C	CE	CE	CE	E
37	7	F	Fairly well	C	E[b]	E[b]	C	CE	CE	CE	CE
38	7	F	Not well	CE	E	E	E	E	E	–	E

Notes:
[a] Informants from the True Jesus Church.
[b] These cells fail to conform to perfect scalability; Interlocutors: 1 = Grandparents and their generation; 2 = Chinese shopkeepers; 3 = Chinese waiters/waitresses; 4 = Parents and their generation; 5 = Teachers at Chinese Sunday School; 6 = Schoolmates at Chinese Sunday School; 7 = Siblings; 8 = Chinese friends

network variable overlaps and interacts with a host of other social variables, but offers, we have argued, a more general and economical way of accounting for language choice if the relationship with these other variables is made explicit (see also Li Wei, 1993; 1996; Li Wei and Milroy, 1995).

Network-specific conversational code-switching patterns

The first part of our analysis of bilingual language behaviour in the Chinese community revealed a sharp intergenerational disjunction in language choice patterns between the children and the older generations, and has suggested that the network variable is a more accurate predictor of language choice than that of generation, with which it is closely associated but not isomorphic. The implicational scales presented in Tables 7.1 and 7.2 not only illuminate the interaction between inter- and intra-speaker linguistic variations, but also locate specifically the contexts (indicated by a CE pattern) where *conversational code-switching* is likely to occur.

Extracts (1) and (2) below are discussed by Pong (1991: 24, 99) as typical of the different kinds of language mixing behaviour of the child and the parent generations. Note, however, that the fluent code-switching of the bilingual teenagers in (1) indicates a language choice pattern which is rather less English-oriented than that of the speakers listed at the very bottom of the scales in Tables 7.1 and 7.2. The parents in (2) regard themselves as monolingual Chinese speakers, so that whatever criteria we use for distinguishing borrowings from single-word code-switching (and we shall not consider this issue further here), it is reasonable to consider the English items *football hooligan* and *pub* as borrowings (see further Poplack and Sankoff, 1984).

(1) *Fieldworker*: Gem nei dei dou wui hao leu wen go ying guog yen zon peng yeo ne wo.
(So you won't consider having an English girlfriend.)

    Anthony: Zou peng yeo wui, *but not a wife.*
(Yes friends, but not a wife.)

. . .

    Anthony: Yeu hou do yeo *contact.*
(We have many contacts.)

    George: *We always have opportunities* heu xig kei ta dei fong gao wui di yen. Ngo dei xi xi dou *keep in contact.*
(We always have opportunities to get to know people from other churches. We always keep in touch.)

(2) *Father*: Bed guo, Ying Guog di heo seng zeo kuai di la. Bin dou yeo Ying Guog gem do *football hooligan.*
(But the teenagers in Britain are very badly behaved. Where else can you find so many football hooligans?)

    Mother: Ni dou di heo seng zung yi yem zeo. So yi ngo m bei di zei neu heu *pub* ga.
(The teenagers here like to drink. That's why I never allow my children to go to pubs.)

These two extracts illustrate contrasting patterns of intergenerational conversational behaviour which partly derive from the language choice patterns we have described in the preceding sections. To a very large extent, these patterns are associated not only with the different socialisation patterns described above, but with differing levels of ability in the two community languages. However, intergenerational differences in the way the two languages are used in conversation are often subtle and seem to be better analysed as *socially symbolic discourse behaviours* rather than as following from these community-level social variables in any obvious way. We shall examine this dimension of code-switching behaviour within a general *conversation analysis* framework (cf. Auer, 1991). Briefly, this involves searching the data for recurrent sequential patterns, which are then interpreted with reference both to the observable behaviour of participants and to generalisations derived inductively from previously observed conversational corpora (see Levinson, 1983; Atkinson and Heritage, 1984; Roger and Bull, 1989). Using this general framework, we shall look in this section at how speakers alternate their two languages in conversation as a procedure for the organisation of preference marking, repairs and insertion sequences.

Preference marking

Consider first the following conversational sequences:[1]

> (3) (Dinner table talk between mother A and daughter B):
> A: Oy-m-oy faan a? Ah Ying a?
>   (Want or not rice?)
> B: (No response)
> A: Chaaufaan a. Oy-m-oy?
>   (Fried rice. Want or not?)
> B: (2.0) *I'll have some shrimps.*
> A: Mut-ye? (.) Chaaufaan a.
>   (What? Fried rice.)
> B: Hai a.
>   (OK.)

In extract (3), a mother, speaking Cantonese throughout, offers her daughter rice. The child first delays her response to the offer, and then in English requests an alternative to rice. Her final acceptance is in Cantonese. In extract (4), B, a 12-year-old boy, is playing with a computer in the family living-room. A is his mother.

> (4) A: *Finished homework?*
>   (2.0)
> A: Steven, yiu mo wan sue?
>   (want to review (your) lessons)
> B: (1.5) *I've finished.*

In this extract, B does not respond to A's question. The mother then switches to Cantonese for a further question, which B apparently understands as an indirect request to review his lessons. His response is marked by a pause as 'dispreferred' and his language choice contrasts with that of his mother. In both (3) and (4), dispreferred responses seem to be marked by code-switching to a contrasting language, as well as by the more usual pause. A rather clear example of this pattern can be seen in (5), where A is the mother, B her nine-year-old daughter and C her 12-year old son:

(5) A: *Who want some?* ⌈*Crispy a.*
    B: ⌊*Yes*
    A: Yiu me?
       (Want some?)
    B: Hai a
       (Yes.)
    (A handing over some spring-rolls to B.)
    A: (To C) *Want some, John?*
    C: Ngaw m yiu.
       (I don't want.)
    A: M yiu a? *Crispy* la.
       (Don't want?)
    C: (Shaking head) mm

In this sequence, B twice accepts A's offer of spring rolls, twice using the same language as A (English and Cantonese respectively) for this preferred response. However, when C declines A's offer we find a pattern similar to the one which is evident in (3) and (4). After a short pause, C selects a language different from the language used for the first pair part; A uses English for the offer whereas C uses Cantonese for the refusal. This example supports Auer's argument that the contrast is more socially meaningful than the actual choice of language. Switches marking dispreferred responses can be in either direction.

Dispreferred responses in monolingual English conversations (e.g. refusals and disagreements, as opposed to acceptances and agreements) are generally marked by various structural complexities including pauses before delivery, 'prefaces' such as *but* and *well*, token agreements, appreciations and apologies (see further Levinson, 1983: 334–5). These three sequences suggest that contrasting choices of language – with the second-part speaker choosing a language different from the first-part speaker – can be used to mark dispreference in bilingual conversation in much the same way as a wide range of markedness features in monolingual conversation. In fact, Auer (1991) argues that code-switching is the most significant discourse marker in bilingual conversations in the sense that marked language choices are more noticeable than other discourse markers (see also Lavandera, 1978; Gumperz, 1982). It is perhaps for this reason that code-switching may even replace some language-specific dispreference markers. For example, although we have shown that pauses accompany code-switching in this conversational context, we find that in our corpus English discourse markers such as *well* and *but* do not. These items commonly occur in monolingual discourse as prefaces to dispreferred second parts of pairs.

A general pattern which emerges from these examples and many others in the corpus is that code-switching to mark a dispreferred second part occurs chiefly in *intergenerational conversation*. Furthermore, it is usually *children* who use English to mark their dispreferred responses to the Chinese first pair parts of their parents or grandparents (although this is not invariably the case, as can be seen in (5) above). Code-switching seldom seems to be used to mark dispreference in conversations between speakers of the same generation and, where it is, the language direction of the switch is rather less predictable. The emergence of a general pattern of this kind lends support to the point made earlier, that the association between conversation structure and language choice varies according to speakers. Thus, in order to understand the social and discourse meaning of code-switching, we need to relate specific interactional strategies to the more general patterns of language choice and language ability at the inter-speaker (or community) level.

Repair

Consider now the following three sequences, which involve older speakers. A and B are both women in their early forties.

> (6) *A*: . . .koei hai yisaang.
>   (He's a doctor.)
>   *B*: *Is he?*
>   *A*: Yichin (.) hai Hong Kong.
>   (Before. In Hong Kong.)

In extract (6), B's utterance, in a language contrastive with that of A's preceding utterance, initiates a self-repair by A, prompting her to specify more accurately that the man mentioned in her first turn was formerly a doctor in Hong Kong, but is not currently a doctor in Britain.

In extract (7), where A and B again are both women, A in her forties and B in her mid-twenties, B similarly marks a repair initiator with a contrasting choice of language. Here she queries the accuracy of A's assertion that the person she is trying to contact on the telephone will ring in a short time.

> (7) *A*: Da m do. Koeige *telephone* gonggan. Koei dang yatjan joi da.
>   (Can't get through. Her telephone is engaged. She'll ring again in a short while.)
>   *B*: *She ring?*
>   *A*: Hai a, ngaw da.
>   (Yes, I'll ring.)

> (8) *A*: *He's a* [ku:]. . . (.) *I don't know how to say* (.) *send message* (.)
>   Nay ji-m-ji a?
>   (Do you know?)
>   *B*: *Oh, courier.*
>   *A*: *Yes, courier.*

In extract (8), A, a woman in her late thirties, initiates a subsequent other-repair by B, a man in his late twenties. Again the repair initiator is marked by a contrasting choice of language, as in the previous two examples. Researchers have frequently observed that code-switching can serve such functions as word-finding, self-editing (with or without discernible errors), repetition, emphasis, clarification, confirmation and so forth. All these uses are parts of a more general repair procedure, examples of which we have presented. Although they are difficult to analyse quantitatively because of the multifunctional nature of specific conversational contributions, the association between code-switching and repair is a common one in our corpus.

The role of code-switching in organising discourse can be seen also in conversation sequences which do not fit the adjacency pairs structure, to which we now turn.

Presequences

Not all conversational sequences can be analysed as paired sets of utterances or as chained to the preceding and following utterances in a linear fashion, as illustrated by our examples so far. The first utterance in (9) is an example of the first part of a 'presequence', a type of conversational structure which prefigures or clears the ground for a later interactional episode. Presequences simultaneously mark the boundary of two interactive episodes (Levinson, 1983), and our data suggest that this boundary is often marked by code-switching. In (9), A is talking with his (female) cousin, B, about one of their friends who has been ill. Both speakers are in their twenties:

> (9) A: *Did you see Kim yesterday?*
> B: *Yeah.*
> A: Mou [mat si. . .
>   (It's not serious. . .)
> B: [Yau di tautung je, Mou mat si ge.
>   ((She) only has a little headache. It's nothing serious.)
> A: Ngaw jing yiu man nay.
>   (I was just about to ask you.)

A's first utterance is a question checking the precondition for his subsequent enquiry about their friend's health. After B confirms that she is in a position to provide this information, A embarks upon his intended enquiry. The boundary between presequence and target sequence is marked by code-switching. In monolingual discourse, presequences are often marked prosodically or phonologically in various ways (Levinson, 1983: 345ff).

In this section we have cited examples designed to illustrate some of the conversational patterns marked by code-switching which recur in our corpus, and we have suggested that code-switching might plausibly be viewed as fulfilling some specifiable conversational functions. Probably because of the contrasting language preferences of the children, on the one hand, and the parents and grandparents, on the other, it seems to be particularly common in intergenerational communication. In addition to the functions of preference marking, marking of repairs and presequence boundary marking illustrated here, code-switching seems to be used to regulate turn-taking in various ways (see Li Wei and Milroy, 1995). As we have hinted, the adoption by individuals of one or another of these discourse strategies seems to a considerable extent to be generation and network specific. For example, parents and grandparents generally do not code-switch during peer conversations, except to mark self-repairs. However, they sometimes switch from Chinese to English when they are addressing children, particularly to mark turn allocation and repair initiators. Children, on the other hand, tend to use English with their peers and to switch to Chinese to mark presequences and embedded sequences. However, it is characteristic of this generation to mark dispreferred responses by switching from Chinese to English.

These intergenerational differences in code-switching practices might be described as interactional reflexes of the network- and generation-specific language choice preferences in the Tyneside Chinese community. Although they can sometimes be related to practical constraints arising from the language preferences and language abilities of different sub-groups, many code-switching practices such as those exemplified in extracts (3)–(8) cannot easily be related to such constraints, and are better interpreted as network-specific strategies of a socially symbolic kind.

Social network and the broader social framework

As well as relating interactional and community levels of analysis, network structure can relate to social, economic and political structure. The main point we need to make here is that the various network types discussed in this chapter do not constitute themselves in a socially arbitrary fashion. Particularly, the characteristic occupational preferences of the economically active Chinese largely determine the nature of the ties which they contract with others. Similarly, the mainly kin-oriented ties which the economically dependent adults contract are a natural consequence of the Chinese family system. The British-born generation, for their part, by attending school and participating in life outside the community, will contract ties with non-Chinese peers.

A coherent theory of language choice and code-switching needs to make explicit the relationship between community networks – 'frames' within which language choice takes place – and large-scale social and economic structure. As Gal (1988) points out, the success, persistence and precise form of the 'opposition' to mainstream values symbolised by minority language maintenance depend not upon community-internal linguistic or interactional factors, but upon the relation of the group to the national economy and to like groups in other cities or states; we need both a socio-political and interactional level of analysis. The outcome in terms of language (or dialect) survival or shift in Belfast may be different from that in Paris or Copenhagen; in Catalonia it may be different from Gascony. It will be constrained by local variations in political, economic and social structure.

What seems to be required is a *social* (as opposed to a sociolinguistic) theory which can associate these network patterns with specifiable sub-groups which in turn emerge from larger scale social, economic and political processes. One useful integrated analysis is proposed by Giddens (1984), but the *life-modes* theory of the Danish anthropologist Thomas Højrup, which is grounded more firmly in systematic ethnographic work, is particularly helpful. Offering an analysis which is designed to be generally applicable to Western Europe but allows for local, historically contingent differences in social and economic systems, Højrup proposes a division of the population into sub-groups which are described in terms of three life-modes. These life-modes are seen as both social and cultural, as necessary and inevitable constituents of the social structure as a whole which spring from economic systems of production and consumption. Thus, like social network types, they are not socially or culturally arbitrary, but are the effect of 'fundamental societal structures which split the population into fundamentally different life-modes' (Højrup, 1983: 47). The precise way in which they split the population will, however, vary between nation-states, depending on local political and economic systems. Højrup's analysis focuses on the differing ideological orientation of the three sub-groups to work, leisure and family, and from the point of view of this research, the distinction between, on the one hand, Life-mode 1, the life-mode of the self-employed, and of the other, Life-mode 2, that of the ordinary wage-earner, is particularly important. The life-mode of a different kind of wage-earner, the high-powered Life-mode 3 executive, is quite different from either of these.

A close-knit family-centred network with a strong solidarity ideology and little distinction between work and leisure activities is characteristic of the self-employed. Conversely, ordinary wage-earners will be embedded in less kin-oriented and generally looser-knit networks. This analysis, to which we cannot do justice here, converges with our own. We would predict a more Chinese-oriented pattern of language choice by speakers who are embedded in close-knit networks, and would expect such a personal network structure to be characteristic of Life-mode 1. Indeed, this seems to be the case. For example, two speakers in our sample are a married couple who are both wage-earners, employed by a local computer company. They interact on a daily basis with English speakers, retaining contact with other Chinese only for a short time on Sundays. Their command of English is very much better than other economically active but self-employed (Life-mode 1) Chinese. Højrup does not see the life-mode of the self-employed as a relic of an earlier period but as highly efficient and competitive given its flexibility of operation and the commitment of the producers. He uses the Danish fishing industry as an example, but his description equally well applies to the Tyneside Chinese family catering businesses.

Conclusion

While we have used the Tyneside Chinese community to illustrate a social network perspective on code-switching and language choice, the analysis presented in this chapter is intended to be of more general application. We have tried to demonstrate that while network interacts with a number of other variables, it is capable of accounting more generally for patterns of language choice than the variables such as generation, sex of speaker, duration of stay and occupation with which it interacts. It can also deal in a principled way with differences within a single generational group. We have also suggested that it can form an important component in an integrated initial theory of language choice: it links with the interactional level in focusing on the everyday behaviour of social actors, and with the economic and socio-political level in that networks may be seen as forming in response to social and economic pressures. We briefly examined this latter link in terms of Højrup's life-modes analysis.

We can conclude by suggesting fruitful directions for future research. To some extent this has been done already in the argument for a more coherent approach to the economic and socio-political context of code-switching, without sacrificing detailed sociolinguistic analysis of code-switching behaviour. What is needed, however, is a more principled analysis of interacting social variables such as sex, age, class, generation cohort and network to see how they interact in their effect on language choice. However, there is a more general point which needs to be emphasised: rather than collecting ever more data which, while intrinsically interesting, cannot easily be interpreted, researchers need to devote some energy to developing a framework within which this interpretation can take place.

Note

1   We have kept the transcription conventions used in our samples of bilingual conversation as simple as possible. The romanised system for transcribing spoken Cantonese was developed by Li Wei (see further Li Wei, 1994) in association with colleagues at the University of Hong Kong. The chief conversational phenomena provided for all our samples in this article are simultaneous speech (marked by [ ) and pauses (marked by (.) to indicate a micropause and by a series of dots to indicate longer pauses).

Source: Li Wei, Milroy, L. and Pong, S.C. (1992) A two-step sociolinguistic analysis of code-switching and language choice. *International Journal of Applied Linguistics* 2(1): 63–86. Reproduced with permission of the authors and Blackwell Publishing.

Postscript

The main objective of our 1992 article was to illustrate the social network approach to language choice and code-switching in bilingual communities. We believed, and still believe, that the social network approach had/has the capacity to provide the macro–micro link in sociolinguistic studies of bilingualism. We felt strongly that systematic analysis of community structures and language choice patterns of bilingual groups should not be entirely separate from detailed analysis of interactional strategies of bilingual speakers. The concept of social networks offered a useful analytic tool of community structures and the power relations between different groups of speakers on the one hand, and of the cultural practices, including language choice and code-switching, and attitudes of the individuals on the other.

The notion of social network had been used by sociologists and anthropologists for many decades prior to its applications in sociolinguistic research. Many anthropological linguists and linguistic ethnographers used social networks in their fieldwork and data collection. They also used it as a metaphor in data interpretation. For example, John Gumperz talked about open and close-knit networks in his studies of multilingual practices in India. The concept of social network only began to be used as an analytic tool by sociolinguists in the late 1970s, initially as an alternative to social economic class as an explanatory factor in studies of linguistic variation and change (e.g. Milroy, 1980).

Susan Gal's work on language shift in the Hungarian–German bilingual community in Oberwart, Austria (1979) was amongst the first to apply the social network concept, as an analytic concept, to a bilingual community. Our work on the Chinese community in Tyneside in the North-East of England followed Milroy's and Gal's examples and tried to account for variations in language choice patterns, across different individuals and generations, by a detailed, quantitative analysis of three different kinds of network types – exchange, interactive and passive.

The advantages of a social network approach, as we saw it, included the fact that an individual's linguistic practices are part and parcel of his or her social network formation. To put it another way, social network development is also a language socialisation process. Social network, therefore, is not an external variable to language behaviour. Furthermore, social network analysis allows us to embed an analysis that focuses on the individual in his or her social group.

The way we approached social network analysis was very similar to that of the British school of social anthropologists (e.g. Clyde Mitchell and Elizabeth Bott). We focused on ego-centred networks and the contents, rather than structures, of network ties. Specifically, we used the notion of 'anchorage' and focused on first order contacts. Since our initial work with the Tyneside Chinese community, we have found that the notion of 'anchorage' has other important implications. For example, we have found that many immigrant families maintain their ethnic language primarily because there is a monolingual grandparent in the family. That grandparent provides the anchor, and when he or she dies the regular use of the ethnic language in the family goes as well. Social network analysis offers a good explanation for this 'grandma' factor.

We have also found that the notion of 'passive' networks of immigrant bilinguals is very useful in helping us to understand the changes over time in the speakers' language socialisation patterns. 'Passive' ties are the people with whom ego cannot interact on a regular basis, but are still considered as important relations. They reflect individuals' psychological orientation and social attitudes. They can be activated at any particular time for a particular purpose. Immigrants who have not adapted well to the new environment tend to maintain strong 'passive' ties. Some re-activate these ties by returning to their places of origin after a period of residence in what they see as a foreign land. They also tend to have a more negative attitude toward the language and culture of the adopted home.

Perhaps the most important strength of the social network analysis is its capacity to offer an explanation for behavioural changes of individuals and groups over time. Once again, the concept of language socialisation is important. Language learning, for example, is a socio-cultural process. Through learning a new language, the speaker develops a new identity and makes new friends. Which language a person decides to learn, how he or she learns and uses it, and what kinds of social contacts the person builds are all closely linked to each other. In our current work, we are aiming to apply the social network concept to studies of bilingual acquisition.

Li Wei, 2006

Li Wei, PhD, is Professor of Applied Linguistics at Birkbeck, University of London, UK. li.wei@sllc.bbk.ac.uk

Lesley Milroy, PhD, is Hans Kurath Collegiate Professor Emeritus of Linguistics, University of Michigan, USA. amilroy@umich.edu

Pong Sin Ching was a postgraduate researcher with Li Wei and Lesley Milroy. She is no longer in academia.

Notes for students and instructors

Study questions

1   What kinds of special communicative effect can be achieved through code-switching?
2   How do you decide which language is 'marked' and which is 'unmarked', in Myers-Scotton's sense of the terms, for specific situations in a specific community?
3   What are the key functions of 'discourse-related' code-switching in Auer's sense of the term?
4   In what way can code-switching be used as an organisational procedure for conversational interaction?

Study activity

Record an informal conversation involving two or more bilingual speakers on to an audio tape recorder. Transcribe the recording in detail, paying particular attention to any gap, false start, overlap and interruption. Examine the language choice of each individual speaker and see how a particular choice may be related to the co-participant's choice of language as well as his or her own in previous turns in the conversation. Can you describe particular instances of code-switching as 'situational', 'metaphorical', 'marked', 'unmarked', 'participant-related' or 'discourse-related'? What problems are there in using these terms? How is code-switching related to the overall organisation of conversation?

Further reading

Blom and Gumperz's approach to code-switching is further developed in J.J. Gumperz, 1992, *Discourse Strategies*, Cambridge University Press. For Gumperz's contributions generally, see *Language in Social Groups: Essays by J.J. Gumperz*, selected by A.S. Dil, 1971, Stanford University Press.

For a more detailed exposition of the 'markedness' model of code-switching, see C. Myers-Scotton, 1993, *Social Motivations for Codeswitching: Evidence from Africa*, Oxford University Press.

A fuller account of Auer's analysis of conversational code-switching is in J.C.P. Auer, 1984, *Bilingual Conversation*, John Benjamins.

A detailed analysis of the code-switching patterns in the Tyneside Chinese community can be found in Li Wei, 1994, *Three Generations Two Languages One Family: Language choice and language shift in a Chinese community in Britain*, Multilingual Matters.

A state-of-the-art collection of sociolinguistic studies on bilingual interaction is given in J.C.P. Auer (ed.), 1998, *Code-Switching in Conversation: Language, interaction and identity*, Routledge. A more recent collection of papers on the pragmatics of conversational code-switching is *Journal of Pragmatics*, 2005, Vol. 37, No. 3, a special issue guest-edited by Li Wei.

Recent debate between the 'markedness' model and the conversational analysis approach to code-switching can be found in: C. Myers-Scotton, 1999, Explaining the role of norms and rationality in codeswitching, *Journal of Pragmatics*, 32: 1259–71; A. Bolonya, 2001, Calculating speakers: codeswitching in a rational choice model, *Language in Society* , 30: 1–28; Li Wei, 2002, 'What do you want me to say?' On the conversation analysis approach to bilingual interaction. *Language in Society* 31: 159–180; Li Wei, 2005, 'How can you tell?' Towards a common sense explanation of conversational codeswitching, *Journal of Pragmatics*, 37: 375–90.

Identity and ideology

Chapter 8

Code-switching and the politics of language

MONICA HELLER

It's not always how you play the game, it's how you use the rules[1]

1 Introduction

In 1977, the government of the province of Quebec passed Bill 101, a law to affirm and support French as the official and dominant language of the province. This law was a key element in Francophones' strategy to overcome two centuries of domination by English-speakers, and it touched on many domains, notably government, education and the workplace. Among other things, it required practitioners of certain professions (such as pharmacy, nursing, engineering) to demonstrate adequate knowledge of French in order to be licensed to practice. For some, this meant passing tests of French proficiency created and administered by the government.

In 1978, an English-speaking gentleman arrived at the office where these tests were administered and presented himself at the front desk, where the receptionist was chatting in French with a co-worker. He asked the receptionist, 'Could you tell me where the French test is?' The receptionist responded in French, 'Pardon?' The man repeated his request in English, 'Could you tell me where the French test is?' The receptionist asked, 'En français?' The man replied, 'I have the right to be addressed in English by the government of Quebec according to Bill 101.' The receptionist turned to her colleague and asked, 'Qu'est-ce qu'il dit?' ('What's he saying?'). In the end, both parties won: the man got his information without having to speak French, and the receptionist was able to show him the right direction without having to speak English.

In this encounter, as in so many others in Quebec (then, and still today), it is possible to see that the struggle between speakers of French and speakers of English is waged not only in the legislature, but also in face-to-face interactions. Indeed, the politics of language permeate not only interactions in the kinds of institutional settings where language is closely and obviously linked to ethnic interests (as in the above example), but also many others which occur regularly in daily life.

The purpose of this chapter is to discuss ways in which the study of code-switching is relevant to the politics of language, by which I mean the ways in which language practices are bound up in the creation, exercise, maintenance or change of relations of power. I am principally concerned here to set out a theoretical framework which situates the study of code-switching within the larger agenda of the study of the politics of language, and which is intended to be useful in framing future research.[2]

I will argue in this chapter that the study of code-switching illuminates language politics only to the extent that it is situated in the broader study of language practices. Code-switching has to be seen as an interactional moment whose significance can only become apparent when linked to other instances of language use. In the first part of the chapter I will develop the theoretical framework which elaborates this view. In this vein, I use code-switching in an extended sense, to refer not only to instances of inter-sentential switching, but also to less structurally integrated instances of language alternation or language choice.

The second part of the chapter focusses on the kinds of questions that can be addressed within that framework, drawing on my own work in Canada.[3] In particular, it will address questions related to: (i) the linguistic resources available to speakers as a consequence both of their own position in the local speech economy and of the nature of the local speech economy as emergent from international networks and social, political and economic relations; and (ii) the ways in which relations of power can be transformed through language practices which draw on those resources.

In this framework language is seen as related to power in two ways. First, it is part of processes of social action and interaction, part of the ways in which people do things, get things, influence others, and so on. Second, language itself thereby becomes a resource which can be more or less valuable, according to the extent that the mastery of ways of using language is tied to the ability to gain access to, and exercise, power.

2 Code-switching, repertoires and resources

Code-switching becomes available as a resource for the exercise of, or resistance to, power by virtue of its place in the repertoires of individual speakers, on the one hand, and of its position with respect to other forms of language practices in circulation, on the other. This view hinges on a notion of code-switching as a means of drawing on symbolic resources and deploying them in order to gain or deny access to other resources, symbolic or material. It builds both on Bourdieu's concepts of symbolic capital and symbolic marketplaces, and Gumperz's concepts of speech economies and verbal repertoires (Bourdieu 1977a, 1982; Gumperz 1982).

I will use Bourdieu's concepts in the following way. I take code-switching as a means of calling into play specific forms of linguistic and cultural knowledge, forms which conventionally possess certain kinds of value. That value is linked to the extent to which those forms facilitate access to situations where other kinds of symbolic and material resources are distributed, resources which themselves have value based on the prevailing modes of organisation of social life in the community (and who controls them). Certainly some resources have a concrete, functional basis to their value (like food); but most are related in more indirect ways to the methods people have of calculating honour, or status or prestige. Their value is in any case a function of processes of power and solidarity, that is, on the one hand, the means to mobilise and allocate resources, and, on the other, the ability to mobilise other people in the name of common concerns which are held to override both what the members of a group might have in common with others and any differences which may exist among them. Solidarity can thus be bound up in the development of ties and cultural practices which help members of an elite to maintain their position of power, or in the development of relations and practices which help members of a subordinate group cope with, or resist, their condition of subordination.

Groups which control valued resources (of whatever kind) also control the 'marketplace' (in Bourdieu's terms) in which they are exchanged, the set of social relations in which the value of resources is defined and resources themselves are exchanged. Beyond sheer force, such marketplaces operate through hegemonic practices, through symbolic domination, through convincing participants that the values and modes of operation of the marketplace are immutable and universal. In the terms of the metaphor of power as game with which I began, specific groups set the rules of the game by which resources can be distributed. In other words, it is necessary to display appropriate linguistic and cultural knowledge in order to gain access to the game, and playing it well requires in turn mastery of the kinds of linguistic and cultural knowledge which constitute its rules. Buying into the game means buying into the rules, it means accepting them as routine, as normal, indeed as universal, rather than as conventions set up by dominant groups in order to place themselves in the privileged position of regulating access to the resources they control. Bourdieu has insisted over and over again that it is precisely through appearing not to wield power that dominant groups wield it most effectively (Bourdieu 1982; Gal 1989).

These notions tie into those of Gumperz in a number of ways. First, both Bourdieu and Gumperz have noticed that linguistic and cultural capital are not equally distributed in any given community, despite the fact that all members of the community might share (at least along some dimensions) the same scale of values, that is, they all might agree on the fact that it is the capital (and other resources associated with it) concentrated in the hands of one group that is what is really valuable in life. In Gumperz's terms, forms of language are distributed unequally across a speech community. Individual members have verbal repertoires which draw on part, but rarely all, of the forms in circulation. Further, it is this unequal distribution as well as the way in which unequally distributed resources are deployed which drives the operation of the marketplace, and hence the reproduction of relations of power. Only some members of a population are in a position to decide what will count as appropriate behaviour in situations where resources are distributed and to evaluate performances there; normally, it is the symbolic capital which dominant groups already possess which is the key to participation and success in the situations they control. As Gumperz and others have shown, an inability to bring to bear appropriate conventions of behaviour on key situations in daily life where crucial decisions about one's acccess to resources are decided (a job interview, an exam., a courtroom trial, etc.) can result in the systematic exclusion of segments of the population from the resources distributed there.

In order to understand the value that code-switching has as a practice, then, it is essential to understand the broader game in which code-switching is merely one set of possible moves. In order to explain code-switching's occurrence, it is equally necessary to grasp the nature of individual repertoires, that is, to understand why it is available as a resource to some and not to others. Similarly, it is necessary to understand how it can be that code-switching as a practice can emerge in specific communities at specific historical moments, and not at others, and how it can either persist or fade away.

Code-switching is thus a form of language practice in which individuals draw on their linguistic resources to accomplish conversational purposes; those resources have value in the terms of the various existing marketplaces. In other terms, those resources constitute the basis of strategies, like code-switching, for playing the game of social life. Language practices are inherently political insofar as they are among the ways individuals have at their disposal of gaining access to the production, distribution and consumption of symbolic and material resources, that is, insofar as language forms part of processes of power.

However, as noted above, linguistic resources are among the symbolic resources which are, generally speaking, not equitably distributed in society. Some people, by virtue of their social position, have access to more- or less-highly valued forms of language, and are more or less able to control the value accorded to linguistic resources in society in general. Equally, to the extent that more than one market is available (or that more than one game can be played), people will have differential access to those games or markets.

Woolard (1985) has pointed out that Bourdieu's notion of marketplace is restrictive in that it assumes a single dominant marketplace. One can argue that Gumperz's notion of speech economy encounters the same conceptual problem. In addition, both suffer from the assumption that marketplaces, or speech economies, are somehow bounded, that it is possible to identify where their limits are. Much recent ethnographic work has pointed to the necessity of rethinking these dimensions of the notions involved.

Woolard's work in Catalonia has addressed the problem of the unified marketplace by showing how different sources of power (economic vs politico-legal) can form the basis of alternative marketplaces, where the different forms of language in circulation (in this case, most relevantly Castilian and Catalan) have different value (Woolard 1985, 1989). My own work in Quebec and Ontario (Heller 1989a, b; Heller 1994; Heller and Lévy 1992a, b) has shown the same kinds of tensions to be operating there, in that marketplaces can splinter and individuals can adopt a variety of strategies in the face of difficult and changing conditions depending on both the resources to which they have access and their individual calculations of strategies which they perceive to be in their best interests. This has notably been the case for the relationship between the historically English-dominated private sector, the new basis of Francophone power in the public sector and Francophones' use of that power-base to gain entry into the private sector. Some individuals find themselves involved simultaneously in social arenas reflecting different 'moments' in this historical transition, such as Franco-Ontarian women married to Anglophone men at a time when Anglophone domination was clear, but who, having raised a family, re-enter the workforce to find that their once-stigmatised French has new value. The new opportunities opened up for them in this way also raise a number of difficult questions, including how to cope with linguistic insecurity constructed through years of subordination and language transfer and how to re-define marital and parental relations in which ethnolinguistic relations of domination no longer so completely overlap gender relations of inequality.

Thus, a number of different scenarios may exist: a community may be dominated by one marketplace, by one game with one set of rules regarding the use and value of the resources circulating there. People have to deal with that situation as well as they can; I will return in the following section to what some possibilities might be. Alternatively, it might be possible to play more than one game at a time; this too will be taken up in the next section. For our purposes now, what is important to recognise is that games are mutable and potentially multiple, as are the nature and value of the resources that are at once at issue there and simultaneously the means of access to further resources.

Empirical work has dealt less successfully with the second problem mentioned, that is, with the impossibility of identifying clear boundaries or limits to the games or markets involved. The most promising leads are emerging through various forms of network analysis, which recognise that social processes emerge from sets of inter-actional experiences which tie together both people and the conditions of their lives. One dimension of networks is therefore the ties which exist among individuals (as mediated by their participation in social institutions; cf. Milroy 1987a; Milroy and Milroy 1992).

Giddens (1979, 1984) and Cicourel (1980) have pointed to other dimensions of networks, which are equally important. Giddens refers to these ties as existing both in space and in time. For him, a central element of social process concerns the ties which exist among events or experiences. Interactions, in his view, have both intended and unintended consequences which affect the lives of participants, as well as the lives of others who may not have been present, across time. Equally, they can best be understood when they are linked to other forms of social interaction which may be concurrent, but geographically removed. To give a simple example, I may receive a telephone call from a colleague at another university requesting a reference for a former student who has applied for a job there. That telephone conversation is tied to past interactions I and my colleagues have had with that candidate as well as to future possibilities that she might actually end up teaching at that university; they in turn, are also undoubtedly linked to interactions which may be occurring simultaneously, for example, exchanges between students and faculty at that university which may inform the hiring committee's ideas about the kind of candidate they want to recruit in order to meet current student needs. They are also linked in broader ways to other interactions and institutionalised pro-cesses: how, say, students who are members of minority groups become qualified for and interested in training and subsequent employment in post-secondary institutions. Marcus (1986) and Gal (1989) have pointed to the necessity in particular of understand-ing the global economic processes in which interactions are embedded: the kind of conversation I have with my colleague, indeed the possibility of having it at all, is bound up in political and economic relations which increasingly tie us to the rest of the world, but in specific, concrete and historically conditioned ways.

In this vein, Cicourel and Giddens have also focussed on how such interactions are shaped by social institutions whose functioning is far beyond the control of any small subset of individuals, and which emerge through a variety of forms of interaction, not merely the face-to-face. The complex relations we build through family, school, law, medicine and the like occur also through text as well as talk, through visual as well as verbal means, and so on.

Perhaps most importantly, Giddens and Cicourel have also drawn attention to the ways in which social processes at once shape, and are shaped by, social interaction. Marketplaces, games, speech economies may exist, and act, in Giddens's terms, as constraints on the possibilities open to any given individual; but they are also products of interaction. Individuals can use the resources they have available to them strategically, to play the game, but more importantly, to use the rules, and, indeed, even to change them. Social process is thus both constraint and possibility, obstacle and opportunity.

The conceptual and methodological challenge posed by such arguments is to be able to identify the linkages which we think exist, and beyond that, to discover the significance of the social processes which are constituted there. If we want to understand how code-switching is linked to relations of power, it is therefore not enough to examine instances of code-switching in specific interactions. It becomes necessary to discover both what the consequences (intended and unintended) of code-switching might be for individuals, and also how code-switching is tied to all the interactions which occur where code-switching does not.

Yet herein lies precisely the reason why code-switching is so compelling as a means of discussing power. For the analyst, it acts as a flag, it signals that here, in this interaction, people are drawing on their linguistic resources in some way which will have an effect both on them and on others. They are using language to take action in a complex world, to react to their experience and to create it anew. (For further discussion, see Heller 1992.)

3 Code-switching and the politics of language use

The framework outlined above makes it possible to use the study of code-switching in certain specific ways in order to shed light on how language use is bound up in the creation, maintenance or change of relations of power. In this section, I will briefly outline what some relevant questions might be, and how some recent work addresses them. Code-switching is clearly a means of drawing on a variety of linguistic resources in the course of a single interaction. The questions it raises are linked both to what speakers are trying to do through code-switching and to what makes it possible to attempt what they are attempting.

In this section, I want to focus both on different ways of dominating and on different ways of coping with conditions of subordination, principally by examining individual and collective strategies which may involve moves towards unified, or, on the contrary, multiple alternative marketplaces. While I will not, in the space available, be able to cover all possible logical or ethnographically demonstrated combinations, I do want to set up a framework which might help us situate current research and guide us in specific directions for further work. My goal, then, is the more modest one of pointing to some ways in which the study of code-switching can form part of a broader understanding of the politics of language use.

One framework that I find useful is drawn from the work of Barth (1969). While Barth did not specifically discuss language practices, his work on the relationship between ethnic boundaries and material and symbolic resources is illuminating. There are three sets of concepts that may be useful in understanding how language can play a role in the unfolding of that relationship.

First, Barth pointed out that ethnic relations depend on a differential distribution of access to and control over resources, or what he termed 'ecological niches'. That distribution, however, can vary along two dimensions, namely, it may be complementary (groups occupy different niches) or competitive (groups vie for control over the same niche), and it may be equal or unequal (the resources controlled and the ability to control them may be differentially valued or differentially effective).

One category of ethnic relations includes, then, contact between groups each of which controls different, complementary, but equally valued resources. However, different and unequal economic relations are more commonly represented in the literature. Gal (1979), McDonald (1990) and Dorian (1981) all provide examples of marginal groups (Hungarians, Bretons, Gaelic-speaking Scots) engaged in farming and/or fishing who come into contact with other, more powerful groups (speakers of German, French and English, respectively) as the latter expand their industrial activities into (from their perspective) more remote areas.

Competitive and equal relations characterise to a certain extent the relationship between the French and the Flemish in Belgium, or the French and the English in Canada, as illustrated, for example, by Quebec companies in which English-speakers retain power due to their accumulated knowledge and current links to North America, while Francophones seek to compete on the same terrain but from the different power-base of recent political mobilisation through the public sector (Heller 1989a).

Finally, competitive and unequal relations obtain between Francophones and Anglophones elsewhere in Canada, or between the Welsh- and English-speaking urbanised middle classes of Wales (cf. Williams 1987). While groups compete for the same resources of industrialised, capitalist society, they usually do not do so from an equal position of strength.

Second, Barth discussed the ways in which processes of domination are tied to stability or change in ecological niches. Under conditions of stability, the issue becomes one of how dominant groups maintain their position of power, and of how subordinated groups, and individual members of those groups, cope with those conditions of sub-ordination. Under conditions of ecological change, however, the issue becomes how individuals and groups cope with conditions of change beyond their control, or how they set off conditions of change themselves. It is also possible to take another angle on this set of problems, and ask what it is that makes for conditions of stability or change.

Third, Barth focussed more narrowly on the strategies disadvantaged social actors adopt, either individually or collectively. In particular, attention centred on instances in which members of one group possess resources of low value, or no longer have access to any resources at all (say, due to some radical ecological imbalance). These strategies can be seen as falling into two broad categories: what the members of that group do when they decide their best bet is to go after the resources of another group, which would correspond to a collective mobilisation with the goal of creating an alternative marketplace, and what they do when they decide that their best bet is to develop an alternative resource base of their own (but which might include a role as brokers). In either case, strategies can be individual or collective: the first category would include individual assimilation or collective incorporation, or potentially individual takeovers and redefinitions of positions of power within the target group as well as collective mobilisation for similar takeovers; while the second would comprise individual or collective brokerage roles, as well as individual pioneering or collective mobilisation for the creation of alternative marketplaces.

In any of these cases, it is clear that language represents one set of potentially valuable resources, specifically insofar as it is bound up with processes of getting access to, and controlling production of, other valuable material and symbolic resources. Code-switching is one way in which it is possible to manipulate valuable linguistic resources, and indeed to manipulate the definition of their value. That is, in order for code-switching to have any meaning at all, it must draw on resources which are some-where separate, either in the lives of individuals or in their distribution in a network of individuals who are otherwise linked. In other words, there has to be some kind of separation somewhere in the various kinds of linkages explored above, whether these are links between people or events, across time or space. Here I am referring to the meaning of code-switching as a communicative practice, and not to the meaning of specific switches.

4 Language practices, code-switching and strategies for power and solidarity

In what follows, I will examine some of the strategies outlined above, in order to provide some examples of the complex interaction between the constraints imposed by social structure and human agency, in terms of the discussion in section 2. In particular, I will focus on the way in which language practices, including code-switching, can become salient means for achieving social, economic and political goals.[4]

I will focus here on the relations of power between Francophones and Anglophones in Canada. The history of these relations is such that it is possible to find examples of the ways in which language played a role in the exercise of domination, and in coping with, or resistance to, that domination on the part of members of the subordinate group, including strategies of assimilation, brokerage and collective mobilisation. Central dynamics have included the increasing integration of Francophones into national and international networks and markets, and a playing-off of political power against power emergent in the economic realm. In this respect, over the course of time, one can see elements of what I described earlier as being cases of unequal and complementary as well as of unequal and competitive relations. One can even see glimmerings of relations which might be described as equal and competitive.

For much of the course of English–French relations, at least until the Francophone mobilisation beginning in the 1960s, in day-to-day terms, domination was exercised through the imposition of British social and cultural practices in sectors of contact between groups, most notably through the imposition of English as the language of public and inter-group private communication. This linguistic domination worked insofar as members of other groups were unable ever to learn to speak English well enough to truly master the game or to get themselves taken seriously as English-speakers (in Bourdieu's terms, to produce the legitimate discourse, or to become legitimate speakers). It also rested on the use of bilingual brokers (generally native speakers of French) who could mediate between Anglophone bosses, for example, and their Francophone workers. It was here, in such circumstances, that one found code-switching practices, which took their significance precisely from their location in the relations of power between Francophones and Anglophones. (Little is known about the practices of the old Francophone elite, which played an important brokerage role as well.)

For most members of subordinate groups, however, the issue became one of coping with conditions of subordination. Until Francophones became increasingly integrated into national markets as a result of industrialisation and other economic shifts after the Second World War, French was principally important in locally circumscribed arenas where certain kinds of resources were circulated, resources which were only valued by the minority and often because they were resources which helped individuals cope with the conditions of their lives. They included, and to this day for Francophones who remain locked in certain subordinate economic niches continue to include, the products of subsistence practices, but also symbolic resources such as emotional support.

We saw this clearly in discussions with some Francophone women in northern Ontario, women who came from families which were part of the industrial workforce and/or engaged in lumbering or (mainly subsistence) farming, and structurally excluded from avenues of social mobility. English in this milieu is clearly a path to social mobility; indeed, social mobility is next to impossible without it. As part of a strategy of upward mobility, these women had in fact married Anglophones. At the same time, French is the language of home and of friendship. Marie, for example, is a Francophone woman married to an Anglophone and living in Sudbury, a town in northern Ontario with a Francophone population of about 30 per cent, most of them working-class. She values English and uses it extensively. However, she, along with many others in her situation, has a strong support network of female kin and friends with whom she speaks French or, more accurately, what some call 'bilingue' and others, including Marie, call 'mélangé' ['mixed'], that is, an English–French code-switching variety. These are the people she turns to when she needs to talk about marital problems or problems with the children (problems which often take on ethnic as well as purely interpersonal dimensions). For example, Marie says, 'Quand on se rencontre on va parler puis ça vient toujours sur ce sujet-là, tu sais, les hommes (rires), et puis on pense pas mal toutes pareil comme tu sais' ['When we meet we'll talk and it always comes to that subject, you know, men (laughter), and we all think pretty much the same like you know']. Later, she says, about these same conversations with her female friends, 'Comme je te dis on va de une à l'autre tu sais . . . puis je te dis c'est bien mélangé . . . ça vient naturel, on sonne pas tellement intelligent, mais en tout cas' ('like I'm telling you we go from one to the other you know . . . and I tell you it's really mixed . . . it comes naturally, we don't sound so bright, but anyway']. In this case, the practice of code-switching among Marie and her friends has to be read as a means by which subordinate Francophones make sense of their position of powerlessness both as Francophones and as women. Through these practices they are able to create and retain vital support networks which enable them to survive the consequences of otherwise playing the game according to the rules set by Anglophones.

In other cases, some individual members of subordinate groups do attempt assimilation, for example through intermarriage, but in any case certainly through language learning. Nadine is a Francophone woman who was brought up in monolingual towns of southern Ontario. She still understands but no longer speaks French, and passes for an Anglophone. Louis, on the other hand, is a Francophone living in Montreal, who had managed to obtain a low management position in a large national brewery owned and operated by an Anglophone family. For most of his career he had to work in English, but he never mastered English well enough to pass as an Anglophone, and never rose very high in the organisation (although he did carve out an important niche for himself as a broker between the Anglophone monolingual bosses and the Francophone monolingual factory workers). In these cases, code-switching may be part of a process of eventually successful assimilation (seen at the level of individuals as a process of language learning or collectively as one of language shift), or alternatively it may be part of a process of assimilation blocked by strong power relations in which code-switching functions to mediate between unequal groups. Louis's inexpert English, for example, marks him as someone who has lived all his life on the edge of both groups, without being able to gain the access to Anglophone networks with which mastery of English is associated.

Finally, groups may react to their conditions of subordination by mobilising, either to take over the dominant group's resources, or to create alternative markets of their own. Native groups in Canada, for example, are currently debating which of these strategies to adopt: some argue that it is best to return to the land, to reinvest in the value of traditional subsistence practices and ways of life. Others argue that it is too late, that the aboriginal population is already too integrated into national and international networks to withdraw, and that it is therefore better to seek exclusive control of some of those resources in that unified marketplace, and hence some measure of possibility of defining the rules of the game to their own advantage. Francophone mobilisation in Canada has certainly taken that route: the goal is to gain access to global networks and globally valued economic resources, but without having to become Anglophones to do so. In these cases, code-switching may be a means of re-defining conventions of language choice as part of a process of re-defining relations of power. In the late 1970s in Quebec, Anglophone domination of public life was exercised in part through the prevailing convention of using English in public encounters. Francophones wishing to contest those relations of power could do so by contesting conventions of language choice. The more radical resisters made radical choices, insisting on unilingual French in place of uni-lingual English. Others attenuated their strategy through code-switching practices which allowed for subtler negotiations towards the same end.

More attention has been given in the literature to strategies of domination, resistance and mobilisation than to strategies adopted by formerly dominant groups in the face of successful mobilisation. Nonetheless, one can expect a number of different strategies to emerge. A recent article in a Canadian news-magazine gave a revealing survey of Anglophone responses to Francophone mobilisation in Quebec (Tombs 1991). These responses include: (i) emigration: rather than learning French in order to cope with the new conditions of the marketplace, some Anglophones take their linguistic capital to a market where it retains its value; (ii) promotion of national bilingualism: by preserving a concept of a unified bilingual marketplace, English retains its value through its link to the rest of Canada, while not claiming pre-eminence over French; (iii) accommodation: acceptance of a devalued status for English and of an augmented value for formerly stigmatised French; (iv) assimilation: rejection of any further use for English; (v) promotion of Anglophone rights: acceptance of a re-defined marketplace as limited to Quebec, but development of an Anglophone niche within that market; and (vi) development of a niche as bilingual brokers between monolingual Francophones in Quebec and monolingual Anglophones in the rest of North America.

Depending on the strategy adopted, code-switching may or may not make sense or be effective. One would imagine that those who leave, or, on the contrary, stay but in order to vigorously promote Anglophone rights, would be the most likely to adopt monolingual language practices. Those who advocate accommodation would probably speak French to Francophones, but would be likely to code-switch among themselves, as presumably would brokers. Those who advocate national bilingualism might adopt code-switching practices in a wide variety of situations. Depending on one's social position, it may or may not be possible to adopt any one of these strategies, with the mastery of specific kinds of linguistic resources that each entails. Those who have had access to

French (through intermarriage, education, work opportunities, etc.) might be less likely to move; it certainly strikes me as no coincidence that the example of brokerage cited by Tombs concerned a man of Irish origin, since the Irish and the French have historically had close (although sometimes conflictive) relations through shared class background and shared religion (and possibly shared interests in symbolic opposition to people of English origin).

The preceding examples also illustrate the methodological importance of seeing code-switching as an interactional moment with links in both time and space to other forms of social interaction, and with consequences for social actors. Yet it is equally important to grasp the significance of the nature of the interaction, for not all interactions have equal weight. As Gumperz (1982) and others have pointed out, the interactions which take place in the important social institutions of our society carry more weight than others.

Thus what code-switching does is to flag to the analyst a moment, a locale, a piece of social process where somehow at least two sets of symbolic and material resources are at issue for the participants. It is as a result a point of entry into understanding the nature and significance of those resources for the different groups of people involved in their production, allocation and consumption, and hence into the nature of the relationship among those groups. It is one way, among others, for people to draw on their linguistic resources to create and deal with the relations of power which frame their lives.

5 Conclusion

In this chapter I have tried to set out a framework for exploring ways in which language practices are bound up in relations of power. I have argued in particular that it is difficult to understand the significance of any given language practice, such as code-switching, without grasping its relationship to other language practices in individual repertoires and in collective speech economies. More importantly, it is essential to link those practices to the ideologies which legitimate the unequal distribution of resources and the value accorded them, and to the real-world consequences they have for people's lives. In particular, it is possible to see in language practices the tension between power and solidarity, and hence ways in which power is maintained or may be successfully resisted or overturned.

In attempting to understand such important processes through an analysis of code-switching, we have in fact had to call into question the distinctions we were making between 'micro' levels of social interaction and 'macro' levels of social processes. If we can use code-switching to understand processes like power and solidarity, it is because code-switching shows us how specific interactions are mediated through social institutions and linked across time and space to other interactions, through their intended and unintended consequences. If we translate the language of 'macro' and 'micro' into the language of constraint and possibility, or, to use Giddens's terms, 'structure' and 'agency', then we can see both how the linguistic resources at issue in any given interaction flow from a particular (and often institutionalised) arrangement of such resources and the way in which individuals are positioned to exploit them, and how the exploitation of those resources in particular ways has consequences for the possibilities which open up in front of social actors (present or absent).

Such a view has particular methodological implications. If one takes as one's point of departure an attempt to understand language as political, then there are at least two ways into the problem. One is to chart out the speech economy and individual repertoires, the institutions and networks and the links between interactions, which characterise daily life in whatever locale one has chosen to focus on. In this approach, one discovers the extent to which language varieties are separated, or, on the contrary, overlap in the ways which lead to code-switching. This can then be explained in terms of the strategies adopted for gaining or maintaining access to resources and of the conditions which render certain strategies feasible or sensible for different people.

A second approach is to take specific language practices and the patterns of their occurrence as a signal that some question of unequal distribution of resources, some form of the process that is the development and exercise of (or resistance to) power, is relevant here, at this moment, in this situation. One can then follow the variety of paths which stem from that interaction: its links to other interactions of similar type, to other interactions participants have elsewhere and in the future, to interactions involving others but which have consequences for these participants or for the shape of this kind of interaction, and so on.

The systematic use of both these approaches is necessary in order to accumulate the kind of ethnographic material on which theory-building relies. Through such ethnographic studies it is possible to understand on the one hand the conditions which allow certain kinds of strategies, and hence certain kinds of language practices, to emerge, and, on the other, the ways in which certain kinds of practices lead to specific consequences in terms of relations of power among groups and members of groups.

Notes

1   From the song 'Love Played a Game' (Bryant, Peebles and Hodges); A. Peebles, 'I'm Gonna Tear Your Playhouse Down', 1985 (Los Angeles, Cream/Hi Records, Inc.).

2   While the paper is devoted to the politics of language use in everyday life, I also intend it to be applicable to the more institutionalised forms that such issues can take, in the form of language policy. In using the term 'language policy' I mean the ways in which governments or para-governmental organisations seek to contribute to the politics of language through conventionalised and institutionalised language practices or statements of preference regarding those practices. Language policies are therefore particular manifestations of the politics of language.

3   Excellent studies have, of course, been carried out in Europe and elsewhere. See, for example, Gal 1979, 1987; Hewitt 1989; McDonald 1990; Rampton 1991; Williams 1987; Mérida and Prudent 1984; Lafont 1977; and Woolard 1985, 1989. The focus on Canada is motivated by my own experience and knowledge. The data I draw on are from research projects funded by the Government of Quebec and the Social Sciences and Humanities Research Council of Canada, whose support I gratefully acknowledge. I am also grateful to the other authors in this volume, and especially to Lesley Milroy, for insightful comments on an earlier version of this paper.

4   Much of this discussion draws on Heller 1982a, 1989a, 1992, 1994 and Heller and Lévy 1992a, b.

Source: Heller, M. (1995) Code-switching and the politics of language. In L. Milroy and P. Muysken (eds) *One Speaker Two Languages*, Cambridge: Cambridge University Press, pp. 158–74.

Postscript

Since this article was written, the various threads it contains have been further developed. The notion of looking at the distribution of code-switching practices from a political economy perspective has led me and others to operationalise some ideas and question others. The major questioning has had to do with the very idea of code-switching. Indeed, once you look at patterns of practice, it is hard to keep your lens on putative linguistic systems. Instead, what emerges is the idea of people as agents, as actors of social life, who draw on complex sets of communicative resources which are unevenly distributed and unevenly valued. The systematicity appears to be at least as much a function of historically rooted ideologies (of nation and ethnicity) and of the ordering practices of social life as of language per se. This perspective then opens up the possibility of looking at bilingualism as a matter of ideology, communicative practice and social process.

The issues of operationalisation have largely been a matter of deciding what counts as data, and of how to collect it, if what we are after is not just local instances, but evidence of distribution and circulation of linguistic resources across time and space, and of their significance in the construction of relations of social difference and social inequality. This has involved borrowing some ideas from the development of multi-sited anthropology, and examining communicative practices within and across sites which can be ethnographically demonstrated to be linked. We have been working with the ideas of *trajectories* (of actors, linguistic resources, discourses, institutions) across time and space, and of *discursive spaces* which allow for, and also constrain, the production and circulation of discourses. These notions are framed in the context of the ways linguistic practices contribute to the construction of social boundaries (in the case of bilingualism that concerns us, these are ethnonational ones), and of the resources those boundaries regulate. They therefore also raise the question of the social and historical conditions which allow for the development of particular regimes of language (to borrow a Foucauldian idea), for their reproduction, their contestation and, eventually, their modification or transformation.

These questions have become particularly salient in the last ten years or so, as the conditions for the reproduction of the ideologies of nation and identity have been altered by the globalised new economy. It has become necessary to see how ideas and practices about language and identity are shifting (towards a greater commodification of both) in complex and interconnected ways; to understand connections across time and space as local resources and practices get bound up in networks far beyond the here-and-now; and to grasp how existing ideas about bilingualism are drawn on to approach new experiences and conditions.

The article reprinted here represents, then, some first approximations of an approach to bilingualism in a changing world, and one in which matters of difference and inequality are more than salient. This approach does end by asking us to question the assumptions underlying the very idea of bilingualism as a question of codes, but in doing so opens us up to discovering how linguistic resources are ordered in the context of historically contingent forms of social organisation.

Monica Heller, PhD, is a Professor in the Centre de recherches en éducation franco-ontarienne, Ontario Institute for Studies in Education and the Department of Anthropology, University of Toronto, Canada. mheller@oise.utoronto.ca

Chapter 9

Language crossing and the problematisation of ethnicity and socialisation[1]

BEN RAMPTON

This paper begins in Section 1 by noting two processes that have been generally over-looked in sociolinguistics. Firstly, the prevailing approaches to ethnicity have tended to neglect the processes through which individuals can either adopt someone else's ethnicity, or get together with them and create a new one. Secondly, socialisation in sociolinguistics is most commonly seen as enculturation into an ingroup, not as a process of learning to like and live with social and ethnic difference. To throw some light on these two processes, the paper turns its focus towards a practice it calls 'language crossing' ('code crossing', 'crossing').

Language crossing involves code alternation by people who are not accepted members of the group associated with the second language that they are using (code switching into varieties that are not generally thought to belong to them). This kind of switching involves a distinct sense of movement across social or ethnic boundaries and it raises issues of legitimacy which, in one way or another, participants need to negotiate in the course of their encounter. A fuller account of the intricate dialectic between language, peer group belonging and ethnic otherness that lies at the heart of language crossing emerges as the paper proceeds. After some methodological pre-liminaries (Section 2) and an outline of some of the ways in which the multiracial peer group I studied can be considered a community (Section 3), the empirical description of crossing itself begins with an initial emphasis on the way that crossing was inte-grated with what was shared in peer group culture (Section 4). The following section (Section 5) turns to the way in which crossing processed ethnic division and race stratification within the peer group, and this is further elaborated in the discussion of socialisation in Section 6. Section 7 contains a conclusion which briefly links crossing's treatment of ethnicity with Bourdieu's discussion of doxa, orthodoxy and heretical discourse.

1. Some problems in sociolinguistic discussion of ethnicity and socialisation

The relationship between language, ethnicity and socialisation has been one of the founding preoccupations of contemporary sociolinguistics, and so far, it has been understood in two main ways.

1.1. Ethnicities

An enormous amount of research has understood ethnicity as the distinctive patterns of language use acquired in the early years at home and in local community networks, and it has looked at the ways that these group specific communicative styles affect interethnic interaction at school and in other public institutions (Labov 1969; Hymes 1972; Cazden *et al* 1972; Gumperz 1982; Heath 1983; Roberts *et al* 1992). One problem with this first approach is that it risks an absolutist view of ethnicity as a discrete, homogeneous and fairly static cultural essence, fixed during the early years. Another problem centres on the relationship of ethnicity to other factors: How far is ethnicity the crucial factor in the development of distinctive patterns of communicative competence and in the production of different levels of educational achievement, and how far is it class or gender (cf eg Bernstein 1975; Maltz and Borker 1982)? Which discursive patterns derive from which identities and in what ways do they interact and exert their influence? In fact, network specific communicative dispositions can play a significant role in the constitution of a wide range of different social identities – on what grounds is priority given to ethnicity (cf Rosen 1985: Heath and McLaughlin 1993: 6; Gilroy 1987)?

These problems in the first sociolinguistic approach to language, ethnicity and socialisation have been identified, and at least partially overcome, by the second, much more semiotic perspective. Here, rather than being seen as a cultural legacy, ethnicity is regarded much more as a socio-cognitive category that is activated in different ways in different contexts (eg Barth 1969a; Moerman 1974; McDermott and Gospodinoff 1981; Giles and Johnson 1981; Woolard 1989). In this second approach, ethnicity is a contrastive, positional construct through which participants create, express and inter-pret a variety of social and political differences, only some of which are connected to early socialisation. Ethnic, class, gender and other identities are seen as situated identities that become interactionally relevant at different times according to varying situational needs and pressures, and one of the most important implications of this approach is that ethnic identities are negotiated rather than fixed, gaining their signifi-cance from the character of the particular interactions in which they are activated.

Although this second approach is often seen as a deconstruction of the first (traditional anthropologists may think it makes sense to ask "Who are the Lue", but contemporary analysts know that one really needs to ask "when and why" (Moerman 1974)), these two approaches are by no means necessarily antithetical (see Gumperz and Cook-Gumperz 1982: 5–6 on how network specific communicative conventions become semiotic resources available for strategic use in intergroup settings), and my own analysis draws elements from both (together with the contested ground that lies between them). There is however one crucial characteristic in this configuration of sociolinguistic views which leaves them unable to do justice to most of the data that I shall discuss in subsequent sections. The anti-essentialism introduced by the contrastive, socio-cognitive approach to ethnicity is generally taken to be the privilege of the analyst. The assumption is that if participants did not feel that it reflected primordial bonds and relatively fixed boundaries, ethnicity would not have any meaning for them as an interpretive category (cf eg Fishman 1977: 17–19, 23; Gumperz and Cook-Gumperz 1982: 6–7; LePage and Tabouret Keller 1985: Ch6; Roosens 1989: 41, 160–1). Ordinary people may see their professional and recreational roles as something they perform, but they are supposed to experience ethnicity as a stable and basic part of their background, not as a negotiated accomplishment.

Because participants are assumed to experience ethnicity as an unchangeable inheritance, sociolinguistics produces an image of *intergroup* communication in which ethnicity is only ever either negative or neutralised. Analysed from the first perspective as an unrecognised but distinctive speech style, ethnicity is liable to lead to communicative breakdown. Analysed from the second perspective as a semiotic category that is either accentuated or attenuated as interaction proceeds, ethnicity entails either race polarisation (eg McDermott and Gospodinoff 1981; Gumperz and Cook-Gumperz 1982: 5), or at best, a rather measured bureaucratic hospitality or tolerance (Gumperz, Roberts and Jupp 1979; Furnborough *et al* 1982). It is as if individuals are faced with just two options: They can either (a) embrace and cultivate their own ethnicity, or (b) deemphasise it and drop it as a relevant category. What is generally missing is a recognition of the possibility that participants might themselves see ethnicity as something 'produced' rather than simply 'given', 'brought about' as much as 'brought along', and they could encounter a third option: (c) taking on *someone else's* ethnicity, or creating a new one. Once it is recognised that non-essentialist experiences of ethnicity may be available to ordinary people, multiracial interaction emerges as an arena in which participants could generate a sense of the historic emergence of new allegiances, cross-cutting kinship descent, reworking inherited memberships (though cf Hewitt 1986; Erickson and Shultz 1981: 30).

This alternative perspective can be linked up with the emergence of what Stuart Hall calls 'new ethnicities' of the periphery:

We are beginning to see constructions of . . . a new conception of ethnicity: a new cultural politics which engages rather than suppresses difference and which depends, in part, on the cultural construction of new ethnic identities . . . What is involved is the splitting of the notion of ethnicity between, on the one hand the dominant notion which connects it to nation and 'race' and on the other hand what I think is the beginning of a positive conception of the ethnicity of the margins, of the periphery . . . this is not an ethnicity which is doomed to survive, as Englishness was, only by marginalising, dispossessing, displacing and forgetting other ethnicities. This precisely is the ethnicity predicated on difference and diversity (Hall 1988: 29; see also eg Donald and Rattansi 1992).

Ethnicity generally involves some combination of a sense of place and of common origin and destiny, shared culture and/or language, a measure of consensus on the evaluation of outgroup 'others', active self-identification with the ingroup, ascription to it by outsiders, and/or some idea of biological kinship and inheritance (cf LePage and Tabouret-Keller 1985: Ch6). There is no reason why all these features should be either synchronised or active simultaneously, and in the emergence of new urban ethnicities predicated on difference and diversity, the processes by which ethnic descent is reworked or deemphasised clearly merit close examination, for reasons that are both ethnographic and political.

1.2. Socialisation

In fact Hall's idea of an ethnicity "predicated on difference and diversity" also makes it important to reconsider the notion of socialisation. Socialisation is sometimes defined as the process by which a person becomes a competent member of society or their social group (eg Cook-Gumperz and Corsaro 1986: 4; Ochs 1988: 5; Schieffelin 1990: 14). But that formulation rather assumes (a) that groups are socio-cultural totalities and (b) that people eventually arrive at an endpoint of expert belonging. What happens if social groups are actually plural and internally fragmented, cross-cut by highly defined (sub-) groupings with cultural resources that many members of the larger group are never likely to be able to either access fully or master properly? Ochs in fact suggests that sociolinguistic studies of socialisation tend to idealise out the plurality of often conflicting practices, values, identities and groupings which children are exposed to from an early age (1986: 10–11), but if we follow Hall's thoughts on a new ethnicity of the margins, these become central.

In trying to understand socialisation into these new mixed ethnicities, two points need to be born in mind. Firstly, this kind of learning to belong in a differentiated community is not a process of taking up a pre-allocated position in a stable and widely accepted social hierarchy. As Hall stresses, ethnic stratification and division are highly contested in contemporary Britain and there is enduring dispute between the absolutist discourses of race and nation on the one hand, and pluralism and egalitarianism on the other. So in the first instance, learning to live with difference is not a matter of enculturation into a well-established ideology of hierarchy, duty and deference.

Secondly, socialisation into culturally heterogeneous peer networks is likely to involve experiences of exclusion that are rather different from the kinds of exclusion most often described in sociolinguistic studies of children's interaction (eg Maynard 1985; Streeck 1986; Corsaro and Rizzo 1990). There, the distinction between 'friend' and 'enemy' is crucial, and accounts of peer group conflict show how the activation of 'us' vs 'them (him/her)', 'friend vs enemy' generates allegiances and builds a sense of local social structure (Maynard 1985: 207, 212; Corsaro and Rizzo 1990: 46, 60). In Zygmunt Bauman's terms,

The friends/enemies opposition sets apart truth from falsity, good from evil, beauty from ugliness. It also sets apart proper and improper, right and wrong, tasteful and unbecoming. It makes the world readable and thereby instructive. It dispels doubt. It enables one to go on. It assures that one goes where one should (1990: 144).

In contrast, in situations where cultural pluralism is acknowledged and accepted, moral judgments are harder to make, because people often feel that there are aspects of their peers' knowledge and activity which they are neither equipped nor entitled to judge. Here, exclusion and difference are much more likely to produce uncertainty. In a sense, everyone is a 'stranger' in the polyethnic peer group: everyone is situated within a particular . . . group . . . But his position in this group is determined by the fact that he has not belonged to it from the beginning, that he imports qualities into it, which do not and cannot stem from the group itself (Simmel 1950: 402).

In fact according to Bauman, the stranger "calls the bluff of the opposition between friends and enemies as the compleat mappa mundi, as the difference which consumes all differences and hence leaves nothing outside itself . . . [Strangers] unmask the brittle artificiality of division" (1990: 145, 148). The "brittle artificiality of division" takes us back, of course, to Hall's new ethnicities, which embrace differences treated as incompatible in "the dominant notion . . . doomed to survive, as Englishness was, only by marginalising, dispossessing, displacing and forgetting other ethnicities".

In sum, in order to understand socialisation into the new ethnicities, we need to examine the ways in which people come to embrace politically fraught differences, the ways in which they manage to develop strong feelings of community which are nevertheless grounded in some permanent uncertainties and an appreciation that they're irremediably incompetent in areas that they really quite care about. We need an account of what happens in socialisation when in opposition to ideologies of hierarchy and division, people learn to live happily with their own exclusion from groups that they actually like and interact with daily.

2. Some relevant evidence

I would like to try to throw some light on the 'new ethnicities' and their implications for socialisation by referring to some sociolinguistic research on multiracial friendship groups in Britain. The research focussed on language crossing among adolescents: The ways that youngsters of Asian and Anglo descent used Caribbean based Creole, the ways Anglos and Caribbeans used Panjabi, and the way stylised Indian English ('stylised Asian English' – 'SAE') was used by all three.

Although quantitative sociolinguistics (Labov 1972; Milroy 1980) served as one initial reference point (see Section 3 and footnote 2 below), the methodologies of ethnographic and interactional sociolinguistics were the most influential, and led to the examination of four closely interrelated dimensions of socio-cultural organisation: (a) language, seen both as a central element in social action, and as a form of knowledge differentially distributed across individuals and groups; (b) the interaction order, particularly as mapped out by Erving Goffman (eg 1983); (c) institutional organisation, encompassing domains, networks, activity types, social roles and normative expectations; and (d) social knowledge specifically as this relates to race and ethnicity. Two years of fieldwork focused on one neighbourhood in the South Midlands of England, with 23 eleven to thirteen year olds of Indian, Pakistani, Afro-Caribbean and Anglo descent in 1984, and approximately 64 fourteen to sixteen year olds in 1987. Methods of data-collection included radio-microphone recording, participant observation, interviewing and retrospective participant commentary on extracts of recorded interaction, and the analysis was centred on about 68 incidents of Panjabi crossing, about 160 exchanges involving stylised Indian English, and more than 250 episodes where a Creole influence was clearly detectable.

We can begin the analysis of empirical data with a brief characterisation of the peer group itself and of the language that its members used in routine interaction.

3. Peer networks and multiracial vernacular English

All of my adolescent informants during 1984 and 1987 were at the same school (Southleigh Middle in 84, and Newton Upper in 87). Most of them lived in the surrounding neighbourhood, many of them had been at school together since the age of five, and nearly all of them knew each other at least a little bit.

Both among the 11–13 year olds at Southleigh and the 14–16 year olds at Newton, there was a general tendency to associate with peers who were of the same sex and ethnic background (cf also Davey 1983; Thomas 1984). In 1987, for example, I most closely observed about 15 friendship clusters, and in about nine or ten of these, one ethnic group could be said to predominate. A number of informants themselves said that people tended to hang around with others from the same background, and adolescents often referred to ethnicity when identifying different network groupings (as being Indian, black, Pakistani and so forth). So ethnic descent was an important organising principle in the associative networks of local adolescents (for detailed discussion of the 1984 data, cf Rampton 1987: Chs 6, 7 and 12).

Even so, in comparison with home and the adult community, school and peer recreation were still important sites for ethnic *mixing*. In 1984, noone associated exclusively with co-ethnics, and while most friendship cliques were *predominantly* co-ethnic in 1987, only a small proportion were exclusively so: Though a particular friendship group might be described as 'black' or 'Indian', this often included one or two people with a different ethnic background. Furthermore, a great deal of general sociability occurred in large, polyethnic, mixed sex crowds, and school provided a number of sites for this kind of wider socialising. Lessons were one important setting: 'When you get to know friends in lessons, you can mess about'; 'I know a lot of others – Leela, Marina, and Julie – but I don't hang around with them out of lessons'; 'I reckon more goes on in lessons than there does in six weeks holiday'. Dinner queues and breaktimes were others, and outside school, many adolescents congregated in large groups in parks and youth clubs.[2]

Analysis of local adolescent networks suggested, then, that a shared ethnic background was of major significance in friendship formation, but that its influence was far from absolute. Subsequent sections will address uses of language which made ethnicity salient, but before then, it is worth stressing that interaction between youngsters from different ethnolinguistic backgrounds also resulted in an ordinary style of English which Hewitt (1986) calls a local multiracial vernacular. Drawing on his own research in mixed white and black areas of London, he writes:

There has developed in many inner city areas a form of 'community English' or multiracial vernacular which, while containing Creole forms and idioms, is not regarded as charged with any symbolic meanings related to race and ethnicity, and is in no way related to boundary maintaining practices. Rather, it is, if anything, a site within ethnicity is deconstructed, dismantled and reassembled into a new, ethnically mixed, community English. The degree of Creole influence on the specific local vernacular is often higher in the case of young black speakers, but the situation is highly fluid and open to much variation . . . [This] de-ethnicised, racially mixed local language [operates as] . . . a constraining, taken-for-granted medium subsisting through all interactions. If there is an 'ethnicity' that is lived in this non-reflexive way it is more likely to reside in the emergent hybrid culture [and language] of black and white urban youth (Hewitt 1989a).

Much the same could be said of the vernacular speech in the neighbourhood I analysed, though here Panjabi was also a significant contributor. As Hewitt notes, it was usually possible to tell where a person's parents came from, but a small quantitative study of two sociolinguistic variables in the relatively informal interview speech of three Caribbean, three Anglo, four Indian and seven Pakistani boys showed a significant degree of confluence and fusion.[3]

To summarise: Ethnic descent was an important factor in friendship formation in this extended adolescent network. But there was also a lot of ethnic mixing, and although it didn't eliminate subtle ethnolinguistic differences, this resulted in a good deal of similarity in the linguistic patterns that adolescents displayed in routine talk. Both the network and phonological data provide evidence of quite a high degree of commonality in peer group culture, and in the next section, this will be elaborated when in some detail, language crossing itself is introduced as a familiar practice in the local adolescent community.

4. Language crossing in the adolescent community

In contrast to the tacit linguistic dispositions and practices discussed above, language crossing was generally rather spectacular. Indeed, in so far as it always involved deviation from the linguistic norms of the speaker's habitual speech, crossing was directly counterposed to the local multiracial vernacular.

Although adolescents differed systematically in their abilities, access and allegiance to Panjabi, Creole and stylised Indian English, these three languages all figured prominently in the local social environment, and adolescents used them as auxiliary adjuncts in a range of activities that formed a basic part of the daily round of peer group recreation: Pool, cards, soccer, chasing games; verbal jokes and ritual abuse; listening to music; banter with the opposite sex; and repartee with adults in authority. For example:

(1) Participants: Raymond [13 mixed Anglo/Afro-Caribbean descent; male; wearing radio-mike], Ian [12 Anglo, male], Hanif [12 Bangladeshi descent, male], others
Setting: 1984. Coming out of lessons into the playground at break. Ian and Ray are best friends. Stevie Wonder is a singer whose song 'I just called to say I love you' was very famous. Ray has a bad foot – cf line 17. (Extr III.13)

1 Ray :IA::N::
2 Hanif: (   )
3 Ian ((from afar)) RAY THE COO:L RAY THE COO:L
4 Hanif: yeh Stevie Wonder YAAA ((laughs loudly))
5 Ray: ⌈It's worser than that
6 Ian ((singing)):   ⌊I just called to say
7 Hanif: ha (let's) sing (him) a song
8 Ian: I hate you

 9 Hanif: ((loud laughs))
10 Anon ((coming up)): (   ) are you running for the school (.)
11 Ray : huh
12 Anon : are ⌈you running for the school =
13 Ray :   ⌊no
14 Anon: = ⌈I am
15 Ian :   ⌊he couldnt run for th-he couldnt ⌈run for the school
16 Ray :   ⌊SHUT UP =
17 Ray : =I couldn-I don wan- ⌈I can't run anyway
18 Hanif: ⌊right we're wasting our ⌈time=
19 Ian :   ⌊I did=
20 Hanif:= ⌈come on   (we're) wasting our time=
21 Ian :   ⌊you come last (   )
22 Hanif: = ⌈mʌmʌmʌ:]
23 Anon :   ⌊I came second
24 Ian((singing)):I just called to say ⌈I got   ⌈a big=
25 Ray: ⌊I hate you
26 Ian : =[lʊɬɑ:]
((Panjabi for 'willy'))
27 Hanif and others: ((loud laughter))
28 Ray ((continuing Ian's song)): so's Ian Hinks (1.5)
29   ((Ray Laughs)) no you haven't you got a tiny one (.)
30   you've only got (a big arse)

In this extract, Ian mixed Panjabi with Stevie Wonder in some jocular abuse directed at his good friend Ray. When he started out in lines 6 and 8, he seemed to be identifying himself with the first person expressed in the song, but when he repeated it in lines 24 and 26, it looks as though he was putting the words in Ray's mouth rather than claiming the 'I' for himself – certainly, Ray's retaliation in line 28 suggests that it was him that had been attributed the item in Panjabi, not Ian. Whatever, Ian came off best in their brief exchange of ritual abuse: Ian's [lʊɬɑ:] upstaged Ray's effort to preempt him in line 25; it was Ian who won an enthusiastic response from third parties in line 27; and in lines 29 and 30, Ray evidently judged his own immediate retort (line 28) as itself rather weak.

Ian only knew a few words in Panjabi, and even then, his grasp was rather insecure ("I understand most of what they're saying when they're saying 'phuddoo' and this to me . . . and 'mari bunji' and all this . . . oh no 'murri bunji', I don't know what that means, I just made that up I think"). Rather than representing the kind of smooth code alternation often found in the speech of fluent bilinguals, the switch in Extract 1 was conspicuously sited in the punchline, and it instantiated a form of agonistic Panjabi code-switching that was widely commented on by my informants (cf Rampton 1991b, 1995: Chs 2.2 and 7). Indeed, in contrast to the highly critical reception of spectacular white incursions into Creole generally given by black (and other) adolescents in Hewitt's data (1986: 150–1, 162; see also Milroy 1980: 60–1), responses to Panjabi switches like these were usually quite enthusiastic (Rampton 1995: 42–3), and indeed as already indicated, in the laughter in line 27, Ian's effort met with acclaim.

A fairly comprehensive account of the factors contributing to Ian's success will only emerge in the next section when the potential problematicity of language crossing is properly addressed. But in the first instance, it is worth underlining the initial value of following Ochs (1988: 6) and seeing the local adolescent peer group as a loosely identifiable socio-cultural collectivity, with a shared set of orientations, practices and standards of competent conduct. Among other things in Extract 1, language crossing was clearly embedded within good friendship, shared knowledge of popular music, and up to a point at least, familiarity and common acceptance of jocular abuse (which in this peer group, adolescents called 'blowing'; cf Labov 1972a; Goodwin and Goodwin 1987). In the course of their recreational activity more widely, individuals negotiated a variety of interactional and institutional identities (eg games player, joker, fellow pupil, opponent in blowing, chaser and chased in tag, attractive member of the opposite sex), and they also built up personal ties of familiarity, esteem, affection or dislike. So when it occurred and made ethno-linguistic inheritance a relevant issue, language crossing was always set within the (generally supportive) context of a range of non-racial identities that had already been activated.

So a common peer group culture played a significant role facilitating language crossing. In fact, crossing's relationship with peer group culture was often more active than this perhaps implies: It was sometimes actually used in interaction to inculcate or restore conduct consistent with 'normal' adolescent propriety. At the start of the new school year, for example, a senior student could turn to a new one and use stylised Asian English to tell them that they should have grown out of chasing games:

(2) Participants and setting: At the start of the school year, Mohan [15 years, Indian descent, male, wearing radio-microphone], Jagdish [15, In, M] and Sukhbir [15, In, M] are in the bicycle sheds looking at bicycles at the start of the new academic year. Some new pupils run past them. (III.3)

1 Sukh: STOP RUNNING AROUND YOU GAYS (.)
2 Sukh: ⎛((laughs))
3 Moh: ⎝EH (.) THIS IS NOT MIDDLE (SCHOOL) no more (1.0)
      [aɪ   dɪs   ɪz ɳɒtʰ mɪd̪   nəʊ mɔ:]
4   this   is   a   re spective (2.0)
      [dɪs   ɪz   ə   ɹə spektɪv
5 : (school)
6 Moh:school (.) yes (.) took the words out my mouth (4.5)

In this extract, Mohan was claiming that the norms of conduct appropriate to secondary pupils during breaktime had been broken, and Goffman's account of remedial inter-changes (1971: 95–187) helps to explain the way that stylised Asian English (SAE) figured in the episode. Goffman argues that two kinds of issue arise when infractions occur. One of these is 'substantive', relating to practical matters such as the offender making amends and the offended showing that they are not going to accept the way they have been treated. The other kind of issue is ritual, which in contrast, is concerned with the way in which participants display their more general respect and regard for social norms and personal preserves (Goffman 1971: 95–98, 100, 116) – here the concern is with "indicating a relationship, not compensating a loss" (1971: 118).

In line 1, the initial noticing of the infraction was announced by a normal vernacular English 'prime' – an attempt to get the (putative) offender to provide a remedy which they might do by desisting, apologising and/or giving an explanation (Goffman 1971: 154ff, 109–114). Propositionally, the utterance in line 3 only reminded the (disappearing) addressee that old rules of conduct no longer applied, but the switch to stylised Asian English made a symbolic proclamation about the transgression's relation to a wider social order. In switching away from his normal voice to SAE, Mohan aligned the offence with a more general social type, so that the offending act was now cast as a symptom. SAE was stereotypically associated with limited linguistic and cultural competence (see below) and the switch implicitly explained the transgression by imputing diminished control and responsibility to the offender.[4] In doing so, it achieved the same effect as a sanction: "The significance of . . . rewards and penalties is not meant to lie in their intrinsic worth but in what they proclaim about the [actor's] moral status . . . and [their] compliance with or deviation from rules in general" (Goffman 1971: 95, 98). (See also Rampton 1995: Ch 6.2.)

Creole could also be used in the affirmation of peer group norms. In the following extract, immediately after visibly coming off worse in a verbal tussle with the teacher, an adolescent turns to his friend and produces some Creole to repair his loss of face:

(3) Participants: Asif [15 years old, Pakistani descent, male, wearing radio-microphone], Alan [15, Anglo-descent, M], Ms Jameson [over 25, An F], and in the background, Mr Chambers [25 + An M]
Setting: 1987. Asif and Alan are in detention. Ms Jameson is saying why she arrived late for the detention, and now she wants to go and fetch her lunch. (II.17)

```
80  Ms J:  I had to go and see the headmaster
81  Asif:   why
82  Ms J:  (              ) (.) none of your business
83  Alan:   a- about us (            )
84  Ms J:  no   I'll be    ⌈back
                ((l.))
85  Asif:                  ⌊hey how can you see the =
                             ((f.))
86          = headmaster when he was in dinner (.)
87  Ms J:  that's precisely why I didn't see him
                ((l.))
88  Asif:   what (.)
89  Ms J:  I'll be back in a second with my lunch  ⌈(        )
90  Asif:                                          ⌊NO [1] =
                                          ((ff.))
91          = dat's sad man (.) (I'll b     ) =
                ((f.))
92          =I     ⌈had to miss my play right I've gotta go
93  Alan:          ⌊(           with mine        )
94          (2.5) ((Ms J must now have left the room))
```

95 Asif   ((Creole influenced)): ll:unch (.) you don't need no =
                ((f.))
                [ll:ʌntʃ]
96   = lunch ⎡ not'n grow anyway ((laughs))
                   ⎢ [natˀn ɡɹəʊ]
97 Alan: ⎢ ((laughs))
98 Asif: have you eat your lunch Alan

Lines 80–88 of this extract involve a verbal tussle in which Asif and Alan use questions to undermine the positions that Ms Jameson stakes out in what she says. Asif's question in line 81 treats the account she gives of her late arrival as inadequate; she rejects his inquiry as illegimate in line 82 but this is then undermined by Alan in lines 83 and 84; and in lines 85–87, Ms Jameson is delayed in the departure she announced in line 84 by a question that upgrades the query over her initial excuse into an explicit challenge. All this time, she has been locked into the interaction by the adjacency structures set up by the boys' questions, but at line 89, she breaks out of this pattern, ignores Asif's line 88 repair initiation, again announces her departure and leaves without saying anything more. With the cooperative exchange structure now disrupted, Asif launches into some 'afterburn'/'muttering':

Afterburn . . . is . . . a remonstrance conveyed collusively by virtue of the fact that its targets are in the process of leaving the field . . . when one individual finds that others are conducting themselves offensively in their current dealings with him . . . he can wait until they have closed out the interchange with him and turned from the encounter, and then he can express what he 'really' feels about them . . . he may turn to a member of his encounter . . . and flood into directed expression (Goffman 1971: 152, 153).

In muttering we convey that although we are now going along with the line established by the speaker (and authority), our spirit has not been won over, and compliance is not to be counted on (Goffman 1981: 93).

In this afterburn, Asif uses some Black English/Creole. Admittedly, it is sometimes difficult to distinguish Creole from the local multiracial vernacular (cf Hewitt 1986: 128–9 and below), and Asif's stopped TH in "dat's sad man" is ambiguous. But in lines 95 and 96, he uses a distinctly Creole unrounded front open vowel in "not" (cf Wells 1982: 576; Sebba 1993: 153–4), and the stretched and heavily voiced L in his first "lunch" maybe connects with a black speech feature noted by Hewitt in South London (1986: 134). Creole (and/or London Black English) synchronises with a turn that refutes any notion of meek pupil submission on Asif's part, and seems to reaffirm his reputation for lively adolescent assertiveness.

    Finally, language crossing was itself sometimes referred to as a sign of local peer group membership:

(4) Setting: 1987 interview
     Participants (and referents): Ben – over 30 years old, male, Anglo descent; Faizal – 14, M, Pakistani descent; Manwar – 14, M, Pakistani descent; Billy and Peter – 14, M, Anglo))

Manwar: we've nicknamed Billy a few . . . I dunno, (for) about a
         year, in our school half, half . . . half-jabber ((= Asian))
Faizal: he's half-jabber now – knows most of the words – and so's
         Peter, he knows quite a lot of ((Panjabi)) words too
Manwar: yeh, these two are one of us

(5) Setting: 1987 interview
     Participants (and referents): Ben – over 30 years old, male, Anglo
     descent; Faizal – 14, M, Pakistani descent; Kuldip – 14, M, Indian
     descent; Peter – 14, M, Anglo

Ben: so who would you say knows most ((Panjabi))
Faizal: Peter
Kuldip: yeh, he knows, he's been in our sort of community
Faizal: he's been our friend long time

(6) Setting: 1987 playback session
     Participants: Ben and Peter (14, M, Anglo)

Peter: **'gora'** – white man ((in Panjabi)) . . . I always call the
         people who didn't go to Southleigh ((local middle school))
         'goras', yet I'm white myself
Ben: the kids who didn't go to Southleigh you say
Peter: yeh, cos we reckon they're, you know, a bit upper class

(7) "all of us you know Asian guys, we can use ((Creole)) well you see, cos
     we've all been talk . . . you know speaking it since Southleigh second
     years ((the age of ten))" [Informant: 15 years old, Pakistani descent,
     male]

In this section, then, we have considered three aspects of crossing's integration
within local peer group culture. Firstly, and rather obviously, crossing was facilitated by
some quite extensively shared orientations, practices and standards. Secondly, it was
sometimes used spontaneously to draw identities and conduct back into line with peer
group norms and ideals. And thirdly, it was explicitly cited as emblem of peer group
belonging. The emphasis so far has been on crossing's relationship with the socially
cohesive aspects of local multiracial peer group life. Commonality has been stressed
more than diversity and difference. It is important now to turn to the way in which
language crossing registered the potential conflicts and divisions that also ran through
the local adolescent community.

5. Language crossing and the evocation of race difference

Both Creole and stylised Asian English carried a complex set of symbolic connotations,
and although a comprehensive account would also need to reckon with their more
intimate family associations (cf Rampton 1995: Ch 2.4), part of their social meaning was
influenced by wider politics of race in Britain. Asian English had quite wide media
currency in stereotypic potraits of British Asians (Dummett 1973: 279; Goffe 1985),

and it frequently conjured 'babu' images of linguistic incompetence and bumbling deference inherited from the days of the British Raj (Yule and Burnell [1886] 1985: 44). The mass public image of Creole was more varied, and its association with music and popular culture gave it considerable prestige among youth (cf Hewitt 1986: Ch 3; Rampton 1995: Chs 2.1 and 9). At the same time, it was also stereotypically associated with tough assertiveness and opposition to authority (Hewitt 1986; Rampton 1995). The result was that in Hewitt's data, black adolescents tended to see white Creole use "(a) as derisive parody, and hence as an assertion of white superiority, and (b) as a further white appropriation of one of the sources of power" (1986: 162). To a considerable degree, in combination stylised Asian English and Creole constituted variations on the victim/problem, clown/threat couplets recurring in the discourses of British racism (Gilroy 1987; Walvin 1987).

These highly problematic symbolic associations immediately complicate the picture of language crossing as a local community practice outlined in the previous section. How could multiracial peer group community be consolidated by the evocation of dangerous images like these? The faultlines of race difference transected the peer group internally and so anyone wanting to use an ethnic outgroup language had to bear in mind the possibility that there might be non-intimate ethnolinguistic inheritors on hand who could take legitimate offence at the expropriation of a valued resource (particularly with Creole), and/or at the reductive imagery which crossing frequently entailed.

There are two answers to this, and they relate back to the two notions of exclusion outlined in Section 1.2 – one hingeing on the 'friend/enemy' dichotomy, and the other involving an interplay between 'strangeness' and 'belonging'. I shall discuss the former only rather briefly, although it is important to recognise the operation of what was in effect an often racist dichotomy for at least two reasons. Firstly, recognition of it helps us to avoid romanticising interracial peer group processes, and secondly, in what follows, it can also serve as a useful reminder that we cannot claim to be dealing with some 'essence of peer group': The focus is on one or two from a wide range of linguistic and cultural practices, some of which promoted and projected particular notions of community and otherness, and some of which didn't.

With regard, then, to the first, 'friends/enemies' notion of exclusion, it became clear during interviews that language crossing was felt to be neither legitimate nor likely among posh whites and youngsters of Bangladeshi descent (even though the radio-microphone data reveals that at least among Bangladeshis, crossing was quite common). This pointed to a sense of class and race stratification that was very influential among my informants. In this folk schema, non-local white boys and Bangladeshis were typified as contrasting points of negative reference that helped to define the 'normal', and they formed a number of polar contrasts between which 'ordinary' adolescents could situate themselves and their friends. Posh Anglos were said to reside in wealthier villages and districts outside the neighbourhood, while Bangladeshis were generally seen as living in much poorer accommodation in the central parts of town. Posh white kids were associated with private school, with high curriculum sets at Newton Upper and with proper English, while Bangladeshis were linked to the local ESL reception centre, remedial classes at Newton and inadequate second language varieties of English. Neither of these class and race stereotypes was unproblematic or uncontested, and when reflecting on it, adolescents generally felt quite guilty about their treatment of Bangladeshis in particular. Even so, the term 'Bengali' was repeatedly used in 'humourously' critical remarks about the conduct of associates, Bangladeshis were endlessly associated with unsociability, unfashionable dressing and other undesirable characteristics, they were almost entirely excluded from my informants' friendship networks, and lastly, they were also subjected to quite aggressive uses of stylised Asian English (eg Rampton 1995: 143–4).

So the account of exclusion in terms of a 'friends/enemies' opposition certainly reflects the way ratified members of the local peer group regarded Bangladeshis and most posh whites,[5] and most of the time with these two groups, peer group members really didn't care whether they used stereotypes that caused offence. This is not however adequate as an account of the way they responded to exclusion and difference, since it only refers to people with whom relations were generally unfriendly, neglecting the fact that most friendship clusters were themselves ethnically mixed. To understand Hall's new ethnicities, we need to dwell at greater length on the interplay between strangeness and belonging, and on the way in which language crossing handled ethnic differences **internal** to the network of recognised peer group members.

The language crossing of adolescents showed sensitivity to the different ethnic backgrounds of their friends in two general strategies. First and most obviously, by **not** crossing in certain contexts (avoidance). Black and white adolescents seldom used stylised Indian English to **target** Panjabi friends, and most whites and Panjabis either avoided Creole or used it in very circumscribed ways when they were in the company of black peers (Hewitt 1986: Ch 5; Rampton 1995: Chs 6 and 8). Secondly, crossing generally only occurred in moments, activities and relationships in which the constraints of ordinary social order were relaxed and normal social relations couldn't be taken for granted.

In extract 1 for example, in combination with friendship and a number of other factors (cf Rampton 1995: Chs 7.3, 7.4, 7.8), the formulaic use of song meant that for a brief interlude, the exchange of abuse was ritual and jocular rather than personal and serious (cf Labov 1972; Goodwin and Goodwin 1987). In the other two examples of spontaneous discourse, crossing was closely tied up with breaches of some kind or other: Mohan's stylised Asian English in Extract 2 rebuked a new pupil's impropriety, and in Extract 3, it was an explicit sense of injustice and injury that led into Asif's semi-resilient Creole in lines 95 and 96. As both Goffman and Garfinkel make abundantly clear, breaches, improprieties and transgressions disrupt our everyday sense of social reality.

In fact in one form or another, routine assumptions about ordinary life seemed to be temporarily relaxed, suspended or jeopardised *whenever* adolescents code-crossed. These interruptions to the routine flow of normal social order took a wide range of different forms, and varied very considerably in their scale and duration. As well as cueing or being cued by delicts, transgressions and ritual abuse, adolescents code-crossed at the boundaries of interactional enclosure, when the roles and identities for ensuing interaction were still relatively indeterminate (Goffman 1971: Ch 7; Laver 1975); in self-talk and response cries, which constituted time away from the full demands of respectful interpersonal conduct (Goffman 1981: 81, 85, 99); in games, where there was an agreed relaxation of routine interaction's rules and constraints (Handelman 1977; Turner 1982: 56; Sutton-Smith 1982); in the context of per-formance art (cf Gilroy 1987: 210–216); and in cross-sex interaction, which in a setting where everyday recreation was single sex and where many parents discouraged unmonitored contact between adolescent girls and boys, itself seemed special, unusually vested with both risk and promise (Foley 1990: 33, 70, 95; Shuman 1993: 146). So in one way or another, crossing was occasioned by (or occasioned) moments and events in which the hold of routine assumptions about social reality was temporarily loosened. In all of these moments and events, "the world of daily life known in common with others and with others taken for granted" (Garfinkel 1984: 35) was problematised or partially suspended (see Rampton 1995 for comprehensive exemplification).

We can summarise this aspect of language crossing by saying that it was profoundly connected with liminality and the 'liminoid' (Turner 1982),[6] and from this, we can draw two inferences. Firstly, its intimate association with liminality meant that crossing never actually claimed that the speaker was 'really' black or Asian – it didn't finally imply that the crosser could move unproblematically in and out of their friends' heritage language in any new kind of open bicultural code-switching. Secondly, crossing's location in the liminoid margins of interactional and institutional space implied that in the social structures which were dominant and which adolescents finally treated as **normal**, the boundaries round ethnicity were **relatively** fixed.

So language crossing cannot be seen as a runaway deconstruction of ethnicity, emptying it of all meaning: Inherited ethnicity was something that adolescents treated as a basic feature of routine social reality, and in this regard, the interactional data corroborated the data on patterns of friendship, as well as a large number of other aspects of local cultural and material life. But this doesn't mean that adolescents submitted reverentially to ethnic absolutism. If what Hall calls the dominant, dispossessing, 'race' and nation notion of ethnicity had been hegemonic, language crossing would have been unacceptable, a ceaseless source of local conflict. It wasn't. Inherited ethnicity certainly wasn't rejected or abandoned, but neither was its influence left unquestioned, invisibly and incontrovertibly pervading common sense. Crossing was one interactional practice in the repertoire of peer group activity that foregrounded ethnicity itself, and in doing so, it at least partially destabilised it.

When adolescents code-crossed with friends, there was in fact a tension in the way that they treated the boundaries round an ethnic category. They both respected and transgressed them, and in this light, crossing can be interpreted as a process of delicate political negotiation. In excess, both an acceptance **and** a disregard for these boundaries could slip into injustice, which can be defined as either (a) treating people the same when in relevant respects they are different, and/or as (b) treating them as different when in relevant respects, they are similar (Halstead 1988: 154). For adolescents in a multilingual peer group, unrestricted use of an ethnic outgroup language could constitute the first kind of injustice; on the other hand, if an individual resisted every temptation to experiment in an outgroup code, they might also find that they had actually succumbed to the second. Crossing generally wove a path between these two forms of racism. Through it, adolescents actively explored the waterline where ethnic and interracial forms and practices overlapped and intermingled with each other and here they challenged (b) – ethnic fixity and division. But at the same time, they normally only brought out their improvisations and new acquisitions in places where it could be safely understood that they weren't making any claims to real, equal or enduring membership of an ethnic outgroup. So in this way, they also avoided (a) – the insensitivity to difference instantiated elsewhere in race relations in 'colour blindness', ethnocentrism and so forth.

Looking back, then, over the account given in this section and the one before it, it is possible to see how language crossing links directly into the tension between similarity and difference pinpointed in Hall's new 'ethnicity of the margins'.

On the one hand, crossing emerges as a practice closely tied to the shared norms, values and activities of a particular cultural collectivity. It required a specific kind of interactional competence to situate the use of outgroup codes in liminal moments and events. Crossing showed sensitivity to a complex set of situational contingencies – the stage and state of talk, the activity type, the institutional setting, the relationship between interlocutors and so forth – and as a skillful, group-specific practice, effective and accepted crossing generally only came with substantial experience of local multiracial peer group life. In this respect, as well as in its explicit function as emblem of group identity, language crossing was intimately associated with belonging in new form of multiracial community.

But at the same time, crossing also invoked difficult and dangerous knowledge of ethnic difference and race stratification, using them to enhance or protect the performance of local adolescent recreation. Evidently, adolescents experienced ethnic division as more than just 'brittle artificiality', but it wasn't treated as absolute, and in code-crossing, they played with the redefinition of group boundaries in discursive acts that involved a complex combination of violation and regard. In this respect, crossing looks like a significant contribution to the emergence of a sense of youth community 'predicated on difference and diversity', and the account given here is one way in which sociolinguistic analysis can illuminate the interethnic processes highlighted in Section 1.1. But what of socialisation?

6. Perspectives on socialisation

So far, my account has emphasised the group dimensions of language crossing – on the one hand, its integration with local culture, its use in the support of adolescent norms, its citation as evidence of peer group membership, and on the other, its engagement with intergroup politics in society at large. The empirical discussion has also taken socialisation rather for granted, treating adolescent community practice only as an endstage of competent conduct. But what did crossing mean for particular speakers, and what did it say about the social development of individuals in a multiracial setting?

A full account of the processes of trial, error and correction involved in white adolescents learning to use Creole is provided by Hewitt (1986: Ch 5). My own analysis of these is less detailed, and I have rather less to say on how individuals actually learnt to cross in ways that were accepted in the local youth community (socialisation into the peer group as a first hand experience). Nevertheless, as a generic practice, language crossing repeatedly foregrounded incompetence, instruction, temporality, personal change and individual social positioning, and through it, at the level of behavioural ideology (Volosinov 1973: 91–2), adolescents continually engaged with central issues in socialisation. To complete the account of how language crossing figured in the attempts that adolescents made to live with difference, it is essential to provide a brief outline of the ways in which crossing into Panjabi, Creole and stylised Asian English displayed a range of subtly differentiated concerns with learning and social development.

With Panjabi, being an effective and accepted crosser generally involved an ability to exploit and enjoy incompetence itself. Adolescents competent and ratified in the ways of multiracial peer group culture often participated in interethnic activities which announced, accepted and indeed sometimes celebrated a lack of linguistic proficiency. For example, in playground interaction among boys in early adolescence, it was quite common for Panjabi bilinguals to invite monolingual friends of Anglo and Afro-Caribbean descent to either say things in Panjabi, or to respond to Panjabi questions[7]. These invitations to use another language normally contained elements which lay just beyond the learner's grasp, and the fact that an important element of what was being said to the second language learner was incomprehensible to them was crucial, generating a great deal of the entertainment (see Rampton 1991a: 230–4, 1995: Ch 7). Learners had to operate just beyond the limits of their linguistic competence, and playfully speaking, their reputations depended on their performance. Here is an example:

(8) Participants: Mohan (male, 13 years, Indian descent, wearing a radio-
     microphone), Sukhbir (M 13 In), Jagdish (M 13 In), David (M 12 Afro-
     Caribbean), Pritam (M In), others
     Setting: Breaktime outside. Mohan, Jagdish and David are best friends

    1 Jagdish ((turning to David, speaking in Panjabi)):
    2   [ə tu lɔɾə di bʊn mʌɾ egə]
            ((Approximate translation: do you want to bum Laura?))
    3 Sukhbir: [ha ha ha ha ha
    4 Others: [((laughter for about three seconds))
    5 David: no I don't think so
    6 Jagdish: DAVID (·) no I said that- that means that you're-
    7   are you going to beat Laura up
    8 David: no=
    9   Sukhbir:= yeh it does, it does ⌈(it does)
   10 David: ((smile voice))   ⌊that- that means [h] are you
   11   going to make her pregnant=
   12   Sukhbir:=NO:: ⌈(   )
   13 Mohan: ⌊no

            ((a few moments later))

   21 Jagdish: SAY IT TO HIM (·) say it to him say it to him
   22   ⌈say it to him [meri mãdi_____]
             ⌈((Panjabi. Trans: my mum's fanny))
   23 Others: ⌊((laughter))
   24 Anon: go on
   25 David: I ⌈don't want to say that
   26 Jagdish: ⌊NO SAY IT TO HIM GO ON say it to him
   27 Anon: ha ⌈ha ha ha ha
   28 Anon: ⌈ go on
   29 David: ⌊(it says- your go-)
   30   it means that ⌈MY mum's got a –
   31 Jagdish: ⌊eh?
   32   no say ((. . . the 'elicitations'; continue))

Here, a minimal and unconfident knowledge of Panjabi was drawn into traditional playground practice, in variations on the verbal routines which the Opies describe as 'incrimination traps' (Opie and Opie 1959: Ch4).[8] Placed in situations of this kind, a number of strategies were available to an L2 Panjabi speaker aware of the insufficiency of their linguistic knowledge, and in this extract, David's could be characterised as a knowing refusal. Another commonly used tactic was to ask a friend:

> (9) "my friend, you know, he swears in Panjabi to English girls, and they go and ask an Indian boy they know, and he tells them and tells them other words and they come and say it to us"

Consultations of this kind were very commonly construed in pupil-teacher terms ("if they're our friends, we teach them it"), although as illustrated in the episode above, you'd be foolish to trust too much in the instruction that these provided:

> (10) "like Ishfaq tells . . . you know Alan Timms, if Alan Timms says 'teach me some dirty words', Ishfaq makes him say swear words to himself ((laughs)), so he's saying it to hims . . . he goes up to Asif and he says it and Asif starts laughing"

Particularly among 11 to 13 year old white and black boys, a high level of incompetence in Panjabi generated a range of entertaining recreational activities, and when asked, they said they wouldn't be interested in attending any formal Panjabi classes. They didn't want to improve their proficiency in Panjabi, and were evidently quite happy to remain permanently as pre-elementary language learners. The rudimentary Panjabi L2 learner was a significant and enjoyable local identity.

Stylised Asian English also made linguistic competence a relevant issue, though in a much more politically charged way than Panjabi. In a great deal of its use, the symbolic meaning of interracial Panjabi was relatively unaffected by the wider context of race stratification. In contrast, as I have already indicated in section 5, SAE often evoked 'babu' stereotypes of deference and incompetence. In addition, Asian English was also associated both with adults who had come to England from India and Pakistani (towards whom informants often expressed solidary sentiments), and with recently arrived Bangladeshi peers (towards whom they were generally hostile – cf Rampton 1988 and 1995: 2.4 on the ambiguous and troublesome – connotations of Asian English).

In all of its connotations, Asian English conjured a past that Panjabi adolescents now felt that they were leaving behind. It evoked an historical time frame of migration and contact and this seemed to impact on the self-voice relationships expressed in spontaneous discourse. Adolescents used SAE in a variety of ways: Probing the inter-group perceptions of adults in authority by feigning mock deference or incomprehension (Rampton 1995: Ch 3; forthcoming); abusing Bangladeshi peers; reprimanding junior pupils; jokily attributing impropriety or incompetence to friends (Rampton 1995: Ch 6). But when they did so, there was generally a clear distinction between self and voice, 'principal' and 'figure' (Goffman 1974): In Bakhtin's terms, the 'double-voicing' was varidirectional (1984: 193).[9] Addressed to another adolescent either in mock or in serious criticism (cf Extract 2), SAE was used as a 'say-for' (Goffman 1974: 535), attributing the persona it evoked to the target, not claiming it for the speaker, and indeed it seemed to achieve its effect as a negative sanction for deviant conduct by threatening the recipient with regression, symbolically isolating them on a path of historical development now abandoned by adolescents who had arrived at an endpoint that they now took for granted.

Admittedly, the claim here for an intimate connection between a practical sense of historical temporality on the one hand, and on the other, the manner in which Asian English was interactionally exploited, requires rather more supporting evidence than there is space to provide here (though cf Rampton 1995: Chs 3, 4 and 6). Even so, it is worth adding that the data on Creole crossing suggested a link of the same kind, even though in its particular character, it seemed to be the exact opposite of SAE. In contrast to Asian English, Creole stood for an excitement and excellence in vernacular youth culture which many youngsters aspired to, and it was even described as 'future lan-guage'. In line with this, Creole crossing generally ressembled Bakhtin's uni-directional double-voicing, and self and voice were often closely entwined. Certainly, there was usually some reservation in the way it was used by whites and Asians, and this was indicated both by the way they avoided it in the presence of black peers and by its location in liminal moments and events. Even so, crossers tended to use Creole to lend emphasis to evaluations that synchronised with the identities they maintained in their ordinary speech, its use lent power to the speaker, and when directed towards deviance, it often expressed approval. Consistent with this, as Hewitt (1986: 148, 151) emphasises and as is illustrated in the discussion of Extract 3, Creole crossing headed towards fusion with, and was often hard to disentangle from, the local multiracial vernacular (cf Bakhtin 1984: 199 on 'uni-directional double-voicing' shifting over into 'direct unmedi-ated discourse').

In sum, as a form of practical consciousness, language crossing displayed a recurrent preoccupation with issues central to the discussion of socialisation. In cross-ethnic Panjabi, adolescents made play with knowledge and ignorance, instruction and deceit. To describe stylised Asian English and Creole, we can borrow Goffman's terms (1967: 56, 77) and say that SAE projected an image of too much deference and not enough demeanour while the Creole persona had an excess of demeanour over deference, and the suggestion is that together they represented poles of fear and desire on a path of historical development, one standing for regression and the other for advance.

But the difference between the way that socialisation was represented in crossing and the way that it is usually discussed in the academic literature lies in the fact that in crossing, hardly anyone finally arrived. Instead, crossing generally constituted multi-racial adolescence as a world of uncertainty and movement, towards and away from other-ethnic inheritances. Certainly, some youngsters aspired to become uncontested members of the black or Panjabi youth community, and some got much closer than others, particularly when the contexts were romance or performance art (cf Hewitt 1986; Rampton 1995: Chs 9.2, 10.6, 10.8 for a discussion of particular cases). But finally, the boundaries round ethnicity were relatively fixed in the social structures that were dominant and which adolescents treated as normal, and although it varied a lot in its insistence and intensity, a sense of anomaly was always close at hand when-ever crossers moved outside the identities displayed in habitual vernacular speech. In fact for many adolescents, this was central to crossing's attraction. Although it needed to be accessed through the proper channels, and although there were clear constraints on the display of its creations, crossing represented an interest in travelling around the borderlands themselves, in being both near and different, close and apart. Crossing revelled in not-yet- or never-to-be-realised potentiality itself.

7. Conclusion

Among sociolinguists, there has been a good deal of debate about whether ethnicity is best seen as a cultural inheritance that participants bring along with them to interaction, or whether it is more properly regarded as a construct that they bring about in inter-actional discourse itself (cf eg Meeuwis and Sarangi 1994). Conceptually, this paper doesn't actually resolve the argument in favour of one term or the other (cf Bourdieu 1977b), but it shifts the floor of the debate and in doing so, throws up empirical phenomena with a social significance that sociolinguistics perhaps hasn't yet fully appreciated.[10]

The paper suggests that at the level of behavioural ideology, there was an unsettled debate about group-membership-as-acquired-disposition and group-membership-as-situated-performance being conducted in the code crossing practices of a multiracial adolescent peergroup. Ethnolinguistic inheritance was forgotten neither in the inter-actional practice and nor in the social organisation of local adolescents, and in their treatment of youngsters with Bangladeshi descent, it was embraced with virulence. But at the same time, through language crossing, youngsters temporarily **denaturalised** both ethnicity and socialisation in a series of acts which thematised change in ethnic identity and cultivated a spectacular, dynamic, heteroglossic marginality. Defined as a discursive practice in which speakers moved across ethnic (or social) boundaries and used languages that weren't generally thought to belong to them, language crossing itself crystallised in adolescent culture something very similar to the tension between ethnicity-as-communicative-inheritance and ethnicity-as-discursive-construct.

If awareness of this tension between the brought-along and brought-about is regarded as an exclusively academic affair, if the interactional negotiation of ethnic category membership is only seen as something which participants do **without** actually knowing, then for participants, experiencing ethnicity in interaction can only involve either the defence or affirmation of 'roots' (hostility or unease in intergroup situations, rapport with the ingroup). There is no scope for seeing how participants could change their ethnic identities: New interactional experiences could only either be assimilated to ethnicity as given, or lead to its internal renovation (or alternatively, be treated as simply irrelevant). The issue of which individuals had the potential to be aligned with which ethnic categories would itself remain unproblematised.

If, on the other hand, inherited ethnicity is foregrounded in a set of activities which actually confront it with the possibility of **negotiated** ethnicities, then plainly, the hold of ethnicity as inheritance is no longer absolute. In Bourdieu's terms, it has lost its authority as doxa, it is no longer "accepted undiscussed, unnamed, admitted without scrutiny", and can instead only hope to become "the necessarily imperfect substitute, **orthodoxy**" (1977a: 169–70).

This is exactly what seemed to happen in language crossing. Ethnic descent was credited with a lot of authority in routine social reality, but it was regularly transgressed in liminal moments and events when adolescents invoked, explored and momentarily inhabited ethnicities other than their own. Metaphorically speaking, crossing stopped ethnolinguistic inheritance from being an unnoticed, all-encompassing superordinate frame, and drew it down into the 'picture' itself (cf Bourdieu 1977b: 168). In this commentary on ethnicity, crossing constituted a form of "political action [which] . . . aims to make or unmake groups . . . by producing, reproducing or destroying the [mental, verbal, visual or theatrical] representations that make groups visible for themselves and for others" (Bourdieu [1981] 1990: 127). More specifically, juxtaposed to ethnic inheritance as an orthodoxy which adolescents themselves often embraced, crossing can be seen as a form of 'heretical discourse' which helped "to sever the adherence to the world of common sense by publicy proclaiming a break with ordinary order" (Bourdieu [1981] 1990: 129; cf Sections 5 and 6 above).

According to Bourdieu, beyond simply problematising the world of common sense, heretical discourse

must also produce a new common sense and integrate within it the previously tacit or repressed practices and experiences of an entire group, investing them with the legitimacy conferred by public expression and collective recognition ([1981] 1990: 129).

It is not possible here to discuss the extent to which language crossing either instituted a new common sense or developed from behavioural to established ideology (cf Rampton 1995: Ch 12). Plainly, crossing itself was not unconstrained as form of public expression, and collective recognition of it was not invariably approving. Nevertheless, it is clear that language crossing has the potential to play an important part in the emergence of 'new ethnicities' 'predicated on difference and diversity', and that as such, it is a practice that merits a lot more sociolinguistic attention.

Conventions used in transcription

Segmental phonetics

[ ] IPA phonetic transcription (revised to 1979)

Conversational features

⎡
⎢   overlapping turns
⎣

=	two utterances closely connected without a noticeable overlap, or different parts of a single speaker's turn
(·)	pause of less than one second
(1.5)	approximate length of pause in seconds
l.	lenis (quiet) enunciation
f.	fortis (loud) enunciation
CAPITALS	fortis (loud) enunciation)
(( ))	'stage directions'
( )	speech inaudible
(text)	speech hard to discern, analyst guess
Bold	instance of crossing of central interest in discussion

Notes

1   An earlier draft of this paper was originally presented at the symposium on "Socialisation, Race, Language" at the XIII World Congress of Sociology in Bielefeld, June 1994, and the research it draws on was funded by the Economic and Social Research Council and the Leverhulme Trust. I am very grateful to Celia Roberts and to an anonymous reviewer for comments on an earlier draft.

2   Admittedly, the social fields that each of these sites made available were constrained in a number of different ways. In lessons, participants were grouped according to an idea of academic ability that wasn't random in the way it is intersected with ethnic descent. Dinner queues only brought together pupils from the same year group. Unofficial social zoning in the upper school recreational areas meant that you couldn't meet a full cross-section of the pupil population if you hung around in only one place. And at the local youth club, you would be much more likely to encounter Pakistani, Anglo and Indian boys than girls, Afro-Caribbeans, Bangladeshis or Italians. Nevertheless, it was within larger gatherings of this kind that male-female relationships were formed, and it was here that network clusters came together, defined themselves and sometimes changed their membership. And though to differing degrees, many of these bigger gatherings were multiethnic.

3   With laterals in post-vocalic, prepausal or preconsonantal environments

- the vocalic L traditionally associated with non-Standard Anglo speech (Wells 1982: 258) was also used by adolescents of Indian, Pakistani and Caribbean descent;
- 'dark' [ɫ] occurred in everyone's speech, inspite of its not typically occurring in Urdu, Panjabi or Creole;
- traditionally Creole and Panjabi clear [l] (Wells 1982: 5, 70; Shackle 1972: 11) was also used postvocalically in the speech of the white informants
- one of whom also used retroflex L, a variant typically associated with Panjabi and Indian English.

Youngsters with a Panjabi background tended to use retroflex L more than white and black informants, but the extent to which they did so appeared to depend on the extent to which they had multiplex network ties with black and/or white peers – Panjabi bilinguals in the most ethnically exclusive ties used retroflex L most – and the white boy who used retroflex L had a greater number of multiplex ties with Panjabi bilinguals than any of the other black or white kids (multiplex ties represented those that involved co-participation in the home and adult community as well as school and peer recreational domains).

With voiced TH in word-initial positions, mean use of the plosive variant [d] seemed to be slightly higher among youngsters of Pakistani descent than in any of the other ethnic subgroups. The association between [d] and a Pakistani background, however, showed up much more clearly in the cross-ethnic ripple effects picked up by the network measure: Among youngsters with black, white and Indian parents, the use of [d] was strongly correlated with the extent to which they had multiplex ties with Pakistani peers (the r co-efficient from a Pearson product moment correlation was 0.86). With the other variants of word-initial (ð), usage was more evenly distributed:

- everyone made a good deal of use of the fricative variant, inspite of its non-occurrence in Panjabi and its apparent rarity in English in India (Wells 1982: 629)
- everyone used zero TH (coalescences and other sandhi forms in post-consonantal environments), inspite of this being described as a London variant by Wells (1982:

329), and inspite of Gumperz's observation that "Indian English speakers . . . pronounce almost all consonants with a higher degree of articulation than native speakers" (1982: 121).

For a more detailed account, see Rampton 1987: Ch 13, 1989.

4 In the interpretation here, SAE is being used as a 'say-for', as a voice deemed representative of the addressee/target rather than the speaker (cf. Goffman 1974: 535 and Section 6). An alternative account might reject this, and propose instead that SAE represented a voice of Panjabi adult authority which, in reprimanding a younger pupil, Mohan was claiming for himself. There are, however, at least four difficulties with such an alternative. In the first place, it presupposes that parents of bilingual Panjabi adolescents reprimanded their children in English rather than Panjabi, despite the fact that informants generally said (a) that Panjabi was used as much at home as English (Rampton 1987: 176–82), and (b) that Panjabi was associated with politeness and respect. Secondly, if SAE was used in criticism as a language of parental authority, why would it be addressed to youngsters, of Bangladeshi descent, about whom Panjabi adolescents didn't feel at all paternal (see Section 5)? Thirdly, how could SAE as a language of authority be reconciled with the image of babu deference and incompetence, which it also often made quite explicit in Panjabi accented utterances like "I no understand English", "excuse me, Miss", and "after you"? And lastly, in interracial arenas, bilinguals occasionally commented rudely on the accented Indian English of adults, and so it couldn't be argued that SAE was universally respected as a language of authority. All in all, the explanation offered in the main body of the text seems more coherent. It is also perhaps worth adding as an afterword that this account does not insist that the symbolic connotations evoked by SAE were invariant – in fact, it can be fitted quite effectively with the way in which SAE's symbolic resonances seemed to vary according to activity type (Rampton 1995: Chs 6 and 9.5).

5 It perhaps ought to be added that in their perception of posh whites, local peer group members sometimes made an exception with girls (cf. Rampton 1995: Ch 2 on this intricate interaction between class, race and gender).

6 'Liminality' is a concept developed by Victor Turner in particular, drawing on anthropological studies of initiation rites in tribal and agrarian societies. These rites have three phases: Separation, in which initiands leave their childhood life behind; transition; and then incorporation, in which they are returned to new, relatively stable and well-defined positions in society, now a stage further on in life's cycle (Turner 1982: 24). Turner concentrates on the transitional middle phase, which he calls 'liminal':

> during the intervening phase of transition . . . the ritual subjects pass through a period and area of ambiguity, a sort of social limbo which has few . . . of the attributes of either the preceding or subsequent social statuses or cultural states . . . In liminality, [everyday] social relations may be discontinued, former rights and obligations are suspended, the social order may seem to have been turned upside down (Turner 1982: 24, 27).

It is not possible to argue directly from this account of traditional ritual to the kinds of urban social relationship addressed in my own research. But Turner extends the notion of liminality into a form that fits more easily with practices common in industrial society, and he calls these 'liminoid' ('-oid' meaning 'like', 'resembling' but not identical). The distinction between liminal and liminoid can be hard to draw, but while, for example, liminal practices tend to contribute to the smooth functioning of social systems, liminoid practices are often creative, containing social critiques and exposing wrongs in mainstream structures and organisation (1982: 45). Similarly, liminality tends to involve symbols with common intellectual and emotional meaning for all members of the group, while "liminoid phenomena tend to be more idiosyncratic, quirky, to be generated by specific named individuals and in particular groups" (1982: 54). For fuller discussion in the context of language crossing, see Rampton 1995: Ch 7.9.

7   Among monolinguals of Anglo and of Caribbean descent, there was a small stock of Panjabi words and phrases in general circulation, and this comprised a selective if rather predictable cocktail of nouns referring to parts of the body, bodily functions, animals, ethnic groups and kin; adjectives describing personal physical attributes; verbs of physical violence and ingestion; and a few other items (cf. Rampton 1991a: 395–6, 1995: Ch 7.1). It was generally some part or parts of this collective lexicon, which few individuals commanded in its entirety, that featured in the utterances that Panjabi bilinguals tried to get their friends to engage with.

8   Typical examples in English would be "Adam and Eve and Pinchmetight went down to the sea to bathe, Adam and Eve were drowned and who do you think was saved?", and

> A: "Count on. I one a rat."
> B: "I two a rat."
> C: "I three a rat."

and so on up to "eight".

9   Double-voicing is a term that Bakhtin uses to describe some of the ways that this heteroglossia acts upon the utterance. With double-voicing, speakers use someone else's discourse (or language) for their own purposes,

> inserting a new semantic intention into a discourse which already has . . . an intention of its own. Such a discourse . . . must be seen as belonging to someone else. In one discourse, two semantic intentions appear, two voices (Bakhtin 1984: 189).

Bakhtin describes several kinds of double-voicing, and one of these is described as 'uni-directional'. With uni-directional double-voicing, the speaker uses someone else's discourse "in the direction of its own particular intentions" (1984: 193). Speakers themselves go along with the momentum of the second voice, though it generally retains an element of otherness which makes the appropriation conditional and introduces some reservation into the speaker's use of it. But at the same time, the boundary between the speaker and the voice they are adopting can diminish, to the extent that there is a "fusion of voices". When that happens, discourse ceases to be double-voiced, and instead becomes 'direct, unmediated discourse' (1984: 199). The opposite of uni-directional double-voicing is **varidirectional** double-voicing, in which the speaker "again speaks in someone else's discourse, but . . . introduces into that discourse a semantic intention directly opposed to the original one". In varidirectional double-voicing, the two voices are much more clearly demarcated, and they are not only distant but also opposed (Bakhtin 1984: 193).

10   There are in fact a number of accounts with a good deal of descriptive similarity to my own account of language crossing: for example, Hill and Coombs 1982; Woolard 1988; and most obviously Hewitt 1986. But in general, the distinctiveness of language crossing is lost, and it is either swallowed up under the rubric of code-switching, or misconstrued as second language acquisition (cf Rampton 1995: Ch 11 for further discussion).

Source: Rampton, B. (1995) Language crossing and the problematisation of ethnicity and socialisation. *Pragmatics* 5(4): 485–513. Reproduced by permission of the author and the International Pragmatics Association.

Postscript

The term 'language crossing' has now gained some currency in sociolinguistics (Duranti 2001) and, overall, I think it has been quite a timely addition to the notion of 'code-switching'. Code-switching research has tended to look for conventional pragmatic and syntactic patterns in the mixed speech of relatively well-established ingroups, and this in turn reflects the wider view (a) that language study is centrally concerned with systematicity in grammar and coherence in discourse and (b) that these properties come from community membership, that people learn to talk grammatically and coherently from extensive early experience of living in fairly stable local social networks. In contrast, in research on crossing, there's as much emphasis on emergence, improvisation and the (partial) denaturalisation of convention as on conventionalisation itself and, with people using varieties associated with minority ethnic outgroups, it's very clear switching occurs between more than just the national standard language(s) and home vernaculars.

The last ten years have seen a substantial growth in empirical studies of language crossing. As well as emerging in sustained interethnic interaction in urban settings, crossing practices can be found in new and popular media (both mainstream and alternative), and they sometimes form a part of the more general commodification of ethnicities in contemporary societies. Ethnic forms, products and symbols are disseminated and often marketised as aesthetic objects, lifestyle options and/or desirable commercial items, and the consumer's personal taste and purchasing power can matter as much as (or more than) interethnic peer-group socialisation. Language frequently serves as a major element in the design and consumption of such products, and the ways in which both members and non-members of the groups represented react to, reject or buy them are bound to be highly diverse. Overall, empirical studies document a wide range of stances on the legitimacy and authenticity of cross-language use (with participants and analysts sometimes disagreeing), and the sense of 'otherness' also varies in salience. For Europe, see Urla 1995, and Pujolar 2001 (Spain), Androutsopoulos 2001, and Auer and Dirim 2003 (Germany), Doran 2004 (France), and Back 1995 (UK); for North America, see Hill 1995, 1999, Zentella 1997, Cutler 1999, Bucholtz 1999, Lo 1999, Ronkin and Karn 1999, Bailey 2000, Sweetland 2002, Ibrahim 2003; for New Zealand, see Bell 1999.

Beyond its connection with research on code-switching, the concept of 'crossing' has implications for our understanding of the learning and teaching of second and foreign languages (S/FLLT). At a fairly general level, the analysis of crossing has contributed to the substantial growth of interest in the social, cultural and ideological dynamics of S/FLLT (e.g. Firth and Wagner 1997; Mitchell and Myles 1998: Ch. 8; Block 2003), while in more specific terms it invites analysts to consider the manner and extent to which S/FLLT encompasses practices where instrumental purposes give way to play and ritual, where indexical and poetic meaning dominate the lexical and referential, and where invention and mixing are celebrated rather than deemphasised (cf. Rampton 1997, 2005: 11.4, 2006: Part II).

Looking beyond specifically bilingual issues for a larger theoretical home in sociolinguistics, I'd continue to see 'crossing' as one variant of Bakhtin's 'double-voicing', which itself connects with 'stylisation' and Richard Bauman's notion of artful 'performance' (e.g. Coupland 2001; Bauman and Briggs 1990). Double-voicing, stylisation and performance are often quite closely integrated into ordinary talk, but, with varying degrees of intensity, all three invite a break with routine habits of interpretation when they occur, bringing specific ways of speaking into the spotlight for evaluation and critique. And far from just focusing on varieties associated with clearly demarcated outgroups, this objectification can also involve speech styles that – at other times – actually form quite an intimate part of the speaker's habitual repertoire: Texan women acting extra-Southern (Johnstone 1999), African-American students exaggerating standard (Clark 2003), Cardiff disc jockeys doing hyper-Welsh (Coupland 2001), and adolescent Londoners putting on ultra-posh and Cockney (Rampton 2006: Part III). Of course there's lots of variation in what these performances signify, but, in playing up the kinds of dialect feature that have traditionally interested Labovian variationist sociolinguists, the study of stylisation promises to build new bridges between interactional and quantitative socio-linguistics, opening new windows on language change (Eckert 2000).

Lastly, in terms of broader intellectual currents within the humanities and social sciences, the evidence on 'crossing' compels us to engage with the profound philosophical reassessments associated with post-structuralism and late-modernity. Zygmunt Bauman, for example, argues that "the reality to be modelled is [actually] . . . much more fluid, heterogeneous and 'underpatterned' than anything that soci-ologists tried to grasp intellectually in the past" (1992: 65), and this resonates with the difficulties that crossing poses for traditional conceptions of 'speech community', 'socialisation' and 'language system' (Rampton 2001, 2006: Ch 1; Pratt 1987). On the one hand, debates in contemporary social science provide concepts – like 'new ethnicities', 'hybridity' and 'liminality' – that help to make better sense of the cultural processes involved in sociolinguistic practices like language crossing, while, on the other, interactional sociolinguistic methods can bring out vivid intricacies in the empirical fine-grain of everyday activity that substantially complicate more abstract (and essentialised) social science theorisations (see e.g. Rampton 1999a, Harris and Rampton 2002).

Ben Rampton, PhD, is Professor of Applied and Socio-Linguistics at King's College London. ben.rampton@kcl.ac.uk

Notes for students and instructors

Study questions

1. What kind of ways can bilingual speakers manipulate their language choice to show resistance, opposition or disagreement to other people's views, attitudes or remarks?
2. Can you identify new multilingual practices, including literacy practices, in your community? How are they related to the ethnic, social and linguistic identities of the language users?

Study activity

Collect information on the official policies and public discourse on bilingualism in a chosen community. Interview some key personnel on their views of bilingualism. Observe and record social interaction of a target group within the community and ask them about their views on bilingualism. Can you see any mismatch between: a) the official policy, public discourse and the actual social practice; b) what people say they do and what they actually do?

If you have access to historical records of language contact in a particular community, can you identify any major changes in language policy and practice? How are the changes related to other social political changes in the community?

Further reading

Key publications on language ideology include B. Schieffelin, K. Woolard and P. Kroskrity (eds), 1998, *Language Ideologies: Practice and theory*, Oxford University Press; R. Bauman and C. Briggs (eds), 2003, *Voices of Modernity: Language ideologies and the politics of inequality*, Cambridge University Press; R. Lippi-Green, 1997, *English with an Accent: Language, ideology, and discrimination in the United States*, Routledge; and J. Milroy and L. Milroy (1991) *Authority in Language: Investigating standard English*, 2nd edn, Routledge.

On language choice as a political strategy, see K.A. Woolard, 1989, *Double Talk: Bilingualism and the politics of ethnicity in Catalonia*, Stanford University Press.

More detailed expositions of Heller's work can be found in M. Heller, 1994, *Crosswords: Language, education and ethnicity in French Ontario*, Mouton de Gruyter; and M. Heller, 1999, *Linguistic Minorities and Modernity: A sociolinguistic ethnography*, Longman.

A more detailed exposition of Rampton's work on language crossing is B. Rampton, 1995, *Crossing: Language and ethnicity among adolescents*, Longman.

Linguistic dimensions of bilingualism

Introduction to Part Two

LI WEI

Part Two focuses on the linguistic aspects of bilingualism. Chomsky (1986a) defined three basic questions for linguistics:

1   What constitutes knowledge of language?
2   How is knowledge of language acquired?
3   How is knowledge of language put to use?

For bilingualism research, these questions need to be rephrased to take in knowledge of more than one language:

1   What is the nature of language, or grammar, in the bilingual person's mind and how do two systems of language knowledge co-exist and interact?
2   How is more than one grammatical system acquired, either simultaneously or sequentially? In what aspects does bilingual language acquisition differ from unilingual language acquisition?
3   How is the knowledge of two or more languages used by the same speaker in bilingual speech production?

The articles reprinted in this part of the Reader cover approaches to bilingualism that are related to this particular agenda of linguistic research. They are further divided into two sections: 'Grammar of code-switching' and 'Bilingual acquisition'.

Grammar of code-switching

The occurrence of code-switching – the alternation of two languages both between and within sentences – has been shown to be governed not only by extra-linguistic (or social and situational) but also by intra-linguistic (or structural) factors. In her agenda-setting article, Shana Poplack (Chapter 10) proposes two grammatical constraints which seem to operate on code-switching:

1   the *free morpheme constraint*, which states that codes may be switched after any constituent in discourse, provided that constituent is not a bound morpheme; and

2   the *equivalent constraint*, i.e. code-switching tends to occur at points in discourse where juxtaposition of two languages does not violate a surface syntactic rule of either language.

Poplack further argues that the equivalent constraints on code-switching may be used to measure degrees of bilingual ability. Using quantitative analysis, she demonstrates that fluent bilinguals tend to switch at various syntactic boundaries within the sentence, while non-fluent bilinguals favour switching between sentences, allowing them to participate in the code-switching mode without fear of violating a grammatical rule of either of the languages involved.

A theoretical model of code-switching which focuses on the production process of bilingual speech is presented in the article by Carol Myers-Scotton and Janice L. Jake (Chapter 11). This model, known as the Matrix Language Frame (MLF) model, is built on the hypothesis that the two languages involved in code-switching do not participate equally, the matrix language (ML) being more dominant and setting the grammatical frame while the embedded language (EL) provides certain elements to be embedded in the frame. Furthermore, only certain EL elements can participate in code-switching: they must be content morphemes *and* they must be congruent with the ML in terms of three levels of structure: lexical-conceptual, predicate–argument and morphological realisation. Myers-Scotton and Jake point out that the analysis of intrasentential code-switching, using the MLF model, provides an empirical window on the viability of key theoretical claims about the structure of language and the nature and organisation of language production.

The chapter by Muysken (Chapter 12) approaches the grammar of code-switching from a different perspective. First it outlines two broad types of code-switching: insertional and alternational. Second, it evaluates existing theoretical models of code-switching by applying and adapting standard grammatical theories to the issue of equivalence. While pointing out that different mechanisms play a role in different code-switching situations, the author argues that a unifying theory of code-switching should be based on generally accepted, standard theories of grammar, rather than specific grammars of code-switching.

Bilingual acquisition

The second section of this part of the Reader focuses on language acquisition of bilingual children. Despite the upsurge of case studies of bilingual children in the 1990s, the central theme has remained largely unchanged: do bilingual children have one undifferentiated linguistic system or two differentiated systems? The first two articles reprinted in this section both focus on this issue.

Volterra and Taeschner's study (Chapter 13) of the simultaneous acquisition of Italian and German by the second author's two daughters, Lisa and Guilia, was the first to propose a developmental model which suggested that bilingual acquisition went through three key stages:

- *Stage I:* The child has one lexical system consisting of words from both languages.
- *Stage II:* The child distinguishes two different lexicons, but applies the same syntactic rules to both languages.
- *Stage III:* The child speaks two languages differentiated in both lexicon and syntax, but each language is associated with the person who uses that language.

Volterra and Taeschner's claims later became known as the 'fused system hypothesis', i.e. bilingual children begin with one mixed linguistic system and gradually learn to differentiate the languages.

Fred Genesee's article (Chapter 14) examines the empirical basis for the 'fused system hypothesis'. He points out the serious methodological problems of some of the studies, and re-analyses selected case studies. He also offers new data from speech perception studies, arguing that young bilingual children are able to differentiate two languages from the earliest stages of bilingual development, and that they can use their two languages in contextually sensitive ways. He points out that code-mixing itself is not good evidence for the unitary system argument. In fact, children's mixing may be related to mixed input by parents. Genesee calls for more serious research on the possible role of parental input in the form of mixed utterances.

Although the one-system-or-two debate continues to attract new empirical studies, researchers have begun to ask broader questions about bilingual acquisition. For example, is bilingual acquisition the same as monolingual acquisition? Theoretically, separate development is possible without there being any similarity to monolingual acquisition. In the meantime, how do the two languages interact in the acquisition process? One area in which bilingual children clearly differ from monolingual children is code-switching. Code-switching, as the articles in the previous section show, provides evidence of the various ways the two languages interact with each other. The last paper in this section, by Jürgen Meisel (Chapter 15), addresses the developmental aspect of code-switching. As the author points out, early code-switching in very young children depends on knowledge of the grammatical properties of the language involved. It is also regulated by principles and mechanisms of language use. The formulation of grammatical constraints needs to have cross-linguistic validity, and the acquisition of such constraints needs to take into account the linguistic development of the child in both languages.

Grammar of code-switching

Sometimes I'll start a sentence in Spanish *y termino en español*: toward a typology of code-switching

SHANA POPLACK

1 Introduction

An overwhelming majority[1] of Puerto Ricans residing in the continental United States currently claim Spanish as their 'mother tongue'. This is true for young as well as older speakers, despite the fact that most of them were either born, raised, or spent a good part of their adult life in an English-speaking society.

Along with signs of vigour and renewal of the language, however, there is also some indication that use of Spanish is on the wane, especially among the younger generations of speakers who were born and raised in New York City (Pedraza, 1978). The present investigation is part of an interdisciplinary study which aims to examine the place of both Spanish and English in a Puerto Rican community in East Harlem through:

1   participant observation of their distribution in the daily life of the community;
2   analysis of attitudes of community members toward each of the languages; and
3   quantitative sociolinguistic analysis of selected linguistic behaviour.

Due, among other things, to a circulatory pattern of migration, this appears to be a stable bilingual community, rather than a transitional one where acquisition of a second language would eventually displace the first (Fishman, 1971). This pattern of displacement of the mother tongue has characterized several early twentieth-century immigrant groups in the United States, and has usually been brought to completion by the third generation. In contrast, the Puerto Rican community under investigation includes third-generation speakers of both Spanish and English.

102nd Street, a block in the heart of El Barrio, perhaps the oldest continuous Puerto Rican settlement in the United States, provides a unique setting to investigate these issues. Block residents are predominantly (95%) Puerto Rican, to the virtual exclusion of all other ethnic groups, an attribute which is not characteristic of the Puerto Rican community in the United States as a whole (Pedraza, 1978). If the Spanish language and Puerto Rican culture are to survive in the United States, their chances of doing so are presumably greatest in such an ethnically homogeneous environment.

This chapter is an attempt to integrate the results of the ethnographic and attitudinal components of the broader study into a specifically sociolinguistic analysis.

2 Code-switching

Long-term ethnographic observation of 102nd Street, carried out by Pedro Pedraza (1978), indicated three modes of communication among block members: English-speaking, Spanish-speaking and code-switching. While use of Spanish predominates in certain domains (such as in the home or while playing numbers), its exclusive use in any of these settings was not observed. Similarly, while use of English predominates in official settings, it is also possible to hear Spanish in these domains. Pedraza further observed that 'there were speakers who code-switched because they lacked full command of Spanish and those who code-switched because they lacked full command of English' (p. 33). However, as we will see, it is only by linking ethnographic observations with linguistic analysis that code-switching behaviour may be most adequately explained.

Code-switching is the alternation of two languages within a single discourse, sentence or constituent. In a report on an earlier study of a balanced bilingual speaker (Poplack, 1978/81), code-switching was categorized according to the degree of integration of items from one language (L_1) to the phonological, morphological and syntactic patterns of the other language (L_2).

Because the balanced bilingual has the option of integrating his utterance into the patterns of the other language or preserving its original shape, items such as those in (1) below, which preserve English phonological patterns, were considered examples of code-switching in that study, while segments such as those in (2) which are adapted to Puerto Rican Spanish patterns, were considered to be instances of monolingual Spanish discourse.[2]

(1) a. Leo un MAGAZINE. [mægəˈziyn]
    'I read a magazine'.
  b. Me iban a LAY OFF. [léy ɔ̀hf]
    'They were going to lay me off'.
(2) a. Leo un *magazine*. [maɣaˈsiŋ]
    'I read a magazine'.
  b. Me iban a dar *layoff* [ˈleiof]
    'They were going to lay me off'.

In the ensuing sections we explore code-switching on a community-wide basis, focusing on speakers of varying bilingual abilities. Inclusion in the sample of non-fluent bilinguals requires modifying our previous definition of code-switching. In the speech of non-fluent bilinguals, segments may remain unintegrated into L_2 on one or more linguistic levels, due to transference of patterns from L_1. This combination of features leads to what is commonly known as a 'foreign accent', and is detectable even in the monolingual L_2 speech of the speaker, as in (3) below, which was rendered wholly in Puerto Rican Spanish phonology:

(3) That's what he said. [da 'waɾi se] (58/100)[3]

In order to consider an utterance such as (3), which occurs in an otherwise entirely Spanish context, as a code-switch from Spanish into English, we have refined the criteria for identifying a code-switch in terms of the type of integration as in Table 10.1.

The example of Type I, *mogueen*, is phonologically (phon), morphologically (morph) and syntactically (syn) integrated into the base language, although etymologically a loan word from English 'mug'. It is here considered an instance of monolingual Spanish discourse. In contrast, Type 4 segments are totally unintegrated into the patterns of the base language. This sort of code-switch occurs most typically in the speech of balanced bilinguals. Type 2 follows English phonological and morphological patterns, but violates English syntactic patterns. The example shown follows the Spanish syntactic pattern of adjective placement. This type of segment is also considered a code-switch into English, although one which violates the 'equivalence constraint'. Although Type 3 involves phonological integration into Spanish (i.e. follows Puerto Rican Spanish phonological rules), it is morphologically, syntactically and lexically English. Thus the example of Type 3 is considered a code-switch into English, rendered with a 'foreign accent'. Spontaneous switches of words, sentences and larger units at a turn boundary, not involving any change in interlocutors, were also considered to be code-switches if they exhibited Types 2, 3 or 4 of integration in Table 10.1.

Table 10.1   Identification of code-switching according to type of integration into the base language *

| Type | Levels of integration into base language | | | Code-switch | Example |
	phon	morph	syn		
1	✓	✓	✓	no	Es posible que te MOGUEEN. (They might mug you.) (002/1)
2	–	–	✓	yes	Las palabras HEAVY-DUTY, bien grandes, se me han olvidado. (I've forgotten the real big, heavy-duty words.) (40/485)
3	✓	–	–	yes	[da 'waɾi se] (58/100)
4	–	–	–	yes	No creo que son FIFTY-DOLLAR SUEDE ONES. (I don't think they're fifty-dollar suede ones.) (05/271)

Note: * We follow Hasselmo (1970) in designating as the 'base' language that language to which a majority of phonological and morphological features of discourse can be attributed.

3   Theoretical background

Much of the literature on code-switching (e.g. Gumperz and Hernández-Chávez, 1970; Gumperz, 1971a; 1976; McClure, 1977; Valdés-Fallis, 1976; 1978) has focused on its social and pragmatic functions. While there is little doubt that functional factors are the strongest constraints on the occurrence of code-switching, it is clear that linguistic factors also play a role. This paper demonstrates how the incorporation of both functional and linguistic factors into a single model is necessary to account for code-switching behaviour.

Although in some of the earlier literature (e.g. Lance, 1975) the occurrence of code-switching was characterized as random, most investigators now appear to agree that in many aspects it is rule-governed, despite the fact that there is little agreement on the precise nature of the rules involved. Proposed grammatical rules have generally taken the form of categorical constraints based on acceptability judgments of invented instances of code-switching (Gingràs, 1974; Timm, 1975; Gumperz, 1976). While acceptability judgments provide a manageable way to tap community grammar norms, their use is questionable in the case of an overtly stigmatized sociolinguistic marker, as is the case of code-switching (Gumperz, 1971a). Moreover, studies of code-switching performance in two widely separated bilingual communities have independently yielded counterexamples to these categorical constraints (Pfaff, 1975; 1976; Poplack, 1978/81).

More importantly, the proposed constraints are not of the general nature one would wish to ascribe to linguistic universals.[4] In Poplack (1978/81) two syntactic constraints on code-switching were suggested, which together were general enough to account for all instances of code-switching in the Puerto Rican data on which that study was based, as well as the Chicano data on which the majority of the code-switching literature is based, and at the same time restrictive enough not to generate instances of non-occurring code-switches:

(a) *The free morpheme constraint*: Codes may be switched after any constituent in discourse provided that constituent is not a bound morpheme.[5] This constraint holds true for all linguistic levels but the phonological, for reasons explained above. Thus, a segment such as (4) may be produced, where the first syllable follows the Caribbean Spanish tendency to aspirate /s/ before voiceless consonants, while the second syllable follows English phonological patterns. This should be seen as aiming for, but missing, an English target, rather than a switch between two bound morphemes. However, items such as (5) where the Spanish bound morpheme *-iendo* ('-ing') is affixed to the English root 'eat', have not been attested in this or any other study of code-switching to my knowledge, unless one of the morphemes has been integrated phonologically into the language of the other.

> (4)   una buena EXCUSE [eh'kjuws]
>   'a good excuse'
> (5)   *EAT – iendo
>   'eating'

Included under this constraint are idiomatic expressions, such as *cross my fingers* [sic] *and hope to die* and *si Dios quiere y la virgen* ('God and the virgin willing') which are considered to behave like bound morphemes in that they show a strong tendency to be uttered monolingually.

(b) *The equivalence constraint*: Code-switches will tend to occur at points in discourse where juxtaposition of L_1 and L_2 elements does not violate a syntactic rule of either language, i.e. at points around which the surface structures of the two languages map onto each other. According to this simple constraint, a switch is inhibited from occurring within a constituent generated by a rule from one language which is not shared by the other.[6] This can be seen in Figure 10.1, where the dotted lines indicate permissible switch points and the arrows indicate ways in which constitutents from two languages map onto each other. The speaker's actual utterance is reproduced in (C).

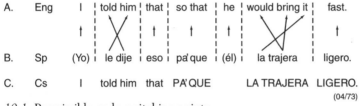

A.   Eng   I   told him   that   so that   he   would bring it   fast.

B.   Sp   (Yo)   le dije   eso   pa'que   (él)   la trajera   ligero.

C.   Cs   I   told him   that   PA'QUE   LA TRAJERA   LIGERO.
(04/73)

Figure 10.1 Permissible code-switching points

An analysis based on the equivalence constraint may be applied to the by now classical examples in (6) which were constructed by Gingràs (1974) and tested for acceptability on a group of Chicano bilinguals.

> (6)   a.   El MAN que CAME ayer WANTS JOHN comprar A CAR nuevo.
>   'The man who came yesterday wants John to buy a new car.'
>   b.   Tell Larry QUE SE CALLE LA BOCA.
>   'Tell Larry to shut his mouth.'

Gingràs claims that (6a), in which codes are switched after almost every other word, is 'in some very basic sense different' from (6b), where the switching occurs between major constituents (1974: 170). While it is true, as we will see below, that major constituents are switched more frequently than smaller ones, we suggest that constituent size only partially explains the difference between the two sentences, and that the important distinction is with respect to the equivalence constraint.[7] The sentence structures in (6a) and (6b) are similar in that both include a verb phrase and a verb phrase complement. In each, the verbs belong to a class which in English requires that an infinitive complementizer rule apply to the verb phrase complement, while Spanish makes use of a subjunctive complementizer in this same construction.

Sentence (6a) violates the equivalence constraint because it applies an English infinitive complementizer rule, which is not shared by Spanish, to the verb phrase complement. Because the code switch did take place in this invented example, an English rule was lexicalized in Spanish, yielding a construction which could not have been generated by a Spanish rule, and which is therefore ungrammatical by Spanish standards. On the other hand, the first portion of (6a) was generated by rules which are shared by English and Spanish (i.e. marked for both L_1 and L_2). The L_1 and L_2 versions map onto each other, constituent-by-constituent and element-by-element. A code-switch may therefore occur at any point within the main clause and the utterance remains grammatical by both L_1 and L_2 standards. Structures in discourse to which a rule from L_1 but not from L_2 must categorically apply were found to be avoided as switch points by the balanced bilingual. There were no cases like (6a) in our data, and furthermore, all 26 of Gingràs' Chicano informants found it to be unacceptable as well. Constituents whose structures are non-equivalent in L_1 and L_2 tend to be uttered monolingually in actual performance. This occurred in (C) in Figure 10.1 (as well as in Gingràs' example (6b)), where the verb phrase complements have undergone the Spanish subjunctive complementizer rule and are also lexicalized completely in Spanish. Ninety-four per cent of Gingràs' informants also found (6b) to be an acceptable utterance.

An additional site of non-equivalence in (6a) is the object noun phrase in the embedded sentence: A CAR *nuevo*. English and Spanish have non-equivalent rules for adjective movement. In English, attributive adjectives typically precede the head noun, whereas in Spanish they typically follow it. A closed set of Spanish adjectives may also precede the noun. Switching an adjective but not the noun within the noun phrase, by following *either* L_1 or L_2 adjective placement rules for adjectives other than those in the closed set, results in a construction which is judged unacceptable by Timm's Chicano informants (1975: 479) and 'fairly unacceptable' by Gingràs' informants (1974: 172). Such constructions occur very rarely in our own performance data.

Simultaneous operation of the free morpheme and the equivalence constraints permits only code-switched utterances which, when translated into either language, are grammatical by both L_1 and L_2 standards, and indicate a large degree of competence in both languages.

One might ask then whether the formulation of these constraints was not simply a consequence of having studied a balanced bilingual speaker: it is not surprising, although it required empirical proof, that an individual with an extensive repertoire in more than one language can manipulate them without violating the grammatical rules of either. But what happens in the case of non-fluent bilinguals? Being clearly dominant in one of the two languages, are they forced to switch into it from time to time because of lack of lexical or syntactic availability when speaking the other?

Weinreich (1953) characterized the ideal bilingual as an individual who 'switches from one language to the other according to appropriate changes in the speech situation (interlocutor, topics, etc.) but not in an unchanged speech situation, and CERTAINLY NOT WITHIN A SINGLE SENTENCE' (p. 73; emphasis added). He further speculated that there must be considerable individual differences between those who have control over their switching and those who have difficulty in maintaining or switching codes as required (p. 73).

The phenomenon of code-switching has been a point of contention in assessing community identity. While intellectuals have seen language mixture as constituting evidence of the disintegration of the Puerto Rican Spanish language and culture (e.g. de Granda, 1968; Varo, 1971), community members themselves appear to consider various bilingual behaviours to be defining features of their identity (Attinasi, 1979). The opinion that code-switching represents a deviation from some bilingual 'norm' is also wide-spread in educational circles today (LaFontaine, 1975). It is our contention here that code-switching is itself a norm in specific speech situations which exist in stable bilingual communities. Furthermore, as we will demonstrate, satisfaction of this norm requires considerably more linguistic competence in two languages than has heretofore been noted.

The present study addresses these issues by analysing the code-switching behaviour of twenty Puerto Rican speakers of varying degrees of reported and observed bilingual ability.

4   Hypothesis

As documented in Poplack (1978/81), a single individual may demonstrate more than one configuration or type of code-switching. One type involves a high proportion of intra-sentential switching, as in (7) below.

> (7) a.   Why make Carol SENTARSE ATRAS PA' QUE (sit in the back so) everybody has to move PA' QUE SE SALGA (for her to get out)? (04/439)
>
>   b.   He was sitting down EN LA CAMA, MIRANDONOS PELEANDO, Y (in bed, watching us fighting and) really, I don't remember SI EL NOS SEPARO (if he separated us) or whatever, you know. (43/412)

We refer to this as a more complex or 'intimate' type, since a code-switched segment, and those around it, must conform to the underlying syntactic rules of two languages which bridge constituents and link them together grammatically.

Another, less intimate type, is characterized by relatively more tag switches and single noun switches. These are often heavily loaded in ethnic content and would be placed low on a scale of translatability, as in (8).

> (8) a.   Vendía arroz (He sold rice) 'N SHIT. (07/79)
>
>   b.   Salían en sus carros y en sus (They would go out in their cars and in their) SNOWMOBILES. (08/192)

Many investigators do not consider switches like those in (8) to represent true instances of code-switching, but rather to constitute an emblematic part of the speaker's monolingual style (Gumperz, 1971a; Wentz, 1977). It will also be noted that their insertion in discourse has few, if any, ramifications for the remainder of the sentence. Tags are freely moveable constituents which may be inserted almost anywhere in the sentence without fear of violating any grammatical rule. The ease with which single nouns may be switched is attested to by the fact that of all grammatical categories, they have been found to be the most frequently switched (e.g. Timm, 1975; Wentz, 1977).

It was found that the choice of intimate versus emblematic code-switching is heavily dependent on the ethnic group membership of the interlocutor in the case of the balanced bilingual, who has the linguistic ability to make such a choice. In-group membership favours intra-sentential code-switching, while non-group membership favours emblematic switching. In other words, that type of switch which all investigators agree to be 'true' instances of code-switching was mainly reserved for communication with another in-group member. In considering whether this pattern holds true more generally, we first note that the type of code-switching used by non-fluent bilinguals must be further constrained by bilingual ability. The research described in the following sections examines the extent to which the bilingual competence evinced by the skilled code-switching behaviour of a balanced bilingual is shared by the non-fluent bilinguals in the same speech community. This will have ramifications for the possible use of code-switching as an indicator of bilingual ability.

With the inclusion of non-fluent bilinguals in the sample, three alternative outcomes may be hypothesized. The speaker may engage in both intimate (intra-sentential) and emblematic switching, regardless of her competence in the two languages, thereby running the risk of rendering utterances which will be ungrammatical for L_1, L_2 or both (and hence providing a principled basis for the claim that code-switching represents a deviation from some norm). On the other hand, the speaker may avoid those intra-sentential switches which are syntactically risky. This might assure grammatical utterances. Such results would weaken the claims that code-switching occurs due to lack of availability in L_2. Logically, there is a third possibility, that the speaker will not switch at all. This need not be considered; although two members of the sample switched only once each in two-and-a-half hours of speech, there was no one who did not switch at all.

5   The sample

5.1   Block description

102nd Street is located in the heart of El Barrio, one of the oldest and until recently the largest Puerto Rican community in the United States. Although Puerto Ricans have now dispersed to other areas of Manhattan and other boroughs in New York City, we estimate that the population on 102nd Street is still at least 95% Puerto Rican.

The block, which is identified by the census to be one of the lowest socio-economic areas of the City, is largely residential. It consists of 16 three- to five-storey tenements housing some 600 people, and is bounded by major avenues on the East and West. There is a small number of commercial establishments on the block, including two *bodegas*, an *alcapurria* stand, two Hispanic social clubs, a numbers parlor, a pet store, a vegetable market, and a plumbing supply shop.

Block life is active. It is not uncommon to see groups of people congregating on the stoops, and in the summer months, children play in the streets and adults set up tables on the sidewalks for domino games.

The block has had a stable Puerto Rican population since the 1930s, and today includes third- and even fourth-generation family members. Although uncharacteristically homogeneous with regard to ethnicity, block residents are heterogeneous with regard to personal history. About half of the block residents were born and raised in Puerto Rico. These are mostly older people, who tend to be Spanish dominant or monolingual. The younger people were generally born and raised in El Barrio, and most are either English dominant or bilingual. This fact and the low median age of the population (three-fourths are under 45 years of age) match the general demographic characteristics of the New York City Puerto Rican population in general (United States Department of Labor, 1975: 44).

Extended participant observation of 102nd Street indicates that block residents may be divided into nine social networks, which though not mutually exclusive, are seen to reappear consistently in the public life of the block. The informants for this study are drawn from two of the more closely observed of these networks.

Half of the sample belongs to a network centered around the *Gavilanes* social club. Participants in this network are linked through friendship or familial ties as well as participation in common club activities. The group is male-dominated, and its members are on public display more than other block residents since they are out on the street for large periods of the day. Members range in age from the early twenties to the fifties and most of the males were employed during the period of observation (1975–1977). (Only one female in the present sample had paid employment during this time.) The group includes both the Island-born and raised, who are Spanish dominant, and New York City-born and raised, who are English-dominant or bilingual. Group members generally accommodate to the older, Island-born members by speaking Spanish.

An additional eight informants belong to a network whose members congregate around the numbers parlor (*Banca*), a center of lively social activity on the block. Calling the numbers and passing them on by word-of-mouth (in Spanish) is a daily event in block life. Like members of the *Gavilanes* group, *Banca* group members range in age from the twenties to the fifties; however, both men and women participate in this network. Friendship and familial ties are less of a factor in linking group members than shared participation in activities in and around the *Banca*. Members of this network were all born and raised in Puerto Rico, and are Spanish-dominant or bilingual. *Banca* members were for the most part unemployed during the period of observation.

Of the two remaining informants, one does not participate in any network significantly more than in any other, and the second is a recent arrival to the block. Both are Spanish-dominant.

5.2 The informants

The twenty informants in the sample were selected primarily on the basis of two parameters: age of arrival in the United States, and (ethnographically) observed language preference. This choice was made in order to study the effects of bilingual ability and community influence on code-switching. Sample members are fairly evenly divided between:

- those who arrived as children or were born in the United States (0–6 years of age), when parental influence on child language use is greatest;
- those who arrived as pre-adolescents (7–12), when peer influence encroaches on parental influence;
- those who arrived as adolescents (13–17), when peer influence on language choice is greatest (Payne, 1976; Poplack, 1978); and
- those who arrived as adults, when patterns of language use tend to have crystallized.

About half of the speakers were observed to be Spanish-dominant; about 10% English-dominant; and the rest bilingual. With some exceptions these observations confirm the speakers' own self-reports (cf. Section 5.4 below).

In addition, several other demographic, ethnographic and attitudinal factors which could affect language use were studied.

5.3   Demographic characteristics of the sample

Eleven of the twenty informants are male, nine are female, and 75% of them are between 21 and 40 years of age. Regardless of age of arrival, all but two have spent ten years or more in the United States, and the majority (60%) has been there for more than twenty years. Since duration of stay is probably overshadowed by other influences on linguistic behaviour after about two years (Heidelberger Forschungsprojekt 'Pidgin-Deutsch', 1977), the level of competence in English of this group is not likely to change much with increased residence in the United States.

Most of the sample (65%) have also spent ten or more years in Puerto Rico, either early in life (only one informant was born in the United States), or including extended sojourns after having migrated to the continental United States. There is some correlation between speaker age and time spent in Puerto Rico: the older speakers are generally those who have spent most time on the Island. However, the majority of the sample (70%) visits the Island infrequently: less than every two years. In sum, it is reasonable to expect that these speakers have all also acquired some competence in Spanish, whether it is put to use at present or not.

Sample members report more years of schooling than the general Puerto Rican population in New York City. Seventy percent have had at least some high school education; this includes 20% who have either graduated high school or had some college education.

Slightly less than half the sample was employed at the time of the study, and these mainly in the service sectors of the workforce: baker, cook, medical technician, counterman, etc. Of these, the majority (70%) is employed off the block.

5.4   Language-oriented characteristics of the sample

The informants responded to a language-attitude questionnaire, designed to tap various aspects of language skill by self-report as well as community attitudes towards Puerto Rican language and ethnicity.

When asked if they considered themselves 'mainly Spanish speakers, English speakers, or bilinguals', slightly more than half (55%) of the sample claimed to be mainly Spanish speakers. The others considered themselves bilingual. No one claimed to be mainly an English speaker, reflecting the underrating on the part of speakers of their English language skills. There is doubtless some correlation between this finding and the fact that all speakers report having learned Spanish in early childhood (between the ages of two and seven), with the majority (75%) having learned it in Puerto Rico. On the other hand, only two informants learned English in early childhood. Sixty percent of the sample learned English between the ages of seven and 21, and all speakers report having learned English in the United States. When asked to rate their competence in both Spanish and English on a seven-point scale, speakers' ratings are consistent with their verbal self-description. Almost all (95%) rate themselves as having more than median proficiency in Spanish, while less than half (45%) claim this for English. If the hypothesis that code-switching is caused by lack of availability in L_2 were correct, it would appear that members of this sample population would favour switching into Spanish from an English base.

5.5 Attitudinal characteristics of the sample

Our language-attitude questionnaire also seeks to tap speakers' feelings towards language as it relates to Puerto Rican culture and ethnicity. Responses to attitude questions are less readily interpretable than reports of language use. On an ethnic-identity scale based on questions about pride in being Puerto Rican, feelings towards assimilation and speakers' characterization of nationality (e.g. Puerto Rican, *Nuyorican*, American, etc.), the majority (65%) revealed clear positive identification as Puerto Ricans. When asked to assess how important the Spanish language is to 'Puerto Ricanness', 90% felt that Spanish is 'important' or 'very important' to being a Puerto Rican. This attitude was summarized by Sally:

> SI TU ERES PUERTORRIQUEÑO (if you're Puerto Rican), your father's a Puerto Rican, you should at least DE VEZ EN CUANDO (sometimes), you know, HABLAR ESPAÑOL (speak Spanish). (34/25)

Nevertheless, a majority (60%) also felt that Puerto Rican monolingual English speakers did not represent a divisive force in the Puerto Rican community in New York City.

When asked if there was 'anything you could say in Spanish that you could not say in English', or vice-versa, 60% of the speakers felt that there was nothing that could be said in one language that could not be translated into the other. For the most part (75%), the speakers in this sample are also aware that code-switching is a frequent and wide-spread phenomenon in their community. When asked if they thought that 'few, some or many speakers mixed languages', three-fourths of the sample thought that many people code-switched. Such awareness of community and individual behavioural norms with regard to code-switching was again voiced by Sally, who provided the title for this paper.

> Sometimes I'll start a sentence in Spanish Y TERMINO EN ESPAÑOL [sic] ('and finish in Spanish'). (34/489)[8]

This opinion corroborates Pedraza's ethnographic observation that a majority of block residents code-switched somewhat or frequently.

In sum, although the Spanish language is overwhelmingly considered an integral part of being Puerto Rican, and in spite of the fact that only a minority feels that one or the other of the languages may be better for saying certain things, ethnographic observation, quantitative sociolinguistic analysis, and speakers' own self-reports all indicate that code-switching is an integral part of community speech norms on 102nd Street. Code-switches provoked by lack of availability or utilized as an emblem of ethnic identity appear, then, to be only weak factors in speakers' perception of their own behaviour.

6 Methodology

6.1 Data collection

The quantitative analyses which follow are based on recorded speech data in both interview and 'natural' settings. Pedraza's membership in the Puerto Rican community and his familiarity with the setting and participants allowed him to enter local network situations, such as domino games or *bochinche* (gossip) sessions, and simply turn on his tape-recorder without causing an apparent break in the conversational flow. In addition, he carried out a 'sociolinguistic interview'[9] with each informant aiming to elicit casual, undirected speech, and administered the detailed attitude questionnaire mentioned above. Our data, then, range from the vernacular speech of informal, intra-group communication, to the more formal discourse used in discussing concepts such as language and culture.

The importance of data-collection techniques cannot be overemphasized, particularly in the study of a phenomenon such as code-switching, which cannot be directly elicited. The actual occurrence of a switch is constrained, probably more than by any other factor, by the norms or the perceived norms of the speech situation. The most important of these norms for the balanced bilingual was found (Poplack, 1978/81) to be the ethnicity of the interlocutor, once other criteria (appropriateness, formality of speech situation) were met. The balanced bilingual speaker switched four times as frequently with an in-group interlocutor as with a non-member and, what is more, used a much larger percentage of intimate switches with the in-group member. Since the data utilized in this study are representative of in-group interaction only, they are presumably characterized not only by a higher rate of code-switching, but also by a larger proportion of intra-sentential switches, than would have been the case if they had been collected by a non-member.

6.2   Coding procedures

Sixty-six hours of tape-recorded speech in which each informant participated in each of the three speech situations provided 1,835 instances of code-switching. Transcription, coding and analysis of the data were carried out with the invaluable collaboration of Alicia Pousada. The informants appeared on tape, either alone or in a group, from a minimum of two-and-a-half hours to a maximum of eleven hours. Each instance of a switch was coded as to its syntactic function in the utterance, along with the syntactic categories of the segments which preceded and followed it. We also noted the language of the switch, whether it was preceded or followed by editing phenomena (hesitations, false starts, etc.), whether it constituted a repetition of the preceding syntactic category, whether it was a single noun switch in an otherwise L_2 base, and if so, whether it was an ethnically loaded item.

In each instance, the largest complete constituent next to the switch in the syntactic derivation of the utterance was considered to be the syntactic category of the segment adjacent to the switch. Thus, *con los puños* in (9a) was coded as a prepositional phrase preceded by an independent clause and followed by a tag. *Promising* in (9b) was coded as a verb preceded by an auxiliary and followed by an object noun phrase, since all of them are dominated by the same verb phrase node. *Que* in (9c) was coded as a subordinate conjunction preceded by an independent clause and followed by a subordinate clause. This method was used to determine syntactic category of the code-switch and segment following it as well.

(9) a. But I wanted to fight her CON LOS PUÑOS (with my fists), you know.
(43/356)

    b. Siempre está PROMISING cosas. (He's always promising things.)
       (04/408)
    c. I could understand QUE (that) you don't know how to speak
       Spanish. ¿VERDAD? (right?). (34/24)

Other segments of varying syntactic make-up, but which exercised a consistent function in discourse, were coded according to that function. Examples of these are fillers, e.g. *este* (umm), *I mean*; interjections, e.g. *¡ay, Dios mio!* (oh, my God!), *shit!*; tags, e.g. *¿entiendes?* (understand?), *you know*; idiomatic expressions, e.g. *y toda esa mierda* (and all that shit), *no way*; quotations, e.g. put down *'menos'* (less). These are segments which are less intimately linked with the remainder of the utterance, insofar as they may occur freely at any point in the sentence. As will be seen, they contrast with the intra-sentential switches, which must obey sentence-internal syntactic constraints.

Certain switched segments were larger than a single constituent, as in (10) below. Hasselmo (1970) has called this 'unlimited switching'. These cases, which were relatively rare, required special coding conventions. The only type with non-negligible frequency involved moveable constituents like *sometimes* and *honey* in (10). Since these constituents do not form an integral part of the syntactic structure of the sentence, they were relegated to the category of intervening material between the switch and the adjacent syntactic categories, and the switches were considered to have occurred between the independent clause and the adverb in (10a), and between the verb phrase and the adverbial phrase in (10b).

    (10) a. No tienen ni tiempo (they don't even have time) SOMETIMES
          FOR THEIR OWN KIDS, AND YOU KNOW WHO I'M TALKING ABOUT.
          (04/17)
        b. Se sentó (he sat down), HONEY, AWAY FROM US. (04/433)

In a case like (11), utterances were divided by sentence boundary. *Pa' muchos sitios* was coded as a switched prepositional phrase in Spanish preceded by an independent clause and followed by a sentence.[10] *With my husband* was coded as a switched prepositional phrase in English preceded by an independent clause and followed by a pause.

    (11) And from there I went to live PA' MUCHOS SITIOS (in a lot of places).
        Después viví en la ciento diecisiete (then I lived on 117th) WITH MY
        HUSBAND. (42/76)

It will be noted that the analysis in (11) involves a change of base language. The first prepositional phrase is considered a switch into Spanish from an English base, while the second is considered a switch into English from a Spanish base. While speakers who are dominant in one language show a strong tendency to switch into L_2 from an L_1 base, more balanced bilinguals often alternate base languages within the same discourse.[11] An example of this can be seen in (12) which represents a single discourse, and where segments to the left of the slashes exhibit a base language different from those to the right of the slashes.

    (12) But I used to eat the BOFE, the brain. And then they stopped selling it
        because TENIAN, ESTE, LE ENCONTRARON QUE TENIA (they had, uh,

they found out that it had) worms. I used to make some BOFE! / Después yo hacía uno d'esos (then I would make one of those) CON-COCTIONS: THE GARLIC con cebolla, y hacía un mojo, y yo dejaba que se curara eso (with onion, and I'd make a sauce, and I'd let that sit) FOR A COUPLE OF HOURS. / Then you be drinking and eating that shit. Wooh! It's like eating anchovies when you're drinking. Delicious! (04/101)

6.3   Non-code-switches

Certain borderline alternations between L_1 and L_2 were excluded from this study. One type involves switched items which have been referred to by Hasselmo (1970) as socially integrated into the language of the community: segments which are repeated often enough in a certain language to be regarded as habitualized. These may or may not be phonologically integrated into the base language; and should not be confused with the types of integration shown in Table 10.1:

> (13)   a.   Ay, ¡qué CUTE [kju] se ve! (34/202)
>   'How cute he looks!'
>   b.   Eso es un TEAM [tiŋ]: 'Palo Viejo'. (37/42)
>   'That's a a team: "Palo Viejo".'
>   c.   En ese tiempo había muchos JUNKIES [jɔŋki]. (34/40)
>   'At that time there were a lot of junkies.'

Switches into L_2 designating food names, proper names and place names were also omitted from this study, except when there was an acceptable L_2 alternative which was not used, e.g. *Puerto Rico* [pɔɔə'əiykow] ~ [pwɛrtə'xikɔ].

Also excluded were translations in response to requests for information, as in (14a), L_2 segments followed by an explanation in L_1, as in (14b), switches accompanied by metalinguistic comments, as in (14c), and instances of 'externally conditioned switching' (Clyne, 1972: 70) in which the interlocutor switched languages within the same discourse and the informant followed suit, as in (14d).

> (14)   a.   *A*:   Lo pusieron un . . . ¿cómo se dice? ¿un tutone?
>   (They gave him a – how do you call it? tuton?)
>   *B*:   TUTOR? (52/229)
>   b.   But I used to eat the BOFE, the brain. (04/101)
>   c.   I'm one of those real what you call in Spanish PENDEJAS (jerks), you know. (04/158)
>   d.   *A*:   I had a dream yesterday, last night.
>   *B*:   ¿DE QUE NUMERO? (What number?)
>   *A*:   EL CERO SETENTA Y CINCO. (Zero seventy-five.) (34/040)

6.4   Quantitative analysis of the data

We are concerned here with both linguistic and extra-linguistic questions, and we shall attempt to incorporate the answers into a single analytic model. The linguistic questions concern the surface configuration of the switches. Are there some sorts of constituents in discourse which can be switched and others which cannot? Are there constituents which tend to be switched into one language rather than the other? In what ways do switched items combine with unswitched portions of discourse?

The extra-linguistic questions concern the code-switchers. Can the community as a whole be characterized by some code-switching type, or are there speakers who favour certain switch types over others? In the latter case, what are the demographic, attitudinal, and social factors which contribute to the occurrence of one type over another, and what is the comparative effect of each?

To answer these questions the following quantitative analyses were performed on the data. The syntactic category of the switched item was cross-tabulated first with the preceding and then the following syntactic category to ascertain whether certain points (as, for example, the point between determiner and noun) in discourse were more favourable to the occurrence of a switch than others. Also cross-tabulated were switched item by language, to see if certain switch types were favoured by one language over another, and switched item by speaker, to see if there was any difference in switching behaviour among speakers.

The cross-tabulations revealed that speakers could be divided into two groups: one which favoured extra-sentential switches, and another which tended towards the intra-sentential, or more intimate type. The code-switching data were subsequently collapsed into two categories: intra-sentential and extra-sentential switches. These categories were then cross-tabulated individually with the demographic, attitudinal and language-oriented characteristics of the informants to discover which, if any, have an influence on the choice of one code-switch over the other. Tests of association were applied to each of these cross-tabulations to determine the significance of the extra-linguistic factors for the occurrence of one code-switching type over the other.

Having thus been able to determine a dependent variable (in this case, code-switch type), its relevant variants (intra-sentential and extra-sentential code-switching), and the total population of utterances in which the variation occurs (i.e. the total corpus of switched items), the significance tests made it possible to suggest which extra-linguistic factors might reasonably be expected to affect the relative frequency of the two types of code-switches. Because these factors may be correlated among themselves within the sample and have correlated effects on code-switching type, it was then necessary to use multivariate statistical techniques to determine which factors made a significant contribution, independent of the effects of other factors, to the choice of code-switch type. Because of the binomial nature of the data and their uneven distribution among the different possible configurations of factors, a maximum likelihood approach was taken for the evaluation of factor effects, together with log-likelihood tests of significance.

7   Results

Perhaps the most striking result of this study is that there were virtually no instances of ungrammatical combinations of L_1 and L_2 in the 1,835 switches studied regardless of the bilingual ability of the speaker.

Our hypotheses as to the nature of syntactic constraints on code-switching in the speech of the balanced bilingual, i.e. the free morpheme constraint and the equivalence constraint, are generally corroborated by the present investigation of both balanced and non-fluent bilinguals. There were no examples of switches between bound morphemes of the type *eat -iendo* mentioned in (5) above. A small number (five, or less than 1% of the data) of switches within idiomatic expressions did occur, however, as in (15a), where a Spanish expression is broken up, and (15b), where an English expression is broken up.

(15) a. Estamos como marido y WOMAN. (We are like man and wife.
        < Sp. Estamos como *marido y mujer*.) (05/141)
     b. Mi mai tuvo que ir a firmar y SHIT pa' sacarme, YOU KNOW. (My
        mom had to go sign 'n shit to get me out, you know.) (07/058)

A small number of switches which violated the equivalence constraint also occurred (11, or less than 1% of the data). The majority (7/11) of these involved adjective placement, a rule which is not shared by L_1 and L_2. This can be seen in (16a), where adjective placement follows Spanish but not English rules, and (16b), where the reverse is true.

(16) a. Tenían patas flacas, pechos FLAT. (They had skinny legs, flat chests.)
        (09432)
     b. I got a lotta BLANQUITO (whitey) friends. (34/274)

A strong tendency to avoid non-equivalence is nonetheless manifested in the fact that 88% (49/56) of the adjectival forms in the corpus are either predicate adjectives, which have equivalent surface structures in Spanish and English, or members of the subset of Spanish adjectives which precede the noun, as in English.

The proportion of switched items which when combined with the rest of the utterance did not follow grammatical rules shared by both L_1 and L_2 is negligible. (Of this small number, NONE of the constructions was idiosyncratic, or based on rules which were not drawn from one or the other of the grammars.) This finding is strong evidence that alternation between two languages requires a high level of bilingual competence. Code-switching involves enough knowledge of two (or more) grammatical systems to allow the speaker to draw from each system only those rules which the other shares, when alternating one language with another. Surprisingly enough, this knowledge appears to be shared by even the non-fluent bilinguals in the sample. The way in which these latter speakers are able to fulfill the requirement of grammaticality, despite their limited competence in one of the codes, is examined in Section 7.5 below.

7.1   Discourse functions of code-switching

The finding that code-switching constitutes the skilled manipulation of overlapping sections of two (or more) grammars is further corroborated by an examination of some of the ways in which a code-switch functions in discourse. One of the characteristics of skilled code-switching is a smooth transition between L_1 and L_2 elements, unmarked by false starts, hesitations or lengthy pauses. When we examine the data we find that the transition between the preceding category and the switched item is made smoothly, i.e. with no editing phenomena, 96% of the time, while the transition between switched item and following syntactic category is made smoothly 98% of the time. Other characteristics of skilled code-switching include a seeming 'unawareness' of the alternation between languages, i.e. the switched item is not accompanied by metalinguistic commentary, it does not constitute a repetition of all or part of the preceding segment, nor is it repeated by the following segment; switches are made up of larger segments than just single nouns inserted into an otherwise L_2 sentence; and code-switching is used for purposes other than that of conveying untranslatable items.

On examining the data for the sample as a whole, we find that these characteristics are strongly in evidence: the switched item only constitutes a repetition of the preceding segment 5% of the time, while the following segment repeats all or part of the switched item only 8% of the time. Single noun switches constitute only 10% of the data; of these, less than one-fourth represent items which are ethnically loaded.

In other words, features known to be characteristic of communication with a non-group member, such as high percentages of single noun switches used to convey notions which are difficult to translate, are not defining features of intra-group communication.

7.2 Linguistic properties of switched segments

Having established that switching occurs in a smooth fashion, we turn our attention to the nature of the switches themselves. Which constituents are switched, and in what ways do they combine with preceding and following segments? Do certain combinations tend to occur more regularly?

Fifteen syntactic categories whose occurrence is dependent on sentence-internal constraints were extracted from the data, along with seven extra-sentential, or freely distributable categories. These appear in Table 10.2.

The relative frequencies with which constituents may be switched, indicated in Table 10.2, largely confirm the findings of other studies (Gumperz, 1976; Wentz, 1977; Poplack, 1978/81). As can be seen, full sentences are the most frequently switched constituent, making up 20% of the data. Extra-sentential code-switching types, which require less knowledge of two grammars since they are freely distributable within discourse, together constitute about half the data.

Among the intra-sentential switches, we find single nouns to be the most frequently switched category, again confirming the findings of other studies. Table 10.2 also reveals a tendency to switch major constituents, which account for about 60% of the intra-sentential data, more frequently than smaller ones. This provides additional support for the equivalence constraint, which predicts that whole constituents will be switched rather than elements within them if the syntactic rule for generating the constituent is not shared by both L_1 and L_2.

7.3 Language of the switch

Table 10.2 also shows the frequencies with which the syntactic categories under investigation are produced in each language. As can be seen, with a few exceptions, segments are about as likely to be switched into English as into Spanish, providing further evidence for the suggestion that the code-switching mode proceeds from a single grammar.

Examining the data in Table 10.2 more closely, we may test whether the rate of occurrence of a given syntactic category of a switch is significantly different from one language to the other. For this we compared a log-likelihood of a rate estimate for the two languages separately compared to that for the combined data. Significantly more

Table 10.2 Code-switching by syntactic category and language *

	Syntactic category of CS (code-switch)	*Number of CS from English to Spanish*	*Number of CS from Spanish to English*	*Percentage of total CS*	*N*
Intra-sentential	determiner	3	0	0.2	3
	(single) noun	34	141	9.5	175
	subject noun phrase	44	25	3.8	69
	object noun phrase	62	78	7.6	140
	auxiliary	0	0	0.0	0
	verb	6	13	1.0	19
	verb phrase	27	13	2.2	40
	independent clause	44	35	4.3	79
	subordinate (and relative) clause	53	23	4.1	76
	adjective	3	12	0.8	15
	predicate adjective	6	37	2.3	43
	adverb	14	33	2.6	47
	preposition	2	0	0.1	2
	phrases (prep. adj. advb. inf)	55	39	5.1	94
	conjunctions (subordinate, coordinate, relative pronoun)	33	16	2.7	49
Extra-sentential	sentence	201	171	20.3	372
	filler	9	11	1.1	20
	interjection	26	89	6.3	115
	idiomatic expression	8	23	1.7	31
	quotation	20	14	1.9	34
	tag	9	403	22.5	412
	Totals	659	1176		1835

Note: *Nouns and verbs were counted as noun phrases or verb phrases respectively if they functioned within the utterance.

switches from Spanish into English were found for four categories: tags, interjections, single nouns, and predicate adjectives. The latter is probably an artifact of sparse data, but the results for tags, interjections, and single nouns have important interpretations.

It is not surprising that bilinguals residing in an English-speaking society should favour English noun switches over Spanish. Interjections and tags, as will be shown in Section 7.5, are precisely the switch types which are favoured by Spanish-dominant speakers. These speakers not only switch almost uniquely into English from a Spanish base, but are also distinguishable from the bilinguals by the type of constituents they switch.

The statistical analysis shows that aside from the four switch types which are favoured from Spanish into English, most of the rest tend to be switched significantly more from English into Spanish. This result is an artifact of the other, however, and when the tag, interjection, and noun switches are removed from the data, almost all of the remaining switches show no significant rate differences between the two languages.

7.4   Combinability of switched segments

In order to ascertain points within the sentence at which segments may be switched, intra-sententially switched items were cross-tabulated with segments preceding and following them. In a 225-cell table generated by the 15 possibilities of syntactic category preceding the code-switch versus 15 syntactic categories for the code-switch itself, about 40% were filled; i.e. 88 different combinations of some constituent and another switched one occurred. Of the non-occurrent combinations, 40% were syntactically impossible (e.g. auxiliary + preposition); the remainder of the cells were empty due most probably to the distribution of the data – cells corresponding to relatively rare switch types and/or relatively rare preceding categories would not be expected to occur with this sample size.

The two most frequently recurring switch points among 681 tokens of intra-sentential code-switch + preceding category were between determiner and noun (19%) and between verb phrase and object noun phrase (12%). This is not surprising since we already have evidence that nouns and noun phrases are frequently switched. Other combinations which recur frequently include independent clause and subordinate clause (4%), verb and predicate adjective (4%), and subject noun phrase and verb phrase (3%). The remaining combinations each represent 2% or less of the data. Similarly, 63 (28%) of the possible combinations occurred among the 729 tokens of code-switch + following category, the overwhelming majority of which also individually represented very small proportions of the data.

Because of the size of the data set, it is statistically unlikely that clearer patterns could emerge from such a large-celled table. With more data we might be able to predict frequencies with which code-switched items precede and follow specific constituents. We hypothesize that such frequencies would simply reflect the frequency of any given combination of constituents (e.g. adverb + adjective, preposition + noun phrase) in monolingual speech. This hypothesis could only be confirmed by evaluating the frequencies of all the possible constituent combinations in a large sample of monolingual speech, a task beyond the scope of the present research.

What information we do have, however, indicates that there is a rather large number of points within the sentence at which it is permissible to switch codes. This is additional evidence that code-switching requires knowledge of two systems. Note that there is about as much intra-sentential as extra-sentential switching (Table 10.2) in the corpus. While extra-sentential switching could presumably be accomplished by alternately drawing on rules from two separate grammars, intra-sentential code-switching would appear to depend on the juxtaposition of constituents too intimately connected to be generated separately by rules from two distinct grammars. This, together with the finding that only a very small number of switches are accompanied by breaks in the speech flow, lends strong support to the hypothesis that code-switching is in fact a verbal mode distinct from English-speaking and Spanish-speaking, yet which consists of the overlapping elements from both.

7.5   Differential behaviour of informants

Let us now examine the individual code-switching behaviour of the informants in the sample.

Table 10.3 shows the frequency with which speakers switch into English. It is striking that the Spanish-dominant speakers switch almost uniquely into English from an unambiguously Spanish base. Bilingual speakers, on the other hand, cluster around the half-way mark, with some switching somewhat more into Spanish from an English base, others the reverse. It is clear that these bilinguals cannot be said to have a single base or dominant language of discourse, but rather two.

Note that three bilingual and two Spanish-dominant speakers (according to self-reports) show patterns which contrast with the other members of their respective

Table 10.3 Percentage of code-switches into English for Spanish-dominant and bilingual speakers

Spanish-dominants

Informant	% of CS from Spanish to English	N
Eli	100%	9
Gui	100	35
Tera	100	1
Isi	100	45
Rosa	100	1
Fela	97	69
Charlie	94	33
Sami	93	93
Chito	92	89
Shorty	71	40
Wilda	63	127
Average	92%	542

Bilinguals

Informant	% of CS from Spanish to English	N	
Cal	100%	35	
Edo	99	212	
Apache	91	63	
Pearl	57	135	
Garra	53	15	
Candy	52	81	
Lola	43	309	
Melo	39	89	
Sally	37	354	
Average	63%	1293	N = 1,835

groups. As will be seen again in the next section, four of these are speakers whose self-report of language dominance conflicted with our ethnographic and linguistic observations in this regard. The fifth, Edo, is in fact bilingual, but has strong feelings towards speaking Spanish, and has been observed to do so almost uniquely when interacting on the block.

7.5.1   Differential behaviour of informants: switch type

Let us now examine another way in which bilinguals differ from Spanish-dominant speakers. The switches in Table 10.2 were listed according to the presumed degree of bilingual proficiency required to produce them, in decreasing order. Lowest on the scale are tag-like switches. These include interjections, fillers, tags, and idiomatic expressions, all of which can be produced in L_2 with only minimal knowledge of the grammar of that language. Next on the scale are full sentences or larger segments, which require much more knowledge of L_2 to produce, although hypothetically, not as much as is required by the third category, intra-sentential switches. As suggested above in order to produce this latter sort of switch, the speaker must also know enough about the grammar of each language, and the way they interact, to avoid ungrammatical utterances.

Figure 10.2 graphs the percentages of each of these switch types for the informants in our sample.[12]

Figure 10.2 shows that reported language ability (which in all cases but four corresponds to observed ability) is an excellent indicator of code-switching patterns. Figure 10.2a shows that most of those who report that they know, feel more comfortable in, and use more Spanish than English, tend to switch into L_2 by means of tag-like constructions, sometimes to the practical exclusion of sentential or intra-sentential switches. Those who claim to be bilingual, on the other hand, show a reversal (Figure 10.2b). They favour large amounts of the switches hypothesized to require most knowledge of both languages, sentential and intra-sentential switches. The most favoured switch type for bilinguals is clearly intra-sentential, while the least favoured is tag-like switching.

The few exceptions to these patterns are represented by the dotted lines on the graphs. Two speakers who claimed to be Spanish-dominant in fact show a similar code-switching configuration to the bilinguals, while two who claim to be bilingual show patterns similar to the Spanish-dominants. Strikingly enough, these are precisely the cases where ethnographic observation and linguistic analysis were previously found to conflict with self-report, because the speakers underrated or overrated their ability in English. Two additional speakers are actually Spanish-dominant, but also show a code-switching pattern similar to that of the bilinguals. They do, however, have a greater degree of competence in English than those who follow the 'Spanish-dominant' pattern. Their switches tend to distribute among the three switch types, rather than show a marked preference for any one, and they may be considered to exhibit code-switching behaviour intermediate to the bilinguals and the more clearly Spanish-dominant speakers.

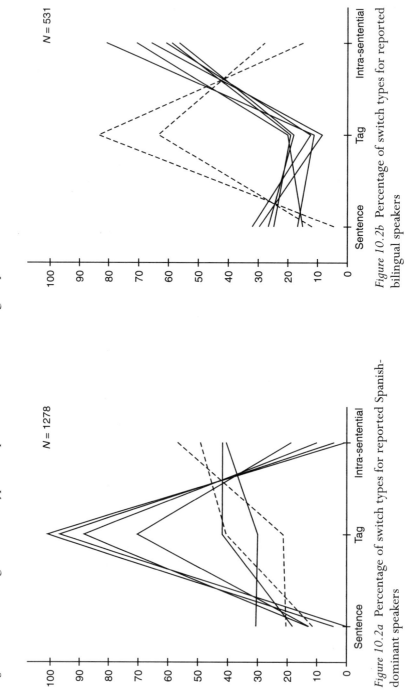

Figure 10.2 Percentages of switch types for Spanish-dominant and bilingual speakers

Figure 10.2a Percentage of switch types for reported Spanish-dominant speakers

Figure 10.2b Percentage of switch types for reported bilingual speakers

8   Contribution of extra-linguistic factors to the occurrence of code-switch type

Having ascertained that reported and observed bilingual ability is an important factor in predicting the type of code-switch that will be uttered (a chi-square test shows this factor to be significant at the 0.001 level), we next attempted to determine which other extra-linguistic factors might have an effect on the occurrence of intra-sentential code-switching. Individual tests were performed on each factor group as well as each pair of factors within each group to determine their significance.

8.1   Sex

The sex of the speaker is a significant factor in predicting code-switch type at the 0.001 level. Women favour intra-sentential switching; over half (56%) of their switches are intra-sentential, while only one-third of the men's switches are of this type.

8.2   Age of L$_2$ acquisition and age of migration to the United States

These two factors were originally examined separately for each speaker. All informants learned Spanish in early childhood, though there was some variation in the age at which English was learned. Since there is a one-to-one correspondence between the age at which the speaker arrived in the United States and the age at which she learned English (not a surprising fact since all speakers report having learned English in the United States), these two factors were subsequently considered as one. On ethnographic grounds we had originally distinguished four ages of arrival/L$_2$ acquisition: early childhood (2–7), pre-adolescent (8–13), adolescent (14–18), and adult (over 18). Tests of association reveal that the difference between learning English/arriving in the United States as an adolescent or as an adult is not significant at the 0.05 level. Consequently, these two age groups were considered together. All the other age distinctions were significant at either 0.001 or the 0.01 levels.

Those speakers who learned both English and Spanish in early childhood, the 'true' bilinguals, show the highest percentage of intra-sentential switching (346/582, or 59%). Those who learned English between the ages of 8 and 13, show only a slightly lower percentage of this type of switch (309/593, or 52%), a small difference, but one which is nonetheless significant at the 0.01 level. Speakers who learned English after the age of 13, however, show a much lower percentage of intra-sentential switches (196/660, or 30%), a drop which is significant at the 0.001 level.

8.3   Reported bilingual ability

As we have already seen in Figure 10.1, reported (and observed) bilingual ability is an excellent predictor of code-switching type. Bilinguals produce a far greater percentage of intra-sentential switches (682/1293, or 53%) than those who are Spanish-dominant (169/542, or 31%). This difference is significant at the 0.001 level.

8.4   Education

Sample members were divided into three categories according to their educational attainment: those who had no more than primary school education (first through eighth grades), those who had some high school but did not graduate (ninth through eleventh grades), and those who graduated high school and/or attended some college. An initial test performed on this factor group revealed that it has an effect on code-switching which is significant at the 0.001 level. Speakers who had primary school education or less tended to switch intra-sententially slightly more (45%) than those who had some high school education (41%). This difference is not significant. High school graduates, however, switched intra-sententially more (60%) than either of the other two groups, a significant difference at the 0.001 level. Upon closer examination, however, it became apparent that although the category contained six speakers, all but five of the tokens (401/406) had been uttered by two bilingual women who had learned English as children. Sex, bilingual ability and age of L_2 acquisition are the three factors we have already seen to be highly correlated with choice of switch type.

8.5   Age

Sample members were divided into two groups: younger speakers (those between 20 and 40) and older speakers (those over 41). Speaker age was found not to be significant in predicting code-switch type.

8.6   Social network membership

All but two informants belong to two ethnographic networks we called the *Gavilanes* and the *Banca* groups, both of which include both Spanish-dominant and bilingual speakers. Network membership is not a significant factor in predicting code-switch type.

8.7   Ethnic identity

People were divided into those who scored low on a composite index measuring positive feelings towards Puerto Rican identity and those who obtained high scores. Those with positive feelings towards Puerto Rican ethnic identity switched codes intra-sententially somewhat more (446/881, or 51%) than those who had negative feelings (405/954). This difference is significant at the 0.001 level.

8.8   Continued contact with Puerto Rico

Sample members were also divided according to relative frequency of return visits to Puerto Rico. Those who return to the Island, where they must speak more Spanish than in New York, more frequently than once every two years, tend to switch intra-sententially far less (71/304, or 23%) than those who visit Puerto Rico less frequently than once every two years (780/1576, or 49%). This difference is significant at the 0.001 level. Further perusal of these categories, however, indicates that all speakers who migrated to the United States in early childhood (and hence tend towards bilingualism) return to Puerto Rico less frequently than once every two years, and that all those who return more frequently are Spanish-dominant, a distinction we have already seen to be significantly correlated with a low incidence of intra-sentential switching.

8.9   Workplace

A distinction was made between those informants who are employed off the block, where they must presumably interact in English, and those who are either unemployed or employed on the block, where they may communicate in English, Spanish or the code-switching mode. Those who work off the block switch intra-sententially only about a third of the time (167/460), while those who remain on the block engage in this switch type half of the time (684/1375), a difference which is significant at the 0.001 level. It is conceivable that those who spend the better part of the day in a speech situation where code-switching is not appropriate get less practice in switching and are therefore less skilled at it. More likely, however, since only Spanish-dominant speakers are employed off the block, it is this characteristic which undoubtedly accounts for the low percentage of intra-sentential switching by these speakers.

9   Multivariate analysis of code-switch type

Situations in which the data is poorly distributed, as is the case for the factors of education, continued contact with Puerto Rico, and workplace, can be as misleading. As we have seen, the apparently significant effect of one factor may really be mainly due to another, language dominance, a fact which is not brought out by looking at one factor at a time. Multivariate analysis can, within limits, separate out these overlapping effects, and extract the independent contributions proper to each of several related factors (Rousseau and Sankoff, 1978; Sankoff and Labov, 1979). It can also provide information on the statistical significance of the distinctions defining each factor group.

Let us now examine the comparative contribution of each extra-linguistic factor found by the factor-by-factor analysis to be significant in the prediction of code-switch type: sex, language dominance of speaker, age of arrival in the United States and age of L_2 acquisition, educational attainment, the speaker's feelings towards his own ethnicity, amount of continued contact with Puerto Rico, and location of work place.

To what extent are these extra-linguistic factors significant when considered simultaneously? To carry out this multivariate analysis we used VARBRUL 2 (Sankoff, 1975) to calculate factor effects and significance levels of factor groups. The factor effects combine to give the probability that a switch will be intra-sentential, according to the

model $\dfrac{P}{1-p} = \dfrac{P_0}{1-p_0} \times \dfrac{P_1}{1-p_1} \times \ldots \times \dfrac{P_n}{1-p_n}$, where P_0 is a corrected mean parameter

and $p_1, \ldots, p_n$ are the parameters representing the effects of factors $1, \ldots, n$ characterizing a given speaker. Factor probabilities vary between zero and 1, with figures higher than 0.5 favouring intra-sentential code-switching, and figures lower than 0.5 favouring extra-sentential code-switching. The higher the figure, the greater the contribution to rule application, so comparisons can easily be made between various factors and factor groups. The program also calculates the log-likelihood of the model under a given configuration of factor groups. Different analyses can then be compared to see whether the various factor groups contribute significantly to explaining the differential use of code-switching types among speakers.

In the preceding section we found seven factors that, when examined one by one, seemed to significantly affect code-switch type. Some of these factors, however, are clearly correlated among themselves. To see which ones could be considered to have an independent contribution to choice of code-switch type, we carried out 128 separate analyses, each one corresponding to a different combination of explanatory factors. By examining the log-likelihoods first of the seven one-factor analyses, then the 21 two-factor analyses, and so on, we could detect which factors contributed a significant independent effect to the explanation of the variation in the data.[13] The result of this was the four-factor analysis depicted in Table 10.4. Each of the four factors here has a strongly significant independent effect on choice of switch type, but the addition of any of the others: ethnic identity, education or continued contact with Puerto Rico, does not significantly increase the explanatory power of the model.

The comparative effect of the factors is of particular interest. As can be seen, reported and observed language dominance is the single factor which most affects the occurrence of this switch type. Bilinguals favour it the most, at 0.68, while those who are Spanish-dominant disfavour it, at 0.32. An almost equal effect is shown by the factor of work place. Those who are unemployed or work on the block, where they engage in this discourse mode with other members of their social network, show a greater tendency to switch intra-sententially than those who work off the block. Table 10.4 shows that those speakers who acquired both languages in early childhood or pre-adolescence, a defining feature of the balanced bilingual, switch intra-sententially more (0.55) than those who learned L_2 at a later age.

Table 10.4 also indicates that women, who are often in the vanguard of linguistic change, favour intra-sentential switching more than men.

10   Discussion

We have shown how to incorporate both linguistic and extra-linguistic factors into a single analytical model to account for code-switching performance. The linguistic constraints on this phenomenon, the free morpheme and equivalence constraints, represent the basis on which the foregoing analysis was carried out.

The extra-linguistic factors contribute variably to the occurrence of one switch type over another. Choice of these factors arises from long-term familiarity with the

Table 10.4 Contribution of extra-linguistic factors to the occurrence of intra-sentential code-switching; corrected mean: 0.36

Sex		Age of arrival L_2 acquisition		Language dominance		Work place	
Female	0.59	Child	0.55	Bilingual	0.68	On-block	0.67
Male	0.41	Pre-adolescent	0.55	Spanish	0.32	Off-block	0.33
		Adolescent	0.40				

members of the speech community, and on the basis of attitudinal and ethnographic studies carried out in the community.

An elementary, but crucial finding of this study is that there are virtually no ungrammatical combinations of L_1 and L_2 in the 1,835 switches studied, regardless of the bilingual ability of the speaker. This corroborates the hypothesis as to the nature of syntactic constraints on code-switching advanced in Poplack (1978/81), for both balanced and non-fluent bilinguals.

By showing that non-fluent bilinguals are able to code-switch frequently, yet maintain grammaticality in both L_1 and L_2 by favouring emblematic or tag-switching, we have also demonstrated empirically that code-switching is not monolithic behaviour. Three types of code-switching emerge in the speech performance studied, each characterized by switches of different levels of constituents, and each reflecting different degrees of bilingual ability. Multivariate analysis of extra-linguistic factors confirms that those speakers with the greatest degree of bilingual ability ('true' bilinguals) most favour intra-sentential code-switching, the type we had hypothesized to require most skill. The two Chicano code-switching studies of Gingràs (1974) and Pfaff (1975; 1976) also indirectly support these findings. Gingràs tested a group of Chicano and non-Chicano bilinguals on the acceptability of a series of constructed intra-sententially code-switched utterances. The Chicano bilinguals showed much higher rates of acceptance of his grammatical code-switches than the non-Chicanos. This led him to posit that there were probably code-switching norms peculiar to the Chicano community. While speech communities may be characterized by different code-switching norms, it was also the case that the Chicano group had learned both languages in early childhood, while the non-Chicano informants all learned English as adults. Bilinguals of the first type are precisely those we have shown to engage most in intra-sentential code-switching, a fact which concords with their high rate of acceptance of such switches. Similarly, of three samples of Chicano speakers studied, Pfaff found that those who engaged most in 'deep-s' (intra-sentential) switching were those whose speech was characterized by use of both Spanish and English.

Previous work (Gumperz 1971a; 1976; Valdés-Fallis, 1978; Poplack, 1978/81) has shown that code-switching may be used as a discourse strategy to achieve certain interactional effects at specific points during a conversation. The findings in the present chapter, together with the ethnographic observations that code-switching is a linguistic norm in the Puerto Rican community, suggest that this use is characteristic only of certain types of code-switching, which we call 'emblematic', including tags, interjections, idiomatic expressions, and even individual noun switches. On the other hand, a generalized use of intra-sentential code-switching may represent instead an overall discourse MODE. The very fact that a speaker makes alternate use of both codes itself has interactional motivations and implications beyond any particular effects of specific switches. Indeed, speaker attitudes toward use of Spanish, English and code-switching reported in Section 5.4 above do not offer any ready explanation for why a particular segment in discourse should be switched. McClure and Wentz (1975) have pointed out that 'there is apparently no real social motivation for, or significance attached to, the practice of code-switching [for example] subject pronouns alone' (p. 266). We agree that there is no 'good reason' (Wentz, 1977; e.g. pp. 143, 218) for switching subject pronouns, or lone determiners, etc. Nonetheless, such segments ARE switched by bilingual speakers. It may well be possible in some cases for the analyst to impute situational motivations or consequences to specific intra-sentential switches, but the evidence presented here suggests that this has little if any pertinence for the speakers themselves. More important, there is no need to require any social motivation for this type of code-switching, given that, as a discourse mode, it may itself form part of the repertoire of a speech community. It is then the choice (or not) of this mode which is of significance to participants rather than the choice of switch points. When these conditions are met, any segment in discourse may be switched, depending on the bilingual ability of the speaker, and provided it obeys the equivalence constraint. Thus, we cannot agree that switches of, say, object pronouns are 'non-sentences' of any language because 'they violate the social motivation for code-alternation in the first place' (McClure, n.d.: 265). They simply violate the equivalence constraint!

The suggestion that code-switching is itself a discrete mode of speaking, possibly emanating from a single code-switching grammar composed of the overlapping sectors of the grammars of L_1 and L_2, is supported by several findings in the present study. We have shown that there is a large number of permissible switch points in the data, rather than a few favoured ones. Switching any given constituent in discourse does not necessarily entail continuation in the language of the switch, unless the surface structures are not equivalent in L_1 and L_2. Hence larger constituents are switched more frequently than smaller ones. It was additionally shown that all constituents are about as likely to be switched into L_1 as into L_2, with the few exceptions contingent upon the bilingual ability of the speaker.

In light of these findings, code-switching behaviour may be used to measure bilingual ability. Bilingual speakers might have expanding grammars of the type depicted in Figure 10.3, representing greater degrees of bilingual acquisition. Further empirical studies of code-switching performance in other bilingual communities would provide comparative data to test these hypotheses.

These findings, taken together and interpreted in terms of the equivalence constraint, provide strong evidence that code-switching is a verbal skill requiring a large degree of linguistic competence in more than one language, rather than a defect arising from insufficient knowledge of one or the other. The rule-governed nature of code-switching is upheld by even the non-fluent bilinguals in the sample. Their behaviour suggests at least enough passive competence in L_2 to switch codes by means of the few rules they know to be shared by both languages. It is also striking that precisely those switch types which have traditionally been considered most deviant by investigators and educators, those which occur within a single sentence, are the ones which require the most skill. They tend to be produced by the 'true' bilinguals in the sample: speakers who learned both languages in early childhood, and who have most ongoing contact with the monolingual English-speaking world.

Code-switching, then, rather than representing deviant behaviour, is actually a suggestive indicator of degree of bilingual competence.

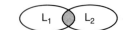

a. Inter-sentential switching   b. 'tag'-switching   c. Intra-sentential switching

Figure 10.3 Representation of bilingual code-switching grammars

Notes

1 92% (Bureau of the Census, 1973).

2 The reverse pattern, the insertion into an English base of Spanish items with English phonological or morphological patterns is non-existent in this community.

3 Numbers in parentheses identify speaker and code-switch.

4 For example, why should it be possible to switch codes between a subject and a verb, but not if that subject is pronominal, as suggested by Gumperz (1976) and Timm (1975)?

5 This constraint is confirmed by data from independent studies (Pfaff, 1975; 1976; Wentz, 1977; McClure, n.d.).

6 A condition similar to the equivalence constraint has been independently suggested by Lipski (1978).

7 Gingràs also claims that it is not obvious whether (6a) should even be considered an example of code-switching, mainly because 'in the formation of the complement it is not clear whether English transformations have applied in an otherwise Spanish structure' (Gingràs, 1974: 168). Whether or not an invented example should be considered a code-switch is questionable; in any event, it is one which is hardly likely to occur in actual speech, as operation of the equivalence constraint demonstrates.

8 This lapsus provides ground for interesting speculation, which we leave to the reader.

9 This questionnaire was developed for the Philadelphia speech community by the Project on Linguistic Change and Variation under the direction of William Labov, and subsequently adapted for use in the Puerto Rican community by the author.

10 Note that the sentence itself contains a switch. The switched segment was only coded for the following syntactic category if the category was produced in the language other than that of the switch. So an example like *Pa' muchos sitios* was not coded for following syntactic category.

11 A construct such as 'language of the sentence', which according to Wentz (1977: 182) is the one in which the determiner and main verb were produced, does not appear to be operative for these data, as they contain a good number of code-switched verbs (60, or 3% of the data) in a language other than that of the determiner.

12 Three Spanish-dominant and one bilingual speaker were omitted from these calculations as they each produced 15 tokens or less.

13 I would like to thank David Sankoff for making available a version of the variable rule program which facilitates this stepwise multiple regression procedure.

Source: Poplack, S. (1980) Sometimes I'll start a sentence in Spanish *y termino en español*. *Linguistics* 18: 581–618, by permission of Mouton de Gruyter.

Postscript

Reprinting a 20-year old paper is a risky business, especially one interpreted or misinterpreted in as many ways as *Sometimes I'll start a sentence . . .* has been. I have none the less accepted the invitation to reproduce it virtually unchanged, with only this brief attempt to situate it in the context of what we know now, thanks to two decades of corroborative research in a variety of bilingual communities and language pairs, about code-switching and lexical borrowing.

Sometimes I'll start a sentence . . . represented a first attempt to delineate, for quantitative analytical purposes, what has turned out to be the fundamental distinction in language mixing: that between code-switching and borrowing. This was manifest in the contrast between those English-origin items which, despite their etymology, function morphologically and syntactically as though they were Spanish (borrowings), and those retaining the inflections and syntactic characteristics of their lexifier language (code-switches) (Section 2, especially Table 10.1). It was also evident in the conception of the *free morpheme constraint* – essentially a preliminary formulation of the claim, now amply confirmed – that the (nonce) borrowings and the (single-word) switches in a corpus of bilingual discourse may be identified and operationally distinguished from each other.

We know much more about the relevant criteria for delimiting borrowing and code-switching now than we did 20 years ago. For example, phonological integration need not go hand in hand with morphological integration, although this was usually the case in the Puerto Rican–English context studied here. In many bilingual communities, phonological integration of loanwords is highly variable, and this is also foreshadowed in Sections 2 and 6.3, disqualifying phonology as a (foolproof) criterion. Moreover, it has now been proved that loanword (vs. code-switch) status can be determined even for items featuring *no* overt linguistic indications (the 'zero forms' recently debated in the literature), at least in the aggregate. The key to disambiguating the status of such apparently ambiguous elements is recourse to the monolingual varieties that combined to produce the mixed utterance. Such comparison has revealed that even uninflected borrowed forms pattern along with their counterparts in the recipient language, which also show variable marking (see the papers in Poplack and Meechan, 1998). Code-switches (single-word as well as multiword code-switches) have similarly been shown to pattern according to the donor, or lexifier, language.

From this perspective, many of the lone other-language forms operationally classified as code-switches in *Sometimes I'll start a sentence* . . . would today be identified as borrowings. Despite the nomenclature, their quantitative patterning (Table 10.2) already revealed them both to outweigh by far the unambiguous multiword switches, and to behave differently from them, as has by now been confirmed for numerous other communities and contexts. For example it is the inclusion of large numbers of lone English-origin nouns (and a lesser number of other lone items) that is responsible for the apparent tendency in Table 10.2 for unidirectional (Spanish–English) 'code-switching'. When the lone items are treated separately from the unambiguous switches, any significant rate differences disappear.

Most of these lone other-language items have since been identified, after Weinreich (1953), as *nonce borrowings*. For such items, the Free Morpheme Constraint turns out to be a consequence of the *nonce borrowing hypothesis* (Sankoff *et al.*, 1990). As originally formulated, however, the free morpheme constraint also suggests that switches should not occur across a morpheme boundary where a morpheme appearing at the end of a multiword fragment in one language is bound to another at the beginning of a multiword fragment in the other language. Although there are still no published reports of the systematic occurrence of this type of counterexample – which would effectively falsify the free morpheme constraint in this context – we have no particular stake in this issue. The constraint was basically intended to account for the disproportionate number – now empirically confirmed in dozens of bilingual communities – of *lone* other-language lexical items in code-mixed discourse (Poplack and Meechan, 1998). This is more precisely formulated as the *nonce borrowing hypothesis*.

What of the *equivalence constraint*, adumbrated in Poplack (1978/81) and first tested empirically on a community-wide basis in *Sometimes I'll start a sentence . . .?* Once lone other-language items are identified as syntactically and morphologically part of the recipient-language fragments in which they are embedded, the analysis of intrasentential code-switching may proceed unimpeded by confusion between switching and borrowing. The equivalence constraint – which has since been formalized (Sankoff and Mainville, 1986) and shown to be a logical consequence of consistency conditions on speakers' production of hierarchically and linearly coherent sentences (Sankoff 1998; 1998a) – turns out to account for virtually all quantitatively significant patterns of switching in most large corpora. Patterns other than equivalence-point switching, such as 'repetition-translation', and 'constituent insertion' (Naït M'Barek and Sankoff, 1988) also occur, but these are confined to specific communities and are observed in only one or two quite specific constructions. It is by first recognizing all the data accounted for by the equivalence constraint that these other patterns are highlighted, detected and described. Thus the major conceptual preoccupations of *Sometimes I'll start a sentence . . .* – the avoidance by speakers of word-order conflicts at switch-points, and their patterned use of the fundamentally different processes of code-switching and borrowing – have provided the essential tools for dozens of studies of bilingual contexts that have followed.

No less important has been the community-based research protocol first exemplified here, inspired by the variation theory paradigm originating with Labov. It is evidenced not only in the delineation of the speech community through innovative participant-observation fieldwork techniques, but also in the quantitative analyses of the data collected there and, especially, adherence to the *principle of accountability* to those data. These have more recently been augmented by techniques of computational linguistics. Such research methods are onerous and often tedious compared with elicitation, intuition or reanalysis of previously published examples, but they continue to furnish the richest and by far the most valid material for the scientific study of bilingual discourse.

October 1999

Shana Poplack, PhD, is Distinguished University Professor of Linguistics, University of Ottawa, Canada. spoplack@uottawa.ca

Matching lemmas in a bilingual language competence and production model: evidence from intrasentential code-switching

CAROL MYERS-SCOTTON AND JANICE L. JAKE

1 Introduction

This chapter has three related goals. First we show that how language pairs behave in code-switching provides evidence for certain types of salient congruence between languages. The analysis assumes the *matrix language frame model* (MLF model) for code-switching and provides elaborations and extensions of this model (Myers-Scotton, 1993a). Second, based on this evidence, we make proposals about the nature and organization of language production. Third, while the chapter focuses its discussion on production, proposals in this area imply details of a model of language competence. Many language production models include three levels; these are the conceptual, functional, and positional levels. At the conceptual level, intentions are "bundled" into semantic and pragmatic features associated with lexemes. At the functional level, morphosyntactic directions encoding the predicate–argument structure are activated. At the positional level, lexemes are realized in a surface structure. Our proposals deal largely with the first two levels and relate specifically to producing bilingual language. However, we argue that the same organization of language production holds for monolingual discourse.

Data discussed here come from code-switching (CS). Most briefly and generally, CS is defined as the use of two or more languages in the same discourse. From a structural point of view, there are two types of CS, intersentential and intrasentential. Our interest here is only in intrasentential CS, because it is only there that the grammars of the two languages are in contact. A more explicit definition of intrasentential CS follows below.

2 Designating the matrix language in CS

Central to our discussion of intrasentential CS is the claim that the two languages involved do not participate equally. One language, which we call the matrix language (ML), is more dominant in ways crucial to language production. This language sets the grammatical frame in the unit of analysis. The other language(s) is referred to as the embedded language (EL). However, both languages are "on" at all times during bilingual production; the difference is a matter of activation level.[1]

Although the subject here is intrasentential CS, it is as well to note that the constituent level that is relevant in the determination of either intersentential or intrasentential CS is the same. This is the CP (complement phrase) or S-bar (S′). The CP as the relevant unit of analysis in intrasentential CS will be discussed below. A CP is a syntactic structure expressing the predicate–argument structure of a clause, plus the additional syntactic structures needed to encode discourse-relevant structure and the logical form of that clause. Because CP explicitly assumes that the unit of structure includes COMP (complementizer) position, it is a more precise term than either clause or sentence.[2] Its use does not assume that the MLF model analyzes CS within a government and binding framework, and, in fact, some of our assumptions differ significantly from those of such a framework. We continue to use the term intrasentential CS because of its widespread use in the CS literature; however, intra-CP switching would be a more appropriate and precise term.

In contrast with intrasentential CS, intersentential CS involves switching BETWEEN CPs that are monolingual. For this reason, describing the INTERNAL structure of the CPs making up intersentential CS in terms of oppositions between an ML and EL is not appropriate.[3]

In order for the identification of an ML vs. an EL to be relevant in intrasentential CS, as we argue, morphemes from more than one language must occur under the same CP. In fact, a precise definition of intrasentential CS is this: if a CP includes morphemes from two or more languages in one or both of these patterns, the result is intrasentential CS: (1) the CP includes a mixed constituent, and/or (2) the CP includes monolingual constituents, but from two or more languages. In such a CP, one of the languages sets the grammatical frame and is the ML. The other language is the EL. This distinction between the ML vs. the EL is the basic principle structuring intrasentential CS within the MLF model (Myers-Scotton, 1993a) and its extended version followed here.

3   The role and nature of the matrix language

The decision of the interlocutors in a discourse to use intrasentential CS (cf. Section 7) is based on social, psychological, and structural factors. Consequently, a definition of the ML is based on a complex interaction of these factors. Two of the definitional criteria have a structural basis. The first criterion is this: the ML is the language that projects the morphosyntactic frame for the CP that shows intrasentential CS. A major aspect of this criterion is operationalized as the *morpheme order* and *system morpheme* principles of the MLF model:

- *The morpheme order principle*: In ML + EL constituents consisting of singly occurring EL lexemes and any number of ML morphemes, surface morpheme order (reflecting surface syntactic relations) will be that of the ML.
- *The system morpheme principle*: In ML + EL constituents, all system morphemes that have grammatical relations external to their head constituent (i.e. participate in the sentence's thematic role grid) will come from the ML (Myers-Scotton 1993a: 83).[4]

Second, the ML is defined generally, but not always, as the source of more morphemes in a sample of discourse-relevant[5] intrasentential CS. The structural basis of these two criteria will become clear under the discussion of the distinction between content vs. system morphemes and the issue of congruence.

Sociolinguistic factors provide a basis for psycholinguistic factors in the second set of definitional criteria. The ML is the unmarked or expected choice as the medium of communication in the interaction type in which the intrasentential CS occurs. Its unmarked status is generally empirically demonstrable: the ML is the language that contributes quantitatively more linguistic material in the entire discourse (including monolingual stretches). Based on this fact, speakers engaged in CS perceive the ML as "the language we are speaking" (cf. Stenson, 1990; Swigart, 1994); often they do not even recognize they are using another language in addition to the ML.[6]

4   The structural constituents in intrasentential CS

In a CP showing intrasentential CS, the distinction between ML vs. EL of the MLF model allows us to identify three types of constituents that are structurally different.[7] By constituent we mean any syntactic S-structure constituent. Within the CP of intrasentential CS, the most relevant constituent is the maximal projection. Two types of possible constituents in such a CP are made up entirely of one language or the other(s). These are either ML or EL islands. A third type of constituent is one consisting of morphemes from both languages, that is, an ML + EL constituent (hereafter a "mixed" constituent). All three types are found in most data sets showing intrasentential CS.[8]

5   Content/system morpheme distinction

In addition to the ML vs. EL opposition, a second crucial opposition in intrasentential CS is the distinction between content and system morphemes. This opposition is relevant to all linguistic structures in a number of ways, as evident in monolingual speech-error data (cf. Garrett, 1988) as well as in other forms of bilingual speech (Myers-Scotton, 1995c). As it is played out in intrasentential CS, this opposition interacts with the ML vs. EL distinction (Myers-Scotton, 1993a; Jake, 1994).

Nouns, adjectives, time adverbials, and most verbs and prepositions are prototypical content morphemes. The feature shared by these lexical categories is that they constitute the predicate–argument structure, by either receiving or assigning thematic roles. Nouns and descriptive adjectives receive thematic roles; verbs, predicate adjectives, and some prepositions assign thematic roles. Discourse markers (e.g. *well, because*) are content morphemes because they assign thematic roles at the discourse level.

Failure to either receive or assign a thematic role prevents a member of these categories from being designated as a content morpheme. For example, the copula and some *do* matrix verbs fail to assign thematic roles. Similarly, some prepositions only assign case, and not thematic role (e.g. English *of* in *student of physics*).

A second feature characteristic of most system morphemes is the feature [+Quantification] ([+Q]). Within the MLF model, a morpheme shows a plus setting for quantification if it restricts possible referent(s) of a lexical category. For example, articles restrict the possible reference of nouns, either to a smaller set (*the boys* vs. *boys*) or to an individual (*the boy*). Similarly, tense and aspect restrict the possible reference of predicates (i.e. verbs and adjectives) (Dowty, 1979). Degree adverbs, such as *very*, also restrict the reference of events and adjectives. More formally, a [+Q] morpheme quantifies (=restricts) across a variable (=category).

6　Congruence and EL participation

The net result of the two principles of the MLF model, the morpheme order principle and the system morpheme principle, is to restrict the role of the EL in mixed constituents in intrasentential CS. Essentially, only EL content morphemes, not system morphemes, may occur, and these must occur in the frame projected by the ML. Example (1) shows content morphemes from English, the EL, inserted into a frame prepared by Irish, the ML.

(1)　Bíonn　sé ag　　CONTRIBUT-áil　do MAGAZINE
　　　be-HAB he PROG contribute-PROG to　magazine
　　　atá PUBLISHED　　in Sasana.
　　　REL/be published in England
　　　'He is contributing to a magazine that is published in England.'
　　　(Irish/English; Stenson, 1990: 176)

However, not even all EL content morphemes can occur freely. A blocking hypothesis states that "a blocking filter blocks any EL content morpheme which is not congruent with the ML with respect to three levels of abstraction regarding subcategorization" (Myers-Scotton, 1993a: 120). Congruence refers to a match between the ML and the EL at the lemma level with respect to linguistically relevant features. Lemmas are entries in the mental lexicon and are discussed below.

In this chapter, we make the discussion from Myers-Scotton (1993a) more specific and introduce additional aspects of congruence. We propose that certain non-uniformities of lexical structure across languages mean that a mixed constituent may pass the blocking filter, but may not pass unscathed. For example, in many languages, the only way an EL verb appears in a mixed constituent is in a construction where an ML auxiliary verb carries all necessary inflections and the EL verb is a bare form. Such examples are discussed below in Section 11.

Various views of congruence have figured in many attempts to explain constraints on intrasentential CS. Many of these were stated in terms of surface structure (Pfaff, 1979; Poplack, 1980; Sridhar and Sridhar, 1980; Woolford, 1983; *inter alia*). Lack of congruence regarding lexical subcategorization has been discussed by others but is generally limited to subcategorization differences between specific language pairs (e.g. Azuma, 1991; Bentahila and Davies, 1983; Muysken, 1991). In this chapter, the nature of congruence as relevant to CS is seen as more complex because a more complex view of lexical structure is assumed (Jackendoff, 1983; Talmy, 1985). Here congruence is examined in terms of the different levels or subsystems comprising content lexemes. In addition, the relation of these subsystems to a model of production of a bilingual utterance is articulated.

7   A language production model: a first sketch

The language production model sketched here is specifically designed to accommodate "system decisions" regarding congruence. One of our hypotheses is that variation in congruence (complete, partial, or absent) in the levels of language restricts and there-fore structures choices in CS. That is, variation in actual CS realizations reflects variation in congruence at more abstract levels of linguistic structure. We will be referring to these levels in terms of three types of structure: lexical-conceptual, predicate–argument, and morphological realization patterns.

The way in which the MLF model, as elaborated here, analyzes intrasentential CS data makes important predictions about how types of linguistic information are organized in language production. In turn, these predictions imply certain aspects of the nature of linguistic competence.

A single mental lexicon is hypothesized for bilinguals, but with entries tagged for specific languages. The entries are not lexemes, but rather *lemmas*, more abstract elements that support the realizations of actual lexemes (Levelt, 1989). (In some cases they support idiomatic collocation of lexemes at the surface level, e.g. *keep tabs on* or *a fly in the ointment*). In this model, lemmas are characterized as containing abstract pragmatic information, in addition to semantic, syntactic, and morphological information. Incon-gruence in pragmatic messages in cross-language lemmas that are otherwise nearly identical often motivates mixed constituents in CS; other types of congruence problems motivate other CS patterns, such as EL islands, we will argue.

The information contained in lemmas is referred to at two levels: the conceptual level and the functional level. The conceptual level (i.e. *conceptualizer*) consists of the lexical-conceptual structure in which universally available semantic and pragmatic information is conflated as specific lexical-conceptual structures (referred to as semantic/pragmatic feature bundles, or *SP feature bundles*), which are necessarily lan-guage-specific. The functional level consists of the *formulator* and the morphosyntactic procedures that are activated by directions from the lemma. The formulator is a sort of "control central" in actual on-line production.

Initially, speakers make selections encapsulating the lexical-conceptual structures they wish to convey; for example, in choosing a lexical-conceptual structure in English to encode MANNER as well as MOTION, a speaker will select the structure supporting *roll* vs. *go*. Selections at this stage are abstract and result in the activation of abstract, but language-specific, lemmas in the mental lexicon.

In addition to lexical-conceptual structure, lemmas contain predicate–argument structure and directions for morphological realization patterns. This is how syntactic and morphological information is coded. When speakers select a particular conflation of semantic and pragmatic information, this involves selection of a language-specific lemma, which in turn specifies a particular predicate–argument structure and certain morphological realization patterns. Table 11.1 provides a schema of language production.

7.1   The nature of lemmas

A lemma can he defined as a carrier of lexical-conceptual structure and an associated predicate–argument structure and concomitant morphological realization patterns.

Table 11.1   Speaker's intentions

Conceptual level:	Universally present lexical-conceptual structure in the conceptualizer.
	"Choices" made: If discourse includes CS, then select ML and semantic/pragmatic feature bundles
	Language-specific semantic/pragmatic feature bundles activate entries in the mental lexicon (language-specific lemmas)
	Language-specific lemmas send directions to the formulator ↓
Functional level:	The "activated" formulator projects
	Predicate-argument structures (e.g. thematic roles) and
	Morphological realization patterns (e.g. word order, case marking, etc.) ↓
Positional level:	Morphological realization (surface structure after move-alpha, agreement inflections, etc.)

What follows develops our view of lemmas and their relation to lexical entries. First, they are not concrete; that is, they are not lexical items with subcategorization features. Rather, they support such items. In order for this to be so, what is their nature? Each one includes the specific bundling of semantic and pragmatic features that encodes the lexical-conceptual structures that represent the speaker's communicative intentions. They also include information as to how these intentions are grammatically realized in a sentence. An example of such morphosyntactic information is lexical category (e.g. Noun vs. Verb) or grammatical gender. Note that such categories are not what speakers select at the conceptual level; rather, speakers are dealing in terms of notions such as "thing" or "process." This information (predicate–argument structure and morphological realization patterns) is something of a default choice; that is, selecting features in the conceptualizer that become a specific semantic/pragmatic bundle in language X entails selecting the predicate–argument structure and its morphological realizations associated with this bundle in language X. Thus, lemmas are what link conceptual intentions (=semantic and pragmatic features) to the predicate–argument structures and morphological realization patterns of a specific language.

7.2   Lemmas and lexical items

Do lemmas support specific lexical items? Yes, and no. In some cases, the abstract feature bundles do match up with a specific lexical entry. For example, an easily accessible concrete entity, such as *nose*, does match a lemma. Yet, this lemma is (most likely) language-specific, because of pragmatic considerations. For any one particular language, then, lexemes for concrete entities are supported by specific lemmas in the mental lexicon. This is also true for many more complex concepts. However, because the semantic and pragmatic features associated with them are more complex and less concrete, there may be less cross-linguistic congruence with the lemmas supporting such concepts than with concrete entities.

When there is sufficient incongruence between an EL lemma and its ML counterpart, inserting the EL lexeme supported by the EL lemma in a constituent framed by the ML may require the types of strategies to be discussed below. Cases of insufficient congruence are what give us an insight into the relative importance of features in lexical entries in defining the entries (in regard to pragmatic/semantic matters) and in allowing for the occurrence of lexemes supported by these entries in specific types of constituents.

When there is a lack of correspondence in pragmatic force between lexemes, this state of affairs will be referred to as a "pragmatic mismatch." Most insertions of single EL lexemes in ML frames are motivated by pragmatic mismatches. That is, from the speaker's point of view, *le mot juste* is an EL lexeme, not the ML counterpart with like semantic features. Some pragmatic mismatches may be general (i.e. based on differences in connotations of semantically congruent lexemes); however, other cases of mismatches may only arise in specific interactions as a result of unique social and psychological factors.

Note how pragmatic mismatches are different from *lexical gaps*, which also may motivate the inserting of EL lexemes in ML frames. When there are gaps in the semantic correspondence between lexemes, we apply the term "lexical gap" to such cases. When the gap is large, such as in the case of EL lexicalizations for objects or concepts new to the ML culture for which the ML has no counterpart at all, the net result is typically a borrowing of the EL lexeme into the ML. For example, lexemes akin to *computer* now occur in many languages; that is, a gap has been closed through lexical borrowing so that both the donor and the recipient languages have lemmas supporting the equivalent lexeme.

In other cases, however, especially when the gap is only partial and thus there is sufficient cross-linguistic congruence, the ML does not borrow the EL lexeme, but bilingual speakers may insert the EL lexeme in CS discourse. For example, in French, *journal* refers to "daily news bulletins." A daily newspaper is a *journal* in French, but so is a daily television news broadcast (cf. *télé-journal*). In contrast, in English, while some daily news "bulletins" are referred to as *journals* (e.g. *The Wall Street Journal*), in English more prototypical as *journals* are academic or scientific publications that appear less frequently than daily. Thus, English *journal* is not an exact counterpart to French *journal*, nor is any other English lexeme. This lexical gap in English relative to the French lexeme *journal* remains, and when speakers engaging in English/French CS want to convey the specific semantic content of this French lexeme, they may insert it in an English frame, as long as the context makes clear that the intended referent is a daily *journal*.

When a lexical gap exists, this means that there is no lemma in the mental lexicon to support an actual surface lexeme. Yet, we argue that the potential to lexicalize any concept exists in any language as what we will call *lexical knowledge*.[9] Such lexical knowledge must be posited to provide for the possibility of languages bringing into existence lemmas to support new lexemes. Further, because in all languages it is possible to express all semantic and pragmatic intentions (while at the same time actual lexicalization patterns differ cross-linguistically), we propose that these intentions, located in the conceptualizer, must be available to all languages for configuring new lemmas. When these intentions are conflated into a "bundle," they can combine with the undifferentiated lexical knowledge present in the mental lexicon. This lexical knowledge includes universal as well as language-specific default information about predicate–argument structures and morphological realization patterns. Universal default aspects of lexical knowledge cover such matters as the unmarked syntactic treatment of nouns and verbs. Language-specific lexical knowledge includes information about the unmarked syntactic realization of thematic roles (e.g. how experiencer is encoded) and the morphosyntactic treatment of these roles. How congruence checks in CS may make use of undifferentiated lexical knowledge (i.e. when there is a lexical gap in the ML) is discussed further in Section 13.

8   The conceptual level

We now discuss in some detail the language production model motivated by our analysis of CS data. At the conceptual level speakers seek linguistic structures that satisfy their intentions. First they make decisions structuring the entire discourse. Second, speakers take account of other aspects of lexical-conceptual structure that apply at the level of specific lexemes; they consider which surface lexemes would best convey the semantic as well as the more purely pragmatic and sociopragmatic features of their intentions.

8.1   Overall discourse-level decisions

In reference to the overall discourse, speakers first consider socio- and psycholinguistic aspects of lexical-conceptual structure. For example, of particular relevance to CS, speakers assess the feasibility of monolingual or bilingual discourse. This means that they take into account attitudes toward the linguistic varieties that the speakers have the potential to employ (i.e. sociolinguistic considerations); they also take account of their perceptions of proficiency of the interlocutors in these same linguistic varieties (i.e. psycholinguistic considerations). One consideration is simply the effect of their producing monolingual vs. bilingual speech. Possible attitudes toward even specific varieties of bilingual production are also considered (e.g. in a particular speech community, is intrasentential CS acceptable?). While interlocutors in a particular discourse setting weigh such matters, they are free to choose modes of speaking that may be characterized by others as marked (vs. unmarked; cf. Myers-Scotton, 1993).

If the interlocutors in a particular discourse choose to engage in bilingual speech involving intrasentential CS, they simultaneously select an ML to frame CPs to be produced. In Section 3, we referred to the socio- and psycholinguistic factors defining the ML. When speakers choose the ML, these are considered, but also salient are the more purely semantic (referential) features of a speaker's intentions. Based on some combination of these considerations, the ML is selected as the frame for the CP to be produced.

8.2   Semantic/pragmatic intentions

Also, again simultaneously, these same features come into play when individual content morphemes (lexemes) are considered to encode specific speaker intentions. That is, speakers consider which surface lexemes would best convey the semantic as well as the more purely pragmatic and sociopragmatic features of their intentions. The lexemes they select can be from either the ML or the EL. Recall, however, that at this abstract level of production, there are no lexemes accessed, but rather lemmas are activated in the mental lexicon that will support surface-level morphemes.

In summary, even though decisions made at the conceptual level refer to intentions, not utterance structures, the results of these decisions determine the language or languages to be activated and set their structural roles.

8.3 Semantic/pragmatic feature bundles

The particular semantic and pragmatic features associated with each lemma entry form its own specific lexical-conceptual structure. As indicated, the model assumes a universal set of semantic and pragmatic features that are available for the lexical-conceptual structuring of lemmas; yet, it also expects their presence and conflation to vary cross-linguistically. We see variation in lexicalization patterns across languages as evidence that there are different configurations of these features across related lemmas in different languages. As noted above, we refer to a lemma's configuration of these features as its *semantic/pragmatic feature bundle* (*SP feature bundle*).

Implicit in our discussion is the hypothesis that the structures appearing in intrasentential CS are evidence of the relative importance of lexical-conceptual DIFFERENCES in the nature of lexical entries. That is, when there is not an exact match across the language pairs involved in CS, there are consequences for the resulting CS structures. These conceptual structure differences may be simply pragmatic or semantic, or semantic with morphological consequences. When there are such differences across the languages involved in CS, the structures that are possible in CS give us information about the relative importance of specific conceptual differences as defining features of a lexical entry.

8.3.1 Differences in semantic/pragmatic features

A number of examples illustrate the nature of semantic/pragmatic features encoded in lexical-conceptual structure and how their conflation into SP feature bundles may differ cross-linguistically. First, in example (2), second-generation Turkish women immigrants in the Netherlands are alternating between Dutch and Turkish in discussing a traditional prewedding event and its attire (Backus, 1994). Related lexemes in Turkish and Dutch referring to "dress" are selected as appropriate at different points in the discourse; in (2a) the Turkish lexeme *elbise* is selected while in (2b) the Dutch lexeme *rok* is selected. Example (2a) occurs when the speakers are focusing on the traditional event, while much later in the conversation, the speakers produce (2b) as part of a general discussion of fashion ranging from velour trousers to LA Gear tennis shoes.[10]

> (2) a. als jij die   trouwjurk   zie-t, en die   KINA
>   if 2S DEM wedding dress see-2S and DEM henna
>   GECE-Sİ   ELBİSE-Sİ,
>   night-POSS dress-POSS
>   'if you see that wedding dress, and the "henna evening" dress,'

b. en die   gaa-t ze   drag-en   onder haar   KINA
   and DEM go-3S she wear-INF under FEM/S/POSS henna
   GECE-Sİ   rok.
   night-POSS skirt
   'and she will wear that under her "henna evening" skirt.'
   (Turkish/Dutch CS; Backus, 1994)

Second, examples (3a) and (3b) and (4a) and (4b) show how semantic differences in the SP feature bundles of conceptually related lexemes have morphosyntactic consequences. For example, how the feature CAUSATION is conflated with other semantic features of a predicate determines the lexical-conceptual structure contained in a lemma (cf. Talmy, 1985). This affects the type of morphosyntactic procedures that the lemma calls from the formulator.

In English, agent causation is not distinguished from autonomous (non-) causation. In contrast, in Spanish and Japanese, the relevant semantic features are conflated into two distinct lexicalization patterns. In Spanish, CAUSATION is inherently part of the lexical conceptual structure of *abrir* 'open'. In order to express an autonomous, non-causative related event, a "morpheme satellite," the reflexive, is called up as part of the morphologically complex entry. In contrast, in Japanese, *aku* 'open' is inherently an autonomous, noncausative event, and a causative verb form *akeru* is required to add a semantic feature to the lexical- conceptual structure of intransitive 'open'.

(3) a. Spanish:
        Abrió la   puerta.   La puerta se   abrió
        [he] opened the door.   the door REFL opened
        'He opened the door.'   'The door opened.'
    b. Japanese:
        Doa   ga   aita
        door   SUBJ open (PAST)
        'The door was open.'
        Kare wa   doa   o   aketa
        he   TOP   door OBJ   open (CAUS PAST)
        'He opened the door.'
        (Talmy, 1985: 85)

Another pair of examples illustrating how semantic features can be conflated differently into SP feature bundles (and consequently realized in lexical entries differently) involves the feature MANNER. English motion verbs can include MANNER as a semantic feature; Spanish motion verbs cannot. In (4a), MOTION and MANNER are conflated into *float*. The PP *into the cave* expresses PATH. In (4b), MOTION and PATH are conflated into *entró*. A present participle *flotando* expresses MANNER.

(4) a. The bottle floated into the cave.
    b. La botella entró a la cueva flotando.
       (Talmy, 1985: 69)

Similarly, one can argue that certain CS examples arise because of lack of congruence in semantic features. For example, the English verb *decide* occurs frequently in

Swahili/English CS conversations (see example (5)), seemingly filling a semantic function not met by a Swahili counterpart. In a Swahili counterpart to *decide* (-*kata shauri*, literally 'cut/reduce problem'), the relevant semantic features of -*kata shauri* express (in Talmy's terms; 1985: 88) "inchoative *entering-into-a-state*." These contrast with those of *decide*, which express "agentive *putting-into-a-state*."

(5) Kwa vile zi-ko   ny-ingi,   si-wez-i   DECIDE
     because   CL10-COP CL10-many 1S/NEG-be able-NEG decide
     i-le   i-na-fa-a   zaidi
     CL9-DEM CL9-NON-PAST-be proper-FV[11] more
     'Because there are many, I can't decide the most proper one.'
     (Swahili/English; Myers-Scotton, 1993a: 114)

8.3.2   SP feature bundle congruence and CS examples

We now consider the consequences for CS structures of cross-linguistic variation in SP feature bundles. Example (6) illustrates a case of sufficient congruence across SP feature bundles to allow for near-complete morphosyntactic integration of an EL content morpheme in a surface string fully inflected by the ML (i.e. a mixed constituent).[12] We posit that English *come* can occur because it is projected from an EL lemma in the mental lexicon that has an SP feature bundle sufficiently congruent with an ML lemma counterpart. The ML lemma that has the most closely related SP feature bundle supports the Swahili verb stem -*j*- 'come'. At this point in our articulation of the model, what is "sufficiently congruent" is unknown. (The presence of "double morphology" (i.e. the English plural morpheme in *books*) is discussed in Section 9.2.)

(6) Leo   si-ku-COME   na   Ø-BOOK-S z-angu.
     today 1S/NEG PAST/NEG-come with CL10-book-s CL10-my
     James a-li-end-a   na-zo   mpaka kesho
     James 3S-PAST-go-INDIC with-CL10(them) until tomorrow
     'Today I didn't come with my books. James went with them until tomorrow.'
     (Swahili/English; Myers-Scotton, 1993a: 80)

8.4   Conceptual structure and compromise CS strategies

Two main alternatives to full ML inflection of an EL morpheme in a mixed CS constituent exist.

First, an EL content morpheme can occur as a *bare form*. That is, although the EL content morpheme does occur in the constituent slot project by the ML, it lacks the ML system morphemes to make it completely well formed according to the ML morphosyntax. (Note that bare forms do not violate the system morpheme principle, which requires that if syntactically active system morphemes are present, they must be from the ML.) We propose that uninflected EL content morphemes occur because there is not sufficient congruence at some level (Myers-Scotton, 1993a: 112–16). In (7), the lexical-conceptual structure of *underestimate* is not totally congruent with a Spanish counterpart. The result is that *underestimate* occurs as a bare form without the second person familiar suffix *-as*.[13] Possible Spanish counterparts have different semantic/ pragmatic bundles; *menospreciar* 'undervalue' has a negative connotation, and *desestimar* has more the sense of 'not esteem'.

(7) Tú lo   UNDERESTIMATE a Chito
you him underestimate   to Chito
'You underestimate Chito.'
(Spanish/English; Pfaff, 1979: 301)

The second alternative strategy is more radical from the standpoint of the ML frame: an EL island is produced. Recall that an EL island consists only of EL morphemes and must be well formed according to EL well-formedness conditions. We hypothesize that the major reason EL islands are formed is a congruence problem across the CS language pair in regard to SP feature bundles. Examples (8), (9), and (10) illustrate such cases. The other major reason for their formation has to do with incongruence regarding predicate–argument structure, and that will be discussed below. Note that these hypotheses depart somewhat from the discussion of EL islands in Myers-Scotton (1993a). The ways in which the ML still frames the entire CP that includes EL islands are discussed in Section 11.5.

In example (8) the English lexeme *nonsense* is the head of an EL island posited to result because of differing SP feature bundles across the languages involved. According to our hypothesis, at the level of the mental lexicon where the lemma supporting *nonsense* is present, there is no ML counterpart in which the relevant semantic and pragmatic features are conflated into a sufficiently congruent SP feature bundle, that is, its lexical-conceptual structure. Still, since an EL rendition of a certain concept is preferred, the EL lemma supporting this concept is activated in the mental lexicon.[14] This lemma activates morphosyntactic procedures in the formulator, such that ML procedures are inhibited for the maximal category projection (here, NP) associated with that lemma. The result is an EL island. As in all EL islands, all of the system morphemes come from the EL.

(8) Wewe u-li-ku-w-a   mlevi   sana jana.
You   2SG-PAST-INFIN-be-FV drunk person very yesterday
Karibu m-kosan-e   na kila mtu.
nearly obj-make mistake-SUBJUNC with every person
U-li-ku-w-a   u-ki-onge-a
2SG-PAST-INF-COP-FV 2SG-ASP-chat-FV
A LOT OF NONSENSE
'You were very drunk yesterday. That you should almost make a fool of yourself with every person. You were talking a lot of nonsense.'
(Swahili/English; Myers-Scotton, 1993a: 44)

In line with our hypothesis, example (9) also arises because the SP feature bundles of the EL lemma are not sufficiently congruent with those of the ML lemma. *Bring it up* occurs as an EL island because the speaker chooses an EL lemma's lexical-conceptual structure. One of the consequences of selecting *bring up* with a pronominal object is that the EL lemma projects a morphosyntactic structure in which the pronominal object of English occurs before the particle satellite. This example illustrates that in EL islands, it is the EL lemma that calls up morphosyntactic procedures in the formulator. Notice that in a mixed constituent, while an EL lemma may support an EL lexeme, provided that the EL lemma is sufficiently congruent with the ML counterpart, it is always this ML counterpart that calls up the morphosyntactic procedures from the formulator, never the EL lemma. Compare (7) above, in which the EL lexeme *underestimate* occurs in a morphosyntactic frame projected by its ML counterpart. Evidence that it is the ML counterpart projecting the frame is that the object pronoun clitic occurs before the inflected verb in (7) while the object pronoun occurs according to English structural constraints in (9).

(9) No va-n   a BRING IT UP
     NO go-3PL to
     'They are not going to bring it up.'
     (Spanish/English; Pfaff, 1979: 296)

Thus, one reason EL islands result is that the speaker's intentions regarding lexical-conceptual structure cannot be adequately realized in the ML (i.e. SP feature bundles do not match sufficiently).

The above examples illustrate EL islands resulting from lack of congruence regarding content morphemes; however, because speakers can also have intentions regarding lexical-conceptual structure conveyed by system morphemes, they may produce EL islands because of congruence problems in such cases.

Quantifiers are good examples of system morphemes that may produce such problems. Quantifiers are system morphemes that clearly have semantic content. Recall that system morphemes with the feature [+ Q] identify a member or members of a set. Thus, in many examples of EL islands, it seems that a motivation for producing the island is to make a contrast to ensure UNIQUE specification of quantification. That is, there may well be a pragmatic or semantic mismatch cross-linguistically in quantifiers. In (10), the speaker's intention seems to be to draw attention to the contrast between her having completed a task as opposed to the addressee's more minimal accomplishments. The English construction, *all the x*, gives the quantifier *all* prominence not afforded by the Swahili counterpart *nguo zote* 'clothes all'. (Neither would a mixed constituent offer prominence to 'all' since it would follow Swahili order, e.g. *clothes zote*.) Her choosing to use English, partly because of the word order it affords, is made at the conceptual level; yet, this has consequences in terms of the morphological realization pattern.

(10) Ni-me-maliz-a ku-tengenez-a vi-tanda ni-ka-WASH
      I have finished to fix [make] PL-bed 1SG-CONSEQ-wash
      ALL THE CLOTHING na wewe bado   maliza na
                       and you   not yet finish with
      KITCHEN. Ni nini u-na-fany-i-a hu-ko?
                is what you are doing there?
      'I finished making the beds and I've washed all the clothing and you aren't yet finished in the kitchen. What are you doing there?'
      (Swahili/English; Myers-Scotton, 1993a: 80)

8.5   The conceptual level and predicate–argument structure

As should be clear, the selection of the SP feature bundles is part of the conceptual level of this language production model. Yet, this selection can have consequences at another level. Recall that lemmas, which are located in the mental lexicon, send directions to the formulator to construct sentential frames at the functional level. The basis for most directions is the predicate–argument structure contained in lemmas. Yet the SP feature bundle may ultimately be the determining factor for some of these directions. The specifics of this argument will not be developed in this chapter; but such examples as the morphosyntactic consequences of selecting the nominalization version of a conceptual structure rather than the verbal version come to mind.

9   Insights into the complexities of lemma entries

CS data also provide empirical evidence about the nature of at least certain lemma entries and their relation to the conceptual structures activating them.

9.1   Nonfinite verb forms and their lemma entries

First, consider nonfinite forms, such as present and past participles. In all CS data sets available, such lexical items, although morphologically complex, act as if they are single units from the standpoint of the constituent frame.

For example, when an EL participle appears in a mixed constituent, evidence of its unitary nature is twofold.

1   The participle always appears in a multimorphemic form, as the verb stem plus the requisite EL affix(es) associated with well-formed participles in the EL. Such "full category-identifying affixation" does not occur for other EL content morphemes in mixed constituents, with the exception of plurals in some cases, as noted above.

2   The formulator treats the EL participle as a "completed content morpheme" of the same order as an EL noun or adjective. That is, no further ML affixes relevant to category membership (i.e. participle, in this case) are applied (cf. for example Ten Hacken, 1994: 311–12). Example (11) illustrates an English past participle (*worried*) in a mixed constituent.

(11) ma ba'tiʔid   innik   WORRIED bas
       no 1S/PRES/think COMP/2S worried   but
       inti   CURIOUS
       you   curious
       'I don't think that you are worried but you are curious.'
       (Arabic/English; Okasha, 1995: 2.50)

Recall that, as formulated in the MLF model, the system morpheme principle refers to "syntactically active" system morphemes. A syntactically active morpheme has relevance in a syntactic category beyond its head. This principle, therefore, allows for the possibility of EL system morphemes, but only if those morphemes do not control the signalling of syntactic relationships of the head in its larger constituent.

The fact that certain EL inflected forms occur in mixed constituents implies that there are two different kinds of procedures operating in the formulator. One is sensitive to directions INTERNAL to a lexical category. This is the procedure that accepts the English past participle *worried* as congruent with an ML modifier. Under this view, EL affixes on nonfinite verb forms are accessed via procedures providing morphology relevant only in a category-internal sense. One way of looking at those affixes that we refer to as category-internal is to say that they are best classified as derivational rather than inflectional. The other procedure in the formulator is sensitive to directions ACROSS lexical categories, including those regarding morphological realization patterns of surface phrase structure. Directions relevant across lexical categories must come only from the ML.

In terms of the inflectional procedures they undergo, participles are treated as single units in CS. Whether the lemma supporting the morpheme is complex or whether two lemmas are involved is open to question.

Yet CS data also provide evidence that the complexity of these lemmas – and presumably other lemmas as well – can vary cross-linguistically. For example, even though the lexical category Infinitive would have seemingly identical SP bundles cross-linguistically, the lemma supporting this category may be different from one language to another The evidence is at the morpheme level. English and French infinitives differ in their realizations in CS mixed constituents when either language is the EL. The French infinitive is always bimorphemic (including an affix which apparently marks Infinitive), as in (12) below. In contrast English infinitives never include the free-form system morpheme *to*, which also marks Infinitive. This pattern suggests two things:

1   The French infinitive lemma entry is complex and distinctive, while the English one is the same as that for the verb stem.
2   English *to* is a system morpheme while the French infinitive marker serves more as a derivational affix.

Thus, the same conceptual structure (Infinitive) has different lemma histories cross-linguistically.

9.2   How does "double morphology" result?

Plurals in a number of language pairs show "double morphology," that is, plural affixes from both the ML and the EL. In fewer cases, infinitives also show infinitival affixes from both languages; this is usually the case when French is the EL, since, as noted above, a French infinitive always appears with the French infinitival affix.

The two different cases of double morphology arise in two different ways. When infinitives in CS show double morphology, it is because the EL lemma entry for Infinitive is the base form in that language. For example, in (12) the entire French infinitive *comprendre* is retrieved as a single unit because there is no other form in French that is congruent with the base form of the Lingala verb stem.

> (12) L'   HEURE ya kala TROIS QUARTS ya ba-JEUNE-S
>   DET hour   of past three   quarters of CL2-young-PL
>   ko-COMPREND-RE   AVENIR te . . .
>   INFIN-understand-INFIN future   not

'In the past three-fourths of the young people did not understand
what their future meant . . .'
(Lingala/French; Bokamba, 1988: 37)

The plural case is more problematic. Myers-Scotton discusses the phenomenon
extensively (1993a: 110–12, 132–6) and concludes that there is "strong implicational
evidence that double morphology may result from misfiring at some point in production" (1993a: 135). Under her argument, the plural affix is encoded in its own lemma
and the EL affix is accessed by mistake when the lemma for the noun itself is called.
Since the grammatical frame in which the EL noun is to appear is under ML control,
the formulator then goes on to call the ML affix. The net result is two affixes for the
same job.

The issue remains, however, what is the nature of the suggested "misfiring" and why
should it come about frequently only with the plural affix and not affixes for inflections
for other properties, such as gender or case?[15] We can make "misfiring" more specific in
the following way. We suggest that plural has a conceptual structure setting it apart
from other nominal affixes whose contribution has to do with structuring the nominal
phrase, not adding semantic weight. While all system morphemes are "indirectly
elected" at the conceptual level by the content lemma that projects them (Willem
Levelt, personal communication), only an ML system morpheme should be elected (i.e.
not a system morpheme from BOTH the ML and the EL). A possible reason both
morphemes appear is that there may be a "mistiming" (rather than a "misfiring") such
that the EL lemma supporting both the nominal concept and its indirectly elected plural
are selected before the ML setting the grammatical frame is activated (Willem Levelt,
personal communication). Then, when it turns out that the ML is not the same language
as that of the nominal concept, in its frame-building function, the ML supplies its own
rendition of plural.

10 Predicate–argument structure and the functional level

Recall that while intrasentential CS requires that morphemes from both languages be
present in the same CP, it is only ML lemmas that send directions to the formulator to
set the CP frame (except internally in EL islands). Setting the frame has several aspects
for intrasentential CS. As in monolingual discourse, it means that the predicate–
argument structure is realized (i.e. a schema with slots for the verb and its arguments)
as well as morphological realization patterns (most crucially the requisite system
morphemes). For the mixed constituents of intrasentential CS, setting the frame also
means inhibiting EL lemmas at the functional level so that only ML lemmas will "call"
procedures in the formulator setting up the schema (i.e. morpheme order and system
morphemes will come from the ML). Yet, lemmas from BOTH languages are activated at
some point in the production process.

Above we suggested how EL lemmas first come into play at the conceptual level.
That is, speaker intentions that involve EL content morphemes activate the EL lemmas
in the mental lexicon that support the morphemes. There, these lemmas are checked
with ML counterparts for congruence with respect to lexical-conceptual structure; that
is, their SP feature bundles are checked.

We now discuss CS data that motivate the claim that another checking procedure must take place before directions are sent to the formulator. The predicate–argument structures supported by EL lemmas and their ML counterparts are checked; that is, their *morphosyntactic feature bundles* (hereafter *MS feature bundles*) are compared.

Suppose that an EL lemma is selected at the conceptual level. If the MS feature bundle of its supported lexeme is congruent with the MS feature bundle of the ML lexeme whose lemma is directing the projection of the sentential frame, then the EL lexeme is morphosyntactically integrated into the ML frame.

As was the case with the conceptual level, there is internal complexity at the functional level. The predicate–argument structure encoded in the lemma "calls" two classes of morphosyntactic procedures in the formulator, an argument introduced in Section 9.1. First, some procedures result in structures internal to a single maximal category (e.g. regarding a noun and certain affixes – possibly those for gender and plural). There is some evidence that not only the ML but also the EL may be involved in calling these procedures that determine category-internal form. Specifically, we have in mind gender as a feature. Further discussion awaits more research, however. Second, there is another class of procedures that is called only by the ML. These determine the morphosyntactic relations between the projections of the various lexical categories. The examples that we cite now to demonstrate the role of congruence between EL and ML lemmas at the predicate–argument structure come from this second class.

Example (13) shows the prototypical case of close congruence between the lemmas underlying the realization of an EL content morpheme (the English verb stem *help*) in an ML frame. In this case, the thematic content of the lexical-conceptual structure and the grammatical argument structure are very similar across the ML and EL. In both the ML (Adaŋme) and the EL (English), a figure is a benefactive and the subject is the actor.

(13) a   ŋɛ   mĩ   HELP-e
      3PL COP 1S/OBJ help-PRES PROG
      'They are helping me.'
      (Adaŋme/English; Nartey, 1982: 185)

Example (13) contrasts with (12) from Lingala/French CS. In (12) the French verb includes the infinitive suffix. We argue that the difference between the EL verb in (12) and (13) lies in the difference between what is perceived as the base form of the verb in the EL (i.e. English and French differ in this regard).

11 Issues of congruence in verb phrase structure

In some cases, an EL verb may be congruent at the conceptual level, but not congruent in terms of the predicate–argument structure.

11.1 Congruence and predicate–argument structure

The lack of congruence between the EL and ML regarding the verbal phrase in example (14) shows clearly that it is the ML that projects the morphosyntactic frame. In this case, the lemmas supporting the notion of *graduate* in the ML (Japanese) and the EL (English) have similar enough lexical-conceptual structures for the EL lemma to project its lexeme in the surface. Yet, these structures are slightly different and this becomes evident when SOURCE is part of the proposition to be expressed. In English to express SOURCE with *graduate* requires a surface form of verb + prepositional phrase (*graduate + from*-NP). Its Japanese counterpart expresses the notion of SOURCE without a prepositional/postpositional contentful phrase; it takes only a direct object with accusative case marking. While this may be only a slight difference, it still means the MS feature bundles of *graduate* are different in English and Japanese.

(14) a. *Watashi wa Waseda-kara   GRADUATE
          1S   TOP   from (ABL)
          shimashita
          did
      b. Watashi wa Waseda-(o) GRADUATE shimashita
                              ACC
          'I graduated from Waseda [University].'
          (Japanese/English; Azuma, 1991: 97–8; also cited in
          Azuma, 1993: 1078–9)

If the EL lemma supporting *graduate* were the one calling morphosyntactic procedures in the formulator for mixed constituents, then a sentence such as (14a) should be possible, since the system morpheme *-kara* 'from' comes from Japanese, and only the content morpheme *graduate* comes from English. Since (14a) is not attested, but (14b) is, such evidence supports the hypothesis that the ML (Japanese here) is the only one sending morphosyntactic directions of any kind to the formulator when mixed constituents are being constructed – even though EL lemmas (*graduate* here) can support content morphemes in these constituents.[16] (The use of an EL content verb with an ML auxiliary verb in a *do* verb construction is discussed in Section 11.2.)

The following example illustrates a similar situation in Turkish/Dutch. The main difference is that both the verb and its grammatical argument, the direct object, are EL lexemes. The Dutch direct object occurs with the ML suffix for accusative and plural, *gesprek-ler-i* 'conversations'. If the frame for this mixed constituent were projected from the EL, then this Dutch noun would occur in a comitative/instrumental PP (with *met*) and with a Dutch plural suffix. However, as is predicted, the formulator has projected an accusative-marked slot for the direct object, in line with the specifications of the ML. This is why the Dutch noun occurs without *met*, but with the Turkish accusative suffix.

(15) POLITIEK GESPREK-ler-i   OPHOUD-EN yap-ın
      political   conversation-PL-ACC stop-INF   do-IMP
      la
      INTENS
      'Stop this about politics, man!'
      (Turkish/Dutch; Backus, 1992: 99)

Example (16) shows how a lexical gap for a verb is handled by Turkish. Turkish has no equivalent for *uitmaken met* 'break up with' in Dutch. The Dutch verb itself is inserted as a nonfinite form into a mixed constituent by using the *do* construction discussed below. The verb "satellite" meaning 'with' (Dutch *met*) is rejected by the

Turkish frame; yet a loan translation of *met* into Turkish is accepted, possibly because Turkish has no competing counterpart; thus, the question of ML congruency for the satellite does not arise. This is a remarkable example from the standpoint of showing the robustness of the ML frame in controlling system morphemes.

(16) O diyor ben UITMAK-EN   yap-tı-m   kız-ınam
      he said I   break up-INFIN do-PAST-1S girl-with
      'He said [that] I have broken up with [the] girl.'
      (Turkish/Dutch; Backus, 1994)

The following Swahili/English example contrasts with the Japanese/English and Turkish/Dutch examples above in that the lack of congruence across lexical categories of verbal complements is solved in a different way – without the system morpheme supporting the ML frame prevailing, but with no EL frame, either.

(17) Mbona ha-wa   Ø-WORKER-S w-a   EAST AFRICA
      why   dem-CL2 CL2-worker-PL CL2-of
      POWER AND LIGHTING wa-ka-end-a   STRIKE
                           3PL-CONSEQ-go-FV strike
      hata we-ngine na-siki-a
      even CL-other 1SG/NONPAST-hear-FV
      wa-sha-wek-w-a   CELL
      3PL-"PERFECTIVE"-put-PASS-FV
      'And why did these workers of the East African Power and Lighting [Company] go [on] strike? – I even hear [that] some of them have already been put [in] cell[s].'
      (Swahili/English; Myers-Scotton, 1993a: 96)

In this example, note the mixed constituents *wa-ka-end-a STRIKE* and *wa-sha-wek-w-a CELL*. The result is now a bare form; both *strike* and *cell* are EL content morphemes uninflected in either the ML or the EL. In the previous two examples, the ML inflections appeared. We propose that the full form vs. the bare form realization can be explained by the difference in the morphosyntactic requirements of the respective MLs. In Japanese, for example, all NPs must be overtly case marked (unless the accusative direct object immediately precedes its verb). In Swahili, however, specific word order and verbal extensions, as well as prepositions and postpositions, are required to realize thematic roles. In (17) word order seems to serve the function of identifying *cell* as locative goal, even though the NP is not well formed in Swahili without some functional element marking its class gender (i.e. an element corresponding to any of classes 16–18, the locative gender classes).

In the Swahili/English example, the MS feature bundle projected by the verb for both languages includes the thematic role of locative. In English, locative thematic roles occur as PPs; in Bantu languages, most locatives are NPs prefixed or suffixed with a locative class (= gender) marker. This example shows a compromise strategy. The EL locative NP occurs with neither the EL preposition nor the ML class marker (-*ni* in this case), with only word order as an indication of role.

11.2   A strategy to include EL verbs as nonfinite forms

Another type of compromise strategy already exemplified above is a *do* construction. This construction consists of the ML verb encoding *do* (or a similar auxiliary verb) inflected with all of the requisite ML system morphemes (tense/aspect, agreement, etc.) appearing with an uninflected EL content verb (often the infinitive). We propose that the structural properties of verbs (what constitutes an inflectible stem) are such that when these languages are MLs, these properties block the occurrence of an EL verb with ML inflections. Thus, if an EL verb best satisfies the speaker's intentions, a compromise strategy is to place it in a frame projected by the ML auxiliary, with the auxiliary taking all verbal inflections.

> (18)   Avan enne CONFUSE paNNiTTaan
> he   me   do-PAST
> 'He confused me.'
> (Tamil/English; Annamalai, 1989: 51, cited in Myers-Scotton, 1993: 113)

Boeschoten (personal communication) argues that such constructions are an areal feature rather than a typological one. He makes two points: first, such constructions are a commonplace strategy for incorporating borrowed lexemes in the geographical area extending from Turkey to India. Second, such *do* constructions are now being found in the Moroccan Arabic/Dutch CS of some Moroccans living in the Netherlands, possibly by analogy with such constructions in Turkish/Dutch CS. Example (19) shows this:

> (19)   baš y-dir   AFKOEL-EN!
> for 3-do/IMPERF cool down-INF
> 'In order to cool (himself) down!'
> (Moroccan Arabic/Dutch; Boumans, 1994: 3)

In many of the data sets in which the *do* construction is attested, the ML is verb-final. One could argue that this typological contrast seems to motivate the use of an ML auxiliary verb (usually *do*) in final position preceded by a nonfinite EL verb that carries the content. Language pairs in which the ML is verb-final showing *do* constructions include various Indian languages/English (both Indo-European and Dravidian), Japanese/English, and Turkish/Germanic languages. Earlier examples from Japanese/English CS (14) and Turkish/Dutch CS ((15) and (16)) include *do* constructions. No cases of EL verbs inflected with ML morphology, if the ML is verb-final, are reported in the literature. However, the *do* construction is also found in other language pairs that do not show this directional contrast in thematic role and case assignment, for example southern Bantu languages (e.g. Shona, Chewa) and English CS as well as Moroccan Arabic/Dutch CS (see (19)).

Thus, as we have suggested above, directionality may be only a surface manifestation of a more basic distinction in what it takes for a verb to qualify for projecting thematic roles onto the sentential frame. Lack of congruence at the level of morphological realization patterns in terms of both thematic role and case assignment seems to promote use of the *do* construction, but more research is necessary.

11.3   When a lexical category is missing

Some passive constructions in CS illustrate the effects of lack of congruence cross-linguistically when verbal derivations are encoded differently, For example, in English, past participles function adjectivally (and are analyzed as adjectives within most generative frameworks, having lost their case-assigning properties). That is, English past participles can be viewed as [+N] and [+V], but Swahili lacks a past participle and Swahili passive verbs are only [+V]. These passive verbs exhibit the same morphosyntactic properties as active verbs; subject morphology and tense/aspect morphology are identical. Furthermore, the passive suffix is a member of the set of verbal suffixes that add to or alter the lexical-conceptual content of the verb stem. Other characteristic members of the set are stative, causative, and applied. Passive combines productively with many of these suffixes to produce modified SP feature bundles (for example, *-andik-* takes the passive suffix for the meaning 'be written', *-andik-w-*; combined with the applied suffix *-andik-i-w-* has the meaning 'to be written for'). In the example below, the lexical-conceptual structure associated with the SP feature bundle of *offered* has been selected. It could be argued that English *offered* fills a lexical gap; yet it seems the better argument is that *offered* and its Swahili counterpart are pragmatic mismatches. The Swahili semantic counterpart is *-nunuliwa* 'be bought for'; however, its use incorporates the sense of 'money being paid' much more so than does *offered*. At any rate, the EL lexeme most closely matches the speaker's intentions and occurs in the sentential frame projected by the ML counterpart lemma. The lexical category of the EL lexeme, however, does not fit into the morphosyntactic frame normally projected in the Swahili passive construction. It does, however, fit into a frame of *copula "be" + predicate adjective* in Swahili.

(20) A-li-ku-w-a   ha-zi-BUY   hi-zo
      3SG-PAST-INF-BE-FV 3SG/NEG-CL10/OBJ-buy those-CL10
      a-li-ku-w-a   a-na-ku-w-a   OFFERED tu
      3SG-PAST-INF-BE-FV 3SG-PROG-INF-be-FV offered   just
      'He didn't buy those, he was just being offered.'
      (Swahili/English; Myers-Scotton, 1993a: 115)

The use of a compromise strategy is common in Swahili/English CS when there is lack of congruence across derived verbal forms, here, a past participle. For example, in "popular Swahili" there is a construction consisting of the locative copula *-ko* inflected for subject plus a predicate adjective. English past participles occur readily in this construction (e.g. *tu-ko confused* 'we are confused'; Myers-Scotton, 1993a: 115). Recall that we argue in Section 9.1 that participles are morphologically complex single units supported by a single lemma.

11.4   Tailoring EL verb stems to meet ML requirements

Another compromise strategy is illustrated in the Swiss German/French example below. In order for French verbs to receive Swiss German subject–verb agreement, they are morphologically adapted to a Swiss German verbal paradigm. This is accomplished by attaching the derivational affix *-ier-* before the normal inflectional agreements. That is, in order for a verb to be recognized as an inflectible stem, it must satisfy certain morphological requirements of Swiss German. Without the German derivational affix, French verbs do not appear to do so, for reasons unknown as yet. Note that while *forcier-* occurs in Standard German, it does not occur in monolingual Swiss German.

(21) Die altere muen die jungere FORCIER-e, no die ander Sproch au no einisch hie und do . . .
'The parents must force the children, to [use] the other language now and then . . .'
(Swiss German/French; Lüdi, 1983)

11.5   EL islands: the radical solution to a mismatch

When predicate–argument structures across languages involved in CS show such incongruence that the types of compromise strategies discussed above do not seem to suffice, then a more radical strategy is followed: EL material selected at the conceptual level appears in EL islands. All EL islands consist entirely of EL morphemes and follow EL well-formedness conditions for internal structural dependency. EL islands that are not internal EL islands (discussed below) are well-formed maximal projections (e.g. NP, PP) in the EL; internal EL islands may or may not be maximal projections. All EL islands are within a CP framed by the ML. This is a more restricted definition of an EL island than that in Myers-Scotton (1993a).

Under the approach followed here, sometimes congruence at the lexical-conceptual structure level provides a match between the EL lemma and its ML counterpart, but the ML morphosyntactic frame does not accept the mapping that the EL lemma would project. For example, in (22) from Shona/English CS, the issue is lack of congruence in how a required locative NP (i.e. the verb is subcategorized for it) is realized in the morphosyntactic frame. In Shona, to convey the idea of movement along a PATH, a motion verb with an applied suffix conveying directionality toward a figure realized as a postverbal NP is required. English conveys such directionality with a PP. Because *ku-transfer* has been realized without the requisite applied suffix, an EL island with PPs is required to convey the notion of PATH. Note that we would argue that while *transfer* DOES trigger a following constituent in English, the trigger is not the surface lexeme *transfer*.[17] Rather, the reason is that *transfer* lacks the applied suffix that would allow for a bare NP complement as projected by the ML counterpart. Thus it is the morphological realization encoding the predicate–argument structure that triggers an EL island. Given *transfer* as a "bare verb" (without the applied suffix), the only alternative is to complete the projection of the locative thematic role with an EL island PP.[18]

(22) . . . WHENEVER munhu kana-ada ku-TRANSFER FROM A CERTAIN DEPARTMENT TO A CERTAIN DEPARTMENT . . .
'. . . whenever a person wants to transfer . . .'
(Shona/English; Crawhall, 1990: tape 16d)

The example above contrasts with the following one from English/Spanish CS. In English, an NP expressing the notion of PATH must be governed by a locative preposition, as in (22). However, an NP expressing the notion of BENEFICIARY (MALEFACTIVE) can be directly governed by its verb, as in *accuse someone*. This contrasts with Spanish, in which a verb cannot directly govern a BENEFICIARY complement. Thus, if a speaker engaging in intrasentential English/Spanish CS selects Spanish to encode the BENEFICIARY, this NP can appear in an EL island, as in (23). The BENEFICIARY NP occurs in a PP EL island, properly governed in Spanish, by the case-assigning preposition *a*.

The argument that Spanish, not English, is the underlying ML was considered, but discarded. On this view, a Spanish verb would project the PP and English *accused* is only an inserted EL lexeme (a sufficiently congruent counterpart of the Spanish verb). But if Spanish were the ML, then there is no explanation for the English pronoun (*he*), which is not congruent with a Spanish counterpart, or the English past tense inflection. Within the model, the only possible explanation is to argue that English is the ML and that there are two Spanish EL islands. The English verb *accuse* projects the beneficiary thematic role, but it need not project the surface phrase structure realizing the role; it can be realized in an EL island. Of course the speaker could have avoided using Spanish altogether. However, he/she has chosen to identify the beneficiary in Spanish; this is a decision made for pragmatic reasons at the lexical-conceptual level. As long as the constituent *a Mister Bigote* is a well-formed maximal projection in Spanish, it qualifies as an EL island. This constituent case-marked by a preposition is predicted (not an NP) because Spanish, not English, calls procedures in the formulator spelling out the morphosyntax. Thus, it is the content lexeme *Mister Bigote* that indirectly elects its requisite system morpheme *a*, not the case-marking preposition that is hierarchically superior in surface phrase structure. As long as the projection of a beneficiary is congruent across Spanish and English (as it is), the Spanish PP following the English verb is possible. The presence of such a mixed CP implies that the realization of thematic roles is somehow a surface phenomenon, separable from the projection of those roles.[19]

(23) He accused A   MISTER BIGOTE DE DOBLE LENGUAJE.
      [to] mister   bigote   of double   language
      'He accused Mister Bigote ["Mister Moustache"] of double talk.'
      (English/Spanish; Moyer, 1992: 55)

Finally, lack of congruence between two languages based on clitic properties of definite articles may explain why NP EL islands occur in an asymmetric fashion. Data from a large corpus of Swiss German/Italian CS (Preziosa-Di Quinzio, 1992) in which at times Swiss German is the ML and at other times Italian is the ML shows such an asymmetry. EL islands consisting of NPs from Italian occur freely, but not such islands from Swiss German when Italian is the ML. The EL island from Italian (DET + N) in (24a) exemplifies the many Italian NP EL islands that occur in this corpus, while (24b) illustrates a German noun occurring with an Italian determiner. There are no instances of German definite DET + N EL islands. This case illustrates lack of congruence at the functional level (morphological realization patterns), but it may also reflect congruence problems at the conceptual level (lexical-conceptual structure).

(24) a. Eba   dann simmer go LE   PENTOLE
          exactly then be-1PL go DET/FEM/PL pan-PL
          bringa
          take-INF
          'Exactly, and then we went to take the pans there.'

b. Gli   italiani   sono cosi
the/MASC/PL italian/MASC/PL be/3PL so
forti   con le   ABCHURZIGA,
strong/MASC/PL with DET/FEM/PL abbreviations,
ga?
huh?
'The Italians are so good at abbreviations, aren't they?'
(Italian/Swiss German; Preziosa-DiQuinzio, 1992: xxx, vii)

11.6   Summary of effects of congruence on resulting phrase structures

All the examples in the preceding parts of Section 11 show some compromise strategy that seems necessary to accommodate the appearance of the EL material. In line with our overall claim, we hypothesize that there is insufficient congruence, regarding some aspect of predicate–argument structure, between an EL lemma and its ML counterpart for the EL lexeme supported by the EL lemma to appear with no modifications in a mixed constituent framed by the ML. In (14) an EL verb is stripped of its satellite (*graduate from* = *graduate*) but otherwise morphosyntactically integrated into the ML frame. In (15) the Dutch noun *gesprek* receives ML accusative marking rather than occurring in a PP headed by *met* 'with' as it would in Dutch. In (16) a "*do* construction" from the ML plus an ML loan translation of the Dutch verb satellite is employed to accommodate a Dutch verb for which the ML shows a lexical gap (i.e. *uitmaken met* 'to break up with' becomes *uitmaken* plus the Turkish suffix for 'with' on the Turkish direct object). Examples (14) through (20) and (22) show EL lexemes occurring in mixed constituents, but as bare forms, under a variety of conditions including the *do*-verb construction. Recall that a bare form is an EL noun or verb that appears in a mixed constituent, but without the requisite ML system morpheme that would make it a fully inflected noun in the ML or a finite verb in the ML. Another strategy for dealing with noncongruent EL material is shown in example (21); a derivational suffix added to an EL verb enables it to be read as an ML verb and therefore to receive ML verbal inflections. Finally, examples (22), (23), and (24) show the most extreme accommodation to lack of congruence between an EL lemma and an ML counterpart. In these cases, accommodating certain types of EL material in a mixed constituent seems impossible; the evidence is that the EL material appears only in an EL island.

12   EL islands further studied

In (6)–(24), we have shown how EL material can be treated in various ways when congruence involving its predicate–argument structure or morphological realization patterns is checked against that of its ML counterpart. As discussed above, one strategy for dealing with insufficient congruence is to produce an EL island that fits the requirements of both the ML and the EL as a maximal projection. Evidence that these islands are under some ML control, even while conforming to the well-formedness conditions of the EL (i.e. morphological realization patterns are those of the EL, not the ML) is twofold:

1   EL islands (which are not internal EL islands) must qualify as maximal projections in the ML as well as in the EL, but they need not be identical syntactic categories, a constraint proposed in Woolford (1983).
2   Placement of EL islands follows well-formedness conditions of the ML, not the EL.

For example, see (25) in which the French PP conforms with Brussels Dutch placement, not unmarked placement in French.

(25) Ja vijf of zes waren er   want die À FRONT DE RUE
      yes five or six were there for who at end   of street
      waren
      were
      'Yes there were five or six, (for) who were at the end of the street.'
      (Brussels Dutch/French; Treffers-Daller, 1993: 223)

There is also another type of EL island. While these islands may be maximal projections within the EL, they are not according to ML well-formedness conditions. Rather, they occur as intermediate constituents within ML maximal projections. For this reason, we differentiate them by calling them "internal" EL islands. Such islands do meet well-formedness conditions of the EL. Yet, because they occur within ML maximal projections, ML morphosyntactic procedures govern into internal EL islands in ways that do not happen with EL islands that are not internal EL islands. Such an internal EL island (*dak la semaine*) is illustrated in (26).

(26) . . . jaɣni   w   kant dak LA SEMAINE djal   tajzawlu
      . . . I mean and it   was that-the-week where they take away
      LES PERMIS
      the driving licenses
      '. . . I mean, and it was [that] the week where they take away the
      driving licenses.'
      (Moroccan Arabic/French; Bentahila and Davies, 1992: 449)

Both *la semaine* 'the week' and *les permis* 'the driving licenses' are EL islands. That is, they are well formed according to French grammatical constraints; consequently, the determiners, which are system morphemes, are from French, not from Arabic, the ML. The one island of interest here is *la semaine* 'the week'. While it is well formed in French, it is within a larger NP constituent for which the ML projects the frame. For an NP introduced by the demonstrative *dak* to be well formed in Arabic, it must be followed by a determiner, not just a noun, resulting in the structure Demonstrative–Definite Article–Noun, or a triple bar structure. Thus, while **dak semaine* would not be predicted, *dak* plus *la semaine* does meet the ML specifications.

Contrastive evidence from other data sets involving French as an EL leads to the argument that while an internal EL island must be well formed in the EL, that is not enough. Rather, its particular form is governed by the constituent frame projected by the ML maximal projection containing it. In two other CS data sets with French as the EL, such internal EL islands as *la semaine* (consisting of a DET + N) do not occur

(Wolof/French in Swigart, 1992); (Lingala/French in Kamwangamalu, 1989). See (27) for how a French noun is inserted into a Wolof frame and (28) for how one is inserted into a Lingala frame. In both cases, the NP has only a double bar structure (i.e. in Wolof the French noun only occurs with a single determiner and in Lingala the French noun has no determiner because there are no definite article determiners in Lingala).

> (27) MÈRE bi, SIX la   am
> mother the six poss/existential has
> 'The mother has six [a young man keeping score during a card game].'
> (Wolof/French; Swigart, 1992: 136)

> (28) O-leki DIRECT na   CHAMBRE À COUCHER . . .
> 2S-go direct   to [the] room of sleeping
> 'You go straight to the bedroom . . .'
> (Lingala/French; Kamwangamalu, 1989: 138)

The argument here is that in these cases the ML frame does not call for a prenominal determiner, as do both Arabic and French. In Wolof, determiners follow their heads and Lingala does not have determiners. Thus, while a mixed constituent in these data sets may well include a French noun, internal EL islands of a French DET + Noun do not occur.

Another reason why an internal EL island of French DET + N is possible in an Arabic frame, but not in either a Wolof or a Lingala frame, is that determiners in Arabic are morphophonemically attached to their heads. Determiners in French are the same. Thus, again French meets Arabic structural requirements, but not those of the other two languages.

Finally, another example shows how the ML frame governs into an internal EL island. The ML in (29a) and (29b) is Turkish. Both instances of a Dutch ADJ + Noun may be considered internal EL islands; they are N-bar projections in Dutch, not maximal projections, and they are part of Turkish maximal projections. But note that the island in (29a) contains an overt agreement suffix on the adjective *blond*, while the one in (29b) does not. In Dutch, definite NPs including a noun from the neuter class take *-e* as an agreement suffix on their adjectives. However, indefinite NPs, as in (29b) in this class have no AGR suffix on adjectives. It seems clear here that whether the Dutch NP is considered definite or indefinite is controlled by a higher-level ML procedure, expressed on the surface by the appearance of either definite or indefinite Turkish specifier lexemes (definite is marked by *o*; indefinite by *birtane*).

> (29) a. Ø   BLOND-E MEISJE afstuder-en   yap-tı
> DET blond-AGR girl   get-degree-INF do-PRET
> 'That blond girl got her degree.'
> b. ENGELS-i   birtane BLOND MEISJE-dan
> English-ACC one   blond   girl-ABL
> alı-yor-dun
> take-IMPERF-2SG
> 'You got the English [lessons] from a blond girl.'
> (Turkish/Dutch; Backus, 1992: 74, 44)

As in other EL islands, the EL directs the formulator to activate the EL morpho-syntactic procedures in such internal EL islands. However, the choice of one EL pro-cedure vs. another is determined by the larger ML frame. The semantic/pragmatic features of the ML phrasal category (NP, here) have certain morphological consequences for the entire NP. Thus, for example, if this SP feature bundle specifies the NP as definite, because the frame has been set at the maximal projection by the ML, the intermediate category (here, N′) also has this feature. Therefore, if the N′ is an internal EL island, it must also have this feature. Further research needs to be done as to what intermediate categories can be internal EL islands and whether morphosyntactic procedures of the ML always have consequences for the morphology of these EL islands.

13   The checking of ML and EL lemmas

While other hypotheses/principles of the MLF model refer to overall structural patterns in intrasentential CS, it is the blocking hypothesis and its "blocking filter" that determine how EL material is incorporated into these patterns. This hypothesis states that if an EL content morpheme has been chosen at the conceptual level as best conveying the speaker's intentions, the EL lemma supporting this morpheme must pass the blocking filter. That is, the EL lemma must be checked for congruency with an ML counterpart in the mental lexicon. The result is a determination of how that EL morpheme can be realized in a CP under ML control.

We propose that congruence checking is possible because whether or not languages show direct lexical correspondences, correspondences do exist (i.e. SP feature bundles), even if they are incompletely specified. As indicated above, our assumption is that the ML projects the frame for entire CP in intrasentential CS. If, at the conceptual level, the speaker has chosen what is assembled as an EL SP feature bundle, then this will activate the EL lemma in the mental lexicon associated with that bundle. Of course an EL lemma also includes the predicate–argument structure and morphological realization patterns associated with such an EL bundle. But because the ML projects the overall CP frame, this EL lemma will be checked against an ML counterpart.

This checking may occur in one of two ways. First, if the counterpart ML lemma does support an ML lexeme, then the ML lemma is necessarily fully specified according to lexical-conceptual structure (i.e. semantic and pragmatic information) and predicate–argument structure and morphological realization patterns (i.e. what directions to send to the formulator).

A second possibility is that the ML lemma does not support an existing ML lexeme; that is, there is a lexical gap in the lexical entries of the ML. Or, speakers as "rational actors" may well exploit differences in SP feature bundles between ML and EL counter-parts (i.e. these are pragmatic mismatches) when they select a particular lexical-conceptual structure (cf. Myers-Scotton, 1993c; Myers-Scotton, 1995). That is, they may choose an EL content morpheme with no close ML surface correspondent. Still, a checking is possible with ML material. In the case of a lexical gap in the ML or a serious pragmatic mismatch, no existing ML lemma is a ready-made counterpart. Yet checking may be done with "unbundled" ML material (i.e. undifferentiated ML lexical know-ledge). Note that while this material is not bundled into specific lemmas, it is proto-typical ML material.

Thus, because congruence is being checked with an EL lemma supporting a content morpheme, checking may be done with the ML lexical knowledge that is associated with content morphemes. Based on the EL lexical-conceptual information that has been activated, it is evident how a content morpheme supported by this lemma would fit into a semantic structure; for example, at the least it is clear whether it would receive or assign thematic roles. Also, because characteristic predicate–argument structure of the ML is available as part of ML lexical knowledge, this means that information about characteristic lexicalization patterns is available.

Thus, whether the ML lemma counterpart of the EL lemma selected (based on speaker intentions) is fully specified (i.e. supports an actually occurring lexeme) or must be matched with ML lexical knowledge, congruence can be checked. As already indicated, the result of this check has consequences for how the EL lexeme supported by the EL lemma in question will appear in intrasentential CS. In the examples of intrasentential CS cited here, we have illustrated degrees of congruence across ML and EL lemmas and their consequences for intrasentential CS. Most of the examples involve cases of congruence across lemmas supporting existing lexemes in both the ML and the EL; however, the case where an ML lexical gap exists has also been illustrated.

14   Summary

We conclude by recapitulating the type of language production model that CS data motivates. At the conceptual level, the speaker makes two types of decisions simultaneously. The first has discourse-general consequences. In brief, discourse decisions answer two related questions. Does the bilingual speaker wish to conduct the current discourse in a bilingual mode? If the answer is yes, then, does the speaker wish to use intrasentential CS? The development of the language production model in this chapter assumes that the speaker has answered yes to both of these questions.

These decisions having been made, the result is that both languages are "on" during production; however, the language to be designated the ML is more activated in specific ways, since it projects the overall frame for the relevant CP. In most discourses, the ML also supplies more of the morphemes than the EL.

The second type of decision made at the conceptual level concerns semantic intentions, as well as those pragmatic intentions in addition to the more specifically sociopragmatic intentions addressed in discourse-level decisions. In general, these intentions relate to answering two questions as well. Which of the languages to be used in bilingual speech will be the ML? Second, which content morphemes best convey specific semantic and pragmatic intentions? The discussion in this chapter has concerned itself largely with the consequences of satisfying these intentions by selecting an EL content morpheme as a potential entry in an ML frame. In summary, then, while lexical-conceptual structure in the conceptualizer is unspecified according to language, once selections are made regarding bilingual vs. monolingual modes, the ML, and the specific semantic/pragmatic feature bundle desired, these decisions are necessarily language-specific.

The intention to select an EL content morpheme activates an EL lemma in the mental lexicon. (Of course, intending to select an ML content morpheme would activate an ML lemma in the mental lexicon.) In order for an EL lemma to support an EL content morpheme in an ML frame, the EL lemma must be checked for congruency with an ML lemma counterpart.

This checking concerns lexical-conceptual structure (respective SP (semantic/pragmatic) feature bundles), but also the predicate–argument structure and morphological realization patterns associated with the lexical-conceptual structure (respective MS (morphosyntactic) feature bundles). These types of structures are what define lemmas.

At the functional level, lemmas send directions to the formulator in order to build the CP frame and support surface level lexemes. The directions calling frame-building morphosyntactic procedures are a response to the predicate–argument structure and morphological realization patterns encoded in lemmas. The evidence from intrasentential CS is that these procedures fall into at least two categories when they apply to mixed constituents. Directions affecting procedures internal to a single maximal category may come from both the ML and the EL. In general, a more systematic investigation of intrasentential CS is needed in order to determine which morphosyntactic procedures affecting surface morphology are sensitive to EL, as well as ML, directions. For example, in relation to double morphology, it seems that the procedure calling plural is one of these.

A second class of procedures is called only by the ML. These determine morphosyntactic relations between the projections of separate lexical categories. For example, while a noun may be marked for plural from both the ML and the EL, the agreement on any modifiers is supplied via directions from the ML.

As indicated above, when a speaker's intentions call for an EL content morpheme at the surface level, this selection activates the EL lemma in the mental lexicon supporting that morpheme. How the EL morpheme may appear in a CP framed by the ML depends on the extent to which there is congruence between its lemma and an ML counterpart in the mental lexicon.

If the ML counterpart supports an existing ML lexeme, its lexical-conceptual structure (i.e. semantic and pragmatic information) as well as its predicate–argument structure and morphological realization patterns are fully specified. These structures are checked against those of the EL lemma's entry.

If there is no existing ML lemma as a counterpart, the EL lemma is matched with relevant prototypical ML material that exists in the mental lexicon in an unbundled state as ML lexical knowledge. In order to form new words (fill lexical gaps) and change the meaning or grammatical patterning of existing lexemes, the existence of prototypical ML material as undifferentiated lexical knowledge, alongside fully specified lemmas, seems necessary. The undifferentiated ML lexical knowledge contains information at the same three levels as lemmas do (lexical-conceptual and predicate–argument structures, and morphological realization patterns). This is sufficient for both frame building and congruence checking.

Thus, based on such information contained in even undifferentiated ML lexical knowledge, congruence checking is possible.[20] If the result of the checking of counterparts is sufficient congruence, then the EL lemma meets the specifications of the ML frame, and the EL lexeme that this EL lemma supports can appear in a mixed constituent in this ML frame. If the result is insufficient congruence, one of a number of compromise strategies is necessary. Many of these have been discussed above, such as "bare" nouns, do-verb constructions and EL islands.

There is a second way in which an EL morpheme may appear in an ML frame.[21] As a discourse decision, the bilingual speaker makes the choice not to engage in intrasentential CS. Thus, the speaker intends to produce a monolingual CP framed by language X, a language chosen because it meets sociopragmatic and semantically based intentions, whatever they may be. Yet, the speaker is not successful in finding *le mot juste* in language X for a semantic/pragmatic feature bundle that he/she wishes to convey (i.e. in this case, finding *le mot juste* involves shifting from monolingual discourse). Thus, the speaker revises his/her plan and attempts to select a content morpheme from language Y (another entry in the speaker's linguistic repertoire). At this point, the speaker must also select either monolingual production in language Y (which may mean a "frame restart" at the conceptual level) or proceed with language X as the frame-building language. If he/she continues with language X, since this language was already framing the CP, the necessary adjustment is slight. Rather than framing a monolingual CP, language X becomes the ML of a bilingual CP, and the result is an instance of intrasentential CS. Further study may show that most of these searches for *le mot juste* result in the speaker staying with the original framing language; psycho-linguistically, this would seem to be the easiest alternative to take. Of course the EL lemma supporting the morpheme from language Y (*le mot juste*) must be checked against its ML counterpart in the manner described above, even though most certainly the ML counterpart may support no actual surface ML morpheme.

Hesitation phenomena indicate that revision is possible at any point in the production process. Revisions are more minor if the speaker has chosen a candidate lexeme from language Y that is congruent with the requirements of an otherwise fully specified frame. Insertion is simply delayed but is accomplished with no change of the frame. More serious are revisions that require "restarting" the frame; these indicate that the predicate–argument structure or morphological realization patterns satisfied by the language X semantic/pragmatic feature bundle that was rejected are not congruent with what is projected by the new candidate from language Y.[22]

15   A window on language production and lexical entries

In this chapter, we have presented evidence from intrasentential CS to motivate a model of language production. We have dealt with only two levels of the model: the conceptual level and the functional level. Of course any complete discussion would also have to treat the surface, or positional, level. Our main interest has been in supporting the hypothesis that various types of congruence explain variation in structures found in intrasentential CS. Congruence involves lexical-conceptual structure, predicate–argument structure, or morphological realization patterns, or some combination of these three levels.

In turn, implicit in our discussion is the suggestion that how congruence issues are resolved in CS provides evidence about the nature of lexical entries. Specifically, this resolution implies how central certain aspects of lexical-conceptual structure and predicate–argument structure are to the specification of lexical entries. Put another way, how an EL content morpheme is accommodated by an ML frame tells us something about which features characterizing that morpheme (ultimately characterizing its supporting lemma) are critical and which may be peripheral in lexical entries. At this stage, we only claim to have shown the effects on CS of different aspects of lexical structure, but we do think it is clear how studying congruence in CS has implications far beyond the nature of CS itself.

Notes

1   Grosjean and Miller (1994) present experimental evidence that while both languages are activated during CS, a complete phonological shift from one language to another is possible.

2   Both "traditional" subordinate clauses and main clauses are CPs; however, most main clauses have a null element in COMP position as in the main clause of [I want [for him to do it]].

3   In contrast with the ML vs. EL distinction, relative dominance of languages at the discourse level does apply to both intersentential and intrasentential CS. First, one language usually contributes more material to the entire discourse (e.g. in intersentential CS, more CPs are in this language). Second, this same language sets various aspects of the discourse frame; however, we will have no more to say about them in this chapter. This more dominant language is often synonymous with "the unmarked choice" of the discourse, while the other language(s) are more or less "marked choice(s)" (Myers-Scotton, 1993; 1993c).

4   The examples below illustrate both the morpheme order and the system morpheme principles. In (a) the modifier of *plate* follows, as is required by Swahili, the ML. Swahili also provides the system morpheme *ma-* on *home*.

> (a)   Hata MIDTERM, wa-ki-pe-w-a   ha-wa-end-i
>   even midterm,   3PL-CONDIT-give-PAS-FV neg-3PL-go-neg/FV
>   ma-HOME. . . .
>   CL6-home
>   a-na-ku-l-a   PLATE m-bili   z-a   murram
>   3S-NON-PST-INFIN-eat-FV plate   CL10-two CL10-of maize
>   'Even at midterm, when they are given [breaks], they don't go home . . . He
>   eats two plates maize.'
>   (Swahili/English; Myers-Scotton, 1993a: 86)

In (b), the French past participle *recalé* precedes Alsatian *wurd*, following the Alsatian ML order, rather than following the inflected auxiliary verb, as would be required by the EL grammar of French. (In Alsatian subordinate clauses, the inflected auxiliary occurs in final position, although it may be followed by adjunct PPs.) In the mixed constituents in this example, the system morphemes come from Alsatian, the ML: the determiner *de*, the preposition plus determiner *am*, and the passive auxiliary *wurd*. The constituent *panne d'essence* is an EL island; in EL islands, all the morphemes, including system morphemes, come from the EL.

> (b)   Noch schlimmer, wenn de CLIENT RECALÉ wurd
>   Still   worse,   when the client   refused become + 35G/PAST
>   am   PERMIS weje   de PANNE D' ESSENCE.
>   to + DEF license because the lack   of   gas
>   'Even worse is when the client has been failed because of the lack of gas.'
>   (Alsatian/French; Gardner-Chloros, Appendix III, cited in Myers Scotton,
>   1993a: 89)

5   "Discourse-relevant" implies coherence; i.e. a relevant sample should include minimally two contiguous CPs, either from a single speaker or from an adjacency pair produced by two speakers.

6   The socio- and psycholinguistic criteria mean that the ML is often the speaker's first language; but this is not necessarily so, most obviously if the different speakers have different first languages. It should be clear that neither is the ML necessarily the speaker's "best" language, by either his/her own assessment or independent evaluation, although it often is.

    ML assignment is not fixed across time or even for a single discourse. If the socio-linguistic and psycholinguistic factors associated with ML choice in a community change over time (e.g. new sociopolitical divisions arise or language policies change, etc.), what was the EL (or another language) may become the ML. Also, in many communities when situational factors are modified (e.g. the topic shifts or participants change, etc.), which language is the ML may change in "on-line" discourse.

7   Note that these are not the only types of constituents that are logically possible. Thus, certain types of constituents are ruled out by the MLF model.

8   There can be characteristic patterns of CS in particular communities or in particular language pairs. For example, intersentential CS may be the dominant or even exclusive pattern. Or, within intrasentential CS, there can be differences in the role of the EL that can be qualitative and quantitative.

    One type of qualitative difference is in the syntactic nature of the mixed constituents. For example, in some languages internal EL islands occur; these may or may not be maximal projections in the EL. However, from the point of view of the ML they are intermediate constituents or nonmaximal projections within an ML maximal projection. In Moroccan Arabic/French CS such islands consisting of Determiner + Noun occur relatively frequently (Bentahila and Davies, 1983; 1992). In some corpora, EL verb stems inflected with ML morphology occur frequently; (e.g. in Swahili/English CS (Myers-Scotton, 1993a) or in Irish/English CS (Stenson, 1990)).

    In addition, some differences are strictly quantitative. For example, how many singly occurring EL morphemes are found in mixed constituents? In some data sets, there are very few (e.g. Swiss German/French in Myers-Scotton and Jake, 1994). In other sets, single EL morphemes are very frequent (e.g. Turkish/Dutch in Backus, 1992).

    Finally, the difference in the role of the EL can be both quantitative and qualitative. For example, are there more EL islands or more mixed constituents? Another source of difference is the syntactic role of EL islands across corpora. However, equivalence, as discussed by Poplack (1980) does not determine what can occur as an EL island. In fact, as we argue here and as Myers-Scotton (1993a: 138) argues, "when there is NOT equivalence (= congruence) of an abstract nature, this is when there is a change in the basic procedures resulting in EL islands."

9   We thank Pim Levelt for suggesting *lexical knowledge* as a cover term for this material.

10   Note that *kina gece-si elbise-si* 'henna evening dress' is an internal EL island, discussed below. Turkish requires possessive suffixes in this type of compound noun construction.

11   FY = final vowel. Bantu languages have a characteristic phonotactics of CVCV.

12   From the standpoint of bilingual language production, whether they are borrowed forms or pragmatic mismatches, or have another semantic/pragmatic history, we argue that singly occurring EL lexemes in mixed constituents undergo the same processes.

    There is only "near-complete" morphological integration because the code-switched verb form lacks the final vowel characteristic of Bantu verbs and required by the Bantu CVCV phonotactics. This final vowel, however, carries no or very little morphological information independent of other elements in the verbal assembly.

13   Another possible analysis of example (7) would be to argue that *underestimate* is an internal EL island. That is, it could be claimed that it is inflected with an English present tense 2nd person suffix, realized as zero. This is implied in Pfaff (1979: 301, note 8). The idea was suggested to us by Mary Sue Sroda. Either as a base form or as an EL island, its treatment in this mixed constituent indicates less than total congruence between the EL lemma supporting the lexeme *underestimate* and an ML counterpart.

14   Reference to studies of expected collocations in English would test the claim that *a lot of nonsense* has a near idiomatic, unitary value.

15   Nominal plural morphemes are not structurally assigned, whereas some gender and case morphemes are. This leaves open the possibility that doubling of other inherently assigned system morphemes may occur. However, we hypothesize that structurally assigned system morphemes cannot double because, although their slot is prepared by the content lemma, structurally assigned system morphemes cannot be spelled out until the functional or positional level where morphological patterns are set. The matching of the SP feature bundle with a lemma takes place at the conceptual level and this is where mistiming can occur, not later in the production process.

16   Azuma (1993) also discusses this example, but to support a somewhat different argument.

17   This use of "trigger" differs from that of Clyne (1987), where triggering depends on the surface occurrence of a form in one language that is similar or cognate with a form in the other and therefore triggers a language switch.

18   The argument that the island occurs because the verb form really is an inseparable phrasal verb (*transfer* + a satellite *from*) does not go through. Recall example (18) where *graduate* appears without *from*.

19   Elsewhere (Jake and Myers-Scotton, 1994) we make a complimentary argument about EL islands in Spanish/English CS data. A quantitative analysis of 259 EL islands that are PPs in Pfaff (1979) shows that only three possible configurations are present in PP EL islands in CS involving these two languages: (1) the entire PP is in Spanish; (2) the entire PP is in English; or (3) there is a Spanish P and an English NP. That is, there are no cases of an English P and Spanish NP complement, even when English is apparently the ML. We explain this anomaly by arguing that Spanish nouns require "tighter" case markers than English prepositions assign, resulting in structural asymmetry in possible EL islands.

20   The matching process in CS has parallels in learner varieties in second-language acquisition. This means that there are natural similarities between CS and interlanguage phenomena. We thank Ad Backus for this suggestion. Jake *et al.* (1995) discuss interlanguage in these terms.

21   We thank Georges Lüdi for reminding us that this provision is necessary to the model.

22   A final comment about the overall model is this: while this information is represented in discrete modules of the grammar (as represented in most generative approaches to grammar), parallel processing of the information contained in these modules characterizes language production. That is, the projection of linguistic information from the lexical-conceptual structure is simultaneous to specification of the predicate–argument structure and morphological realization patterns in terms of many different modules of the grammar. Information regarding thematic roles, case, and government for example, is being processed at the same time.

Source: Myers-Scotton, C. and Jake, J. (1995) Matching lemmas in a bilingual competence and production model. *Linguistics* 33: 981–1024. Reproduced by permission of the authors and Mouton de Gruyter.

Postscript

Looking back, we still find the arguments and insights in "Matching" (Myers-Scotton and Jake, 1995) meet our understanding of how language production works and the constraints on code-switching (CS). Here we have two goals. Most importantly, we show how a new model, the 4-M model, makes it possible to discuss CS structure more precisely. Serendipitously the 4-M model captures more formally certain aspects of morpheme classification that the MLF model already expressed intuitively. However, first we address some ambiguities in "Matching". One concerns the scope of the MLF model. The model applies only to classic CS. This is CS in which only one language, the ML, is the source of both the abstract and the surface morphosyntactic frame. In this type of CS, the ML does not change within the bilingual CP although it may change between CPs. In contrast, in composite CS, not only do morphemes come from both languages, but also part of the abstract framing structure comes from the EL. Some readers find another ambiguity in the system morpheme principle; the 4-M model clarifies that this principle applies to only one type of system morpheme. A third ambiguity concerns EL islands. Our discussion emphasized mis-matching of semantic and pragmatic features. Structural factors, such as differences in morphological realization patterns, also can promote EL islands (cf. Myers-Scotton and Jake, 2001).

Some researchers think the 4-M model is a revised version of the MLF model. But it is not. Instead, it is a model of morpheme classification that applies to language in general, not just CS. Because of its wider relevance, the 4-M model connects a theory of grammar with language production and processing in ways that extend beyond the MLF model and, therefore, beyond CS.

Under the 4-M model, the four types of morphemes are content morphemes and three types of system morphemes. The model uses the term "morpheme" for both the abstract entries in the mental lexicon – lemmas – and the surface-level realizations of these lemmas. Content morphemes are directly elected by speaker intentions at the conceptual level, as already indicated in "Matching". As stated in any discussions of the MLF model, content morphemes also are defined as receiving or assigning thematic roles. Nouns and verbs are prototypical content morphemes. Like content morphemes, early system morphemes are conceptually activated; other system morphemes may convey conceptual material, but they are structurally assigned. However, early systems do not participate in the thematic grid. They are indirectly elected by their content morpheme heads to more fully realize the semantic/pragmatic feature bundle activating their heads. Early system morphemes include many determiners and the prepositional satellites of verbs in English, such as *throw away*. The other two types of system morphemes are called late system morphemes. They are activated at the level of the formulator and are only salient when larger constituents are assembled in language production. Bridge late system morphemes join together elements within a phrase. The most obvious example is the associative markers in many languages, such as *of* in *child of Alice*. Outsider late system morphemes are critical to indicating grammatical relationships between phrases. Subject–verb agreement affixes and clitics are called outsiders because they depend on information about their form that is outside of where they appear in the clause.

The 4-M model is relevant to CS because the distinctions underlying this classification system provide a principled explanation for the distribution of different morpheme types. The 4-M model implies a differential access hypothesis that states that, from the production standpoint, the major division between morpheme types is not between content and system morphemes, but between those that conceptually activated (content and early system morphemes) and those that are structurally assigned (late system morphemes). See Myers-Scotton (2005a). This distinction makes it possible to explain CS phenomena, such as morpheme doubling (i.e. equivalent morphemes from both languages). The occasional doubling of system morphemes is limited to early system morphemes that are accessed with their EL content morpheme heads. To date, the most significant implication of the 4-M model for CS is that it makes it clear how the system morpheme principle of the MLF model applies. Example (1) shows Xhosa–English CS, with Xhosa as the ML. There are two English constituents, a singly occurring lexeme, the verb *treat*, and a preposition phrase (EL island), *like human beings*. The English verb agrees with the Xhosa subject. Its prefix is an outsider system morpheme from the ML, Xhosa, as required by the system morpheme principle.

(1) Aba   ba-ntwana   ku-funek-a   ba-*treat*-w-e *like human beings*.
    CL2/DEM   CL2-child   INF-need-INDICATIVE CL2-treat-PASSIVE-SUBJUNC
    "These children need to be treated like human beings."

(Myers-Scotton, 2005b)

In some sense, the system morpheme principle loses prominence to a more general principle that was not noted in "Matching", the uniform structure principle (cf. Jake, Myers-Scotton and Gross, 2002; Myers-Scotton, 2002):

A given constituent type in any language has a uniform abstract structure and the requirements of well-formedness for this constituent type must be observed whenever the constituent appears. In bilingual speech, the structures of the Matrix Language are always preferred . . .

(Myers-Scotton, 2002: 8)

The first sentence states the obvious: languages have structure; but the second captures the generalization that bilingual speech shows asymmetries that favor the matrix language in order to preserve and make transparent the uniform structure of any CP.

Example (2) illustrates the strength of the uniform structure principle. Even though the nouns in this associative construction are both from English, the associative marker comes from Xhosa, the ML. That Xhosa provides the uniform structure in this bilingual example is obvious. The head of the associative construction is also inflected with Xhosa, showing that the noun class system of Xhosa controls the subject–verb agreement.

(2) . . . i-*rate*   y-e   *crime*   i-nyuk-ile
        CL9-rate   CL9-ASSOC   crime   CL9-go up-PERF
". . . [the] rate of crime is high."

(Myers-Scotton, 2005, unpublished data)

As argued in "Matching", an understanding of congruence, now supplemented by the 4-M model and the uniform structure principle, makes sense of bilingual speech.

Carol Myers-Scotton

Carol Myers-Scotton, PhD, is Distinguished Professor Emeritus of Linguistics at the University of South Carolina, USA. carolms@sc.edu

Janice L. Jake teaches English and Linguistics at the Midlands Technical College, South Carolina, USA. jakej@midlandstech.edu

Chapter 12

Code-switching and grammatical theory

PIETER MUYSKEN

In the last fifteen years, a large number of studies have appeared in which specific cases of intra-sentential code-switching were analysed from a grammatical perspective, involving a variety of language pairs, social settings and speaker types. It was found that code-switching is a quite normal and widespread form of bilingual interaction, requiring a great deal of bilingual competence. In individual cases, intra-sentential code-switching is not distributed randomly in the sentence, but rather it occurs at specific points.

Where much less agreement was reached is with respect to general properties of the process. Various 'constraints' and 'models' regulating intra-sentential code-switching (the type most interesting from the grammatical perspective) have been proposed and tested, with the result that some cases appear to fall under one constraint, and others under another. This is by itself unsatisfactory. We do not know in any systematic way how different the models proposed are, neither intrinsically nor in their predictions. It should be mentioned at this point that many of the studies do not make the constraints or models very explicit, limiting themselves to descriptive statements. Therefore, an account is needed of the grammatical notions relevant to code-switching. These notions can then be used both to characterise specific instances of intra-sentential switching and to relate the various proposals in the literature to each other.

I will organise this chapter around five main questions:

(i)   to what extent is code-switching seen as alternational and symmetrical (and hence involving properties of both languages involved) or insertional (and hence primarily governed by features of one dominant language)?

(ii)   to what extent are restrictions on the code-switching process seen as absolute or relative?

(iii)   to what extent is the relevant syntactic representation of the switch point seen as involving syntactic dependency?

(iv)   to what extent are sentential and lexical phenomena seen in the same perspective?

(v)   to what extent does equivalence between patterns or elements of the languages involved play a role, and how should this equivalence be characterised?

Before treating these five questions one by one, it is important to discuss further the relation between grammatical theory and code-switching. There are at least two connections between the two. First, I think this type of research is crucial for linguistics as a scientific discipline. What makes code-switching so special that it warrants relatively complex and time-consuming, hence costly, research is the following: one of the crucial questions in modern linguistics is the division of labour between the lexicon and the grammar of a language. To what extent do we rely on properties of individual words, when we produce and comprehend utterances, and to what extent on general rules of the language we speak? Related to this question – and for many researchers the same question phrased differently – is the following: can we reduce the differences between languages to lexical differences? If so, all that is specific about a language is its lexicon, and the lexicon plays a very major role in sentence production and comprehension. In the latter case, we should note, there *are* no rules specific to the language we speak, independent of lexical items. This complicated cluster of questions has produced much research and a so far inconclusive debate in the linguistic literature. I think the study of code-switching and language contact can uniquely contribute to elucidating and perhaps ultimately resolving these issues. When sentences are built up with items drawn from two lexicons, we can see to what extent the sentence patterns derive from the interaction between these two lexicons.

Second, the sociolinguistic study of code-switching cannot proceed without a solid, theoretically based 'structural analysis'. To understand which cases are of the same type, and which are different, to see which patterns are exceptional or marked and which are not, to be able to do quantitative research, for all this we need to know what the structural features of the patterns are. The present chapter discusses some of the descriptive tools that can be used for the analysis.

Clearly we should aim for universal explanations when looking for grammatical constraints. Much recent research into code-switching constraints is characterised by an attempt to relate two observations: (a) in different contact situations different switch patterns are found; (b) the differences are related, at least in part, to typological characteristics of the languages involved.

We can imagine two approaches to account for this.

(A) A model that believes there is a general set of constraints on code-switching, constituted, for example, by structural equivalence (Poplack 1980), or government

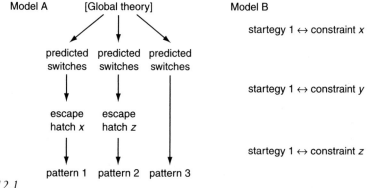

Figure 12.1

(Di Sciullo, Muysken and Singh 1986), or a matrix language/embedded language asymmetry (Myers-Scotton 1993a). In model A, the assumption is that the global theory makes a more limited set of switch sites available in specific instances than would be desirable. In those cases, escape hatches are needed, making additional switch sites possible.

(B) In model B, implicit in at least some of the recent work by Poplack and associates, different switching strategies occur – flagging, constituent insertion, etc. – governed by constraints specific to those strategies. There is no specific relation between linguistic properties of the languages involved and the choice of the strategy. What unifies both approaches is that both end up with a series of different language-mixing patterns or strategies.

In my view, it is methodologically desirable to aim for approach A, for three reasons. First, A makes a unified account possible. Second, in B it is not clear why in a given situation one strategy is preferred over another. Third, in the absence of a global theory, the relation between specific strategies and constraints remains unclear.

Model B has advantages over A if it turns out that the choice of a specific switching or mixing pattern is not motivated by structural considerations, and a combination of both models is called for if it is only partially motivated by structural considerations.

Keeping these observations in mind, we will now consider the five principal issues in the grammatical analysis of code-switching.

1 Is code-switching alternational or insertional?

Other authors might come up with a different general picture, but one could say that there are two dominant approaches to intra-sentential code-switching: those in terms of the *alternation* of the languages involved in the switch, and those in terms of a single-language matrix structure into which *insertion* of a constituent from another language takes place. Under this latter view we can conceive of the process of code-switching as something akin to borrowing: the insertion of an alien lexical or phrasal category into a given structure. The difference would simply be the size and type of element inserted, e.g. noun in borrowing vs noun phrase in code-switching.

It is clear there is alternation between codes in, for example, inter-sentential switching, and insertion with single borrowed elements. The question is whether we can establish objectively which process we are dealing with in the other cases. Some criteria:

(i)   when several constituents in a row are switched, which together do *not* form a constituent, alternation is more likely – otherwise we would have to assume multiple contiguous insertions; conversely, when the switched elements are all single, well-defined constituents, e.g. noun phrases or prepositional phrases, insertion is a plausible option.

(ii) when the switched element is at the periphery of an utterance, alternation is a clear possibility; conversely, when the switched string is preceded *and* followed by material from the other language, insertion may be more plausible, particularly if the surrounding material is grammatically linked in some kind of structure.

(iii) longer stretches of other-language material are more likely to be alternations.

The modality of these criteria makes it clear that there will be many undecidable cases. Is a subject in language A followed by a verb phrase in language B a case of alternation, of subject insertion, or of verb phrase insertion? For many language pairs the order of subject and verb phrase will be identical, so the clause as a whole may not belong to one language.

Consider a few examples:

    (1) Yo anduve *in a state of shock* pa dos días.
          'I walked in a state of shock for two days.' (Pfaff 1979: 297)

Here the temporal expression *pa dos días* is clearly related to the verb *anduve*. Similarly:

    (2) es una *little box* asina y ya viene . . .
          [It is a little box like this and it comes already . . .] (Lance 1975: 145)

Here the post-nominal determiner *asina* is clearly related to the article *una*.

However, there is not always such a relation. A few cases to illustrate this include:

    (3) [A] Right to 104th Street [B] *donde tenía una casa* [C] which were furnished rooms.
          [Right to 104th Street where I had a house which were furnished rooms.] (Sankoff and Poplack 1981: 35)

Here the Spanish fragment (B) modifies *Street* in (A) and the second English stretch (C) modifies *casa* ('house') in (B). Clearly the English fragments (A) and (C) are not syntactically related. Similarly:

    (4) [A] Why make Carol *sentarse atras [B] pa'que* everybody has to move [C] *pa'que se salga*.
          [Why make Carol sit at the back so that everybody has to move so that she can get out.] (Poplack 1980: 589)

Here the sentence fragment (B) is a complement to (A), and (C) is a complement to (B). Notice that the first Spanish fragment here contains both a verb phrase, *sentarse atras*, and purposive complementiser, *pa'que*. Neither between the English fragments nor between the Spanish ones is there a particular grammatical relation. A final example:

    (5) [A] *Se me hace que* [B] I have to respect her [C] *porque 'ta* . . . older.
          [It appears to me that I have to respect her because [she] is . . . older.]
          (Lance 1975: 143)

Again, (B) is a complement to (A), and (C) modifies (B). Notice that *porque 'ta* (because [she] is) does not form a unique constituent, excluding other elements – in this case 'older'.

It is clear that this type of data cannot be handled very well in a model which takes insertion into a matrix and a dependency relation between matrix and inserted material as its primes. Rather, the type of data has led to the idea that order equivalence across the switch point is what constrains code-mixing here.

1.1 Determining the base-language

In those cases where it is reasonable to assume that there is a base-language (also termed: matrix language) in a code-switched sentence, as in insertion models (e.g. Myers-Scotton 1993a), how do we determine which one it is? The answer to this question is in part empirical, in part theoretical in nature.

A discourse-oriented way of determining the base-language is: the language of the conversation. A statistical answer would be: the language in which most words or morphemes are uttered. A psycholinguistic answer could be: the language in which the speaker is most proficient. None of these answers is particularly satisfactory from the point of view of grammatical analysis. From that perspective, two types of answers have been given. In a model that attaches great importance to a parsing procedure from left to right, the first word or set of words in the sentence determines the base-language (such a model is reported on in Joshi 1985), triggering a set of analytic rules. Whatever insights this yields, care should be taken that switched left-peripheral interjections, exclamatives or adverbial adjuncts are not taken as the first element. These elements do not in any way determine the structure of the rest of the sentence.

In a structurally oriented model, some element or set of elements determines the base-language: often the main verb, which is the semantic kernel of the sentence, assigning the different semantic roles and determining the state or event expressed by the clause, is taken to determine the base-language. Plausible though adoption of the main verb as determining the base-language may be, in many languages there is a strategy to incorporate alien verbs, e.g. through agglutinative prefixes, as in Swahili, or through an auxiliary verb such as 'do', as in Hindi. In these cases, taking that borrowed verb as determining the base-language is clearly not correct. In the Matrix Language Frame model proposed by Myers-Scotton, the grammatical morphemes have to be from the base-language.

In the perspective of the government model (Di Sciullo *et al.* 1986; see section 3), there need not be a single base or matrix language for the clause. Still, there is a notion of base or matrix present in that model: each governing element (e.g. verb, preposition, auxiliary) creates a matrix structure. If the chain of government were unbroken, the highest element in the tree would determine the language for the whole tree; this would often be the inflection on the finite verb, as in the theory proposed by Klavans (1985) and taken up by Treffers-Daller (1991). In subordinate clauses, this would be the complementiser.

1.2 Function and content morphemes

In much of the literature on code-switching, and particularly in insertional models, the distinction between function and content morphemes plays an important role (Joshi 1985; Myers-Scotton 1995a). There is no single valid criterion for distinguishing these two classes: rather, different sub-classes can be distinguished on the basis of at least four different criteria. A first one is 'open' versus 'closed' class. Nouns and verbs typically belong to open classes, pronouns typically to closed one. Adjectives in many languages form an open class, but in some a small closed one. There is often only a limited number of co-ordinating conjunctions and adpositions in a language, but equally often elements could still be added to these categories.

A more precise criterion would therefore be whether a given closed class is *paradigmatically* organised, i.e., whether the elements in it are defined in opposition to each other (present vs past, singular vs plural, definite vs indefinite etc.). Pronoun and tense systems particularly tend to be tightly organised paradigmatically.

A third criterion may be *role in structuring the clause*. Some elements, such as subordinating conjunctions and agreement and tense markers, play a central role in the clause; others, such as diminutive markers and degree adverbs, a more peripheral role.

Finally, an important distinction is that between *bound* and *free* morphemes. In many, but not all, languages – e.g. the Northwest Coast Amerindian languages form an exception – the bound morphemes are function elements.

Given these different criteria different sub-classes can be distinguished in the categorial systems of various languages, in a way that needs to be made more precise. The same holds for the role these sub-classes play in theories of switching. The Matrix Language Frame model rests on the assumption that code-switched sentences have one base-language, or matrix language. This matrix language determines the order of the elements in mixed constituents and provides the 'system morphemes' (function morphemes) in such constituents.

2 Absolute or relative restrictions

Many models propose principles ruling out certain types of switch, but what is the nature of the predictions made? Poplack (1980), working in the variationist framework, proposes general constraints which are supposed to hold for the majority of cases. Di Sciullo *et al.* (1986) make absolute, all-or-nothing, claims. In more recent work exploring the implications of the theory of government for code-switching, however – e.g. Treffers-Daller (1991) – a probabilistic perspective is taken. Rather than just trying to predict which switches are disallowed, an attempt is made to establish which kinds of switches are the more frequent ones. Sankoff and Poplack (1981) explored this direction as well, but interpreted the results as showing that there were no fundamental differences in probability for any switch site, and did not return to it in later work. Myers-Scotton (1993) proposes to account for the unmarked cases of code-switching, allowing the socially marked cases to fail the predictions made.

At the present stage my own bent is towards probabilitistic statements. Absolute constraints, that could be invalidated by as few as one counterexample, are less appropriate for performance data, particularly data which arise from quite complex factors, not all of which are always under control. Just making a general statement about which type of switch is not likely to occur, as in the Poplack (1980) paper, misses the point that some types of switches are less frequent than others, within a given corpus.

Statements in terms of markedness as a yes/no factor, as in the work of Myers-Scotton (1995a), seem somewhat unsatisfactory to me, for three reasons: (i) it is hard to argue for the (un)markedness of any single instance of switching; (ii) so far there is little indication that the patterns of code-switching in communities where code-switching is not a discourse mode are highly unusual; (iii) suppose the restrictions on code-switching are in part due to factors determined by our grammatical competence. Then we should look to what extent rules of our grammar are violated in stylistically marked registers of the monolingual speech mode. The answer is: not a great deal.

There are specific stylistically marked syntactical patterns, but they do not depart from our grammar as a whole in significant ways. Hence there is no immediate reason to expect socially marked code-switching to do so.

I want to stress here that it is as important to consider the non-occurring switches as the ones that do occur. In which places in the sentence do we find that speakers refrain from switching? From the perspective of structural analysis these would correspond to the starred examples in a Chomskyan article, and from that of Labovian sociolinguistics, to the non-application cases. Nortier (1990: 124–40), for instance, shows that in her corpus there are switches at every conceivable juncture in the sentence (although not always equally frequently), but this has not been demonstrated for other cases of switching.

A very complicated issue concerns the relation between qualitative structural and quantitative distributional analysis. Since intuitions about code-switching are not always reliable (and we do not know when they are and when they are not), and psycho-linguistic experimental techniques to study grammatical factors in code-switching are not yet well developed, we have to work with natural speech data. Since we do not know how the grammar and the lexicon interact with other psychological faculties to produce actual speech, we clearly cannot ignore phenomena such as frequency of occurrence and regularity. This would lead us to take the frequent types of switches as the main body of evidence, and to consider the infrequent ones as possibly fluke phe-nomena, performance errors and the like (*pace* the need to consider non-occurring switches).

Two (possibly related) complications arise, however. First, frequency may result from the conventionalisation of a certain type of switch, rather than from a crucial grammatical factor. Second, we do not yet know enough about the relation between frequently distributions of specific grammatical patterns in monolingual speech data and properties of the grammar to handle frequency in bilingual data with any assurance.

3 Head/dependent relations: the syntactic government model

In some perspectives on code-switching the relation between a lexical element and its syntactic environment plays an important role, e.g. Bentahila and Davies (1983) and Di Sciullo *et al.* (1986). The idea behind these perspectives is that a lexical item will often require specific other elements in its environment, and this requirement may be language-specific and can be formulated in terms of the head-complement relations of X-bar theory.

The traditional assumption behind X-bar theory is that syntactic constituents are endocentric, i.e., that their properties derive from those of their head. Thus a noun phrase inherits many of its features from the head noun; the internal constituency of a verb phrase in terms of number of objects, etc., derives from the properties of the verb. Another way of saying this is that the head noun or head verb project their features in the phrase, but not beyond it. The central notions involved here are exploited in the code-switching literature under the government constraint: not only the categorial and semantic features of a lexical head are projected in the constituent, but also its language index.

The relation between a head and its syntactic environment is thus circumscribed by the relation of government. For code-switching the government constraint was formalised in Di Sciullo *et al.* (1986) as follows:

(6) * [X^p Y^p], where *X* governs *Y*, and *p* and *q* are language indices

The nodes in a tree must dominate elements drawn from the same language when there is a government relation holding between them. In this formalisation the notion of government was taken willy-nilly from Chomsky (1981), where the general structural dependence on a syntactic head within a maximal projection was meant, e.g. between *see* and *THE BOOK* or between *on* and *THE BENCH* in *did you see THE BOOK* and *on THE BENCH.*

For the purposes of the government constraint, this notion was inappropriate in two ways. First, the class of governors included not only content words (such as verbs and prepositions) but also functional categories such as inflection, the comple-mentiser, etc. Thus the frequent switches between, for example, the inflected verb and the subject or between the complementiser and the clause were ruled out. In spite of the theoretical appeal of this constraint and of its empirical success, it has the drawback that it must explain why the following government relations fall outside the constraint:

(7) between INFL and the subject:
     Les canadiens^f *scrivono* '*c*'^i.
     'The Canadians write "c".'
(8) between Det/Q and N:
     a. Io posso fare i^i *cheques*^f.
     'I can make [out] the checks.'
     b. Mettava tanto^i *maquillage*^f sulla faccia^i.
     'She put so much make up on her face.'.
     (Di Sciullo *et al.* 1986: 13–15)
(9) between V and Adv:
     Uno no podía comer carne^s *every day*^e.
     [We couldn't eat meat every day.] (Sankoff and Poplack 1981: 27)

For (7) there was no real explanation. (8) was explained by assuming that government is minimal and that minor categories mark the phrase they are contained in by their index without governing their complement (not in accordance with Aoun and Sportiche 1983). The assumption that government is minimal, i.e. holding only on the level of V' (the minimal verb phrase), was meant to explain (9) as well.

Second, the domain of government was too large, including in principle the whole maximal projection. Thus switches between determiners or quantifiers and the noun they modify or between the verb and a locational adverb are predicted to be ungrammat-ical as well, again contrary to the evidence. For this reason the government constraint was modified in Muysken (1990):

(10) *[X^p Y^q], where *X* L-marks *Y*, and *p* and *q* are language indices
      (1990: 124)

L-marking is a more restricted notion of lexical government by a non-function word under thematic marking. The domain of lexical dependency is a proper subdomain of the domain of structural dependency: government, in exactly the right way. L-marking corresponds to the notion of government in the grammatical tradition. The notion of L-marking has the theoretical attraction that the language indices needed to account for the possible patterns are induced from the lexicon. In this revised view code-switching is possible where the chain of local dependencies resulting from L-marking is broken. If we assume that INFL does not L-mark (to account for (7)), that determiners and quantifiers are heads (hence determiner phrase, quantifier phrase) but not L-markers (so that the switches in (8) are not excluded), and that V does not L-mark time adverbs (as in (9)), then it accounts for the cases listed.

Even in this more limited form the government constraint is simply too strong, whatever its initial appeal. Counterexamples abound, for example in Nortier (1990), where the government constraint is explicitly tested on data from Moroccan Dutch–Arabic switching. Verbal and prepositional object noun phrases are often in a different language from their governing verb or preposition. Crucial counterexamples include (with the number of incidences in Nortier's corpus given in parentheses):

(11) [a] žib li-ya *een glas water of zo.*   (7)
           'Get for-me a glass of water or so.'
      [b] anaka-ndir *intercultureel werk.*   (14)
           'I I-am-doing intercultural work.'
      [c] wellit *huisman*   (10)
           'I-became "houseman".' (Nortier 1990: 131)

We get seven cases of switching between indirect and direct object (11a), no less than fourteen cases of switching between verb and direct object (11b), and ten cases involving a predicate after a copula-type verb, (11c). I should also mention the occurrence of ninety-seven switches of object noun phrases involving a single noun.

The data in (11) are particularly damaging since switching between subject and verb is, if anything, less frequent in Nortier's corpus than switching between object and verb. We also find fifteen cases where a Dutch noun phrase is the complement of a Moroccan Arabic preposition, as in (12).

(12) [a] u dewwezna f-*zelfde tijd.*
           and we-spent in same time
      [b] ka-yxxes bezzaf dyal *generaties voorbijgaan*
           it-must much of generations pass (Nortier 1990: 139)

These data clearly show that the government constraint, even in the revised form of Muysken (1990), cannot be maintained. The distribution of switched noun phrases is much wider than predicted. A way to salvage what is valuable in the government constraint is presented in section 5 below. What is valuable in it is that it predicts in a general way that the looser the syntagmatic relation is in a sentence, the easier it is to switch. This prediction is borne out by all available data.

It may be worthwhile to discuss the relation between government models and the model elaborated by Myers-Scotton (1993a). Both models share the idea of an asymmetry between a matrix and an embedded language. For the purpose of the discussion let us call the matrix language the governing language. Where the two models differ is in what counts as a governor. While the government model, particularly in its later versions, specifically excluded functional elements from being relevant governors in terms of code-switching constraints, as outlined above, the Myers-Scotton models are focussed on functional elements as governors for code-switching. It is fair to say that this latter option must be much closer to the truth.

4 Similarities between sentential and lexical phenomena

In many situations of intense language contact, a number of phenomena involving 'mixing' are going on at the same time: lexical borrowing, code-switching, interference, calquing, relexification, semantic borrowing, L1 transfer in L2 learning, possibly convergence. It is not always possible to decide beforehand what is what and therefore it is important to depart from a set of clear cases, abstracting away from the others, and setting up models which will divide, perhaps artificially, the domain of study into distinct sets of phenomena (e.g. borrowing and code-switching, or syntactic convergence and code-switching).

This procedure of abstraction will be justified if it is possible in the next stage of research either to unify the initially separate domains at a higher level of abstraction or to make strong empirical claims about the properties of the distinct sets of data, allowing one to subsequently classify the unclear cases. Thus it appears that at present the general contours of the phenomenon of lexical borrowing are becoming firmly established; this will allow us to separate it from phenomena such as calquing, if these are indeed systematic.

4.1 The borderline between borrowing and switching

Code-switching is the use of two languages in one clause or utterance. As such code-switching is different from lexical borrowing, which involves the incorporation of lexical elements from one language in the lexicon of another language. Here I will try to deal with this distinction in somewhat more precise terms; the notions of word, and the above-word and below-word levels, play a central role.

Code-switching can be conceived of as involving words with different language indices, marked with p and q subscripts here, inserted into a phrase structure (13), where the brackets labelled S mark the clause level, while lexical borrowing can be conceived of as involving formatives (F) inserted into an alien word structure (14) (the word structure is alien because it behaves externally like an element from the host language):

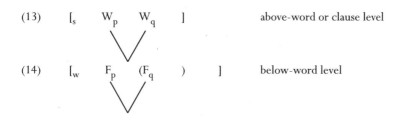

(13) $[_S$ W$_p$ W$_q$ $]$ above-word or clause level

(14) $[_W$ F$_p$ (F$_q$) $]$ below-word level

Here the brackets labelled *W* mark the word level. I will use the term sub-lexical for mixing below the level of insertion of a word into a syntactic tree; and the term supra-lexical for mixing at the level of insertion into a tree and in the syntactic projection of a word. Thus a word can be inserted into a syntactic tree as, say, English, even though some of its components are French. This conception has several interesting results.

There are two dimensions to what I will pre-theoretically call lexical interference (both code-switching and borrowing): (a) whether a particular case occurs at the supra-lexical or sub-lexical level, in the sense just described; and (b) whether it involves being listed (Di Sciullo and Williams 1989) or not.

The dimension of listedness refers to the degree to which a particular element or structure is part of a memorised list, which has gained acceptance within a particular speech community. We can arrange linguistic elements on a scale running from essentially creative to essentially reproductive.

Jackendoff (1975) and others have pointed out, of course, that these two dimensions are not entirely separate. The sub-lexical mode is primarily reproductive (listed), the supra-lexical, syntactic mode primarily creative. Nonetheless, there are many languages, for example polysynthetic and agglutinative languages, in which processes of word-formation can be highly creative. Similarly, there are aspects of phrase structure, most clearly in idioms and collocations, which are to some extent reproductive. For this reason, it is better to see these dimensions as separate.

When we look at linguistic interference in terms of these dimensions, the following picture emerges:

(15) | | not-listed | listed |
|---|---|---|
| supra-lexical | code-switching (a) | conventionalised code-switching (b) |
| sub-lexical | nonce loans (c) | established loans (d) |

Most code-switchings are of course spontaneously formed in discourse, (a). There is recent evidence, however, in work of Poplack and Sankoff, that certain patterns of switching are more frequent in one speech community, other patterns in another speech community (the language pair involved being the same). In this case one might speak of conventionalised code-switching, (b).

The phenomenon of nonce loans, (c), was first described by Haugen (1950) and has recently been taken up in work of Poplack and Sankoff (see also Poplack and Meechan 1995); elements are borrowed on the spur of the moment, without yet having any status in the receiving speech community. Finally, established loans, (d), are a familiar phenomenon.

Taking this set of distinctions into account, we can now turn to the problem that has dominated the field in recent years: the demarcation between borrowing and code-switching. In Poplack and Sankoff (1984), which summarises much earlier work, the following distinctions were listed between code-switching and borrowing:

(16) | | borrowing | code-switching |
|---|---|---|
| no more than one word | + | − |
| adaptation: phonological | $\pm/+$ | $\pm/-$ |
| morphological | + | − |
| syntactic | + | − |

frequent use	+	−
replaces own word	+	−
recognised as own word	+	−
semantic change	+	−

Notice that we can identify the phenomena associated with lexical borrowing with those associated with ordinary morphological derivation. It has often been noted that lexical borrowing, in contrast with code-switching, involves gradual semantic specialisation over time, blurring of morpheme boundaries, lexical unpredictability, etc. These strikingly resemble the properties of derivational morphology. Both can be viewed as the consequences of lexicalisation typical of sub-lexical structures. Code-switching has the ordinary, supra-lexical, productive properties of syntax.

Much of the recent and very productive work in generative morphology, however, is based on the premise that there is a common set of formal principles to morphological and syntactic structure, such as headedness, government, etc., independent of the phenomenon of lexicalisation. Similarly, we may explore the possibility that parallel constraints govern borrowing and code-switching.

4.2 Morphological typology

Morphological typology plays a role in code-switching as far as we consider the type of word-internal mixing involved in morphologically integrated borrowing as a type of code-switching. Here I will illustrate the issues involved in trying to unify the grammatical constraints on borrowing with those on code-mixing, in terms of the notion of local coherence imposed by language indices. Code-mixing can be conceived of as involving words with different language indices inserted into a phrase structure tree, while lexical borrowing can be conceived of as involving formatives inserted into an alien word structure. Following the general notions of government or L-marking elaborated above, borrowing is predicted to be easier when the components of a word are more loosely connected, as in agglutinative or compounding morphology.

The unified perspective adopted here allows us to link the ways in which elements are borrowed to the morphological typology of languages. Several cases come to mind. In Hindi and other languages of the Indian subcontinent it is possible to form complex verbs by appending a semantically neutral verb 'do' to a content word. This morphological possibility makes it extremely easy to borrow verbs:

(17) *onti* kare
      [to hunt]   SRANAN
      bewijs kare
      [to prove]   SRANAN/DUTCH BORROWING

These examples are from Surinam Hindustani (Kishna 1979). The verb *kare* 'do' is the morphological head of the construction, and assigns its Hindustani language index to the whole verb, without internally imposing lexical restrictions ('L-marking' in the framework of Chomsky 1986a) on the alien element (Muysken 1993). Similar constructions are found in examples from Tamil (Sankoff *et al.* 1990) and from Navaho (Canfield

1980). In the analysis proposed here, these cases are made possible because the auxiliary verb does not L-mark, i.e. does not specifically select, its complement.

A second case involves highly agglutinative languages. In these languages elements can easily be incorporated and can receive affixes productively. Consider a Finnish example:

(18)   Misis K. oli housekeeper-*iina*
      Mrs. K. was   [essive case]
      [Mrs. K. was the housekeeper]   (Poplack *et al.* 1987: 38)

There is L-marking on the phrasal level, which is unproblematic because the noun is Finnish externally, but there is no L-marking between the case affix and the noun.

We predict that fusional languages are highly resistant to borrowing, since there the shapes of the formatives are highly interdependent. This prediction is borne out. In fusional languages we see the typical noun/verb asymmetries in borrowability most clearly: nouns, which can generally occur uninflected, are frequently borrowed, while verbs rarely are.

5   Equivalence

In much work on language contact, at least since Weinreich (1953), and including, for example, the tradition of contrastive grammar research, the notion of equivalence plays an important role. The guiding assumption is that equivalence between the grammars of two languages facilitates bilingual usage, be it second language learning, lexical borrowing, or code-switching.

There can be equivalence of categories (lexical elements, phonemes, phrase structure nodes, morpho-syntactic features) or of relations between categories, in structuralist terms. The latter are either syntagmatic (e.g. word-order or agreement rules) or paradigmatic (equivalent oppositions).

5.1   Categorial equivalence

Here I will consider just word-order equivalence and categorial equivalence. Word order equivalence is a sub-case of categorial equivalence, under the government theory, since the rightward governing verb is not directly equivalent to a leftward governing verb, just like a postposition (governing leftward) is not immediately perceived as the categorial equivalent of a preposition (governing rightward). In the Sankoff and Poplack (1981) and Sankoff and Mainville (1986) formalisations there is the preliminary idealisation of categorial equivalence: there is assumed to be a match between both the terminal and the non-terminal nodes in the syntactic tree of the languages involved in the switch. It has been pointed out before that this idealisation is unwarranted; in fact there is no exact match between categories in different languages. Well-documented problem areas in categorial equivalence include clitic versus non-clitic pronouns, types of determiners and demonstratives, and types of auxiliary elements.

We may need to conceive of equivalence not only as a grammatical notion, but also from a psycholinguistic perspective. This allows us to treat processes of code-switching in diachronic and sociolinguistic terms. Assume that one bilingual speech community does not recognise the categories from different languages as equivalent, and another one does. This will have immediate impact on code-switching patterns, of course. We can think then of the recognition of categorial equivalence as the first step in the process of syntactic convergence. A category often recognised as equivalent may be 'noun', and frequently also 'noun phrase' will be recognised as such, whereas conjunctions are perhaps less likely to be interpreted as equivalent. In addition, phonological and mor-phological factors (e.g. similar paradigms) may be involved in furthering the recognition of equivalence.

5.2 Word order equivalence

The word order equivalence constraint was given an informal formulation in Poplack (1980) – switching is only possible at points where the order of linguistic elements in both languages is the same – and was then formalised in Sankoff and Poplack (1981) and in Sankoff and Mainville (1986). In the latter work the following formalisation of the constraint is presented:

Given a 'set E of immediate descendants of the node directly above the two con-stituents', then 'the symbol for any nodes in E to the left of the boundary between the two constituents must precede the symbols for all nodes in E to the right of the boundary, in the right side string of the two rules from the two grammars'. (Sankoff and Mainville 1986: 6)

Thus the formal definition of the word order equivalence constraint is in terms of the immediate daughters of a given phrase structure node. The precise definition of word order equivalence is crucial, as can be seen when we compare Dutch and English word order in the light of the equivalence constraint (Adelmeijer 1991). In simple main clauses, surface strings are similar:

(19) Mary eats apples. / Marie eet appels.

In informal linear terms a switch would be allowed at every point, then, in these sentences. Notice, however, that many grammarians, adhering to different theoretical models, assign rather different structures to these sentences. In some Government and Binding analyses, for instance, the English verb *eats* occupies the auxiliary position, and the Dutch verb has been moved into the complementiser position (e.g. Koster 1978). The English subject is in its canonical position, while the Dutch subject has been moved into sentence-initial position. A switch between subject and verb would not be possible under the more formal configurational definition in terms of sister nodes.

The opposite result is found when we take main clauses with a fronted adverbial. In English this element will precede the subject, while in Dutch it will occur in pre-verbal first position instead of the subject:

(20) Now Mary eats an apple. / Nu eet Marie een appel.

Under a purely linear conception of equivalence, a switch would not be allowed after *now* / *nu*; the element following differs in both languages: the subject in English, the finite verb in Dutch. Under the more formal conception of equivalence in terms of sister constituents, there is equivalence between the clausal constituents following the fronted adverbial, and hence switching would be allowed.

One of the conceptual problems with the notion of word order equivalence is that the order of elements in the sentence is expressed in phrase structure configurations, but results from the interaction of a number of independent principles (see particularly the work of Stowell (1981), Travis (1984) and Koopman (1984)). Some of these principles include:

(21) directionality of government (Case, Theta)
[NP V], * [V NP] under leftward government
[P NP], * [NP P] under rightward government

(22) adjacency or other locality conditions on government
[V NP X], * [V X NP], since case assignment is local

(23) iconicity
[E1 E2], * [E2 E1], where E1 and E2 are coordinate events and E1 preceded E2 in time

(24) Considerations of given/new, functional sentence perspective, topic/comment, etc.
[given information   new information]

(25) prosodic considerations
[short constituent   long constituent]

Now with respect to these principles (and undoubtedly there are more), two things may be said. First, they do not form a natural class, and derive from different components of linguistic theory in the wide sense. Second, only the first two are likely to be language specific, generally speaking, and hence pertinent to the equivalence constraint. Notice now that (21) and (22) are directly determined by government.

Thus a formulation of the equivalence constraint that realistically covers word order differences involves the notion of government. The constraint at the intersection of the earlier approaches may then be formulated as:

(26) * [Xp, Yq], where X L-marks Y, p and q are language indices, and there is no equivalence between the category Y in one language and the category Y in the other language involved.

To see what this means we must return to the issue of equivalence. The linear notion of equivalence would translate in this framework as Xp governing leftward or rightward.

6 Conclusion

A more general way of approaching equivalence in code-switching research is through the notion of neutrality. If we take a strong system-oriented view and conceive of the juxtaposition of material from different languages in one utterance as theoretically problematic — when the grammar of each single language is viewed as a system *où tout se tient* [everything holds together], in Saussure's terms — then we can imagine there to be various strategies to make mixing, juxtaposition, less offensive. In other words, code-switching is impossible in principle, but there are numerous ways that this fundamental impossibility can be circumvented. Something that should be ruled by the very coherence imposed by the sentence seen as syntagmatic unit, is made possible in any of four ways, thus neutralising the system conflict:

(i)   switching is possible when there is no tight relation (e.g. of government) holding between two elements, so-called paratactic switching;
(ii)   switching is possible under equivalence;
(iii)   switching is possible when the switched element is morphologically encapsulated, shielded off by a functional element from the matrix language;
(iv)   switching is possible when at the point of the switch a word could belong to either language, the case of the homophonous diamorph (e.g. *in* in English, German or Dutch).

The loose, associative, style of this survey of grammatical notions relevant to the analysis of code-switching is not accidental. It reflects my perception of the present state of the field as characterised by pluralism and the growing recognition that various mechanisms may play a role in different code-switching situations.

Source: Muysken, P. (1995) Code-switching and grammatical theory. In L. Milroy and P. Muysken (eds) *One Speaker Two Languages*, Cambridge: Cambridge University Press, pp. 177–98. Copyright © 1995 Cambridge University Press, reproduced with permission of the author and publisher.

Postscript

Since the publication of my original article, 'Code-switching and grammatical theory', a number of new developments have taken place in the grammatical study of code-switching and -mixing.

In the first place, more refined typologies have emerged, reflecting the growing diversity and complexity in the language interaction data encountered as more studies were brought to an end. In Muysken (2000) a three-way distinction was proposed between insertion, alternation and congruent lexicalisation. The latter notion refers to intimate code-mixing where the languages are quite similar. Similarly, in the work of the research groups of Carol Myers-Scotton and Shana Poplack more refined typologies have been presented. A comparative overview is given in Table 12.1.

Table 12.1 Schematic comparison of code-switching and -mixing typologies in three traditions (adapted from Muysken 2000: 32)

Myers-Scotton	Muysken (2000)	Poplack
ML + EL constituents	Insertion	(Nonce) borrowing
EL-islands		Constituent insertion
ML-shift	Alternation	Flagged switching
ML-turnover		Code-switching under equivalence
(Style shifting)	Congruent lexicalization	(Style shifting)

A particular concern in these typologies has been the relation between code-mixing and language change. In a number of communities, switching and mixing phenomena are part of overall processes of language change. This influences our formal account of the process of mixing itself.

A second development has been towards more fine-grained grammatical distinctions, e.g. in the domain of functional categories. Examples are the account in Muysken (2000: 154–83), where the distinction between lexical and functional categories is assumed to be gradual rather than absolute. Myers-Scotton and researchers in her group have further developed the lexical-functional distinction in their 4M model (Myers-Scotton 2003; Myers-Scotton and Jake (eds) 2000).

Third, the rise of the Minimalist Program in Chomskyan linguistics has triggered a number of attempts to apply this theory to code-mixing data, notably by MacSwan (2000, 2005).

In my own interpretation of where the grammatical study of code-switching and -mixing is going, two issues stand out.

First is the role of the typological properties of the languages involved in the mixing. (a) Does the presence of considerable inflectional morphology lead to different mixing patterns from those of relatively isolating morphology? The impression one gains from mixing involving the Chinese languages, Malay varieties and various West African languages (often paired with English) is that more intimate mixing patterns are more frequently encountered than elsewhere. (b) How important are word order similarities and differences? It appears that mixing involving languages with different word orders often leads to the creative use of various 'strategies of neutrality'. (c) Does the head marking versus dependent marking distinction influence code-mixing patterns to any extent? Recent work by Patrick McConvell and associates on code-mixing involving various Australian languages (McConvell and Meakins 2005) suggests this to be the case. (d) What is the role of intonation and tone, in addition to syntactic structure? Work reported on by Michael Clyne (2003) stresses the role of tone in Vietnamese-English code-mixing, suggesting the importance of phonological (PF) planning in constraining code-switching and -mixing.

Second, can we really distinguish grammatical constraints on code-switching and mixing from processing constraints, i.e. is there a distinction between competence and performance? In this question, issues both concerning the syntax/processing interface in sequencing and sentence planning and concerning the language label of specific syntactic nodes and items play a role.

In all this research, there is the issue of sources of evidence. There is a wide gap between the Labovian tradition of accountable analysis of naturalistic speech data, stressed in the work of Poplack and associates, on the one hand, and the tradition in which grammaticality judgements play an important role, as in the work of MacSwan and many others. Ultimately, neither tradition will give us the answers needed. The grammaticality judgements research is simply not reliable; the basis for these judgements varies widely between different communities. The naturalistic corpus research is more reliable, but quite costly, and often does not yield all the necessary data. A way out of this dilemma is the development of reliable experimental techniques, which need to be shown to replicate naturalistic language behaviour but at the same time allow one to test more complex grammatical issues. This is the focus of my current (2006) research in this area.

Pieter Muysken, PhD, is Professor of Linguistics at Radboud University Nijmegen, the Netherlands. P.Muysken@let.ru.nl

Notes for students and instructors

Study questions

1 Give three examples of 'insertional' code-switching and three examples of 'alternational' code-switching involving the languages you know to illustrate the 'free morpheme constraint' and the 'equivalent constraint'.

2 What are the criteria for the identification of the 'matrix language'?

3 How do the concepts of 'system morpheme' and 'content morpheme', as defined by Myers-Scotton and Jake, apply to a language other than English that you know?

Study activity

Using a sample of code-switching data – either collected by yourself or documented in detail by others – find out to what extent the grammatical constraints proposed by Poplack and others work. How do the examples of code-switching in the sample fit into the Matrix Language Frame (MLF) model? Can the same examples be explained by standard grammatical theories with minimal modification?

Further reading

For an overview of the grammar of code-switching, see S. Poplack, 2001, Code-switching (linguistic), in N. Smelser and P. Baltes (eds), *International Encyclopedia of the Social and Behavioral Sciences*, Elsevier Science, pp. 2062–5; C. Myers-Scotton, 1997, Codeswitching, in F. Coulmas (ed.), *The Handbook of Sociolinguistics*, Blackwell, pp. 217–37; or J. MacSwan, 2004, Code-switching and grammatical theory, in T.K. Bhatia and W.C. Richie (eds), *The Handbook of Bilingualism*, Blackwell, pp. 238–311.

For further discussion of Poplack's approach to grammatical constraints on code-switching, see S. Poplack, 1978/81, Syntactic structure and social function of code-switching, in R. Duran (ed.), *Latino Discourse and Communicative Behaviour*,

Ablex, pp. 169–84; D. Sankoff and S. Poplack, 1979/81, A formal grammar for code-switching, *Papers in Linguistics* 14: 3–46; S. Poplack and D. Sankoff, 1984, Borrowing: the synchrony of integration, *Linguistics* 22: 99–135; S. Poplack, 1993, Variation theory and language contact: contact, concept, methods and data, in D. Preston (ed.), *American Dialect Research*, John Benjamins, pp. 251–86; and S. Poplack and M. Meechan (eds), 1998, *Instant Loans, Easy Conditions*, Kingston Press. A state-of-the-art collection of studies which apply Poplack's model is published in a special issue of the *International Journal of Bilingualism* 2 (2).

A fuller exposition of the MLF model can be found in C. Myers-Scotton, 1997a, *Duelling Languages: Grammatical structure in code-switching*, Oxford University Press; and C. Myers-Scotton and J.L. Jake (eds), 2000, *Testing a Model of Morpheme Classification with Language Contact Data*, Kingston Press. A state-of-the-art collection of studies which apply Myers-Scotton's model is published in a special issue of the *International Journal of Bilingualism* 4 (1). See also: C. Myers-Scotton, 2005a, Supporting a differential access hypothesis: codeswitching and other contact data, in J. Kroll and A.M.B. de Groot (eds), 2005, *Handbook of Bilingualism*, Oxford University Press, pp. 326–48.

Other studies of the grammar of code-switching include: C. Pfaff, 1979, Constraints on language mixing: intrasentential code-switching and borrowing in Spanish/English, *Language* 55: 291–318; A. Bentahila and E.E. Davies, 1983, The syntax of Arabic-French code-switching, *Lingua* 59: 301–30; E. Woolford, 1983, Bilingual code-switching and syntactic theory, *Linguistic Inquiry* 14: 520–36; A.K. Joshi, 1985, Processing of sentences with intrasentential code-switching, in D.R. Dowty, L. Karttunen and A.M. Zwicky (eds), *Natural Language Parsing*, Cambridge University Press, pp. 190–205; A.M. Di Sciullo, P. Muysken and R. Singh, 1986, Government and code-switching, *Journal of Linguistics* 22: 1–24; S. Berk-Seligson, 1986, Linguistic constraints on intrasentential code-switching, *Language in Society* 15: 313–48; H.M. Belazi, E.J. Rubin and J. Toribio, 1994, Code-switching and X-bar theory: the functional head constraint, *Linguistic Inquiry* 25: 221–37; S. Mahootian and B. Santorini, 1996, Code-switching and the complement/adjunct distinction, *Linguistic Inquiry* 27: 464–79; R.M. Bhatt, 1997, Code-switching, constraints and optimal grammars, *Lingua* 102: 223–51; and J. MacSwan, 2000, The architecture of the bilingual language faculty: evidence from codeswitching, *Bilingualism: Language and cognition* 3 (1): 37–54.

Book-length studies of the grammatical structures of code-switching include: J. Nortier, 1990, *Dutch-Moroccan Arabic Code-Switching among Moroccans in the Netherlands*, Foris; J. Treffers-Daller, 1993, *Mixing Two Languages: French-Dutch contact in a comparative perspective*, Mouton de Gruyter; A. Backus, 1996, *Two in One: Bilingual speech of Turkish immigrants in the Netherlands*, Tilburg University Press; H. Halmari, 1997, *Government and Code-Switching: Explaining American Finnish*, John Benjamins; L. Baumans, 1998, *The Syntax of Codeswitching: Analysing Moroccan Arabic/Dutch conversation*, Tilburg University Press; J. MacSwan, 1999, *A Minimalist Approach to Intrasentential Code-Switching*, Garland; and P. Muysken, 2000, *Bilingual Speech: A typology of code-switching*, Cambridge University Press.

Bilingual acquisition

Chapter 13

The acquisition and development of language by bilingual children

VIRGINIA VOLTERRA AND

TRAUTE TAESCHNER

Introduction

The form of bilingualism which is considered in this study involves the simultaneous acquisition of two languages from 1;0 to 4;0. The subjects in our study were exposed almost equally to the two languages concerned from birth, and the language acquisition process took place within the environment of the children's families. In all the cases considered, the two languages spoken by the children's parents were differentiated in the sense that one parent spoke one language and the other parent the other language. We were aware of the fact that this kind of bilingualism involves various problems from the social, pedagogical and psychological points of view, but in our study we intend to consider only linguistic development. The basic questions we wish to answer are: (1) What are the linguistic stages through which a child passes in order to acquire simultaneously two languages in early childhood? (2) what are the strategies used by the child during the acquisition process?

Method

The data which we use in this study derive both from the results of longitudinal research conducted by the authors of this paper and from Leopold (1970). The latter used as his principal source detailed and accurate notes from his diary, taken over a period of seven years and describing the bilingual development of his oldest daughter, Hildegard. She grew up in an English-speaking environment, and English was spoken by her mother while Leopold spoke to her in German. The data collected by the authors concern two sisters (Lisa and Giulia) living in Rome, who had been exposed to two languages since birth; their father always spoke Italian to them while their mother spoke only German (see further, Taeschner 1976a, b). Monthly recordings of 30 minutes each in an alternate language environment were performed. Lisa was observed from 1;5 to 3;6, and Giulia from 1;2 to 2;6. The recordings were exhaustively transcribed, including everything that was said by the adults present, and notes on the behaviour of the children. Other data were collected without the use of tape recorder by taking note of the new words and constructions used by the children which were considered to be relevant to our research. A detailed lexical and syntactic analysis of the data was then performed. We are concerned here just with the children's productions.

Results

In the gradual learning process through which a child becomes bilingual from early infancy three stages can be distinguished.

(1) In the first stage the child has one lexical system which includes words from both languages. A word in one language almost always does not have a corresponding word with the same meaning in the other language. In fact, in this stage the language development of the bilingual child seems to be like the language development of the monolingual child. As a result, words from both languages frequently occur together in two- to three-word constructions. It is very difficult to describe syntactic rules and to make any definite conclusions about syntax, in this first stage, as the child does not yet use enough two- and three-word sentences.

(2) In the second stage the child distinguishes two different lexicons, but applies the same syntactic rules to both languages. For almost any word in one language, the child has a corresponding word in the other language. Moreover, words drawn from the two lexicons no longer occur together in constructions.

(3) In the third stage the child speaks two languages differentiated both in lexicon and syntax, but each language is associated with the person using that language: 'une personne – une langue' (Ronjat 1913).

The first stage

The data on which the first stage is based are set out in Tables 13.1 to 13.4; all three subjects used words belonging to both languages. Although the number of words may appear quite large, only the italicized items can be considered as corresponding to each other in the two languages. However, taking into consideration these words, and the context in which they were said, we can note that

(1) the children often do not appear to consider such words as exactly corresponding to each other;

(2) some words not considered corresponding in adult speech show a certain correspondence in our bilingual children, just as we might find in the case of the monolingual child;

(3) monolingual children also show a few synonyms in their early vocabulary.

Table 13.1   Number of words in each child's productions, first stage[a]

Lisa (1; 11)			Giulia (1; 6.15)			Hildegard (1; 6)		
I	G	IG	I	G	IG	E	G	EG
38	25	24	27	33	22	36	24	29

[a] I = Italian words, E = English words, G = German words, IG (EG) = 'words which are closely akin in form and meaning in both languages' (Leopold 1970: 150).

Table 13.2   Words used by Lisa, first stage

Italian	German	Italian-German
aaino (bavaglino)	Aie (Seife)	baubau/wauwau
aaila (aereo)	Beine	bu (rumore)
belle	Bobo (Bonbon)	bata (basta)
bui (buio)	Bo (Bock)	caca
cucu tètè	guguck da	cocò
coa (ancora)	Blle (Blume)	Dodo (Rodolfo)
chiai (occhialli)	Baum	Giulia
chiaie (chiavi)	Bauch	lata/lade (cioccolato)
chechea (acqua)	*Wasser*	Lalla (Daniela)
chi è	Chku (Schuhe)	Lia (Lisa)
cotto (biscotto)	*Keh* (Keks)	miao
cata (cane)	daki (danke)	Mamma
caa (cara)	haia haia (schlafen)	mu
chie (scrivere)	ist	Nanna (Anna)
chiu (chiudere)	Kih (Kaese)	popò
chio (anch'io)	Kita (Kinderì)	Papa
cotta (scottare)	Koka (Kartoffel)	Paola
carta	nyam nyam (essen)	tatau (ciao)
dito	Puppe	tum (cadere)
da (dare)	Taila (Tasche)	to-to
la	*da*	tic-tic
laila (lascia)	Titi (Brust)	tata
latte	Tuta (Lutscher)	onc-onc
lata (l'altra)	upa (hoch genommen werden)	palle/balle
nonno	ja	
nonna		
no		
sti (sì)		
tona (viziatona)		
tia (zia)		
ti (tira)		
tu		
totto (capotto)		
totto (rotto)		
tita (matita)		
qua/qui		
pappo (tappo)		
più		
pila		

Table 13.3 Words used by Giulia, first stage

Italian	German	Italian-German
acqua	auch	Auto
ada (guarda)	aizi (anzihen)	Anna
api (aprire)	Bonbon	Bata (basta)
ancoa (ancora)	Baume (Baum)	bum
bua	Bauch	babau
baba (barba)	Baby	caca
bimba	Buch	Chichì
bella	Bitte	Dodo (Rodolfo)
balla	badi-badi (baden)	Mami
buon natale	baite (arbeiten)	Nado/Nase
cane	Beine	nyam-nyam
cate (carta)	dicke	ò! ò!
cotta (scotta)	*heiss*	O.K.
cara	Donner	Oi
datsie (grazie)	*dane* (danke)	Pipì
da (dare)	guguck da	Paola
fatto	feitich (fertig)	Papi
cotto (biscotto)	Hale (Haare)	tatau (ciao)
mela	haia haia	titè
la	*da*	tati
Nonno	kalt	Taute (Traute)
Nonna	Kuchen	tò-tò
no	kin-kinny (trinken)	
pela (pera)	*nei*	
pettapetta (aspetta)	Kaese	
più	komm	
palle	Milch	
pane	Nenni	
panna	Puppi	
qua	sitzi-sitzi (sitzen)	
tato	wo	
tutto-tutto	*alle-alle*	
tovato (trovato)	upa (hoch genommen werden)	
toia (togliere)		
zita		
zia		
uva		

Table 13.4   Words used by Hildegard first stage

English	German	English-German
pretty	Bild	Mamma
there	*da*	piep-piep
down	Ball	nenene
hot	Blumen	tick-tack/tick-tock
Gertrude	*Gertrud*	njam-njam
thank you	*danke*	Opa
bye bye	kiek	Papa
peek-a-boo	kritze	bimbam
up	schoen	pieks
yes	*ja*	quak-quak
snow	*Schnee*	wauwau
all	Tante	baby
brush	ist	Carolyn
hello	bitte	muh-moo
high-chair	es	pfui/pooh
I	heiss	Bad/bath
mitten	klingeling	kitty
naughty	mehr	Bett/bed
night	auf	Marion
see	atsch	Apfel-apple
you	Bauch	auto
away	Bleistift	Mann/man
bottle	Nackedei	Rita
box	nein	aus/out
buggy – cake – cookie		Buch/book
toothbrush		Dodo
dolly – no – more – oil		mein/mine
duck – heart – light		Milch/milk
		Schuh/shoe

Taking up point (I), let us consider the Italian word *là* 'there' and the German word *da* 'there' of Lisa. At the first stage, Lisa uses the word *là* for things that are not visible at the time of speaking, while she uses *da* for things that are present and visible to her. For example (Lisa to Mother):

(1) Lisa (1; 10)
    L: Miao miao.   while coming from outside and going to her mother.

    M: Wo ist miao? ('where is meow?')
    L: Là miao. ('there meow')   while pulling her mother outside. Outside, the conversation continues.

    M: Wo ist miao? ('where is meow?')
    L: Da ist miao. ('there is meow')

We can represent this relationship between the words *là* and *da* as follows:

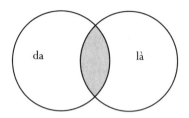

Concerning point (2), let us now consider the example of *da* and *daki*. The word *da* is the third person singular of the Italian verb *dare* 'to give'. *Daki* derives from the German word *danke* 'thanks'. Lisa uses the word *daki* when she wants to thank somebody, to give something to somebody, or to get something from somebody. For example:

(2) Daki Buch. ('thanks book')   her mother had just given her a book
(3) Daki. ('thanks')   while giving the pencil to her mother
(4) Mamma tita daki.   she wants her mother to give her the pencil
    ('Mommy pencil thanks')

When Lisa was 1;10 she learned the Italian word *da* which is in a relationship of correspondence with *daki*, but she used it only to give something to somebody. For example:

(5) Da.   offering a sweet to her mother

We can represent the relationship between the words *daki* and *da* as follows:

This is the relationship which we usually find within a lexical system. For Lisa, *daki* seems to be more generalized while *da* is more restricted. The same kind of relationship is found also in the Italian monolingual child Claudia (see Ferguson and Slobin 1973): Claudia uses the word *tazie* (from *grazie* 'thanks') when giving something to or receiving something from her mother, e.g. *Tazie a mamma* 'thanks to mommy', and asking for something from her mother, e.g. *Tazie a Claudia* 'thanks to Claudia', and she uses *da* when giving something to her mother, e.g. *Mamma da* 'Mommy give', and asking for something from her mother, e.g. *Dai a mamma* 'give a Mommy'. So we see that such words may not be synonymous but may have a relationship of hyponymy, for both bilingual and monolingual children.

For the other italicized examples we found a difference in the frequency of use: Lisa's *cotto*, *chechea* and *ja* are very frequent while she has just a few examples of *kek*, *Wasser* and *sti*. Giulia uses almost always *no* and *datsie* while *nei* and *danne* are seldom.

So we see that all the words of the child's speech appear to form one lexical system. Therefore the use of one language or the other depends upon what the child wants to say and not so much on the language spoken to him. In this phase the few two- to three-word constructions appear as a mixture of words taken from both languages, and it is difficult to make any assessment concerning syntax. In practice, the bilingual child speaks only one language which is a language system of his own (cf. Leopold 1970, Vol. I: 179, where a similar conclusion is arrived at).

The second stage

In the second stage the child reaches the point where he can be said to possess two lexical system, in the sense that the same object or event is indicated with two different words pertaining to the two languages. It is interesting to analyse the process by which the child reaches the stage in which he chooses the words from the two languages and what factors influence his choice. Let us consider an example.

Lisa at age 2; 5 learned the Italian word *occhiali* 'glasses' very early, as her father wears glasses. One day her mother draws a picture of a woman wearing glasses and teaches her the word *Brillen* 'glasses'. She then tells Lisa to show the drawing to her father and to tell him what it represents:

(6) F: Cos'è questo? ('what is this?')
    L: Brillen (and she repeats *Brillen* many times and never *occhiali*).

Then Lisa sees her father's glasses and says:

    L: Occhiali.
    M: Was is das hier? ('what is this?')   pointing to the father's glasses
    L: Occhiali.

Then the mother points to the glasses in the drawing and asks:

    M: Was ist das hier? ('what is this?')
    L: Brillen.

Lisa asks her mother to draw other *Brillen*, which the mother does. At a certain point Lisa says:

    L: Occhiali, occhiali!

Then the mother shows Lisa the glasses which she had drawn in the beginning and Lisa says:

    L: Brillen.

Then after a little while she says again:

    L: Brillen occhiali.

And going to the father she repeats:

    L: Occhiali Brillen.   while showing the drawing

Later the mother tells Lisa that *occhiali di Papi* 'Daddy's glasses', corresponds to *Papi's Brillen*, because in referring to the real glasses Lisa insists on calling them *occhiali* and not *Brillen*. After a while Lisa is convinced and says:

L: Papi's Brillen.

Half an hour later the mother asks:

M: Lisa, was ist das hier? ('what is this?')   pointing to the father's glasses
L: Occhiali occhiali, occhialen occhialen; occhiali Brillen

From the above example one can note that Lisa is already able to generalize in the sense that she understands that *Brillen* is the same as *occhiali*. In her everyday use, however, she remains strongly influenced by the context in which she first learned the word. The factors which influence the use of a word and which distinguish *occhiali* from *Brillen* seem to be the pragmatic conditions in which the word was learned.

The same rigidity and influence of context can be seen in Giulia and Hildegard:

(7) Giulia (2; 2)
    G: Mami, was das da? ('Mommy, what's that?')   pointing to a hair pin
    M: Das ist eine Klammer. ('this is a hair pin')
    G: Klammer Klammer.   (and she repeats it many
                                                   times)
    About a month later the father, holding a hair pin, says:
    F: Questa è una molletta. ('that's a hair pin')
    G: No, non è molletta, è eine Klammer. ('no, that's not a *molletta*, it is *eine
       Klammer*')

Leopold (1970, Vol. 4: 44) writing about Hildegard, who had heard for the first time some stories from a German book, notes that: 'She tells her mother the stories in English, adorned with a few German words, especially nouns, but also some verbs like *weinen*'. And we know from preceding examples that Hildegard also used the corresponding English word *cry*.

As may be seen from these examples, the process of generalization implies a great effort on the cognitive level. The child must detach one word from a certain specific context and identify that word with the corresponding word in the other language. We have evidence that children quickly achieve this generalization. Very soon the child is able to translate from one language into the other:

(8) Lisa (2;5)
    L: La panna da oben ada. ('the cream up there, look')
    M: Ja die Sahne ist da oben. ('yes, the cream is up there')
    L: Dillo dillo. ('say it say it')
    M: Die Sahne ist da oben.
    L: No, la panna è là su. ('no, the cream is up there')

(9) Giulia (2;2)

G: Metti tavolo di Giulia. ('put table of Giulia') she wants her mother to put some cups on the table

M: Wo soll ich's hintun? ('where shall I put them?')

G: Das da, das da auf Tisch von Giulia. ('that there, that there on table of Giulia')

(10) Hildegard (3; 0)

H: Nose.

F: Wie heisst das auf Deutsch? ('what is the name in German?')

H: Nase.

In spite of these examples of exact translations, we found also in the same period that children in a single sentence keep mixing words of the two languages:

(11) Lisa (2;5)

Spetta lass zu Lisa komm ida, bene? Bene. ('wait, let closed, Lisa comes back, O.K.?')

(12) Lisa (2;7)

Mami vuole Stickzeug, vuole Arbeit, si? ('Mommy wants knitting, wants work yes?')

(13) Giulia (2;2)

Giulia gemacht a casetta per a böse Wolf. ('Giulia made a little house for the bad wolf')

(14) Giulia (2;5)

Mami ich will prendere ja? ('Mommi I will take it, yes?')

(15) Hildegard (3;3)

I can't give you any Kuss because I have a Schmutznase.

(16) Hildegard (3;9)

Look how many Platz there is; is this viel?

We can explain these apparently conflicting results by the fact that corresponding words are normally learned some time apart from each other, and that each word tends to be tied to the particular context in which it was learned.

It is only when the knowledge of the two linguistic codes becomes greater and the generalization process becomes habitual that the child learns to distinguish between the two lexical systems. He recognizes that a group of words belongs to the same lexical system and uses only such words in a sentence. When this happens most of the child's sentences are in one or the other language, the choice depending on the person with whom he is speaking. It is at the end of this stage that bilingual children amaze observers because of their extraordinary skill in passing from one language to another during the same verbal interaction:

(17) Lisa (3;3)

Lisa talking to an Italian friend asks:

Dov'è Kitty? ('where is Kitty?')

Immediately after, without waiting for an answer, Lisa asks her mother:

Wo ist Kitty? ('where is Kitty?')

(18) Giulia (2;3)

  Quetto parla no. ('this speaks no') looking at and speaking to an Italian boy while on a bus

  Das hier splecht nicht. ('this here speaks not') looking at her mother and pointing to the boy

  Quetto è buono. ('this is good') and again she talks to the boy

  Das hier lieb. ('this here is good') looking and talking to her mother and pointing to the boy

(19) Hildegard (3;3)

  This is a wasser . . . water. playing with her cousin who does not know German

But this exceptional flexibility on the lexical level may not be found on the syntactic level. In fact, subsequent to the acquisition of two separate lexical systems, the child may still apply the same syntactic rules to the two languages. This can be verified by the data on Lisa (which happen to be syntactically quite rich). Lisa uses some constructions that have completely different syntactic rules in German and Italian (see Schwarze (1974) for a comparative analysis). Let us consider three differences:

(1) In German the idea of possession is expressed through the possessive case while Italian uses the preposition *di*: cf. *Maria's Haare* vs. *I capelli di Maria*.

(2) In German the adjective comes before the noun while in Italian it comes after (see D'Addio (1974) for exceptions): cf. *Ich kaufe ein enges Kleid* vs. *Compro un vestito stretto*.

(3) In German the negative element follows the verb; in Italian it precedes the verb: cf. *Karl trinkt nicht* vs. *Carlo non beve*.

From the data collected one can see that, at least for a period of time, Lisa differentiates the two languages on the lexical level but applies the same syntactic rules to them. From Tables 13.5 to 13.7 it can be seen that Lisa acquires the rules only gradually. For a long period of time, until the age of 2;9, she appears to have acquired only one syntactic system.

  To express the idea of possession she uses the same strategy in both German and Italian, e.g.

(20) Giulia Buch. ('Giulia book') Giulia giamma. ('Giulia pyjamas')
  Lisa Hose. ('Lisa pants') Lisa bicicletta. ('Lisa bicycle')

During the same period, Lisa regularly uses adjectives before nouns in German, e.g. *ein schoen Blume* 'a nice flower', *klein ladio* 'little radio', while we have no examples of Italian sentences with adjectives. Only at 2;9 do we find the first examples of both construc-

Table 13.5 Possession constructions in Lisa's data

	German	Italian	
N + (s) + N	N + (von) + N	N + N	N + (di) + N
1;8	Kita Kita Giulia		
1;9 Giulia Buch			
Giulia . . . Beine			
1;10 . . . Giulia Haia Haia		Miao bua	
Guia Beille		Mamma, Paola tita	
Mamma Nyam Nyam cotta			
2;1 Mami Baby		Giulia popò	
2;3 Giulia Buch		Giulia agiama	
Lisa Schuhe			
Giulia Hand			
2;4 Giulia Dodoi		Guarda Giulia bua	
		Lisa bicicletta	
2;6 Nein, Lisa Arbeit		Mami bottone	Quetto da Giulia?
Lisa fertig Lisa Arbeit		Giulia attenta bua	Da Mamma questto?
Giulia camicina blau		Lisa letto	Da Mamma
Mammi Nase		Giulia penna . . .	
Giulia Nase			
Tante Hanny macht Lisa Hose			
Tante Hanny Lisa Hose macht			
Lisa Buch			
Lisa Baum			
2;8 Lisa Arbeit	Shappen Lisa	Lisa gomma	. . . a penna di Lisa
2;9 Giulia Buch	Quetto von Giulia		Quetto è di Giulia
Di Lisa Haare			Quetto libro di Giulia
			Di Lisa
			Quetta è di Giulia
		Quetto è di Giulia libro	Sono i capelli di Lisa
2;10	E qui von Mami		Sai quella è la stellina di nonna
			Ricordi stellina di nonna
			Testa di Giulia
			La favola di Lisa
3 Nur Lisa Mami Baby, Giulia Mami Hund			
3;3 Lisa Schlappen	Von Lisa klein klein	Anna di la casetta	
3;4			

Table 13.6   Adjective constructions in Lisa's data

| | German | | Italian | |
	Adjective + N	N + Adjective	Adjective + N	N + Adjective
2;3	Schöne Blume			
	Schöne Blume			
2;4	Ein schön Blum, Mamma			
2;8	Klein Ladio			
	Auch Lisa blaune Haare			
	Blonde Haale			
2;9			Mangia ham buono la mela	Cip, cip uno solo rosso
			Glande pescelino fa pipì	Pipì fa ein Flsh pesceli no glande
			Guarda che bello sole, hai visto?	
2;10	Klein Boot			
2;11	Die schön Schwein			
	Armes Schwein			
3;2				Pallone gran grande
3;3	. . . so viele Kinder	Von Lisa klein		Questa è Lisa piccolina
	Papi hat kurze Haare	klein		
	Ein kleines Haus			
	Armer Federico			
	Klein Lisa			
3;4	Das alles Haus		Questa tutta casa	
	Ein grosser Vasino			
	Ein Buch mit so viele Geschichte			
3;5	Armes Schwein guck			
	Grün Mer, blau Mer			
3;6	Der kleine Badezimmer	Und die Zieglein marron und klein klein	. . . tanti uomini	. . . bambini tanti
	Ein hübsche Kandele		Dov'è il grosso lupo?	tanti, le donne tanti . . .
	. . . grün Bleistift, ich will rot Bleistift	Lisa will nur Schuhe dunkel-braun	Il grosso lupo è . . .	Si, le onde grandi
	Der grosse böse Wolf	Des Reis gut	Quel bianco pecora	E lì un sole rosso rosso
	Ist die liebe Sonne da		. . . grande bastone	Il riso buono
	Ein grosser Vasino			Io ho fatto due muri grandi
	Der weisse Glas, der grün Glas			

Table 13.7   Negative constructions in Lisa's data

| | German | | Italian | |
	V + Negative	Negative + V	V + Negative	Negative + V
1;5				Non c'è più eh!
1;9	Ta da daki noo!			Non è qua
2;4			Fa pilli pilli no	Io non vuole
			Lisa cade no	
2;6				No, non vuole
2;7	Lisa haia haia machen no		Giulia vuole haia no	N'c'è più Lisa
	Kein giogioletto kaputt nein		Questa non è la bottiglia no	Questa non è la bottiglia no
	Radio no, badi badi no		Lisa va da là no	
			Questo è tuo no . . . lompe no	
2;8			Non fa totò no	Non fa totò no
				In vase non c'è più vase
				Quella non è a penna di Lisa
				No, non c'e più
				Quella non fa, non fa
2;9			Non è morto	Non è morto
			Chicchi no	Chicchi no
			Fa rompe no	
3;2	Noch nicht gekommen			
3;3	Giulia will nicht weiter schlafen	Onkel Karlos nicht versteht Italienisch		Papi non è munto
3;4	Lisa hat kein Topolino, kein Giogioletto	Nicht meine Schlappen anziehen Giulia hm?		Lisa non ha ii giogio
	Mami erzähl eine Geschichte no no no			
3;5	Ist nicht Cremina			
3;6	Ist nicht da	Und nicht kommt Mami		Ecco non c'è l'auto
	Ist nicht da die Sirene	Nein, ich nicht will		Si, non c'è la pecora
	Warum ich will nicht grün Bleistift . . .	Ich nicht bin müde		Anch'io non la so contare
	Lisa hat nicht Haare	Ich nicht will der		Così anche non va bene
	. . . und schwarze ist nicht da	weisse Glas ich will den grün Glas		Non ci sta dopo

tions, e.g. *Cip Cip uno solo rosso* 'Bird one only red', *Grande pesciolino fa pipì* 'big fishie does a pee pee'. As far as negation is concerned, during this period there are not many examples in German. In the Italian data there are a few sentences in which the negation precedes the verb[1] but a large number of sentences in which the negation follows the verb, which is a construction never used by Italian-speaking adults, e.g. *Fa pilli pilli no* 'plays no', *Lisa cade no* 'Lisa falls no', *Lisa va da la no* 'Lisa goes there no'.

At first we are tempted to say that Lisa adopted the adult German syntactic rules and applied them to Italian. But considering Lisa's negative sentences, we see that her rule is to put the negation at the end of the sentence, e.g. (at 2;7) *Lisa haia haia machen no* 'Lisa sleep does no', *Lisa va da la no* 'Lisa goes there no'. Had Lisa applied the adult German syntactic rule for negation she would have had a different word order; a German-speaking adult would have said: *Lisa macht nicht haia haia* 'Lisa does not go haia haia' and *Lisa geht nicht dort hin* 'Lisa does not go there'. In the course of normal monolingual language acquisition, Italian children often adopt the same construction that Lisa used: they put the negation at the end of the phrase. For example, *sporco no* 'dirty no', *aabiae no* 'angry no', *piove no* 'rains no', while an Italian adult would say *non è sporco* 'it is not dirty', *non ti arrabbiare* 'don't get angry', *non piove* 'it is not raining'. So we rather think that, in this period, Lisa, like the monolingual children, uses a consistent syntactic system of her own instead of imitating the adult system (Slobin 1975). She is therefore using two lexicons but one and only one syntax.

The third stage

In the third stage the bilingual process of learning is practically complete. The child speaks both languages correctly at both lexical and syntactic levels. Referring to the three constructions seen before, Lisa uses two syntactic rules differentiated for each language, e.g.

> (21) (2;9)
> Giulia Buch. ('Giulia book') Sono i capelli di Lisa. ('They are hair of Lisa')
> (3;3)
> Ein kleines Haus. ('a little house') Questa è Lisa piccolina. ('this is Lisa small')
> (3;6)
> Ist nicht da. ('is not there') Così anche non va bene. ('so also not goes well')

It is certainly not an easy process. As can be seen from Tables 13.5 to 13.7 there still are, in the same period, many examples of interference, and these continue for quite some time. In the previous stage, interference was observed on the lexical level; in this stage there is still interference, but on the syntactic level, e.g.

> (22) Lisa (2;9)
> Quetto è di Giulia libro[2]. ('this is Giulia's book') modelled on the German
> sentence *Das ist Giulia's*
> *Buch*

(3;6)

Lisa will nur Schuhe dunkelbraun. ('Lisa wants only shoe brown')	modelled on the Italian sentence *Lisa vuole solo scarpe marroni*
Quel bianco pecora. ('the white lamb')	modelled on the German construction *Das weisses Lamm*
Ich nicht bin müde. ('I not am tired')	modelled on the Italian sentence *Io non sono stanca*

This interference is particularly observed when the child is put into a situation of conflict. She may have to switch rapidly from one language into another because she interacts simultaneously with persons speaking different languages, or she has to express in one language something that she is accustomed to express in the other language (for example when she has to tell a story in Italian from a German book).

In the same period Lisa has to learn a series of very complex rules which are differentiated for both languages. To minimize the risk of interference she must try to keep the two languages separate as far as possible. It is at this stage that she more rigidly associates the languages with different persons ('une personne – une langue'). The act of labelling a person with one of the two languages makes the choice of the words and rules a kind of automatic process, thus reducing the effort she has to make, e.g.

(23) (3;6)

    An Italian friend talks to her in German. Lisa immediately becomes upset and begins to cry. The mother tries to calm her and says: *Virginia spricht Deutsch*! 'Virginia speaks German'. Lisa slaps her mother.

(24) (3;11)

    The father, who is talking to Lisa, uses a short German sentence. Lisa reacts immediately:

    L: No, non puoi. ('no, you can't')
    F: Ich auch . . . spreche Deutsch ('also I speak German')
    L: No, tu non puoi! ('no, you cannot')   extremely upset

As the syntactic differences become more and more apparent to the child, the tendency to label people with definite languages decreases. She accepts the possibility of speaking either of the two languages with the same person, including the one which is not normally spoken by that person.

At the end of this stage, the child is able to speak both languages fluently, i.e. with the same linguistic competence as a monolingual child, with any person. It is only at this point that one can say a child is truly bilingual.[3]

Notes

1   These few sentences do not lessen the force of our argument, because *non c'è piu* is used by Lisa (and by many other Italian children) as if it were just one word. So the verbs *è* (with this meaning) and *vuole* are used by Lisa until 2; 9 only with this kind of negation and never alone. For this reason, in these cases the negation does not precede the verb, but is an indispensable part of the predicate.

2   This is a clear example of transition from Stage II to Stage III: Lisa uses the Italian preposition but in the German word order. This word order could be found in Italian only when *di* + N is not a noun modifier but the predicate of the sentence, as in Lisa's example *Perchè è di Lisa la bicicletta*.

3   Lisa is now in the third stage. A comparative study of language acquisition between monolingual and bilingual children is in preparation by the authors.

Source: Volterra, V. and Taeschner, T. (1978) The acquisition and development of language by bilingual children. *Journal of Child Language*, 5: 311–326. Copyright © 1978 Cambridge University Press, reproduced with permission of the author and publisher.

Postscript

'The acquisition and development of language by bilingual children' was one of our very first published papers, a brief exposition of what would later on be expanded and discussed in the book *The Sun is Feminine* (Taeschner, 1983). The idea expressed in the original paper has been, in the years, of inspiration for other authors as well as for ourselves and we have applied these concepts to other related research areas.

Searching with Google, more that 200 quotations could be found for the 'classic' Volterra and Taeschner article, with authors providing evidence in favor of or against the model we proposed. In this postscript we are not entering into the debate but prefer to comment on the development of our thinking on bilingualism since the publication of the original piece.

In the paper we claimed that when children are exposed to two languages from birth they seem to use a single lexical system which includes words from both languages. A word in one language often does not have a corresponding word with the same meaning in the other language. Only in a second stage does the child learn to distinguish between the two lexical systems.

In a similar way monolingual children acquiring their first spoken language around one year of age make extensive use of the gestural modality in their efforts to communicate, and also here it was observed that their gestural and spoken productions tended to refer to different referents. The finding of a minimal overlap between early words and gestures for a very short period was observed not only in single case studies (Caselli 1994) but also in larger samples of children (Casadio and Caselli 1989; Iverson, Capirci and Caselli 1994). Progressively children start to use gestures and words with corresponding meanings (sometime simultaneously) and it is only in a subsequent phase, in the second year of life, that the spoken modality becomes the predominant mode of communication.

The extent to which the gestural modality becomes elaborated for linguistic purposes depends on the nature of the input to which the child is exposed: children exposed to a sign language acquire it following rates and stages similar to those followed by children acquiring a spoken language. The topic of 'Sign language acquisition and bilingualism' (Volterra 1990) became another interesting research area. Given that in many countries the tendency to expose deaf children to a bilingual or a bimodal input was growing, it was necessary, for theoretical as well as for practical reasons, to clarify the distinction between bilingual and bimodal exposure (Volterra, Taeschner and Caselli 1984; Caselli *et al.* 1994).

The child will overcome the tendency to build one linguistic system (whether in sign or spoken languages) when coming in contact with an adequate linguistic input in production as well as in comprehension. Grammont's fundamental principle 'une personne – une langue' (in Ronjat 1913) is in general applied by parents only for production and not for comprehension, i.e. each parent speaks to his/her child in one language but understands both. This parental behaviour will lead the child to become a 'passive' bilingual in that the child will understand both languages but speak just one. If the goal is to help the child to become an active bilingual speaker the adult should pretend not to understand the other language. This principle together with other positive conditions has been applied to education for the teaching/learning of a foreign language. Research conducted in different countries and with various languages has shown that children between 3 and 9 years of age can learn a foreign language in kindergarten or primary school with a *magic teacher* who is pretending to understand only the foreign language and who is applying a narrative format approach (Taeschner 1991, 2005; Taeschner, Testa and Cacioppo 2001; Taeschner, Pirchio and Francese 2003; Springer 2004).

Taking into account similarities and differences of bilingualism applied to hearing versus deaf children, a similar educational model has been successfully applied to bilingual experiences carried on in mainstream Italian schools (Ardito and Mignosi 1995; Ardito 1998; Teruggi 2003).

Children learn more than one language when the right input conditions are respected, and we should be able to create such conditions in order to give any child such a chance. Our later research focused precisely on these conditions, with the goal of giving theoretical and practical indications to parents, teachers and other professionals.

Virginia Volterra, PhD, is Research Director of the Institute of Cognitive Sciences and Technologies, CNR, Rome. virginia.volterra@istc.cnr.it

Traute Taeschner, PhD, is Professor of Psychology at the University of Rome, Italy. traute.taeschner@uniroma1.it

Chapter 14

Early bilingual language development: one language or two?

FRED GENESEE

IT IS COMMONLY THOUGHT that children learning two languages simultaneously during infancy go through a stage when they cannot differentiate their two languages. In fact, virtually all studies of infant bilingual development have found that bilingual children mix elements from their two languages. Researchers have interpreted these results as evidence for an undifferentiated or unitary underlying language system. In this chapter I will examine the empirical basis for these claims and I will argue that they are questionable because of serious methodological shortcomings in the research. I will then offer some tentative evidence based on speech perception studies and re-analyses of selected bilingual case studies that young bilingual children are psycholinguistically able to differentiate two languages from the earliest stages of bilingual development and that they can use their two languages in functionally differentiated ways, thereby providing evidence of differentiated underlying language systems.

Before proceeding, it is necessary to define some terms that will be used in the remainder of this chapter. BILINGUAL DEVELOPMENT/ACQUISITION will be used to refer to simultaneous acquisition of more than one language during the period of primary language development. FIRST LANGUAGE DEVELOPMENT/ACQUISITION will be used when acquisition of only one language from birth is in question. SECOND LANGUAGE ACQUISITION will be used to refer to acquisition of a second language after the period of primary language development. Finally, the term MIXING will be used to refer to interactions between the bilingual child's developing language systems. Mixing has been used by other researchers to refer to the co-occurrence of elements from two or more languages in A SINGLE UTTERANCE. The mixed elements may be phonological, morphological, lexical, syntactic, phrasal or pragmatic. The definition is problematic when discussing childhood bilinguals because it pertains only to two-word and multi-word stages of development, thereby eliminating a consideration of mixing during the one-word-stage. For reasons that will become clear later, it is desirable to extend the definition of mixing to include single-word utterances from two languages during the same stretch of conversation between a child and caregiver.

Bilingual mixing

The majority of empirical investigations of bilingual development have found mixing (for a summary of early research see McLaughlin, 1984). Phonological, lexical, phrasal, morphological, syntactic, semantic and pragmatic mixing have all been reported. Examples of each type will be described.

Phonological mixing in the form of loan blends has been reported by Murrell (1966) and Oksaar (1971). Loan blends are words made up of phonemic segments from two languages. For example, Oksaar has recorded the loan blend *kats* from an Estonian/ Swedish bilingual child: it consists of the Swedish word for 'cat' (*katt*) and the Estonian word for 'cat' (*kass*). Mixing of grammatical morphemes has been noted by Murrell (1966), Oksaar (1971), Burling (1978), Lindholm and Padilla (1978), and Redlinger and Park (1980). Redlinger and Park report instances of morphological mixing by a German/English bilingual: *pfeift*ING ('whistling') and *Die Mädchen's going night-night* ('The girl's going night-night'). Bergman (1976) reports that her Spanish/English bilingual daughter used the English possessive morpheme *'s* in Spanish utterances, apparently in imitation of her nursery school teacher's use of this mixed form.

By far the most frequent type of mixing to be reported involves whole lexical items, both content and function words (see Swain and Wesche, 1975; Burling, 1978; Leopold, 1978; Lindholm and Padilla, 1978; Redlinger and Park, 1980; Vihman, 1982; 1985; Goodz, 1989). Some investigators have found that content words, and especially nouns, are the most frequently mixed lexical items (Swain and Wesche; Lindholm and Padilla), while others have found that functors are the most frequently mixed (Redlinger and Park; Vihman, 1982; 1985). Redlinger and Park have reported specifically that adverbs, articles, pronouns, prepositions and conjunctions occurred in mixed utterances in descending order of frequency. Examples of lexical mixing can be found in Appendix 14.1.

Mixing at the level of the phrase has also been found. Redlinger and Park (1980) gave an example for a German/Spanish child: *Putzen Zähne* CON JABON ('Brushing teeth with soap'). Lindholm and Padilla (1978) cited an example from a Spanish/English bilingual child: *I ask him* QUE YO VOY A CASA ('I ask him that I go home'). They also reported that when phrasal mixing occurred, the structural consistency of the utterances was maintained so that there were no lexical redundancies or syntactic errors (see also Padilla and Liebman, 1975). To the extent that this is generally true, it would argue against an interpretation of mixing in terms of linguistic confusion.

Swain and Wesche (1975) have reported examples of syntactic mixing, or what they refer to as structural interactions, in the case of a three-year-old French/English boy:

1   *They open,* THE WINDOWS? (use of the noun apposition construction from French in an otherwise English utterance);
2   *A house* PINK (colour adjectives follow the noun in French).

Swain and Wesche also report instances of semantic mixing: *You want to* OPEN *the lights?* (in French, the verb *open* is used in comparison with the English verb *turn on* when referring to lights). It is difficult to interpret such utterances unequivocally as linguistic creations by the child that reflect an underlying lack of differentiation of language systems, since this usage is heard sometimes even among native English speakers in

Quebec, where the Swain and Wesche study was conducted. It is possible that bilingual children mix because they have heard mixing by their parents or other speakers in the environment. This raises an important methodological issue that will be discussed in more detail later – it is necessary to study the language models to whom bilingual children are exposed in order to understand all possible sources of mixing.

An example of pragmatic mixing to elicit parental attention can be found in Goodz (1989). She reports that Nellie, an English/French bilingual, being concerned that her French-speaking father would take away a recently acquired set of barrettes, admonished him to leave them alone, initially in French (*Laisse les barrettes, touche pas les barrettes, Papa*), and then desperately in English (*Me's gonna put it back in the bag so no one's gonna took it*).

Rates of mixing vary considerably from study to study and from case to case. Mixed utterances are reportedly more frequent in early stages of bilingual development and diminish with age (Fantini, 1978; Volterra and Taeschner, 1978; Redlinger and Park, 1980; Vihman, 1982). Summarizing the results from four case studies, Redlinger and Park found 20% to 30% mixing during Stage I (Brown, 1973), 12% to 20% during Stage II, 6% to 12% during Stage III, and 2% to 6% during Stages IV and V. Vihman (1982) reports that the use of mixed utterances by her Estonian/English bilingual son dropped from 34% at 1;8, to 22% at 1;9, to 20% at 1;10, to 11% at 1;11 and to 4% at 2;0.

Reported rates of mixing are difficult to interpret or compare across studies owing to:

1   differential exposure to the languages in question;
2   the possibility of unequal or inequitable sampling of the child's language use in different language contexts and/or with different interlocutors;
3   the lack of an acceptable metric of language development with which to identify children at comparable stages;
4   different operational definitions of mixing; and
5   different language histories.

It is important to point out at this time that adult bilinguals also mix languages in the same sentence, a phenomenon referred to as code-mixing (Sridhar and Sridhar, 1980). Studies of code-mixing in adults show it to be a sophisticated, rule-governed communicative device used by linguistically competent bilinguals to achieve a variety of communicative goals, such as conveying emphasis, role playing, or establishing socio-cultural identity. It has highly structured syntactic and sociolinguistic constraints. In particular, mixing of linguistic elements from one language into another is performed so that the syntactic rules of BOTH languages are respected (Poplack, 1979/80). Poplack cites evidence to the effect that intra-sentential mixing increases in adult bilinguals as their competence in the two languages increases. Adult bilinguals also switch between languages as a function of certain sociolinguistic factors, such as the setting, tone and purpose of the communication or the ethnolinguistic identity of the interlocutor. This language behaviour is referred to as CODE-SWITCHING (Sridhar and Sridhar, 1980). What is thought to distinguish bilingual children's mixing from adult mixing is the lack of systematicity or compliance to linguistic rules in the case of children.

The period of language mixing just described is generally reported to be followed by linguistic differentiation. Investigators studying children with different language histories have reported that differentiation occurs during the third year of life (Murrell, 1966; Imedadze, 1978; Vihman, 1982). At this time, the child is thought to have developed or to be developing two separate representations of his/her language systems or, alternatively, to have overcome the linguistic confusion characteristic of the earlier stage. He or she begins to switch systematically between languages as a function of the participants, the setting, the function of the message (e.g. to exclude others), its form (e.g. narration), and to a lesser extent, the topic of conversation. Bilingual children are reported to be especially sensitive to their interlocutors so that initially when differentiation occurs they tend rigidly to use the language they associate with the speaker even though he or she may express a willingness to use the other language (Fantini, 1978; Volterra and Taeschner, 1978).

In sum, the fact that mixing of two languages occurs during bilingual development has been reported and is accepted by all investigators. More questionable are the explanations of it.

The unitary-language system explanation

Language mixing during the early stages of bilingual development has been interpreted in general terms as evidence of a unitary-language system with undifferentiated phonological, lexical and syntactic subsystems (except see Bergman, 1976; Lindholm and Padilla, 1978; Pye, 1986; Goodz, 1986; 1989). For example, Leopold, in one of the first and still most comprehensive studies of bilingual development, concluded that 'Words from the two languages did not belong to two different speech systems but to one . . .' (in Hatch, 1978: 27). In 1977, Swain postulated a 'common storage model' of bilingual development according to which all rules of both languages are initially stored in a common location. Even rules that are specific to each language are initially stored in common storage and subsequently tagged as appropriate for a particular language through a process of differentiation. More recently, Redlinger and Park (1980) write 'These findings suggest that the subjects were involved in a gradual process of language differentiation and are in agreement with those of previous investigators supporting the one system approach to bilingual acquisition' (p. 344). Volterra and Taeschner (1978) have interpreted mixing in terms of a three-stage model:

1   initial unification of both lexical and syntactic subsystems;
2   differentiation of the lexicon but continued unification of syntax;
3   finally, differentiation of both the lexicon and syntax.

The title of Swain's (1972) thesis – *Bilingualism as a first language* – exemplifies the unitary-system interpretation of early bilingual development.

There are empirical reasons to question this interpretation The evidence cited by the respective investigators is simply not sufficient to support such an interpretation. In order to uphold the unitary-system hypothesis one would need to establish that, all things being equal, bilingual children use items from both languages indiscriminately in all contexts of communication. In other words, there should be no differential distribution of items from the two languages as a function of the predominant language being used in different contexts. In contrast, support for the differentiated-language systems hypothesis would require evidence that the children use items from their two languages differentially as a function of context. Even in cases where the child might be more proficient in one language than the other, which is common, it would be possible to test the differentiated-systems hypothesis by observing the distribution of items from the weaker language. In particular, if the differentiated-language systems hypothesis were true, one would expect to find more frequent use of items from the weaker language in contexts where that language is being used than in contexts where the stronger language is being used, even though items from the stronger language might predominate in both contexts.

In fact, most proponents of the unitary-system hypothesis do not present or analyse their data by context. Therefore, it is impossible to determine whether the children are using the repertoire of language items they have acquired to that point in a differentiated way. For example, the evidence cited by Volterra and Taeschner (1978) in support of stage I of their model consists simply of isolated examples of lexical mixing in utterances addressed to the child's German-speaking mother. No evidence of language use with the child's Italian-speaking father is given. Redlinger and Park (1980) calculated the rate of mixing for four different bilingual children over a period varying from five to nine months and found a decline in mixing over time. No systematic data of differential mixing of each language as a function of language context are provided. Evidence of declining rates of overall mixing does not constitute sufficient proof that the child has only one language system. Mixing may decline with development, not because separation of the languages is taking place but rather because the children are acquiring more complete linguistic repertoires and, therefore, do not need to borrow from or overextend between languages.

Some investigators have examined mixing as a function of interlocutor or context, but their analyses are incomplete or questionable. Vihman (1985), for example, reports the percentage use of English in English contexts versus an Estonian context, but she does not report corresponding values for Estonian. That the child used English utterances in the Estonian context, which was the home, is perhaps not surprising given that the child's sister and parents all spoke English and were undoubtedly overheard using English in their home in Palo Alto, California (see also Pye, 1986). More convincing evidence of a unitary language system would include examples of Estonian multiword utterances in English contexts (the daycare centre, for example). Swain (1972) cites evidence of mixing in bilingual children who were asked to translate messages from one monolingual adult stranger to another, neither of whom spoke the other's language. Mixing under such conditions may reflect the peculiarities of such language use rather than lack of differentiation of language *per se*. In the absence of sound and complete data on language use in different language contexts, an explanation of bilingual mixing in terms of undifferentiated language systems is open to serious question.

Other explanations of mixing

A number of other more specific explanations of bilingual mixing have been suggested. By far the most frequent of these is that bilingual children mix because they lack appropriate lexical items in one language but have them in the other language and, effectively, they borrow from one language for use in the other (see, for example,

Fantini, 1978; Lindholm and Padilla, 1978; Volterra and Taeschner, 1978; Redlinger and Park, 1980). Vihman (1985: 313) has argued that this is an unsatisfactory explanation of mixing, and that, alternatively, mixing declines as the child 'comes to recognize adult-imposed standards of behaviour and shows awareness of his own ability to meet them'. If this is indeed the case, then differentiation would be more an issue of developing sociolinguistic competence than of underlying psycholinguistic separation of the language systems.

Mixing has also been reported in cases of overly restricted use of specific lexical items. Imedadze (1978) and Swain and Wesche (1975) have suggested that in some cases bilingual children identify a referent with the lexical item in the language that was first or most frequently used to label it. They might insist on using that word at all times when talking about that referent regardless of the linguistic context. A particularly striking example is described by Volterra and Taeschner (1978: 317–18) in which a German–Italian girl insisted on using the Italian word *occhiali* to refer to her Italian-speaking father's eyeglasses when speaking with her German-speaking mother. The mother had to make repeated attempts to get the child to refer to her father's glasses as *Brillen* when speaking German.

Yet a third explanation of mixing has been suggested in terms of structural linguistic factors (Tabouret-Keller, 1962; Murrell, 1966; Vihman, 1985). Vihman, for example, claims that her bilingual son used English function words in otherwise Estonian utterances because the English words were simpler and more salient than the corresponding Estonian words.

In contrast to the unitary-language system explanation which implicates the nature of the representational system underlying the bilingual child's developing language competence, these more specific explanations implicate the nature of the acquisitional process underlying bilingualism. All three of these explanations of bilingual mixing can be interpreted in terms of acquisitional processes that have been identified in monolingual acquisition. Thus, instances of mixing due to lexical borrowing could be viewed as overextensions of the type observed in monolingual children (Griffiths, 1986), with the difference that bilingual children overextend inter-lingually as well as intra-lingually while monolingual children overextend intra-lingually only. In the case of first-language acquisition, it has been observed that particular overextensions of nominals usually cease once the child has learned what mature speakers of the language would consider a more appropriate word (Griffiths, 1986). In other words, monolingual children make use of whatever vocabulary they have acquired; as their vocabulary grows, they use increasingly appropriate, less overextended words. This also seems a reasonable interpretation of bilingual overextensions (see also Goodz, 1989) and, in fact, accords with the tendency for bilingual children to mix less as their proficiency increases, as noted earlier.

Overly restricted use of particular lexical items has been observed in monolingual children in the form of underextensions (Stross, 1973; Reich, 1976). Anglin (1977) has suggested that in fact underextensions are more frequent than overextensions in monolingual development, but they often go unnoticed because they do not violate adult usage. It has been suggested further that 'the characteristic early path is for nominals to be underextended first and only later to apply to a wider range of entities (perhaps then going as far as overextension)' (Griffiths, 1986: 300). Bilingual children may overextend longer than monolingual children because they hear more instances of particular nominals being used in specific contexts (e.g. the German nominal for 'glasses' being used in German contexts or with German-speaking interlocutors), whereas monolingual children are likely to hear the same nominals used in extended contexts (e.g. *glasses* used in all contexts in which the referent occurs). Moreover, bilingual children's use of specific nominals in specific language or interlocutor contexts is accepted by bilingual parents, whereas monolingual parents are not as likely to accept underextended usage, if they notice it.

Finally, Slobin (1973) has argued for a set of universal operating principles which every child brings to bear on the problem of language acquisition, and for a number of language-specific strategies which are involved in the acquisition of aspects of a given native language. According to Slobin, the order of development of various grammatical devices is determined by the child's cognitive and perceptual development and by characteristics of the languages to be learned. It follows that children learning two languages simultaneously may be expected to mix aspects of their languages because of acquisitional strategies that are independent of language representation *per se*. More specifically, language mixing might occur in any given utterance of a bilingual child, even though his/her two languages are represented separately, for two possible reasons. In one case, mixing might occur because the language system in use at the moment is incomplete and does not include the grammatical device needed to express certain meanings. If a device from the other language system that serves the same purposes were available, it might be used at that moment. In the other case, the grammatical device required to express the intended meaning is available in the language currently in use, but it is more complex than the corresponding device in the other language system and its use strains the child's current ability. Therefore, the simpler device from the other system might be used at that moment. In both cases, developing bilingual children can be seen to be using whatever grammatical devices they have in their repertoire or whatever devices they are able to use given their current language ability. In neither of these cases is it necessary to assume that the languages are represented in a unified system.

Issues concerning acquisitional strategies in bilingual development are independent of the issue of language representation. That particular acquisitional strategies may result in differences in the utterances of bilingual and monolingual children obscures what is perhaps a more important implication, namely that bilingual development is characterized by the same processes of acquisition as monolingual development. Indeed on theoretical grounds one would expect bilingual and monolingual acquisition during infancy to be the same (see Genesee, 1987). To date, researchers have not seriously examined the nature of bilingual acquisition in infancy and, in particular, whether it is the same as or different from monolingual acquisition. There has been much speculation about a possible relationship between bilingualism and metalinguistic awareness and the effect this might have on language acquisition (Cummins, 1976; Diaz, 1983; Hakuta, 1986). While there is some evidence of such relationships, it is inconsistent and pertains to older bilinguals, either school-age children or adults (Ben-Zeev, 1977; Ianco-Worrall, 1972), and not infant bilinguals.

The role of input

Notwithstanding the possible significance of specific acquisitional processes in accounting for some instances of mixing, an alternative general explanation of mixing that has not been examined seriously is that bilingual children's mixed utterances are modelled on mixed input produced by others (see also Goodz, 1989). Modelling could affect the child's language mixing in two ways – in specific ways, such that particular instances of modelled mixed utterances are used by the child, or in a general way, such that frequent mixing by adults or linguistically more mature children will result in the child mixing frequently and generally. Bergman's speculation, noted earlier, that her daughter's use of the English possessive marker *'s* in otherwise Spanish utterances could be traced to her nursery school teacher's use of this same construction is consistent with the first possibility. Also in this regard Goodz (1989) cites evidence of parents using mixed utterances in response to their children's language choices. She notes that parents might thereby present specific examples of mixing that children are particularly sensitive to since they are made in response to the children's solicitations.

Certainly one would expect children exposed to frequent and general mixing to mix frequently, since there is no reason for them to know that the languages should be separated. Indeed, there are fully formed dialects which consist of elements of two languages (e.g. so-called Spanglish in the southern US, or Franglais in Quebec). Conversely, it is commonly advocated, although not well documented, that the best way to avoid bilingual mixing in children is to have each parent speak only one language to the child – the so-called rule of Grammont, after the individual who first espoused this principle (Ronjat, 1913). In fact, it appears from the published evidence that more mixing does occur among children who hear both languages used freely and interchangeably by the same interlocutors (Murrell, 1966; Redlinger and Park's case Danny 1980), and less in children who hear the languages separated by person and/or setting (Fantini, 1978; Redlinger and Park's case Marcus 1980).

It is difficult, however, to ascertain the exact relationship between input and rate or type of mixing from the available research, since descriptions of the language-input conditions are either totally lacking (Padilla and Liebman, 1975; Lindholm and Padilla, 1978) or, at best, are general and impressionistic (Volterra and Taeschner, 1978; Vihman, 1982). In a study of parental language use in bilingual families, Goodz (1989) found that even parents 'firmly committed to maintaining a strict separation of language by parent, model linguistically mixed utterances to their children', but are unaware of doing so. Thus, impressionistic reports are probably inaccurate. Garcia (1983) has studied what he refers to as bilingual switching in 12 children in interaction with their mothers. The children were aged 2;0–2;8 at the beginning of the study, which lasted 12 months, and the mothers were part-time teachers in their children's co-operative pre-school where the study took place. He found that switching could be classified as serving three different communicative functions – instructional, translation or other – and that it occurred relatively infrequently (11%). It is difficult to know whether these results are typical of younger bilingual children and of less linguistically sensitive mothers in more natural, home conditions.

The most extensive study to date of the relationship between parental mixing and children's mixing is that of Goodz (1989). She has studied some 17 children raised in French/English bilingual families longitudinally for over three years in some cases. Of particular relevance to the present discussion, she reports that the frequency of occurrence of children's mixed utterances is correlated with the frequency of occurrence of parental mixing, especially in mother–child dyads. Parental mixing may occur for a number of different reasons, all of which are motivated to maintain and encourage communication:

1   use whatever lexical items the child understands;
2   as part of linguistic expansions and repetitions of their children's two- and three-word utterances; and
3   to attract attention, emphasize or discipline. Goodz points out that children may be particularly attentive to such parental mixing given its communicative context and intention.

There are reasons to believe that all of the children examined by the research under review here heard some mixed input – a number of researchers indicate obliquely that the parents did not separate their languages completely, and others even allude to the possible role of mixed input as an explanation of mixed output, thereby implying that mixed input was present (e.g. Tabouret-Keller, 1962; Burling, 1978; Redlinger and Park, 1980; Vihman and McLaughlin, 1982). The problem is that virtually all researchers to date (cf. Goodz, 1989) accept their own general impressions or parental reports that the languages are used separately, and on this basis do not seriously consider mixed input as a major contributor to the children's use of mixed utterances. Evidence that mixing by bilingual children can be traced in part to mixed input would weaken arguments that mixing during early bilingual development NECESSARILY reflects an underlying undifferentiated language system. Bilingual children with differentiated language systems may still mix because the input conditions permit it or because the verbal interaction calls for it. We will see examples of this shortly. Clearly, careful, detailed research examining input to bilingual children is needed (see Goodz, 1989).

The unitary-language system hypothesis re-examined

So far I have argued that the extant evidence on bilingual development is inadequate to conclude, as most researchers have to date, that bilingual children have an undifferentiated representation of their two languages. The question arises: what kind of evidence would be necessary? First, since one cannot examine the underlying representation of language directly, evidence for differentiation would necessarily be based on functional separation of the languages, that is, how the languages are used. Second, data on language use would need to be collected in different language contexts in order to determine the relative functional distribution of elements from the two languages, as already noted. Third, detailed documentation of the input conditions, both during specific interactional episodes and more generally, is needed in order to correlate the incidence and type of mixed output with mixed input. Finally, as was also noted earlier, children who mix during the early stages of bilingual development do so less with age as their lexical systems and presumably their other linguistic subsystems expand, making overextensions and overgeneralizations between languages less necessary. Therefore, it would be necessary to examine their language use prior to this stage of development; that is, from the one-word stage on.

In the absence of adequate data, how plausible is the differentiated-language systems hypothesis and what do existing data tell us? Differentiation of two languages during bilingual development minimally requires that children be able to discriminate perceptually between the spoken languages. Research on the perceptual abilities of infants suggests that they possess many, if not all, of the necessary prerequisites for speech perception (Jusczyk, 1981) and that they are capable of fairly sophisticated perceptual discriminations (Jusczyk, 1982). In this regard, Jusczyk (1982: 361) has commented that 'today, some researchers in the field . . . have been moved to comment that the most interesting kind of result would be to discover some aspect of speech perception that infants were incapable of'.

Relevant to bilingual development, Trehub (1973) has found that infants of 6–17 weeks are able to differentiate phonetic contrasts in languages (Czech and Polish) that they have never been exposed to. Also, Mehler *et al.* (1986) report that 4-day-old infants from French-speaking families were able to discriminate between French and Russian and that they showed a preference for French. That this was not simply a novelty effect is suggested by an earlier study by Mehler *et al.* (1978) in which 4- to 6-week-old infants were found to discriminate between their mothers' voices and those of strangers, but only if the speech was normally intonated; they were unable to make this discrimination when both voices were monotone. Thus, it would appear that it is the linguistic properties and qualities of speech, or at least their complex acoustic properties, that infants are sensitive to. These studies do not tell us whether children can differentiate between two languages they have heard, which is the appropriate test case for bilingual children, but they are certainly suggestive of such discriminative capacity. At the very least, the extant evidence suggests that bilingual-to-be infants are capable of discriminating between different unfamiliar spoken languages at the point in development when they begin to utter single words.

Re-examination of a number of published language samples of interactions between children and their parents suggests that in fact bilingual children may use their languages differentially. Three such samples will be examined briefly at this time (Murrell, 1966; Volterra and Taeschner, 1978; Redlinger and Park, 1980). These interactions have been reproduced in Appendix 14.1. The point of this re-examination is not to prove the differentiated-language systems hypothesis, since the available data are inadequate, but rather to establish its tenability.

Volterra and Taeschner (1978) (see Appendix 14.1) report a conversation between a German/Italian bilingual girl, Lisa, and her German-speaking mother, along with three isolated utterances by Lisa to her mother. Lisa was 1;10 at the time of the recordings. With the exception of Lisa's use of *la* (Italian for 'there'), all items used by Lisa could be German. The authors interpret Lisa's use of *da* in the last utterance as mixing from Italian *dare* ('to give'); an alternative interpretation is that it is the German *da* ('there'), which Lisa had used previously.

Redlinger and Park (1980) report conversations between a German/Spanish bilingual boy, Marcus, and both his German-speaking father and Spanish-speaking mother (see Appendix 14.1). Marcus was between 2;4.23 and 2;5.20 and had an MLU [mean length of utterance] of 2.21 at the time of the recording. German was used by the parents with one another; the father used only German with Marcus; and the mother used predominantly Spanish (70%); the family resided in Germany. It can be conjectured from the parents' reported language use that Marcus had learned more German than Spanish, and indeed, German predominated in both conversations. Of particular interest is Marcus's use of Spanish – he used four different Spanish lexical items with his Spanish-speaking mother and only two with his German-speaking father.

These data could be interpreted as functional differentiation of his limited Spanish. The authors' interpretation was that 'Marcus appeared to have basically one lexical system consisting of words from both languages' (p. 340).

Finally, Murrell (1966) reports conversations between a Swedish/Finnish/English trilingual child, Sandra, and the author and her mother (see Appendix 14.1). According to the author 'At the nursery only Finnish was spoken. Her mother spoke mostly Swedish to her at home, while I spoke partly Swedish and partly English. Her mother and I spoke mostly English together' (p. 11). The recordings were made almost three months after the family had moved to England when Sandra was between 2;3.25 and 2;4.1. Examination of the transcripts indicates that Sandra's lexical usage with the author is predominantly in English. The only non-English lexical items used by Sandra are references in Finnish to a cat in a picture (*kia*) and responses in Swedish to utterances initiated by the author in Swedish. To illustrate this, in Appendix 14.1 transcript (3b), turn S1, Sandra utters a word (*kekka*) that the author interprets to be Swedish ('to lick') but acknowledges that it might have been the corresponding English verb. As a result of this interpretation, apparently, the author responded in SWEDISH in turn F1 to the child's otherwise ENGLISH string of lexical items. Sandra then responded in Swedish (*kikka*) in turn S2. The author then responded in turn F2 in Swedish (apparently intending to provide a corrected imitation of Sandra's previous Swedish utterance) AND in English (apparently providing an English translation of his own previous utterance). Sandra then proceeded with a combination of English and Swedish in turn S3. In short most, and it could be argued all, of the child's Swedish utterances are made in response to Swedish modelled by the author; otherwise, the child used English. Even the child's use of the Finnish lexical item *kia* is equivocal in that it might actually function as a proper noun or name for her cat. Contrary to evidencing a lack of linguistic differentiation, Sandra appears to have used Swedish and English differentially in contextually sensitive ways during the same conversation with an interlocutor who switches back and forth, somewhat in confusion.

Analysis of Sandra's conversation with her mother yields a similar impression. In this case, Sandra uses predominantly Swedish except for three English-content words (i.e. *pull*, *bucket* and *faggit*) and the demonstrative adjective *that*. The child's use of *faggit* here is not at all clear from the transcript. It is not clear whether the child is really confused over the use of English *bucket* for spade and Swedish *ambare* for bucket as the author's notations would seem to imply or, alternatively, whether she is not underextending her use of the English lexical item *bucket* to a specific referent (i.e. a 'spade'); admittedly this is an incorrect lexical usage.

The preceding analysis focused on differentiation of language according to lexical distribution. One final piece of evidence which focuses on the use of different syntactic features will be offered here in support of the differentiated-language systems hypothesis. Meisel (1990) reports on the syntactic development of two French/German bilingual children. The children were observed between 1;0 and 4;0. The parents claimed to use their respective native languages exclusively with their children. Meisel examined the children's use of word-order sequences and verb inflections in French and German; these syntactic features were examined because they differ in mature forms of the target languages and in monolingual children's acquisition of the target forms. In brief, Meisel found that the bilingual children used different word orders in French and German as soon as they produced multiword utterances, and they correctly inflected verbs to agree with subjects according to the rules of each language as soon as they consistently filled the subject slot in their utterances.

Conclusion

In sum, I have argued that, contrary to most interpretations of bilingual development, bilingual children are able to differentiate their language systems from the beginning and that they are able to use their developing language systems differentially in contextually sensitive ways. As well, I have suggested that more serious research attention needs to be given to parental input in the form of bilingual mixing as a possible source of influence in children's mixing. Evidence that children's mixing may indeed be related to mixed input by parents was presented. This evidence, however, was limited to lexical mixing, and more attention to phonological, morphological and other kinds of mixing by parents and children is clearly needed. The available evidence is obviously inadequate to come to confident conclusions regarding these points, and my re-examination of other researchers' transcriptions must be regarded as preliminary and tentative pending more adequate research. What is clear from this review is that the case for undifferentiated language development in bilingual children is far from established.

Appendix 14.1

(1)   Volterra and Taeschner (1978: 355–16)

Lisa with German-speaking mother

(a)   L: Miao miao.
         M: Wo ist miao? ('Where is meow?')
         L: *La* miao. ('There meow.')
         M: Wo ist miao? ('Where is meow?')
         L: Da ist miao. ('There is meow.')
(b)   L: Daki Buch. ('Thanks book.') (*Her mother had just given her a book.*)
(c)   L: Daki. ('Thanks.') (*while giving the pencil to her mother.*)
(d)   L: Mama tita daki. ('Mommy pencil thanks.') (*She wants her mother to give her the pencil.*)
(e)   L: *Da.* (authors: interpret this as variant of Italian *dare* 'to give'; could be German *da* 'there') (*offering a sweet to her mother.*)

(2)   Redlinger and Park (1980: 340–41)

(a)   *Marcus with German-speaking father*
         F: Und was macht er hier? ('And what's he doing here?')
         Ms: Haare putzen ('Hair cleaning.')
         F: Ja, er wäscht die Haare, und dann auch? ('Yes, he washes his hair, and then also?')
         Ms: ¡Jabón! ('Soap!')
         F: Bitte? ('What?')
         Ms: ¡Jabón! ('Soap!')
         F: Mit der Seife. Und was macht er denn hier? ('With the soap. And what is he doing then here?')
         Ms: Putzen Zähne *con jabón*. ('Brushing teeth with soap.')
(b)   *Marcus with Spanish-speaking mother*
         M: ¿Qué hacen los niños? ('What are the children doing?')
         Ms: Müd. Die Kinder da müde. ('Tired. The children there tired.')

M: ¿Están cansados? No juegan los niños? ('Are they tired? Aren't the children playing?')

Ms: Das *no juegan*. ¡*Arboles!* ('That not playing. Trees!')

M: ¿Qué hay en los árboles? ('What are on the trees?')

Ms: *Manzanas.* Hund schlafen. ('Apples. Dog sleeping.')

(3)   Murrell (1966: 19–22)

Sandra with father
Situation: *Looking at two pictures, the first (a) showing a woman with a cat, the second (b) showing the same cat, this time covered with milk, and a dog licking the milk off the cat's back.*

(a)   F1:   What else have you got there? ('What other pictures have you got there?')

S1:   [ˌmami]
   See comment on S3.

F2:   Is that Mummy?

S2:   [n̩ ˈkʰin̩ˌɛə]
   ([n̩] often preceded utterances at this stage (it did not apparently derive from Finnish *on* 'is' or English *and*)

F3:   Kia.

S3:   [n̩ ˈkʰia ˌmami]
   With [ˈkʰia] compare S2. This utterance meant 'Kia's mummy', i.e. 'the cat's owner'. The word *mummy* was still used to designate any older female in cases where a relationship was implied.

F4:   Pussy-cat.

(b)   S1:   [n̩ ˈdɛə [ˈ. . .] ˈbɔββa . . . ˈkʰekka . . . ˈuːː ˈkʰia]
   [dɛə] English *there* (Swedish *där*). S2 [ˈbɔββa] English *bow-wow*, Swedish *vovve*. Swedish *slicka* '(to) lick' (the English word was less well known than the Swedish). [uːː] was an exclamation of feigned shock and disapproval and real delight at seeing the cat covered with milk.

F1:   Vad gör han?
   Swedish 'What's he doing?' (I did not understand [ˈkʰekka] but assumed, partly because of the form [ˈbɔββa], that it was Swedish rather than English she was speaking.)

S2:   [ˈkikka]
   Swedish *slicka* (the gemination and final [-a] suggest the Swedish word).

F2:   [ˈkʰɪk . . . he's licking.
   I may have thought she was using English *kick*.

S3:   [ˌlikiŋ . . . [ˈʋaɣʋa] ˈkikkan ˈkikin [ˈʋaɣʋa ˈkikiŋ [ˈʋaɣʋa ˈkikiŋ] [ˈʋaɣʋa]
   Swedish *vovve* 'bow-wow'; cf. S1. The diphthong now more closely resembles my own (dialect) equivalent of standard British-English /ɑu/; but
   cf. Finnish *hauva* 'Bow-wow' and Finish *vauva* 'baby'. All four words were at first used indiscriminately for both 'dog' and 'baby'.

F3:   Licking pussy-cat.
   I repeat the verb and add the object.

S4:   [ˈkiki ˈbɔββa]
   The final nasal is lost in [ˈkiki]. The diphthong in [ˈbɔββa] suggests the English word. She is now excited, whereas in S3 she was speaking more deliberately. She assumes I have contradicted her, that I mean it is the cat that is doing the licking.

F4:   Bow-wow licking pussy-cat.
   I misunderstand her, too prematurely attributing to her a knowledge of English syntax. Two-item utterances were still maximal and the order arbitrary.

Sandra with Swedish-speaking mother

Situation: *looking at two pictures, the first (c) showing a monkey pulling a girl's hair, the second (d) showing the girl with a bucket.*

(c) *M1*: Och vad är det?

Swedish 'And what's that?'

S1: [ˈɑːpa]

Swedish *apa* 'monkey'.

M2: Apa. Vad gör apan?

Swedish 'Monkey. And what's the monkey doing?'

S2: [ˌpu ˌsika ɟje]

English *pull*, Swedish *flicka* 'girl' and Swedish *håret* 'the hair'. (= 'He's pulling the girl's hair.')

M3: Ja, han drar flickan i håret, så dum apa! Fy! dum apa.

Swedish 'Yes, he's pulling the girl's hair [lit. 'the girl in the hair'], what a naughty monkey! Tut, tut! naughty monkey.'

S3: [ˈeː hɛ e ˈkɔkkea]

Finnish *ei saa koskea* 'mustn't touch'

M4: Ei saa koskea . . . 'ei ta kokia'.

Her mother repeats the sentence in its correct form and then in mimicry of a common version of the child's.

S4: [ˌei saː ˈkɔkkia]

(d) *M1*: Vad har flickan?

Swedish 'What's the girl got?'

S1: [ˌemˌen ˈembala]

Swedish *ämbare* 'bucket'.

M2: Och vad har hon mera – i andra handen?

Swedish 'And what else has she got – in her other hand?'

S2: ˌbakit . . . 'dat ˌembala]

English *bucket* and English *that*. Both *bucket* and *ämbare* were used for both 'bucket' and 'spade', but here she seems to be making a distinction between *bucket* (= 'spade') and *ämbare* (= 'bucket').

M3: Det år *spade*.

Swedish 'That's 'spade'.'

S3: [ˈpaːde]

M4: Det där är *ämbare*.

Swedish 'That's "bucket".'

S4: [ˈembala . . . ˌfaggit]

The child repeats the Swedish word, then, after a pause, the English.

Source: Genesee, F. (1989) Early bilingual language development: one language or two? *Journal of Child Language* 16: 161–79. Copyright © 1989 Cambridge University Press, reproduced with permission of the author and publisher.

Postscript

It has been almost 20 years since 'Early bilingual development: one language or two?' first appeared in the *Journal of Child Language* (*JCL*). Considerable research on bilingual first language acquisition has been conducted since that time, certainly enough to re-examine the main claims made in the article and to assess our current understanding of the issues raised by it. The main argument in the 1989 *JCL* article was that earlier claims that children who acquire 'two languages simultaneously during infancy go through a stage when they cannot differentiate their two languages' (p. 161) were empirically questionable and that, to the contrary, evidence available at the time provided support for the counter-claim that such children 'are able to differentiate their language systems from the beginning' (p. 174). In question in the article were the extent to which such children could be said to be bilingual or, in the parlance of the day, 'to know two different languages' and, also, the nature of the evidence that is necessary and sufficient to support claims about unitary versus differentiated language systems in young bilinguals. In hindsight, I think these questions were both the 'right ones' and overly simplistic.

The nature of the young bilingual child's knowledge (or underlying representation) of language seems to have been the 'right' question because it was a focal issue at that time and continued to occupy a focal position in much thinking about bilingual first language acquisition, not only in research circles but also among laypersons who were raising or caring for bilingual learners. In support of the claim in the *JCL* article (as well as parallel claims by Meisel, 1989, at the same time), there has been considerable evidence that is compatible with the notion that young bilingual children have knowledge of two languages, not one single hybrid language, at least from the one-word stage of development onward (Meisel, 2001). Earlier claims that simultaneous bilinguals go through an initial monolingual stage were often based on their code-mixing (e.g. Volterra and Taeschner, 1978). Much evidence has been accumulated since 1989 that bilingual children can use their languages in a differentiated and appropriate fashion with different interlocutors (e.g. Genesee, Boivin and Nicoladis, 1996). This evidence is difficult to reconcile with the unitary language system hypothesis. Subsequent research also showed that bilingual children's code-mixing is formulated according to the grammatical constraints of the participating languages (e.g. Paradis, Nicoladis and Genesee, 2000; Köppe, 2006), evidence, again, that is difficult to reconcile with the notion of fused language systems. Yet other research that has focused on functional aspects of bilingual first language learners' language development has revealed that, rather than being a sign of underlying cognitive fusion of two languages, code-mixing is largely a performance-based phenomenon and reflects children's communicative competence (Genesee, 2002) and socio-cultural factors operating in the learning environment. Lanza (1997), for example, has argued that the frequency of individual bilingual children's code-mixing can be linked to language socialization patterns in the home and, likewise, Genesee and his colleagues have shown that bilingual children's code-mixing is sensitive to variation in their interlocutor's mixing and, at the same time, can be constrained by feedback from interlocutors that it is inappropriate or ineffective.

More direct evidence that simultaneous bilinguals know two languages comes from research on their syntactic development. There is general agreement from such studies that bilingual children's rates and patterns of syntactic development resemble those of monolinguals learning the same languages for the most part and under conditions of adequate input (see Genesee and Nicoladis, in press; Meisel, 2001). That bilingual children appear to develop differentiated morpho-syntactic systems for the most part opened up research to other questions, such as the extent to which and the linguistic conditions under which the grammars of bilingual children interact during development (see Döpke, 2001, for a review). To date, research indicates that bilingual children evidence some instances of cross-linguistic transfer during development, but these appear to both linguistically and developmentally circumscribed. Research on these issues continues.

Taken together, the results of these studies paint a different picture of bilingual development that differs quite significantly from that which was contained in earlier studies. At the same time, however, recent research on early speech perception and production in young bilingual children indicates the picture may be more complex than that painted by research on functional language use and lexical and morphosyntactic development (Sebastián-Gallés and Bosch, 2005; Genesee and Nicoladis, in press). Indeed, asking whether bilingual children possess differentiated language systems may not even be the most useful question to ask when it comes to examining these aspects of bilingual acquisition, and research on bilingual first language acquisition has moved in different and more varied directions. More specifically, for example, there has been a burgeoning interest in the language development and precursors of language development in bilingual first language learners during the pre-verbal and very early verbal stages of development. This research is examining the perception of segmental and supra-segmental features of dual language input by children exposed to two languages from birth in comparison to that of monolingual learners. Interesting similarities and differences are emerging from this, as yet nascent, body of research. Researchers have also examined bilingual first language acquisition in children at risk – for example, children with language impairment (Paradis et al., 2003) and Down syndrome (Kay-Raining Bird et al., 2005). This latter line of research is interesting because it promises to extend our understanding of the boundaries of children's capacity for language learning even further than that revealed by typically developing children.

Fred Genesee, PhD, is Professor of Psychology at McGill University, Canada. genesee@psych.mcgill.ca

Code-switching in young bilingual children: the acquisition of grammatical constraints

JÜRGEN M. MEISEL

Code-switching is a well-studied phenomenon. Yet despite the wealth of existing studies, a number of problems related to code-switching are not well understood. One such area that needs further investigation is the acquisition of the kind of knowledge that enables the bilingual individual to use code-switching adequately and successfully. One would like to know more about questions like the following: How and when do children acquire grammatical constraints on code-switching? Do children violate such constraints at certain stages of language development? Similarly for sociolinguistic aspects of code-switching: When and how do children acquire the pragmatic competence that enables them to switch adequately?

In this paper, I study the development of certain grammatical phenomena in bilingual speech, especially during early phases, that is, before age 3;0 (3 years; 0 months).[1] The question to be raised in this paper is when and how bilingual children acquire the necessary knowledge that enables them to use code-switching adequately, without violating the constraints that govern adult switching.

Some terminology, definitions, and concepts

Let me begin by briefly stating how I understand some of the terms that are crucial for this discussion. Given the terminological confusion in this area of research, this should help to avoid misunderstandings, although I do not attribute specific importance to the particular choice of labels used here.

I call *bilinguals* those individuals who acquired their two languages in early child-hood, that is, who were exposed to both languages from early on, say before age 3;0 (cf. McLaughlin, 1984). As for those acquiring the second language (L2) later on, I refer to them as child or adult *L2 learners*. As suggested in Meisel (1989), I will use the term *(language-) mixing* to refer to all instances where features of two languages are juxta-posed, within a clause or across clause boundaries, irrespective of the etiology of these phenomena. If, however, the causes for specific instantiations of mixing can be traced back to a failure in separating the two grammars, this will be called *fusion*. Fusion, in other words, is a phenomenon related to grammatical competence; that is, the bilingual individual has integrated parts of the grammar of L_a into the grammar of L_b. *Code-switching*, on the other hand, is defined as a specific skill of the bilingual's pragmatic competence, that is, the ability to select the language according to the interlocutor, the situational context, the topic of conversation, and so forth, and to change languages within an interactional sequence in accordance with sociolinguistic rules and without violating specific grammatical constraints. Note that code-switching as well as fusion lead to language-mixing, although they are substantially different in nature. In fact, language differentiation is a necessary prerequisite for code-switching. By definition, one can only switch from one system into the other if the two are distinct.

There exists one more kind of mixing, which may be called *code-mixing*. This term refers to those instances where the speaker violates the constraints on code-switching that normally govern the linguistic behavior of the bilingual community. These constraints can be defined in terms of grammar, discourse organization, or social rules. Borderline cases arise where it is difficult to decide whether one has to do with code-switching or with code-mixing – for example, when mixing is used if an expression is not immediately accessible in the other language. In other words, it is available in principle, but it is momentarily not accessible or is difficult to retrieve. In spite of such problematic cases, these definitions should prove useful in distinguishing rule-governed from nonsystematic cases of mixing. Note that, according to these definitions, both code-switching and code-mixing are performance phenomena, whereas fusion is explained in terms of the grammatical competence of the bilingual.

Code-switching at preschool age

Although studies dealing with code-switching at preschool age are not abundant, certain problems have been investigated in some detail, leading, for example, to a reasonably good understanding of what triggers code-switching and what communicative functions it serves at this age.

In fact, all studies seem to agree that, initially, the interlocutor is the most important single factor in the developing language decision system (see Grosjean, 1982, p. 204). This includes cases where a person influences the child's choice merely by his or her presence in the room (Saunders, 1988, p. 70), and the interlocutor may well be an animal or a toy. Another factor mentioned in most studies is that children mix as a kind of *relief strategy* when an expression in one language is not easily retrieved or if a true equivalent does not exist in the other language, as in the case of culturally bound expressions. Other factors determining language choice and switching familiar from the study of adult speech – for example, the topic of the conversation – soon begin to influence the children's linguistic behavior (see Saunders, 1988). As for the question when all this happens, two age ranges appear repeatedly in the literature, namely, 2;0–3;0 and 5;0–6;0. According to these findings, children are able to use code-switching as early as age 2;0–2;6, but they apparently acquire the more subtle pragmatic or sociolinguistic abilities only later, some as late as age 5;0 or after.

Early switching thus does not yet serve the full range of functions observed in adult usage. In fact, language-mixing before approximately age 2;6–3;0 differs not only in function but also in form from what we are used to calling code-switching. It is therefore not clear whether language-mixing up to age 2;6–3;0 may indeed be compared to adult code-switching, or whether these mixes must be regarded as cases of lexical transfer, as unsuccessful switches, or code-mixing. To decide on this issue, we need to know more about the structural properties of switches, about the kind of knowledge manifested by this type of language use, and about skills required for the child to be able to actually use this knowledge. Intrasentential switches are of specific importance here, for they are likely to be most strictly constrained by structural properties. I refer here to the grammatical characteristics of the mixed element itself, as well as to the switch point and the morphosyntactic properties of the entire sentence. Quite strikingly, however, little is known about the development of the grammatical aspects of code-switching, and information is especially scarce concerning the earliest phases, which deserve special attention. Most studies begin at around or after age 3;0, and only a few deal with grammatical aspects (e.g., Bergman, 1976; de Houwer, 1990; Lanza, 1990; Lindholm and Padilla, 1978; Petersen, 1988; Redlinger and Park, 1980; Taeschner, 1983; Veh, 1990; Vihman, 1985).

With respect to the properties of the switched elements themselves, the available literature indicates that bilinguals before age 3;0 tend to insert single lexical items from one language into the other, mostly nouns (see Kielhöfer and Jonekeit, 1983; McClure, 1977; among others). Yet this does not necessarily stand in conflict with what we know about adult code-switching. Poplack (1980), for example, reports in her seminal paper that Spanish-English adults use nouns and noun phrases (NPs) rather frequently in intrasentential switching. Similar results are reported by Berk-Seligson (1986) in a study in Spanish-Hebrew bilingualism. She finds that 50% of intrasentential mixing concern nominal elements (40% single nouns, 10% NPs). Not only do both studies agree that N and NPs are of particular importance, they also concord in the claim that verbs are much less likely to be mixed into the other language. This, too, is found in child bilingualism. The percentages of mixes by grammatical category given by Redlinger and Park (1980, p. 345) for three children indicate that nouns appear most frequently in this context, at an average of 40.3%, whereas verbs account for only an average of 6% of mixing. Let me add that Redlinger and Park (1980) found virtually no phrasal mixes, and the few that did occur were almost exclusively subject NPs. The findings by Lindholm and Padilla (1978) are also in accordance with these observations; they give the following numbers for mixes in the speech of five Spanish-English children (the two figures refer to mixes from English into Spanish and from Spanish into English, respectively): N (71/12), V (3/3), conjunction (5/3), adjective (2/0), and phrasal mixes (4/8). Note, again, that phrasal mixes occur only rarely.

The results obtained by Vihman (1985) seem to differ significantly from those of the other studies mentioned so far. She finds that in 151 mixed utterances of an Estonian-English boy, there appear 23 (different) nouns, 24 verbs, 1 adjective, and 24 *function words*. The latter show up in 88 (58%) of the mixed utterances. The class of so-called function words, however, is defined in negative terms: It contains everything but N, V, and Adj. In other words, it consists mainly of adverbials, determiners, particles, deictic elements, auxiliaries, and quantifiers. Based on these four classes alone, she concludes that function words, not nouns, are most frequently mixed into the other language by very young bilinguals. I find this classification highly questionable on linguistic as well as psycholinguistic grounds, but I will not go further into this discussion. I will return, however, to Vihman's claim that intrasentential code-switching can be characterized by the predominance of single noun switches whereas code-mixing[2] is characterized by the preponderance of mixed function words.

In conclusion, one finds that all the studies mentioned agree that syntactic categories do not appear randomly in mixed elements. Rather, their distribution suggests that grammatical properties of the mixed expression are relevant from early on. Most notably, phrasal switches occur infrequently, and nouns and noun phrases are encountered most frequently, especially as compared to verbal elements.[3]

Whether these generalizations apply to the earliest occurrences of language-mixing, however, is still a matter of controversy and cannot be decided without taking into consideration the developmental aspect of the problem. Most studies on child bilingualism, in fact, confirm that mixing is more common during very early phases of bilingual language development. This has repeatedly been interpreted as evidence in favor of the claim that early mixing is code-mixing and not yet code-switching. Note that this does not support the *one system hypothesis* (cf. Taeschner, 1983, and Volterra and Taeschner, 1978), which holds that bilingual children go through a developmental phase during which they have only one grammar and only one lexicon available. This corresponds to what has been called fusion, and I have shown elsewhere (Meisel, 1989) that this hypothesis lacks empirical as well as theoretical support; see Genesee (1989) and de Houwer (1990), who arrive at similar conclusions. The reasoning here is indeed that switching, defined as rule-governed linguistic behavior, requires elaborate grammatical knowledge about both languages; and since young children apparently still lack this kind of grammatical competence, their mixes cannot be classified as instances of code-switching.

Let me point out an implication of this *grammatical deficiency hypothesis* that may have been overlooked and that, at any rate, has not been made explicit, namely, that it predicts a U-shaped developmental pattern in the frequency of mixes in the course of early bilingual acquisition. High frequency of mixing due to limited competence in both languages should be expected to decrease as the child acquires knowledge about the two lexicons and the two grammars; but it may increase again, once the child has acquired sufficient knowledge in order to use adultlike code-switching. Note that the predicted increase is merely a behavioral possibility; it need not happen with each individual and would depend on whether the children use code-switching freely or they are reluctant to do so. Vihman (1985), in fact, did find a pattern of this kind. The Estonian-English child she studied slowly gave up mixing English words into Estonian after age 2;0, but the frequency increased again after age 3;0. Vihman interprets this as indicating that mixing during later phases represents code-switching whereas earlier instances are of a different nature.

A further prediction of the deficiency hypothesis is that mixing is expected to be related to whether the competence in using both languages is well balanced or not. Various studies have observed that early mixing consists mostly of inserting elements from the stronger language into the weaker one (cf. Kielhöfer, 1987, and Petersen, 1988) even though mixing into the stronger language is also possible. As for adult bilingual language use, Poplack (1980) reports that speakers who are dominant in one language do switch to the weaker language, but that these are typically not intrasentential switches. On the other hand, she also found that balanced bilingualism favors code-switching. The greater the competence in both languages, the more frequently the adult speakers use code-switching. And it is used more frequently by individuals who learned the L2 early, at age 2;0–6;0, that is, by bilinguals who acquired both languages simultaneously. Interestingly enough, intrasentential switching, which requires specific grammatical knowledge, is used significantly less frequently by those learners who acquired the L2 after the age of 13. Similar observations have been made about children by McClure (1977): Nonbalanced bilinguals switched less often than children who were more or less equally proficient in both languages, and they tended to switch only single words.

In sum, balanced bilinguals tend to use code-switching more frequently,[4] and their mixed utterances differ in kind from less proficient or nonbalanced speakers; mixing occurs intrasententially, it is not restricted to single words, and it avoids transfer of bound grammatical morphemes. Note, however, that the theoretical status and the implications of these findings are by no means clear. Does "a large degree of competence in both languages" (Poplack, 1980, p.588) indeed refer to grammatical competence? Kielhöfer and Jonekeit (1983) make a suggestion that might contribute to a clarification of this point. They argue for the impact of what they call "training effects" on code-switching. This is based on the observation that after extended periods of time spent in a monolingual environment with the weaker language, bilingual children do better in switching than before. This seems to suggest that the notions of good linguistic knowledge and balanced bilingualism are related to the speakers' experience in using both languages and consequently to the ease with which grammatical knowledge is implemented during speech. In other words, what has changed is not that the children acquired new knowledge but rather that they became more confident in manipulating their knowledge. In this sense, then, balanced bilingualism is a performance phenomenon.

I thus want to propose the hypothesis that increasing and decreasing frequencies of mixing are performance phenomena rather than the result of developing grammatical competence alone. In other words, I want to claim that the weaker language is the one used more reluctantly and with less developed performance skills. Grammatical knowledge, however, is also a necessary prerequisite for code-switching. Switching as rule-governed behavior requires pragmatic as well as grammatical competence. In other words, whereas the *frequency* of mixing is primarily dependent on community norms and performance factors, the specific *type* of mixing, especially sentence-internal switches involving more than single words, requires grammatical knowledge in addition to the skills necessary to put it into use.

Grammatical constraints on code-switching revisited

The preliminary conclusion based on the discussion so far is that due to functional and formal properties of early mixing the possibility cannot be excluded that during an initial period children may be code-mixing. But early during their 3rd year of life, they begin to use code-switching, even though it may still differ in some respects from adult usage. This leads to the question of whether early code-switching is already subject to structural constraints. The discovery that seemingly random linguistic behavior is indeed constrained by, among other things, grammatical principles has been a major step toward a better understanding of adult code-switching. This is due to work by, among others, Gingràs (1974), Timm (1975), Pfaff (1979), Poplack (1980), Sankoff and

Poplack (1980), Woolford (1983), Joshi (1985), di Sciullo, Muysken, and Singh (1986), and Klavans (1985).[5]

In the ensuing discussion, I will concentrate on three of the structural constraints that have been proposed in the literature, for these are, in my opinion, the most promising generalizations about grammatical aspects of code-switching for the present purpose of explaining bilingual children's language mixes. This choice is primarily motivated by the fact that they refer to a kind of linguistic knowledge that may reasonably be expected to become available to the child during the age period studied here. The first two constraints are the *free morpheme constraint* and the *equivalence constraint* as formulated by Poplack (1980, pp. 585f.):

The free morpheme constraint. Code may be switched after any constituent in discourse provided that constituent is not a bound morpheme.

The equivalence constraint. Code-switches will tend to occur at points in discourse where juxtaposition of L_1 and L_2 elements does not violate a syntactic rule of either language, i.e. at points around which the surface structures of the two languages map onto each other.

The third is the *government constraint* put forth by di Sciullo et al. (1986). As opposed to most other attempts to capture structural properties of code-switching, it is not restricted to linear properties of language. By referring to more abstract morphosyntactic properties, di Sciullo et al. (1986) hope to be able to replace a number of specific constraints (e.g., the clitic constraint; cf. Pfaff, 1979) by this one. The government constraint is stated as follows: If X governs Y, . . . X_q . . . Y_q . . . (p. 5), where q is a "language index," indicating that items X and Y are drawn from the same lexicon. Stated differently, it says that if X governs Y, then switches should not happen between X and Y; that is, Y must be from the same language as X. Government is defined in the following way:

> X governs Y if the first node dominating X also dominates Y, where X is a major category N, V, A, P and no maximal boundary intervenes between X and Y. (p. 6)

A comprehensive discussion of the implications and consequences of these constraints is clearly beyond the scope of this paper.[6] I will therefore only point out two conclusions that can be drawn from findings of previous studies that are, in my opinion, reasonably well founded and that are relevant for the study of early bilingualism. Subsequently, I will discuss very briefly some empirical and theoretical shortcomings of these three constraints, leading, most importantly, to a revision of the government constraint.

The first important result is that grammatical constraints on code-switching apply to surface structure properties of the languages involved. Virtually all authors who explicitly discuss this issue, with the exception of Woolford (1983) and possibly Joshi (1985), agree on this point.

The second point concerns what has been called the *grammatical coherence* of constructions. Although perhaps not all authors mentioned would prefer to express it this way, one may indeed generalize that these constraints serve to capture coherence defined in terms of grammatical relations.[7] Di Sciullo et al. (1986) even claim that government is the "syntagmatic coherence principle . . . *par excellence*" (p. 4, emphasis in original). But this is clearly too strong a generalization, for both linear sequences and structural relations contribute to creating coherence; one does not exclude the other. Note that even certain syntactic operations – for example, Case assignment – make use of notions like adjacency, directionality, distance, and so forth. Parsing as well as generating surface structures obviously relies even more crucially on linear sequencing.

Empirical validity and theoretical implications of proposed constraints

The empirical testing of the proposed constraints has yielded encouraging results, even though a look at the relevant literature reveals that every single constraint ever proposed has been challenged, usually by citing empirical counterexamples. I want to maintain, however, that since the proposed constraints make correct predictions for the over-whelming majority of cases, a number of apparent counterexamples should not induce us to reject these generalizations immediately. Instead, a sound research strategy appears to be to examine whether it might be possible to reformulate a constraint in a more adequate fashion and/or to scrutinize the data to determine whether they indeed represent counterexamples. I am not suggesting that conflicting data should be ignored. Rather, they must be collected to serve as the object of further research. Yet at the same time I do want to maintain that serious critics of grammatical constraints will have to do more than simply point to utterances that cannot be accounted for in a straightforward manner. In this spirit, I will mention briefly some of the achievements of the constraints under discussion and some of their remaining shortcomings.

The free morpheme constraint has been corroborated empirically in a large number of studies – for example, Bentahila and Davies (1983) for Arabic-French, Berk-Seligson (1986) for Spanish-Hebrew, and Clyne (1987) for German-English and Dutch-English, to mention only some more recent works. Some counterexamples are documented by several authors, yet these typically appear in data from speakers where one language is strongly dominant; in this case, the dominant-language bound morphemes may cooccur with lexical items from either language. Note that Petersen (1988) and Lanza (1990) also demonstrate that dominance leads to mixing of bound morphemes.

The main objection to the equivalence constraint is that it is not sufficiently restric-tive; that is, it predicts the possibility of code-switching at a number of points where it actually never happens, as far as we know from the available data. There can be no doubt, I believe, that this weakness needs to be remedied. A straightforward solution appears to be to assume that constraints conspire: Possible switchpoints, as far as structural equivalence is concerned, may be ruled out by other structural properties creating coherence. It nevertheless seems to be possible to violate the equivalence constraint in certain cases. There is at least one such problematic case, N + Adj versus Adj + N constructions. If one of the languages places adjectives postnominally and the other one prenominally, switching should be excluded. Yet switches of this type do occur, though not very frequently, and need to be explained.

The government constraint is surprisingly reliable in some areas, but it fails totally in others. This is an indication, I believe, that it suffers from important shortcomings, although it represents a step in the right direction, capturing essential properties of grammatical restrictions on code-switching. As already mentioned, it does not seem either necessary or indeed possible to replace all constraints by a single one. The point is to define coherence; government may well be the single most crucial factor in this respect, but it is definitely not the only one. Moreover, the definition of government employed by di Sciullo et al. (1986) is not quite satisfactory for theoretical reasons. They define government referring to "the first node dominating X," and they list only lexical categories as possible governors. This is somewhat surprising, for they are aware of more recent and, I maintain, more adequate definitions of government that include INFL as a possible governor and that extend the domain of government to "the first maximal category," recognizing m-command rather than c-command as the pertinent structural configuration (see di Sciullo et al., 1986, p. 9f and footnote 4; see also Haegeman, 1991, p. 404, for a recent discussion of these notions).

A major problem for the constraint as formulated by di Sciullo et al. (1986) is that, as they themselves recognize, switching between subject and verb is predicted to be possible whereas it is excluded between verb and object. If anything, the facts exhibit the reverse pattern: Switches do occur between subject and verb, but certainly less frequently than between verb and object. This objection has been raised by a number of researchers (see Clyne, 1987; Klavans, 1985; Romaine, 1989). If, following Chomsky (1986b), we accept m-command as the relevant structural configuration for government, and INFL as the head of S, the problem is remedied because subjects are then governed by INFL and objects are governed by V. This is illustrated by Figure 15.1, which gives an idea of the structure generally assumed for SVO languages like English and French;[8] at surface structure, then, subjects are placed in SpecIP and are thus governed by INFL.

Interestingly enough, revising the government constraint in this fashion leads to a conclusion similar to the one suggested by Klavans (1985): "(a) each sentence has a matrix language (L_m), and (b) the L_m in each S is determined by the INFL bearing element of the verb" (p. 218). Even if one rejects the notion of matrix language as developed by Klavans, the observation that the finite verb is of special importance seems to be warranted; that is, ". . . the verb exerts some sort of special control over switching."[9]

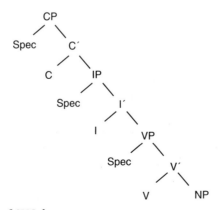

Figure 15.1 Structure of SVO languages.

Another problematic prediction made by di Sciullo et al. (1986) is that switching should occur after, not before, the complementizer. Various empirical studies (e.g., Sankoff and Poplack, 1980) confirm that switches happen after COMP, but there are also examples for switching before COMP. As for coordinating conjunctions, the prediction is that switches occur before the conjunction. This seems to be correct, but it is not obvious how this follows from the government constraint.

To conclude this short survey, I would like to mention the results of a recent study by Reidegeld (1992). In addition to testing various constraints against the data available in published sources, the author elicited acceptability judgments by 10 French-German bilinguals and 10 German learners of French of 40 sentences containing code-switching.[10] The sentences had to be rated on a scale ranging from 1 (perfectly accept-able) to 5 (totally impossible). For a number of structures, the results are quite unambiguous. Switching between clitic and verb is strongly rejected, for both subject and object clitics (average rating 4.6). Similar results are obtained for switching after a coordinating conjunction (rated 4.25, as opposed to 1.85 for the switch-point preceding the conjunction) and after the complementizer (4.6, compared to 2.3 preceding COMP). Note that the latter result clearly contradicts the predictions by di Sciullo et al. (1986). This may well be a case where government cannot be assessed independently of the equivalence constraint. The examples in (1) yielded ratings of 2.7 for (1)(i) and 4.8 for (1)(ii).

(1) (i) *Der Fahrprüfer*   *merkte* QUE J'ETAIS TRES NERVEUSE
          The driving examiner noticed THAT I WAS VERY NERVOUS
     (ii) *Der Fahrprüfer*   *merkte* daß J'ETAIS TRES NERVEUSE
          The driving examiner noticed that I WAS VERY NERVOUS
          "The driving examiner realized that I was very nervous"[11]

Switching between determiner and noun is also easily accepted. In other cases, judgments are not as clear. The least consistent ratings are given to switches between subject and verb; they vary from 2.8 to 3.8 for individual sentences and exhibit unusual intragroup variation among the informants.

Summary and discussion

The principal goal of this section has been to attain a more comprehensive and precise understanding of what characterizes code-switching, especially its formal properties. This should enable us to determine whether language-mixing during early bilingual development may justifiably be regarded as code-switching. There is evidence that as early as age 2;6, possibly even 2;0, children's mixed discourse is shaped by pragmatic and grammatical principles similar to those underlying adult speech. Yet the issue is still controversial. This is partly due to the fact that the body of generally accepted knowledge about the underlying regularities of adult switching is still quite limited. In addition, since pragmatic and grammatical competence, as well as social and linguistic behavior of children, is different from that of adults, the question arises whether this is only an indication of age-dependent limitations, or whether it reflects a qualitatively different underlying system – or whether there is no system at all.

The picture of grammatical constraints on code-switching that has emerged here can be described as follows. First, these constraints apply at surface structure. This, however, still leaves open the question as to their theoretical status. Many researchers apparently view them as constituting a grammatical (sub)system, arguing about whether one should assume the existence of a special grammar, that is, a third grammatical system, in addition to the two that the bilingual already possesses. This strikes me as rather awkward. These constraints do not possess, as far as I can see, any properties of grammatical principles, neither universal nor parameterized. It is, furthermore, totally unclear to which grammatical module they could belong or how they could constitute a specific "code-switching module." Clyne (1987) remarks that it is "a matter of doubt if the notion of grammaticality can be applied at all to data as variable as code switching" (p. 744), suggesting that these constraints reflect acceptability rather than grammaticality judgments. In other words, code-switching is a performance phenomenon, as I have tried to argue throughout the first part of this paper. Grammar as a theory about the competence of a speaker constrains the kinds of language uses possible, but, by definition, there is no such thing as a "grammar of code-switching."[12]

My second point, thus, is that grammatical constraints on code-switching should be regarded as principles of language processing and use that reflect but are not themselves principles of Universal Grammar. In this, they may be compared to parsing principles or to operating principles, as suggested by Slobin (1985a). This view entails a number of consequences that are empirically testable. One is that we should not expect them to operate in a categorical fashion. UG principles, if stated correctly, will ideally never be violated. Constraints on code-switching, however, can be violated; this happens, for example, in cases of *flagged switching*, where the speaker temporarily suspends the rules of the game. Violations are predicted to lead to increased costs; for example, more difficulty for the hearer to process them, decreasing acceptability, and so forth. Note that, as has been suggested already, switching at certain points may imply violation of more than one constraint; as with Slobin's operating principles, multiple violations are not categorically excluded but further increase costs dramatically.

I would like to hypothesize that the various constraints are not all equal in this respect. The hierarchy of constraints follows from the strength of coherence that they impose on a sequence of grammatical elements. The more they contribute to creating coherence, the more difficult it should be to violate them. The hypothesis is that word-internal coherence is the strongest. On the sentence level, abstract grammatical relations such as those defined in terms of government impose tighter connections than linearization principles, which are directly accessible through observation of surface patterns. In other words, the bound morpheme constraint, referring to the output of the lexical component of grammar, will be more resistent to violations than the government constraint, which refers to structural configurations in the sentence, and the equivalence constraint, which refers to linear configurations, may well be the most vulnerable.

To some extent, corroboration of these claims has already been found in the preceding discussions. They indicated that the verb plays an especially important role in this sense; this can be explained by the fact that it determines the argument structure of the sentence, assigns theta roles and Case, and so on. Similarly, INFL, which is the head of the sentence, assigns Nominative Case, and so forth. The union of the two, that is, the finite verb incorporated into INFL, consequently creates a particularly tight network. All this, however, will have to be worked out in more detail in a yet-to-be-developed theory of code-switching.

Let me finally mention a third point that has consequences for bilingual language acquisition. If the theory of code-switching such as the one just outlined is basically correct, it follows that both grammatical competence and performance skills are equally necessary. Remember that balanced bilinguals appear to code-switch more frequently. They also switch in a way that reflects grammatical knowledge; that is, they frequently use intrasentential switches, they use phrases instead of single words, they avoid switching of bound morphemes, and so forth. One can therefore predict that for children to be able to code-switch in a way similar to adults, the training effect will be as important as their access to grammatical knowledge about their languages.

The DUFDE study (German and French – simultaneous first language acquisition)

In what follows, I will present some findings based on an analysis of the language use of children acquiring two first languages simultaneously, German and French. This study is part of a larger research project on the simultaneous acquisition of German and French by children of preschool age.

A total of 13 children have been studied longitudinally by our research group DUFDE.[13] They have been videotaped every 2nd week while interacting with adults and occasionally with other children. The recordings consist mainly of free interaction in play situations; they last for approximately 60 min each, half in German and half in French. The well-known principle of "une personne – une langue" (Ronjat, 1913) is observed. This means that two researchers participate in each recording, one speaking only French with the child, the other consistently sticking to German. Both linguistic and nonlinguistic interactions and the relevant contexts are transcribed. At least one recording per month is transcribed and analyzed. If preliminary analyses indicate that important changes in the linguistic behavior of the child occurred during this period, more than one recording per month is included in the analysis.

The present analysis focuses on the speech of two children, A and Iv. Iv was 1; 3,24 (1 year; 3 months, 24 days) and A was 1;4 at the beginning of the data collection period. Both children are growing up in middle-class families in Hamburg, Germany. French is the native language of both mothers; the fathers' first language is German. Each parent uses his or her native tongue when communicating with the children. The language of communication between father and mother is usually German, but Iv's parents also speak French with each other. For both children, French initially appears to be the dominant input language, and during this period it is also the language preferred by the children. This clearly changes over time.

A, a girl, is an elder child. Her mother, a French and Malagasy bilingual herself, took care of her until she was 4;0. As of the age of approximately 3;0, A has spent weekday mornings in a day-care center where she only speaks German. She speaks French with her mother, with French friends in Germany, and during stays in France. The family spends approximately 6 weeks every year in France. A's younger brother was born when she was 2;8 years old, and she addresses him in French as well as in German. Initially, both languages seem to have been equally well developed. After age 2;6, German began to be the more dominant language for the child.

Iv, a boy, is also a first-born child. He speaks French to his mother, who takes care of him most of the time, German to his father, whom he sees during evenings and on weekends, and to his sitter, who takes care of him three times a week. Iv's mother takes him to France to see his grandparents and other relatives about twice a year. She also makes efforts to ensure that he has sufficient opportunities to speak French by maintaining contact with French-speaking friends in Hamburg. Beginning at the age of 3;0 years, he began participating in a German-speaking playgroup, where he met a German boy who became his best friend. Iv's two languages have always been well in balance, except for a short period at age 2;3, when, according to our analyses, his French was weaker.

As should be apparent from the short description of the methods of data collection, the setting is such that it does not stimulate code-switching. One reason for this is that, in general, we try to stick to the "one person, one language" principle. During early phases, however, the mother has to be present. Once the child is acquainted with the interviewers, the mother is normally not present anymore. Exceptions to this rule do, however, occur: (a) Occasionally, the child insists the mother be present; (b) sometimes the mother walks into the room, gets involved in the ongoing activities, and remains there for a while; and (c) the child may turn to the interviewer not engaged in the interaction, who is handling the video equipment and is thus present in the room. This person may also interfere with the ongoing activities, although we tried to avoid this.

Apart from these particularities of the situation, the setting is basically monolingual in nature. In other words, it does not favor code-switching. We should thus expect to find less frequent switches than would occur in a truly bilingual setting and less intrasentential switching, which is discouraged in both families. But for our purposes, these data may prove to be particularly well suited. If the child switches in a situation that we have defined as monolingual, one may hypothesize that a very strong factor is at play, that is, that there is a strong motivation for switching – unless, of course, the child simply cannot do otherwise and is mixing freely.

Some empirical results

In this section, I want to present a short description of the development of language-mixing by children studied in the DUFDE project. This will allow us to answer some of the questions raised earlier. As mentioned before, I will focus on the early age period (1;4–3;0), but I will add some observations concerning later developments.

Mixing into the weaker language: German into French

A's linguistic productions were analyzed beginning at age 1;4 up to age 3;1. Her corpus includes 23 videorecordings, two sessions per month from 1;5 to 2;1 and one per month from 2;2 to 3;0.[14] Iv's speech was analyzed from age 1;5 up to age 3;1. Again, the corpus includes all recordings up to age 2;0, and one per month thereafter. Single-element and intrasentential mixes for A are shown in Table 15.1 and for Iv in Table 15.2.

Table 15.1 A's mixes of German into French

Age	da	das	dies	ja/nein	alle	auf/zu/ab	so	doch	auch	Adj	N
1;5,9	2			1							
1;6,6	1									1	
1;7,2				1	3						
1;7,26	1	1		1		1					
1;8,9	2	2							1		1
1;8,23	3	3		3	1		1	1			
1;9,7		2		5	3						
1;9,21				5							1
1;10,3		1	1	2				1			3
1;10,18	2	1	1	3	2	1					
2;0,10	2			6					1		
2;0,17	4					1					1
2;1,10	2										
2;2,22	1			1			1				
2;3,16	1										2
2;5,18	1	2					1				
2;6,18	1	1									1
2;8,19	5										
2;10,27				2	1						
2;11,27											1

Table 15.2 Iv's mixes of German into French

Age	da	das	dies	ja/nein	part	so/fertig	auch	noch	und	Adv	Adj	N	V
1;9,28				1									
1;10,12	1	1	1										
1;10,30											1	1	1
2;0,2		7											
2;0,29	1	1										3	1
2;2,7	6	9		2	1	1	1	2		1	2	3	1
2;3,5	6	13		2	1	2	3	4	5	2		6	6
2;4,9	2	5				2		1		1	1	7	3
2;5,7	1	1	1	1		1		1				2	1
2;6,6		1				1		1		2		3	5
2;7,17										1			
2;8,15	1												
2;9,18													
2;10,24													
2;11,21													3
3;1,3													2

Analysis focused on types of mix rather than tokens; if an item occurred repeatedly over a series of turns, only the first occurrence was counted.

The first question I want to raise is: *How much* is mixed? Both children exhibit an interesting pattern in their linguistic behavior as far as mixing is concerned. Initially, the frequency of mixing increases, only to drop fairly rapidly after a certain period of time. A uses 2–10 (partially or totally) German utterances per French recording session and 0–4 French utterances during German sessions. In other words, German expressions appear more frequently in the French context than vice versa. By approximately age 2;1, mixed utterances are used less frequently, never rising above 3% of the total number of utterances. In the case of Iv, the picture is somewhat different. Initially, he uses few mixes. The frequency then increases, by age 1;11, roughly parallelling, however, the overall increase in number of utterances per recording. During this period, one finds more French elements in German contexts (11–15 per recording) than vice versa (2–9 German elements in French contexts per recording). During the subsequent age period, ranging from 2;2 to 2;3, the number of mixes increases dramatically (French into German: 12–23; German into French: 15–44), but at age 2;5,7 it drops again, even more suddenly, in fact, than it had increased. By age 2;7, intrasentential mixes have virtually disappeared from Iv's speech.

More interesting than the number of mixes is a qualitative analysis of the kinds of mixes used, for frequency counts hide some of the most salient features of the children's linguistic behavior. Asking *what* is mixed reveals that a limited number of lexical items account for the majority of the instances of mixing. As far as German expressions in French contexts are concerned, the following items apparently play a special role: *ja/nein* ("yes/no"); deictic elements, *da/das/dies* ("there/that/this"); particles, *auf/zu/ab* ("on(open)/closed/off"); adverbials like *alle* ("all gone"), expressions of completion of action, *so/fertig* ("done/finished"); contradicting expressions, *doch* ("yes, I do"); and *auch* ("me, too"). Note that this set of elements is almost identical in the language use of both children.

The pattern that emerges when one examines the occurrence of these elements shows that they appear early and that their use fades out after a certain period of time. For Iv the change occurs at age 2;3, and he stops using them at around age 2;5. For A they begin to disappear at about age 2;0–2;1, although with her this process is slower than with Iv; but after 2;6, only *da* and *ja/nein* are used in one more recording. A few occurrences still persist in her speech, mostly uses of *da*, until about 2;11. Deictic elements and yes/no are the most frequent and the most persistent features among those under discussion.

The question, then, is *why* yes/no, deictic expressions, and others are used in this way. Note that they appear in all of the studies discussed in the preceding sections. In fact, A and Iv also use the French negative *non* in German contexts; in A's speech, the use of *non* accounts for as many as 10 out of 24 examples of French expressions in the German recording sessions during a time span ranging from 1;5,9 until 2;10,27. Observations of this kind show that these mixes cannot be explained by lack of knowledge of the respective lexical item in the other language. This claim is corroborated by the fact that a few other items are used in a similar fashion; that is, they are mixed from language L_a into L_b, and the corresponding element of L_b is mixed into L_a. This is, for example, the case with French *un autre/encore* and German *noch* ("another one, more"). All this indicates that these elements express pragmatic functions, such as deictic reference, assertion and negation, completion of action, and contradiction, which, for the child, are apparently not tied to the domain of one of the two languages. Note also that these are high-frequency elements in early speech.[15]

These mixes are reminiscent of the type of mixing known as *tag* switching (Poplack, 1980) in adult bilingual communities, that is, code-switching of elements with loose or no grammatical links to the rest of the sentence – in other words, with little grammatical coherence.[16] According to Vihman (1985), the kinds of mixes discussed here are of the type that indicates code-mixing rather than switching. Given, however, that they can also be interpreted as tag switches, this is not a necessary conclusion. Although such mixes do not represent evidence that grammatical constraints on switching are already available to the children, they are not instances of violations of constraints, either, for they do not break up grammatically coherent constructions. All one can say, at this point, is that A's mixes resemble tag switching up to approximately age 2;0; afterward, she still uses them occasionally, until approximately 2;6. Iv, on the other hand, uses them roughly until age 2;3.

So far, I have not yet discussed the use of adjectives, nouns, verbs, and adverbials in early mixing by the two children. Adjectives, in fact, only play a minor role in this context. Only two adjectives, for example, were observed in A's speech, *heiß* ("hot") at age 1;6,6 and *gut* ("good") at age 2;0,10. A closer examination reveals that they appear in situations that happen repeatedly; the routine action and the word seem to be closely tied together and are, in this case, part of the German domain. A similar situation is found in Iv's data; he mixes three German adjectives into French: *rot* ("red"; *un autre ROT*, "another RED (ONE)") at 1;10,30, *wach* ("awake"; *nounours WACH*, "bear AWAKE"), at 2;2,7, and *kaputt* ("broken"; *un autre KAPUTT*, "another (one) BROKEN") at 2;4,9. The adjective *nounours* is actually used like a proper name, referring to Iv's toy teddy bear, and is therefore not uniquely labeled as French. What is important to observe with these examples is that the verbal element, probably the copula "is," is omitted in all cases, a phenomenon typically encountered in the speech of children at this age, monolingual as well as bilingual. It is precisely this element, however, that imposes restrictions on switching in adult language use, namely, as the governing element in terms of the government constraint. Consequently, these are instances of nonapplicability rather than of violation of grammatical constraints.

Iv alone mixes adverbials and verbs into French during the period investigated. The adverbials are all locative and directional expressions: *darein* ("into that"), *darauf* ("on top of that"), *raus* ("out"), *drin* ("inside"), *darunter* ("under that"), and *unten* ("down there"). Again, these are not tightly linked parts of grammatical structures.

German nouns are mixed fairly frequently into French, especially by Iv. For an extended period of time, these are single nouns, since the children do not yet use determiners at all, or at least not systematically. What motivates these mixes is not clear. The words may not be available in French, although this is hard to believe in cases like *auto* ("car"), *bett* ("bed"), and so on, and it is definitely not true for *ente* ("duck") in A's data since the French equivalent *canard* appears during the very same recording session. Similar examples are found in Iv's data – for example, *teddy* / *nounours* appearing each in the other language. Remember that Vihman (1985) suggested that nouns are mixed as a result of code-switching, as opposed to code-mixing in the case of so-called function words. Our data thus do not support the claim that early mixing is code-mixing, since it is not restricted to these types of function words; instead, nouns, adjectives, and verbs may also appear in the children's mixed utterances. One can therefore conclude, again, that grammatical constraints do not apply because grammatical elements, which in adult language crucially contribute to the structural coherence of a construction, are missing – in this case, determiners.

This type of mixing prevails in the two children's language use until approximately age 2;6 (A) and 2;3 (Iv). At this point of linguistic development, one observes qualitative changes. Iv, for example, initially only uses single word switches, with the exception of *das ist* ("that is"), which, however, must still be regarded as an unanalyzed formula. Yet by 2;3,5, he also uses multiword switches, such as *ich will NONOURS* ("I want TEDDY") and *l'eau, DE SCHIFF SCHWIMMT l'eau* ("the water, THE SHIP SWIMS (on) the water"). Note that the determiner is still missing in the first example, as is the preposition in the second, again an element that is potentially of crucial importance in defining coherence. A does not yet use similar constructions, but this is due to the fact that multiword utterances are very rare in her speech during the period under investigation; A's mean lengths of utterances[17] values still remain below 2.0. There is evidence, however, for A, as well, that she uses adultlike code-switching no later than age 2;3. One piece of evidence is that she does not use intersentential mixing into French involving entire sentences between ages 1;9,21 and 2;3,16. From then on, such examples appear regularly, and they are used adequately; that is, these utterances are directed toward a German-speaking person.

Mixing into the dominant language: French into German

Let us now look at French lexical material mixed into German. As far as A is concerned, a rather different picture emerges; she hardly mixes at all, as shown in Table 15.3. Only between ages 1;6 and 2;1 does one find some instances, and the most frequently encountered element is the aforementioned *non* ("no"). These examples all have to be interpreted in the same fashion as their German counterparts discussed before. There also exist a few French nouns in the German context: *chat* ("cat") at age 1;9,7, *canard, coq, poule* ("duck, rooster, chicken") at 1;10,3, and *fourchette* ("fork") at 2;0,17. It appears that A did not know the German equivalents in these cases and filled the lexical gaps with French words. The verbs *dessine* ("draw a picture") (1;9,21) and *attache* ("fasten") (2;0,17) are apparently motivated in the same way. The verbal element encountered at age 1;6,6 is the past participle *cassé* ("broken").

Interestingly enough, one also finds instances of mixing used adequately according to the adult norms. These utterances are all directed toward her mother or toward some other French-speaking interlocutor in a German context: *maman* ("Mommy") (repeatedly), *cassé* ("broken") (1;6,6), *maman du thé* ("Mommy tea") (1;7,2), *pomme* ("apple") (1;9,7), *maman thé* (1;9,21), and *Pascale regarde!* ("Pascale, look!") (2;6,18). Note that these are all intersentential switches where grammatical constraints do not apply, but these cases confirm the finding mentioned earlier that, from very early on, children choose the language according to the interlocutor. Let me add that A also used two intrasentential switches during this period, *nein CANARD* ("no DUCK") (1;10,3) and *ja und ein CEINTURE* ("yes and a BELT") (2;8,19), both involving single nouns.

In Iv's case we find a similar pattern as in French (see Table 15.4). Mixes begin approximately at age 1;10. Negation (*non*), *ça* ("that"), *encore* ("more"), and also the past

Table 15.3   A's mixes of French into German

Age	Neg	N	V	S
1;5,9				
1;6,6	1		1	
1;7,2	1			1
1;7,26	4			
1;8,9	1			
1;8,23				
1;9,7		2		
1;9,21			1	1
1;10,3		3		
2;0,10	1			
2;0,17		1	1	
2;1,10	1			
2;2,22				
2;3,16				
2;5,18				
2;6,18				1
2;8,19		1		

Table 15.4   Iv's mixes of French into German

Age	Neg	Ça	Past Participle	Encore	Adv	Adj	N	V
1;9,28	1							
1;10,12							1	
1;10,30		2		2	1		5	
1;11,17	1	3	1				2	
2;0,2				2	1		4	2
2;0,29		2		1		2	6	2
2;2,7	3		1	2			8	10
2;3,5		1		3	1		8	
2;4,9	3		3			1	5	1
2;5,7			2			1	3	3
2;6,6					1		1	2
2;7,17					1			
2;8,15	1							
2;9,18				1				
2;10,24								
2;11,21								
3;1,3		2					1	

participles *parti* ("gone"), and *tombé* ("fallen") belong to the by now familiar group of elements mixed. Note that the negative is mixed into both languages, as are *ça* ("that"), corresponding to German *da/das/diese*, and *encore* ("another one, more"), corresponding to *noch*. The past participles should also be assigned to this group; *parti* is the equivalent of German *weg* ("all gone"), and *tombé* ("fallen") replaces German adverbials like *runter, unten* ("down"). The first three uses of mixed adverbials are instances of *dedans* ("in, inside"). They are characteristic of the period from approximately age 1;10 until 2;4; after that, they disappear abruptly.

Let us now turn to the mixes involving nouns, verbs, and adjectives. Only four adjectives occur: *das PETIT tiger* ("that LITTLE tiger"), *BEAU, ne?* (BEAUTIFUL, isn't it?") (2;0,29), *jetz der TROP PETIT* ("now this (one) TOO SMALL") (2;4,9), and *rouge* ("red") (2;5,7). The first one, meaning "this is a little tiger," is excluded by the government constraint, but not by the equivalence constraint, and bilingual judgments diverge considerably as to the acceptability of this sentence type (see Reidegeld, 1992, p. 107). In the third example, as in the first, the verbal element is missing again. At any rate, concerning the question whether this is evidence for code-mixing or for code-switching, the set is simply too small to serve as the basis for far-reaching conclusions.

Nouns are mixed more frequently, but this is also true of adult usage, as has been pointed out repeatedly before. There seem to exist different reasons for this kind of code-mixing of nouns. First of all, 12 of the 44 instances involve *nounours* ("bear"), which, as already mentioned, is a special case, almost resembling a proper name and functioning like a loan word in this case. This is not to say that no German equivalent exists; in fact, *nounours* and *teddy* appear during the same recording. Similarly, the children refer to their mothers as *maman* and *Mama*. But although they have two labels available, they tend to use each of them in both linguistic contexts. This merely reflects language use in the family where adults also use *nounours* when speaking German. Other French nouns apparently fill lexical gaps, just like German nouns in French (e.g., *chapeau*, "hat"). The fact that these items appear in various recordings is a further indication that the German equivalent is not familiar. Structural properties, too, support the claim that these instances of mixing are not yet constrained by grammatical cohesiveness. The first nominal mixes consist of single nouns, exclusively. By 2;0,2 one finds *das N* ("that (is) N") and N + V (subject + verb) patterns, plus the example *das NOUNOURS DORT* ("the TEDDY SLEEPS"), this is to say, the first switch between article and noun. Note that this is yet another particularity of this lexical item (*nounours*). Otherwise, more complex structural contexts start being used at age 2;3,5 when *das* + NP sequences emerge (e.g., *das UN AUTRE FIL*, "this (is) ANOTHER THREAD"). This is clearly not merely a case of filling in a noun when the German expression is not easily retrieved. It would, indeed, be an example for the incriminated switches between subject and verb — had the verbal element not been omitted again. From age 2;5,7 onward, French nouns are mixed into a German NP (e.g., *'s ein TOUR*, "(it')s a TOWER"); *das ein GARÇON*, "that (is) a BOY").

Surprisingly, at first glance, there exist many verbal elements mixed into German in Iv's data. Yet 7 of the 20 occurrences are instances of *dort* ("sleeps"). *Répare* ("fix") also appears repeatedly, namely, in 6 of the 10 examples at age 2;2,7. In other words, verbal mixes are restricted to a very small set of lexical items. Before age 2;4, all but one (*DONNE darauf* "give (= put) on top of this" at 2;2,7) of these examples are structurally of the type N + V (= S + V); that is, they are inserted after a German subject. By 2;4 one also finds French verbs combined with German objects.

The developmental pattern for both verbal and nominal mixes thus is the same; they begin to be used as of approximately 1;10 and 2;0, respectively, their frequency then increases rapidly until 2;3–2;4, and after 2;6 they disappear.

Grammatical development and the acquisition of grammatical constraints

The last problem I want to address here concerns the proposed grammatical constraints discussed earlier. I have argued that they should be regarded as principles of language processing reflecting, among other things, principles of UG, instantiated in the grammars of the two languages of the bilingual individual. They define coherence of surface structures and predict that the stronger the coherence of a sequence of elements is, the less likely it is that switching will occur within that sequence. Although grammatical relations are not the only defining factors of coherence, they contribute in an essential way. In what follows, I will therefore concentrate on them.

Let us return briefly to the question of which grammatical relations are most relevant for the purpose of defining coherence. As has become apparent in the preceding discussion, government is likely to be a particularly important one. Note that, contrary to the suggestion by di Sciullo et al. (1986), our definition of government relies on m-command. More importantly, INFL is not only included in the set of possible governors; it may also well be the most crucial one for the present purpose. Throughout this paper it has been reported repeatedly that the verb plays a particularly important role in defining constraints on code-switching. But this generalization refers, in fact, to finite verbs, in other words, to the verb incorporated into INFL. There is some evidence, again in contradiction with di Sciullo et al. (1986), that COMP may serve a similarly important function (see Reidegeld, 1992). For reasons of space, I cannot go further into this. If, however, this suggestion can be maintained, one might hypothesize that certain functional categories crucially define coherence as used in this context, that is, the functional categories that, universally, can host verbal elements like INFL and COMP, as opposed to nominal ones like DET. In other words, the functional categories dominating VP (see Figure 15.1) provide the grammatical glue for the lexical elements in VP.

Returning now to developmental aspects of the problem, these hypotheses predict that children should begin to observe grammatical constraints on code-switching once their grammars contain functional categories of the sort just mentioned. This remark refers to a theory of early grammatical development suggested by Radford (1986, 1990) and others (see Meisel, 1992, for some recent contributions to this debate). According to this view, early sentence structures resemble adult VPs; that is, they initially lack INFL and COMP, which are implemented only later into the children's grammars. As for the children whose language use is discussed here, this happens approximately at age 2;4–2;5 for Iv (Meisel, 1999a, 1994a) and at age 2;6 for A (Stenzel, 1994). Let us, then, look again at intrasentential switches after this point of development, when children have access to functional categories, in order to test the hypothesis that these grammatical developments enable the bilingual child to observe grammatical constraints on code-switching.[18]

In one respect, mixing after ages 2;5 and 2;6, respectively, is not entirely different from that at earlier occasions, for nouns are still the most frequently encountered elements. Yet switching now occurs regularly between the determiner and the noun:

(2) (i) *moi je va   à la   KÜCHE*(Iv 3;1,3)
       me I goes to the KITCHEN
       "I go to the kitchen"
    (ii) *il y   a   beaucoup de BERGE* (Iv 3;1,3)
        it there has many   of MOUNTAINS
        "There are many mountains"
    (iii) *tu   veux que je te   donne des DATTELN?* (Iv 4;2,4)
         you want that I to you give of DATES?
         "Do you want me to give you some dates?"
    (iv) *ja   und ein CEINTURE ein ein-* (A 2;8,19)
        yes and a BELT   a a [interrupts]
        "Yes and a belt, a, a . . ."

As has been pointed out before, switching is indeed predicted to occur at this point. But entire noun phrases, prepositional phrases (see (3)(i)), and bare nouns (see (3)(ii)) are mixed into the other language, as well, although less frequently. Since this happens mainly with objects and never with subject-NPs, it is in accordance with the government constraint as proposed here, yet it provides further evidence against the version suggested by di Sciullo et al. (1986).

(3) (i) *on va maintenant ZUM KRANKENWAGEN* (Iv 2;11,21)
       we go now   TO THE AMBULANCE
       "We now go to the ambulance"
    (ii) *je veux MILCH* (A 3;7,2)
        I want MILK
        "I want milk"

A problematic case is given in (4) where the switch occurs after the subject pronoun. This is, however, the only example of this kind in our data;[19] furthermore, the child, in this situation, has been asked by the German adult to ask a question of the French adult. It seems that Iv simply failed to switch in time, as indicated by the pause he makes, rendered in our transcription by a comma.

(4) *DU   DU, aimes ça la   soupe* (Iv 2;8,15)
       YOU YOU like   that the soup?
       "Do you like soup?"

Interestingly enough, French clitics are never mixed into a German sentence. Yet there exist two cases in A's data where a German verb appears in a French utterance together with a clitic pronoun, clearly violating the government constraint:

(5) (i) M: *je t'avais interdit de monter sur le radiateur/absolument interdit/ compris?*

> Mother: "I had told you not to sit on the radiator. Absolutely not. Got it?"
>
> A: *mais mais mais je p- mais PAPA   a   dit   je peux me   SETZEN*
>   but but but I c- but DADDY has said I can clitic SIT
>   "But but but I c- but Daddy said I can sit down" (A 3;7,13)

(ii) A: *Sonja a-   je SCHENK   ça* (A 3;2,24)
      Sonja has- I GIVE   this
      "Sonja has- I give this as a present"
      Sonja a quoi?

    French adult: "Sonja did what?"

  A: *SCHENK ICH SCHENK DAS*
     GIVE   I   GIVE   THAT
     "Give, I give this as a present"

These examples are problematic for several reasons. First of all, (5)(i) represents a case of switching between subject and verb; also, *me SETZEN* and *je SCHENK* are instances of switching between clitic and verb. Some contextual factors may help to explain these uses. *Papa*, used with its German pronunciation, and the name of the German friend Sonja may have triggered these mixes, as is also suggested by the fact that in (5)(ii) A solves the problem by switching entirely into German. Furthermore, several of the children studied seem to have problems finding an equivalent for *schenken* ("give a present") because the French *donner* ("give") does not unambiguously convey this meaning, and they may not know the expression *faire un cadeau*, which more closely expresses the meaning of the German verb. But the fact remains that these constructions violate grammatical constraints on code-switching. Note that A otherwise only switches nonfinite verbs, mostly German infinitives placed in final position. Iv, in fact, does not switch verbal elements after age 2;6; there is only one exception – see (6)(ii), (6)(i) otherwise representing the last occurrence.

(6) (i) *VEUX   pienen (= spielen) mit   das* (Iv 2;6,6)
      WANT to play   with that
      "I want to play with this"

   (ii) *du   willst TE   VOIR?* (Iv 3;8,29)
      you want YOURSELF TO SEE? (in a mirror)
      "Do you want to see yourself?"

(6)(ii) is another case where the German adult urged Iv to ask a question of the French adult, and there is again a pause and a delay in switching. These examples are instances of switching between the finite and the nonfinite verb, a pattern not violating the constraints because the finite verbal element is in INFL, the nonfinite verb and its complements remaining in VP. Lindholm and Padilla (1978), McClure (1981), and Taeschner (1983) also reported examples of this kind. Iv does not use more constructions of this type; A uses three of them, (5)(i) and (7)(i)–(ii).

(7) (i) *et   puis Patti a   SEIN ARM   GEBROCHEN* (A 3;7,13)
     and then Patti has HIS   ARM BROKEN
     "And then Patti has broken his arm"

(ii) *il a   GEWONNEN* (A 4;3,24)
    he has WON
    "he has won"

As for other potentially problematic switching points, no instances appear in our data. There is only one example of switching between adjective and noun in Iv's speech. Switching immediately before or after a complementizer is not attested, nor between the negated verb and French *pas* or German *nicht* ("not"). The nonoccurrence of mixing of this type may well indicate that the children avoid violations of grammatical constraints. This is confirmed by the fact that Iv occasionally violates the bound morpheme constraint combining German verb stems with French affixes or a German and a French stem, but this only happens up to age 2;5, not afterward: *reitÉ* ("ridden") (Iv 2;0,29), *REsucht* ("looks repeatedly for something") (Iv 2;4,9), and *ANmise* ("put on") (Iv 2;5,7). Note that, much later, he occasionally mixes within compounds, but he then indicates that he is aware of the fact that he is violating norms.

(8) (i) *wart ich mach mir   ein ein MONSIEUR hut* [laughing] (Iv 4;8,17)
        wait I   make myself a   a   MAN   hat
        "Wait, I will make a man's hat for myself"
  (ii) *maman   on met- on met les- les SACHEN de ski* (Iv 4;11,14)
        Mommy   we put- we put the- the stuff   of ski
        "Mommy, we put- we put the ski stuff in"

In sum, then, except for the counterexamples mentioned, no violations of grammatical constraints could be found in our data, once the children have access to functional categories in their grammars. Veh (1990) did, however, find hesitations, interruptions, and repetitions in mixed utterances, indicating a lack of training. Iv, for example, tends to repeat the switched element, and he only does so after age 2;6.

(9) *elle connaît- DIE- DIE WEIß   DAS   NICHT* (Iv 3;8,1)
    she knows- SHE- SHE KNOWS THAT NOT
    "She knows- she- she doesn't know this"

I interpret these findings as confirming the hypotheses developed in this paper that children, once they have access to crucial properties of grammars, quite consistently avoid violations of grammatical constraints on code-switching even though they still show signs of insecurity for some time when code-switching.

Conclusion

In this paper I have tried to summarize some crucial facts on what is known about early language-mixing in bilingual children, focusing on grammatical aspects of very early bilingualism, before age 3;0. This has led me to conclude that constraints on code-switching cannot only be defined in terms of grammatical properties of the languages involved; rather, they should be regarded as principles of language processing. Code-switching thus requires grammatical knowledge as well as a certain amount of experience in using the two languages. The central concern of the paper then has been to find out in more detail what grammatical constraints on code-switching are and what it takes for children to be able to observe them.

One finding has been that grammatical constraints apply to surface structure properties of the languages involved. Secondly, they are crucially dependent on what has been called the "grammatical coherence" of constructions. I have argued that both linear sequences and structural relations define coherence. Another suggestion has been that constraints may conspire: Possible switch-points, as far as structural equivalence is concerned, may be ruled out by government relationships creating coherence. A crucial point here is that these constraints are defined as principles of language processing. As such, they may in fact be violated in language use, unlike principles of grammar.

As for bilingual language development, the conclusion has been that early mixing is characterized by mixes of elements that are only loosely connected to others by grammatical relations; grammatical constraints thus do not apply in these cases. Grammatical constraints on code-switching can only operate once the child has access to certain properties of grammars, most importantly to functional categories. These hypotheses have been corroborated by an analysis of the language-mixing behavior of two bilingual children acquiring French and German simultaneously. Significant quantitative as well as qualitative changes were detected, and these occurred precisely during the age period following the point of grammatical development at which functional categories have been shown to become accessible.

Notes

I am grateful to Susanne E. Carroll, Georg Kaiser, Regina Köppe, Axel Mahlau, and Birgitta Veh for their comments on an earlier version, as well as to the anonymous reviewers of *SSLA*. I would furthermore like to acknowledge the support of the Deutsche Forschungsgemeinschaft in the form of several research grants (1986–1992) to the author of this study. I also want to thank Shona Whyte for her very helpful editorial assistance.

1   Köppe and Meisel (1995) offer a summary of current knowledge on code-switching in bilingual first language acquisition.

2   Vihman (1985) actually uses the term "language mixing" and defines it as fusion (in my terminology). I do not believe that she really gives evidence for fusion, but I will not pursue this question at this point (see Meisel, 1989).

3   This is not necessarily the case. Romaine (1989, pp. 120ff.) reports a situation (Panjabi-English) where verbal elements are switched frequently. It is possible that these cases should be regarded as loans rather than as code-switching.

4   Again, this is an option, not a necessity, because whether an individual uses code-switching freely depends on a number of other factors as well, such as community norms, for example.

5   Quite recently, a further approach to code-switching has been suggested by Myers-Scotton and her associates, the frame-process or matrix language frame model (see Myers-Scotton, 1991, 1992a). The claim is that, in combination with her so-called markedness model, it can account for intrasentential code-switching in all attested cases. I believe that the extraordinary power of this model is also its weakness. Contrary to what is claimed by the proponents of the model, determining the matrix language correctly in each case is highly problematic. It remains to be seen whether these models do indeed have any explanatory value. Providing a detailed critique would take us too far afield.

6 Clyne (1987) reviews some of these proposals, and Romaine (1989, pp. 110–164) offers a state-of-the-art discussion of this controversy.

7 This is quite obvious in the case of the free morpheme constraint and also for the clitic constraint (see Pfaff, 1979, p. 303), which states that clitics are realized in the same language as their hosts.

8 For the present purpose, one can ignore the so-called split INFL hypothesis (see Pollock, 1989), which posits several maximal projections of functional categories, including AGRP and TP.

9 Similar arguments are made by Joshi (1985).

10 Shortcomings of this kind of data collection procedure are well known (see Pfaff, 1979; Sankoff and Poplack, 1980), but although such data can hardly be used to refute hypotheses based on spontaneous data, they can help to clarify certain issues that remain opaque in naturalistic studies.

11 Switched elements are reproduced in capital letters in all linguistic examples.

12 Joshi (1985), although arguing differently, arrives at the same conclusion.

13 DUFDE = Deutsch and Französisch-Doppelter Erstspracherwerb (German and French – Simultaneous Acquisition of Two First Languages). During the period when this paper was written, the researchers in this team were Caroline Koehn, Regina Köppe, Natascha Müller, and Achim Stenzel.

14 The first recording is excluded because no mixes occurred, and no recordings were made between age 1;10,18 and 2;0,10, because the family spent a longer holiday in Madagascar with the mother's family.

15 Note that the appearance of German *da* in both languages can perhaps be explained as resulting from a pragmatically motivated strategy using this element, which is universally available rather than being transferred from German (see Williams, 1992).

16 This similarity was pointed out by one of the *SSLA* reviewers.

17 I am well aware of the fact that computing mean lengths of utterances (MLU) values is not the optimal instrument to assess grammatical development. Yet MLU values are widely used and therefore permit comparisons among a large number of studies. When I refer to grammatical development in this paper, this is really based on detailed analyses of developmental patterns in different areas of grammar (see the contributions to Meisel, 1990a).

18 In this discussion I rely to a large extent on the study by Veh (1990), who analyzed Iv's data up to age 5;2 and A's up to age 4;4.

19 Note that the government constraint predicts that switches should not occur after subjects that appear in the specifier position of the phrase where the finite verb occupies the head position, that is, in IP for languages like French or in CP in verb-second languages like German. If, however, the subject has been moved out of this category, into the specifier of CP in French, for example, switching is tolerated. One should thus expect cases of code-switching after subjects to occur. Only a careful syntactic analysis will reveal, then, whether the constraint has indeed been violated.

Source: Meisel, J.M. (1994) Code-switching in young bilingual children: the acquisition of grammatical constraints. *Studies in Second Language Acquisition* 16: 413–41. Copyright © 1994 Cambridge University Press, reproduced with permission of the author and publisher.

Jürgen M. Meisel, PhD, is Professor of Romance Languages and Linguistics at the University of Hamburg, Germany. jmm@uni-hamburg.de

Notes for students and instructors

Study questions

1 What factors can cause a child to mix two languages in an utterance? Why is code-mixing *not* good evidence for the ' "fused" system hypothesis'?

2 What error patterns can you observe in each of the languages of a developing bilingual child? Are they different or the same as the error patterns of normally developing monolingual children in the matching languages?

3 Does bilingual children's code-switching observe the same grammatical constraints as that of bilingual adults?

Study activity

Observe a bilingual child in different situations (e.g. at home with parents, with siblings, outside home with other children, and with other adults). Pay special attention to his or her language choice with different people. Note down the occasions when the child makes a 'wrong' choice, i.e. using Language A when the addressee only understands or prefers Language B. Is there any particular reason for the 'wrong' choice (e.g. accidental, deliberate)? Does the child realise he or she has made a 'wrong' choice? What does the child do when he or she realises he/she has made a 'wrong' choice?

If time permits, design a case study of a bilingual child under the age of three. Either ask the parents to keep a weekly record of (1) their own language choice to the child and (2) the child's speech over an extended period of time (no less than six months) or tape-record the child's speech at weekly intervals. (If the keeping of a weekly record is not realistic, negotiate with the family to see how often they can keep such a record.) Analyse the speech data of the child, paying particular attention to any sign of under-differentiation (i.e. when two features in Language A for which counterparts are not distinguished in Language B are confused) and over-differentiation (i.e. the imposition of distinctions from Language A on the system of

Language B in which they are not required) of his or her two languages. To what extent can the child's mixing of two languages be attributed to the language mixing in the parents' speech?

Further reading

A comprehensive review of the field of bilingual language acquisition can be found in A. De Houwer, 1995, Bilingual language acquisition, in P. Fletcher and B. MacWhinney (eds), *The Handbook of Child Language*, Blackwell, pp. 219–50. J.M. Meisel, 2004, Bilingual child, in T.K. Bhatia and W.C. Ritchie (eds), *The Handbook of Bilingualism*, Blackwell, pp. 91–113, offers an up-to-date account of the theoretical issues in the study of childhood bilingualism.

An early classic is W. Leopold, 1939–49, *Speech Development of a Bilingual Child: A linguist's record*, 4 volumes, Northwestern University Press.

Recent studies that specifically address the issue of language differentiation in bilingual children include: F. Genesee, E. Nicoladis and J. Paradis, 1995, Language differentiation in early bilingual development, *Journal of Child Language* 22: 611–31; R. Köppe, 1996, Language differentiation in bilingual children, *Linguistics* 34: 927–54; M. Deuchar and S. Quay, 1998, One vs. two systems in early bilingual syntax: two versions of the question, *Bilingualism: Language and cognition* 1: 231–43.

Book-length studies of language acquisition of bilingual children include: J.M. Meisel (ed.), 1990, *Two First Languages: Early grammatical development in bilingual children*, Foris; A. De Houwer, 1990, *The Acquisition of Two Languages from Birth: A case study*, Cambridge University Press; S. Döpke, 1992, *One Parent One Language: An interactional approach*, John Benjamins; J.M. Meisel (ed.), 1994, *Bilingual First Language Acquisition: French and German grammatical development*, John Benjamins; G. Extra and L. Verhoeven (eds), 1994, *The Cross-Linguistic Studies of Bilingual Development*, North-Holland; J. Lyon, 1996, *Becoming Bilingual: Language acquisition in a bilingual community*, Multilingual Matters; E. Lanza, 1997, *Language Mixing in Infant Bilingualism: A sociolinguistic perspective*, Oxford University Press; M. Deuchar and S. Quay, 2000, *Bilingual Acquisition: Theoretical implications of a case study*, Oxford University Press.

A state-of-the-art collection of studies on the language acquisition of bilingual children is given in A. De Houwer (ed.), 1998, *Bilingual Acquisition*, Kingston Press, also available as a special issue of *International Journal of Bilingualism* 2(3).

Psycholinguistic and neurolinguistic dimensions of bilingualism

Introduction to Part Three

LI WEI

Part Three of the Reader focuses on the psycholinguistic and neurolinguistic aspects of bilingualism. It consists of two sections: 'Bilingual processing' and 'The bilingual brain'.

Bilingual processing

Bilingual speech production and perception has been a very active area of psycho-linguistic research. There is now wide recognition that learning and using more than one language is a natural circumstance of cognition. Research on bilingualism there-fore provides crucial evidence regarding the universality of cognitive principles, as well as an important tool for revealing constraints within the cognitive architecture. The first two articles in this part of the Reader, by David W. Green (Chapter 16) and Kees de Bot (Chapter 17), present two theoretical models of bilingual speech production. Green examines the way in which bilinguals control the use of their two languages. In view of the fact that bilingual speakers can choose which language they want to use in a given context, he suggests that the bilinguals' languages are organised in separate sub-systems which can be activated to different extents. He argues that a bilingual speaker who wishes to speak a particular language must ensure that activation exceeds that of competing languages. Green pays much attention to the resources that are needed to regulate, or control, the activation levels. The theoretical framework proposed by Green is meant to account for the performance of normal as well as brain-damaged bilinguals.

The model presented in de Bot's article is based on Levelt's (1989) 'Speaking' model, in which a number of information-processing components, or levels, are postulated. Because Levelt's model has a firm empirical basis, de Bot's adaptation made very few changes to the original. It is concluded that the first component, the conceptualiser, is partly language-specific and partly language-independent. Further it is hypothesised that there are different formulators for each language, while there is one lexicon where lexical elements from different languages are stored together. The output of the formulators is sent to the articulator, which makes use of a large set of non-language-specific speech motor plans. The adapted version of Levelt's model provides a good explanation of various aspects of bilingual speech production, especially with respect to code-switching and the storage and retrieval of lexical elements.

The article by Kroll and de Groot (Chapter 18) offers a critical review of psycho-linguistic models of bilingual memory. It examines the evidence for the various views on how the memory stores are connected and what the implications are for bilingual word processing, more precisely for the way forms are mapped to meaning and vice versa. The authors discuss in some detail the revised hierarchical model, which assumes directionality and differential strength of the connections between the memory stores, resulting in asymmetries in the memory structures, and the new conceptual feature model, which posits 'distributed' meaning representations. The developmental dimension and the inherent competitions of these models have powerful explanatory powers for bilingual behaviour.

The last article in this section, by François Grosjean (Chapter 19), reviews a number of psycholinguistic studies of bilingual speech production and perception which have apparently given rise to conflicting results. Grosjean discusses how differences in methodology – criteria for subject selection, the language used with subjects, stimulus characteristics, task demands, and so on – are at the root of the conflicts. He proposes the concept of 'language mode', which assumes that the language system of the bilingual is organised into two subsets that can be activated and deactivated independently of one another, or activated simultaneously, each to a particular degree. In the bilingual mode, both of the bilingual speaker's two languages are activated, although one to a relatively higher level than the other, whereas in the monolingual mode only one language is activated and the other is deactivated as best as possible. Grosjean argues that psycholinguistic research on bilingual production and perception needs to take the notion of 'language mode' seriously in order to have clear, interpretable and comparable results.

The bilingual brain

One of the most controversial and most discussed issues in bilingualism research has been the brain organisation of the bilingual speaker. In particular, there have been sustained claims that the languages of bilingual speakers are less asymmetrically represented in the cerebral hemispheres than the language of unilingual speakers. The first two papers in this part address this issue.

In Chapter 20 Loraine K. Obler, Robert J. Zatorre, Linda Galloway and Jyotsna Vaid review the literature on lateralisation for language in bilinguals, which seems to suggest conflicting positions. One is that left hemispheric dominance, which is clearly evident in most monolinguals, applies to bilinguals too. A second proposes weaker left lateralisation for language in bilinguals, while a third maintains that there is differential lateralisation for the two languages. Obler *et al.* discuss a broad range of methodological parameters which need to be considered in carrying out, analysing and interpreting studies of language lateralisation in bilinguals. These include issues of subject selection, language and stimulus selection, testing procedure, data analysis and theoretical questions around interpreting dichotic and tachistoscopic measures of lateralisation.

While Obler *et al.* plead for caution in research design and conclusion, Michel Paradis (Chapter 21) calls for a complete stop to what he regards as a fruitless pursuit. In his article, Paradis critically reviews previous studies on language lateralisation in bilinguals and points out the many methodological flaws. He urges researchers to 'move on to something more productive'. However, evidence seems to suggest that inappropriately designed experiments and implausible interpretations have continued to appear and, as Paradis has already warned in his article, recommendations have continued to be made for applications of the alleged findings of increased participation of the right hemisphere to foreign language teaching, the treatment of mental illness or the rehabilitation of bilingual aphasia.

The advent of new research technologies has enabled neuroscientists to begin to address some of the theoretical and methodological issues in bilingualism research. It is fair to say that, until recently, neuroimaging studies have by and large failed to connect to theoretical debates in the behavioural and clinical literature on bilingualism. Nevertheless, studies of the bilingual brain using non-invasive, functional neuroimaging technologies are on the increase. The last chapter of the section (Chapter 22), by Jubin Abutalebi, Stefano F. Cappa and Daniela Perani, presents an overview of the most relevant results that have so far been achieved in the field of the exploration of the cerebral basis of bilingualism using functional neuroimaging techniques and discusses what conclusions may be drawn from these studies. It lays the foundation for a new era in neurolinguistic research on bilingualism.

Bilingual processing

Control, activation, and resource: a framework and a model for the control of speech in bilinguals

DAVID W. GREEN

ONE EXPLANATION FOR THE effects of brain damage on speech is that it destroys, or isolates, one or more of the components of the system required for intact performance. Such an explanation lacks generality. It does not account for the speech errors of normal speakers and it fails to explain certain phenomena within the clinical literature itself, such as the recovery patterns of two bilingual aphasics recently reported by Paradis *et al.* (1982). This chapter develops a framework which accommodates the performance of normal as well as brain-damaged individuals, and it provides a specific model of the bilingual speaker. The framework and model describe a conceptual nervous system and make no claims as to the nature of the underlying neural mechanism.

The chapter presents three main ideas. The first is that the impaired performance of aphasic patients, and of bilingual aphasics specifically, reflects a problem in controlling intact language systems. Problems of control also seem the best way of explaining the kinds of speech error observed in normal bilinguals. Hence such an idea offers a way to accommodate both normal and pathological data.

The second idea concerns how control is effected. It is assumed that speech production can be understood in the same way as skilled action in general. In particular, the selection of a word, like the selection of a particular action, involves regulating a single underlying variable of the amount of activation. Choosing an appropriate word requires ensuring that its activation exceeds that of any competitors.

The third idea is that regulation involves the use, and hence possible depletion, of the means to increase or to decrease the activation of some internal component. Most functional models of speech production ignore this energy dimension and yet we would not normally consider the description of a working device as complete without some account of how it is powered. (A blueprint for a car ignores the fuel and braking systems at some peril.) A system needs energy to work and operating it consumes energy. Thus, if the means required to regulate a system are insufficient for whatever reason then, even though the system is intact, control will be imperfect. Brain damage, it is suggested, affects the availability of resources. These three ideas (control, activation, and resource) allow an explanation of the recovery patterns of the bilingual aphasics reported by Paradis *et al.*

The chapter considers each of these ideas in turn and develops a specific model within the overall framework. It begins by considering a functional model of bilingual performance based on certain typical case reports and then describes the data reported by Paradis *et al.* which are so problematic for such a model.

Albert and Obler (1978) cite the case reports of a number of brain-damaged polyglot speakers who understood speech in all their languages but who were either unable to speak, or who had severe difficulty in speaking, at least one of them (e.g., Cases 14, 41, 81, and 94). Such patterns indicate that the subsystems mediating the comprehension and production of language are separable and that different functional systems underlie different languages. Figure 16.1 presents a simple model for a bilingual speaker compatible with such data and it is apparent that the destruction or isolation of one output system is a reasonable explanation of the effects of brain damage on such patients. Such a model is a variant of the kind of model proposed by Morton (1980) and restricts itself to the recognition and production of words. Although not included in the figure it is perfectly possible to complicate the output systems by separately specifying the syntactic, prosodic, and lexical components. Information from these converges at the stage of phonological assembly. Such a model can be used to account not only for the selective loss of a language but also for the recovery of a lost language. It can be assumed that the individual has either relearned or is using a novel strategy which bypasses the damaged subsystem, or even that damage has allowed a previously subordinate system to take over. However, major fluctuations in performance within brief periods of time are outside its scope. Just such fluctuations have been reported by Paradis *et al.* The case of A.D. is the better documented of the two cases cited and so her report is used to illustrate the phenomena of interest.

A.D. was a 48-year-old nun, fluent in French and Arabic, who was in charge of various child care clinics in Morocco. She spoke French with the other sisters and the doctors, and Arabic with the nursing aids, patients, and the local population. Following a moped accident, she suffered a right-parietal fracture and, in consequence, a contusion in the left temporoparietal area. After a period of total aphasia and a period where

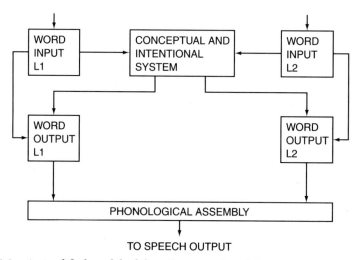

Figure 16.1   A simplified model of the subsystems for a bilingual speaker

she spoke only a few words of Arabic, she was flown to a hospital in France, where the phenomena termed "alternate antagonism" and "paradoxical translation" were observed.

Eighteen days after the accident, she showed little spontaneous use of French but she was able to name objects in Arabic and to speak Arabic spontaneously. On the following day, naming and spontaneous speech were good in French and poor in Arabic. This pattern, "alternate antagonism," coincided with good comprehension in both languages.

Correlated with this pattern was the second phenomenon of "paradoxical translation." On the day when she could speak Arabic spontaneously, i.e., 18 days postonset, she was unable to translate into it, even though she was able to translate from Arabic into French, which was the language she was unable to speak spontaneously. On the following day, when her spontaneous speech in Arabic was poor, she was able to translate into Arabic but was unable to translate into French which she could use spontaneously.

As Paradis et al. point out, the phenomenon of "alternate antagonism" establishes the functional dissociation of the two languages. Indeed, A.D. exhibits a "double-dissociation" – a fundamental type of evidence for neuropsychology (Shallice, 1979). The two phenomena cannot be explained by the destruction, or isolation, of an output component, rather, as Paradis et al. phrase it, one language becomes "restrictively inaccessible" for a period of time but only under certain conditions.

The idea of control: errors and impairment

Temporary disruption of varying degrees of severity is a feature of the speech of normal monolingual and bilingual speakers. Indeed normal speech can be seen as the successful avoidance of error. Transient failures include errors where we blend two or more words together. Within a language we find blends such as "strying" (blended from "trying" and "striving") and across languages we find ones such as "Springling" (blended from "spring" and "Frühling"). In such cases, it is evident that the normal speaker can recognize that an error has been made and can also produce an appropriate utterance. There is no reason to suppose that some part of the speech system has been destroyed or isolated. On the contrary, the error is best seen as one of a failure to exercise full control over an intact system. A number of factors such as temporary distraction or stress may occasion such a failure and a number of detailed accounts of specific phenomena have been developed that explain how they may arise (e.g., Shattuck-Huffnagel, 1979; Butterworth, 1981). What is important for present purposes is that such errors occur as a result of a problem in controlling intact systems.

If a problem of control can offer a way to explain normal speech errors it may also account for aphasic performance. Freud ([1891]1953) noted that the paraphasias observed in aphasic patients do not differ from the incorrect use and distortion of words healthy persons can observe in themselves when they are tired or distracted. Recent support for the idea comes from analyses of the neologisms of jargon aphasics that indicate that these may reflect a strategy for coping with *temporary* difficulties in retrieving words (Butterworth, 1985). At least, for temporary problems (i.e., ones where on other occasions a person does use the right word), it seems reasonable to suggest that the difficulty arises from a problem of controlling an intact system. This claim is sufficient for present purposes, but in order to apply it we need to consider how such control is exercised.

The idea of activation

The notion that the internal representation of words can vary in their level of activation is a relatively common assumption in recent theorizing. Combined with the notion that a word must reach a certain threshold of activation in order to become available as a response, it is possible to explain why, for example, speakers pause longer before producing less predictable words (Goldman-Eisler, 1958) – the less predictable word is at a lower level of activation. In the case of naming an object the appropriate name must be activated and come to dominate over other possible candidates. A picture of a car, for instance, may lead to the internal representations of the names for "car," "cab," "truck" becoming active since they all share some of the perceptual and functional properties that define a car. The appropriate name comes to dominate other possible candidate names by reducing their level of activation, i.e., by suppressing or inhibiting them. Empirical and experimental evidence further suggests that this process of word production may be divided into a stage at which the speaker activates words of a certain meaning and a second stage where the actual sound or phonological form of these is retrieved (see, for example, Garrett, 1982; Kempen and Huijbers, 1983) though for reasons of simplicity, these stages are not separately illustrated in the figures. On occasions two names labeling the same referent or idea may both reach threshold and give rise to a blend. Our primary concern is not the mechanics of producing words from a single language system but the nature of the control requirements when two such systems are involved.

Since a normal bilingual speaker can elect to speak one language rather than another it might be thought that this is achieved by completely deactivating the nonselected language. In fact, some early accounts did presume some internal on–off switch (e.g., Penfield and Roberts, 1959); others (e.g., Ervin and Osgood, 1954) raised the issue but failed to offer any sufficient explanation. In fact, experimental evidence using a variety of techniques, such as a bilingual version of the Stroop test (Preston and Lambert, 1969) and a lexical decision task (Altenberg and Cairns, 1983), indicates that in normal bilinguals although only one language may be selected, the other is nonetheless active, at least when both languages are in regular use. In the case of naming, one consequence of such activation is that bilinguals take longer to name any single object (Mägiste, 1979). The joint activation of both systems is also apparent in the case of errors of interference. A French–English bilingual talking to his son who speaks only English and pointing to a truck says: "Look at the camion" where "camion" is pronounced as if it were an English word (Grosjean, 1982). Indeed the effort to avoid interference can be extremely demanding (see Clyne, 1980a) and become almost impossible under severe stress (Dornic, 1978).

However, delay or interference are not the only outcomes of knowing two languages. Where two bilinguals share the same two languages they can switch between them (see Sridhar and Sridhar, 1980). In code-switching, elements from one language are embedded in those of another. At least part of the reason for such switching is the availability of expressions in one language compared to another. Speakers can output whichever expression first achieves threshold. Hence, code-switching need not involve dysfluency.

But why should a nonselected language remain active? It may be used frequently in daily life and its activation will, accordingly, be maintained both because the language is spoken and because it is heard. It would also continue to receive input from the conceptual system. However, it seems implausible to assume that a language system remains active when unused for long periods. Unused, its level of activation is likely to fall. We may distinguish, then, between three states of a language system, viz.:

1   selected (and hence controlling speech output);
2   active (i.e., playing a role in ongoing processing); and
3   dormant (i.e., residing in long-term memory but exerting no effects on ongoing processing).

These three states have been identified previously by Norman and Shallice (1980) and Shallice (1982) in the context of nonverbal motor skills. Our primary concern, of course, is to deal with circumstances in which both languages are active, or conceivably active, and here the idea that naming and speech production involves controlling the activation of the internal representations of words is useful because it offers a general way to account for both the fluent and the dysfluent aspects of normal speech in bilinguals.

The idea of a resource

In order to be able to activate or to suppress the activity of a component in a system it is necessary that some means exist for doing so. Within the activation framework (e.g., Collins and Loftus, 1975) it has been assumed that activation is limited and therefore that only one part of a system can be highly activated at any one time. Other researchers have postulated that each cognitive processor (e.g., a device for recognizing words or for producing them) has its own limited pool of resources (e.g., McLeod, 1977; see also Navon and Gopher, 1979). The present proposal links the resource idea to the actual process of controlling or regulating a system. A resource may be used either to excite a system (an excitatory resource) or to inhibit one (an inhibitory resource) and any act of control consumes resources. The resource idea makes explicit the fact that a system needs energy to operate — a fact which is invariably ignored in functional models of language and cognition. Now an inevitable consequence of the resource notion is that unless resources are replenished at the right rate, control will be impaired. We presume, then, a "resource generator" that manufactures such resources at a certain rate.

Controlling two language systems: an inhibitory control model

Where a person wishes to speak one language only, this language must be selected and the output from the other language system inhibited. Such selection and suppression requires that the relevant outputs be identified.

One solution to this problem, and the one adopted here, is to suppose that words possess particular "tags," where a tag can be thought of, following Albert and Obler (1978), as "a feature label associated with each individual item." (Such tagging may not be restricted to distinguishing words or structures in different languages. Some form of tagging may also be used to label vocabulary or structures associated with particular "registers" or styles of speech within a language.)

Since a bilingual can speak one or other language and can translate from one to the other, or switch between them, there must be a device (a "specifier") that specifies how the system must be controlled if a person is to act in one or other of these ways. The general scheme is presented in Figure 16.2.

Let us consider first of all the control requirements for speaking one language (L1) rather than the other language (L2). It is evident that the devices for recognizing words in L1 must be active and that the device for producing them must be selected. Selection is partially a matter of increasing the activation of L1 but, principally, it is a matter of suppressing the activation of L2 words so that words from that system do not get produced. The output from L2 could be suppressed within the system itself (internal suppression) or by the L1 system externally suppressing the activity of L2 (external suppression). Internal suppression, indicated in Figure 16.2 by an inhibitory loop, restricts the retrieval of word sounds from L2. External suppression, indicated by an inhibitory link to the output of L2 at the stage of phonological assembly, suppresses the activation of L2 words at the assembly stage.

It is proposed that the suppression of L2 is achieved *externally* in spontaneous use. This proposal predicts that dysfluencies in L1 will occur whenever there is an L2

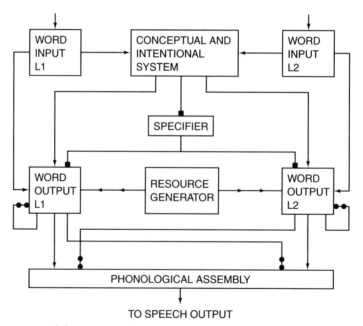

Figure 16.2   An inhibitory model for a bilingual speaker within the control, activation and resource framework

Notes: →, flow of activation; ▬■, control instructions; →→, resource input; ▬●▬●, inhibitory control.

expression of a concept which is more available than one in L1. For instance, L2 may possess a single word or idiom which expresses an idea that demands a novel phrase in L1. In order to produce the L1 phrase, the alternative in L2 must be suppressed.

In the case of code-switching, there need be no external suppression of L2 at all; at least in the simplest case, such as continuous word association, the output can be free to vary according to which words reach threshold first. Indeed in this circumstance, mixing languages is certainly no slower than producing associations in only one language (Taylor, 1971). In the case of normal speech a word cannot be produced unless it fits the syntax of the utterance. Accordingly, for example, an adverb will not be produced in a slot requiring a noun. Switches then will obey the syntactic properties of the two languages although no special device or grammar is required to achieve this goal. Code switches most often involve single words, especially nouns (Pfaff, 1979), though ones involving phrases or entire clauses also occur. In these latter cases, we suppose that structures from L2 reach threshold earlier. Since any words produced must meet the structural conditions, such a scheme predicts that code switches will preserve the word order in both languages (see Chapter 10 of this volume).

A more complex form of regulation is needed in the case of translation. Both language systems are required and when translating from L2 to L1 the output system for L2 must be suppressed. In principle, such suppression may be achieved internally or externally (as noted above). In practice, however, since translation into L1 requires that the speaker does not simply repeat the message in L2, it is proposed that suppression of the output from L2 is achieved internally in the same way as a monolingual speaker might avoid simply repeating a word or a phrase just heard. To recap, when speaking L1 spontaneously, L2 is *externally* suppressed, whereas when translating from L2 to L1 the output of L2 is *internally* suppressed.

Since distinct inhibitory means are used in spontaneous speech and in translating, it follows from the claim that resources are consumed in such activities that speaking may be affected by the nature of the previous activity. For example, in a paced task where the rate at which resources are used exceeds the rate at which they are replaced, there should be a "fatigue effect." A bilingual will be slower to name pictures in L1 after a session of such naming compared to a session where L2 names had to be translated into L1. In the latter case no L1 inhibitory resources would have been used to regulate the L2 system and hence would be available for naming in L1 in the second session.

The model outlined above can be generalized to account for language control in trilingual or polyglot speakers. In fact, these groups provide a further way of testing the model. As the number of languages increases, so should the problems of control. For instance, the time required to name simple objects should be greater for the trilingual compared to the bilingual speaker, as L1 must externally suppress the activity of the third language (L3) system as well as that of L2. Translation would involve the same control requirements for translating L1 into L2 (i.e., internal suppression of L1) but, in addition, L2 must externally suppress L3. Assuming that the rate of generating inhibitory resources is the same for bilingual and trilingual speakers, when the latter are engaged in translation they should suffer impaired performance earlier than bilingual speakers. It may be that there is some limit on the number of language systems that can be active at the same time, which would reduce the problem of control. But such an empirical constraint is not part of the current model.

More generally, if other nonlinguistic systems also consume the resources provided by the generator then the use of such systems would affect the control of speech. So, for example, as stress or anxiety increase, speech should be disrupted especially in a person's weaker language. As remarked earlier, empirical research supports this expectation (Dornic, 1978). A further factor which may exert a profound effect on the availability of resources is brain damage.

Alternate antagonism and paradoxical translation: control and the limitation of resources

Brain damage may limit the availability of both the means to excite as well as the means to inhibit a system. This assumption is compatible with accounts of the working brain proposed by Luria (1973) and the account of memory disorders discussed by Talland (1965). Without sufficient activation no output could be achieved. On the other hand, unless there are sufficient means for L1 to inhibit L2, the person would be unable to use L1 spontaneously since the output of this system would be unable to dominate that of L2. This line of reasoning underlies some of the predictions of the model for normal speakers as well. In general, the kinds of output produced depend on the relative balance of the means to excite or to inhibit a system. Assume, though, that there are sufficient resources to activate the various systems but that brain damage in aphasics limits, at least initially, the availability of the means to inhibit these systems. Difficulties in inhibiting responses have been mooted before as one of the aspects of aphasia (Hudson, 1968; Yamadori, 1981). Such a view allows the inhibitory control model to explain in a unified way both of the central phenomena (alternate antagonism and paradoxical translation) reported by Paradis *et al.* (1982).

Suppose that there is an initial imbalance in the amount of inhibitory resource available to the two systems such that L1 has more of these means than L2 but that both receive resources. We have, then, the state depicted in Figure 16.3. According to the present framework, L1 can be used spontaneously because it can externally suppress outputs from L2, whereas L2 cannot meet this requirement and externally suppress L1. Since operating L1 consumes resources, and given the rate at which resources are generated is less than the rate at which they are consumed, the inhibitory resource available to L1 will cease to be adequate. Meanwhile, the inhibitory resources available for use by L2 will increase. Behaviorally, this entails a shift from A.D. being able to use L1 spontaneously to a state where she can only use L2 spontaneously. Similarly, if the rate of generation continues to be insufficient to replenish resources as they are consumed, L2 will in turn cease to dominate and the system will flip back into the previous state where L1 but not L2 could be used spontaneously. Thus, a limitation on the inhibitory means available to a system can explain the pattern of alternate antagonism. It is a strong claim of the present account that even when one language cannot be used spontaneously, it is not because it is inactive but because it is unable to suppress sufficiently the activation of the other system.

The claim that L2 output is in fact active is consistent with the second phenomenon of paradoxical translation in which A.D. was unable to translate into the language which she used spontaneously but could translate into the one she could not use. How might this pattern be explained by the model? On the one hand, translation into L1 (the language of spontaneous use) would be precluded when L2 could not suppress its own

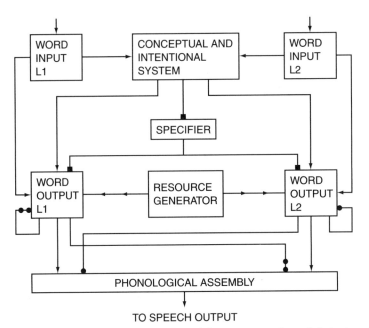

Figure 16.3   A state of the system in the inhibitory control model during alternate antagonism and paradoxical translation

Notes: →, flow of activation; ⁻■, control instructions; →→, resource input; ⁻●⁻● adequate inhibitory control; ⁻●, inadequate inhibitory control.

activity sufficiently. On the other hand, when L1 can suppress its own activity, L2 would be free to translate. On this account, then, at one time each language system was able to externally suppress the other system as well as to internally suppress its own activity, whereas at another time it could meet neither of these control requirements. Thus, both alternate antagonism and paradoxical translation can be seen as outcomes of a system with limited inhibitory resources.

These phenomena are really a subset of those that could be produced by a system with insufficient regulatory means. There is no necessary reason why a system that can suppress the activity of another need have the means to suppress its own activity sufficiently to allow translation. External and internal suppression are distinct forms of control and adequacy in that one does not guarantee adequacy in another. Table 16.1 documents the alternative outcomes when there are adequate or inadequate means of internal and external control for two languages.

The third row in the table corresponds to the case of paradoxical translation. When, as in the fourth row, only one language can be used spontaneously, but the means for internal suppression in that language are inadequate, we have an outcome in which the speaker can only translate into the language of spontaneous use (nonparadoxical translation). Where neither language can suppress its own output sufficiently, translation is precluded entirely and we have the outcome such as that listed in the second row. Later in her recovery A.D. evinced both of these phenomena.

The present model then explains such outcomes by postulating an underlying problem of control whose precise outcome depends on the relative availability of

Table 16.1   Speech outcomes for two languages as a function of the adequacy (+) or inadequacy (−) of the means for internal and external suppression

Suppression				
External		Internal		
L1	L2	L1	L2	Outcome
1 +	+	+	+	Spontaneous use of both languages and translation in either direction
2 +	+	−	−	Spontaneous use of both languages; translation impossible
3 +	−	+	−	Spontaneous use of one language and paradoxical translation
−	+	−	+	
4 +	−	−	+	Spontaneous use of one language and nonparadoxical translation
−	+	+	−	
5 +	−	−	−	Spontaneous use of one language; translation impossible
−	+	−	−	
6 −	−	−	−	No output although systems are active

inhibitory means. Although a variety of outcomes can thereby be accommodated, each outcome is a direct consequence of a failure of a specific control requirement.

Some generalizations, predictions, and limitations

One of the surprising claims of the model is that the absence of speech following brain damage does not entail that some subsystem has been destroyed (see row 6, Table 16.1). The regulatory means, specifically the inhibitory resources, may be inadequate. If this is the case, then there should be evidence of activity (for example, EEG recordings) in those areas normally associated with language production. But such a measure is unlikely to tell us about the status of a specific language system. In cases where, following damage, only one language is recovered (selective recovery; Paradis, 1977), if the nonrecovered language is active then this fact should be detectable using such tasks as bilingual Stroop, since a color word in L2 (the nonrecovered language) should interfere with naming the ink color in L1.

In the case of antagonistic recovery, the disappearance of one language (L2) may be attributed to inadequate means to suppress the other system and this problem would be revealed by increasing problems in performing a bilingual Stroop task in L2 in the presence of an L1 color word. Mixing and differential recovery patterns may also be explained on the basis of insufficient inhibitory means. In the case of mixing it is a lack which extends to both systems, whereas in the case of differential recovery it is restricted largely to one system. The most widespread recovery pattern is one where both languages recover in parallel (see Paradis, 1977). If such recovery reflects the gradual increase in inhibitory means then recovery should be accompanied by a gradual decrease in bilingual Stroop interference as the means for suppressing alternative names improves.

We have supposed that recovery solely produces a change in the availability of inhibitory resources. As these increase it becomes possible to regulate active systems more effectively. The crucial determinant of the output of the system is this balance of the means to excite and the means to inhibit. But a change in excitatory means would also influence this balance. Perhaps as recovery progresses other areas become activated and require regulation. The problem of control is still one of the relative sufficiency of inhibitory means, but the model would need extending to incorporate such changes in excitatory means. However, such an extended model would still remain part of the general framework being proposed.

Conclusion

One of the primary aims of this chapter has been to describe a framework based on the ideas of control, activation, and resource which can increase the scope of functional models and establish a link between the normal and the pathological. The framework predicts that there are at least some cases in which language impairment following brain damage is not caused by the destruction or isolation of some functional subsystem but is the result of a problem in regulating the activity of an intact system. No speech can mean no activity, but the present framework encourages the search for cases where such activity does in fact exist. The major problem in coping with the effects of brain damage on this view is one of reestablishing control over intact systems. The longitudinal study of the recovery patterns of bilingual aphasics promises to provide insight into the means by which a person regulates alternative systems of expression.

Many alternative models are possible within this framework and one, in particular – an inhibitory control model – was proposed which makes specific predictions about both normal and pathological performance.

Postscript

The 1986 paper proposed a framework for thinking about recovery patterns in bilingual aphasics that would be sufficiently general to cover the process of speech production in normal bilinguals. In addition to the core distinction between conceptual and linguistic systems, there were three key ideas: the notion that the internal representation of words variesy in their its level of activation, that the production of a word involves a process of selection and control which requires that words in different languages are distinguished in some way (via a language tag) and that control is effected by excitatory and inhibitory means. Use depletes such means and leads to problems of control that may account for both errors and slips of the tongue in normal speakers and specific patterns of recovery in bilingual aphasics.

In order to speak one language rather than another, or translate between languages, a conceptual-intentional system spelled out, via a mechanism termed the specifier, how the language system should be configured and, via links from the conceptual system to the lexical systems of L1 and L2, what messages were to be expressed. Both lexical systems are active where the languages are used regularly (though one could become dormant if not used over a period of time). In order to speak one language rather than another, activation was raised in the selected language and outputs from the nonselected language suppressed. Two loci of inhibition were identified: one in which the non-selected system inhibited its own outputs (as in translation) and a second one in which outputs from the non-selected system where inhibited by the selected language system at the stage of phonological assembly (as in spontaneous production). By distinguishing different loci of inhibitory control, the inhibitory Control (IC) model offered an account of the patterns of recovery in which ability to speak in one language was dissociated from the ability to translate into it. Such an account was premised on the notion that impaired performance reflected a problem of control arising from constraints on inhibitory resources.

Green (1998a, b) extended the cognitive side of the IC model by unpacking the nature of the 'specifier' in the original model. The configuration of processes and representations needed to perform a language task is termed a task schema. If a task had been performed before then, a pre-existing task schema is activated, i.e., a pre-existing control configuration is reinstated. A translation schema, for instance, involves binding an input word form in L1 (say) to an output word form in L2 with the constraint that they share the same meaning.

More than one schema might be activated, as in the case of the verbal Stroop task where the schema to name the colour in which a word is written may compete with that for reading the word aloud, and compete to control output. The intended schema would seek to inhibit the non-intended schema and further excitatory input from the intentional system might be required to allow it to do so.

As in the 1986 model, lexical representations in both languages are active. However, the site of inhibitory selection for words was restricted to the lemma level and was primarily held to be reactive. That is, inhibition was applied on a needs-only basis. As in the earlier model, control involves multiple levels with a proactive aspect (configuring processes and representations) and a reactive aspect (inhibiting non-intended competitors).

Both patient data and neuroimaging data are consistent with the notion that control involves a number of levels: involving both cortical (e.g., prefrontal regions) and subcortical structures – the basal ganglia (e.g., Abutalebi, Miozzo and Cappa, 2000; Price, Green and von Studnitz, 1999). However, the notion that words in both languages can compete for selection remains controversial. Certainly, neuroimaging data support the view that the representations of words in a second language converge with those in the first language as proficiency increases (e.g., Green, 2003). There is also general agreement that representations in both languages are activated in response to language input, but researchers disagree whether only words meeting the current language goal compete for selection (see Costa and Caramazza, 1999; Roelofs, 2003). Such a view predicts that naming a picture in L1 on a study trial should not affect the time to name that picture on a test trial, but it does (Wodniecka et al., 2005).

The precise mechanism of language selection also remains open to debate. If there is competition for selection, it is unclear whether the activation level of words in the non-selected language isare driven down or whether selection operates on the outputs of the lexical system and affects the process of selecting the item for entry into the response system or filters out representations that lack the requisite tag just prior to output (see, for example, von Studnitz and Green, 2002; Dijkstra and van Heuven, 2002; and French and Jacquest, 2004, for a discussion).

The view that selection operates by inhibiting non-target representations at some stage remains contentious and unresolved. Certainly it is possible to construct cognitive computational models of lexical production (i.e., existence proofs) that do not appeal to inhibitory processes. But if we are to have theories that apply to normal bilinguals and to individuals with brain- damage we need to build models that are plausible from a neurocomputational point of view and such models cannot ignore the importance of inhibitory interneurones Ö estimated to account for nearly a quarter of the total cell population of the neurons in the cortex. More generally, thinking about the resources required to control a system paves the way for pharmacological interventions to aid recovery (Green, 2005). Fabbro, Skrap and Aglioti (2000) reported the case of a bilingual aphasic with a lesion in the frontal lobe whose only deficit was an inability to avoid switching into a non-target language. Such a problem might reflect reduced dopamine needed to inhibit the non-target language and be ameliorated by a dopamine agonist.

David W. Green, PhD, is Senior Lecturer in Psychology at University College London, UK
d.w.green@ucl.ac.uk

Chapter 17

A bilingual production model: Levelt's 'speaking' model adapted

KEES DE BOT

WHILE RESEARCH INTO BILINGUALISM increased dramatically in the 1980s, there was remarkably little research aimed at the development of a model of bilingualism. The linguistic performance of bilinguals has been used to support syntactic theories – for example, Woolford's (1983) study of government and binding and code-switching and White's research into the relationship between Universal Grammar and second language acquisition (1989) – but there are no theories about the bilingual speaker that aim at a description of the entire language production process. There are of course partial descriptions of the process, as in Krashen's Monitor theory (1981), Bialystok's Analysis/Control approach (Bialystok, 1990), and the global description of the production process in Færch and Kasper (1986), but a full model which covers the whole process from message generation to articulation is still lacking.

In this article it is assumed that the single most important entity we are concerned with in model-construction is the individual speaker in whom we see all factors and influences combined. In language behaviour research there have traditionally been reasonably sharp dividing lines between linguistic, psycholinguistic, and sociolinguistic research. In a good production model these dividing lines fade; the model should be able to cope with universal characteristics of language as well as cognitive processes and situational factors in interaction and their consequences for language use. The individual speaker is seen as someone in whom all sorts of influences on language use are expressed, influences of a microsociological nature (influences resulting from the situation in which interaction takes place) as well as those of a macrosociological nature (such as language repression and language contact). In such an approach, societal concepts such as language vitality, ethnicity, and social mobility have, to use Hakuta's words (1986: 192) 'psychological reality as concepts in bilingual individuals'.

Levelt's 'Speaking' model (1989) is very promising in all respects. Although the model has been developed explicitly to describe the unilingual speaker – the only thing that has anything at all to do with multilingualism is a reference to Perdue (1984) – it might also be useful, after adaptations, to describe the bilingual speaker. Clearly, many aspects of speaking are the same for monolingual and bilingual speakers, and a single model to describe both types of speaker is to be preferred over two separate models for different types. It could be argued that because every unilingual speaker has the potential to become bilingual, the validity of a model can be tested by examining whether it is suitable for bilingualism. Or, to push this point even further: given the fact that bilingualism or multilingualism is the rule all over the world and unilingualism the exception, especially if we include bidialectism as a form of bilingualism, one could argue that the basic model should be concerned with bilingualism, with an option to have a unilingual version.

As Meara (1989) points out, there is a real need for a model to describe the bilingual language user. Even if the model used may ultimately turn out to be inadequate, it can still serve to structure and organize research and data: 'Using a model as a starting point makes clear what problems we are addressing, what problems we are ignoring, and forces us to make explicit some of our central assumptions' (Meara, 1989: 12).

There are several reasons for taking Levelt's model as a starting point. The model is based on several decades of psycholinguistic research and is based on a wealth of empirical data, obtained through experimental research and the observation of speech errors. The present model is a further development of earlier proposals by Garrett (1975), Dell (1986), and Kempen and Hoenkamp (1987). A major advantage of the model is that it is not restricted to parts of the production process: its strength lies in the integration of the different parts.

In the following sections I will give a brief and global description of Levelt's model, subsequently I will consider how such a model should be adapted to make it suitable to describe the bilingual speaker, and finally some alternatives are presented for parts of the model. A full description of the model in only a few pages is impossible: it takes Levelt (1989) some 500 pages of rather dense text to present the model in full.

The bilingual version of the model presented here is not completely new or unique. It shares a number of characteristics with earlier proposals by Macnamara (1967), Dechert (1984), Hieke (1986), and Perecman (1989).

Levelt's model

The model aims at describing the normal, spontaneous language production of adults. It is a 'steady-state' model, and not a language learning model, and it hardly says anything about language perception. The model is not concerned with reading and writing and it is not aimed at the explanation of language disorders of a central or peripheral nature.

A distinction is made between declarative knowledge – which includes encyclopaedic knowledge (conceptual and lexical knowledge in particular) and situational discourse knowledge – and procedural knowledge, which is relevant to the processing of declarative knowledge. Procedural knowledge forms part of the different processing components. A final general characteristic is that the same lexicon is used for production and perception.

Figure 17.1 presents a blueprint for the speaker. Boxes represent processing components, circles and ellipses represent knowledge stores. In this model the following components are distinguished:

- *A knowledge component* which is more or less separate from the production system and where general knowledge of the world and more specific knowledge about

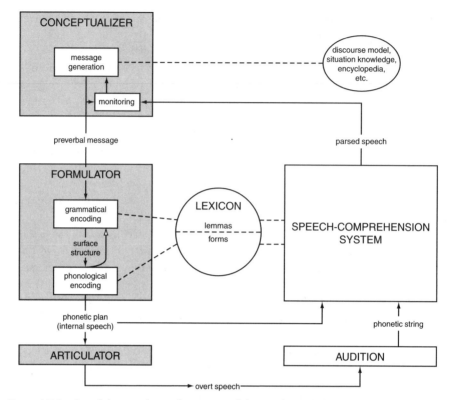

Figure 17.1   Levelt's speech production model (Levelt, 1989: Fig. 1.1.)

the interactional situation is stored. Levelt's description of this part of the model is not very extensive, and it is not really clear what it actually does or does not contain.

- *A conceptualizer*: this is where the selection and ordering of relevant information takes place and where the intentions the speaker wishes to realize are adapted in such a way that they can be converted into language. The output of this component is so-called 'preverbal messages', in other words messages which contain all the necessary information to convert meaning into language, but which are not themselves linguistic. In the planning of preverbal messages two stages can be distinguished: macroplanning and microplanning. Macroplanning involves the elaboration of communicative goals/intentions and the retrieval of the information needed to express these goals, while microplanning is 'the speaker's elaboration of a communicative intention by selecting the information whose expression may realize the communicative goals' (Levelt, 1989: 5).

- *A formulator*, where the preverbal message is converted into a speech plan (phonetic plan) by selecting the right words or lexical units and applying grammatical and phonological rules. According to several researchers (Kempen and Huijbers, 1983; Levelt and Schriefers, 1987) lexical items consist of two parts: the lemma and the morpho-phonological form or lexeme. In the lemma, the lexical entry's meaning and syntax are represented, while morphological and phonological properties are represented in the lexeme. In production, lexical items are activated by matching the meaning part of the lemma with the semantic information in the preverbal message. Accordingly, the information from the lexicon is made available in two phases: semantic activation precedes form activation. The lemma information of a lexical item concerns both conceptual specifications of its use, such as pragmatic and stylistic conditions, and (morpho-)syntactic information, including the lemma's syntactic category and its grammatical functions, as well as information that is needed for its syntactical encoding (in particular: number, tense, aspect, mood, case, and pitch accent). Activation of the lemma immediately provides the relevant syntactic information which in turn activates syntactic procedures. The selection of the lemmas and the relevant syntactic information leads to the formation of the surface structure. While the surface structure is being formed, the morpho-phonological information belonging to the lemma is activated and encoded. The phonological encoding provides the input for the articulator in the form of a phonetic plan. This phonetic plan can be scanned internally by the speaker via the speech-comprehension system, which provides the first possibility for feedback.

- *An articulator* which converts the speech plan into actual speech. The output from the formulator is processed and temporarily stored in such a way that the phonetic plan can be fed back to the speech-comprehension system and the speech can be produced at normal speed.

- *A speech-comprehension system* connected with an auditory system which plays a role in the two ways in which feedback takes place within the model: the phonetic plan as well as the overt speech are guided to the speech-comprehension system to find any mistakes that may have crept in.

In order to try to clarify the workings of this model I will illustrate the various components by using an example. Imagine we want to say: *The train from Amsterdam arrives at platform four*. We know from our knowledge of the world that trains regularly arrive at platforms and stop there, and that there is more than one platform. The communicative intention is pre-processed in the conceptualizer, after which the contextual information is passed on to the formulator in manageable chunks in the preverbal message. How this information is passed on is not exactly clear. It is possible that we have some sort of mental image of trains, platforms, and arrivals which is then transformed into interpretable information. The preverbal message also contains information about topic and comment assignment. In other words, it specifies whether the sentence will become *It is on platform four that the train from Amsterdam will arrive* or *It is the train from Amsterdam that will arrive on platform four*. Now the formulator becomes involved in the process. An important characteristic of this model is that the lexical items needed in the utterance are retrieved first and that the characteristics of these items determine the application of grammatical and phonological rules. In other words, the selection of the verb *arrive* automatically entails that there is a subject, something or some one that arrives, but that there is no object, and that adverbials of time and place are optional. Furthermore, information has been processed which says that only one train will arrive, so the verb is provided with the relevant morphological information which ensures the correct use of the inflectional suffix (*–(e)s*). Selecting these items also entails that information about their pronunciation is included so that what comes out of the formulator is a grammatical unit, as well as clues as to the pronunciation of the words of that sentence. The phonetic plan is temporarily stored in the buffer and fed back to the speech-comprehension plan, and sent on to the articulator which makes sure it is actually pronounced by activating and driving the entire speech mechanism, which leads to the production of the sentence *The train from Amsterdam arrives at platform four* with the right segmental and suprasegmental cues.

In the model, production takes place 'from left to right', i.e. the next processor will start working on the output of the current processor even if this output is still incomplete. In addition, there is no need to look back continually in time to see what has already been produced. This means that when a part of an utterance has left the conceptualizer and is being formulated, it cannot in any way influence the construction of parts that follow: each part of the utterance that leaves the conceptualizer passes through the whole system more or less by itself; without taking account of what may follow later on. Furthermore, production is incremental, so as soon as the information which goes with one part of the utterance is passed on to the formulator, the conceptualizer does not wait for that chunk to go through the whole system but immediately starts on the next part. In this way various parts of the same sentence will be at different processing stages: when the first part is being produced by the articulator, the last part may not have left the conceptualizer. Consequently the different components are at work simultaneously. Processing is largely automatic. Greatest attention is paid to conceptualizing and some attention is paid to the feedback mechanisms, but the remainder functions without conscious control. Production has to be incremental, parallel, and automatized in order to account for the enormous speed at which language is produced.

Requirements which a bilingual version of this model should meet

The requirements which a unilingual version of the model should meet are already relatively high, and a bilingual version has to meet additional requirements. In general it should provide an explanation for all phenomena associated with balanced and non-balanced bilinguals' speech. To be more specific, the most important demands are as follows:

- The model must account for the fact that the two language systems can be used entirely separately or mixed depending on the situation. Extensive literature on code-switching (for reviews, see Giesbers, 1989; Nortier, 1989) shows that all degrees do occur: from complete separation to extensive mixing of the two systems. The issue of code-switching will be dealt with later on in this article.
- Cross-linguistic influences have to be accounted for in the functioning of the model. There is a host of literature on cross-linguistic influences (see, for example, Kellerman and Sharwood Smith, 1986; Odlin, 1989). Research in this field was, of course, not set up to test the present model, but the outcomes of that research should not be at odds with the model.
- The fact that a bilingual uses more than one language should not lead to a significant deceleration of the production system. It is very likely that the production system has sufficient over-capacity to deal with language production

problems. Mägiste (1986) observed a slight slowing down in language processing of multilinguals in a very demanding experimental setting, but there is no research which compares the speed of normal language production of unilinguals and bilinguals.

- Assuming that people seldom achieve 'total' bilingualism, the model should be able to deal with the fact that the speaker does not master both language systems to the same extent. First and second language proficiency can vary from very low to (near-)native. These differences in proficiency can be the result of incomplete acquisition, but also of loss of language skills in the first or the second language (cf. Weltens, 1989; de Bot and Clyne, 1989). It would be reasonable to assume that the extent to which the speaker has command of the two systems has consequences for the organization within the model and the way in which the model works.

- The model should be able to cope with a potentially unlimited number of languages, and must be able to represent interactions between these different languages. Typological differences between languages should therefore not cause problems. The languages of a bilingual may be typologically closely related or completely unrelated. However, this does not imply that the structural differences between the bilingual's languages are irrelevant for the workings of the model.

Single or double components?

For each of the components represented in Figure 17.1, the question should be asked whether these components are able to play their role in the production of the bilingual's speech without fundamental changes being made to them. Our aim is to keep the original model intact as much as possible and to revert to adaptations only if empirical findings on language production cannot be explained with the existing model. As compared to unilingual speech, the amount of empirical research on bilingual language production is rather sparse. For different components relevant data is still missing, therefore the model as described below invokes at least as many questions as it answers.

The knowledge component and the conceptualizer

We assume that the knowledge component is not language specific, and that a single system will suffice. This system is aware, for example, that conventions in conversation in Thailand are different to those in Great Britain and will supply the conceptualizer with the appropriate information. There is a crucial question to be asked here: which part of the system is involved in choosing the language to be used in an utterance, and what information is this choice based on? One possibility would be to assume that the knowledge component is involved in this choice: it contains a 'discourse model', a list of limiting conditions for the speech which is to be generated. We may assume that the choice of language depends on these conditions. However, the role of the knowledge component is not very clear.

Indirectly, Levelt gives some indication as to the place where the choice is made: he repeatedly points to the use of 'registers' which he defines as 'varieties which may have characteristic syntactic, lexical and phonological properties' (1989: 368). In adopting such a broad definition registers are no longer clearly distinguishable from 'varieties' and 'languages'. The same idea is found in the work of Paradis (1987) who also assumes that there is no difference, theoretically, between the different registers used by a unilingual speaker and the languages spoken by a multilingual speaker. Although Levelt explicitly refuses to go into the question of whether the use of a register is conceptually conditioned (Paradis, 1987: 183), the description of 'registers' (Paradis, 1987: 368) leads unambiguously to the conclusion that information about the register is already present in the preverbal message and subsequently plays a role in the selection of register-specific lexical items as well as the way in which these items are encoded. For the moment we therefore assume that information about the language to be chosen is included in the preverbal messages. This assumption is supported by the fact that in conversation between bilinguals, the language choice expresses communicative intentions and therefore carries meaning (Giesbers, 1989: 317).

Levelt assumes that the conceptualizer is language-specific (1989: 103–4). He argues this point by referring to differences in concepts between languages. In the case of spatial reference, for example, Dutch, like English, only makes one conceptual distinction (proximal/distal: *hier/daar* (*here/there*), *dit/dat* (*this/that*)) where Spanish makes two such distinctions (proximal/medial/distal: *aquí/ahí/allí*). These distinctions would have to be defined in the preverbal message. Because Dutch does not make these distinctions and Spanish does, the preverbal messages for the same speech intention should be different for each of these two languages. One possibility is to assume that the first of the two processes that take place in the conceptualizer, the macroplanning, is not language-specific, while microplanning is language-specific, in accordance with Levelt's proposals. It could of course be argued that the preverbal message should contain all the possible relevant information for all possible languages, thus the proximal/medial/ distal distinction for Spanish, tense and aspect for languages like English and Dutch, and shape characteristics for Navaho. Although this is not impossible in principle, it is not a very economic solution. It is more likely that in the first phase, the macroplanning, the language to be used is selected on the basis of information from the discourse model and that accordingly language-specific encoding takes place in microplanning.

A language production problem that unilinguals are not often faced with, but which is quite normal for non-balanced bilinguals, is that a concept has to be expressed in a particular language which does not have the lexical items needed to express that concept, or for which the relevant item cannot be found (in time). This will lead to problems in the formulator during the grammatical encoding stage, i.e. when the lemmas are selected from the lexicon. In the present version of the model this problem is still unsolved, not only for bilingual but also for unilingual production. In one way or another the conceptualizer should 'know' that a given concept cannot be lexicalized properly, but it is absolutely unclear how this takes place. At the same time, studies using introspective techniques suggest that foreign language learners anticipate lexical problems and use different strategies to avoid them (Poulisse, 1990).

The formulator and the lexicon

For both procedural grammatical/morpho-phonological knowledge and for declarative lexical knowledge there must be systems for every language that can be called upon. There are two explanations we can think of to account for this:

1   There is a separate formulator and a separate lexicon for each language. This solves the problem of having to separate the two systems. It will cost some storage capacity, but it is economical because there is no need to have a system that controls the co-ordination and separation of the two languages. It is, however, unclear how the two languages can be used simultaneously, during code-switching for example.

2   There is one large system which stores all the information, linguistically labelled in some way, about all the different languages. The problem which results from this solution is that it does not explain how the systems are separated in bilinguals without this causing apparent problems.

When we take into account research which has been done on storage and retrieval of lexical and syntactic information by bilinguals, we could imagine a probable solution somewhere between these two extremes. Elements/knowledge of the two languages may be represented and stored separately for each language or in a shared system depending on a number of factors. The most important of these seem to be the linguistic distance between the two languages and the level of proficiency in the languages involved. Although linguistic distance is a notion which still remains problematic (for a discussion, see Hinskens, 1988), it does seem possible to place languages along a continuum based on formal characteristics such as the number of cognates in languages or sets of shared syntactic characteristics.

It would not be unreasonable to assume that the linguistic difference between Dutch dialects is smaller than the distance between the standard Dutch variety and other standard languages, and that French is more closely related to Dutch than Moroccan Arabic. Based on neurolinguistic research, Paradis (1987: 16) formulates the hypothesis of coherence between linguistic distance and separate or joint storage as follows: 'According to such a view cerebral representation of bilingualism would be on a language pair-specific continuum, ranging from a bi- or multiregister unilingualism to a bilingualism involving two related languages.' So this means that the speaker who speaks two closely related languages will for the most part use the same procedural and lexical knowledge when speaking either of the two languages, while in the case of languages which are not related, an appeal is made to much more language-specific knowledge.

The level of proficiency is an obvious factor where separate or jointly stored knowledge about the two languages is concerned (Grosjean, 1982; Hakuta, 1986). A person who knows a few words and sentences in a foreign language will not have a separate system for this. The first-language system is flexible enough to add an additional register to those already in existence. How the organization of the two languages develops as second language proficiency increases remains a crucial question. There has been very little research into the relationship between the level of proficiency and the organization of the bilingual lexicon. Kerkman (1984) found that balanced bilinguals (lecturers of English at university) store the two languages separately to a greater extent than non-balanced bilinguals (students of English at secondary school and at university). It is, however, not exactly clear what 'stored separately' means. This point will be discussed later on in this chapter.

The mental lexicon

Information about the words in a speaker's language is stored in the mental lexicon. The right words, that is to say the lexical items which express the intended meanings, are retrieved based on the conceptual information which is contained in the preverbal message. A lexical item is retrieved on the basis of its meaning. In the lemma the relevant syntactic information is activated, and in the form part of the item the relevant morphological and phonological information is activated as well. It is assumed that idioms and phrases can be entries in the mental lexicon.

The link between meaning and syntactic information in the lemma is a crucial aspect of Levelt's model. If the syntactic information does not become available via the meaning, the surface structure cannot be constructed. This essential point is also important when the model is applied to bilingualism: if we do not take a very Whorfian position, the idea could be defended by stating that the meaning part of the lemma is not language-specific, and could therefore be shared by more than one language. At the same time meaning and syntax are so closely linked that single storage is only conceivable when lemmas are exactly similar in both meaning and syntax in both languages. The situation is somewhat different for the morpho-phonological information of the lexical item which is retrieved during the formation of the surface structure: there may be single or dual storage depending on the similarity of form of the two items. For example: when a Dutch/German cognate like *Antwort/Antwoord* is retrieved, different lemmas may be called upon because of differences in syntax (gender), despite the great similarity in form. Usually these different lemmas will be connected with different morpho-phonological forms, but this is not necessarily the case. When two lexical items only differ syntactically, then a reference to the same form is conceivable. In the same way as ambiguous words in a language are connected with the same form from different lemmas, reference to cognates may take place from language-specific lemmas to forms that are not language-specific. These considerations make it clear that the prevailing ideas about the organization of the bilingual lexicon in terms of one or two lexicons are gravely oversimplified.

A lot of research has been done to answer the question of how the bilingual lexicon is organized, ever since Kolers' work in the early sixties (Kolers, 1963). For Kolers the question was simply: are the words of two different languages stored in one big container or in two separate ones? The answer to this question is not simply 'one' or 'two', because various factors appear to play a role in the way in which words are stored. Now the question is no longer whether the systems are separated or not, but under what conditions and for which parts of the lexicon they are separated. Based on neuro-linguistic research with bilinguals, Paradis (1987) mentions four different options to explain storage of the two languages in the brain.

1   *The 'Extended System Hypothesis'*: there is no separate storage for each language; elements from a second language are simply stored with what is already there.

2   *The 'Dual System Hypothesis'*, which assumes that there are separate systems for each language, with separate sets of phonemes, rules, and words.

3   *The 'Tripartite System Hypothesis'*, which assumes that language-specific elements are stored separately and joint elements, such as cognates, together.

4   The *'Subset Hypothesis'*, which assumes the use of a single storage system where links between elements are strengthened through continued use. This implies that, in general, elements from one language will be more strongly linked to each other than to elements from another language, which results in the formation of subsets which appear to consist of elements from the same language, and which can be retrieved separately. At the same time links between elements in different languages will be just as strong as links between elements in one language in bilingual speakers who employ a 'code-switching-mode', and who live in a community where code-switching is a normal conversational strategy.

The Subset Hypothesis is in line with Levelt's description of items in the mental lexicon in general: '[A lexical item] may have particular pragmatic, stylistic, and affective features that make it fit one context of discourse better than another' (Levelt, 1989: 183).

The Subset Hypothesis is closely related to current models of the lexicon which are based on 'activation spreading' (for a survey, see Dell, 1986). In an approach such as this the basic question of whether there are one or two systems has become irrelevant. Research should be aimed at factors which influence the extent of the relationship between elements and how these links work: the extent to which the elements are semantically related doubtless plays a role, but the question remains whether relationships between elements in different languages are equally close in both directions. It is possible that a non-balanced bilingual speaker of Dutch (first language, i.e. L1) and English (second language, i.e. L2) is less inclined to think of the Dutch *paard* (horse) when faced with the English *horse* than vice versa (for a discussion, see Kerkman and de Bot, 1989; supportive evidence is also provided by Keatly *et al.*, 1989).

The enormous speed at which speech is processed, in relation to the size of the data-set (i.e. the total of the declarative and procedural knowledge) on which production is based, is one of the most important issues in the construction of a speech production model. This is especially true for lexical processes. It is not known, and not very easy to measure, how big the average speaker's lexicon actually is. Oldfield (1963) estimates that the average first-year university student in Great Britain has a passive lexicon of about 75,000 words at his disposal. Although the number of words we use actively is smaller, the active lexicon may still consist of about 30,000 words. The language user continually has to make the right choice from this enormous collection of words. When we consider that the average rate of speech is 150 words per minute, with peak rates of about 300 words per minute, this means that we have about 200 to 400 milliseconds to choose a word when we are speaking. In other words: 2 to 5 times a second we have to make the right choice from those 30,000 words. And usually we are successful; it is estimated that the probability of making the wrong choice is one in a thousand.

The above-mentioned is relevant for the hypothetical unilingual speaker. The situation is even more complex for the bilingual speaker. Even if we assume that the bilingual's lexicon is smaller for each language than the unilingual's lexicon, and that a proportion of the words are the same in different languages (cognates such as *television* or *multinational*), the total lexicon, even the active lexicon, would easily contain more than 60,000 elements. In order to get an idea of the complexity of the task one might think of someone who has to find a specific marble of a particular colour in a container with 60,000 different marbles 2 to 5 times a second.

Obviously, it is not the case that for the word selection process each individual lexical item is looked at to see if it is suitable every time a choice has to be made. There is no doubt that our brain is a very powerful calculator, but this is probably too demanding a task. The lexicon must be organized in such a way that a choice can be made quickly and accurately. In order to achieve this, irrelevant words have to be eliminated as quickly as possible in the search process. One possibility is that for the bilingual, the lexical items from one language can be retrieved as a separate set. The question is how this is achieved. In order to find the answer, it would be useful at this point to examine a few contemporary theories about the lexicon (for a survey, see Kerkman, 1984). A distinction is made between active and passive models. In active models the characteristics which words should comply with are defined, and subsequently the lexicon is scanned until the right candidate is found. An active retrieval process like this is very time-consuming because the entire lexicon has to be scanned. There are alternative versions of this active model, one alternative being, for example, that words are ordered according to frequency of occurrence, or on the basis of semantic field characteristics. Such orderings make lexical searches far more efficient: after all, we usually use frequent words because we talk about a limited number of topics. Yet this type of model does not seem very suitable because it is reasonably slow.

A more promising type of model is the passive model. The workings of this type can be explained as follows. A lexical element has a number of characteristics and must be stimulated to a certain level in order to become activated. The lexical element has detectors for all these characteristics which continuously monitor the preverbal message to see if these characteristics are present. If this is the case, the element is stimulated. As soon as a number of characteristics belonging to one element are asked for, it will become active: it will present itself as a candidate for a given slot. For example: suppose we are looking for the word *sampan*. This word has many characteristics, such as 'inanimate', 'made of wood', 'ship', 'sailing the Sea of China', but for some people also 'one of those words they use in the tip-of-the-tongue experiments'. If these characteristics are asked for, each characteristic stimulates a number of lexical items, but it is only when the number of characteristics is sufficiently large that the search is completed and *sampan* is retrieved. These types of models, of which Morton's 'logogen model' (Morton, 1979) is the best known, are called passive because there is no active lexical search: candidates automatically present themselves as a result of the information that is given. Passive models have an important advantage: they are extremely fast; by giving a number of characteristics, the number of possible candidates is narrowed down very quickly. Although this solution also presents some problems (for example, the Hypernym problem, see Levelt, 1989: 212–14), it is by far the best model available at the moment.

The main question to be answered with respect to the bilingual lexicon is: how does the selection of lexical items take place in bilinguals? This entails the question of how the systems are kept apart or mixed depending on the situation. A major advantage of the Subset Hypothesis presented earlier in this article is that the set from which the choice has to be made has been reduced dramatically as a result of the fact that a particular language/subset has been chosen. Research on code-switching, cross-linguistic influences, and aphasia has shown however that bilinguals cannot simply switch their language 'on' and 'off'. Green (1986) makes a plausible suggestion by saying that language spoken by bilinguals or multilinguals can have three levels of activation:

1   *Selected*: The selected language controls the speech output.
2   *Active*: The active language plays a role in ongoing processing, works parallel to the selected language and does the same things in fact, but has no access to the outgoing speech channel.
3   *Dormant*: A dormant language is stored in long-term memory, but does not play a role in ongoing processing.

Depending on the situation (the discourse model) languages are selected, active or dormant. One language is always selected, but more than one language can be active or latent. In many situations there is only one selected language and a number of latent languages. During speaking, the words will initially be chosen from the selected language, or from the active language if necessary, and as a last resort from the dormant language, with considerable loss of time as a result. Extreme cases of dormant languages are the mother tongues of immigrants, like the Dutch in Australia: the Dutch immigrants have spoken English almost exclusively for years and they are faced with retrieval problems when they attempt to reactivate their knowledge of the mother tongue. Once they succeed, it is surprising how much knowledge of the language they have retained (de Bot, 1990).

Green's idea of different levels of activation is in line with Færch and Kasper's (1986) suggestions for 'primary' (≈ selected) and 'secondary' (≈ active/dormant) knowledge. An important aspect of Green's proposals is that the active language does everything the selected language also does: it selects lexical items, forms sentences, generates surface structures, and eventually even makes a phonetic plan. The only difference is that the phonetic plan of the active language is not fed into the articulator. Phenomena associated with fluent and frequent code-switching can be explained as a result of this type of parallel production. The notion of parallel production is supported by findings from unilingual research into ambiguous words and speech errors which shows that more candidate-items are available in speaking (Swinney, 1979). For bilinguals Macnamara had already suggested this solution in 1967: 'The most likely solution [for code-switching] is that the bilingual has the capacity to activate the L2 system, carry out the semantic encoding, the selection of words and the syntactic organization while more or less mechanically producing in L1 material which has already been prepared for production' (Macnamara, 1967: 70). Similar ideas have been put forward by Lipski (1978) and Altenberg and Cairns (1983).

Summarizing, a useful extension of the model would be to assume that there is a separate system for every language as far as the processing components in the formulators are concerned. Lexical items are selected from one common lexicon in which items are connected in networks which enable subsets of items to be activated. One such subset can be the items from a specific language.

Following Green's ideas, we assume that there are two speech plans. In order to explain why a particular language is used at a specific time we have to assume that for each part of the preverbal message information is included as to the language in which this part should be articulated.

One of the most salient characteristics of a non-balanced bilingual is the occurrence of lexical retrieval problems. Those problems can have various causes: the words may never have been acquired in the first place or retrieval takes more time than the production system will allow ('speech need'). Based on research by Levelt and Maassen

(1981) and Bock (1986; 1987), Levelt assumes that during production retrieval problems are not directly reported to the conceptualizer, in other words, when the preverbal message is being generated, the possibility that one or more of the lexical items needed may not be available (on time) is not taken into account. With respect to the form characteristics of a lexical item which has already been activated the situation is probably different: it would appear that problems during phonological encoding lead to a revision of syntactic frames in such a way that the time involved in generating speech is not affected. Whether feedback takes place directly or via the speech plan's internal feedback mechanism is not very clear. Lexical retrieval problems are fairly rare in a unilingual non-aphasic speaker. For a bilingual speaker who does not have a perfect command of one of the languages these problems are commonplace, and the question is whether a bilingual speaking-model can do without a mechanism that provides information about the availability of lexical items (i.e. both lemma and form characteristics) when the preverbal message is being generated. The alternative is that for each item that cannot be found a new feedback loop has to be initiated which inevitably leads to a major delay in speech production. The existence of a checking system like this will be brought to light by adapted versions of Levelt and Maassen's and Bock's experiments.

Languages differ in both the nature and size of the lexicon, not only because the number of lemmas may be different but also because the morphological characteristics of a language lead to a higher or lower lexical productivity in a particular language. In agglutinative languages such as Turkish and Finnish (as opposed to English) there will be fewer letter/sound combinations which have the status of 'lexical item', because in those languages stem–suffix combinations, which may be constructed every time they are used, express the meaning and function of lexical items in languages like English. It is not clear when a string of letters/sounds is assigned the status of 'lexical item'. It is conceivable that a certain combination which 'started off' as a stem–suffix combination eventually becomes an independent lemma through frequent use and because of reasons of efficiency. In a number of ways the production process of 'conservative' languages such as English is different from that of agglutinative languages. These differences in the relationship between lemma/information about meaning and morpho-phonological information provide support for the postulation of separated formulators for each language.

Phonological encoding and articulation

The next step in the production process is the phonological encoding. For unilingual speakers there is substantial evidence to show that sounds are not the units of speech planning. It is more likely that speech is encoded and produced in larger units. Levelt assumes that syllables are the basic units of articulatory execution. In fact, phonetic plans for words consist of a number of syllable programs. The speaker has an inventory of syllables that need not be generated from scratch every time a word is produced. Syllable programs are stored for articulatory patterns. The phonetic plan consists of a string of syllable programs. The number of syllable programs for a specific language is not too large. It is estimated that a non-syllabic language such as English has between 6,000 and 7,000 different syllables that actually appear in words. This concerns a count on written language, however, so it does not take into account all sorts of allophones which result from regional and social variation. This number of syllables is small enough to allow for their storage in the lexicon. For syllabic languages such as Chinese, the number of syllables is much smaller.

For the bilingual speaker the situation may depend on the level of proficiency attained in the two languages. Syllable programs are typically automatized, and the level of automaticity is likely to be correlated with level of proficiency. For the more advanced bilingual it is not inconceivable that there is one large set of syllable programs for all languages. The number of different syllables to be stored may become very large, but analogous to what has been said before about the lexicon, syllable programs that are the same for two languages will not be stored twice, while language-specific ones will be uniquely represented. A question not easily answered is, what is meant by 'the same for two languages'. Syllables are supposed to be the smallest relatively invariant articulatory units in speech production (Fujimura and Lovins, 1978), but it is unclear how invariant syllables are for the bilingual. Flege (1986) presents data that suggest that bilinguals tend to classify sounds from the second language in categories of the first language as much as they can.

In his chapter on articulation Levelt, after considering a number of theories, opts for a 'model referenced control' model. In this model, speakers have an internal model ('sensory images') of the sounds which are to be produced (or actually of the syllables, the units of speech production). The speaker has an internal model of his own speech system and knows how it should be adjusted in order to produce a particular sound. The sound itself does not actually need to be pronounced to achieve this. The speaker is able to simulate the sound internally and to check whether the chosen configuration is applicable in the situation or phonological context. Any possible deviations from the normal situation, such as talking while smoking a pipe, are accounted for when the system is adjusted. The internal model is not a system of innate values, but it is based on extensive experience in listening to one's own speech. Oller and MacNeilage (1983) show that the model has not yet been perfected in four- to nine-year-olds and that deviations from the normal situation do not always result in optimal accommodation.

The bilingual speaker must have models for all sounds/syllables in the different languages. If the units of production were sounds, then it is unnecessary to assume double/separated systems for the articulator: the existing collection of normalized sounds in L1 can be extended with additional sounds when a new language is acquired, and it is not inconceivable that the L1 norms apply to the L2 as long as possible. This could mean that for the advanced L2 speaker, the sounds which are similar in the two languages are represented by one single norm, while language-specific sounds develop their own norm. Cross-linguistic influence at the phonological level can be explained by the fact that the L1 norm is maintained when L2 sounds are being realized. The quality of the L2 norm will depend on the frequency of use of the language, the amount and quality of language contact, and the extent to which subtle differences between L1 and L2 sounds can be perceived. It is interesting to note that we do not know whether the absence of a perfect model for an L2 sound has repercussions for speech planning at other levels: does (the awareness of) the absence of a particular norm lead to the avoidance of word forms in which this sound occurs? As indicated above, Levelt's model is characterized by the absence of direct feedback mechanisms. It will have to be made clear experimentally whether this type of form-driven avoidance does in fact take place.

Prosody is one of the most important characteristics of speech. Information about prosodic aspects is generated mainly by the formulator. The phonological encoding module (see Figure 17.1) contains a prosody generator. This generator processes four types of input:

- 'intonational meaning', which includes the meaning of a particular intonational pattern, in particular the illocutionary functions;
- information about the surface structure, including the assignment of stress;
- information about the metrical structure of utterances;
- information about the segmental structure of utterances.

Based on information from these four sources, the prosody generator constructs a temporal structure and a pitch contour for the utterance. It is not known how the different components lead to the choice of a specific pitch contour (Levelt, 1989: 398). It seems likely that a choice is made from a restricted set of relevant pitch movements ('nuclear tones'). This set may be different for different languages or for different dialects of one language (Pijper, 1983; Willems, 1983).

How should this part of the model be adjusted to make it suitable to be used for bilingual speakers? The prosody generator's input is largely language-specific. The relationship between certain intonational patterns and their related meanings/connotations (for example, 'disbelief', 'joy') are different in each language (Keijsper, 1984; Bolinger, 1989: 26). Languages also differ with respect to metrical rules. A well-known distinction in this respect is the difference between 'stress-timed' languages like Dutch and English and 'syllable-timed' languages like French, Spanish, and Hungarian (Dauer, 1983). Information on the surface structure and segmental structure is also to a considerable extent language-specific. And, finally, the intonation contours from which the prosody generator can make a choice show differences between languages. If there were separate systems for the above-mentioned components for each language then it would be reasonable to assume that these systems would not influence one another; they function only when 'their language' is asked for. Although relatively little research has been carried out to examine cross-linguistic influences in prosody, and research in this field has been rather impressionistic (for a survey, see de Bot, 1986), it is clear that this dual system hypothesis is hardly tenable. Successive bilinguals in particular, that is to say people who were not brought up bilingually, appear to have many intonational characteristics from their L1 in their L2. Their foreign accent is highly determined by prosodic cues. The undeniable fact that only very few bilingual speakers completely master the prosodic aspects of the two languages must be accounted for in a bilingual model. A tentative conclusion would seem justified for the articulator. There is only one articulator for bilingual speakers which has an extensive set of sounds and pitch patterns from both languages to work with. The extent to which these sounds and patterns are more or less perfect models depends on the frequency and quality of contact with the L2. Extensive evidence of cross-linguistic influences at the pronunciation and phonological level suggests that L1 models continue to play a role even when the speaker has excellent command of the L2. This evidence makes the existence of two separate systems very improbable.

If we propose that each language has its own formulator, it would seem natural to assume a separate speech-comprehension system for each language as well. A discussion on this topic is outside the scope of this chapter.

Testing the adapted model against the requirements

Earlier in this chapter we set a number of requirements which the bilingual model should meet. In this section we explore to what extent the adapted model meets these requirements.

Separation of systems, code-switching, and cross-linguistic influence

By assuming that there are separate formulators and lexical subsets for each language and by adopting Green's ideas regarding the activation of different languages, it is plausible that the bilingual can keep the two language systems separate.

Accounting for the fact that bilinguals are capable of switching from one language to another very quickly and without much difficulty is less easy. Very relevant in this respect is Giesbers' study (1989). In his investigations into code-switching between a dialect and the standard language he tries to link different types of code-switching to components of a language production model, in his case the model developed by Kempen (Kempen and Hoenkamp, 1987). This model shares many of the characteristics of Levelt's model. One essential difference is that Kempen assigns an important role to the system which monitors all the subsystems' output, while Levelt assumes that it is only in the last/lower stages of the production process that monitoring or feedback takes place.

Giesbers distinguishes three basic forms of code-switching:

- intended, situationally motivated switches;
- contextual switches which are connected with the topic of conversation; and
- performance switches which include code-switching as a speech style or a speaking-mode.

Intended switches result from a choice at the conceptual level: through the choice of the language additional information is conveyed. Contextual switches originate in the grammatical encoding component and occur more particularly during the selection of lemmas. In Kempen's model this takes place in the 'lexico-syntactic module'. One of the mechanisms could be that the level of activation of particular lexical items in another language than the one being spoken is increased to such an extent by the conversational topic for example, that these lexical items will become more readily available. Another possibility is that the discourse model conveys the information that the conversational setting allows for any switching to take place, and that accordingly in the macroplanning no strict indications as to language choice are added, which may lead to more or less random switching. Performance-switches are justified by Kempen's morpho-phonological module which corresponds to Levelt's phonological encoding component. Giesbers assumes that these performance-switches are the result of form characteristics being more or less randomly linked to lemmas in the surface structure. In their research on L2 production by Dutch learners of English, Poulisse and Bongaerts (1990) found the same type of switches, which they call 'automatic switches'. Although Giesbers' pro-posed linking of types of code-switching and modules in the language production system is definitely a crucial step forward, this does not mean that all problems are automatic-ally solved. As he indicates himself, a sharp division between types cannot always be maintained (Giesbers, 1989: 319), and there are sentences in his corpus which seem to indicate that the switching occurring in these utterances was planned at the conceptual level even though they have the form of a non-intended switch. Contextual switches present an additional problem. There must be a specific subset in the lexicon in which lexical elements within one language can be activated but also a subset which contains lexical elements from different languages. This means that there must be separate subsystems which decrease or increase the extent of code-switching depending on the conversational setting and topic. If we adhere to the subset hypothesis we can provide an explanation for what happens with so-called triggerwords. These words which appear to trigger code-switching because they are similar in form in different languages typically figure in more than one subset/network and activation of this subset in language A leads to activation of another subset which includes this word in language B. Or, to put it more simply, the wrong turn is taken at the crossing.

In research on code-switching, several universal linguistic constraints have been postulated. Clyne (1987) reviews these constraints and concludes that basic assumptions for them are wanting and that therefore the basis for most of these constraints is rather weak. This also holds for what has been called the 'equivalence constraint', which postulates that the syntax on either side of a switch must be grammatical for the language concerned. In his study on bidialectal code-switching, Giesbers (1989) found that in general the equivalence constraint was met in his corpus, while Nortier's (1989) study on Dutch/Moroccan-Arabic code-switching showed that this constraint was not valid for her data. For languages that are structurally similar, as in Giesbers' study, there is equivalence, which is not very surprising, while for less related languages there is no equivalence.

One of the explanations given by Clyne for the occurrence of equivalence in code-switched sentences is that bilinguals actively converge in order to facilitate code-switching. In the terms of the present model this could suggest that in cases where a speaker can make a choice between two possible constructions in a language, that construction will be selected that is closest to the equivalent in the other language.

Many instances of cross-linguistic influences are related to code-switching and cannot be simply separated from this on theoretical or empirical grounds. Theoretically it is possible to restrict the term code-switching to cases where the speaker has a good command of both languages and is thus able, in principle, to convey the relevant information in both languages. In her research on Dutch/Moroccan-Arabic code-switching, Nortier (1989) showed that for a large proportion of the L2 words that appear to cause a switch to L1, her informants actually used these words correctly in other parts of the conversation. It could still be the case that these words were not readily available at that very moment, but they were certainly neither lost, nor never acquired.

Cross-linguistic influences can be indicative of a lack of knowledge. When the knowledge of the L2 is insufficient, the speaker may 'borrow' from the L1.

Slowing down of the production process

Slowing need not occur as a result of more than one language being active in the model as we have described it. Separately used the languages do not get in each other's ways or paths. In addition, languages may differ by convention with respect to the speed of delivery. Möhle (1984) has shown that native speakers of French take longer to describe a given set of cartoons than native speakers of German, and her conclusion is that French speakers are apparently faced with more processing problems than German speakers. This interpretation is not really convincing. The stylistics of German and French may simply differ for that kind of language-use situation. Direct comparisons of native speakers and less proficient speakers of the language is complicated by the fact that L2 learners may indeed have processing problems that cause a deceleration of the speech rate, but at the same time these learners may not be fully acquainted with stylistic conventions. For code-switching comparable problems arise. There has been no research into the difference in the rate of production for subjects who do or do not code-switch. Research by Giesbers (1989) on timing aspects of bidialectal code-switching suggests that there is indeed a tendency to pause before switches, but the same holds for other structural aspects. In fact, he concludes that pausing behaviour is not typically different for code-switching sites. Furthermore a slower speech rate could be part of the 'code-switching mode'. In such a mode the slower rate does not result from capacity problems the system might have; it is instead a more or less consciously chosen style.

Lower speech rates for bilinguals as compared to monolinguals are to be expected for the 'minor' language. For perceptual tasks such a difference in speed has been reported repeatedly in the literature. It is quite obvious that a lower level of proficiency leads to less automatized processing and accordingly to a lower speech rate.

Unequal command of the two languages

As indicated, the model is not aimed at describing and explaining the acquisition process; it is a 'steady-state' model. It should be capable, however, of describing the bilingual system at any moment and at all stages of development. The model does not have to justify how development from stage A to stage B takes place. The majority of bilinguals will not have a complete command of both languages, whatever that may mean. If the above-mentioned extensions to the model (in particular the doubling of the formulator and the development of language-specific subsets in the lexicon) turn out to be valid, then we must determine which level of proficiency brings about the doubling of components (or conversely: which changes in the processing allow the development of higher levels of proficiency). It is clear that when the speaker has very little knowledge of the L2 he can still make utterances in that L2 by making some (internal) extensions to the L1 system. In this way it is plausible to think that it is only the morpho-phonological information for lexical items in the L2 which is L2 specific, while syntactic information from the L1 translation equivalent is activated.

The number of languages and typological differences

In principle the model is infinitely extendable to accommodate any number of additional languages, if we assume that each language has its own microplanning and formulator. The tiny amount of research that has been done into polyglots suggests that a good command of a large number of languages is possible (cf. the classic case studies of aphasics examined in Paradis, 1987).

I have indicated before, as regards typological differences, that the possibility that an individual speaks two typologically unrelated languages justifies the assumption that there is a separate formulator for each language. It would seem unlikely that languages which differ in the way in which intentions are formed syntactically, in particular with respect to the amount of semantic information conveyed through morphological means, can be processed by the same system.

How the model can be applied to explain various kinds of language disorders is outside the scope of the model we have described. However, it is useful to note that a considerable number of possibilities offered here have come about as a result of research into disorders (in particular the work done by Paradis and Green).

Conclusion

In this article an attempt is made to adapt a recent model of language production, Levelt's 'Speaking' model for bilingual speakers Given the adequacy of the model for unilingual language production, it was intended to change the model as little as possible.

The conclusion is drawn that with respect to the conceptualizer, Levelt's ideas had to be modified: rather than assuming that the conceptualizer is completely language specific, it is likely that in the first of the two production phases in the conceptualizer, the macroplanning is not language-specific, whereas in the second phase, the micro-planning is language-specific. In the conceptualizer communicative intentions are given form in the preverbal message, which contains information about the language in which (part of) an utterance is to be produced. Through this information the relevant language-specific formulator is activated. In the formulator the preverbal message is converted into a speech plan very much in the same way as unilingual processing takes place in Levelt's model. There is one lexicon where lexical elements in different languages are stored together. It has been suggested that the relationship between the lemma and form characteristics in bilinguals is not one to one as in the unilingual case: a lemma can be linked to various form characteristics depending on the language or languages involved. Within the lemma, meaning and syntactic information may not be inextricably linked. The different formulators submit their speech plan to an articulator which is not language specific and which stores the possible sounds and prosodic patterns of the languages.

As indicated, the empirical basis for an evaluation of a bilingual production model is rather small at the moment. Therefore, the proposed model should be seen as a first attempt that will be adapted by future research and by reinterpretation of research findings from the past.

Source: de Bot, K. (1992) A bilingual production model: Levelt's 'speaking' model adapted. *Applied Linguistics* 13: 1–24, by permission of the author and Oxford University Press.

Postscript

Just as the basic elements and structure of the original Levelt (1989) model have not changed dramatically in the last 15 years, so the basics of the bilingual version of the model have not been challenged fundamentally, though of course so many years of research in a very active field have produced much more in-depth knowledge of processes on bilingual production. The main points of the bilingual version of the Levelt model were the following:

A bilingual model is not fundamentally different from a monolingual model since monolinguals also use different styles and registers, so there is no need to assume additional components. At the same time, how styles and registers fit in the monolingual models is unclear: in a way the bilingual versions of the model solve some of the unresolved issues of the monolingual versions in this sense.

At the conceptual level a distinction is made between macro-planning and microplanning. It has been argued that macro-planning is non-language specific, while microplanning is language specific (de Bot and Schreuder, 1993). This is different from the original Levelt model and the 1992 bilingual model in which the conceptualizer was assumed to be completely non-language specific.

Language choice is part of the communicative intention and is therefore part of the information in the preverbal message. Several studies have pointed to the existence of some sort of language cue or tag in the preverbal message to allow for the selection of elements from a specific language (Poulisse and Bongaerts, 1994; La Heij, 2005).

Separate languages are subsets of a larger language system. These subsets are based on use and accordingly vary in level of activation. This idea has been proposed by Paradis and is further elaborated in his 2004 book. As yet, no alternatives have been proposed for this.

There are different formulators for different languages. This aspect has been challenged by different authors. Poulisse (1999) has argued that for cognate languages different formulators would show considerable overlap, and de Bot (2004) moved away from the idea of different formulators altogether by postulationg different subsets at the lexical, syntactic and phonological level.

One issue that has attracted considerable attention in recent years is to what extent language activation in bilingual processing is selective or non-selective, that is: when one language is used in production or perception, is the other language completely switched off, playing no role in language processing, or are both languages active though to different degrees? Studies using traditional experimental techniques, such as Stroop, cross-linguistic priming, picture word interference tasks and the study of the effect of lexical neighbors on retrieval in both languages, have convincingly shown that that bilingual processing is basically non-selective (see Dijkstra and van Heuven (2002) for an overview on language comprehension and Costa (2005) and Meuter (2005) on language production). In addition, neuro-imaging techniques have supported the non-selective position (see Abutalebi et al. (2005) for an overview).

The study of code-switching and cross-linguistic influence in language production has continued to attract attention, and one of the important findings is that the cognitive mechanism that controls language selection in bilinguals is probably non-language specific or at any rate it seems to be located in brain areas that are generally considered not to be involved primarily with language processing (Jackson et al., 2001; Rodriguez-Fornelis et al., 2005). For code-switching, the rather simplistic idea of activation and inhibition of languages as subsets has to be replaced by more sophisticated models that take into account the switch costs that come with switching. Meuter and Allport (1999) have shown that switch costs are not symmetrical: it takes more time and effort to switch from the weaker L2 to the stronger L1 than the other way around.

In addition to experimental and neuro-imaging data, there are now more data based on corpora of spontaneous speech, which of course are essential for our understanding of the normal speech production process. Following the research tradition in language production studies that focus on speech errors, and thatwhich has been the basis for most models of monolingual speech production, Poulisse (1999) studied slips of the tongue in L2 and made her dataset available in print, which will allow other researchers to use her data. For the study of code-switching, Broersma and de Bot (2006) provide quantitative data on a code-switching corpus rather than providing typical or interesting examples only as is normally the case in studies of code-switching. The testing of a hypothesis on code-switching using quantitative analyses of corpus data is definitely an interesting development that should be pursued further.

An altogether different issue is to what extent existing models can deal with development. The Levelt model and its bilingual version are basically static models that describe a steady state of a system in time. There now is a tendency in cognitive science to move from such static models to more dynamic and adaptive models (Port and van Gelder, 1995; van Gelder, 1998). The assumption that a language userÒs system is stable and unchanging is clearly wrong: through use, input and output, the system will be in constant flux, and models that cannot deal with such dynamism may well be less valid thant they seemed. This is not a problem specific to bilingual production models, but a problem for all psycholinguistic models that are based on operations on static representations. In models of cognition based on a dynamic systems approach, it is not clear whether such static representations actually exist. Attempts to locate them in the brain have failed so far, and we may need to start thinking about alternative models that take into account the dynamic character of knowledge. This may lead to models that deviate significantly from what we are used to, and to different approaches to the study of processing in which change over time is part of the models.

Kees de Bot, PhD, is Professor of Applied Linguistics at the University of Groningen, the Netherlands.c.l.j.de.bot@rug.nl

Lexical and conceptual memory in the bilingual: mapping form to meaning in two languages

JUDITH F. KROLL AND
ANNETTE M.B. DE GROOT

A central issue in theories of bilingual language representation concerns the mapping of form to meaning. Past research on this topic sought to determine whether word forms and concepts in two languages are represented independently or integrated within unitary lexical and conceptual memory systems. Although an indeterminate conclusion concerning this question initially led some to argue that it was not possible to resolve the issue empirically (e.g., Glucksberg, 1984), recent work suggests that the earlier claims of representational indeterminacy failed to take into account distinctions between levels of representation. If one assumes that lexical-level representations are functionally independent for words in two languages (an assumption that seems to be required for languages in which word form is not similar) but that conceptual representations are shared (as they appear to be for words in the first language and pictured objects), it is possible to interpret the earlier contradictory evidence for the two alternative positions (Potter, 1979; Snodgrass, 1984). In general, evidence gathered from tasks that focus on lexical-level processing tends to support the independence view (e.g., Gerard and Scarborough, 1989), whereas evidence gathered from tasks that require semantic-level processing tends to support the integrated view (Durgunoglu and Roediger, 1987). However, although the assumption of two levels that correspond to form and meaning provides an initial framework for thinking about bilingual representation, it does not determine the specific nature of the mappings between from and meaning within or across languages.

In this chapter, we review current research on the representation of words and concepts in bilingual memory. Because a number of tutorial chapters on this topic have appeared recently (e.g., Chen, 1992; De Groot, 1993, 1995; Kroll, 1993; Kroll and Sholl, 1992), the present chapter focuses on research that we believe has significant implications for ultimately resolving the issue of how word forms are mapped to meaning in two languages. Because the architecture of the bilingual's mind may be a reflection of the level of expertise in the second language and the context in which the second language was acquired, we examine the cognitive processes that are engaged in bilingual tasks by individuals at early stages of second language acquisition, by individuals who are relatively fluent bilinguals, and by individuals who are relatively fluent in a second language and are attempting to acquire a third language. What should be clear from this brief description is that we do not restrict the discussion to the performance of *balanced* bilinguals (who are, in fact, extremely rare) but, instead, define bilingualism in the broadest possible terms, including all individuals who actively use, or attempt to use, more than one language, even if they have not achieved fluency in the second language (L2). Bilingual groups are distinguished on the basis of their L2 proficiency. A further caveat is that we focus primarily on adult second language learners and bilinguals. Because lexical and conceptual development co-occur in early childhood, and because there may be critical period effects that influence the course of language acquisition (e.g., Johnson and Newport, 1989), the topic of childhood bilingualism raises issues beyond the scope of the present tutorial.

Levels of representation for words and concepts

Linguists and psycholinguists often distinguish two levels of meaning. One level consists of the semantic specifications that are taken to be part of the lexical representation. This level of representation constrains the way in which the meanings of words are accessed for the purpose of comprehending and producing syntactically well-formed utterances. The other level represents the conceptual information that includes real world knowledge and the meanings of the objects and events to which words refer. Research on the representation of words and concepts in the bilingual departs from this traditional dichotomy by making the assumption that lexical representations do not include meaning but only aspects of word form. According to this perspective, all meaning is grouped within the conceptual representation (e.g., Potter, So, Von Eckardt, and Feldman, 1984) or a third level of representation is proposed to handle some specific lexical-semantic functions (e.g., the lemma level in Levelt's, 1989, model). The proposal of a lexical representation devoid of meaning may be, in part, a reflection of the emphasis in research on this topic to use bilingual word and picture tasks that are performed outside of sentence context. However, the general assumption that there are independent levels of representation for word form and meaning is not restricted to bilingual research. Recent monolingual work on word and picture recognition (e.g., Besner, Smith, and MacLeod, 1990; Glaser, 1992; Vitkovitch and Humphreys, 1991), language production (e.g., Levelt et al., 1991), and neuropsychology (Anderson et al., 1992) make similar claims.

Word association versus concept mediation: the developmental hypothesis

The first explicit test of alternative hypotheses for mapping first and second language words to concepts was reported by Potter et al. (1984). The two models they contrasted are shown in Fig. 18.1. They are both *hierarchical* models in the sense that they distinguish between word representations and concept representations. According to the word association model, words in the second language (L2) access concepts via words in the first language (L1). In contrast, the concept mediation model allows direct access to concepts for words in both languages. Potter et al. (1984) tested these alternatives by comparing more and less fluent bilinguals on word translation and picture-naming tasks.

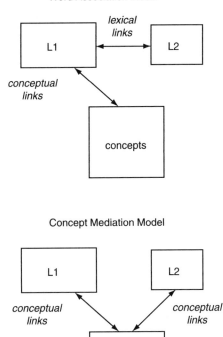

Figure 18.1. The word association and concept mediation models (adapted from Potter et al., 1984). In the word association model, second language words are associated to their translation equivalents in the first language. In the concept mediation model, each language accesses the same shared concepts.

A great deal of research on picture naming suggests that it is accomplished via concept mediation; lexical entries for the names of pictures only appear to be available subsequent to conceptual access (e.g., Potter and Faulconer, 1975). If bilingual translation is also accomplished conceptually, translation and picture-naming tasks should take equally long to perform. However, if translation can take advantage of a word association mechanism that by-passes the necessity for retrieving the concept, translation should be faster than picture naming. Potter et al. found that the two tasks were performed in approximately the same amount of time, supporting the concept mediation alternative. Furthermore, they found that both more and less fluent bilinguals appeared to conceptually mediate L2.

Subsequent research on translation and picture naming extended the logic of Potter et al.'s (1984) study to show that second language learners who are at earlier stages of acquisition than the less fluent group in that study perform in accord with the predictions of the word association model. Less fluent individuals are faster to translate words than to name pictures in the second language (Chen and Leung, 1989; Kroll and

Curley, 1988). Lexical mediation through L1 appears to characterize the performance of nonfluent bilinguals, whereas concept mediation appears to characterize the performance of more fluent bilinguals. Results of Stroop studies, examining interference within and across languages, also support a developmental process from lexical to conceptual processing with increasing expertise in L2 (Chen and Ho, 1986; Mägiste, 1984; Tzelgov, Henik, and Leiser, 1990).

Evidence for the developmental hypothesis

If there is a developmental shift from lexical to conceptual mappings for L2 words with increasing fluency, it should be possible to observe differential involvement of lexical and conceptual processes in the performance of more and less fluent bilinguals. In general, studies using a wide variety of methods to test this hypothesis have found converging support for it.

One source of evidence that suggests that less fluent bilinguals rely on lexical mediation to understand second language words comes from research on cross-language transfer concerning the role of cognates in second language learning. Although cognate status has been defined in a variety of ways in the literature on bilingual language processing, cognates are generally taken to be words that share aspects of both form and meaning across languages (e.g., *tomato* in English and *tomaat* in Dutch). Because cognates are relatively transparent at the lexical level, they provide a means for less fluent bilinguals to use the second language prior to the ability to conceptually access the meanings of L2 words. Hancin-Bhatt and Govindjee (1999) have shown that the degree of transfer from L1 to L2 depends on the similarity of phonology in the bilingual's two languages with languages that share phonology supporting the greatest transfer.

Although a cognate strategy during early stages of second language acquisition (or when acquiring difficult new vocabulary during later stages) may facilitate the acquisition of some kinds of linguistic knowledge in L2 (for example, see Hancin-Bhatt and Nagy, 1994, concerning the acquisition of derivational morphology), it may be a strategy that has only short-term benefits (see also Meara, 1993, for a discussion of the implications of the presence of cognates for L2 learning). For one thing, languages that share aspects of word form are likely to include false as well as true cognates (e.g., the word *red* in Spanish means *net* in English, not *red*). A cognate strategy, although lexically efficient, may not be reliable. Dufour, Kroll, and Sholl (1996) examined the role of cognate status in the translation performance of less and more fluent English–French bilinguals. The results showed that all bilinguals translated cognates more rapidly than noncognates, replicating previous reports of a cognate advantage in translation (e.g., De Groot, 1992a; De Groot, Dannenburg, and Van Hell, 1994; Kroll and Stewart, 1994; Sánchez-Casas, Davis, and García-Albea, 1992), but the advantage for cognates was greater for the less than for the more fluent bilinguals, suggesting that less fluent bilinguals were more reliant on a lexical translation strategy.

To examine the lexical mediation hypothesis more directly, Talamas, Kroll, and Dufour (1995) asked more and less fluent English–Spanish bilinguals to perform a translation recognition task (De Groot, 1992a) in which they had to decide whether two words, one in each language, were translation equivalents. The conditions of interest in this study were the trials on which the two words were not translation equivalents. These *no* trials included cases in which the incorrect translation was similar in form to the correct translation (e.g., *hambre* vs. *hombre* in Spanish), similar in meaning (e.g., *mujer* vs. *hombre* in Spanish), or unrelated. Talamas et al. found evidence for interference (i.e., longer response latencies) for both form-related and meaning-related trials relative to unrelated controls. However, the magnitude of the form and meaning interference was a function of fluency in L2. Less fluent bilinguals produced a large form interference effect but a small meaning interference effect. The opposite was true for more fluent bilinguals, whose performance was more disrupted by similarity in meaning than in form. The results supported the hypothesis that bilinguals shift from reliance on lexical form to reliance on meaning with increasing fluency in the second language. Furthermore, they are consistent with the classroom observation that students at beginning levels of L2 study are more likely to make form-based errors in translation than students at more advanced levels (Talamas et al.). Related studies by Cziko (1980) and McLeod and McLaughlin (1986) also provide support for the claim that increasing fluency in the second language is associated with a reduction in reliance on form and an increase in reliance on meaning.

Two approaches have been taken to determine whether second language learners are conceptually mediating their second language. One approach is to ask individuals to perform a task that, by its very nature, requires conceptual processing. If they are conceptually mediating L2, it should be possible for them to perform the task. If they are not able to conceptually mediate, and, if the conditions of the experiment do not allow participants to resort to translation strategies, then performance should be generally poor. However, the way in which a second language learner or less fluent bilingual solves the problem of accessing the required information in such a task may also reveal the manner in which the conceptual connections are eventually established. A second approach is to manipulate a variable that is believed to reflect access to semantic or conceptual memory and to determine whether performance in both languages is sensitive to that factor.

One way to require conceptual access is to ask participants to categorize exemplars as members of specified semantic categories (e.g., to decide whether *apples* are a type of fruit). Past studies that have examined within- and across-language categorization have shown that fluent bilinguals can categorize as rapidly and accurately within as across their two languages (Caramazza and Brones, 1980; Potter et al., 1984; Shanon, 1982). This result has been interpreted as support for the view that the fluent bilingual's two languages are conceptually mediated by a common semantic representation. However, many of these studies used a paradigm in which the interval between the presentation of the category name and the exemplar was relatively long, thus permitting or encouraging a translation strategy.

More recently, Dufour and Kroll (1995) replicated the concept mediation results for fluent English–French bilinguals in a categorization task in which the interval between the category name and exemplar was brief, providing more compelling evidence for the concept mediation hypothesis. Dufour and Kroll included a less fluent comparison in this experiment and predicted that less fluent bilinguals, who would presumably have to rely on a lexical translation strategy, would have particular difficulty in the categorization task when the exemplar followed the category name by only a brief interval. If less fluent bilinguals must resort to a translation strategy, then the conditions that require the most translation, when both category name and target word appear in L2, should produce the longest categorization latencies. Contrary to the predictions based on a translation strategy, they found that less fluent English–French bilinguals were able to categorize under short SOA conditions and under conditions in which both the category name and the target word appeared in L2 (French). However, the pattern of categorization for the less fluent bilinguals differed from the one produced by the more fluent bilinguals, such that they were slower to categorize when the language of the target mismatched the language of the category name. This pattern of categorization latencies held, even when the category names were presented in L1, a condition in which all participants were presumably able to comprehend the presented information. On the basis of this result, Dufour and Kroll argued that L1 may activate conceptual memory to the point where a less fluent bilingual's relatively weak L2 may not be able to provide the necessary lexical support. Having concepts active, for which no readily available word is known in L2, may serve to inhibit access to those concepts for which L2 words exist. Thus, it may be possible for the less fluent bilingual to direct conceptual access on the basis of a limited L2 but, at the same time, not be able to use conceptual information to retrieve L2 words. Because it is the latter process of L2 lexicalization that is required in production tasks, such as translation and picture naming, it may be possible for individuals at this level of L2 acquisition to use conceptual information in comprehension and recognition tasks, whereas the very same information may not be used if production is required. (See McLeod and McLaughlin, 1986, for a similar argument concerning the degree to which proficiency generalizes across tasks.) Overall, these findings support the claim that the nature of conceptual processing changes with increasing L2 proficiency.

Additional evidence to support the claim that fluent bilinguals are able to conceptually mediate their second language comes from semantic priming tasks in which the languages of the prime and target are manipulated. If bilinguals are able to access concepts for L2 words, and, if concepts are shared across their two languages, then semantic priming should be observed within both L1 and L2 and also across languages. The results of a large number of cross-language semantic priming studies generally support the conclusion that fluent or relatively fluent bilinguals are able to conceptually mediate L2 because priming is typically observed both within and between languages (e.g., Altarriba, 1990; Chen and Ng, 1989; De Groot and Nas, 1991; Frenck and Pynte, 1987; Kirsner, Smith, Lockhart, King, and Jain, 1984; Meyer and Ruddy, 1974; Schwanenflugel and Rey, 1986; Tzelgov and Henik, 1989). However, recent studies that have attempted to carefully control methodological aspects of the semantic priming paradigm have reported some limits to the extent of cross-language priming, even when bilinguals are highly proficient in L2 (e.g., De Groot and Nas, 1991; Keatley and De Gelder, 1992; Keatley, Spinks, and De Gelder, 1994). We return to these exceptions at a later point. For now, the point of these semantic priming studies is to demonstrate that fluent bilinguals are able to take advantage of semantic context, even when it appears in the other language. Few of these studies have examined less fluent bilinguals, making it impossible to assess the prediction that less fluent individuals will fail to demonstrate cross-language priming.[1]

De Groot and Hoeks (1995) used the concreteness effect in translation (De Groot, 1992a; De Groot et al., 1994) as an index of conceptual mediation in Dutch trilinguals who speak English as a relatively fluent second language and French as a nonfluent third language. De Groot (1992a) had previously demonstrated that fluent bilinguals translate concrete words more quickly than abstract words and suggested that the difference in translation performance for concrete and abstract words reflects a difference in the degree of conceptual feature overlap, with concrete translation equivalents sharing a larger number of conceptual features than abstract translation equivalents (see also Taylor, 1976). If access to shared conceptual features and subsequent retrieval of the translation in L2 occurs only when individuals are relatively fluent in both languages, then it should be possible to demonstrate conceptual mediation for the stronger of a trilingual's nonnative languages, but not for the weaker. That is, it should be possible to observe fluency differences within as well as across individuals. This is precisely the result that De Groot and Hoeks (1995) reported: Dutch–English–French trilinguals produced the standard concreteness effect in translation when translating from Dutch to English (L1 to L2) but not when translating from Dutch to French (L1 to L3).

A final source of evidence regarding changes in representation and processing as a function of increasing L2 proficiency comes from training studies that have sought to simulate aspects of L2 learning in the laboratory over a few relatively brief sessions with a small set of materials. Chen (1990) trained a group of native Chinese speakers on a set of French words either by having them learn the translation of the French word in Chinese or by associating the new French word with a picture of the object to which it referred. The study showed that, early in acquisition, the conditions of training produced different results, with superior performance when the modality at test matched the modality at study. Later in training, there were few differences between the groups, the data patterns suggesting concept mediation for both. Concept mediation thus appears possible, at least for a very limited vocabulary, after even short term exposure to second language words.

Kroll and Sankaranarayanan (1996) recently extended Chen's (1990) study by showing that the dependency on modality during early stages of acquisition can be overcome if new second language vocabulary is associated to unique cues, similar to those that might be encountered in an immersion environment. Unusual orientations of objects were used to provide such a cue. Past research (e.g., Palmer, Rosch, and Chase, 1981) has shown that pictures of objects are named more slowly when they are oriented in a noncanonical presentation. If the noncanonical orientation slows not only recognition of the object but also the retrieval of the corresponding concept and name (in L1), then associating a noncanonical view with a new L2 word might effectively inhibit the first language's *claim* to conceptual memory. A group of native English-speaking participants was taught 40 new words in Dutch. Half of the participants learned the Dutch words by associating them to their English translations, and the remaining participants associated the Dutch words to pictures of the objects to which they referred. Half of the pictures were presented in canonical orientation, and half were presented in noncanonical orientation. There were two important results. First, the participants who were trained with pictures were better able to later name the pictures in Dutch and translate words from English to Dutch than the individuals trained with words. The fact that the superiority of picture study held, even when participants were tested on word translation, suggests that the advantage conferred by picture study occurred at a conceptual level. Second, and most interesting, was that learning new Dutch words, by associating them to noncanonical views of objects, produced superior performance in a later test of picture naming and word translation relative to Dutch words learned by association to normally oriented objects. The fact that the advantage for Dutch words associated to noncanonical objects during study was observed in translation (where the perceptual cues were absent) as well as in picture naming provides additional support for Chen's (1990) conclusion that, under some circumstances, it is possible to observe concept mediation early in learning.

The findings we have reviewed suggest that there are changes in bilingual representation and/or processing with increasing expertise and that these different states may simultaneously exist within the very same individual, as the trilingual data suggest. In the next section, we discuss two alternative proposals for the ultimate form of representation in the fluent bilingual. The two proposals, although not mutually exclusive, focus on different aspects of lexical and semantic processing in the bilingual. One, the revised hierarchical model (Kroll and Stewart, 1990, 1994), examines the consequences of the developmental sequence described previously. The other, the distributed conceptual feature model (De Groot, 1992a, 1992b, 1993), focuses on the characteristics of words that may constrain the form of lexical and conceptual representation across languages.

The revised hierarchical model

The research reviewed earlier suggests that second language learners initially access meaning for second language words through the first language and only later become able to conceptually mediate L2 directly (Chen and Leung, 1989; Kroll and Curley, 1988). The shift from reliance on L1 to direct conceptual processing of L2 with increasing fluency may also have the consequence of creating an asymmetry in the strength of lexical-to-conceptual connections between the first and second languages (Kroll, 1993; Kroll and Sholl, 1992; Kroll and Stewart, 1994). Because the second language depends initially on the first language for access to meaning, the lexical-level connections from L2 to L1 will be stronger than the corresponding lexical-level connections from L1 to L2. Because L1 initially holds privileged access to meaning, the strength of the conceptual connections will be stronger for L1 than for L2.

To accommodate these differences in lexical and conceptual representation for a bilingual's two languages, Kroll and Stewart (1990, 1994) proposed a revised hierarchical memory model. The model, shown in Fig. 18.2, depicts the asymmetries

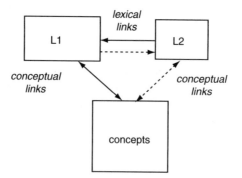

Figure 18.2. The revised hierarchical model (adapted from Kroll and Stewart, 1994). Words in each language (L1 and L2) are interconnected via lexical-level links and conceptual links. The lexical-level links are stronger from L2 to L1 (solid line) than from L1 to L2 (dashed line), but the conceptual links are stronger for L1 (solid line) than for L2 (dashed line).

described earlier. The model assumes that both lexical and conceptual links are active in bilingual memory but that the strength of those links differs as a function of fluency in L2 and the relative dominance of L1 to L2. As shown in the figure, L1 is represented as larger than L2 because the model assumes that, for most bilinguals, even those who are relatively fluent, more words are known in the native language than in the second language. Lexical associations between L2 and L1 are stronger than those from L1 to L2 because that is the direction in which second language learners first acquire the translations of new L2 words. The link between words and concepts, however, is stronger for L1 than for L2. When a person acquires a second language beyond a stage of very early childhood, there is already a very strong link between the first language lexicon and conceptual memory. During early stages of second language learning, second language words are attached to this system primarily by lexical links with the first language. As the individual becomes more proficient in the second language, direct conceptual links are also acquired. However, the lexical connections do not disappear when the conceptual links are established; they appear to remain as viable connections (De Groot, 1992a).

Kroll and Stewart (1994) and Sholl, Sankaranarayanan, and Kroll (1995) tested predictions of the revised model for bilingual translation performance. According to the model, translation from L1 to L2 should be more likely to engage conceptual processing than translation from L2 to L1 because L1 can more readily activate concepts than L2 can. Likewise, L2, by virtue of its initial lexical-level connections to L1, should allow rapid lexical-level translation from L2 to L1 without recourse to meaning. Thus, L2 to L1 translation should be faster than L1 to L2 translation and also less sensitive to the effects of semantic factors. Kroll and Stewart reported support for each of these predictions in an experiment in which fluent Dutch–English bilinguals performed each direction of translation for words in semantically categorized or randomly mixed lists. Words were translated more rapidly and accurately from L2 to L1 than from L1 to L2, and only the L1 to L2 translation task was affected by the semantic context of the list. Other translation studies have reported a similar asymmetry (e.g., Keatley, Spinks, and De Gelder, 1992; Roufca, 1992; Sánchez-Casas, Suarez-Buratti and Igoa, 1992).

Sholl et al. (1995) tested the further prediction that only translation from L1 to L2, the direction of translation hypothesized to be conceptually mediated, would resemble picture naming, a task also believed to require conceptual access (Glaser, 1992; Levelt et al., 1991; Potter and Faulconer, 1975; Vitkovitch and Humphreys, 1991; Wheeldon and Monsell, 1992). Bilingual subjects named pictures in each of their languages during study and translated words in each direction of translation at test. Some of the words at test were repeated concepts that had been named as pictures during study. The results showed that at test L1 to L2 translation was primed by the prior picture-naming task, but L2 to L1 translation was not. These findings lend strong support to the claim that connections between words in a bilingual's two languages and concepts are asymmetric and, in particular, that L2 processing is less likely to engage meaning than L1. The pattern of results also suggests that the translation asymmetry cannot be due entirely to production difficulties in L2. Naming a picture in L1 at study produced significant facilitation in later translation from L1 to L2, despite the absence of a common production at study and test (see also Snodgrass, 1993, for a discussion of this issue).

Other evidence for the revised hierarchical model

A source of converging evidence for the revised hierarchical model comes from the exceptions to the general cross-language semantic priming results described earlier. Many of the past studies of cross-language semantic priming can be criticized on methodological grounds because they included a high proportion of related trials and a long interstimulus interval between prime and target words that may have encouraged subjects to develop expectations for the upcoming targets. The use of long prime-to-target intervals in the bilingual experiments is particularly problematic because, in some of these experiments, participants may have been encouraged to translate the prime and/or target into the same language (see Neely, 1991, for a general discussion of the factors that may exaggerate the magnitude of priming). In a bilingual semantic priming task, if participants can translate, on even a small proportion of trials, then the observed cross-language priming may reflect only the presence of within-language priming in the cross-language conditions.

Recent studies that have carefully controlled the characteristics of the priming paradigm to optimize automatic aspects of processing and minimize the contribution of expectation and strategy have not found cross-language priming under all conditions. For example, using a masked priming paradigm, in which participants are not even necessarily aware of the bilingual nature of the task, De Groot and Nas (1991) found evidence for cross-language semantic priming in Dutch and English only when translation equivalents in the two languages were cognates, sharing lexical form as well as meaning. A cross-language translation priming effect materialized for both cognates and noncognates, although it tended to be smaller for the latter type of words. A recent study by Gollan, Forster, and Frost (1996) showed that masked cross-language translation priming was not restricted to languages that share the same script; for Hebrew and English, there was significant masked priming for both cognate and noncognate translations, but the effect was much larger and more reliable from L1 to L2 than the reverse.

Using the standard priming paradigm but carefully controlling the conditions of presentation, Keatley et al. (1994) reported that, even when bilingual participants are highly fluent in both languages, there are asymmetries in the magnitude of semantic priming. Keatley et al. found priming only from L1 to L2, but not from L2 to L1. Similar asymmetric priming results have been described by Altarriba (1990), Kroll et al. (1992), and Tzelgov and Eben-Ezra (1992).

The observed asymmetries in priming are consistent with the predictions of the revised hierarchical model because L1 words are more likely to activate their respective meanings than L2 words and are thus more effective primes. However, Keatley and De Gelder (1992) have also shown that the cross-language priming effect from L1 to L2 can be eliminated when fluent bilingual participants are forced to speed their responses in a lexical decision task. Under these speeded conditions, Keatley and De Gelder observed semantic priming for within-language conditions only. Cross-language priming occurred only in a condition in which the prime and target were translation equivalents. (See Keatley et al., 1994, for the description of a lexical network model in which conceptual representations are not assumed. This model, like Paivio's, 1971, 1986, dual code model, assumes that cross-language interactions are restricted to lexical associations.)

In a related negative priming paradigm, in which the effects of unattended semantically related flanking words were examined, Fox (1996) found that only L1 words produced cross-language semantic effects on the processing of L2 target words; cross-language semantic effects were not obtained in the L2 to L1 direction. These results are consistent with the predictions of the revised hierarchical model and formally similar to the asymmetries reported earlier in the semantic priming paradigm. However, a further result in the Fox study did not support the predictions of the model. When the unattended words were translations of the target rather than words semantically related to the targets, there were significant effects for both cross-language directions, but they were still larger from L1 to L2 than from L2 to L1. According to the model, L2 words should be *more* likely to activate their respective translations than L1 words, thus, the effect observed with semantically related words should have been reversed for translation equivalents. Similar results have been reported in studies of translation priming (e.g., Altarriba, 1992; Chen and Ng, 1989; Jin, 1990; Keatley et al., 1992): L1 words produce larger translation priming for L2 words than the reverse, although significant translation priming is also found in the L2 to L1 direction.

The problem in interpreting the priming results is that, for bilinguals who are dominant in L1 (which is most of the bilingual population), there will be more information available from an L1 prime than from an L2 prime. Taken together with the fact that, on average, an L1 target will also be recognized more rapidly than an L2 target, it makes sense to expect that L1 will be more effective as a prime but less influenced as a target. That is, L1 words are functionally more frequent than their L2 translation equivalents. Because recognition will be slower for L2 than for L1, it is also more likely that meaning will have been activated by the time the L2 word is identified. The observed asymmetries in priming, with larger effects from L1 to L2 than from L2 to L1, although consistent with the predictions of the revised hierarchical model, may also reflect the limitations of the primed lexical decision paradigm for investigating this issue.

Challenges to the revised hierarchical model

A number of recent papers have challenged the view that translation from L2 to L1 (backward translation) is accomplished via a lexical route. De Groot et al. (1994) used regression methods to determine whether predictor variables related to a word's meaning (e.g., concreteness, context availability, definition accuracy) could account for translation performance in both directions of translation. Their results showed that, indeed, both directions of translation were affected by meaning variables, apparently providing evidence against the strong claim that translation from L2 to L1 is always accomplished lexically. However, some of the correlations between the meaning variables and translation performance were higher for forward translation (from L1 to L2) than for backward translation. The opposite pattern, higher such correlations for backward translation, never occurred. A similar finding was obtained in two recent studies whose primary purpose was to disentangle the effects of word concreteness and context availability in bilingual processing, more specifically, in word translation (Van Hell and De Groot, 1996; cf. the monolingual study of Schwanenflugel, Harnishfeger, and Stowe, 1988). A concreteness effect occurred in both translation directions but was slightly larger in forward translation. These findings support a weak version of the revised hierarchical model, holding that processing the first language is more likely to engage meaning than does processing the second language.[2]

Evidence that might be seen as more damaging to the revised hierarchical model comes from a recent study by La Heij, Kerling, and van der Velden (1996) who, contrary to the predictions of the model, observed semantic context effects in both directions of translation and, if anything, evidence for more semantic involvement in backward than in forward translation. La Heij et al. presented pictures as context along with target words to be translated. In one condition, the pictures depicted an entity belonging to the same category as the referent of the word to be translated (e.g., the word *shark* accompanied by a picture of a whale). In a second condition, the entity depicted by the picture was unrelated to the word's referent. The authors found that both directions of translation were facilitated by the presence of a semantically related context. Furthermore, no translation asymmetry was observed in the size of the context effect, and, in one experiment (Experiment 3), translation from L1 to L2 was faster than translation from L2 to L1. In another experiment (Experiment 4), there was also a hint of this effect, but it did not generalize over subjects.

Because the revised hierarchical model was designed to account for out-of-context translation performance, the La Heij et al. (1996) data are not problematic if one assumes that context provides the semantic support to allow an otherwise weaker L2 to access meaning.[3] The bilinguals who participated in La Heij et al., as, in fact, those in De Groot et al. (1994) and Kroll and Stewart (1994), were drawn from a population of relatively fluent Dutch–English bilinguals capable of reading and speaking at high levels in their L2. The minimal context used in the La Heij et al. study, in the form of a pictured object, might suffice to boost the process of accessing meaning from L2 and, thus, eliminate the asymmetry. The translation asymmetry and the corresponding evidence for lexically mediated processing from L2 to L1 may, therefore, occur only in the absence of context. If this were not the case, then these apparently fluent bilinguals would have great difficulty using their second language under normal conditions that are more contextually rich than most experiments.

Some support for this view comes from Stroop-type translation experiments in which an L2 word is presented for translation, followed after a brief SOA by an L1 distractor word (La Heij et al., 1990; Mazibuko, 1991). According to the revised hierarchical model, no Stroop interference should result from a semantically related L1 distractor word if L2 to L1 translation is lexically mediated. However, both of these studies reported significant semantic interference for semantically related words, suggesting that, in the presence of the L1 context, backward translation is conceptually mediated.

A number of other recent translation studies, however, suggest that not all of the inconsistencies in the results concerning translation direction can be resolved this way. De Groot and Poot (1997) had three groups of Dutch–English bilinguals translate words from Dutch (their L1) to English (their L2) and vice versa. The groups differed in their level of proficiency in English (and in age): One group consisted of university students, drawn from the same population as the participants tested in La Heij et al. (1996), Kroll and Stewart (1994), and De Groot et al. (1994); the second and third groups consisted of secondary-school pupils in the 5th and 3rd years, respectively. The results of that study were, in fact, very similar to those of La Heij et al., even though translation occurred out of context. In the group comparable to those tested in La Heij et al., Kroll and Stewart (1994), and De Groot et al. (1994), no translation asymmetries occurred: Statistically, translation was as fast in the forward direction as in the backward direction (as in De Groot et al, 1994, Experiment 1, and in Van Hell and De Groot, 1996), although, in absolute terms, a nonsignificant benefit was observed for *forward* translation (cf. La Heij et al., Experiment 4). Furthermore, equally large effects of a semantic variable, word concreteness, were obtained in both translation directions. This pattern held for various types of words, for instance, for both cognates and noncognates.

The data patterns for the lower proficiency groups in the study by De Groot and Poot (1997) are even more problematic for the revised hierarchical model. In both groups, the concreteness effect was, statistically, as large in backward translation as in forward translation (and tended to be larger in backward translation). This pattern again held for various types of words, cognates as well as noncognates. Furthermore, now a clear directional asymmetry in RT, opposite to that predicted by the revised hierarchical model, was obtained. For both participant groups, translation RT was considerably slower for backward translation. This latter is not an isolated finding. It has also been reported before for this population of Dutch university students (De Groot et al., 1994, Experiment 2; La Heij et al., 1996, Experiment 3; Swaak, 1992).

Further support for the idea that effects of meaning variables are often immune to translation direction was obtained in a correlational study that included a number of these variables as predictor variables and that employed translation recognition as the test task (De Groot and Comijs, 1995). In this study, the first word of a test stimulus always preceded the second by some hundreds of milliseconds, and the language of the first and second words within the stimuli was varied. The translation-direction manipulation of the common translation (production) task was, thus, mimicked to a certain extent. The meaning variables affected translation-recognition performance in both directions, and to the same extent.

From the effects of semantic manipulations in this latter set of studies, it appears that, at least for Dutch–English bilinguals beyond the very initial stages of English training, translation processes are often, qualitatively, the same in both translation directions: Conceptual memory appears implicated in both directions and to the same extent. At present, it is not at all clear why the data of the studies already discussed, dealing with conceptually very similar issues, do not converge more closely. Of course, albeit conceptually very similar, the studies differ from each other in the ways in which the theoretical questions have been implemented, in terms of the participants, the stimulus materials, the experimental procedure, or a particular combination of these three. The choices made on each of these three dimensions may interact in complex ways, the details of which are not yet understood. That such factors affect performance is, of course, widely known, and, indeed, some indications that they have played a role in the data patterns obtained in the present research area are already available. It will be particularly critical in future research to determine the relations between the conceptual variables that have been examined in these bilingual studies. It may be the case that the semantic organization of a list (the conceptual variable in the Kroll and Stewart, 1994, study), word concreteness (the conceptual variable in many of De Groot and her colleagues' experiments), and semantic context (the conceptual variable in the La Heij et al., 1996, study and in experiments on bilingual semantic priming), though all legitimate semantic variables, may influence different processing loci during translation.

An analysis of the La Heij et al. (1996) study illustrates the manner in which seemingly small methodological differences may have important consequences. La Heij et al. used a procedure in which bilingual participants were first familiarized with the set of pictures to be used as context and with the words to be translated. In addition, the to-be-translated words appeared a number of times during the course of the experiment in different conditions. It is well known that there are repetition priming effects that may affect performance under these conditions (e.g., Scarborough, Cortese, and Scarborough, 1977), at the least producing very fast response latencies. And indeed, the translation RTs in the La Heij et al. study were noticeably fast, relative to other translation studies. However, Sholl et al. (1995) and Kroll, Elsinger, and Tokowicz (1994) have also shown that a single repetition of a concept prior to translation will reverse the translation asymmetry. In these studies, participants named pictures or translated words during a study phase. In a later test phase, they translated words in both directions of translation that included some words that had previously been named during study. It is, therefore, possible that the failure to observe differential effects for the two directions of translation in the La Heij et al. study is due to the effects of repeating concepts across conditions. The absence of an out-of-context condition in that study also makes it impossible to know whether the high frequency words used in those experiments would have produced a translation asymmetry.

As to the choice of participants and the role of choice in translation performance, a study by Janine Swaak, performed in part in the laboratories of both of the present authors, is informative (Swaak, 1993). In one of our laboratories, she tested Spanish–English bilinguals; in the other, she tested Dutch–English bilinguals. The task she used in both experiments of the study was translation recognition, in both directions, and with a clear interval (500 milliseconds) between the first and second word in each translation pair. The procedural details of the experiment that she performed first (Spanish–English) and the characteristics of its stimulus materials were imitated as closely as possible in the second experiment. An attempt was made to match the L2 proficiency levels of the participants in the two experiments, but the data (both RT and percent errors) clearly suggested that this attempt had failed. The L2 proficiency level of the Dutch–English bilinguals turned out to be higher than that of the Spanish–English bilinguals. Particularly interesting for our present purposes is that the data patterns of the two groups were qualitatively different. To mention a few differences: The lower proficiency group showed the regular concreteness effect in forward translation but the reverse effect (faster responses to abstract words) in backward translation, whereas the higher proficiency group showed equally large concreteness effects in both translation directions (with, in both cases, the concrete words producing the fastest responses); the main effect of concreteness was not reliable in the lower proficiency group, but it was in the higher proficiency group; there were some signs that the concreteness effect in forward direction in the lower proficiency group depended on word type (cognates showed a much smaller effect than noncognates), whereas the effect in the higher proficiency group was much more even across the various word types.

Swaak's (1993) data thus suggest that the choice of participants may influence the pattern of results in these studies. But other factors, for instance those just mentioned, are likely to play a role, too. Perhaps the strongest argument that other factors must be relevant as well is that Kroll and Stewart (1994), in the study that gave rise to the revision of the original hierarchical model, tested subjects from the same population of Dutch–English bilinguals used by La Heij et al. (1996), De Groot et al. (1994), and De Groot and Poot (1997; their highest proficiency group). Yet, even though Kroll and Stewart obtained support for the strong version of the model (only involvement of conceptual memory in forward translation), De Groot et al.'s (1994) data suggest a slightly larger involvement of conceptual memory in forward than in backward translation, and the remaining two studies obtained support for the idea of qualitatively similar translation in the two directions, that is, for a *symmetrical* model.[4]

Although the evidence reviewed raises a question as to whether the asymmetry at the center of the revised hierarchical model can be generalized beyond limited conditions, some very recent neuroimaging evidence (Klein, Milner, Zatorre, Meyer, and Evans, 1995) supports the findings of an asymmetry in the direction predicted by model. It will remain to be determined which conditions constrain the form and direction of the asymmetries predicted by the revised hierarchical model for bilinguals at different stages of L2 proficiency. If bilinguals are capable of accessing conceptual memory equally well for both of their languages, once they are beyond an early stage of L2 acquisition, or for some subset of materials, as some of the evidence just reviewed suggests, then an important focus in this area of research will concern the form of concepts and modeling of activation of meaning for words in different languages. The next model we consider, the conceptual feature model, addresses this issue.

The conceptual feature model

An alternative approach to modeling the representation of words and concepts in bilingual memory is to focus on those aspects of words that appear to be associated with lexical or conceptual processing. De Groot (1992a, 1992b, 1993; De Groot et al., 1994) has developed this approach by examining the effects of a host of variables thought to reflect lexical and conceptual levels of processing in bilingual performance in translation production and translation recognition (see also Jin, 1990, and Sánchez-Casas, Davis and García-Albea, 1992, for related studies). Two central findings in this work are that concrete words and cognates are translated faster than abstract words and noncognates. To accommodate these effects, De Groot (1992b) proposed a conceptual feature model in which words in each of the bilingual's two languages activate conceptual features that are assumed to be distributed, such that particular concepts correspond to sets of activated features (see Taylor and Taylor, 1990 for a similar view on bilingual memory representation, and Masson, 1991, for a similar view on monolingual memory representation). The model, shown in Fig. 18.3, provides an account for the observed

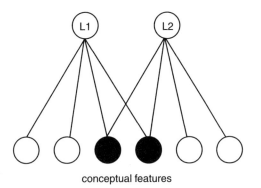

conceptual features

Figure 18.3. The distributed conceptual feature model (adapted from De Groot, 1992b).

concreteness effects in translation and other bilingual processing tasks. Because concrete words refer to perceptual referents that are, for the most part, shared across languages, they will access similar or identical subsets of conceptual features, regardless of the language in which they are presented. Concrete words can be thought to possess true, or close, translation equivalents across languages. In contrast, abstract words that may be more dependent on context for their interpretation (Schwanenflugel et al., 1988; Schwanenflugel and Shoben, 1983) are more likely to differ across languages in that they share fewer conceptual features than do concrete words. In this respect, abstract words may not possess close translation equivalents across languages, but translations that are only roughly similar. If the process of translation is conceptually mediated (e.g., De Groot and Poot, 1997; La Heij et al., 1996; Potter et al., 1984), then access to shared conceptual information will be more available for concrete than for abstract words. Additional support for the view that conceptual overlap is the basis of shared meaning across languages comes from a recent study that demonstrated that semantic similarity was more critical than association value in producing cross-language priming under masked conditions (Williams, 1994).

De Groot (1992a, 1992b, 1993) proposed a similar explanation to account for the advantage of cognates in translation. Superficially, it might seem that cognate words would be translated more rapidly than noncognate words because translation might be able to occur at a lexical level. Some evidence for this claim is provided by a translation recognition study that showed that the degree of meaning overlap between translation equivalents affected performance for noncognates but not for cognates (Sánchez-Casas, Suárez-Buratti, and Igoa, 1992). Indeed, it does make sense to think that the translation of cognates might be influenced more by lexical than by conceptual factors. However, in the studies by De Groot and her colleagues described previously, cognate translations were still shown to be influenced by the concreteness of the target words, a variable thought to reflect conceptual rather than lexical processing. And in the Kroll and Stewart (1994) study, cognates were translated more quickly than noncognates, but a translation asymmetry was observed in both cases, and category interference, a reflection of semantic processing, was present for cognates as well as noncognates in forward translation. These results suggest that cognates engage conceptual processes and that some part of the facilitation for cognate translation may be attributable to a higher level of conceptual feature overlap across translation equivalents for cognates than for noncognates. In some languages, cognates tend to be words that are borrows or loans from the other language, in which case the translations would share very close conceptual as well as lexical form.

Extensions of the conceptual feature model

At present, the proposed conceptual feature model is neutral on the issue of whether, in addition to facilitating access to translation equivalents, the overlapping features assume special importance in bilingual language processing. It is unclear as to whether the conceptual features represent units whose joint activation determines conceptual overlap in a purely quantitative sense or whether, within the conceptual representation, there are differences in the weights assigned to particular features and corresponding assumptions made about the degree of intercorrelation between features. For example, if one were to distinguish defining and characteristic features, as others have, in modeling semantic memory (e.g., Smith, Shoben, and Rips, 1974), the impact of which particular features overlap for a given translation pair might be significant. Similarly, the observed differences in translation for concrete and abstract words may be understood in terms of differential representation of perceptual features for concrete and abstract words. A recent neuropsychological study by Breedin, Saffran, and Coslett (1994) described a patient who showed a reversal of the normal concreteness effect, such that his performance was superior for abstract concepts. Breedin et al. argued that a specific impairment to concrete concepts reflected damage to a distinctly perceptual component of the semantic representation. If concrete translation equivalents across languages activate a large pool of shared semantic features, it is possible that overlapping perceptual features are the source of their meaning similarity.

A similar idea was described by McRae, De Sa, and Seidenberg (1993), who proposed that the conceptual features of exemplars of animate categories are more highly correlated or densely represented than the features of exemplars of inanimate categories. Sholl (1995) tested the McRae et al. proposal by examining animacy effects in bilingual picture naming and translation tasks. The interesting result, for the purpose of the present discussion, is that animacy had a clear effect on translation: Animate concepts were translated more rapidly than inanimate concepts. Because both the animate and inanimate concepts were concrete nouns, this result might suggest that concreteness alone does not determine the degree of conceptual overlap across languages. However, it is also possible that any variable that reflects access to conceptual memory will produce a corresponding effect in translation. Although reports by bilinguals that it is often difficult to come up with an exact translation for a given word are consistent with the idea of degrees of overlap among conceptual features, the available empirical results do not yet allow us to readily distinguish between alternative models.

A related focus in the current literature on bilingual word recognition concerns the issue of whether shared lexical-level units are distributed in a manner analogous to the conceptual features of the De Groot (1992a, 1992b, 1993) model. Recent work by Grainger (1993; Grainger and Dijkstra, 1992) suggests that, for languages that share aspects of lexical form, there may be parallel activation of shared lexical units. Up to this point in the discussion, we have assumed that word forms in a bilingual's two languages are stored separately because a fair amount of research on the bilingual lexicon supports that assumption (Brown, Sharma, and Kirsner, 1984; Gerard and Scarborough, 1989; Kirsner et al., 1984; Scarborough, Gerard, and Cortese, 1984). However, it may be useful to consider how a model might incorporate distributed features at both the lexical and conceptual levels. The model shown in Fig. 18.4 extends the notion of distributed conceptual features to a lexical level of distributed features. The general architecture of this model resembles models proposed by Dell and O'Seaghdha (1992) and Levelt et al. (1991) for speech production. (Note that only one layer of lexical features is depicted, but one could easily assume a multilayered arrangement corresponding to different aspects of lexical form.) In addition to the language-independent (shared) lexical- and conceptual-feature levels, a language-specific lemma level is proposed. We assume that a lemma-type representation (e.g., Bock and Levelt, 1994; Kempen and Huijbers, 1983; Levelt, 1989; Roelofs, 1992) includes the lexical entry itself and mediates between activation of lexical and conceptual features and higher level language processes. Although there is some disagreement about the

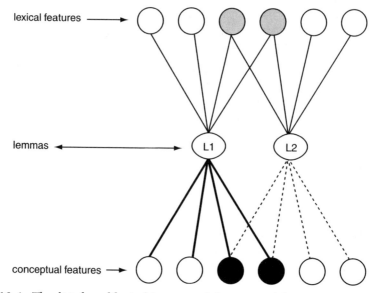

Figure 18.4. The distributed lexical/conceptual feature model. Words in each language can share aspects of word form (lexical features) and/or aspects of meaning (conceptual features). Language-specific lemmas form the interconnection between the lexical-conceptual mappings to and from syntax.

exact nature of the lemma representation, we will make only the general assumption that the lemma includes some syntactic and semantic information.

As we noted at the beginning of this chapter, much of the research on bilingual representation (other than the work on bilingual speech production) has ignored the debate on lemma-level representation, presumably because the out-of-context nature of the tasks that have been used to test these models has not required a commitment to the semantic and syntactic constraints that operate during actual sentence processing. However, bilingual models also have an additional problem that complicates these issues beyond the monolingual case. In addition to all of the lexical, semantic, and syntactic factors that must be specified, the bilingual's language mode varies, such that, at any given moment, he or she may speak and comprehend sentences in one, or the other, or both languages. The interactive models that have been proposed for bilingual language processing (e.g., the Bilingual Interactive Activation model (BIA) of Grainger and Dijkstra, 1992) solve this problem in different ways, with or without the inclusion of language-specific language nodes (see also Poulisse, 1993 and De Bot and Schreuder, 1993, for models of bilingual production that differ in the level at which language is specified).

In the present scheme, we assume that lemmas are not necessarily a form of symbolic representation that function as an interface between the lexical and conceptual features on one hand, and semantic or syntactic constraints on the other, but rather a means to represent the patterns of activation between word forms and meanings. In the absence of context, the lemma level may reflect only these form/meaning mappings. In the presence of context, the lemma may also reflect syntactic-level processes that selectively weight the activation of lexical and conceptual features. The assumption of a language-specific lemma level in the present model may allow the bilingual's two languages to be influenced by one another and to share access to a common pool of lexical and conceptual features but, at the same time, enable functional autonomy when only one language is active. Furthermore, this arrangement can distinguish the situation in which an individual is acquiring new vocabulary in L1 from the case in which the new vocabulary is associated with a new language; the same set of lexical and conceptual features may be activated in each case, but the mapping between these levels and the lemma level will differ, and, hence, the conditions under which they are activated will differ.

According to the model shown in Fig. 18.4, the level of facilitation and/or interference observed across languages will be a function of not only the degree of feature overlap, as the earlier distributed models assumed, but, more importantly, a function of the degree to which there are consistent mappings from word forms to meanings within and across languages. There is some support for this view in the literature on bilingual word recognition and lexical access. For example, Grainger and Beauvillain (1987) reported that in tasks such as bilingual lexical decision, there are costs associated with language mixtures, reflected by increased processing time. However, these costs are not observed when the words in each language are orthographically unique to that language. A similar result has been reported by Li (1996) for spoken word recognition in code-switched sentences. These findings show that it is not the language mixture per se that incurs a processing cost, but the extent to which word forms activate both languages simultaneously. When lexical forms uniquely specify one language or the other, it is possible to consistently map lexical units to meaning via one language alone.

The model may also be able to explain some previously puzzling results concerning the apparent language specificity of lexical representations between languages. Data from tasks such as cross-language repetition (= translation) priming have, for the most part, failed to observe cross-language priming. The reasonable conclusion, on the basis of these results, is that the two languages are represented separately at the lexical level. However, other studies (e.g., Altenberg and Cairns, 1983; Grainger and Dijkstra, 1992; Nas, 1983) have demonstrated lexical-level influences from one language to the other, creating difficulty for this claim. By distinguishing a level of lexical features from the lemma level, we can account for these apparently discrepant results. Because the lemma level is sensitive to syntactic constraints as well as to the mapping between lexical and conceptual features, it will necessarily be language specific. Tasks in which only a single language is presented at a time (as in most of the repetition priming studies that have failed to find cross-language priming), or in which the dominant language is the focus of attention, will likely be associated with relatively high levels of activation for the lemma associated with that language. Tasks in which both languages are simultaneously active, or in which the weaker of the two languages is emphasized, will give rise to activation of both lemmas and corresponding activation of lexical features across languages. In addition, when tasks require conceptual processing, the resulting lexicalization processes will typically favor L1, producing an increase in the likelihood of cross-language influence from L1 to L2.

Additional evidence for the importance of consistent mapping of lexical and conceptual features comes from a study in which fluent Spanish–English bilinguals read high and low constraint English sentences that contained a high or low frequency target word in English or Spanish (Altarriba, Kroll, Sholl, and Rayner, 1996). In one experiment,

Altarriba et al. monitored eye movements while bilinguals read the sentences, and, in another experiment, they measured naming latencies for the English and Spanish target words. When the sentence and the target word appeared in the same language, they found the standard pattern of results associated with sentence constraint and word frequency: Eye fixations were briefer and naming latencies shorter for highly constrained sentences and high frequency targets. However, when a Spanish target appeared in an English sentence, the pattern of results was quite different, such that high frequency target words were more difficult to process than low frequency target words in highly constrained sentences. Although the conceptual features per se may have been similar for the Spanish and English target words (they were all concrete nouns), the combination of high constraint, coupled with the priming of lexical features associated with the predicted English word in an otherwise English sentence, may have served to interfere with recognition of the Spanish word. Interestingly, the same effect did not hold when the Spanish word was low frequency, suggesting, again, that what is critical is the mapping process and not simply activation of each level independently.

How can the distributed lexical/conceptual feature model shown in Fig. 18.4 account for the asymmetries handled within the revised hierarchical model? We assume that the weaker mappings from form to meanings in L2 in early stages of second language acquisition, together with less developed knowledge of L2 syntax, will create a pattern of processing that will functionally mirror the asymmetry described by the revised hierarchical model. Studies of transfer at the lexical and syntactic levels suggest that, initially, L2 is processed as if it were L1, to the extent that there are some shared cues in the two languages (Durgunoglu and Hancin, 1992). Like the competition model, the distributed feature model predicts that performance should be best when it is possible to form consistent mappings between levels for a given language. An interesting implication of this view is that it provides a theoretical basis on which to consider the effects of context of acquisition. Immersion learning, widely held to provide a superior context for L2 acquisition, may provide the unique cues for L2 that allow consistent mappings to form. In contrast, classroom learning may foster continued reliance on L1.

Conclusions

In this chapter, we reviewed recent evidence concerning the relations between lexical and conceptual memory in the second language learner and the more fluent bilingual. Although theory development on this topic is still at an early stage, we believe that recent efforts toward conceptualizing the mapping of word forms to meanings in two languages as a distributed architecture will provide a productive way to understand the mapping problem itself and the dynamic changes it undergoes with increasing proficiency in the second language. It holds the additional promise of providing a framework within which performance on out-of-context bilingual tasks, such as translation, picture naming, and single word priming, may be related to bilingual performance in contexts that are linguistically complex and more representative of second language use. In future research, we hope to explore the implications of this perspective.

Acknowledgments

The writing of this chapter was supported in part by NSF Grant SBR-9496344 to Judith F. Kroll. We thank David Rosenbaum for helpful comments on an earlier version of the manuscript.

Notes

1   An exception is a sentence priming study by Kroll and Borning (1987) in which sentence fragments in English were completed by target words in English or Spanish that rendered the sentences meaningful or not. Fluent English–Spanish bilinguals were faster to make lexical decisions for related than for unrelated target words, regardless of the language of the target. Less fluent bilinguals showed effects of target relatedness only for English targets, suggesting that they were unable to conceptually mediate Spanish.

2   In the De Groot et al. (1994) study, the direction of translation was manipulated between participants, whereas, in the Kroll and Stewart (1994) study, it was manipulated within participants. Because studies of bilingual language processing suggest that mixing languages sometimes incurs a processing cost, particularly for the weaker language, it may be that backward translation is more likely to be conceptually mediated in the absence of forward translation trials. It is unlikely that this is the only factor accounting for the observed differences, however, because a recent study by De Groot and Poot (1997) found concreteness effects in both directions of translation, even though direction was manipulated within participants.

3   This explanation is analogous to the context availability account of concreteness effects offered by Schwanenflugel and Shoben (1983) and Schwanenflugel, Harnishfeger; and Stowe (1988). According to the context availability model, abstract words have a conceptual representation that is more diffuse and, therefore, more dependent on context. In comparison, concrete words are hypothesized to have a more unitary representation that is less dependent on the presence of context. The empirical support for this proposal comes from the demonstration (Schwanenflugel et al., 1988; Schwanenflugel and Shoben, 1983) that concreteness effects disappear following context.

4   Support for the view that the particular choice of stimulus materials can also affect the data pattern is provided by a reanalysis of a subset of the data of De Groot et al. (1994), the study that provided support for a weak version of the asymmetry model (a slightly larger influence of meaning variables in forward than in backward translation). All stimulus words of De Groot and Poot (1997), the study that showed no trace of an asymmetry, had been among the much larger set of stimulus materials in the study by De Groot et al. It would be revealing to see whether the data associated with exactly this stimulus set, extracted from the larger data set of De Groot et al., would show a pattern of results similar to that of De Groot and Poot, that is, no asymmetry. If so, the small asymmetries observed in De Groot et al. would have to have been due to specific characteristics of the remaining stimulus materials, whatever these characteristics may be. Indeed, the relevant reanalysis of the subset of the earlier data set showed no trace of the asymmetries predicted by the revised hierarchical model: Forward translation was not slower than backward translation (in fact, it was faster), and the concreteness effect was equally large in forward and backward translation.

Source: Kroll, Judith and de Groot, Annette (1997) Lexical and conceptual memory in the bilingual: mapping form to meaning in two languages. In Annette de Groot and Judith Kroll (eds)

Tutorials in Bilingualism: Psycholinguistic perspectives, Mahwah, NJ: Lawrence Erlbaum, pp. 169–200, by permission of the authors and Lawrence Erlbaum Associates.

Postscript

We wrote this chapter ten years ago with the goal of summarizing what we then knew about how bilingual memory is organized to allow both proficient bilinguals and second language learners to map words to their corresponding concepts in each language. A focus in the work in each of our research groups has been on how bilinguals are able to translate from one language to the other and how the process of translation reveals the architecture of the bilingual lexicon. The questions that initially defined this investigation were structural. Does the bilingual have one or more representations at both the lexical and the conceptual level? To what extent are concepts shared across the bilingual's two languages? Do the mappings between words and concepts in the two languages change as individuals acquire greater skill in the second language?

In the decade since our chapter appeared, a great deal of research has been conducted on the bilingual lexicon. The more recent work has focused not only on representation but also on access. A particular concern is how activity of information associated with each language is initiated in both comprehension and production (e.g., Dijkstra and van Heuven, 2002; Kroll, Sumutka, and Schwartz, 2005). The recent studies provide overwhelming evidence to suggest that, even when bilinguals read, listen, and speak in one language only, the other language is active to some degree (e.g., Costa, 2005; de Groot, Delmaar, and Lupker, 2000; Jared and Kroll, 2001; Marian and Spivey, 2003). How that activity is modulated to permit selection of the intended language is a problem that has been hypothesized to engage attentional control mechanisms that effectively inhibit the unintended language (e.g., Green, 1998a). Understanding the cognitive consequences associated with the acquisition of these control mechanisms and identifying the manner in which they influence processing in simple tasks, such as speaking the name of a word in one language or the other, and in complex cross-language tasks, such as simultaneous translation and interpretation, are questions that frame the current research agenda (e.g., Bialystok, 2005; Christoffels and de Groot, 2005).

What are the implications of the current research on parallel activation of the bilingual's two languages for the lexical-conceptual feature model of form-meaning mapping presented in our 1997 chapter? One of the controversies that we discussed in the chapter and that has continued in the subsequent literature concerns the question of how early in second language acquisition learners are able to engage conceptual processes directly. We believe that a straightforward answer to this question has not been available because the point at which learners are able to utilize conceptual information in the L2 depends on the way in which conceptual information is used in particular tasks, the type of conceptual information available, and the context of learning. The same learner may have the ability to understand the meaning of L2 words in comprehension tasks but may not be able to translate into the L2 (e.g., Sunderman and Kroll, 2006; Kroll, Michael, Tokowicz, and Dufour, 2002), may be able to acquire and process concrete words and cognates more easily than abstract words and noncognates (e.g., de Groot, 1993; de Groot and Keijzer, 2000), and may be more likely to process words conceptually when immersed in the L2 than not (e.g., Linck and Kroll, 2005). A comprehensive model of how the linkages between form and meaning are modulated with increasing skill in the L2 and under different circumstances is only beginning to emerge from the current research.

Perhaps the most critical aspect of the model proposed in our 1997 chapter was the idea that, at the levels of both lexical form and concepts, the representations are distributed, without a clear separation across languages. Word forms and meanings may be computed differently in the L1 and L2 to give rise to distinct lexical items and concepts, but the pool of orthographic, phonological, and semantic features that are sampled in the computation of lexical and conceptual representations is fundamentally shared across languages. In the recent literature on bilingual word recognition, this proposal has been developed and articulated most clearly by the work of Ton Dijkstra and his colleagues (e.g., Dijkstra and van Heuven, 1998, 2002), who have proposed an integrated bilingual lexicon, first in the bilingual interactive activation (BIA) model, which has been implemented as a computer simulation, and then in the updated BIA+ model. In brief, the idea is that during word recognition there is a data-driven process whereby all shared information across words in the bilingual's two languages is activated. The activated information competes and is hypothesized to be resolved by a later process that takes into account the expectations and context in which the words have been read. Related proposals have been developed for production (e.g., Costa, 2005; Hermans, Bongaerts, de Bot, and Schreuder, 1998), although the conceptually driven nature of production changes the form in which cross-language competition is manifest and the way in which it is resolved.

If the bilingual lexicon is not segregated by language, then a number of additional problems require attention. Among these, there is the question of whether there is similar cross-language activation for bilinguals who speak and read two languages that do not share the same script. The evidence regarding cross-language activation in different-script languages is only beginning to emerge, but the available findings suggest a remarkable degree of parallel activation even in the face of dramatic language differences (e.g., Gollan, Forster, and Frost (1997) for Hebrew-English bilinguals; Hoshino and Kroll (2005) for Japanese-English bilinguals; Jiang (1999) for Chinese-English bilinguals). If cross-language activation is not reduced or eliminated by script differences in out-of-context word recognition and production, then we might expect that a richer sentence context might be required. Quite counterintuitively, the few recent studies that have investigated this issue in sentence context (e.g., Schwartz and Kroll, 2006; Van Hell, 1998) suggest that sentence context per se does not eliminate the activity of the unintended language. Only when the sentence constrains the meaning of the target word is the activation of the unintended language reduced.

A complete understanding of how bilinguals negotiate the competition across their two languages is a topic that is now being actively pursued in many laboratories, not only at the level of the lexicon but also at the level of the syntax and phonology. We believe that this work demonstrates the richness of bilingualism, not only as a pursuit on its own, but also as a model for the way in which cognitive systems develop and interact.

Judith F. Kroll, PhD, is Liberal Arts Research Professor of Psychology and Linguistics at Pennsylvania State University, USA. jfk7@psu.edu

Annette M.B. de Groot, PhD, is Professor of Experimental Psycholinguistics, University of Amsterdam, the Netherlands. A.M.B.deGroot@uva.nl

Chapter 19

The bilingual's language modes[1]

FRANÇOIS GROSJEAN

Bilinguals who have reflected on their bilingualism will often report that they change their way of speaking when they are with monolinguals and when they are with bilinguals. Whereas they avoid using their other language with the former, they may call on it for a word or a sentence with the latter or even change over to it completely. In addition, bilinguals will also report that, as listeners, they are sometimes taken by surprise when they are spoken to in a language that they did not expect. Although these reports are quite anecdotal, they do point to an important phenomenon, language mode, which researchers have been alluding to over the years. For example, Weinreich (1966) writes that when speaking to a monolingual, the bilingual is subject to inter-locutory constraint which requires that he or she limit interferences (Weinreich uses this as a cover term for any element of the other language) but when speaking to another bilingual, there is hardly any limit to interferences; forms can be transferred freely from one language to the other and often used in an unadapted way. A few years later, Hasselmo (1970) refers to three sets of "norms" or "modes of speaking" among Swedish–English bilinguals in the United States: English only for contact with English monolinguals, American Swedish with some bilinguals (the main language used is Swedish), and Swedish American with other bilinguals (here the main language is English). In the latter two cases, code-switching can take place in the other language. The author also notes that there exists two extremes in the behavior of certain bilinguals, one extreme involves minimal and the other maximal code-switching. A couple of years later, Clyne (1972) talks of three communication possibilities in bilingual discourse: in the first, both codes are used by both speakers; in the second, each one uses a different code but the two understand both codes; and, in the third, only one of the two speakers uses and understands both codes whereas the other speaker is monolingual in one of the codes. Finally, Baetens Beardsmore (1982) echoes these views when he writes that bilinguals in communication with other bilinguals may feel free to use both of their language repertoires. However, the same bilingual speakers in conversation with monoglots may not feel the same liberty and may well attempt to maximize alignment on monoglot norms by consciously reducing any formal "interference" features to a minimum.

What is clear from all of this is that, at any given point in time and based on numerous psychosocial and linguistic factors, the bilingual has to decide, usually quite unconsciously, which language to use and how much of the other language is needed – from not at all to a lot. If the other language is not needed, then it will not be called upon or, in neural modeling terms, activated. If on the other hand it is needed, then it will be activated but its activation level will be lower than that of the main language chosen. The state of activation of the bilingual's languages and language processing mechanisms, at a given point in time, has been called the language mode. Over the years, and in a number of publications, I have developed this concept. Already in Grosjean (1982: chapter 6), the bilingual's language behavior was presented in two different contexts: when the bilingual is speaking to a monolingual and when he or she is speaking to a bilingual. The notion of a situational continuum ranging from a mono-lingual to a bilingual speech mode was presented in Grosjean (1985). In the monolingual speech mode, the bilingual deactivates one language (but never totally) and in the bilingual mode, the bilingual speaker chooses a base language, activates the other lan-guage and calls on it from time to time in the form of code-switches and borrowings. The notion of intermediate modes and of dynamic interferences was presented in Grosjean (1989); the latter were defined as those deviations from the language being spoken due to the involuntary influence of the other deactivated language. The expression "language mode" replaced "speech mode" in Grosjean (1994) so as to be able to encompass spoken language, written language as well as sign language, and the current two-dimensional representation of the base language and the language mode was introduced in Grosjean (1997) as was the notion that language mode corresponds to various levels of activation of the two languages. Finally, in Grosjean (1998) perception was taken into account, and the many problems that arise from not controlling the language mode sufficiently in bilingualism research were discussed.

Researchers in bilingualism will need to take into account language mode for a number of reasons: it has received relatively little attention in bilingualism research; it gives a truer reflection of how bilinguals process their two languages, separately or together; it helps us understand data obtained from various bilingual populations; it can partly account for problematic or ambiguous findings relating to such topics as language representation and processing, interference, code-switching, language mixing in bilingual children, bilingual aphasics, etc.; and, finally, it is invariably present in bilingualism research as an independent, control or confounding variable and hence needs to be heeded at all times.

In this chapter, language mode will be described, the factors that influence it will be spelled out, and the impact it has on language behavior will be examined. Next, existing evidence for the bilingual's language modes in language production, language per-ception, language acquisition and language pathology will be described. Language mode as a confounding variable will then be evoked and suggestions for controlling it will be proposed. Finally, future research topics related to language mode such as assessment, processing mechanisms, highly language dominant bilinguals and modeling will be considered.

1 Language mode

Description

Language mode is the state of activation of the bilingual's languages and language processing mechanisms at a given point in time. Given that activation is a continuous variable ranging from no activation to total activation and that two languages are concerned,[2] language mode is best visualized in a two dimensional representation such as that in Figure 19.1. The bilingual's languages (A and B) are depicted on the vertical axis by a square located in the top and bottom parts of the figure, their level of activation is represented by the degree of darkness of the square (black for a highly active language and white for a deactivated language) and the ensuing language mode is depicted by the position of the two squares (linked by a discontinuous line) on the horizontal axis which ranges from a monolingual mode to a bilingual mode. Three hypothetical positions are presented in the figure, numbered 1 to 3. In all positions it is language A that is the most active (it is the base language, i.e. the main language being produced or perceived at a particular point in time) and it is language B that is activated to lesser degrees. In position 1, language B is only very slightly active, and hence the bilingual is said to be at, or close to, a monolingual language mode. In position 2, language B is a bit more active and the bilingual is said to be in an intermediate mode. And in position 3, language B is highly active (but not as active as the base language) and the bilingual is said to be in a bilingual language mode. Note that in all three positions, the base language (language A) is fully active as it is the language that governs language processing. Examples taken from production and perception will illustrate these three positions on the continuum. As concerns production, bilingual speakers will usually be in a monolingual mode when they are interacting with monolinguals (speakers of language A in Figure 19.1) with

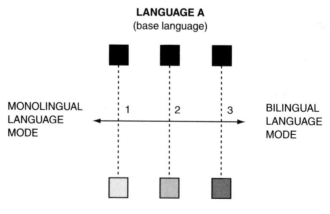

Figure 19.1 Visual representation of the language mode continuum. The bilingual's positions on the continuum are represented by the discontinuous vertical lines and the level of language activation by the degree of darkness of the squares (black is active and white is inactive). This figure first appeared in F. Grosjean (1998) Studying bilinguals: methodological and conceptual issues. *Bilingualism: Language and cognition* 1 (2): 131–49. It is reprinted with the permission of Cambridge University Press.

whom they simply cannot use their other language (language B). When they are in this kind of situation, they deactivate their other language (most often unconsciously) so that it is not produced and does not lead to miscommunication. Speakers will be in an intermediate position (such as position 2) when, for example, the interlocutor knows the other language but either is not very proficient in it or does not like to mix languages. In this case, the speaker's other language (language B in the figure) will only be partly activated. And speakers will be in bilingual mode (position 3) when they are interacting with other bilinguals who share their two languages and with whom they feel comfortable mixing languages. In this case, both languages are active but one language (language B in the figure) is slightly less active than the other language (language A) as it is not currently the main language of processing. The same applies to bilingual listeners. In position 1, for example, a bilingual may be listening to a monolingual who is using language A and who simply does not know language B. In position 2, the same person may be listening to another bilingual who very rarely code-switches and borrows from the other language, and in position 3, the listener may be listening to mixed language being produced by his or her bilingual interlocutor.[3]

Language mode concerns the level of activation of two languages, one of which is the base language, and hence two factors underlie the concept. The first is the base language chosen (language A in the above figure) and the second is the comparative level of activation of the two languages (from very different in the monolingual mode to quite similar in the bilingual mode). As these two factors are usually independent of one another (for possible exceptions, see section 4), there can be a change in one without a change in the other. Thus, the base language can be changed but not the comparative level of activation of the two languages (e.g. a bilingual can change the base language from A to B but remain in a bilingual mode). Similarly, there can be a change in the comparative level of activation of the two languages without a change in base language (e.g. when a bilingual goes from a bilingual to a monolingual mode but stays in the same base language). Since these two factors are always present, it is crucial to state both when reporting the bilingual's language mode. Thus, for example, a French–English bilingual speaking French to a French monolingual is in a "French monolingual mode" (French is the base language and the other language, English, is deactivated as the mode is monolingual). The same bilingual speaking English to an English monolingual is in an "English monolingual mode". If this person meets another French–English bilingual and they choose to speak French together and code-switch into English from time to time, then both are in a "French bilingual mode". Of course, if for some reason the base language were to change (because of a change of topic, for example), then they would be in an "English bilingual mode", etc. Saying that a bilingual is in an English language mode leaves totally open whether the mode is monolingual or bilingual. It should be noted that the expressions, "language set", "language context" and even "language mode" have been used in the literature to refer to the base language the bilingual is using (or listening to) but they do not tell us anything about the comparative level of activation of the bilingual's two languages (for use of such terminology, see for example, Caramazza, Yeni-Komshian, Zurif and Carbone, 1973; Elman, Diehl and Buchwald, 1977; Beauvillain and Grainger, 1987, etc.).

Factors that influence language mode

Any number of factors can help position a bilingual speaker or listener at a particular point on the language mode continuum, that is, set the activation level of the bilingual's languages and language processing mechanisms. Among these we find the participant(s), that is the person(s) being spoken or listened to (this includes such factors as language proficiency, language mixing habits and attitudes, usual mode of interaction, kinship relation, socioeconomic status, etc.), the situation (physical location, presence of mono-linguals, degree of formality and of intimacy), the form and content of the message being uttered or listened to (language used, topic, type of vocabulary needed, amount of mixed language), the function of the language act (to communicate information, to request something, to create a social distance between the speakers, to exclude some-one, to take part in an experiment, etc.) and specific research factors (the aims of the study taking place [are they known or not?], the type and organization of the stimuli, the task used, etc.). Thus, a monolingual mode will arise when the interlocutor or the situation is monolingual and/or other factors require that only one language be spoken to the exclusion of the other. This is the case, for example, when a bilingual adult or child is speaking with, or listening to, a monolingual family member or friend, or when a bilingual aphasic is speaking to a monolingual examiner, etc. Of course, no physical interactant need be present for a bilingual to be in a monolingual mode. If a bilingual is reading a book written in a particular language, watching a TV program in just one language or, more experimentally, taking part in a study in which only one language is used and where there is absolutely no indication that the other language is needed (but see below for the very real difficulty of creating this situation), then the bilingual is probably in a monolingual mode. The same factors apply for any other position on the continuum. Thus, if two bilinguals who share the same languages and who feel comfortable mixing languages, are interacting with one another, there is a fair chance that they will be in a bilingual mode. This will be reinforced if, for example, the topic being dealt with is one that cannot be covered without having recourse to the other language in the form of code-switches and borrowings. A bilingual mode will also arise when a bilingual child is interacting with a bilingual parent (or adult), when a bilingual is simply listening to a conversation which contains elements of the other language or, more experimentally, when the study concerns bilingualism, the stimuli come from both languages and the task asked of the participants requires processing in the two languages. As for intermediate positions on the continuum, they will be reached by different combinations of the above factors. If the bilingual's interlocutor is not very proficient in the other language (but still knows it a bit), if he or she does not like to mix languages, if the topic has to be covered in the base language but the other language is needed from time to time (e.g. in the case of a bilingual child speaking one language to a bilingual researcher about a topic usually talked about in the other language), if the situation is more formal, if only a few stimuli in an experiment are similar in the two languages (e.g. cross-language homographs, cognates), etc., then we can expect an intermediate language mode. Movement along the continuum, which can happen at any given point in time depending on the factors mentioned above, is usually an unconscious behavior that takes place smoothly and effortlessly. It is probably akin to changing speech style or register based on the context and the interlocutor.

Impact on language behavior

The impact a particular language mode has on language behavior is quite varied. Among these we find the amount of use of the other (guest) language during language production and language perception, the amount and type of mixed language used, the ease of processing of the two languages and the frequency of base language change. In the monolingual mode, the language not being processed is deactivated (some researchers such as Green (1986, 1998a) would even say that it is inhibited). This in turn prevents changing base language as well as producing mixed speech, i.e. code-switches and borrowings or, at least, reducing them drastically. However, dynamic interferences may still take place, that is speaker-specific deviations from the language being spoken due to the influence of the other deactivated language. (Note that interferences can also occur in the bilingual mode but they are more difficult to separate from other forms of language mixing such as code-switches and borrowings). As for the impact on listening in the monolingual mode, the bilingual will not make much use of the deactivated language (if any) and this may speed up the processing of the base language (but this still has to be proved experimentally).[4] As concerns the bilingual mode, both languages will be active but one language (language B in Figure 19.1) will be slightly less active than the other language (language A) as it is not currently the main language of communication. In production, bilinguals usually first adopt a base language through the process of language choice (language A in our case) and, when needed, they can bring in the other language, often referred to as the guest language, in the form of code-switches and borrowings. A code-switch is a complete shift to the other language for a word, a phrase or a sentence whereas a borrowing is a morpheme, word or short expression taken from the less activated language and adapted morphosyntactically (and sometimes phonologically) to the base language. Borrowings can involve both the form and the content of a word (these are called nonce borrowings) or simply the content (called loan shifts). It should be noted that given the high level of activation of both languages in the bilingual mode, not only can code-switches and borrowings be produced but the base language can also be changed frequently, that is the slightly less activated language becomes the base language and vice versa. A change of topic, of situation, of interlocutors, etc. may lead to a change in base language. In our example, language B would then become the most active language (it would be represented by a black square) and language A would be slightly less active (the black square would contain white diagonal lines). When this happens repeatedly within the same interaction, it gives the impression that the two languages are equally active but there is evidence in the sociolinguistic and psycholinguistic literature that, at any one point in time, one language is always more active than the other and that it is this language that governs language processing. As concerns perception, both languages will be processed in the bilingual language mode but the base language will usually play a greater role (see Grosjean, 1997, for a review of work on mixed language processing). Finally, the impact of an intermediate mode will be somewhere in between: more code-switching and borrowing than in the monolingual mode, some flagged switches, fewer dynamic interferences, some involvement of the other language during perception, etc.

Additional points

Several additional points need to be made concerning language mode. First, it should be noted that bilinguals differ among themselves as to the extent they travel along the language mode continuum; some rarely find themselves at the bilingual end (for example, bilinguals who rarely code-switch, sometimes on principle, or who do not hear mixed language very much) whereas others rarely leave this end (for example, bilinguals who live in communities where mixed language is the norm). Second, movement along the continuum can occur at any time as soon as the factors underlying mode change, be it during a verbal exchange between bilinguals or, in a more controlled situation, during an experiment. In addition, the movement usually takes place unconsciously and can be quite extensive. Thus, for example, if a bilingual starts off speaking to a "monolingual" and then realizes, as the conversation continues, that he/she is bilingual, there will invariably be a shift towards the bilingual end of the continuum with such consequences as change of base language, code-switching, etc. During perception, if bilingual listeners who start off in a monolingual mode determine (consciously or not) as they go along, that what they are listening to can contain elements from the other language, they will put themselves in a bilingual mode (at least partly), that is, activate both their languages (with the base language being more strongly activated). This is also true of readers, whether they are reading a continuous text or looking at individual lexical items interspersed with items from the other language. Simply knowing that there is a possibility that elements from the other language will be presented (in an experiment, for example) will probably move the bilingual away from the monolingual endpoint of the continuum. Just one guest word in a stream of base language words may well increase this displacement. Third, the minimum and maximum possible levels of activation of the other language (language B) are still not totally clear and remain an empirical issue. Currently, and as can be seen at the two extremes of the continuum in Figure 19.1, it is proposed that the other language is probably never totally deactivated at the monolingual end and that it very rarely reaches the same level of activation as the base language at the bilingual end (except, of course, when there is a change of base language). As concerns the lack of total deactivation, there is considerable evidence in the literature that bilinguals make dynamic interferences (ephemeral deviations due to the influence of the other deactivated language) even in the most monolingual of situations. This can only happen if the other language is active to some extent at least. As for the unequal activation of the two languages in the bilingual language mode, linguists working on code-switching and borrowing have often reported that the base language usually governs the language production process (it is the "host" or "matrix" language) and hence it is used much more than the other. Of course, one can think of exceptions where the two languages could share the same level of complete activation. This may be the case, for example, in an experiment where the participants are told, or find out, that the stimuli presented belong to either of the two languages. More interestingly, simultaneous interpreters need both languages to the same extent: input is in one language and output in the other (this special case will be evoked later in this paper). Finally, the case of non accommodation in language choice should be mentioned, that is, when bilingual A speaks language X and bilingual B speaks language Y. Here both languages may be activated to the same level, unless one chooses to talk in terms of input and output processing systems being activated to different extents. These exceptions aside, the base language is normally more active than the other language.

2 Evidence for language mode

Even though the concept of language mode has been alluded to by several researchers over the years, it has not been the object of systematic study until quite recently. However, if one combines earlier research in which language mode is varied in an indirect, non explicit way with more recent research that manipulates it explicitly, one can find strong evidence for the phenomenon. In what follows, research that pertains to language production, language perception, language acquisition and language pathology will be surveyed.

Language production

In one of her first publications, Poplack (1981) reports on a 35-year-old member of El Barrio (a Puerto Rican neighborhood in New York) who was tape-recorded in four different sessions where the base language was English: "Formal" in which she responded orally to a questionnaire given to her by a bilingual member of her community; "Informal" in which she had a conversation concerning topics of interest to her with the same person; "Vernacular" where she was recorded while doing errands and chatting with passersby in her neighborhood, and finally, "Informal (non group)" where she conversed with an English–Spanish bilingual who was not a member of her community. Although language mode was not manipulated directly, the informant was probably at the bilingual end of the language mode continuum in the "Informal" and "Vernacular" sessions (she was with members of her community with whom she code-switched frequently) whereas she was in an intermediate mode in the other two sessions. In the "Formal" session she probably felt that the formality of responding to a questionnaire was not conducive to code-switching, and in the "Informal (non group)" session, she felt she did not know the other interviewer well enough to code-switch as much with her as with an in-group member. In both these cases, therefore, she probably deactivated her Spanish to some extent and was in an intermediate mode. The code-switching patterns reported by the author confirm the impact of language mode on language production: there were about four times more code-switches per minute in the "Informal" and "Vernacular" sessions than in the "Formal" and "Informal (non group)" sessions.

More recently, Treffers-Daller (1998) has examined explicitly the effect of a speaker's position on the language mode continuum in terms of language choice and code-switching. She placed the same speaker, a Turkish–German bilingual, in three different positions by changing the context and the interlocutors, and she found quite different results. In the first context, which corresponds to a position to the right of the monolingual mode endpoint, the bilingual was speaking to members of a German-speaking family in Turkey who knew some Turkish. As a consequence, about three quarters of the speaker's utterances were in German and not much language mixing occurred (they mainly concerned borrowings). In the second context, which corresponds to an intermediate mode, the same bilingual, in Germany this time, was speaking to a Turkish–German bilingual he did not know very well. The author noted more changes of base language than in the first context and although the amount of mixed utterances was not much greater, these were quite different. They consisted of peripheral switches that filled a pragmatic function and that contained various types of pauses (this behavior has been called flagged switching). As for the third context, which corresponds to the bilingual end of the language mode continuum, the same bilingual interacted with a very close bilingual friend in Turkey. Here most utterances were in Turkish and there was much more language mixing than in the other two contexts. In addition, the code-switches were both intra- and intersentential and they were produced without hesitations or special highlighting (these have been called fluent switches). Based on these results, Treffers-Daller concludes that the language mode continuum concept may offer a new approach to study variable code-switching patterns within and between communities (e.g. Poplack, 1985; Bentahila and Davies, 1991) because it can help predict the frequency and type of switching that takes place.

In a laboratory based study, Grosjean (1997) manipulated the language mode French–English bilinguals were in when retelling French stories that contained English code-switches. The participants were told they were taking part in a "telephone chain" experiment whose aim was to examine the amount of information that could be conveyed from one person to another. The three French interlocutors they had to retell the stories to were described to the participants before the experiment started by means of short biographical sketches. (They were not actually present in the room during the experiment). The first person (referred to as "French") had just arrived in the United States to do a postdoc. He could read and write English quite well but still had difficulties speaking it. He was still adapting to life in America and spoke French at home. Faced with this kind of interlocutor, it was hypothesized that the participants would be in a monolingual mode as the interlocutor could not understand English very well. They would only speak French to him and do very little language mixing. Any code-switching that took place would have to be explained. The second person ("Bilingual A") had lived in the States for seven years and worked for a French government agency. He taught French and organized French cultural events. His children went to a bilingual school and he only spoke French at home although he was bilingual in French and English. It was hypothesized here that the participants would be in an intermediate language mode. Although Bilingual A knew English well it was inferred from the description given that he did not code-switch much. Thus, it was expected that the amount of code-switching would be kept down (although there would be more than for the first interlocutor) but what code-switching did take place would not be explained. Finally, the third person ("Bilingual B"), was a more traditional immigrant bilingual who had also been in the States for seven years. He worked for a local electronics firm, had French and American friends and spoke both languages at home. His children went to the local school. It was hypothesized that with this interlocutor, the participants would be in a fully bilingual mode and that they would code-switch as much as necessary with him. The results confirmed the hypotheses. In effect, the three dependent measures obtained (number of guest language syllables, number of base language syllables, and number of hesitations produced) were all affected by the language mode the speakers were in. The number of guest language syllables (code-switches, borrowings) increased significantly as the participants moved from a monolingual to a bilingual mode whereas the number of base language syllables decreased as did the number of hesitations.

Language perception

There has been far less (if any) systematic research on language mode in the domain of perception. Consequently, evidence for its impact in this modality has to come from studies that have manipulated the variable inadvertently. One example comes from two studies in the domain of speech perception. Caramazza *et al.* (1973) tested English–French bilinguals on VOT continua (ba-pa; da-ta; ga-ka) and obtained identification curves in an English and in a French language set. The language sets were obtained by changing the experimenters (one English speaking, one French speaking), the settings, the language of the instructions and the initial production task. (We should note that manipulations of this type determine what the base language will be, English or French in this case, but do not necessarily deactivate the other language). Although the authors expected the bilinguals to behave like French listeners when in a French language set and like English listeners in an English language set (i.e. show a perceptual boundary shift), they obtained similar functions for the two languages. These were situated in an intermediate position between the functions obtained with monolingual speakers of each language set. The authors concluded that the bilingual participants were responding to the stimuli themselves and were not influenced by language set. A few years later, Elman, Diehl and Buchwald (1977) decided to investigate this question further but this time to make sure that the language set was firmly established. Thus, in addition to using naturally produced stimuli, the test tapes contained an assortment of one or two syllable filler words along with the stimuli. In addition, each item was preceded by a sentence in the appropriate language (in this case, English and Spanish). This time, the authors did find a boundary shift, with ambiguous stimuli perceived significantly more as English, or as Spanish, depending on the language set the listeners were in. How can these contradictory results be interpreted in terms of language mode? It is proposed that in the first study, the language set manipulation undertaken at the beginning of testing was not sufficient to keep the bilingual listeners at the monolingual endpoint of the continuum. In effect, they were probably in, or they quickly moved to, a bilingual mode when asked to identify the experimental stimuli (especially as the latter were language-neutral synthetic speech). Hence the bilingual participants produced compromise (bilingual) results that were intermediate between those of the two monolingual groups. However, in the second study, there was constant language specific information (through the natural stimuli, the carrier sentence and the filler words) which activated one language much more than the other and hence kept the bilinguals at the monolingual end of the continuum. The stimuli were thus processed more "monolingually" in Spanish or English and this led to a boundary shift.

Language mode was manipulated both by top-down and bottom-up information in the two speech perception studies we have just seen, whereas in a lexical access study conducted some years later by Grainger and Beauvillain (1987), it depended on bottom-up information only. In this study, French–English bilinguals were asked to do a lexical decision task on two types of lists: "pure" lists which contained words from one language only and "mixed" lists which contained words from both languages. The authors found that the participants were some 36 msec faster   the pure list condition than in the other condition. We can interpret this result in the following way. In the pure list condition, the bilinguals were close to the monolingual end of the continuum (they didn't attain it though as they knew the study dealt with bilingualism) and hence their lexical search/look-up task was made easier as one lexicon was much more active than the other. In the mixed condition, however, the bilinguals were at the bilingual end of the continuum. Both lexicons were active as words could come from either and hence lexical decision took more time. It should be noted that in a second experiment, the authors found that the list condition effect was significant only in the absence of language specific orthographic cues. This in no way weakens the explanation just given as language mode is just one of many variables that will account for the time it takes to recognize a word.

Finally, in a very recent study, Dijkstra, Van Jaarsveld and Ten Brinke (1998), bring further, albeit indirect, evidence for the effect of language mode during perception. They tested Dutch–English bilinguals (dominant in Dutch) in three experiments and manipulated word type, language intermixing, and task. In what follows, only the first and third experiments will be examined as they pertain more directly to the language mode issue. In the first, the participants saw English/Dutch homographs and cognates, English control words and English nonwords. They were asked to do an English lexical decision on the items presented, that is indicate whether the items were English words or not, and they were tested in an English language set. Although cognates were responded to significantly faster than control words (570 and 595 msec respectively), no difference was found between homographs and their controls (580 msec in both cases). In the third experiment, participants once again saw homographs (no cognates though) as well as English and Dutch control words and English and Dutch nonwords. On this occasion they were asked to do a general lexical decision, that is indicate whether the items were words in English or in Dutch. This time, the authors did find a homograph effect in English: participants reacted to homographs faster than to English control words (554 and 592 msec respectively) but not to Dutch words (554 msec). A language mode account of these results is as follows. In Experiment 1, the participants were positioned towards the monolingual end of the continuum without reaching it totally though as they knew they were being tested as bilinguals. They only heard English words and nonwords (although some words were homographs and cognates) and they were asked to decide whether the items were English words or not. Thus although their Dutch was partly active (which would explain the cognate effect) it was not sufficiently active to create a homograph effect. However, in Experiment 3, the participants were definitely at the bilingual end of the continuum. Not only were the words and nonwords both English and Dutch but the participants were asked to do general lexical decision, that is search/look-up both their lexicons to accomplish the task. As both lexicons were active, they probably considered homographs as Dutch words and hence reacted to them as quickly as to regular Dutch words. This would explain the lack of difference between homographs and Dutch control words but the significant difference between homographs and English control words. The latter, it should be recalled, belonged to their weaker language and hence were reacted to more slowly.

Language acquisition

As will be seen later, language mode has rarely been controlled for in bilingual acquisition research. However, more recent studies have started to manipulate this variable and they have produced converging evidence for its importance. In one such study, Lanza (1992) recorded a two-year-old Norwegian–English bilingual child (Siri) interacting either with her American mother or her Norwegian father, both of whom were bilingual. What is interesting is that the mother frequently feigned the role of a monolingual and did not mix languages with Siri. The father, on the other hand, accepted Siri's language mixing and responded to it. Lanza studied the interactions between Siri and her parents in terms of a monolingual–bilingual discourse context continuum on which she placed various parental strategies. For example, "Minimal grasp" and "Expressed guess" are at the monolingual end (they were precisely the strategies used by the mother) and "Move on" and "Code-switching" strategies are at the bilingual end (they were the ones used by Siri's father). These strategies produced very different results: Siri did much more content word mixing with her father (who was open to code-switching) than with her mother (who did not respond to it), and this over the whole period of study (from age 2;0 to 2;7). What this means in terms of language mode is that Siri was herself probably in different modes with her two parents – she leaned towards the monolingual end with her mother (but never reached it as she did switch with her sometimes) and she was at the bilingual end with her father.

Although Nicoladis and Genesee (1998) have not managed to replicate Lanza's finding with English–French bilingual children in Montreal, they do not seem to question the parental discourse strategies proposed by Lanza nor the results she obtained. Instead they offer other reasons for finding different results such as the different sociolinguistic context, the fact that the Montreal children may not have understood the parental strategies, or the difference in language proficiency of the children in the two studies. In fact, Genesee, Boivin and Nicoladis (1996) have published some rather compelling evidence that bilingual children are very sensitive to the language behavior of the adults they are with. They recorded four English–French bilingual children (average age 2;2) as they spoke to their mother, to their father or to a stranger who only spoke their weaker language. On the level of language choice, they found that each child used more of the mother's language (be it French or English) with the mother than with the father, more of the father's language with the father than with the mother, and that they accommodated to the stranger as best they could by adopting the stranger's language as the base language, at least in part, or by mixing more. As concerns language mode, it would seem that only two of the four children had enough competence in the two languages to benefit fully from movement along the language mode continuum (Jessica and Leila). If for these children one takes the amount of weaker language used by the parent (e.g. the amount of English spoken by a French dominant parent) to which one adds the amount of mixed utterances, and one then correlates this value with the equivalent amount obtained from the child when speaking with that parent, one obtains a very high 0.85 correlation. This indicates that the more a parent switches over to the other language during communication, the more the child does so too. This finding is very similar to Lanza's (1992). In terms of language mode, children are more in a monolingual mode with parents who do not mix language much (all other things being equal) whereas they are more in a bilingual mode with parents who mix languages to a greater extent (or at least accept language mixing).

Language pathology

Studies that have examined bilinguals that suffer from some form of language pathology (aphasia, dementia, etc.) have also rarely manipulated language mode or controlled for it. Thus claims that language mixing is due to the patient's pathology may have to be revised if language mode is a confounding factor (as it often is; see the next section). Just recently, Marty and Grosjean (1998) manipulated language mode in a study that examined spoken language production in eight French–German aphasic bilinguals. The patients were asked to undertake various language tasks: place one of several cards in a specified position on a board, describe a postcard in enough detail so that it can be found among several similar postcards, take part in a topic constrained interaction and, finally, talk freely about any topic which comes to mind. The critical independent variable was the patient's interlocutor. The first was a totally monolingual French speaker who did not know any German whatsoever (unlike in many other studies where the interlocutor knew the other language but pretended not to) and the second was a French–German bilingual. The patients were told about their interlocutors' language background prior to testing and they interacted with them a bit at that time. The results clearly differentiated pathological from non pathological mixing. Five of the eight aphasics did not mix their languages with the monolingual interlocutor (they only used her native language), one did so extremely little (it was probably due to stress or fatigue) whereas two did so quite extensively. It was concluded that of the eight aphasics, six patients could still control their language mode and adapt it to the interlocutor whereas two could no longer do so.

In sum, there is increasing evidence, direct and indirect, that language mode plays an important role in language processing as well as in language acquisition and language pathology.

3   Language mode as a confounding and a control variable

Given that language mode plays an important role in all types of bilingual language behavior, it is important that it be controlled for if it is not the main variable being studied. Unfortunately, this has not been the case in many past studies. The consequence is that the data obtained is both very variable, due to the fact that participants are probably situated at various points along the continuum, and at times ambiguous given the confound between this factor and the variable under study. In this section, issues in bilingualism research that are affected by language mode will be presented and examples of how the variable can influence them inadvertently will be discussed. Ways of controlling language mode will then be proposed.[5]

Language mode as a confounding variable

One issue influenced by language mode concerns the type of data obtained in descriptive studies. For example, researchers who have examined bilingual language production have often reported instances of interference. The problem is that it is not always clear what is meant by this term (also called transfer or transference). As indicated earlier, for Weinreich (1966), interferences are instances of deviation from the norms of either language which occur in the speech of bilinguals as a result of their familiarity with more than one language. Haugen (1956) refers to interference as the overlapping of two languages, Mackey (1968) talks of the use of features belonging to one language while speaking or writing another, and for Clyne (1967) transference is the adoption of any elements or features from the other language (he uses the term as a cover term for language contact phenomena). A direct result of this broad view is that the interferences observed in linguistic studies correspond to interferences but also often to borrowings and even code-switches. As stated in Grosjean (1998a), we will never get to the bottom of this terminological problem, and we will never isolate interferences from code-switches and borrowings in bilingual speech, if we do not take into account (and do not control for) the language mode bilinguals and language learners are in when they are being studied (i.e. observed, recorded, tested, etc.). Very often the bilinguals' inter-locutors know the language not being spoken (the one causing the interference) and hence bilinguals are in an intermediate mode if not in a bilingual mode when being recorded. When interferences occur in the bilingual mode, which they also do, they are very difficult to separate from other forms of language mixing, especially borrowings. What might appear to be an interference could also be a guest element or structure produced by the speaker who is aware that his or her interlocutor can understand mixed language. (The same point is made by Poplack, 1985).

A similar problem concerns "intentional" and "unintentional" switches in second language production. Poulisse and Bongaerts (1994), for example, define unintentional switches as cases which were not preceded by any signs of hesitation and did not stand out from the rest of the utterance by a marked intonation. The problem is that it is not clear what language mode their second language learners were in when they tested them. If they were not in a monolingual mode, then their switches may not have been unintentional (at least not all of them). In fact, we are told that these switches contain a large proportion of editing terms which the speakers used to comment on an error made or on an inappropriate word used, and/or to warn the listener that what followed should be interpreted as a repair of what preceded. This would seem to indicate that the interviewers could indeed understand the other language and that the learners were at least partly in a bilingual mode. The same argument can be made about "fluent" and "flagged" switches. Poplack (1985) defines the former as switches with smooth transitions and no hesitations whereas the latter are switches that draw attention to themselves by repetition, hesitation, intonational highlighting and metalinguistic com-mentary. Poplack compares the fluent switches found in the Puerto Rican community in New York and the flagged switches obtained in Ottawa-Hull and recognizes that the difference in type could be due, in part at least, to the data collection technique used in each case – an informal participant observation technique in New York and a more formal random sampling technique in the Ottawa-Hull region. In terms of language mode, participants were probably in a totally bilingual mode in New York and in an intermediate language mode in Ottawa-Hull.

Another issue that is affected by language mode concerns whether bilinguals have an integrated semantic memory for their two languages (also called a shared or a common store) or whether they have two separate, independent semantic systems. Several studies have addressed this question and some (e.g. Schwanenflugel and Rey, 1986; Fox, 1996, etc.) come to the conclusion that bilinguals have a shared representational system. The problem is that it is difficult to tease apart in their results what is due to the representational issue and what is caused by the language mode variable. The bilingual participants were probably not in a monolingual mode when they took part in the studies. They knew they were being tested as bilinguals and they saw words in the two languages. Because of this, they had probably activated both their languages (consciously or unconsciously) and were thus in a bilingual mode. This would invariably lead to results indicating a shared system. A related issue concerns the presence or absence of language-selective access during visual word perception. Beauvillain and Grainger (1987), for example, found evidence for non-selective access when bilinguals were shown interlexical homographs. The problem though is that the bilingual participants in their experiment needed their two languages to do the task: they had to read a context word in one language and then decide whether the next word, always in the other language, was a word or not in that language. In order to do this, they had to activate both their languages and hence were in a bilingual language mode. (As they were tested as bilinguals, they were probably already in a bilingual mode before the experiment even started). It is no surprise therefore that a result indicating non-selective processing was obtained (the same comment can be made about another well known study which examined the same question, that of Altenberg and Cairns, 1983). In sum, if one is interested in such issues as the independence or the interdependence of the bilingual's language systems, selective versus non-selective processing, one versus two lexicons, etc., one should be careful not to activate the other language with the stimuli or the procedure used. When this occurs, it becomes difficult to disentangle what is due to bilingual representation and processing, and what is due to the bilingual language mode the participants are in. In addition, strict dichotomies such as selective vs. non-selective processing probably have little psychological reality if one thinks of the bilingual moving along the language mode continuum in his/her everyday life. Processing may be selective (or very close to it) when the bilingual is in a monolingual mode, partly selective when the mode is intermediate and non-selective when the mode is bilingual.

A last issue pertains to the amount of language mixing that is produced by certain types of bilinguals. For example, in the bilingual language development literature, it has been proposed that children who acquire two languages simultaneously go through an early fusion stage in which the languages are in fact one system (one lexicon, one grammar, etc.). They then slowly differentiate their languages, first separating their lexicons and then their grammar. Evidence for this has come from the observation of language mixing in very young bilingual children and from the fact that there is a gradual reduction of mixing as the child grows older. However this position has been criticized by a number of researchers (e.g. Meisel, 1989; Genesee, 1989, among others) and one of the points made each time (in addition to the fact that translation equivalents may not be known in the other language) is that the children were often in a bilingual mode, i.e. the caretakers were usually bilingual themselves and they were probably overheard using both languages, separately or in a mixed form, by the children, if not actually mixing their languages with them (see Goodz, 1989). In addition, the context in which the recordings were made for the studies probably induced language mixing as it was rarely (if ever) monolingual (see, for example, Redlinger and Park, 1980 and Vihman, 1985). The children in these studies were thus probably in a bilingual context which induced a bilingual mode and hence language mixing. In another domain, the amount of language mixing produced by bilingual patients suffering from some type of language pathology (e.g. aphasia, dementia) has been used as an indication of their pathology (e.g. Perecman, 1984; Hyltenstam, 1991; Ludérus, 1995). However, as argued in Grosjean (1998), most of the patients recorded were at least partially in a bilingual mode when being recorded (and sometimes even in a fully bilingual mode). It is no surprise therefore that they switched to the other language if this improved communication between the interviewer and themselves.

Language mode as a control variable

Until more is known about language mode (see next section), it is safer to control it by putting bilinguals in a monolingual mode or in a bilingual mode in preference to an intermediate mode (Grosjean, 1998). As concerns the monolingual mode, two inappropriate approaches must be avoided. The first is to simply put the participants in a "language set" (also called erroneously by some a "language mode") by giving them instructions in one language, getting them to do preliminary tasks in that language, occasionally presenting reminders in that language, etc. What this does is to activate a particular base language (the variable depicted on the vertical axis in Figure 19.1) but it does not guarantee a particular position on the monolingual–bilingual mode continuum. A second inappropriate approach, which has been used a lot with bilingual children, second language learners and aphasic or demented patients, has been to hide the experimenter's or interviewer's bilingualism. This is a very dangerous strategy as subtle cues such as facial expression and body language can give away the interlocutor's comprehension of the other language. In addition, it will not prevent occasional slip-ups such as responding in the "wrong" language or showing in one's response that what has been said in that language has been understood. The solution to positioning the bilingual at the monolingual endpoint of the continuum is unfortunately not quite as easy as one would like it to be. For interview situations, if the researcher is interested in observing how a bilingual can produce just one language (something a bilingual often has to do), then the interviewer must be completely monolingual in that language (and not feign to be). In addition, the situation must be monolingual and there must not be any other person present who knows the other language. For more experimental situations, the difficulty is how to prevent the bilingual from activating, to some extent at least, the other language. If interest is shown in the participant's bilingualism, if he or she is tested in a laboratory that works on bilingualism, if the experimenter is bilingual, if the participant sees or hears stimuli from both languages, and if the task requires both languages (e.g. the bilingual Stroop test, bilingual word priming, bilingual association production, bilingual category matching, word translation, etc.) then any one of these factors is sufficient to put the participant in a bilingual mode, in part at least, and hence activate the two languages, albeit to differing degrees. One solution that comes to mind is to intermix bilingual participants in with monolingual participants in a monolingual experiment (for example, a study that is part of a course requirement) and once the experiment is done, and after the fact only, so as to avoid the Rosenthal effect, to go back into the list of participants and extract the bilinguals. As concerns the bilingual endpoint of the language mode continuum, care will have to be taken that the participants are totally comfortable producing, or listening to, mixed language. This can be done by having bilingual experimenters or interviewers who belong to the same bilingual community as the participants and, if possible, who know them well. They should interact with the participants in mixed language and the situation should be conducive to mixed language (no monolinguals present, a relaxed non-normative atmosphere, etc.).

4 Further research on language mode

In this last section, several aspects of language mode that need to be investigated further will be mentioned briefly. They concern the assessment of language mode, the bilingual's processing systems, the case of highly language dominant bilinguals, and modeling.

Assessing language mode

As we have seen in this chapter, many different factors influence language mode. They range from factors that concern participants (language proficiency, language mixing habits and attitudes, usual mode of interaction), to situational factors (physical location, presence of monolinguals, formality), to factors that deal with form and content (language used, topic, amount of mixed language) and with the language act (communicate information, create a social distance, etc.), all the way to specific research factors (aims of the study taking place, type and organization of the stimuli, task used, instructions, etc.). Future research will have to isolate these factors, determine their importance, and ascertain how they interact with one another to activate or deactivate the bilingual's languages to varying degrees and hence change the bilingual's position on the language mode continuum. Researchers will also have to examine the maximum movement possible on the continuum for various types of bilinguals. As we saw above, bilinguals differ among themselves as to the extent they travel along the language mode continuum; some rarely find themselves at the bilingual end (the other language is never very active) whereas others rarely leave this end (the other language is always very active). And within a bilingual, the minimum and maximum possible levels of activation of the other language can also vary. Another issue concerns a hypothetical resting mode for any bilingual individual, that is the language mode the bilingual returns to in between language activities. Does this notion have any reality or is the bilingual constantly traveling along the continuum? Finally, to complicate things further, people who use three or more languages in their everyday lives will need to be accounted for. For example, one can certainly imagine a trilingual in a monolingual, a bilingual or a trilingual mode. Figure 19.2 depicts each of these three modes. In the top part of the figure, the trilingual is in a monolingual mode; language A is active and the other two languages are only very slightly active. In the middle part of the figure, the trilingual is in a bilingual mode; language A remains the base language, language B is active (but less so than language A) and language C is very slightly active. Finally, in the bottom part of the figure, the same trilingual is in a trilingual mode where language A is the base language and languages B and C are also active. What has just been said about trilinguals is true of quadrilinguals. For example, a quadrilingual can be in a language B monolingual mode where language B is being used (it is the base language) and languages A, C and D are very slightly active. This same person, in another situation, can be in a quadrilingual mode where, for example, language B is the base language and languages A, C and D are also active. If all this is possible, which it probably is, the language mode concept will have to be extended and its various manifestations in these kinds of multilinguals will have to be investigated. This said, it would be a mistake to put the language mode variable aside in bilingualism studies as long as it has not been described fully and a metric has not been developed for it (as a continuous variable affected by a host of

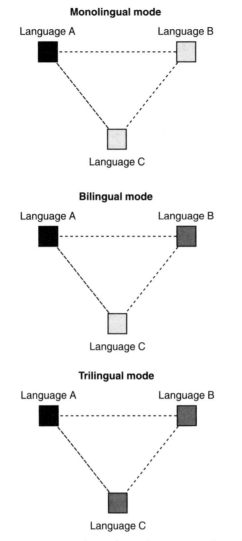

Figure 19.2 Visual representation of a trilingual in a monolingual mode (top part), bilingual mode (middle part) and trilingual mode (bottom part). The level of activation of a language is indicated by the degree of darkness of the squares (black is active and white is inactive). Language A is the base language in each case.

factors, one may never be). Language mode is a variable that is constantly present, whatever the bilingual research question being studied, and it therefore needs to be taken into account at all times.

Language mode and the processing mechanisms

So far language mode has been defined as a state of activation of the bilingual's languages and language processing mechanisms at any given point in time. To simplify things, no difference has been made in terms of mode between language knowledge and language processing, and in the latter case, between the input and output mechanisms. However, it could be that one will need to differentiate these three components at some time. For example, as concerns processing, a bilingual can be speaking one language and listening to another (such as when two interlocutors do not accommodate to a common base language). A simple account of this is that the language mode is the same in the input and output systems but that the base language is different. But things become more complex if the interlocutor's input is monolingual in nature (it contains no language mixing) but the speaker's output involves language mixing (or vice-versa). In this case, different language modes will have to be attributed to the input and output systems. The case of simultaneous interpreters is akin to this situation. What language mode are interpreters in when they are doing simultaneous interpretation? A suggestion made in Grosjean (1997a) is that the input and output processing mechanisms of each language are indeed separated here. First, as can be seen in Figure 19.3, the interpreter is in a bilingual mode and both languages are active. However, one language is *not* more active than the other as is normally the case in the bilingual mode. Both the source language and the target language are active to the same extent (black squares in the figure) as both are needed, for perception and production respectively. Second, input and output components have been added to each language (circles in the figure) and it is their level of activation that varies. Although the two languages are equally active, the processing mechanisms are not. In this way, the interpreter will be able to input the source language (and to a lesser extent the target language, see below) and to output the target language only. Third, the input component of the source and of the target language are both active. At least three reasons require that the input component of the target language also be active: the interpreter must be able to monitor his/her overt speech (Levelt, 1989), the client's occasional use of the target language must be processed

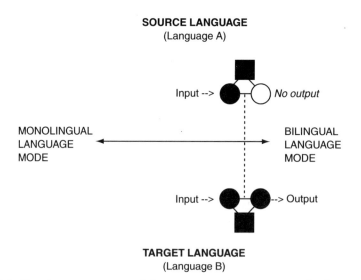

SOURCE LANGUAGE
(Language A)

Input --> ⬤─○ No output

MONOLINGUAL
LANGUAGE
MODE

⟵──────────⟶

BILINGUAL
LANGUAGE
MODE

Input --> ⬤─⬤ --> Output

TARGET LANGUAGE
(Language B)

Figure 19.3 Visual representation of the interpreter's position on the language mode continuum when doing simultaneous interpreting. Both languages are active (black squares) but they differ as to the level of activation of their input and output mechanisms (represented by circles).

(interpreters report that this indeed takes place), and a fellow interpreter's cues must be heard. Fourth, the target language output mechanism is active whereas the source language output mechanism is not (it may be totally deactivated or, quite exceptionally, inhibited). In sum, the two languages are in a bilingual mode (both are active), the output mechanisms are in a monolingual mode (only one language is normally output) whereas the input mechanisms are in a bilingual mode (input takes place in the source and sometimes in the target language). How inactive the source output mechanism should be is discussed in Grosjean (1997a).

Highly language dominant bilinguals

Language mode will also have to be studied in bilinguals who are highly dominant in one language, such as members of minority groups who rarely use the majority language, bilingual children who are strongly dominant in one language, second language learners (on the condition that they make regular functional use of their second language),[6] etc. It has been reported repeatedly in the literature that these types of bilinguals do more language mixing when speaking their weaker language than their stronger language. Thus, Genesee, Nicoladis and Paradis (1995) and Nicoladis and Genesee (1998) report that bilingual children code-mix more when talking with the parent who speaks their non-dominant language (irrespective of whether the parent code-mixes in return); Lanza (1992) reports that the Norwegian–English bilingual child she studied (Siri) did more function word mixing with her English speaking mother, indicating thereby the child's dominance in Norwegian; Poulisse and Bongaerts (1994) report that the use of unintentional switches is L2 proficiency related (more proficient learners produce less of them) and, even in perception, Elman, Diehl and Buchwald (1977) report a 0.52 correlation between the degree of bilingualism and the amount of identification shift for the ambiguous VOT stimuli. This would mean that bilinguals who are highly dominant in one language may simply not be able to control language mode in the same way as less dominant or balanced bilinguals. Although they may deactivate their stronger language in a monolingual environment that requires only the weaker language (for example, it is of no use speaking Italian to an English speaker who knows absolutely no Italian), that language will simply not be developed enough or active enough to allow them to stay in a monolingual mode. Future research will have to investigate the underlying mechanisms that make a stronger language "seep through" despite the fact that it has been deactivated. It will also have to isolate which part of behavior is due to competence (i.e. the representation or grammar of the weaker language) and which part is due to performance (i.e. the system's inability to activate or deactivate a language or processing mechanism at any particular point in time). Finally, attention will have to be paid to bilinguals who through some kind of pathology (aphasia, dementia, etc.) lose their ability to move along the language mode continuum. Some can no longer leave the monolingual mode (they cannot mix languages anymore) whereas others are in a constant bilingual mode and hence mix their two languages when it is not appropriate.

Modeling

Models of bilingual competence, bilingual production and perception as well as bilingual language acquisition will have to take into account language mode. For example, De

Bot's (1992) global model of bilingual language production has played an important role in bilingualism research in recent years but it does not yet give a clear account of how language choice takes place (i.e. how the base language is chosen), how the language mode is set, and the impact it has on processing. Some models may have a harder time integrating language mode, in particular the bilingual language mode where both languages are active but one slightly less so than the other. For example, Green's (1998) Inhibitory Control (IC) Model supposes that a word from a chosen language is output by suppressing lemmas with the incorrect language tags. This can account for production in the monolingual mode but it is problematic when the mode is bilingual. In this case, it is often the most active word that is output, irrespective of language. Admittedly, Green does agree that code-switching would involve a cooperative rather than a competitive relationship between the word production schemas but this needs to be spelled out. Green (p.c.) proposes that this might take place either by reducing the strength (gain) of the inhibitory relations directly or by inhibiting the inhibition. In the domain of perception, models that contain inter-language inhibition will have a problem accounting for the perception of code-switches and borrowings in the bilingual language mode. Thus, in the Bilingual Interactive Activation (BIA) model (Dijkstra and van Heuven, 1998), one language is normally deactivated during the word recognition process by means of top-down inhibition from the other language node and lateral interlanguage word level inhibition. This will produce satisfactory results for word recognition in the monolingual mode but it will be less than optimal when mixed language is being perceived. In this latter case, it would be better if both languages were active with one more active than the other (see the base language effect described in Grosjean, 1988, 1997). BIA has the possibility of presetting a language node from external sources at the beginning of word recognition but invariably, during the actual recognition process, the built-in cross-language inhibitory mechanisms will cause one language to be inhibited unless, of course, these mechanisms are switched off. (It should be noted that Woutersen (1997) proposes a model of the bilingual lexicon that contains language nodes and where the bilingual can be in differing language modes; it is unclear however how the model would be implemented computationally). To our knowledge, the only bilingual word recognition model that currently simulates language mode is the Bilingual Model of Lexical Access, BIMOLA, first proposed by Grosjean (1988). The computational version (Léwy and Grosjean, in preparation) consists of three levels of nodes which use localist representations (features, phonemes, and words), and it is characterized by various excitatory and inhibitory links within and between levels. Among its particularities we find shared phonetic features for the languages (in this case, English and French), language independent, yet parallel, processing at the higher levels (phonemes and words), as well as the absence of cross-language inhibition processes. It does not resort to the concept of a language node as proposed by the BIA model but relies instead on overall language activation as an emergent phenomenon. Both the base language setting (a discrete value) and the language mode setting (a continuous value) can be set prior to simulation.

Conclusion

This chapter has examined the many facets of language mode, a concept that has received relatively little attention in bilingualism research. This is unfortunate as taking language mode into account offers many advantages. It gives a truer reflection of how bilinguals process their two languages separately or together, it helps to understand data obtained from various bilingual populations, it accounts for problematic or ambiguous findings in the literature, and it can serve as a control variable in studies examining other topics. Language mode will invariably be present in bilingual research be it as an independent variable, a control variable, or unfortunately, a confounding variable. Giving it the importance it deserves will facilitate our work as researchers and will further our understanding of the bilingual person.

Notes

1   Preparation of this chapter was made possible in part by two grants from the Swiss National Science Foundation (1213–045375.95 and 3200–049106.96). The author would like to thank the following for their valuable comments on earlier drafts of the paper: Michael Clyne, Kees de Bot, Jean-Marc Dewaele, Ton Dijkstra, James Flege, David Green, Marc Grosjean, Nicolas Léwy and Juergen Meisel. Additional thanks go to Jacqueline Gremaud-Brandhorst, Lysiane Grosjean and Delphine Guillelmon for their careful reading of the manuscript. Requests for reprints can be sent to: François Grosjean, Laboratoire de traitement du langage et de la parole, Université de Neuchâtel, Avenue du Premier-Mars 26, 2000 Neuchâtel, Switzerland.

2   At this stage, only the regular use of *two* languages in relatively stable bilinguals will be considered. People who use three or more languages in their everyday life will be evoked in the last section.

3   As much of the psycholinguistics of bilingualism has concerned language perception (spoken or written) in the laboratory, it is important to stress that depending on the stimuli presented (monolingual or bilingual), the task used, the laboratory setting and the instructions given, a bilingual listener in an experiment can be situated at any point along the language mode continuum but is usually at the bilingual end. We will come back to this in a later section.

4   To my knowledge, no experiment aimed at this question has given all the necessary guarantees that the participants were in a truly monolingual mode.

5   For a more extensive discussion of these topics, see Grosjean (1998).

6   It is difficult to know how the language mode concept applies to "traditional" language learners who acquire their second language in a formal school environment. Those who interact in their L2 in a natural environment can be accounted for more easily.

Source: Grosjean, F. (2001) The bilingual's language modes. In Janet Nicol (ed.) *One Mind Two Languages*, Oxford: Blackwell, pp. 1–22. Reproduced with permission of the author and Blackwell Publishing.

François Grosjean is Professor and Director of the Laboratoire de traitement du langage et de la parole (Language and Speech Processing Laboratory) at the Université de Neuchâtel, Switzerland. francois.grosjean@unine.ch

Notes for students and instructors

Study questions

1 What are the three levels of activation, as identified by Green? What is the role of the *specifier*?
2 Review Levelt's original 'speaking' model. What changes has de Bot made to Levelt's model to accommodate bilingual speech production?
3 What are the key differences between the distributed lexical/conceptual feature model and the revised hierarchical model?
4 What is *language mode*? How does *language mode* differ from Fishman's concept of *domain*?

Study activities

1 Ask a bilingual speaker to retell two pieces of personal experience with traditional cultural festivals, one for each of his/her language cultures, to two imagined monolingual friends, one in each of his/her two languages. That is, the bilingual speaker tells the same experience twice, once in each language. Can you detect any difference in the *amount* and *type* of code-switching in each of the retells? Relate the findings to the notion of *language mode* discussed by Grosjean.
2 Select two groups of second/foreign language learners (learning the same second/foreign language and having the same first language/mother tongue), one beginner's group and one advanced group. Present them with 10 sentences in their first language, either on computer screen or on paper. Ask the learners to translate the sentences orally. Measure the speed of their translation and analyse the accuracy. For more accurate measures of the speed, you will need a specially designed computer program. Compare the results between the two groups of learners to see if the advanced learners produce faster and more accurate translations. Relate the findings to the control, activation and resources model proposed by Green and/or the revised hierarchical model.

Further reading

For a general introduction to bilingual speech production and perception, see Chapter 3 of S. Romaine, 1995, *Bilingualism*, 2nd edn, Blackwell.

For individual studies, see A.M.B. de Groot and J.F. Kroll (eds), 1997, *Tutorials in Bilingualism: Psycholinguistic perspectives*, Lawrence Erlbaum; E. Bialystok (ed.), 1991, *Language Processing in Bilingual Children*, Cambridge University Press.; J.L. Nicol (ed.), 2001, *One Mind Two Languages: Bilingual language processing*, Blackwell.

A state-of-the-art overview of the psycholinguistic studies of bilingualism is J.F. Kroll and A.M.B. de Groot (eds), 2005, *Handbook of Bilingualism: Psycholinguistic approaches*, Oxford University Press.

The bilingual brain

Chapter 20

Cerebral lateralization in bilinguals: methodological issues

LORAINE K. OBLER, ROBERT J. ZATORRE, LINDA GALLOWAY AND JYOTSNA VAID

THE QUESTION OF INTEREST regarding cerebral lateralization for language in bilinguals is whether it differs from that in monolinguals. If lateralization is the same in both groups, one could expect it to be so for both languages of the bilinguals; if not, there are a number of theoretical possibilities; namely:

1   language is more left lateralized in the bilingual than in the monolingual
     (a)   for one language or
     (b)   for both; or
2   language is less left lateralized for the bilingual than for the monolinguals
     (a)   for one language or
     (b)   for both languages.

As with the studies of cerebral lateralization for language among children, elderly individuals, women, and musicians, conflicting findings have been reported around the issues of lateralization for language(s) in bilinguals. While lateralization data from bilinguals have been construed to support most of the theoretical possibilities mentioned above, the crux of recent debate has been whether or not there is greater right-hemisphere participation in the processing of one or both languages in the bilingual than in the monolingual. In order to appropriately interpret apparently contradictory findings, it becomes necessary to discuss a number of variables of potential importance to studies of cerebral lateralization with bilinguals. These include methodological variables such as subject selection, language and stimulus selection, test procedures, and data analysis, as well as theoretical questions around interpreting dichotic and tachistoscopic measures of lateralization. Many of the issues which arise in the literature on bilinguals have not yet been resolved with respect to monolingual subjects. Hence in this chapter we have undertaken to document a broad range of parameters which must be considered in carrying out, analyzing, and interpreting studies of language lateralization in bilinguals, with the conviction that focus on bilinguals will shed light on issues pertinent to testing lateralization in other normal and exceptional populations.

Subject selection

Handedness

It has repeatedly been observed that the "standard" pattern of left-hemisphere (LH) superiority for verbal, and right-hemisphere (RH) superiority for visuospatial processing more strongly characterizes right- than left-handed individuals, and, in particular, right-handed individuals with no family history of left-handedness (Andrews, 1977). Whether the factor of handedness has a similar effect in monolinguals and bilinguals, or whether it interacts with parameters of bilingualism to exert a different effect is a question of theoretical interest.

Unfortunately, evidence bearing on this issue is minimal, insofar as all but two of the experimental studies in the bilingual laterality literature considered only right-handed individuals. (It is doubtful, however, whether any of the early studies employing right-handers screened familial sinistrality.) Moreover, two methodologically similar studies in which the factor of handedness was specifically examined differed in their results with respect to handedness. In a tachistoscopic task, Gaziel *et al.* (1978) found no significant differences in the performance of right- and left-handed Hebrew–English bilinguals on either of their languages. Orbach (1967), however, obtained group differences related to handedness and interacting with language; his 21 strongly left-handed subjects (native speakers of Hebrew who were proficient in English) showed a significant right-visual-field effect (RVFE) for English stimuli, and a nonsignificant left-visual-field effect (LVFE) in Hebrew. By contrast, his 25 right-handers with the same language history showed significant RVFEs in both languages, greater for English than for Hebrew.

Gender

Evidence has accumulated in the literature on monolinguals suggesting that the standard pattern of cerebral lateralization is more characteristic of males than females (Waber, 1977; McGlone, 1978). Although similar evidence has been obtained in the bilingual literature as well (Gordon, 1980; Vaid and Lambert, 1979), the potential contribution of the factor of gender differences in lateralization has generally been ignored. A majority of the bilingual literality studies do not report whether or not significant gender differences were present. Indeed, a third of all the studies do not even report the gender composition of their subject samples. Of those studies in which gender composition was reported, less than one-third employed an equal number of males and females; where the gender ratio was unequal, it was in the direction of more females than males in three-quarters of the studies. In view of this bias in the literature, it is possible that at least some of the claims of differential lateralization made in the bilingual literature (e.g. Obler *et al.*, 1975) may be attributable to gender differences rather than, or in addition to, effects associated with bilingualism per se.

Age at the time of testing

Since it remains unresolved whether there is a developmental course toward left lateralization in childhood or in aging (Clark and Knowles, 1973; Borod and Goodglass, 1979; Johnson *et al.*, 1979), it would be premature to conclude that a finding which holds true for one group of bilinguals will necessarily hold true for bilinguals of different ages (but see Piazza and Zatorre, 1981).

Level of second-language proficiency

A great number of studies in the bilingual laterality literature have not specified the criteria, if any, used to screen individuals for proficiency in their two languages. In the earliest study, native English speakers were selected as subjects on the basis that "they had some knowledge of Yiddish" (Mishkin and Forgays, 1952). Recent studies have not necessarily used more objective criteria for subject selection. As a result, subjects within and across studies may have varied considerably in their levels of second-language proficiency.

Proficiency has itself become the focus of several recent investigations which have centered around the "stage hypothesis" first suggested by Obler *et al.* (1975) and then amended by Krashen and Galloway (1978; Galloway and Krashen, 1980). The hypothesis maintains that bilinguals will initially rely to a greater extent on the RH but will, with increasing second-language proficiency, engage the LH in second as in first-language processing. This hypothesis is consistent with demonstrated RH linguistic capabilities (Galloway, 1980; Galloway and Krashen, 1980) and compatible with general processing strategies of the RH (Vaid and Genesee, 1980).

A direct test of the stage hypothesis of Albert and Obler (1978) would require comparing the neuropsychological performance of second-language learners of varying ages and at different stages in their acquisition of the second language with that of monolingual and balanced bilingual controls. Such a test has yet to be undertaken. However, studies that have employed a cross-sectional paradigm to examine the question of right-hemispheric involvement in the initial stages of second-language acquisition lend some support to the stage hypothesis (Silverberg *et al.*, 1979; Schneiderman and Wesche, 1980; Hardyck, 1980). The findings of several other studies are inconsistent with the predictions of the hypothesis as stated, finding no differences between early and late learners (Galloway, 1980; 1980b; Gordon, 1980; for a review, see Vaid and Genesee, 1980).

Krashen and Galloway (1978; Galloway and Krashen, 1980) have proposed a modified version of the stage hypothesis whereby the second language, L_2, would be less lateralized than the first language, L_1, only among adults acquiring the second language in a naturalistic setting without any formal language instruction. Their test of this, however (Galloway, 1980; Galloway and Scarcella, 1982), did not yield evidence in support of this modification.

Age of L_2 acquisition

A number of studies employing proficient and nonproficient bilinguals have tended to confound the variable of proficiency with that of age of second-language acquisition (Obler *et al.* 1975; Albert and Obler, 1978). Whereas proficient bilinguals in these studies had typically acquired both languages during infancy, nonproficient bilinguals had begun second language acquisition during adolescence and/or in adulthood. However, as recent studies of proficient early and late bilinguals have demonstrated, age of onset of bilingualism may also be a factor responsible for differential hemispheric processing of language. Early bilinguals showed faster averaged evoked responses (AERs) in the left hemisphere on a language recognition task, whereas late bilinguals (who had acquired their second language in adolescence) evinced faster AERs in the right hemisphere for both languages (Genesee *et al.*, 1978). This finding has subsequently been replicated in an evoked-responses study of late Polish–Russian bilinguals (Kotik, personal communication). A similar early–late group difference was obtained from a monaural Stroop study of French and English balanced bilinguals (Vaid and Lambert, 1979). The Sussman *et al.* (1982) study of interference in tapping rate by concurrent speech production in fluent bilinguals likewise showed a strong tendency for more left-hemisphere dominance in subjects who were bilingual from birth, and more right-hemisphere language processing in subjects who learned their second language later. How the purported effects of second language proficiency (as discussed in the previous section) interact with the factor of age of onset of bilingualism is, as yet, unclear.

Manner of L₂ acquisition

The putative differential laterality of bilinguals would imply that lateralization for language is not entirely determined at birth. If we assume language experience may influence laterality, we must then ask:

1   Whether a second language is learned formally or acquired naturalistically.
2   The extent to which individual differences in learning style may interact with lateralization.
3   If a second language is learned in a classroom, what instructional method is used predominantly, e.g. one emphasizing the visual modality (reading) vs. one exclusively relying on the auditory modality.

With regard to the issues of formality and individual learning style, some researchers hypothesize that individuals with more "analytic" cognitive styles would presumably show a greater left lateralization, perhaps reflecting their use of a conscious monitor in second-language processing, as compared to children, who acquire the second language informally (Krashen and Galloway, 1978). One might imagine, likewise, that formal teaching could speak to more analytically inclined students, while informal acquisition would succeed with those less analytically inclined. Two studies with L₂ learners (Krashen *et al.*, 1974; Hartnett, 1975) reported that direction of conjugate lateral eye movements correlated with success in a particular method of instruction in the second language; specifically, individuals who tended to look more consistently toward the right (taken to indicate more left-hemisphere involvement, Kinsbourne, 1972 vs. Gardner and Branski, 1976) also tended to adopt a deductive, "analytic" approach to L₂ learning.

With respect to the method of L₂ instruction, it has been suggested that reading and writing may contribute to increased left-hemisphere control of language (cf. Wechsler, 1976; 1977). In the case of bilinguals who learned one of their languages via the written mode, as did Kotik's (1975) subjects, one would, accordingly, expect greater left lateralization of that language as compared to the language acquired and used auditorily.

Environment of L_2 learning

One must consider whether the learner is in a second-language environment, where the target L_2 is also the predominant language used in the L_2 performer's surroundings (e.g., an Icelandic student in the U.S.), or in a foreign language environment where the target L_2 is not the predominant language around the L_2 performer (e.g., an American studying Yoruba at a U.S. university). Suggestions are found in several studies of a lower overall language laterality in relatively advanced L_2 performers in a second-language environment (Galloway, 1977; 1980a). For example, Gordon's dichotic listening study (1980) found that Americans who learned Hebrew after puberty in Israel showed a trend toward a lower laterality in both Hebrew and English. In contrast, a comparable group of native Hebrew speakers, who had studied English after puberty as a foreign language in Israel, did not evidence lower overall language laterality. However, native Hebrew speakers who had spent many years abroad in English-speaking countries and/or were currently using English extensively (e.g., communicating with a spouse at home) also showed lower laterality scores in both languages.

Language stimuli

Familiar methodological issues arise in selecting word stimuli for laterality studies in monolinguals; the stimuli must be adequately screened in terms of word length, frequency, grammatical class, abstractness, imageability, and phonetic composition. In the case of studies of bilingual laterality, difficulties may arise in preparing comparable sets of stimuli from structurally different languages, especially regarding such dimensions as word length or phonetic composition. To the extent that the stimulus sets are not comparable, differences in lateralization patterns across languages may simply reflect such stimulus differences. Moreover, as language pairs will differ with respect to their genetic relatedness (e.g., Spanish and French are more related than are Spanish and Turkish), it is unrealistic to assume that any particular pairing of two languages is representative of all bilingual combinations. Similarly, orthographic differences between languages (e.g., type and/or direction of script) may contribute to the overall pattern of lateralization observed (Albert and Obler 1978; Vaid, 1981a). It has also been proposed that certain languages reflect more appositional (or "gestalt"), as compared to propositional (or analytic) cultural, modes of thinking (Rogers *et al.*, 1977; Scott *et al.*, 1979) which, in turn, may be reflected in differential hemispheric processing in bilingual speakers of these languages.

Testing procedures

Technical issues

Certain technical issues must be considered since, if stimuli or procedures differed for the two language conditions, artifactual response asymmetries or lack of dominance might result. Eye fixation must of course be controlled in tachistoscopic testing. If the decision is made to require report of a central digit, the "overlearned" status of L_1 numbers even in highly fluent bilinguals must be evaluated. Stimulus duration and displacement of stimuli from center must be equal, as must size of stimulus, tasks which are complicated if two very different orthographies are being studied. Orientation of display may interact with the direction of reading in a given language on tachistoscopic tasks (Bryden, 1970). In the bilingual laterality literature, only Gaziel *et al.* (1978) have contrasted vertical and horizontal displays. With their balanced Hebrew–English bilinguals, they found no visual effect for either language with vertical presentation, and a trend toward RVFE for each language with horizontal presentation.

In dichotic listening, temporal alignment of stimuli is crucial, as it happens that when one word in a dichotic pair precedes another by an interval as short as 20 msec, an accuracy advantage accrues to the delayed stimulus (Berlin *et al.*, 1973). This lag effect could well cancel or interact with the ear advantage of interest, thus making results very difficult to interpret. Of course, when one stimulus tends to predominate in a dichotic pair for any of several reasons (e.g., clarity of one stimulus over another, amplitude, degree of fusion, dichotic masking, etc.; see Repp, 1977), this effect will also interact with any ear advantage that may be present, underscoring the importance of having each dichotic pair appear in both channel-ear assignments. When word length differs between two languages, a dichotic test pitting one language against the other would thus be impossible.

Task differences

Level of processing

Task differences enter not only into comparisons between studies, but also within a single study if, for example, the fact that one language is less well known may mean it is being processed differently (Hardyck, 1980; Schneiderman and Wesche, 1980). As to differences among studies, one must ask what levels of processing are accessed by a task. For example, word recognition, word identification, or language recognition (e.g, reporting whether the stimuli were French or English words) may differ with respect to the type of processing they demand (see Vaid, 1981).

Perception vs. production

Most studies in the laterality literature have presented stimuli to subjects and asked for recognition, recall, etc. These studies are measuring predominantly perceptual capabilities. Productive abilities are also important, however, and tasks can be designed to measure them. This issue may be particularly important in comparing experimental results to clinical results. For example, studies of polyglot aphasia (Albert and Obler, 1978; Galloway, 1980) have suggested some laterality differences between bilinguals and monolinguals. However, the aphasia reports focus on production much more than perception. Therefore, caution must be exercised in comparing experimental results with clinical studies. The only lateralization study to date in the bilingual literature using a production paradigm is that of Sussman *et al.* (1982), who measured finger tapping rates with concurrent verbalization. It is unclear at this point whether their finding of greater right-hemisphere participation in language of bilinguals is due to the use of production in their experiment or to some other variable. Again, an experiment separately testing perceptual and productive tasks would be very helpful in disentangling these variables.

Language set

If two languages are mixed during presentation, subjects with greater proficiency in one language may process all stimuli as if they were in that language. Thus one would not want to claim there was no differential lateralization between the two languages merely because in the testing situation stimuli were not being treated as belonging to two different languages.

Memory constraints

If recall is immediate, the subject may be reading out of a short-term sensory store with little phonetic or semantic processing, whereas with a few seconds' delay, short-term memory proper may come into play. A less than balanced bilingual subject may process the items in his/her two languages differently to the extent that they require different levels of effort in processing.

Dependent measure

Various studies have used different response measures, e.g., accuracy, reaction time, errors, and order of report by ear/visual field. Future studies should investigate more than one response measure in a given study of bilingual laterality, since response time and accuracy means, for example, may give conflicting pictures of performance. Moreover, responses should be analyzed both qualitatively and quantitatively, since the types of errors subjects make may reveal important information about the processing strategies they are employing.

Practice effect

Since left lateralization may increase over the course of a test (Samar, 1980), or with practice with stimuli (Bentin, n.d.), we must question whether studies showing *no* differences in lateralization between the two languages (e.g., Barton *et al.*, 1965) achieved this finding because of much prestudy familiarization with a limited number of stimuli. Note, however, that Schneiderman and Wesche (1980) found differential results despite a very limited stimulus corpus and considerable prestudy familiarization.

Monolingual controls

It should be pointed out that many of the problems described thus far might be greatly alleviated in a bilingual experiment by the appropriate use of monolingual controls. If an interesting effect is found among a bilingual group then the use of a monolingual control group would permit an experimenter to ensure that methodological problems were not confounding the results. Unfortunately, it is often difficult or impossible to obtain matched controls in this situation, since in predominantly bilingual societies, monolingualism may reflect learning disabilities or severe educational deprivation.

Analysis

Measurement and reliability

An issue which can only be touched on here is the use (or lack of use) of *a laterality index* as a measure of hemispheric specialization (Marshall *et al.*, 1975; Repp, 1977; Bryden, 1980), rather than some raw score or simple difference score. Such indices should indeed be used, as without them comparisons across groups (especially groups of bilinguals whose proficiency in their two languages may differ significantly) are questionable at best. A second analytical issue has to do with the *reliability* of dichotic and tachistoscopic tests. Low test–retest reliability may well introduce artifacts into comparisons across subject groups and across languages. The reliability of dichotic tests with monolinguals has been reported to be anywhere from .74 (Blumstein *et al.*, 1975) to .80 (Ryan and McNeill, 1974). To the extent that they may employ differing strategies, bilinguals may be less reliable than other groups if they are more proficient in one language than the other. Moreover, if reliability is low then it makes little sense to single out a few subjects from a group just because they may have an interesting laterality pattern in their two languages, as only the group effect can be considered stable (Hamers and Lambert, 1977). Repp (1977) points out that a remedy for low reliability is to increase the length of the test; however, then factors such as fatigue and over-familiarity with the stimulus set enter.

Continuous vs. discrete laterality effects

A further analytical issue involves the question of degree of laterality effects. If significant differences are found in degree (but not direction) of laterality between two groups or between languages, this does not guarantee that such differences reflect the underlying functional lateralization. Indeed, as Colbourn (1978) has pointed out, it is not necessarily valid to assume a one-to-one correspondence between the magnitude of an observed effect and the corresponding cerebral function it purports to measure. Colbourn believes it may be more prudent to consider the outcome of an experiment in terms of right, left or no difference rather than as a matter of degree. There are many reasons for differences to appear in estimates of a continuous variable, and these reasons (some of which are discussed elsewhere in this chapter) must be taken into account before the conclusion can be drawn that true differences in laterality exist.

Multiple independent significance tests

If a standard statistical test is significant at the $p = .05$ level, we may claim that such a result would be due to chance about one time in 20. The problem is that with more than a single comparison, multiple independent tests will yield true significance levels much less stringent than .05. For example, the probability that at least one comparison of two will be significant is .0975 if each is set to .05. An experiment with, say, six comparisons of interest will yield a true significance level of .26 if six independent tests are performed, each with the significance level set at .05. Therefore, if a significant result is found we can in no way conclude that such a result was not due to chance. Although this is an elementary problem, it appears repeatedly in the lateralization literature in bilinguals as well as monolinguals (Obler and Albert, 1978; Gordon, 1980).

One solution to this problem is obvious and simple: either set the significance level for each test at a much more stringent level, or perform some test such as the analysis of variance which takes all factors into account. The analysis of variance has the added advantage that it allows tests of interaction effects, which may not be apparent with multiple independent tests. A second solution is to run independent replication studies of only those effects that are significant.

Interpretation of nonsignificant intrahemispheric differences results

In cases where no laterality difference is found, the lack of significant results would be important if it were substantiated, since it could indicate equal processing of language in both hemispheres. However, caution must be exercised in interpreting nonsignificant laterality results, for they can arise from any of the numerous technical and methodological issues noted above. Moreover, there are also several statistical reasons for nonsignificant results. Foremost among these are violations of the assumptions underlying parametric tests, viz., normality and homogeneity of variance. Violation of either of these assumptions would be likely to obscure a result and make tests invalid. (In such cases nonparametric techniques may be preferable as there is no dependence on normality or homogeneity of variance.) Other reasons for overall negative results could simply be high dispersion of scores and ceiling and floor effects. The former problem can often be tackled by judicious elimination of outlying scores; also, certain transformations (e.g., logarithms) often help to reduce excessive variability. Ceiling and floor effects can only be corrected by adjusting the difficulty of the task.

The "language-as-fixed-effect fallacy"

Results of an experiment using a set of stimuli chosen from a larger group of possible stimuli must be generalizable to that larger set and not just to the specific examples that were used in the experiment (Clark, 1973). The majority of studies in the field of laterality and bilingualism have not utilized appropriate statistics for this purpose, and therefore their results are not, strictly speaking, applicable to new sets of stimuli. Furthermore, by failing to consider the variance attributable to words, artifactual results can be obtained. Consider, for example, a typical tachistoscopic experiment in which bilingual subjects are given two tests, one in each of their languages, with the appropriate counterbalancing. The analysis of variance should have the following three factors: visual field (fixed, with two levels, right and left), language (fixed, if only the two languages are of interest, and two levels), and also the third factor which must be taken into account: words. Since different words are presented on each trial they too will be a source of variance Further, words must be considered a random factor because the particular words chosen for an experiment can only be a small subset of all the words in a language. (Note that this is independent of whether or not the words were chosen randomly.) Moreover, the words factor must be nested into the language factor because each language (necessarily) has a different set of words; therefore, there can be no interaction of words with language (i.e., the unique effect due to words cannot be separated from an effect due to language). The correct variance components due to each factor and the expected mean squares are given in Table 20.1 for the more general case of an experiment with p languages, q words, r visual fields, and n

Table 20.1 Within-subject variance components for a tachistoscopic experiment using
p languages, q words, r visual fields, and n subjects; words are nested within
the language factor; both words and subjects are considered to be random
factors

Factor	Expected mean squares
Language (L)	$\sigma_e^2 + rn\sigma_{W\times S}^2 + qrn\sigma_{L\times S}^2 + rsn\sigma_W^2 + qrsn\sigma_L^2$
Words within language (W)	$\sigma_e^2 + rn\sigma_{W\times S}^2 + rsn\sigma_W^2$
Visual field (V)	$\sigma_e^2 + n\sigma_{W\times V\times S}^2 + pqn\sigma_{V\times S}^2 + sn\sigma_{W\times V}^2 + pqsn\sigma_V^2$
Language × Visual field (L × V)	$\sigma_e^2 + n\sigma_{W\times V\times S}^2 + qn\sigma_{L\times V\times S}^2 + sn\sigma_{W\times V}^2 + qsn\sigma_{L\times V}^2$
Words × Visual field (W × V)	$\sigma_e^2 + n\sigma_{W\times V\times S}^2 + sn\sigma_{W\times V}^2$
Language × Subject (L × S)	$\sigma_e^2 + rn\sigma_{W\times S}^2 + qrn\sigma_{L\times S}^2$
Words × Subject (W × S)	$\sigma_e^2 + rn\sigma_{W\times S}^2$
Visual field × Subject (V × S)	$\sigma_e^2 + n\sigma_{W\times V\times S}^2 + pqn\sigma_{V\times S}^2$
Lang. × Visual field × Subject (L × V × S)	$\sigma_e^2 + n\sigma_{W\times V\times S}^2 + qn\sigma_{L\times V\times S}^2$
Words × Visual field × Subject (W × V × S)	$\sigma_e^2 + n\sigma_{W\times V\times S}^2$
Experimental error (e)	σ_e^2

subjects, with words nested within language, and with words and subject being random
factors.

If the words factor is ignored the F ratio for the visual field factor, would be:

$$F = \frac{MS_V}{MS_{V\times S}}$$

Note that this ratio would leave two sources of variance in the numerator: one
attributable to visual field, and one to the interaction of words and visual fields. Thus,
a significant F ratio might be obtained even though the variance due to the visual
field factor may have been very small or zero. The appropriate F ratio can be constructed from several of the mean squares, but it must result in only one source of
variance remaining in the numerator. This statistic is known as a quasi-F, and in this case
it would be:

$$F'' = \frac{MS_V + MS_{W\times V\times S}}{MS_{W\times V} + MS_{V\times S}}$$

The degrees of freedom for this test may be calculated from formulas given by
Clark (1973) or from any standard text (such as Winer, 1971). Using the appropriate
test here allows the obtained result to be generalizable to a new set of stimuli. Some
conflicting results in the bilingual literature may be due, then, to this lack of generaliz-
ability. Also, if the words factor is ignored or treated as a fixed effect in the above
example, it could result in a spurious language × visual field effect, which would lead to
the erroneous conclusion that the two languages were differently lateralized, when in

fact the contribution of the variance due to words may be the reason for the obtained significant effect.

Interpretation

As with monolinguals, questions arise with bilinguals as to the discrepancy between lateralization as evidenced (or not evidenced) via instrumental measures compared with lateralization as evidenced via sodium amytal testing or incidence of aphasia. These discrepancies may reflect the insensitivity of the paradigms involved (Colbourn, 1978), or the added complexity of tasks beyond "pure" language processing, or the fact that we tend to generalize from tasks employing single words to speak about language in general (Galloway, 1980). Findings of differential lateralization for a set of language stimuli or for a group of bilinguals cannot be understood as "greater right-hemisphere participation in language processing than normal," i.e., than in monolinguals until all artifactual explanations can be ruled out. In the event that greater right-hemisphere involvement in L_2 acquisition and use can reliably be demonstrated, it will prove of interest to determine the extent to which "linguistic" capacities of the right hemisphere are being tapped; we may find as some suspect (e.g., Genesee *et al.*, 1978) that the right hemisphere contributes cognitive abilities such as effort (Hardyck, 1980), or specialization for novel stimuli (Bentin, n.d.) which while not strictly "linguistic," may be necessary to, or at least linked to, linguistic processing. In any event, the complexity of the factors involved in study of language lateralization in bilinguals must certainly caution us not to assume that any given study can speak for all bilingual individuals, nor for all bilingual populations.

Source: Obler, L.K., Zatorre, R.J., Galloway, L. and Vaid, J. (1982) Cerebral lateralization in bilinguals. *Brain and Language* 15: 40–54. Copyright © 1982 with permission of the authors and Elsevier.

Postscript

This article served the function, as had the conference out of which it arose, of demonstrating that lateral dominance was too coarse a measure to apply interestingly to understanding the bilingual brain. As well, it raised to neurolinguists' attention those participant variables that need to be reported in any study of bilingualism (or multilingualism or bidialectism, concepts hardly meaningfully dissociated from bilingualism in the 1980s). While some study of lateral dominance continues in the neurosciences generally (as evidenced in the continued contributions in the journal *Laterality*), in recent decades it has been eclipsed by techniques that permit more refined behavioral and brain-based understanding. Most crucially these include the burgeoning neuroimaging studies that appear to provide knowledge of both brain areas – cortical and subcortical – involved in language processing, and of temporal processes that subserve them. The focus, thus, has turned from how lateral dominance may distinguish bilinguals' brains from those of monolinguals, or early from late bilinguals, to questions concerning regions of interest within the dominant hemispheres of these populations, and questions of differential temporal processing among bilinguals with different language-learning (and, increasingly, language-use) histories.

Proficiency achieved, too, has taken on a larger role in distinguishing bilingual populations of interest, with addition of foci on near-native and nativelike L2 speakers, and on talented and particularly untalented L2 learners and acquirers.

Loraine K. Obler

Loraine K. Obler, PhD, is Distinguished Professor of Speech and Hearing Sciences at the Graduate School and University Center, the City University of New York, USA. Loraine.Obler@gmail.com

Robert J. Zatorre, PhD, is Professor of Neurology and Neurosurgery at the Montreal Neurological Institute, Canada. robert.zatorre@mcgill.ca

Linda Galloway was a research associate of Loraine K. Obler's. She no longer works in academia.

Jyotsna Vaid, PhD, is Professor of Psychology at Texas A & M University, USA. jxv@psyc.tamu.edu

Chapter 21

Language lateralization in bilinguals: enough already!

MICHEL PARADIS

THE OBSTINACY WITH WHICH psycholinguists continue to look for differences in hemispheric asymmetry between bilinguals and unilinguals is nothing short of astounding. Given the dead-end that the issue is faced with after over two decades of contradictory results, why would researchers want to carry out one more of the same type of inconclusive experiments? Yet the topic seems as popular as ever and scores of experiments continue to be submitted for publication with increasingly implausible interpretations, and, more disturbingly, with recommendations for application of the alleged finding of increased participation of the right hemisphere to foreign language teaching, the treatment of mental illness, or the rehabilitation of bilingual aphasia.

It is not the intention of this chapter to provide one more review of the literature on language lateralization in bilinguals. The reader will find comprehensive treatments in Vaid and Genesee (1980), Vaid (1983), and, more recently, critical reviews in Mendelsohn (1988) and Solin (1989). Suffice it to say that laterality differences have been reported for very specific subgroups of bilinguals and/or under very specific conditions, such as only for early (Orbach, 1967) or for late (Sussman et al., 1982; Albanèse, 1985) bilinguals, early or late bilingual women but only late bilingual men (Vaid and Lambert, 1979), or only when eyes are closed (Moss et al., 1985). Decreased asymmetry has been claimed to hold (exclusively) for just about every possible subgroup of bilinguals and its opposite: proficient late bilinguals having learned their second language formally (Bergh, 1986) as well as only those late bilinguals that are at the beginning stages of acquiring their second language informally (Galloway and Krashen, 1980). In other words, one author claimed to have found differences only in proficient late bilinguals (as opposed to beginners) who have learned their second language in a formal setting, and another found no difference in such a group (nor in beginners) but found differences only in those at the beginning of an informal acquisition of a second language. Not only can we not generalize to all bilinguals from any given subgroup, but given the contradictory nature of the results on the same type of bilingual subgroups, we cannot even generalize to any subcategory of bilinguals, no matter how subcategorized by sex, degree of proficiency, age, and manner of acquisition. We must not forget that, in addition to the contradictory results among studies that did find some difference between bilinguals and unilinguals, about an equal number of studies found NO difference.

If the experimental paradigm is considered a variable (and within the paradigm methodical, procedural, or statistical considerations) that explains the contradictory results, then the validity of the various paradigms (dichotic listening, tachistoscopic presentation in half visual fields, task-sharing experiments, EEG [electroencephalo-gram]) that yield these results must be seriously questioned. How could they be a reflection of laterality of language function if so many variables can have an effect on the results? On what basis could we select the one that would be indicative of the actual state of affairs? Equal involvement in each language, and more as well as less involve-ment of the right hemisphere have been claimed for the first language (L1) only, for the second language (L2) only, and only for early or late stages of informal acquisition or of formal learning.

For instance, Bergh (1986) interprets the results of his study as showing right-hemisphere (RH) participation in L2 processing increasing as a function of increasing proficiency in a formally learned L2. These results are in direct conflict with the predictions of the manner-of-acquisition hypothesis and the modified stage hypothesis. The former predicts that formally learned languages will not be less lateralized than L1 (only those acquired informally will); the latter predicts that greater participation of the right hemisphere will obtain only at the EARLY stages of INFORMAL acquisition of an L2. Yet both had claimed empirical support. Such reports contribute to the widening of the credibility gap associated with dichotic, tachistoscopic, and time-sharing studies of bilingual cerebral laterality of language functions. Such a situation invites one to seriously question the validity and reliability of the paradigm.

Evidence contradictory to the stage hypothesis abounds (see Vaid, 1983). There is now also evidence inconsistent with both the manner of acquisition and the stage of acquisition (Bergh, 1986). Not to mention all the studies that have reported no difference between various sub-populations of bilinguials and unilinguals (e.g., Barton et al., 1965; Kershner and Jeng, 1972; Kotik, 1975; Schönle, 1978; Walters and Zatorre, 1978; Carroll, 1980; Gordon, 1980; Hynd et al., 1980; Piazza and Zatorre, 1981; Soares and Grosjean, 1981; Galloway and Scarcella, 1982; Soares, 1982; Rapport et al., 1983; McKeever and Hunt, 1984; Soares, 1984; Hoosain and Shiu, 1989) or even GREATER asymmetry in bilinguals (Starck et al., 1977; Ben Amar and Gaillard, 1984). Yet in the face of such ever-increasing contradictory evidence, in spite of repeated denunciations of the lack of validity and reliability of current procedures, including those made by the very experimenters themselves (see Obler et al., 1982; Vaid, 1983: 328; Mendelsohn, 1988; Solin, 1989; Sussman, 1989; Zatorre 1989), and remarks about the lack of significance of the published data on bilingual crossed aphasia (by those same authors who then go on and report old selected cases at length in support of their experimental findings), and in the view of recently published reports of unselected cases of crossed aphasia showing no greater incidence in bilinguals than unilinguals, dichotic, tachisto-scopic, and tapping experiments nevertheless continue to be published at an alarming rate. What is the rationale for continuing to run and to publish experiments that the experimenter KNOWS yield uninterpretable conflicting results and ADMITS are neither reliable nor valid?

There was a time when it was possible to legitimately seek for subgroups within the bilingual population once it had been shown that the differential RH participation hypothesis did not hold for bilinguals at large. But why should we now wish to show at all cost that there must be some small subset of bilinguals such as proficient female late acquirers in informal settings, provided they keep their eyes closed (Moss *et al.*, 1985) or block one nostril (Shannahoff-Khalsa, 1984), when it is conceded that "it is questionable whether, even if properly tested, the predicted differences in the extent of hemispheric involvement in the two languages of bilingual subgroups can be reliably detected by current procedures, especially since the size of ear or visual field asymmetries may be influenced by factors other than degree of cerebral lateralization" (Vaid, 1983: 328). On the basis of statistical reanalysis of available data, Sussman (1989) concludes that previous findings and theoretical conclusions based on time-sharing laterality results may be meaningless, and he seriously questions the continued use of the time-sharing paradigm as a behavioral index of language lateralization. In addition, experiments with commisurotomized patients have shown that following section of the corpus callosum, under dichotic stimulation, the left ear score drops to near zero whereas in monaural stimulation it is normal (Milner *et al.*, 1968), which strongly suggests that the left ear score reflects the amount of information successfully transferred from the left ear to the left hemisphere – not information processed by the right hemisphere.

The interpretation of all these results as based on the unproven premise that reduced difference between the ears, or between half visual fields, or between tapping disruption, is indicative of increased RH participation or of a more bilateral contribution from both hemispheres. If left ear or right visual field scores were an index of RH linguistic processing, how would one interpret the 40–45% correct answers generally reported from the LEFT ear or visual field? How would one account for intraindividual variation over time within the same session or between sessions? When a difference between groups (unilinguals vs. bilinguals) is detected, what could the difference be indicative of, as opposed to when no difference is detected (i.e., in about half the studies) or when the difference is supposed to be present only in one specific population (e.g., late bilinguals) in one study, and the reverse (i.e., only in early bilinguals) in another?

It can no longer be assumed to be the case that "taken together, the available clinical and experimental studies suggest that competence in more than one language may influence brain functioning so that it differs from that characterizing speakers of a single language" (Vaid, 1983: 315). Most authors who speculate on a greater participation of the right hemisphere are aware of (and even explicitly mention) the reasons why the literature on which such a presumption is founded is not reliable. Obler *et al.* (1982) and Zatorre (1989) are even cited for providing methodological, theoretical, and statistical problems with these studies, but then authors go ahead anyway. Likewise, mention is made that published selected clinical cases are of no statistical use, but then authors go on to cite percentages anyhow.

In support of the manner of acquisition hypothesis, Hartnett's (1975) study is often cited by authors who have not read the original thesis, but only its published abstract. Had they read the original thesis, they would have realized to what extent the results were unreliable because of severe shortcomings in the areas of design, execution, data analysis, and interpretation (see Stieblich, 1983: 1–5 for details). Likewise, Nair and Virmani's (1973) study has been cited by many authors over the past 10 years as reporting a high incidence of crossed aphasia among bilinguals without having been read, for if these authors had read the original study rather than relying on the incidental misquoting of it in 1978, they would have realized that there was no way that one could have derived any percentage of bilingual crossed aphasics among the reported cases, since the number of bilinguals in their sample is nowhere mentioned.

As for the evidence from clinical reports, it is not just "equivocal" (Vaid, 1983: 317) with respect to the role of the right hemisphere in language mediation, it is simply *nonexistent*. There is not a shred of clinical evidence in support of less asymmetry of language representation in bilinguals for either or for both of their languages. There is NO statistically significant higher incidence of crossed aphasia in bilinguals than in unilinguals (for a review, see April and Han, 1980; Chary, 1986; Solin, 1989). Karanth and Rangamani (1988) report an incidence of crossed aphasia that is actually lower in bilinguals than in unilinguals. That study has been replicated by Rangamani (1989) on an unselected sample of CVA [cerebrovascular accident] patients, reporting crossed aphasia in 2/12 unilinguals and 0/26 bilinguals. Wada testing results are equally clear: both languages are affected only by left-hemisphere (LH) injection (e.g., Rapport *et al.*, 1983).

Given the extreme degree of variation within and between individuals, within and between groups of similar populations, and given that all available clinical evidence (incidence of crossed aphasia, Wada test) unequivocally shows identical LH involvement for both languages, whatever these experimental studies show, it is unlikely to be a lesser asymmetry of language cerebral representation and/or processing.

What is it then that these studies report a greater right-hemisphere participation of? One may in fact seriously question whether any of these paradigms are an index of *language* lateralization, when the stimuli used are nonsense syllables or isolated words. To start with, it seems legitimate to ask oneself what could possibly be the nature of this alleged increased participation of the right hemisphere. At least four possibilities come to mind (Paradis, 1987).

Let us call the first *the redundant participation hypothesis*. According to this hypothesis, both hemispheres process information in identical ways, though the participation of the left hemisphere may be quantitatively greater. The processing by the right hemisphere is redundant and hence the removal of the right hemisphere is of little consequence for language.

Another possibility would be *the quantitatively complementary participation hypothesis* according to which, as above, each hemisphere processes the same stimuli in the same way, with greater participation of the left hemisphere. However, there is a mass effect and the whole is necessary for normal language processing. A lesion to homologous parts of either the right or the left hemisphere will cause qualitatively identical deficits proportional to the extent of the damage.

One can also conceive of *a qualitatively parallel participation hypothesis*. According to this hypothesis the same stimulus is processed in a qualitatively different way by each hemisphere. Each hemisphere processes all aspects of a stimulus in accordance with its own inherent mode of functioning. The participation of the right hemisphere is thus qualitatively complementary to that of the left hemisphere in processing utterances.

Still another plausible candidate is *the qualitatively selective participation hypothesis*. Each hemisphere, in accordance with its intrinsic functional capacities, specializes in the processing of a different aspect of a complex stimulus. In this case, as in the previous one, the participation of the right hemisphere is qualitatively complementary to that of the left hemisphere. However, while in the qualitatively parallel participation hypothesis complementarity is with respect to each aspect of an utterance, in the qualitatively selective participation hypothesis it is with respect to the utterance as a whole.

The qualitatively parallel participation hypothesis predicts that a lesion in the right hemisphere will affect all aspects of the utterance (albeit in a specific way, distinguishable from the effects of a homologous left-hemisphere lesion; e.g., global vs. analytic-sequential decoding of the meaning of a word or phrase), whereas the qualitatively selective participation hypothesis predicts that a right-hemisphere lesion will affect certain aspects of the utterance (a homologous left-hemisphere lesion will affect the other aspects of the utterance; e.g., prosody related to emotional states vs. grammatical stress pattern of lexical tone).

The redundant and the quantitatively complementary participation hypotheses assume an identical processing of the same aspects of an utterance; the qualitatively parallel participation hypothesis assumes a different processing of the same aspects while the qualitatively selective participation hypothesis assumes a different processing of different aspects. Among the most often mentioned intrinsic processing modes attributed to each hemisphere, one finds the analytic/global, sequential/concomitant, logical/analogical, context-independent/context-dependent, and deductive/inductive. Aspects of an utterance that have been involved as likely to be processed separately by each hemisphere are, among others, grammatical/paralinguistic, phonemic/prosodic, and syntactic/pragmatic.

To the extent that right-hemisphere damage is known to cause speech, language, and communication deficits (Alexander, Hiltbrunner and Fischer, 1989) bilinguals will exhibit such symptoms, but only to the extent and in the same form that unilinguals will. Subsequent to right-hemisphere lesions bilinguals may be expected, as unilinguals, to exhibit impairment of affective prosody, of the ability to handle humor, sarcasm, irony, inference, analogy, nonexplicit speech acts, and, in general, any nonliteral meaning. But they should not be expected to exhibit impairment in linguistic aspects of prosody or in grammatical usage; at any rate, not to a greater extent than that which has been reported in unilinguals (Joanette et al., 1983; 1990).

Now, it happens that language teachers are turning more and more to the neuro-psychological literature for guidance. This is a commendable endeavor that may ultimately prove fruitful. However, one cannot be too cautious in applying to classroom methodology what are at best hypothetical and often quite controversial theoretical constructs. In the face of contradictory experimental results and the total absence of clinical evidence, the claim of lesser asymmetry of language representation and/or processing in bilinguals is absolutely unfounded, and should therefore not serve as a basis for researchers in neuropsychology to make any recommendation in the fields of pedagogy, psychiatry, or language therapy.

For example, Shannahoff-Khalsa (1984) reports having observed alternating periods of greater relative amplitudes of EEG activity in one hemisphere, and then in the other. At the same time, measures of airflow in the right and left nostril have shown a similar alternation between the use of each nostril. Rhythms of the nasal cycle and hemispheric cycle have been observed to be tightly coupled. Since this balance of hemispheric dominance can be shifted by forcibly altering the phase of the nasal cycle, it is suggested that we could exert control over cognitive functions by forced breathing through the right nostril to increase our mathematical capacity, or through the left nostril to enhance our creativity. It might nevertheless be premature to recommend that foreign language teachers require their students to block their left nostril to activate their right hemisphere in the hope of forcing language processing in that hemisphere (or the reverse).

Even if it were the case that the right hemisphere played a major role in the acquisition and/or learning of a second/foreign language, it might very well do so in spite of whatever method of presentation of the second/foreign language is used. One cannot force a language to be represented or prevent it from being represented where it is natural for it to be represented (save for the removal of the left hemisphere early in life – which I hope no one would advocate!).

Song, dance, instrumental music, or blocking one's left nostril will not force the grammar to be processed and/or represented in the right hemisphere, if that is not where it is naturally processed and/or represented. The mode of presentation might at best encourage particular processing strategies, but even these are not demonstrably beneficial. The fact (if it is a fact) that second language learning usually does involve the right hemisphere is no assurance that utilizing the right hemisphere is the most efficient way of learning a second language. Indeed it might be a main factor in failure to acquire native-like proficiency since, once higher proficiency has been attained, greater asymmetry is reported. Goodglass (1978: 103) suggests that, while in the early stages of first language acquisition neurons are recruited bilaterally, in the course of language development, the most compact, rapidly acting systems of the left hemisphere survive, while the slower, less efficient components of the neural network of the right hemisphere drop out of the processing of language. It might then be considered more efficient to try to get the left hemisphere to process the second language as soon as possible (if one knew how to do that).

But even if it were beneficial for the second/foreign language to be processed in the right hemisphere, one might argue that any competing right-hemisphere function concurrently activated might be a hindrance (as the time-sharing tasks experimental paradigm would indicate if it were valid; finger tapping is reported to be more disrupted when it is performed by the right hand by right handers). The moral should then be: "Do not overload the right hemisphere with materials (melody, choreography, etc.) that might require its attention." To the extent that the right hemisphere is normally engaged in (first) language processing, it will be engaged in second/foreign language processing as well – but no more. If it is a question of the extent to which certain bilinguals tend to use RH-based strategies in language processing (Gordon and Weide, 1983; Vaid, 1983), then we no longer are looking at a phenomenon characteristic of bilinguals *per se* (or groups of bilinguals) but of some unilinguals as well. The extent of reliance on strategies of the right hemisphere is a function of individual cognitive style, and there is no evidence that this style is more prevalent among bilinguals than unilinguals.

Has the inadequacy of dichotic, tachistoscopic, and time-sharing paradigms in reflecting laterality of language functions in bilinguals not yet been sufficiently attested? How many additional repeated failures to demonstrate differential laterality in increasingly specific subgroups of bilinguals will it take for neuropsychologists to move on to something more productive?

Source: Paradis, M. (1990) Language lateralization in bilinguals. Reproduced from *Brain and Language* 39: 570–86. Copyright © 1990 with permission of the author and Elsevier.

Postscript

Since the 'Enough already!' paper was published, a number of researchers have acknowledged that a plethora of methodological problems affect the experimental procedures used to measure language laterality in bilingual speakers. Nevertheless, they carry on in the hopes that better control over participant variables, better choice of stimuli, more appropriate tasks, or better statistical procedures would do away with the increasingly multidimensional contradictory results (Berquier and Ashton, 1992). Richardson and Wuillemin (1995) declare that they accept Paradis's (1995) comments and share much of his skepticism; admit that the task they use is an impoverished measure, that the stimuli are hardly representative of 'language' and that the method they use is subject to many criticisms; but insist that the inference they draw from their results, namely that there is right hemisphere involvement in processing later-learned languages in multilinguals, is warranted. The problem is not one of making right or wrong inferences from the data obtained with such measures, but of not being able to make *any* inference from findings that are not known to be valid. Experimentation is pointless unless the nature of what is alleged to be lateralized is clearly defined and the validity of the measures employed has been established. Neither condition is generally met. In their comments on the Paradis (1990) paper, Berquier and Ashton (1992) explain away the contradictory results by stating that studies using different tasks should not be compared. But the problem is that these studies, using divergent procedures, all claim to speak to the lateralization of 'language.'

The rationale for suspecting differential laterality is predicated upon Lenneberg's (1967) laterality shift hypothesis, which has repeatedly been shown to have no foundation in fact (Krashen, 1973; Kinsbourne and Hiscock, 1977; Seron, 1981). Granted, the right hemisphere is often involved to a greater extent in the use of a weaker second language – not to subserve any part of the language system (phonology, morphosyntax, lexicon, or semantics) but to subserve pragmatics. No amount of refinement of the process of listening dichotically to syllables, digits or words, or tachistoscopic presentation of isolated written words is likely to reveal the greater right-hemisphere involvement caused by greater reliance on pragmatic cues to compensate for gaps in implicit linguistic competence.

More importantly, all these studies have deliberately ignored the real issue that needs to be addressed before any claim can be made at all: the lack of validity of the notion that degree of right ear or right visual half-field advantage corresponds to the degree of laterality of whatever is claimed to be lateralized. Until it is shown that this paradigm is valid, any improvement in methodology is absolutely irrelevant. The Loch Ness Monster approach is doomed to failure, however well designed the study may be in all other respects. It is like attempting to treat a dead patient with the most efficacious medication available in the most technically advanced facility. Unless the patient is alive, any attempt at improving treatment is useless. Unless a procedure is valid, any attention to methodological detail is a waste of time and energy.

And yet, researchers have drawn attention to the lack of validity of these psychometric tools from the beginning, and have not ceased to do so (Satz, 1977; Colbourn, 1978, 1981; Paradis, 1990, 1992, 1995, 2003, 2004), but to no avail. Although 'it has never been demonstrated that there is any specific form of relation between surface measures of laterality and underlying cerebral organization aside from the original notion of a gross attachment of function to the different hemispheres' and that the ratio interpretation of laterality measures is without foundation since it has not been shown that the degree of ear or visual field advantage actually reflects the degree of lateralization of the task in the brain (Colbourn, 1981: 93); that even proponents of the paradigm concede that there are no validated tasks to assess lateralization of functions (Voyer, 1998); and the sizable literature on polyglot aphasia, supported by evidence from crossed aphasia and lateral dominance studies in non-brain-damaged bilingual individuals, suggests that the left hemisphere is dominant for all languages of most polyglots (Goral, Levy, and Obler, 2002), just as it is for the language of most unilinguals, researchers continue to churn out studies and journal editors continue to publish them as if they were valid. Berquier and Ashton (1992) attributed the shortcomings of the bilingual laterality literature to 'the youth of the field.' But fifteen years later, the state of affairs has hardly changed.

There are, admittedly, obvious methodological flaws, such as not using a unilingual control group and hence not being able to show whether the experimental bilingual group actually differs from unilinguals (Wuillemin et al., 1994; Evans et al., 2002); claiming to measure laterality of language when using single words as stimuli (Wuillemin, et al., 1994; Evans et al., 2002); and using inconsistent procedures across studies. These shortcomings could be avoided and would indeed greatly improve the design of the studies, as Berquier and Ashton (1992) suggested, but it would all be moot as long as the paradigm has not been validated. And, so far, no study has even attempted to demonstrate validity. So could someone please tell us why research teams go through the trouble of running experiments based on a paradigm they know has never been validated and in the full knowledge that there is no external evidence (such as clinical, neuroimaging, etc.)? Is this accepted practice in any other area of experimental psychology? If the answer to the last question is 'yes,' then we may as well publish papers on intelligent design in scientific journals.

Michel Paradis, PhD, is Professor Emeritus of Neurolinguistics at McGill University, Canada. michel.paradis@mcgill.ca

Chapter 22

The bilingual brain as revealed by functional neuroimaging

JUBIN ABUTALEBI, STEFANO F. CAPPA AND DANIELA PERANI

Until recently, the study of the representation of multiple languages in the human brain relied primarily on clinical case studies of aphasic patients. These "lesion" studies, carried out to investigate the clinical features of bilingual aphasia, have provided a complex pattern of results. In particular, recovery studies have clearly indicated that one of the polyglots' languages may recover in a different manner from the others (Pitres, 1895; Albert and Obler, 1978; Paradis, 1983). Indeed, it is not infrequent for a brain lesion to leave a bilingual patient impaired in only one language, while sparing the other. Yet some reports have shown more complex dissociations. A given patient can be impaired in the first language, but not in the second language on one day, while showing the reverse pattern the next day. These stunningly heterogeneous patterns of language recovery in bilinguals have hampered the researchers' effort to define the general rules and the determinants of language organization in the bilingual brain. The hypotheses of differential hemispheric lateralization, and/or of differential localization within the dominant hemisphere have dominated the discussion (see for review Paradis, 1998; Fabbro, 1999).

This panorama was enriched in the late 1970s by the studies of language representations in bilinguals with electrical cortical stimulation, resulting in the temporary inactivation of a brain region. This technique, developed by Penfield and Roberts to map the language areas in epileptic patients selected for neurosurgical treatment (Penfield and Roberts, 1959), was used by Ojemann and Whitaker (1978) to map naming sites in the lateral cortex of the dominant cerebral hemisphere of bilingual patients. In all patients studied, each language involved some "common" sites of naming interference and some "specific" area in which naming was interrupted only for one language. In the following years, Ojemann's efforts were basically addressed to discovering the reasons for this differential organization of the bilingual brain. The results of Ojemann's research may be summarized by his statement to one of his bilingual patients asking whether naming areas for the second language would be somewhat smaller:

they're slightly larger than those for the first language. In other words, the second language can be disrupted from a nickel-sized site rather than a dime-sized site. It's often hard to separate "when you learn it" from "how good you get", but the first language may be somewhat more compactly organized than later ones – its naming sites are not spread out as widely. (cited from Calvin and Ojemann, 1994, pp. 221)

Recently, the advent of noninvasive neuroimaging techniques, such as positron emission tomography (PET), functional magnetic resonance imaging (fMRI), event-related brain potentials (ERPs) and magnetoencephalography (MEG), has permitted the investigation of language organization in healthy individuals. In this paper, we present a brief overview of PET and fMRI techniques and of their contribution to the field of neurolinguistics. This is followed by a review of the studies which have been specifically addressed to the question of the cerebral organization of multiple languages. In particular, the review is focused on the potential role of two variables which may act on language representations of bilinguals: the degree of proficiency in each language and the age of second language (L2) acquisition.

Functional neuroimaging and language organization in the human brain

In the last 15 years, cognitive neuroscientists studying the neural correlates of mental operations have extensively adopted functional neuroimaging techniques to localize the components of cognitive processing in the human brain, and to image their orchestration as humans perform a variety of cognitive tasks. If a cognitive process can be sustained for only a few seconds, the snapshot revealed by PET or fMRI can show us which parts of the brain are active and to what degree (see Perani and Cappa, 1998, for a review). Functional imaging, used in conjunction with experimental cognitive tasks (Posner, Sandson, Dhawan and Shulman, 1989), has been extremely successful in establishing functional specialization as a principle of brain organization in man. In such studies images of blood flow are collected in at least two different conditions (e.g. while listening to a story and while at rest). The perfusion data are then compared, in order to find areas where the experimental task is associated with increased cerebral blood flow in comparison with the control task. These areas of increased perfusion are typically referred to as "activations".

For this purpose, the PET technique employs radioactive labeled biological probes to perform radioassays with exquisite sensitivity. For instance, the regional cerebral blood flow (rCBF) can be measured using tracers such as labeled ^{15}O water. This allows PET to assay biological systems *in vivo*, providing information about brain function which is complementary to the anatomical information portrayed by structural imaging techniques, such as magnetic resonance imaging (MRI) and computed tomography (CT). Indeed, combining functional PET data with the high resolution anatomical maps produced by MRI provides powerful data sets to investigate structure/function relationships in the brain.

Functional magnetic resonance imaging is a more recent technique, based on the measurement of MRI signal changes associated with alterations in local blood oxygenation levels. As in the case of the PET technique, fMRI assesses localized increases in blood flow. In particular, the signal changes result from small differences in the magnetic signal caused by variations in the oxygenation state of the venous compartment. Using this totally noninvasive method, it is possible to localize functional brain activation with an accuracy of millimeters and a temporal resolution of about three seconds. Besides these advantages in spatial and temporal resolution when compared to the PET technique, the fact that no radionuclides are used makes it feasible to repeat experiments several times on the same subject. Using fMRI, it is therefore possible to use more complex experimental designs. However, fMRI has some limits. For instance, crucial structures of the brain (in particular, the inferior temporal gyrus and the temporal pole) may not be visualized due to interference with the magnetic field. This is because the air enclosed in adjacent structures (the middle ear and the mastoid bone) creates serious interference with the magnetic field, resulting in a loss of their visualization.

In recent years, a large number of functional neuroimaging studies have been devoted to the investigation of language organization in the intact human brain. Briefly, imaging studies employing these techniques have confirmed the importance of classical language-related areas within the perisylvian cortex of the left hemisphere; however, language-related activation is observed also outside these regions, in the middle and inferior temporal gyri and temporal pole, in the lingual and fusiform gyri, in middle prefrontal areas (dorsolateral prefrontal cortex) and the insula (see reviews in Price, 1998 and Indefrey and Levelt, 2000); furthermore, right hemispheric activation in mirror regions is observed during the performance of most language tasks. These "language-related" areas, located outside the classical language zone, appear to be specialized for specific components of language processing, such as lexical semantics, as indicated also by recent lesion data (Warrington and Shallice, 1984; Alexander, Hiltbrunner and Fischer, 1989; Hillis and Caramazza, 1991; Damasio et al., 1996; Thompson-Schill, Swick, Farah, D'Esposito, Kan and Knight, 1998). In general, the functional role of the language-related areas appears to be characterized in terms of linguistically relevant systems, such as phonology, syntax and lexical semantics, rather than in terms of activities, such as speaking, repeating, reading and listening (Neville and Bavelier, 1998). The areas related to linguistic processing in the normal human brain appear to be not only more extended, but also less fixed than previously thought. For example, even when the task and experimental design are held constant, dramatic changes in language-related brain activation can be observed as a consequence of increased familiarity with the task. Striking evidence was provided by Petersen and coworkers (Petersen, van Mier, Fiez and Raichle, 1998) who investigated the effects of practice on a verbal task using PET. The neural differences putatively related to processing differences between a high and a low practice performance of verb generation were highlighted by this study, in which decreasing brain activity in the left frontal lobe was observed following practice. That experience alone may decrease brain activity in the left prefrontal cortex was highlighted by a further recent PET study (Petersson et al., 1999), investigating the recall of abstract designs. Specifically, practice-related decreases were observed in the left dorsolateral frontal cortex (Brodmann areas 9, 10 and 46). These data are consistent with similar practice-related changes previously observed in a verbal learning paradigm (Raichle et al., 1994), where the above-mentioned prefrontal brain areas were active in the learning phase but not in the well-practiced automatic condition.

Functional neuroimaging studies and bilingualism

As mentioned above, studies of bilingual and polyglot aphasia have provided evidence that a bilingual may selectively lose one of his/her languages, while the other is spared, suggesting that the neural representation of different languages is differentially organized. Functional neuroimaging studies of normal adult bilinguals have begun, in the last five years, to address this issue, taking into account the possible influence of several factors. For example, the greater ease with which infants, compared to adults, acquire a second language is uncontroversial. In particular, it was stated that the age of L2 acquisition plays a crucial role in the concept of "critical period" (Lenneberg, 1967). Indeed, the phonological and morphological components seem particularly deficient when L2 is learnt later in life, whereas the lexicon seems to be acquired with less difficulty after puberty. This fact entails the hypothesis that the neural representation of an L2 may differ as a function of its age of acquisition.

This and other hypotheses have been tested with functional neuroimaging. The studies are here divided in two groups: those investigating language production and those investigating language comprehension in bilinguals. This broad subdivision is based on the paradigms used for the imaging experiments, which include a number of diverse behavioral tasks, ranging from lexical retrieval to sentence comprehension. While some of these can be clearly considered to focus on, respectively, output (word generation) or input processes, the distinction is not directly applicable to others, such as word repetition and translation. Nonetheless, this atheoretical and, to a certain degree, arbitrary subdivision appears to have interesting implications for the interpretation of language-specific differences in activation of the bilingual brain (see below).

Language production in bilinguals

Several functional neuroimaging studies of language production, investigating the hypothetical differential cerebral representation in bilinguals, are now available in the literature (Klein, Zatorre, Milner, Meyer and Evans, 1994; Klein, Milner, Zatorre, Meyer and Evans, 1995; Yetkin, Yetkin, Haughton and Cox, 1996; Kim, Relkin, Lee and Hirsch, 1997, Chee, Tan and Thiel, 1999, Price, Green and von Studnitz, 1999). It is noteworthy that in all reports subjects were divided only on the basis of their age of L2 acquisition (see Table 22.1 for details), and never according to the level of proficiency in L2. A further important variable is that different experimental designs and modalities have been used to study language production in bilinguals. For instance, the landmark PET investigation by Klein and colleagues (Klein *et al.*, 1994) used a word repetition task (several trials, respectively for each language) in the first language acquired (L1) and L2 to elucidate whether production in a second language involved the same neural substrates as in the first language. The bilingual population of this study was represented by a group of late Canadian bilinguals who were native English speakers but learnt French after age five (mean age 7.3 years), with a high proficiency as established by a prescreening language examination. Klein and colleagues demonstrated that the pattern of rCBF distribution was similar across the two languages, suggesting that repetition involves largely overlapping neural structures. The only difference was found in the selective activation of the left putamen. This subcortical structure was found to be activated only when subjects repeated words in their second language. The authors suggested a crucial role for the left putamen as a function of the increased demands on articulation processes, when producing an L2 learnt late in life. This hypothesis may be supported by lesion studies of the so-called "foreign accent syndrome" associated with

Table 22.1 Language production in bilinguals

Study	Task and methods	Group of study	Main results
Klein *et al.*, 1994	PET investigation of repetition of words in L2 compared to that in L1	Homogeneous group of 12 highly proficient bilinguals who learned L2 after age 5	Increasing activity in the left putamen when repeating words in L2
Klein *et al.*, 1995	PET investigation of phonological and semantic word generation in L1 and L2 and a word translation task	Homogeneous group of 12 high proficient bilinguals who learned L2 after age five	No evidence that a language learnt later in life may be differently represented from the native language
Yetkin *et al.*, 1996	fMRI study of word generation in L1, L2 and L3	Dyshomogeneous group of five multilinguals fluent in L2 but not in L3	Activations were greatest for the languages in which subjects were least fluent
Kim *et al.*, 1997	fMRI investigation of sentence generation task in L1 and L2	Dyshomogeneous group of six early bilinguals and six late bilinguals	Common areas of left frontal lobe activation for L1 and L2 in early bilinguals and spatially separated areas for late bilinguals
Chee, Tan and Thiel, 1999	fMRI study of cued word generation in L1 and L2	Homogeneous group of 15 early bilinguals and nine late bilinguals	Similar pattern of brain activations for early and late bilinguals
Price *et al.*, 1999	PET investigation of written word translation from L1 to L2 and vice versa	Homogeneous group of six late bilinguals	Activation of the anterior cingulate and bilateral subcortical structures while translating

left subcortical damage (Blumstein, Alexander, Ryalls, Katz and Dworetzky, 1987; Gurd, Bessel, Bladon and Bamford, 1988), in which monolingual patients acquired a so-called "foreign accent" when speaking. The possible role of subcortical structures of the dominant hemisphere in the control process of bilingual language production will be further discussed below.

The task used in Klein *et al.*'s experiment allows us to draw only limited conclusions about the cerebral organization of bilinguals, since lexical-semantic access is not necessarily involved during repetition tasks. For this reason, the same authors performed a second study of language production in the same experimental group of highly proficient bilinguals (Klein *et al.*, 1995). The subjects were asked, during rCBF measurement by PET, to generate words selectively in L1 or L2 using three different types of strategy: rhyme generation, based on phonological cues; synonym generation, requiring semantic search; and translation, requiring lexical access in the other language. The word repetition task in each language was used as a baseline and subtracted from the experimental conditions. Compared to the baseline, each word generation task yielded significant activations in the left dorsolateral frontal cortex (Brodmann area (Ba) 9, 45, 46 and 47). Indeed, irrespective of task requirement (rhymes or synonyms) and language used, a considerable overlap was observed in frontal areas. Once again, the authors noted a selected activation in the left putamen, only when subjects generated words in L2. In particular, L2–L1 subtractions for all three conditions revealed a consistent rCBF increase in the left putamen. Within the activated system, the left inferotemporal regions (Ba 20/37) and the left superior parietal cortex (Ba 7) were always involved irrespective of language and task, with the only exception of rhyme generation in L2. Since no evidence of a differential neural substrate subserving language processing was found, the authors concluded that a similar, distributed network of brain areas is engaged in within and across language production in highly proficient bilinguals, despite the late acquisition of L2 (in this case, after age five).

In another fMRI experiment based on word generation (phonemic verbal fluency) in multilinguals, Yetkin and colleagues (Yetkin *et al.*, 1996) reported larger foci of brain activation for the "less fluent" languages. The experimental group was composed of heterogeneous subjects, "fluent" in at least two languages and "non fluent" in a third language. The languages ranged from Indo-European languages (English, German, Russian, Norwegian, French, Spanish) to Ural-Altaic languages (Turkish, Japanese, Chinese). "Fluent" was defined as speaking the language currently and for at least five years, whereas "non fluent" was used for languages studied for two to four years, and without regular use in the everyday life. Thus, in this study, an interesting variable was taken into account, namely the effect of the exposure to a language. For all languages, activations were primarily observed in the left prefrontal cortex, in particular in the inferior frontal, middle frontal and precentral gyri. Additional foci of brain activation were reported, such as in the supplementary motor area and parietal lobe, but the precise localizations (for instance, by using stereotactical coordinates) of these activations were not further specified. Noteworthy is that in all the subjects the extension of focal brain activation was greater for L3 than for L2 and L1, whereas the average activation was less for L1 than for L2, but the difference did not reach statistical significance. These results highlight an interesting hypothesis about the effect of current exposure to a language: when a language is not used regularly, a larger neural network may be necessary for its processing. However, these findings are difficult to interpret, given the lack of control of important variables such as the age of language acquisition and proficiency, which cannot be equated with language "fluency". We should also criticize the fact that the authors labeled English always as L1, despite the fact that the native language was Turkish in subject 2 and Chinese in subject 5.

Two further studies, which addressed the issue of the age of L2 acquisition, produced different results.

Kim and coworkers used fMRI to study the representation of L1 and L2 while bilingual subjects were engaged in covert language production (Kim *et al.*, 1997). The volunteers had to describe what they had done during the morning, afternoon or evening of the previous day, using covert speech. Twelve proficient bilinguals were studied. Of these, six had been exposed to L1 and L2 during early infancy, while six began learning L2 after puberty. The volunteers were bilinguals for widely different pairs of languages, ranging from Indo-European to languages from the Far East. The main result of the study was that in late learners, L1 and L2 were represented in spatially segregated parts of the left inferior frontal cortex (Broca's area). In contrast, overlapping parts of Broca's area were activated for both languages in early learners. The regions activated by L1 and L2 within Wernicke's area overlapped in both groups of subjects, regardless of the age of L2 acquisition. The conclusion was that age of acquisition is a major factor in the cortical organization of second language processing. It must be underlined however that the production of extended speech relies heavily on lexical-semantic and conceptual processing; in contrast, most of the linguistic processing limitations observed in bilinguals are related to phonological tasks, or to morphosyntactic processing. The subtle differences in Broca's area activation may reflect these differences at the phonological and syntactic level. A problem for the interpretation of this study is that no special procedure to assess proficiency was described. Since there is a general negative correlation between age of acquisition and proficiency (Johnson and Newport, 1989), these two variables are confounded in this experiment.

More recently, Chee and his group using fMRI (Chee, Tan and Thiel, 1999) found no difference within the left prefrontal cortex when comparing word generation in early bilinguals (L2 acquisition before age 6) and late bilinguals (L2 acquisition after age 12). Fifteen early bilinguals (Mandarin–English) were compared to nine late bilinguals (Mandarin–English), when producing words cued by a word stem presented visually on a screen. Again, for this single word production task, the most robust foci of brain activity were located in the left prefrontal cortex, along the inferior and middle frontal gyri (Ba 9/46 and Ba 44/45). The authors expected that the neural processing of Mandarin might require processing resources distinct from English, since Mandarin has an ideographic writing system. However, the pattern of brain activation in response to Mandarin words was similar to that observed for English, and further, this was true for both early and late bilinguals.

The reason for the discrepancy between the studies of Kim and colleagues (extended language production) and Chee and colleagues (word stem completion) might be related to the subjects' *different level of proficiency in each language*. As mentioned above, in Kim's study the differential activation in Broca's area for the second language in late bilinguals could have been due to inferior proficiency in the second language. On the other hand, Singapore, from where Chee's subjects were chosen, constitutes a real integrated bilingual society, in which bilingual speakers can be expected to be highly proficient in each language. In other words, these studies leave open the possibility that language proficiency, rather than age of acquisition, may be the crucial factor in determining the neural organization of language processing in bilinguals.

Finally, a recent PET investigation (Price *et al.*, 1999) addressed the mechanisms of word translation from L1 to L2 and vice versa in bilinguals. Price, Green and von

Studnitz studied six subjects, whose first language was German and who became fluent in their second language (English) late, after around the age of nine. Subjects were studied with PET while they read or translated written words, one at a time. In distinct blocks, the words were presented only in German, only in English or in alternation between the two languages. This experimental design allowed the authors to evaluate in the same study the brain areas subserving translation, language switching, perception and production in L1 and L2. Rather surprisingly, the regions that were found to be most active during translation were located outside of the classical language areas. Translating, when compared to reading, activated mainly the anterior cingulate and bilateral subcortical structures (the putamen and the head of the caudate nucleus). Price and colleagues attributed this to the need for greater coordination of mental operations for translation, during which the direct cerebral pathways for naming words must be inhibited, in favor of less automated circuits. This hypothesis was recently raised also in neuropsychological lesion studies in bilinguals, indicating that damage to subcortical structures may interfere with the complex mechanism implicated in the selection of languages. Aglioti and coworkers described the case of a bilingual suffering left subcortical damage (capsulo-putaminal lesion), which inhibited language changes when speaking (Aglioti, Beltramello, Girardi and Fabbro, 1986; Aglioti and Fabbro, 1993). Abutalebi and colleagues (Abutalebi, Miozzo and Cappa, 2000) also reported the case of a polyglot who was no longer able to speak in one language, showing pathological language mixing, due to a lesion located in the head of the caudate nucleus in the left hemisphere. It has thus been hypothesized that the bilinguals'/polyglots' lexical representations may be selectively accessed under the control of neural routes involving a cortical-subcortical circuit where the left basal ganglia may represent the "supervisor" of language output in bilinguals. A further interesting finding of Price's study was the activation of Broca's area and supramarginal gyrus during language switching. It is noteworthy that Poetzl and Leischner had suggested a central role for this region in language switching, on the basis of defective switching performance by patients with supramarginal lesions (Poetzl, 1925, 1930; Leischner 1943).

In conclusion, the majority of the neuroimaging experiments on language production in bilinguals are based on single word processing, in particular on word generation (fluency) tasks. The fluency tasks have been largely employed for language activation studies in monolinguals, which have shown a consistent pattern of activation with the involvement of the left dorsolateral frontal cortex (Frith, Friston, Liddle and Frackowiak, 1991; Poline, Vandenberghe, Holmes, Friston and Frackowiak, 1996). The generation of words according to a cue is a complex task, which involves multiple cognitive processes, such as lexical search, lexical retrieval and speech production. A crucial aspect of the task is the type of cue: for example, in the case of initial letter fluency, the characteristics of the search process are very likely different from conditions in which a semantic cue is given (Martin, Wiggs, Ungerleider and Haxby, 1996). Anatomo-functional differences have been reported between phonemic verbal fluency (initial letter fluency) and semantic verbal fluency within the left frontal lobe (Paulesu et al., 1997; Mummery, Patterson, Hodges and Wise, 1996). Indeed, phonemic fluency has been reported to engage the left inferior frontal gyrus extensively, including the posterior frontal operculum (Ba 44). On the other hand, during semantic fluency there was a discrete activation of more anterior frontal regions (Ba 45 and 46). Functional studies of brain representation of different languages should also take carefully into account these cognitive aspects.

Considering the limitations of the cognitive paradigms employed so far in the research addressing language production in bilinguals, which questions have been answered? Is there a unique common neural network, or rather spatially segregated networks subserving two (or multiple) languages in the human brain? What are the determinants of a common or differential cerebral organization of language in bilinguals?

Leaving aside the substantial differences, the pooled results of these studies seem to indicate the following. No differences in brain activation were present when very early bilinguals produce in L1 or L2 (we might assume that these subjects were highly proficient for both languages). A common neural network also subserves language production tasks in late bilinguals, if they are highly proficient in both languages (Klein et al., 1995; Chee, Tan and Thiel, 1999). On the other hand, in late bilinguals, spatially separated regions were activated within Broca's area for L1 and L2, in the study of Kim and coworkers; however, we do not know if this differential cerebral organization is a consequence of the age of L2 acquisition or rather of a reduced proficiency or low exposure. Interestingly, Yetkin's study provides evidence that when a language is spoken less fluently, a larger cerebral activation can be observed in comparison with languages spoken more fluently. We do not know, however, if this could be ascribed to high/low proficiency or high/low exposure. Taken together, these findings appear to indicate that attained proficiency, and maybe language exposure, might be more important than age of acquisition as a determinant of the cerebral representation of languages in bilinguals/ polyglots. Further investigations, taking into appropriate consideration at least these three important linguistic criteria (age of L2 acquisition, degree of language proficiency, and preferential exposure to a language) are necessary in order to draw stronger conclusions.

Language comprehension in bilinguals

Studies of language comprehension in bilinguals with functional neuroimaging have provided a more coherent picture of language organization in the bilingual brain. Five neuroimaging investigations of language comprehension are summarized in Table 22.2 (Perani et al., 1996, 1998; Dehaene et al., 1997; Chee, Caplan et al. 1999; Price et al., 1999), and with one exception (Price et al., 1999) all are based on sentence comprehension tasks.

The first three studies examined linguistically well-defined bilinguals who were asked to listen to stories alternatively in L1 and L2 while being scanned. In these three studies, subjects were grouped on the basis not only of the age of L2 acquisition but also of the degree of language proficiency as assessed by a psycholinguistic evaluation. In the first, Perani and coworkers (Perani et al., 1996) studied with PET nine late bilinguals (Italian–English) who had low proficiency in their L2, English, which they had studied at school for at least five years. Interestingly, none of them had spent more than one month in an English-speaking environment and, therefore, mastered L2 poorly. Partially different cerebral substrates were active for L1 and L2 when compared to the baseline condition (attentive rest condition). Areas activated by L1 comprised classical left peri-sylvian language areas, including the angular gyrus (Ba 39), the superior and middle

Table 22.2 Language comprehension in bilinguals

Study	Task and methods	Group of study	Main results
Perani *et al.*, 1996	PET investigation while subjects were listening to stories in L1, L2 and in a third unknown language	Homogeneous group of nine low proficient late bilinguals	More extensive activations when processing the native language in comparison to L2. Same activation pattern for L2 and the unknown language
Dehaene *et al.*, 1997	fMRI scanning while subjects were listening to stories in L1 and L2	Homogeneous group of eight low proficient late bilinguals	Differential brain activation for late L2 learners (including the right hemisphere)
Perani *et al.*, 1998	Two PET studies of two groups of subjects listening to stories in L1 and L2	Two homogeneous groups of bilinguals: nine highly proficient but late bilinguals and L2 highly proficient but early bilinguals	Attained proficiency might be more important than age of L2 acquisition as a determinant of cortical representation of L2
Chee, Caplan *et al.*, 1999	fMRI investigation of visually presented sentence-comprehension in L1 and L2	Homogeneous group of 14 early bilinguals	Common patterns of brain activity during the conceptual and syntactic processing of written language
Price *et al.*, 1999	PET study of single word comprehension in L1 and L2	Homogenous group of six late bilinguals	Comprehension of words in L1 yielded greater activity in the left temporal lobe than did words in L2

temporal gyri (Ba 21 and 22), the inferior frontal gyrus (Ba 45) and the temporal pole (Ba 38). Several homologous areas (Ba 21, 22 and 38) were also activated in the right hemisphere. In contrast, the set of active language areas was considerably reduced when applying the same analysis to the second language. Specifically, only the left and right superior and middle temporal areas remained active. This was the first in vivo evidence for a different functional representation of L1 and L2 in comprehension, when a crucial variable such as language proficiency is taken into account. One of the crucial areas of differential activation was, rather unexpectedly, the temporal pole. Activation of this region has been seldom reported in the functional imaging studies on language and memory. However, more recent studies have shown that the anterior part of the temporal lobe is activated by tasks requiring semantic processing; in particular, listening or reading sentences or a continuous text (Mazoyer *et al.*, 1993; Bottini *et al.*, 1994; Fletcher *et al.*, 1995; Perani *et al.*, 1996), rather than unconnected verbal material, is associated with the activation in this area. It is possible that these regions might be involved in processes associated with the sentence or even the discourse level, such as integration with prior knowledge, inference and anaphoric reference. In addition, the temporal poles might be recruited on the basis of increasing memory demands, when the subjects are engaged with the natural task of listening to some simple narrative.

The same experiment was repeated using fMRI in a comparable group of experimental subjects (eight late bilinguals, with French being here the maternal language and English the second language) scanned while listening to short stories alternatively in French and English (Dehaene *et al.*, 1997). The authors partially confirmed the previous results of the Perani *et al.* study since listening to the stories in L1 engaged a totally comparable set of left-sided brain areas, with in addition similar, although much weaker, activation in the right hemisphere, whereas this pattern radically changed when subjects processed L2. The only difference from the previous PET study was the lack of activation in the left temporal pole, due to the above-cited technical limitations of fMRI. It is noteworthy that a detailed single subject analysis showed a quite disparate pattern of brain activity, indicating large intersubject variability. Indeed, listening to L2 engaged a highly variable network of left and right temporal and frontal areas among the subjects, in some individuals restricted only to right hemispheric regions. On the basis of these results, the authors confirmed that while the processing of L1 essentially relies on the dedicated left cerebral network, the processing of an L2 acquired late in life and mastered with reduced proficiency, may be organized within a highly variable cerebral substrate, with a possible participation of right hemispheric structures.

A third study was aimed at evaluating the effect of *early* and *late* acquisition of L2 in *highly proficient* bilinguals (Perani *et al.*, 1998). A group of Italian–English late bilinguals who acquired L2 after the age of ten, but attained high proficiency, and a group of Spanish–Catalan early bilinguals who acquired L2 before the age of four were studied with PET. The differing cortical responses observed when low proficiency bilinguals listened to stories in L1 and L2 were not found in either of the high proficiency groups. Indeed, several brain areas, comparable to those observed for L1, were activated by L2 in these groups. A formal comparison between the groups of highly proficient Italian–English bilinguals of this study was made with the low proficient Italian–English bilinguals of the previous PET investigation. This was in order to isolate the role of proficiency per se. In the highly proficient bilinguals, the results showed significantly greater activation in the temporal poles bilaterally, in the left superior temporal sulcus and in the middle temporal gyrus bilaterally (see Figure 22.1 and Table 22.3).

This series of experiments provides evidence of considerable plasticity in the network that mediates language comprehension in the bilingual brain. The main result is that, while listening to stories in L1 and in L2 yields very different patterns of cortical activity in low proficiency subjects, no major differences are present in high proficiency

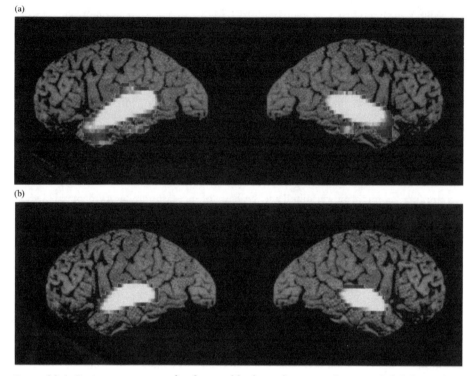

Figure 22.1 Brain areas activated in low and high proficiency Italian–English bilinguals in the comparison between the experimental condition (listening to stories in English) and the baseline (attentive silence). The results, displayed on a three-dimensional cortical reconstruction of the human brain as implemented in SPM96 (Wellcome Department of Cognitive Neurology, London, UK), show the differing cortical responses in low proficiency and high proficiency groups for listening L2 (English): a larger activation in the temporal poles bilaterally and in the left temporal lobe is evident in the high proficiency group (a) (see Table 22.3 for anatomical details).

Table 22.3   Brain areas activated in high proficient late acquisition bilinguals (HPLA) and not in low proficient late acquisition bilinguals (LPLA) during processing of L2 (see Perani *et al.*, 1998)

Brain region	x	y	z
L temporal pole (Ba 38)	−34	8	−32
L middle temporal gyrus (Ba 21/20)	−32	−6	−20
L superior temporal sulcus (Ba 22/21)	−32	−52	16
L insula	−32	−18	24
R temporal pole (Ba 38)	38	18	−24
R middle temporal gyrus (Ba 21/20)	52	−4	−28
R lingual gyrus (Ba 18)	28	−62	4

Differences in activation as revealed by the interaction effect: HPLA (English–Silence) − LPLA (English–Silence), x, y, z: stereotactic coordinates, Ba: Brodman area subjects, regardless of age of acquisition. The languages spoken by the low and high proficiency volunteers were identical, and so was the procedure. Hence we must conclude that the degree of mastery of L2 is responsible for the observed differences between the groups: auditory language comprehension in proficient bilinguals who have learned L2 after the age of ten relies upon a macroscopic network of areas that is similar for L1 and L2 groups. In addition, the highly similar pattern of activation observed for L1 and L2 in Italian–English and in Catalan–Spanish high proficiency bilinguals suggests that, at least at this level of the resolution afforded by PET methodology, linguistic distance does not appear to play a major role in determining the degree of overlap of L1 and L2 when proficiency is very similar.

In a recent fMRI investigation language comprehension was studied in bilinguals using two orthographically and phonologically distant languages – English and Mandarin (Chee, Caplan et al., 1999). Visually presented sentence comprehension was the main focus of this study, which showed significant activations in the left inferior and middle frontal gyri, in the left superior and middle temporal gyri, the left temporal pole, the anterior supplementary motor area and, bilaterally, superior parietal regions and occipital regions. Also with these two orthographically and phonologically distant languages, striking overlapping brain activity pattern was present for both languages, as indicated by the direct contrasts (English versus Mandarin and vice versa) which yielded no significant differences.

At the single word level, the study of Price et al. (1999), in which six late bilinguals were investigated using PET, provided comparable results. The language areas in the left temporal lobe were more activated when processing the mother language when compared to a less known language. Indeed, comprehension of words in L1 yielded a greater activation in the temporal pole than comprehension of the words in L2.

To summarize, neuroimaging studies of language comprehension in bilinguals appear to give more consistent results than production studies. In *early bilinguals*, who received equal practice with their two languages from birth, a single and common neural machinery appears to be responsible for the processing of both languages (Perani et al., 1998; Chee, Caplan et al., 1999). This neural machinery extends along a left-sided network, comprising all the classical language areas. In the temporal lobe, these include the superior and middle temporal gyri, the angular gyrus, and the temporal pole, a structure which seems specifically engaged by sentence and discourse level processing. In the frontal lobe, in particular the prefrontal areas involved in lexical monitoring, such as the inferior and middle frontal gyrus (Thompson-Schill, D'Esposito, Aguirre and Farah, 1997; Thompson-Schill, D'Esposito and Kan, 1999). In the case of *late bilinguals*, the degree of language proficiency seems to be a critical factor in shaping the functional brain organization of languages, since *highly proficient* late bilinguals activated strikingly similar left hemispheric areas for L1 and L2 (Perani et al., 1998), whereas *less proficient* subjects have different patterns of activation for their two languages (Perani et al., 1996; Dehaene et al., 1997; Price et al., 1999). Thus, increasing language proficiency appears to be associated at the neural level with the engagement of a common network within the dedicated language areas.

Conclusions

Given the extent of the phenomenon of bilingualism, it is clear that related questions deserve serious attention, whether they are theoretical or practical in nature. How do bilingual people understand and produce language? Are there fundamental differences from monolingual speakers? How do people learn and acquire a second language? These are just a few of the many questions that can be raised in this respect.

In this paper we have reviewed the functional imaging literature on language processing in bilinguals. Functional neuroimaging with PET and fMRI offers us a direct window into the complex mechanism of interaction among language systems in the human brain, and thus appears to be a valuable tool to attempt to delineate the general principles of cerebral language organization in bilinguals. What we may conclude from these studies is the fact that the bilingual brain cannot be considered as the sum of two monolingual language systems, but is rather a unique and complex neural system which may differ in individual cases. There are several factors which appear to affect the bilingual language system: of these, on the basis of the available evidence, proficiency seems to be the most important one. In the case of word generation and of production tasks in general, there is some evidence that an inferior performance is associated with differences in cerebral activation in anterior brain structures, such as Broca's area and the basal ganglia. In the case of comprehension, the proficiency-related differences involve the temporal lobes, in particular the temporal pole. It is interesting to underline that the differences appear to be in different directions: more extensive cerebral activations being associated with production in the less proficient language, smaller activations with comprehending the less proficient language. It may be speculated that this puzzling result may reflect the inherent differences of these aspects of linguistic processing. In the case of "difficult" tasks such as word generation, this difference may be attributed to the effortful recruitment of additional resources. On the other hand, in the case of sentence comprehension the automatic nature of the processing may be reflected in more limited elaboration of the linguistic material presented in the less proficient language. Another possibility, suggested by the single subject study of Dehaene et al. (1997), is that the limited extent of the activation in the case of comprehension may reflect heterogeneous and inconsistent patterns of cerebral activation.

On the other hand, the role of age of acquisition seems to be less prominent, in particular in the case of comprehension tasks. It must be underlined that the neuroimaging data do not question the claim that age of acquisition is a major determinant of proficiency in L2. Indeed, many studies have found that the late learners are typically less proficient than early learners (Johnson and Newport, 1989; Flege, Munro and MacKay, 1995; Weber-Fox and Neville, 1996). What functional imaging has shown is that, when proficiency is kept constant, age of acquisition per se does not seem to have a major impact on brain representations of L2, at least at the macroscopic (brain area) level.

Finally, the available evidence on the possible influence of language exposure is too limited to venture any speculation on its role: future studies should try to take into account this potentially important factor, and allow its consideration separately for the other two.

Postscript

In the original paper "The bilingual brain as revealed by functional neuroimaging" we attempted to achieve the challenging task of reviewing functional brain imaging studies that had been so far published. The field was young and only a few studies were available. Following the analysis of the available evidence we came to the conclusion that at least the degree of language proficiency may affect the neural representation of languages, independently of the age of L2 acquisition. Indeed, more extensive cerebral activations were associated with language production in the less proficient language, and smaller activations with comprehending the less proficient language.

Since the publication of the original paper many new studies have been performed and among them studies with intriguing new experimental paradigms (see for a recent review Perani and Abutalebi, 2005). For instance, the study of Wartenburger *et al.* (2003) disentangled semantic processing from grammatical processing and, interestingly, it was shown that age of L2 acquisition may have a crucial role for the neural underpinnings of L2 representation. Indeed, in line with theories claiming a "critical period" for L2 acquisition, only in the case of an L2 acquired very early in life did the neural substrates for L1 and L2 grammatical processing clearly overlap, thus suggesting that grammatical processing may be based on competence that is neurologically "wired in". On the other hand, it has been confirmed that for lexical-semantic aspects both the degree of L2 proficiency and the degree of language exposure represented the main determinants of the neural representation of L2.

Researchers have also started to investigate the neural correlates of L2 acquisition. Given the acquisition of L1 during childhood, an adult second language learner meets the task of fitting an L2 within an already well-organized neurolinguistic system with its consolidated computational devices. Conceivably then a different system is used compared to that of native speakers of that language (e.g. Albert and Obler, 1978). Vocabulary acquisition is likely to engage episodic memory systems with eventual transfer to systems that represent the meanings of words in L1. As far as grammatical processing is concerned, the case for a distinct system seems even stronger (e.g. Paradis, 1998, 2004; Ullman, 2001, 2004). L1 is acquired implicitly, mediated perhaps by an innate language learning mechanism only triggered during a critical period, whereas L2 may be acquired explicitly via formal instruction. Consequently, production in L2 may be mediated by explicit, metalinguistic knowledge that is declaratively represented rather than by implicit grammatical competence that is procedurally represented. However, it is worth underlining that recent brain imaging studies have so far contradicted the assumption that L2 is necessarily acquired through different brain areas (see Perani and Abutalebi (2005) for review). Accordingly, grammatical processing of L2 is acquired and carried out through the same computational brain devices underlying L1 grammatical processing. Indeed, during grammatical tasks in bilinguals, the brain structures traditionally associated with grammatical processing (e.g. Broca's regions, basal ganglia) are also involved when performing the tasks in L2 (even for those subjects who acquired L2 late in life (Sakai *et al.*, 2004)). Nevertheless, there may be differences between L1 and L2, but these are rather in terms of additional resource demands within the same neural system (e.g. more extended brain activity for L2 in and around the same area mediating grammar in L1: Broca's area in the specific case).

A future goal is that studies investigating the neural basis of L2 processing may benefit from longitudinal investigations addressing the natural course of L2 acquisition (i.e. follow-up studies in L2 teaching classrooms). Language acquisition per se was mostly investigated through artificial language acquisition paradigms or during the acquisition of distinct L2 components generally achieved in brief time periods (e.g. learning to conjugate a set of L2 verbs in one month). Although these studies may be very informative they do not represent the natural course and environment of L2 acquisition. Scanning L2 learners twice (i.e. at the early beginning of L2 learning and after two years of L2 teaching) would allow the direct investigation of neural plasticity related to the acquisition of L2 in the same subject and could also provide significant neurobiological evidence to fields dealing with language education.

One major drawback of the current neuroimaging work on bilingualism is that it tends to focus only on which particular brain structures are active, but an important future goal is to examine how these structures work together. Indeed, it seems that the brain imaging literature on bilingualism is fixed more on representational issues in terms of the neuroanatomy of L2 rather than being interested in its processing. This is also due to the fact that neuroimaging studies often lack a theoretical account such as those offered by psycholinguistics. Consider, for example, psycholinguistic accounts that assume competition between L1 and L2 in word production. Behavioral research has sought to understand the nature of such competition, especially in the context of lexical retrieval. Many researchers agree that competition may take place at least when producing words in a weaker language. Interferences from the stronger non-target language (L1 in this case) may take place and this is especially because lexical access in L1 is more automatic. Together with David Green, we have recently described in a theoretical work that neuroimaging data may provide good evidence in favor of the claim that there is competition to control output in L2 vs L1, i.e. to achieve language selection. The anatomical differences (i.e. more extended left prefrontal cortex activity for L2) we often observe in word production tasks when the degree of L2 proficiency is not comparable to L1 proficiency provide a good example. It would be erroneous to state that in the latter case L2 lexical items have a more widespread representation in the prefrontal cortex. Instead, given the control functions of the prefrontal cortex, these patterns may reflect the cognitive dynamics of processing a weaker L2 (i.e. to manage the competition between a stronger and more automatic language such as L1 and a weaker language such as an L2 mastered with a low degree of proficiency). With growing proficiency, the bilingual speaker does not have to rely on such control mechanisms as demonstrated by the absence of the "left prefrontal effect" in high proficient bilinguals. Hence, given a suitable interpretive framework, neuroimaging data can be embedded into psycholinguistic accounts of language control and selection mechanisms.

Notwithstanding, in general in the field of bilingualism relatively little work has been done in attempting to integrate functional neuroimaging evidence with coherent psycholinguistic frameworks. One of the major future goals could be that of creating a strong interplay between psycholinguistics and neuroscience to the mutual advantage of both research traditions.

Jubin Abutalebi

Jubin Abutalebi, MD, is a neurologist and Assistant Professor at the Psychology Faculty of the University Vita Salute Raffaele in Milan, Italy and Associate Researcher at the Interdisciplinary Center for Cognitive Sciences at the University of Potsdam, Germany. abutalebi-jubin@hsr.it
Stefano F. Cappa, PhD and Daniela Perani, PhD, both work in the Psychology Faculty of the University Vita-Salute San Raffaele and Scientific Institute San Raffaele, Milano, Italy. cappa.stefano@hsr.it; daniela.perani@hsr.it

Notes for students and instructors

Study questions

1   In Obler *et al.*'s view, how do the following variables affect experimental results on language lateralisation in bilingual speakers:
     (a)   age of acquisition;
     (b)   manner of acquisition;
     (c)   test language stimuli; and
     (d)   experimental task?
2   What are the reasons for Paradis to suggest that language lateralisation in bilinguals is a 'dead-end issue'?
3   What is the evidence for Abutalebi *et al.* to argue that language proficiency is the most important factor in shaping the cerebral representation of the bilingual?

Study activity

Review the literature on language lateralisation in bilingual speakers and sort the studies according to the subjects and experimental paradigms used. Can you see any patterns which may suggest a link between the experimental results and the methods chosen?

Further reading

A general introduction to the bilingual brain can be seen in Chapter 3 of S. Romaine, 1995, *Bilingualism*, 2nd edn, Blackwell; and also in F. Fabbro, 1999, *The Neuro-linguistics of Bilingualism*, Psychology Press.

A collection of earlier studies of the bilingual brain is M.L. Albert and L.K. Obler, 1978, *The Bilingual Brain*, Academic Press.

For state-of-the-art accounts of neurolinguistic studies of bilingualism, see M. Paradis, 2004, *A Neurolinguistic Theory of Bilingualism*, Benjamins.

Conclusion

Methodological issues in the study of bilingualism

LI WEI

The papers collected in this Reader represent a diversity of approaches to various aspects of bilingualism. I have deliberately excluded work on language planning, language attitude and bilingual education, as there are already good collections of papers on these topics (e.g. Garcia and Baker, 1995; Coupland and Jaworski, 1997; Trudgill and Cheshire, 1997). Consequently, most of the papers included in this Reader focus on the language behaviour of bilingual speakers. I have tried to highlight the various theoretical stances of the papers in my sectional introductions. The differences in theoretical stances often lead to the use of different methods in data collection and data analysis. In this final chapter of the Reader, I discuss some of the methodological issues in the study of bilingualism.

It should be pointed out that this chapter is not a user's manual for any specific method, such as questionnaire, interview, tape-recording, transcription or quantification. There are abundant guidebooks on research methods for teachers and students to take their fancy. My main aim here is to raise a number of questions which I believe need to be considered either when we are preparing a study or when we are reading other people's findings.

Who is the researcher?

The identity of the researcher is extremely important, as it affects the aims and objectives of the research, the relationship with the people being studied and the choice of theoretical and methodological perspectives. Unfortunately, we do not always think about this question when we read other people's findings, or for various reasons the identity of the researcher is not made explicit in the research report. In studying the language behaviour of bilingual speakers, it is particularly useful to consider the following issues:

- Is the researcher monolingual or bilingual (in the appropriate languages for the study)?
- What is the ethnic origin and nationality of the researcher?

- Is the researcher male or female?
- What age group does the researcher belong to?
- What is the educational level of the researcher?
- What is the disciplinary background of the researcher (e.g. linguistics, psychology, neuroscience, speech therapy, sociology, education, administration and government, etc.)?
- What is the researcher's attitude towards bilingualism?

In the existing literature, there is very little detailed documentation of how the linguistic background and competence of the researcher affects his or her relationships with the people and their language behaviour being studied, although it is generally accepted that, if the linguistic competence of the researcher is compatible with that of the people being studied, data collection should be smoother and more successful. Native competence certainly helps the research to reveal some of the minute linguistic details, particularly of non-standard language varieties (e.g. Trudgill, 1974). It may well be, however, that the number of researchers who can claim such competence is relatively small and that the majority of the existing studies of the language behaviour of bilingual speakers are carried out by non-native speakers of one of the languages. Some researchers are lucky enough to obtain sufficient funding to employ a team of temporary assistants to carry out data collection and data analysis. However, problems of comparability may then arise, as different researchers may impart their own perspectives to the phenomenon being investigated into the data collection and analysis. While such different perspectives are themselves interesting and provide valuable information worthy of studying, they create difficulties in interpreting the research findings.

Sometimes even if a researcher with the appropriate linguistic background is located, he or she may not be of the ethnic origin or nationality appropriate or necessary for the study. This often happens when the language boundary crosses ethnic or religious boundaries, i.e. the same language is used by members of different ethnic or religious groups. Bilingual researchers with North American or European nationalities may not be readily accepted by some of the people being studied in Africa, South-East Asia or the Middle East even though they may be of the same ethnic origin.

The effects of the age, gender and educational background of the researcher on the data that he or she collects and ultimately analyses have been discussed extensively by sociolinguists (e.g. Milroy, 1987). It is important to remember that there is no ideal candidate for carrying out bilingualism research. Successful investigation requires the researcher's sensitivity to the context of the study, willingness to overcome difficulties, and honesty about his or her identity, attitude and research agenda.

Two related examples from our work with the Pakistani and Chinese communities in Tyneside in the north-east of England may serve to illustrate the points I have made so far. Suzanne Moffatt, a white female researcher of university education, was a non-native speaker of Panjabi who was particularly interested in the bilingual behaviour of young children at the critical kindergarten stage, when they were faced with their first extensive exposure to English. She had previously travelled to Pakistan and had extensive personal contacts within the Pakistani community in Tyneside, partly due to her job as a community speech therapist. Nevertheless, it was impossible to claim the identity of a community member on the grounds of ethnic origin and religious beliefs.

She had the further difficulty of having to deal with the male folks of the community who tended to be heads of the household. Subsequently she decided to concentrate on a variety of situations in kindergarten and infant school, where she doubled as a teacher's helper and was, in fact, accepted as such. Her social role was quite clear and she was able to carry out a participant observation study which gave her systematic evidence of the language-switching behaviours of young incipient bilinguals (for a fuller description of this study and discussions of the findings, see Moffatt, 1990).

In the meantime, I myself was interested in the language shift from Chinese mono-lingualism in the grandparent generation to English-dominant bilingualism in the British-born children's generation which was taking place within the Tyneside Chinese community. Although I was of the same ethnic origin as members of the local Chinese community, my first language was Mandarin and I had only a working knowledge of Cantonese, the lingua franca of the community. Like Suzanne Moffatt, I had built up extensive personal contacts within the community during a three-year period of residence in Tyneside prior to our study. Because I was the only Chinese in the area who had a degree in English language and literature at the time, I was often asked by the families to help with English language problems when they went to see their doctors and solicitors. I also taught in the Chinese community language school and helped organise Mandarin Chinese and English language classes there. Where my situation differed from that of Suzanne Moffatt was that I did have access to the family setting which was usually closed to outsiders. In fact, I was often invited to their homes for meals; many of them offered me lodging, daily necessities and even odd jobs in their restaurants and takeaways! However, I did also have certain difficulties which Suzanne Moffatt did not encounter. Intra-generational interaction amongst Chinese adults was normally exclusively in Chinese, and intergenerational communication between adults and children was in both English and Chinese. Since I was accepted by most families as a friend of the parent generation, my use of English was confined to conversations with the British-born children. Most adults refused to speak to me in English, even if it meant that they sometimes had to switch to Mandarin, a non-native variety of Chinese to them, to accommodate my needs. Indeed, our assessments of the English language abilities of the adult Chinese in Tyneside had to be carried out by a non-Chinese researcher (see further discussions in Li Wei, 1994; Milroy, Li Wei and Moffatt, 1993). The main point that I want to make with these two related examples is that there is no point in trying to conceal the 'incompatible' aspects of one's identity in data collection. Instead, we should take into consideration the effect of the researcher's identity during data analysis and make it explicit in the discussions of the findings.

As well as the linguistic background, age, gender and educational level of the researcher, the issue of the disciplinary background of the researcher is equally impor-tant, not because different disciplinary traditions tend to have different research methods (e.g. sociologists tend to use questionnaires and interviews, and psychologists controlled experiments, and linguists tape-recordings of conversation) but because their views are not always in agreement on what language is. For example, psychologists and neuro-scientists may see languages as fairly clearly defined, discrete systems, each having its own name tag; in contrast, linguists, especially those with a sociolinguistic inclination, see language boundaries as fuzzy and problematic (see discussions in the section 'Language as a socio-political issue' of the Introduction). Even among the broad category of linguists, some maintain a distinction between 'language' and 'speech', whereas others believe such a distinction is unnecessary and fallacious. Consequently, some researchers insist that bilingual speakers possess two more or less discrete grammatical systems, while others argue that bilinguals have their own coherent system which cannot be judged by any monolingual norm (see Chapters 10–15 in this volume). In practice, some researchers attempt to study bilinguals in two separate monolingual modes as well as a bilingual mode, while others believe such an endeavour is completely fruitless and misguided (see Chapter 16 in this volume).

Perhaps the most important issue related to the identity of the researcher is his or her attitude towards bilingualism. This is not a simple matter of seeing bilingualism as advantageous or disadvantageous to the individuals and the society. It is much subtler. Depending on their social and professional positions and personal interests, some bilingual researchers may believe that a generally positive portrayal of the speakers' bilingual ability is more desirable, and their investigations are designed in such a way that the results will highlight 'better' skills of bilingual speakers. Others may insist that only certain types of bilingualism are acceptable. For instance, some bilingual researchers believe that speakers with high proficiency levels in both of their languages do not engage in code-switching; in other words, code-switching is a sign of linguistic deficiency. It is therefore important to have a clear understanding of the ideology of the researcher when reading published research. This leads us to our second question about research objectives, which is clearly affected by the researcher's ideology.

What does the analyst want to find?

Although most published papers and books on bilingualism give fairly clear descriptions of the aims and objectives of the studies being reported, we, as readers, do not often make the link between the research agenda and the researcher's identity, background, personal interests and attitudes towards bilingualism. However, it is quite clear from the vast quantity of published work that, from a socio-political point of view, bilingualism research can never be truly 'value-free'. During my own fieldwork in the Tyneside Chinese community, I came across two groups of community leaders with rather different views: one group wanted to emphasise the problems and disadvantages of being speakers of a 'minority' language in an English-dominant environment; they wanted the central and local governments to provide more support by funding community language schools, translating policy documents and public notices into their language and providing bilingual assistants in public services. In contrast, the other group of community leaders wanted to highlight the success story of the Chinese community: their self-reliance and self-sufficiency, assimilation into the mainstream society and harmonious relationships both within the community and with other social groups. Both groups tried to influence our research agenda by giving us only the examples that they thought would support their views. I have also encountered researchers who had already decided even before the study began that bilingual children, especially those from an ethnic minority background, would have serious difficulties at school because their English was not up to standard. They then set out to find evidence only to confirm their ideas. It is therefore necessary both for those who are planning a research project and for those who are reading published results to be aware of such ideological influences on the aims and objectives of the research.

In addition, researchers of different disciplinary backgrounds often have different research agendas, even though they may be working with the same language pairs, the same speakers or the same data corpus. For example, a number of researchers have looked at Spanish–English bilingualism in the US. Coming from a variationist tradition, Poplack and her associates have used quantitative methods to examine grammatical structures of mixed-code utterances. They maintain there is a distinction between 'borrowing' and 'switching' and such a distinction shows different degrees and processes of integration (see, for example, Chapter 10 in this volume). Zentella (1997), on the other hand, adopts the 'interactional sociolinguistics' (Gumperz, 1982) approach and focuses on code-switching as an act of identity in a New York Puerto Rican community. In the meantime, Pearson and her team have developed a bilingual vocabulary checklist and other measures to investigate lexical development of Hispanic children (e.g. Pearson *et al.*, 1993; Pearson, 1998). Kroll and her associates also included Spanish–English bilinguals in their studies of bilingual memory. They asked the speakers to perform translation recognition tasks to examine the lexical mediation hypothesis, i.e. less fluent bilinguals were more reliant on a lexical translation strategy (for a review, see Kroll and de Groot, 1997). It is only natural that findings from these studies are not always compatible, as the research questions and methods of data collection and analysis are so radically different. When reading such work, we need to be particularly aware of the fact that researchers from different disciplinary backgrounds may use the same terms – such as *process* or *strategy* – with rather different meanings. A lot of the arguments among researchers on bilingualism about findings and interpretations are in fact a result of having different terminologies and research agendas.

Differences in the research agendas lead to different choices of a specific media for research. For example:

- studies of the language development of bilingual children can be based on parental diaries, video-recording or audio-recording of children's play and conversation, or standardised tests and checklists;
- studies of the language attitudes and language ideologies can be based on analyses of written documents or interview data;
- studies of language processing of bilingual speakers, on the other hand, are normally based on experiments.

There is no one method that is intrinsically better than others. Good methods are those that are appropriate for the research agenda and can provide evidence for answering the research questions.

We should be particularly aware of the possibility that style of research (e.g. ethnographic, experimental, survey, systematic observation) and use of tools (such as questionnaires, interviews, tape-recordings, tests, attitude scales) can carry with them a political ideology, a view of the person and a philosophy of knowledge. For example:

- surveys often aim for participative democracy, whereas experiments are often about control;
- qualitative ethnographic observation aims for a holistic view of the person, while quantitative variationist studies tend to fragment the person into variables;

- tape-recordings and detailed transcription of them aim for a 'mirror reflection', or a 'positivist' picture, of what actually happens, whereas in-depth interviews and critical analyses of them want to (re)construct particular versions of experience and reality.

We should also be aware of the fact that some researchers from specific disciplinary backgrounds (e.g. cognitive science, artificial intelligence) are carrying out research on bilingual speakers not with any interest in their bilingualism per se, but in order to validate theoretical models for some other purposes and contexts. Some of their findings may be interesting and relevant to bilingualism research generally, but they should be read with particular caution, as their methodologies are often driven by agendas which are not related to bilingualism at all.

Who is the speaker?

Researchers from different disciplinary backgrounds also sometimes use different terms for the same referent. As we have seen in the articles collected in this Reader, socio-linguists usually refer to the people whose language behaviour is under investigation as 'speakers', while psycholinguists call them 'subjects' or 'participants'.

Although most researchers have certain criteria for choosing the speakers, these are not always explained clearly, nor are they always taken into account during data analysis. Grosjean (1998: 133) suggests that the following questions should be considered in choosing the speakers:

- *Language history and language relationship:* Which languages (and language skills) were acquired, when and how? Was the cultural context the same or different? What was the pattern of language use? What is the linguistic relationship between the bilingual's languages?
- *Language stability:* Are one or several languages still being acquired? Is the bilingual in the process of restructuring (maybe losing) a language or language skill because of a change of linguistic environment? Has a certain language stability been reached?
- *Function of languages:* Which languages (and language skills) are used currently, in what context, for what purpose and to what extent?
- *Language proficiency:* What is the bilingual's proficiency in each of the four skills (listening, speaking, reading and writing) in each language?
- *Language modes:* How often and for how long is the bilingual in a monolingual mode (i.e. when only one language is active) and in a bilingual mode (i.e. when both languages are active)? When in a bilingual mode, how much code-switching and borrowing is taking place?
- *Biographical data:* What is the bilingual's age, sex, socio-economic and educational status, etc.?

Although Grosjean formulated these questions primarily to help experimental psycho-linguists with their research design, they should be considered carefully by everyone who does or reads bilingualism research. Often, conflicting study results are a con-sequence of using different types of speakers for the study. Theoretical models built on the basis of one group of speakers do not always work on other groups of speakers.

Researchers from a sociolinguistic background may also be interested in power and status relationships between speakers, and their subjective constructions of their language situation, as well as the biographical data. Such information is sometimes the subject of investigation in itself, but would impact on the data collected and the conclusions made.

What is the relationship between the researcher and the speaker?

A related question is that of the relationship between the researcher and the speaker. We have mentioned earlier that the researcher's identity, such as linguistic profile, ethnic origin, age, gender, occupation and education, can significantly affect the research agenda. Perhaps the most significant and noticeable effect of the researcher's identity is on the relationship that he or she can build up with the speaker whose language behaviour he or she intends to study. The fact that Suzanne Moffatt was a white, female, non-native Panjabi speaker from an educated background determined that she could not possibly be an 'insider' of the Pakistani community in Tyneside; and the fact that I was ethnically Chinese and spoke the language meant that I could not pretend to be completely detached from the local Chinese community. This does not mean that Suzanne Moffatt could not make friends with the Pakistani families; in fact, she was highly successful in building up an appropriate relationship with the children and their families which gave her a large amount of extremely interesting and useful data. However, I had to be very careful not to let my personal relationships with the Chinese families interfere with the research in a negative way (e.g. I was sometimes asked to do things for the families which either cost valuable research time or affected my relationships with other families in the community). The important point here is that we need to establish an appropriate and mutually acceptable relationship with the people whose language behaviour we are studying, which will be beneficial not only to the individuals involved but also to the fulfilment of the research aims and objectives.

There seems to be a tradition in the study of childhood bilingualism that the researchers are in fact parents of the children whose language development is being observed. Parents as researchers have the advantage of being able to make video-recordings and audio-recordings and/or to keep a diary record over an extended period of time, which a researcher without this relationship may not be able to do. It is nevertheless important for parent-researchers to state explicitly their relationships with the children under investigation, the context of the study, and the normal, daily routine activities of the family which may not be recorded for analysis. It is equally important to avoid idiosyncratic interpretations of the data which are not apparent to the general reader.

At a more micro level, we need to be particularly aware of the fact that the speaker's language behaviour is subject to change according to the relationships with the researcher and with any other people present. Bell (1984) calls this 'audience design', i.e. speakers choose their language and style primarily in response to audience types (e.g. addressee, auditor, overhearer and eavesdropper), including their social characteristics (e.g. age, gender, ethnicity and occupation) and their relationships with the speaker (e.g. stranger, acquaintance, colleague, neighbour, friend and family).

What is the research context?

The context of research includes the wider socio-political background as well as the more immediate physical setting of the study. Changes in the socio-political climate often lead to changes in research priorities. When new immigration legislation was introduced in the USA and Britain in the 1950s and 1960s, there was an upsurge of interest in ethnic minority communities. Military conflicts, natural disasters and economic crises, which contributed to language contacts in the first place, may also prompt renewed interest in bilingualism. The development of information and communication technologies and the reforms of the educational systems may also lead to increased awareness of the multilingual nature of modern life. Funding opportunities for bilingualism research may change drastically as the socio-political context changes. Certain types of research may be favoured at one time, but neglected or even forbidden at another. Some researchers are better, or quicker, than others in developing research projects which suit the current policy initiatives. It would be useful to bear in mind the wider context and conditions of the research when reading the findings and arguments.

The wider social context also has an impact on the specific research methods we use for studying the language behaviour of bilingual speakers. In some societies, one-to-one interviews are not an acceptable form of investigation unless the person being interrogated has committed a criminal offence, while in some others interviews are preferred over written questionnaires. In some cases speakers need to be paid to participate in laboratory experiments, while in others payment of any kind is not acceptable. In Singapore, a postal questionnaire survey can obtain a return rate of up to 98 per cent, especially if the research is funded and supported by government agencies. In most other countries a 30–40 per cent return would be considered a success for a questionnaire study. These 'external' factors need to be considered in both designing a research project and reading study results.

At a more immediate level, bilingualism research can be conducted in various physical settings, ranging from laboratory conditions to community-based participant observations. The specific setting of the study is determined by the aims and objectives of the research. It is important to remember that the same speakers may display very different behaviours in different settings. For example, results from a laboratory experiment on the reaction time of the bilingual speaker to language switching must be interpreted as such and should not be understood as indicating their naturally occurring code-switching behaviours in face-to-face interaction.

There are of course many other issues that need to be considered. But the central methodological question in bilingualism research, especially research on the language behaviour of the bilingual speaker, is that of the 'representativeness' of the data. Ideally, the data being collected and ultimately analysed should be characteristic of the normal behaviour of the speaker in everyday life. However, as Labov (1972: 209–10) points out, there exists a basic scientific quandary in linguistic research where, in almost every possible situation, there is one variable that cannot be controlled in every possible way, namely the observer-researcher himself or herself. If language varies as much as it does, the presence of an observer will have some effect on that variation. Labov calls this the 'observer's paradox', that is, the aim of linguistic research is to find out how people talk when they are not being systematically observed, but the data are available only through systematic observation. Bell (1976: 187–91), drawing extensively on the work of Labov, suggests eight principles as worthy of consideration in linguistic research. Although the eight principles are phrased in terms of sociolinguistic research, particularly studies of language variation and change, they are nevertheless important to all types of research on bilingualism.

The eight principles are:

1   *The cumulative principle:* The more that we know about language, the more we can find out about it, and we should not be surprised if our search for new knowledge takes us into new areas of study and into areas in which scholars from other disciplines are already working.

2   *The uniformation principle:* The linguistic processes which we observe to be taking place around us are the same as those which have operated in the past, so that there can be no clean break between *synchronic* (i.e. descriptive and contemporary) matters and *diachronic* (i.e. historical) ones.

3   *The principle of convergence:* The value of new data for confirming or interpreting old findings is directly proportional to the differences in the ways in which the new data are gathered; particularly useful are linguistic data gathered through procedures needed in other areas of scientific investigation.

4   *The principle of subordinate shift:* When speakers of a non-standard (or subordinate) variety of language, e.g. a dialect, are asked direct questions about that variety, their responses will shift in an irregular way towards or away from the standard (or superordinate) variety, e.g. the standard language, so enabling investigators to collect valuable evidence concerning such matters as varieties, norms and change.

5   *The principle of style-shifting:* There are no 'single-style' speakers of a language, because each individual controls and uses a variety of linguistic styles and no one speaks in exactly the same way in all circumstances.

6   *The principle of attention:* 'Styles' of speech can be ordered along a single dimension measured by the amount of attention speakers are giving to their speech, so that the more 'aware' they are of what they are saying, the more 'formal' the style will be.

7   *The vernacular principle:* The style which is most regular in its structure and in its relation to the history of the language is the *vernacular*, that relaxed, spoken style in which the least conscious attention is being paid to speech.

8   *The principle of formality:* Any systematic observation of speech defines a context in which some conscious attention will be paid to that speech, so that it will be difficult, without great ingenuity, to observe the genuine 'vernacular'.

My main purpose in this chapter is to raise awareness of the various methodological questions that need to be considered in both designing and reading bilingualism research. Bilingualism has become an enormous, multidimensional and multidisciplinary research area. Researchers of diverse interests and agendas are using a variety of methods to study different aspects of bilingualism. Confusions and misunderstandings are only natural, given the diversity and multiplexity of bilingualism research. However, it is hoped that an awareness of the identity of the researcher, the aims and objectives of the research, the characteristics of the speaker, the relationship between the researcher and the speakers, and the research context will help to reduce confusions and misunderstandings and produce less ambiguous and more *truthful* research results.

Notes for students and instructors

Study questions

1   What are the advantages and disadvantages of being a member of the bilingual speech community when carrying out research on the language behaviour of the speakers in that community?
2   How do ideological and socio-economic changes in society affect the agenda of bilingual research?
3   In what way does the research agenda of the investigator affect the methods he or she chooses to use?

Study activity

Carry out a critical analysis of a chosen piece of research on the language behaviour of bilingual speakers. Can you identify the identity of the researcher, the objectives of the research, the methods used, and the socio-political context in which the research was done? How do the presentation and interpretation of research findings reflect the researcher's own beliefs and attitudes towards bilingualism?

Further reading

A new, comprehensive guide to research methods for bilingualism and multilingualism is Li Wei and Melissa Moyer (eds), 2007, *Blackwell Guide to Research Methods in Bilingualism and Multilingualism*, Blackwell. It contains detailed discussions of principles of research, and how research questions and methods are interlinked, as well as specific methods for data collection and analysis. It also contains a useful 'Project ideas' section for students who are planning research projects on bilingualism and multilingualism from different perspectives.

Ideological issues in linguistic research and how they affect the specific methods used in research are discussed in D. Cameron, E. Frazer, P. Harvey, B. Rampton and K. Richardson, 1992, *Researching Language: Issues of power and methods,* Routledge.

A general introduction to specific research methods in linguistics (including sociolinguistics and psycholinguistics) is A. Wray, K. Trott and A. Bloomer, 1999, *Projects in Linguistics: A practical guide to researching language,* Arnold.

RESOURCE LIST

This section contains lists of key reference books, textbooks, academic journals, book series, research tools, websites and electronic mailing lists for students' use. There are many more research publications that students of bilingualism will find useful. These can be found in the comprehensive Bibliography.

Key reference books

A comprehensive, accessible account of bilingualism can be found in C. Baker and S. Prys Jones, 1998, *Encyclopaedia of Bilingualism and Bilingual Education*, Multilingual Matters.

State-of-the-art handbooks of bilingualism include: T.K. Bhatia and W.C. Ritchie (eds), 2004, *The Handbook of Bilingualism*, Blackwell; and J.F. Kroll and A.M.B. de Groot (eds), 2005, *Handbook of Bilingualism: Psycholinguistic Approaches*, Oxford University Press.

Practical guides for professionals (e.g. speech therapists, doctors, psychologists, counsellors, teachers) working with bilingual children include: F. Genesee, J. Paradis and M.B. Crago, 2004, *Dual Language Development and Disorders: A handbook on bilingualism and second language learning*, Brookes; and C. Baker, 2000, *The Care and Education of Young Bilinguals*, Multilingual Matters.

Very useful and practical advice for bilingual families can be found in C. Baker (2000a) *A Parents' and Teachers' Guide to Bilingualism*, 2nd edn, Multilingual Matters; E. Harding-Esch and P. Riley (2003) *The Bilingual Family: A handbook for parents*, 2nd edn, Cambridge University Press; and U. Cunningham-Andersson and S. Andersson, 2004, *Growing Up with Two Languages: A practical guide*, 2nd edn, Routledge. A Spanish version of the Baker volume is available: *Guia Para Padres Y Maestros De Ninos Bilingues* (2001), translated with addition by Alma Flor Ada, published by Multilingual Matters.

Key textbooks

There is a range of introductory texts on bilingualism. S. Romaine, 1995, *Bilingualism*, 2nd edn, Blackwell, is probably the most comprehensive, covering all aspects of bilingualism, ranging from the bilingual brain and code-switching to bilingual education and attitudes towards bilingualism. A more recent textbook is C. Myers-Scotton, 2005, *Multiple Voices: An introduction to bilingualism*, Blackwell. Other textbooks include J. Hamers and M. Blanc, 2000, *Bilinguality and Bilingualism*, 2nd edn, Cambridge University Press.

P. Muysken, 2000, *Bilingual Speech: A typology of code-mixing*, Cambridge University Press, offers a good survey of the structural aspects of bilingual speech. More general introductions to language contact, from a linguistic perspective, include: S. Thomason, 2001, *Language Contact: An introduction*, Edinburgh University Press; D. Winford, 2002, *An Introduction to Contact Linguistics*, Blackwell; and C. Myers-Scotton, 2004, *Contact Linguistics: Bilingual encounters and grammatical outcomes*, Oxford University Press.

An introductory text, focusing on bilingual education, is C. Baker, 2006, *Foundations of Bilingual Education and Bilingualism*, 4th edn, Multilingual Matters. It has a companion reader: O. Garcia and C. Baker (eds), 1995, *Policy and Practice in Bilingual Education*, Multilingual Matters.

An introduction to social aspects of language contact is J. Edwards, 1994, *Multilingualism*, Routledge.

F. Fabbro, 1999, *The Neurolinguistics of Bilingualism*, Psychology Press, is an introductory textbook on neurolinguistic aspects of bilingualism.

An earlier introductory text written from a bilingual speaker's point of view and in a highly readable style is F. Grosjean, 1982, *Life with Two Languages*, Harvard University Press.

Key journals

The *Journal of Multilingual and Multicultural Development* (Multilingual Matters, Clevedon) is a long-established international journal, focusing particularly on the sociological and socio-linguistic aspects of language contact. It is published six times a year.

The *International Journal of Bilingualism: Cross-disciplinary cross-linguistic studies of language behaviour* (Kingston Press, London) is an international, refereed quarterly journal which is devoted to the study of language behaviour of bilingual and multilingual individuals. It also covers cross-linguistic studies of language development and impairment.

Bilingualism: Language and cognition (Cambridge University Press), published three times a year, focuses on bilingualism from a cognitive science perspective. It contains keynote articles with invited commentaries, research articles and notes.

The *International Journal of Bilingual Education and Bilingualism* (Multilingual Matters, Clevedon) focuses particularly on bilingual education and other applied areas of bilingualism research. It is published three times a year.

A new addition is the *International Journal of Multilingualism* (Multilingual Matters, Clevedon), which focuses on three or more languages in contact.

The *Bilingual Research Journal* is the official publication of the National Association for Bilingual Education in the USA and is published (electronically) by the Center for Bilingual Education and Research of Arizona State University (http://brj.asu.edu).

The following journals often carry articles on various aspects of bilingualism:

- *Applied Linguistics* (Oxford University Press)
- *Applied Psycholinguistics* (Cambridge University Press)
- *Brain and Language* (Academic Press)
- *English World-Wide* (John Benjamins)
- *International Journal of Applied Linguistics* (Novus Press)
- *International Journal of the Sociology of Language* (Mouton de Gruyter)
- *Journal of Child Language* (Cambridge University Press)
- *Journal of Language, Identity and Education* (Lawrence Erlbaum)
- *Journal of Multilingual Communication Disorders* (Taylor & Francis)
- *Journal of Neurolinguistics* (Elsevier Science)
- *Journal of Psycholinguistic Research* (Plenum Press)
- *Journal of Sociolinguistics* (Blackwell)
- *Language and Education* (Multilingual Matters)

- *Language, Culture and Curriculum* (Multilingual Matters)
- *Language in Society* (Cambridge University Press)
- *Language Learning* (Blackwell)
- *Language Problems and Language Planning* (John Benjamins)
- *Multilingua* (Mouton de Gruyter)
- *Studies in Second Language Acquisition* (Cambridge University Press)

Relevant book series

Multilingual Matters, published by Multilingual Matters, is a companion series of the *Journal of Multilingual and Multicultural Development* and focuses on the sociological and sociolinguistic aspects of language contact.

Bilingual Education and Bilingualism, published by Multilingual Matters, is a companion series of the *International Journal of Bilingual Education and Bilingualism* and focuses on bilingual education and applied areas of bilingualism research.

Studies on Bilingualism, from John Benjamins, publishes research monographs and general texts on various aspects of bilingualism.

Child Language and Child Development: Multilingual and multicultural perspectives, published by Multilingual Matters, focuses on the language development of bilingual children and children speaking languages other than English.

Cambridge Approaches to Language Contact, published by Cambridge University Press, publishes general texts on linguistic aspects of language contact.

Research tools

The LIDES Coding Manual, compiled by the LIPPS Group (Language Interaction in Plurilingual and Plurilectic Speakers), is a document for preparing and analysing language interaction data, published in 2000 by Kingston Press as a special issue of the *International Journal of Bilingualism*.

Child Language Data Exchange System (http://childes.psy.cmu.edu/) contains a database of bilingual child language acquisition and offers tools for analysing child language data.

Websites, electronic mailing lists and other resources

The Bilingual List (BILING@asu.edu), run by the Center for Bilingual Education and Research of Arizona State University, is the most popular electronic discussion service for bilingualism research. To view the archive and manage your subscription, see http://lists.asu.edu/archives/biling.html.

The Code-Switching Forum (code-switching@yahoogroups.com) is an e-discussion group for people with a specific interest in code-switching (http://www.groups.yahoo.com/group/code-switching).

The Linguist List is a worldwide electronic discussion forum on a variety of issues related to language and linguistics. For further information, see: http://www.linguistlist.org/.

iLoveLanguages, formerly the Human Languages Page, is a comprehensive catalogue of language-related Internet resources, with more than 2,400 links (http://www.ilovelanguages.com/).

The National Association for Bilingual Education's homepage (http://www.nabe.org/) contains information about NABE and links to important websites.

The Bilingual Families Web Page provides practical information about raising children with two languages (http://www.nethelp.no/cindy/biling-fam.html).

Bilingual Education Resources on the Net (http://www.estrellita.com/bil.html) offers links to other pages which have information on bilingual education.

The Center for Applied Linguistics (USA), http://www.cal.org, offers useful links.

The National Centre for Languages, UK, formerly the Centre for Information on Language Teaching (CILT), http://www.cilt.org.uk/, offers useful links.

The *Bilingual Family Newsletter* (Multilingual Matters, Clevedon) is an informal publication, six issues a year, exchanging news and views from bilingual people. It contains useful advice and lists of contacts (http://www.multilingual-matters.com).

GLOSSARY

acculturation   The process whereby an individual adjusts to a new culture, including the acquisition of the language(s) of that culture. See also *assimilation*.

achieved bilingualism   Acquisition of bilingualism later than childhood. See also *late bilingualism*.

additive bilingualism   A situation in which a bilingual's two languages combine in a complementary and enriching fashion.

ambilingualism   Same as *balanced bilingualism*.

anomie   A bilingual's state of anxiety resulting from an inability to resolve the conflicting demands from two cultures.

ascendant bilingualism   A situation in which a bilingual's ability to function in a second language is developing due to increased use.

ascribed bilingualism   Acquisition of bilingualism early in childhood. See also *early bilingualism*.

assimilation   A process whereby an individual or group *acculturates* to another group, often by losing their own ethnolinguistic characteristics.

asymmetrical bilingualism   Same as *receptive bilingualism*.

attrition   The gradual loss of a language within a person over time.

baby talk   Distinctive linguistic characteristics found in the speech of adults when addressing very young children.

back translation   A translation that is translated back into the original language, usually to assess the accuracy of the first translation.

balanced bilingualism   A situation in which a bilingual's mastery of two languages is roughly equivalent. Also called *ambilingualism*, *equibilingualism* and *symmetrical bilingualism*.

base language   The language which provides the morphosyntactic structure of an utterance in which *code-switching* and *code-mixing* occur. Also called *matrix language*.

BICS   Basic Interpersonal Communicative Skills.

biculturalism   A situation in which a bilingual individual or group identifies with and participates in more than one culture.

bidialectalism   Proficiency in the use of more than one dialect of a language, whether regional or social.

bilinguality   A psychological state of the individual who has access to more than one linguistic code as a means of social communication.

biliteracy   Reading and writing in two languages.

borrowing   The taking over of linguistic forms (usually lexical items) by one language from another, either temporarily or permanently. See also *loan blend*.

CALP   Cognitive/Academic Language Proficiency.

CAT   Computerised Axial Tomography.

code alternation   A general term for the communication strategy of alternate use of two languages in the same utterance or conversation, cf. *code-mixing* and *code-switching*.

code-mixing   A communication strategy used by bilinguals in which the speaker of language X transfers elements or rules of language Y to X (the *base language*); it is unlike *borrowing*, however, in that these elements are not usually integrated into the linguistic system of X.

code-switching   A bilingual communication strategy consisting of the alternate use of two languages in the same phrase or utterance.

codification   A systematic description of a variety of a language, e.g. vocabulary, grammar.

cognate   A linguistic form which is historically derived from the same source as another.

community language   A language used by speakers of a specific, usually minority, community. See also *heritage language*.

compound bilingualism   A situation in which a bilingual's two languages are learnt at the same time, often in the same context.

consecutive bilingualism   Same as *successive bilingualism*.

continuum   Continuous linguistic variation between two or more languages or speech varieties; at each pole of this continuum are situated two distinct linguistic entities which may be mutually unintelligible.

co-ordinate bilingualism   A situation in which a bilingual's two languages are learnt during childhood in different and separate contexts.

corpus planning   Language planning which focuses on the linguistic aspects of a language.

covert bilingualism   A situation in which a bilingual conceals his or her knowledge of a given language due to an attitudinal disposition.

critical age   Age at which acquisition or learning is achieved in an optimal way; before that age the individual has not reached the necessary maturation stage; after that age he or she has partially or totally lost the capacity for acquisition or learning. Also called *optimal age* and *sensitive age*.

deculturation   The process by which an individual adapts to a new culture at the expense of his or her first.

diagonal bilingualism   A situation in which someone is bilingual in a non-standard language or a dialect and an unrelated standard language.

diglossia   A situation where two different varieties of a language or two distinct languages co-occur in a *speech community*, each with a distinct range of social functions.

domain   A group of social situations typically constrained by a common set of behavioural rules.

dominant bilingualism   A situation in which a bilingual has greater proficiency in one of his or her languages and uses it significantly more than the other language(s).

dormant bilingualism   A situation in which a bilingual has emigrated to a foreign country for a considerable period of time and has little opportunity to keep the first language actively in use.

double immersion   Schooling where subject content is taught through a second and third language.

early bilingualism   A situation in which someone has acquired two languages early in childhood. See also *ascribed bilingualism*.

embedded language   The language which provides lexical items which are inserted into the utterance in which *code-switching* and *code-mixing* occur.

enculturation   A part of the socialisation process by which a child acquires the rules of behaviour and the values of his or her culture.

endogenous language   A language that is used as the mother tongue within a speech community.

equilingualism   Same as *balanced bilingualism*.

ERPs   Event-related evoked potentials.

ethnolinguistic   A set of cultural, ethnic and linguistic features shared by a cultural, ethnic or sub-cultural social group.

exogenous language   A language not used as the mother tongue but only as an official or institutionalised language in a speech community.

first language   The linguistic code(s) corresponding to the individual's first language experience; also the linguistic code(s) used as the *mother tongue* by most members of a speech community.

fMRI   Functional Magnetic Resonance Imaging.

foreign accent syndrome   A phenomenon associated with aphasia in monolinguals where the speaker produces non-native-like intonation patterns.

foreign language   Second and subsequently learnt language(s) which are not widely used by the speech community in which the learner lives.

foreigner talk   A bilingual communication strategy in which the speaker simplifies his or her mother tongue to make himself or herself understood by another speaker who has limited competence in it.

functional bilingualism   A situation in which a speaker can operate in two languages with or without full fluency for the task in hand.

heritage language   Native language of ethnic minority communities. See also *community language*.

horizontal bilingualism   A situation in which someone is bilingual in two distinct languages which have a similar or equal status.

immersion   An educational programme in which a second language is used as a medium of instruction.

incipient bilingualism   A situation in which someone is at the early stages of bilingualism where one language is not fully developed.

independence   A psychological state which enables a language mechanism or a linguistic code to function independently of another language mechanism or linguistic code.

interdependence   Relationship between two linguistic systems or psychological mechanisms which means that one cannot function or develop without reference to the other.

interference   A situation in which one piece of learning or one association inhibits another.

interlanguage   Successive stages in the processes of acquisition of a second language in which the linguistic productions of the learner represent systematic approximations to the target language.

language aptitude   A particular ability to learn a language as separate from intelligence and motivation.

language awareness   A comprehensive term used to describe knowledge about and appreciation of the attributes of a language, and the way a language works and is used in society.

language dominance   One language being the stronger or preferred language of an individual.

language loyalty   The purposeful maintenance and retention of a language when it is viewed as being under threat.

language maintenance   The continued use of a language, particularly amongst language minorities.

language shift   Process in which a speech community gives up a language in favour of another one.

late bilingualism   A situation in which a bilingual has become a bilingual later than childhood. See also *achieved bilingualism*.

lateralisation   Functional specialisations of the two cerebral hemispheres of the human brain.

localisation   Functional specialisations of specific cerebral networks of the human brain.

leaky diglossia   A situation where one variety or language spreads into the functions formerly reserved for another.

lect   A collection of linguistic phenomena which has a functional identity within a speech community.

lingua franca An auxiliary language used between groups of people who speak different native languages for the purpose of routine communication.

linguistic community Same as *speech community*.

loan blend A type of *borrowing* in which the loan word is modified according to the rules of the borrowing language.

machine translation Translation from one language to another by computer.

majority language A language used by a socio-economically dominant group in society, or one which has received a political or cultural status superior to that of other languages in the community.

matrix language Same as *base language*.

maximal bilingualism A situation in which a bilingual has near-native control of two or more languages.

metalinguistic Using language to describe language. Thinking about one's language.

minimal bilingualism A situation in which a bilingual has only a few words and phrases in a second language.

minority language A language used by a socially subordinate group, or one which has received a social or cultural status inferior to that of another (dominant) language in the community.

monocultural Individual/group identifying with and being identified by only one culture. Also called *unicultural*.

monolingual Individual/group having access to only one linguistic code. Also called *unilingual*.

mother tongue Same as *first language*.

MRI Magnetic Resonance Imaging.

native language The language or languages which have been acquired naturally during childhood.

native speaker An individual for whom a particular language is a *native language*.

natural bilingualism A situation in which a bilingual has not undergone any specific training and is often not in a position to translate or interpret with facility between two languages. See also *primary bilingualism*.

official language A language which is legally adopted by a state as its language of communication.

optimal age Same as *critical age*.

partial immersion Immersion programme in which both the first and the second language are used as media of instruction.

passive bilingualism Same as *receptive bilingualism*.

PET Positron Emission Tomography.

pluralism A cultural and linguistic policy by which ethnolinguistic minority groups are integrated into the wider society while being allowed to maintain their linguistic and cultural characteristics to varying degrees.

preferred language The language chosen by a bilingual speaker in a given situation from among his or her *repertoire*.

primary bilingualism A situation in which two languages have been learnt naturally, i.e. not via school teaching. See also *natural bilingualism*.

productive bilingualism A situation in which a bilingual not only understands but also speaks and possibly writes in two or more languages.

receptive bilingualism A situation in which a bilingual understands a second language, in either its spoken or its written form, or both, but does not necessarily speak or write it. Also called *asymmetrical bilingualism* and *passive bilingualism*.

recessive bilingualism A situation in which a bilingual begins to feel some difficulty in either understanding or expressing himself or herself with ease, due to lack of use.

repertoire The range of languages or varieties available for use by a speaker, each of which enables him or her to perform a particular social role; the range of languages or varieties within a *speech community*.

second language The language learnt by an individual after acquiring his or her first or native language. A non-native language which is widely used in the speech community.

secondary bilingualism A situation in which a bilingual's second language has been added to a first language via formal instruction.

semilingualism A situation in which a bilingual has insufficient knowledge of either language.

sensitive age Same as *critical age*.

simultaneous bilingualism A situation in which a bilingual's two languages are present from the onset of speech.

source language The language in which a message is transmitted and which is decoded by the interpreter/translator with the aim of recoding it in another language. The first language of the second language learner.

speech accommodation The process by which interlocutors modify their speech style or switch codes in order to converge towards, or diverge from, each other in communication interactions.

speech community Any regionally or socially definable human group identified by the use of a shared linguistic system or systems and by participation in shared sociolinguistic norms. Also called *linguistic community*.

standard language A language variety which has been accorded a status which is socially and culturally superior to other varieties and is used officially.

standardisation The attempt to establish a single standard form of a language, particularly in its written form, for official purposes, literature, school curriculum, etc.

status planning Language planning which focuses on the existing status relationships between languages in contact in a given territory.

submersion A form of education in which children are schooled in a language other than their mother tongue.

subordinate bilingualism A situation in which a bilingual exhibits *interference* in his or her language usage by reducing the patterns of the second language to those of the first.

subtractive bilingualism A situation in which a bilingual's second language is acquired at the expense of the aptitudes already acquired in the first language.

successive bilingualism A situation in which a bilingual's second language is added at some stage after the first has begun to develop. Also called *consecutive bilingualism*.

switch mechanism A psychological mechanism by which the bilingual is enabled to shut out one of his or her linguistic systems while using another.

symmetrical bilingualism Same as *balanced bilingualism*.

target language The language into which a message in another language is translated or interpreted. The language which is the goal of second language acquisition.

teacher talk A variety of communication used by teachers in the classroom, specific to the needs of instruction and learning.

territorial bilingualism Co-occurrence of two or more languages which have official status within a geographical area. Co-existence of two or more unilingual areas within a single political structure (e.g. unilingual regions in a multilingual state).

transfer The effect of one language on the learning or production of another.

translation equivalent A linguistic unit in one language corresponding to that in another language at the semantic level.

transliteration The notation of one language in the writing system of another language.

unicultural Same as *monocultural*.

unilingual   Same as *monolingual*.

variety   Any system of linguistic expression whose use is governed by situational variables, such as region, occupation, etc.

vernacular   The indigenous language or dialect of a *speech community*.

vertical bilingualism   A situation in which someone is bilingual in a standard language and a distinct but related language or dialect.

BIBLIOGRAPHY

Abdulaziz, M.H. (1972) Triglossia and Swahili–English bilingualism in Tanzania. *Language in Society* 1:197–213.

Abdulaziz, M.H. (1982) Patterns of language acquisition and use in Kenya: rural-urban differences. *International Journal of the Sociology of Language* 34: 95–120.

Abutalebi, J., Cappa, S. and Perani, D. (2005) What can functional neuroimaging tell us about the bilingual brain? In J.F. Kroll and A.M.B. de Groot (eds), *Handbook of Bilingualism: Psycholinguistic approaches*. Oxford: Oxford University Press, pp. 497–515.

Abutalebi, J., Cappa, S.F. and Perani, D. (2001) The bilingual brain as revealed by functional imaging. *Bilingualism: Language and cognition*, 4 (2): 179–90.

Abutalebi, J., Miozzo, A. and Cappa, S.F. (2000) Do subcortical structures control language selection in bilinguals? Evidence from pathological language mixing. *Neurocase* 6: 101–6.

Adelmeijer, L. (1991) The level of code-switching. Unpublished MA thesis in Linguistics, University of Amsterdam.

Aglioti, S., Beltramello, A., Girardi, F. and Fabbro, F. (1996) Neurolinguistic and follow-up study of an unusual pattern of recovery from bilingual subcortical aphasia. *Brain* 119: 1551–64.

Aglioti, S. and Fabbro, F. (1993) Paradoxical selective recovery in a bilingual aphasic following subcortical lesion. *NeuroReport* 4: 1359–62.

Albanèse, J.F. (1985) Language lateralization in English–French bilinguals. *Brain and Language* 24: 284–96.

Albert, E.M. (1972) Cultural patterning of speech behaviour in Burundi. In J.J. Gumperz and D. Hymes (eds) *Directions in Sociolinguistics*. New York: Holt, Rinehart and Winston, pp. 72–105.

Albert, M.L. and Obler, L.K. (1978) *The Bilingual Brain: Neuropsychological and neurolinguistic aspects of bilingualism*. New York/London: Academic Press.

Alexander, M.P., Hiltbrunner, B. and Fischer, R.S. (1989) Distributed anatomy of transcortical sensory aphasia. *Archives of Neurology* 46: 885–92.

Alexander, M.P., Benson, D.F., and Stuss, D.T. (1989) Frontal lobes and language. *Brain and Language* 37: 656–91.

Alfonzetti, G. (1992) *Il discorso bilingue*. Milan: F. Angeli.

Altarriba, J. (1990) Constraints on interlingual facilitation effects in priming in Spanish–English bilinguals. Unpublished dissertation, Vanderbilt University, Nashville.

Altarriba, J. (1992) The representation of translation equivalents in bilingual memory. In R.J. Harris (ed.), *Cognitive Processing in Bilinguals*. Amsterdam: Elsevier, pp. 157–74.

Altarriba, J., Kroll, J.F., Sholl, A. and Rayner, K. (1996) The influence of lexical and conceptual constraints on reading mixed-language sentences: evidence from eye-fixation and naming times. *Memory and Cognition* 24: 477–92.

Altenberg, E. and Cairns, H. (1983) The effects of phonotactic constraints on lexical processing in bilingual and monolingual subjects. *Journal of Verbal Learning and Verbal Behavior* 22: 174–88.

Al-Toma, S.J. (1957) The teaching of Classical Arabic to speakers of the colloquial in Iraq: a study of the problem of linguistic duality. Doctoral dissertation, Harvard University.

Alvarez, C. (1990) The institutionalization of Galician: linguistic practices, power, and ideology in public discourse. PhD thesis, University of California at Berkeley.

Alvarez-Cáccamo, C. (1998) From 'switching code' to 'code-switching': towards a reconceptualization of communicative codes. In J.C.P. Auer (ed.), *Code-Switching in Conversation: Language, interaction and identity*. London: Routledge, pp. 29–50.

Anderson, S.W., Damasio, H., Damasio, A.R., Klima, E., Bellugi, U. and Brandt, J.P. (1992) Acquisition of signs from American Sign Language in hearing individuals, following left hemisphere damage and aphasia. *Neuropsychologia* 30: 329–40.

Andrews, R. (1977) Aspects of language lateralization correlated with familial handedness. *Neuropsychologia* 15: 769–78.

Androutsopoulos, J. (2001) From the streets to the screens and back again: on the mediated diffusion of ethnolectal patterns in contemporary German. In *Essen: LAUD 2001*. Paper 522. Essen: Linguistic Agency, University of Essen.

Angermeyer, P. (2002) Lexical cohesion in multilingual conversation. *International Journal of Bilingualism* 6: 361–93.

Anglin, J.M. (1977) *Word, Object, and Conceptual Development*. New York: Norton.

Annamalai, E. (1989) The language factor in code mixing. *International Journal of the Sociology of Language* 75: 47–54.

Aoun, J. and Sportiche, D. (1993) On the formal theory of government. *Linguistic Review* 2: 211–36.

Appel, R. and Muysken, P. (1987) *Language Contact and Bilingualism*. London: Edward Arnold.

April, R.S., and Han, M. (1980) Crossed aphasia in a right-handed bilingual Chinese man: a second case. *Archives of Neurology* 37: 342–6.

Ardito, B. (1998) *Giochi di segni e parole: Un manuale per leggere e scrivere con bambini sordi e udenti dai 3 ai 7 anni* [Sign and word games: a manual for reading and writing with deaf and hearing children aged 3 to 7]. Milano: Franco Angeli.

Ardito, B. and Mignosi E. (1995) *Vivo una favola e imparo le lingue: Come giocare a parlare con bambini sordi e non* [I live a tale and learn languages: how to play talking with deaf and hearing children]. Firenze: La Nuova Italia.

Arnberg, A. (1987) *Raising Children Bilingually: The pre-school years*. Clevedon: Multilingual Matters.

Atkinson, J.M. and Heritage, J. (eds) (1984) *Structures of Social Action: Studies in conversation analysis*. Cambridge: Cambridge University Press.

Attinasi, J. (1979) Results of a language attitude questionnaire administered orally to an ethnographically chosen sample of 91 residents of a block in East Harlem. New York, 1977–78. Unpublished ms.

Auer, J.C.P. (1981) Bilingualism as a members' concept: language choice and language alternation in their relation to lay assessments of competence. *Papiere des SFB 99*, Constance, No. 54.

Auer, J.C.P. (1983) Zweisprachige Konversationen. *Papiere des SFG 99*, Constance, No. 79.

Auer, J.C.P. (1984) *Bilingual Conversation*. Amsterdam: John Benjamins.

Auer, J.C.P. (1984a) On the meaning of conversational code-switching. In J.C.P. Auer and A. Di Luzio (eds), *Interpretive Sociolinguistics: Migrants – children – migrant children*. Tübingen: Narr, pp. 87–112.

Auer, J.C.P. (1987) Le transfert comme stratégie conversationnelle dans le discourse en 'L2'. In G. Lüdi (ed.) *Devenir bilingue – parler bilingue: Actes due 2e colloque sur le bilinguisme, Université de Neuchâtel, 20–22 Septembre 1984*. Tübingen: Max Niemeyer Verlag.

Auer, J.C.P. (1988) A conversation analytic approach to code-switching and transfer. In M. Heller (ed.), *Codeswitching*. Berlin: Mouton de Gruyter, pp. 187–214.

Auer, J.C.P. (1991) Bilingualism in/as social action. *Papers for the Symposium on Code-switching in Bilingual Studies: Theory, significance and perspectives, Vol.2*. Strasbourg: The European Science Foundation.

Auer, J.C.P. (1991a) Italian in Toronto: A preliminary comparative report. *Multilingua* 10: 403–40.

Auer, J.C.P. (1992) Instead of an introduction: on contextualizing language. In J.C.P. Auer and A. Di Luzio, *Contextualising language*. Amsterdam: Benjamins, pp. 1–38.

Auer, J.C.P. (1995) The pragmatics of code-switching: a sequential approach. In L. Milroy and P. Muysken (eds), *One Speaker Two Languages*. Cambridge: Cambridge University Press, pp. 115–35.

Auer, J.C.P. (1999) From codeswitching via language mixing to fused lects: toward a dynamic typology of bilingual speech. *International Journal of Bilingualism* 3 (4): 309–32.

Auer, J.C.P. (ed.) (1998) *Code-Switching in Conversation: Language, interaction and identity*. London: Routledge.

Auer, J.C.P. and Di Luzio, A. (1983) Structure and meaning of linguistic variation in Italian migrant children in Germany. In R. Bäuerle, Ch. Schwarze and A. von Stechow (eds), *Meaning, Use and Interpretation of Language*. Berlin, pp. 1–21.

Auer, J.C.P. and Di Luzio, A. (1983a) Three types of variation and their interpretation. In L. Dabène, M. Flasaquier and J. Lyons (eds), *Status of Migrants' Mother Tongues*. Strasbourg: ESF, pp. 67–100.

Auer, J.C.P. and Di Luzio, A. (eds) (1984) *Interpretive Sociolinguistics: Migrants – children – migrant children*. Tübingen: Narr.

Auer, J.C.P. and Di Luzio. A. (1992) *Contextualising language*. Amsterdam: Benjamins.

Auer, J.C.P. and Dirim, I. (2003) Socio-cultural orientation, urban youth styles and the spontaneous acquisition of Turkish by non-Turkish adolescents in Germany. In J. Androutsopoulos and A. Georgakopoulou (eds), *Discourse Constructions of Youth Identities*. Amsterdam: John Benjamins, pp. 223–46.

Azuma, S. (1991) Processing and intrasentential code-switching. Unpublished doctoral dissertation, University of Texas at Austin.

Azuma, S. (1993) The frame–content hypothesis in speech production: evidence from intrasentential code switching. *Linguistics* 31: 1071–93.

Back, L. ([1995] 2003) X amount of Sat Siri Akal! Apache Indian, reggae music and intermezzo culture. In A. Ålund and R. Granqvist (eds), *Negotiating Identities*. Amsterdam: Rodopi, pp. 139–68. Reprinted in R. Harris and B. Rampton (eds) (2003) *The Language, Ethnicity and Race Reader*, London: Routledge, pp. 328–45.

Backus, A. (1992) *Patterns of Language Mixing*. Wiesbaden: Harrassowitz.

Backus, A. (1994) Turkish/Dutch corpus. Unpublished data.

Backus, A. (1996) *Two in One: Bilingual speech of Turkish immigrants in the Netherlands*. Tilburg: Tilburg University Press.

Baetens Beardsmore, H. (1982, 2nd edn 1986) *Bilingualism: Basic principles*. Clevedon: Multilingual Matters.

Bailey, B. (2000) Language and negotiation of ethnic/racial identity among Dominican Americans. *Language in Society* 29 (4): 555–82.

Baker, C. (1995, 2nd edn 1996, 4th edn 2006) *Foundations of Bilingual Education and Bilingualism*. Clevedon: Multilingual Matters.

Baker, C. (1995, 2nd edn 2000) *A Parents' and Teachers' Guide to Bilingualism*. Clevedon: Multilingual Matters.

Baker, C. (2000) *The Care and Education of Young Bilinguals*. Clevedon: Multilingual Matters.

Baker, C. (2001) *Guia Para Padres Y Maestros De Ninos Bilingues*, translated with addition by Alma Flor Ada. Clevedon: Multilingual Matters.

Baker, C. (2006) *Foundations of Bilingual Education and Bilingualism*, 4th edn. Clevedon: Multilingual Matters.

Baker, C. and Prys Jones, S. (1998) *Encyclopedia of Bilingualism and Bilingual Education*. Clevedon: Multilingual Matters.

Bakhtin, M. (1984) *Problems in Dostoevsky's Poetics*. Minneapolis, MN: University of Minnesota Press.

Bakker, P. and Mous, M. (eds) (1994) *Mixed Languages: Fifteen case studies in language intertwining*. Amsterdam: Institute for Functional Research in Language and Language Use.

Balken, L. (1970) *Les effets du bilinguisme français–anglais sur les aptitudes intellectuelles*. Bruxelles: Aimav.

Barber, C. (1952) Trilingualism in Pascua: social functions of language in an Arizona Yaqui Village. Unpublished MA Thesis, University of Arizona, Tucson, AZ.

Barker, G.C. (1947) Social functions of language in a Mexican–American community. *Acta Americana* 5: 185–202.

Barnes, J.A. (1954) Class and committees in a Norwegian island parish. *Human Relations* 8: 39–58.

Barth, F. (1964) Ethnic processes in the Pathan–Buluchi boundary. In *Indo–Iranica: Mélanges présentés à Georg Morgestierne à l'occasion de son soixante-dixième anniversaire*. Wiesbaden: Otto Harrassowitz.

Barth, F. (1966) *Models of Social Organisation*. Royal Anthropological Institute of Great Britain and Ireland Occasional Papers, London.

Barth, F. (1969) (ed.) *Ethnic Groups and Boundaries*. Boston, MA: Little, Brown.

Barth, F. (1969a) Introduction. In F. Barth (ed.), *Ethnic Groups and Boundaries*. London: Allen & Unwin, pp. 9–39.

Barton, M., Goodglass, H., and Shai, A. (1965) Differential recognition of tachistoscopically presented English and Hebrew words in right and left visual fields. *Perceptual and Motor Skills* 21: 431–7.

Bates, E. (1976) *Language and Context: The acquisition of pragmatics*. New York: Academic Press.

Bates, E. and MacWhinney, B. (1982) Functionalist approaches to grammar. In E. Wanner and L.R. Gleitman (eds), *Language Acquisition: The state of the art*. Cambridge: Cambridge University Press, pp. 173–218.

Bauman, R. and Briggs, C. (1990) Poetics and performance as critical perspectives on language and social life. *Annual Review of Anthropology* 19: 59–88.

Bauman, R. and Briggs, C. (eds) (2003) *Voices of Modernity: Language ideologies and the politics of inequality*. Cambridge: Cambridge University Press.

Bauman, Z. (1990) Modernity and ambivalence. *Theory, Culture and Society* 7: 143–69.

Bauman, Z. (1992) *Intimations of Post-Modernity*, London: Routledge.

Baumans, L. (1998) *The Syntax of Codeswitching: Analysing Moroccan Arabic/Dutch conversation*. Tilburg: Tilburg University Press.

Beauvillain, C. and Grainger, J. (1987) Accessing interlexical homographs: some limitations of a language-selective access. *Journal of Memory and Language* 26: 658–72.

Belazi, H.M., Rubin, E.J. and Toribio, J. (1994) Code-switching and X-bar theory: the functional head constraint. *Linguistic Inquiry* 25: 221–37.

Bell, A. (1984) Language style as audience design. *Language in Society* 13: 145–204.

Bell, A. (1999) Styling the other to define the self: a study in New Zealand identity-making. *Journal of Sociolinguistics* 3 (4): 523–41.

Bell, R.T. (1976) *Sociolinguistics*. London: Batsford.

Belliveau, J.W., Kennedy, D.N. Jr, McKinstry, R.C., Buchbinder, B.R., Weisskopf, R.M. and Cohen, M.S. (1991) Functional mapping of the human visual cortex by magnetic resonance imaging. *Science* 254: 716–19.

Ben Amar, M., and Gaillard, F. (1984) January–June. Langage et dominance cérébrale chez les monolingues et les bilingues au seuil de l'école. *Les Sciences de l'Education pour l'ère nouvelle* 1–2: 93–111.

Bentahila, A. (1983) *Language Attitudes among Arabic–French Bilinguals in Morocco*. Clevedon: Multilingual Matters.

Bentahila, A. and Davies, E.E. (1983) The syntax of Arabic–French code-switching. *Lingua* 59: 301–30.

Bentahila, A. and Davies, E. (1991) Constraints on code-switching: a look beyond grammar. *Papers for the Symposium on Code-Switching in Bilingual Studies: Theory, significance and perspectives*. Strasbourg: European Science Foundation, pp. 369–404.

Bentahila, A. and Davies, E.E. (1992) Code-switching and language dominance. In R.J. Harris (ed.), *Cognitive Processing in Bilinguals*. Amsterdam: Benjamins, pp. 443–58.

Bentin, S. (n.d.) Right hemisphere role in reading a second language. Unpublished manuscript.

Ben-Zeev, S. (1977) The influence of bilingualism on cognitive development and cognitive strategy. *Child Development* 48: 1009–18.

Bergh, G. (1986) *The Neuropsychological Status of Swedish–English Subsidiary Bilinguals*. Göteborg: Acta Universitatis Gothoburgensis.

Bergman, C.R. (1976) Interference vs. independent development in infant bilingualism. In G.D. Keller, R.V. Taeschner and S. Viera (eds), *Bilingualism in the Bicentennial and Beyond*. New York: Bilingual Press.

Berk-Seligson, S. (1986) Linguistic constraints on intrasentential code-switching. *Language in Society* 15: 313–48.

Berlin, C.I., Lowe-Bell, S.S., Cullen, J.K. and Thompson, C.L. (1973) Dichotic speech perception: an interpretation of right ear advantage and temporal offset effects. *Journal of the Acoustical Society of America* 53: 699–709.

Bernstein, B. (1961) Social structure, language and learning. *Educational Research* 3: 163–76.

Bernstein, B. (1964) Elaborated and restricted codes: their social origins and some consequences. *American Anthropologist* 66, 6 Part II: 55–69.

Bernstein, B. (1971) *Class Codes and Control*, vol. 1. London: Routledge & Kegan Paul.

Berquier, A. and Ashton, R. (1992) Language lateralization in bilinguals: more not less is needed. A reply to Paradis (1990) *Brain and Language* 43: 528–33.

Besner, D., Smith, M.C. and MacLeod, C.M. (1990) Visual word recognition: a dissociation of lexical and semantic processing. *Journal of Experimental Psychology: Learning, memory, and cognition* 16: 862–9.

Bhatia, T.K. and Ritchie, W.C. (eds) (2004) *The Handbook of Bilingualism*. Oxford: Blackwell.

Bhatt, R.M. (1997) Code-switching, constraints and optimal grammars. *Lingua* 102: 223–51.

Bialystok, E. (1990) *Communication Strategies. A psychological analysis of second language use*. Oxford: Basil Blackwell.

Bialystok, E. (2005) Consequences of bilingualism for cognitive development. In J.F. Kroll and A.M.B. de Groot (eds), Lexical access in bilingual production. *Handbook of Bilingualism: Psycholinguistic approaches*. New York: Oxford University Press, pp. 417–32.

Bialystok, E. (ed.) (1991) *Language Processing in Bilingual Children*. Cambridge: Cambridge University Press.

Bierbach, C. (1983) 'Nun erzähl' mal mas!' Textstruktur und referentielle Organisation in elizitierten Erzählungen italienischer Kinder. In E. Gülich and T. Kotschi (eds), *Grammatik, Konversation, Interaktion*. Tübingen: Niemeyer.

Bierwisch, M. and Schreuder, R. (1992) From concepts to lexical items. *Cognition* 41: 23–60.

Blakemore, D. (2002) *Relevance and Linguistic Meaning: The semantics and pragmatics of discourse markers*. Cambridge: Cambridge University Press.

Blanc, H. (1964) *Communal Dialects of Baghdad*. Cambridge, MA: Harvard University Press.

Blank, M. (1980) Measuring lexical access during sentence processing. *Perception and Psychophysics* 28: 1–8.

Block, D. (2003) *The Social Turn in Second Language Acquisition*. Edinburgh: Edinburgh University Press.

Blom, J.-P. and Gumperz, J.J. (1966) Some social determinants of verbal behavior. Unpublished paper presented at the annual meeting of The American Sociological Association.

Blom, J.-P. and Gumperz, J.J. (1972) Social meaning in linguistic structure: code-switching in Norway. In J.J. Gumperz and D. Hymes (eds), *Directions in Sociolinguistics*. New York: Holt, Rinehart and Winston, pp. 407–34.

Bloom, L. and Lahey, M. (1978) *Language Development and Language Disorders*. New York: Wiley.

Bloomfield, L. (1927) Literate and illiterate speech. *American Speech* 2: 432–9.

Bloomfield, L. (1933) *Language*. New York: Holt.

Blumstein, S., Goodglass, H. and Tartter, V.C. (1975) The reliability of ear advantage in dichotic listening. *Brain and Language* 2: 226–36.

Blumstein, S.E., Alexander, M.P., Ryalls, J.H., Katz, W. and Dworetzky, B. (1987) On the nature of foreign accent syndrome: a case study. *Brain and Language* 31: 215–44.

Bock, J. (1986) Meaning, sound and syntax: lexical priming in sentence production. *Journal of Experimental Psychology: Learning, Memory, and Cognition* 12: 575–86.

Bock, J. (1987) An effect of the accessibility of word forms on sentence structures. *Journal of Memory and Language* 26(2): 119–37.

Bock, K. and Levelt, W. (1994) Language production: grammatical encoding. In M.A. Gernsbacher (ed.), *Handbook of Psycholinguistics*. San Diego, CA: Academic Press, pp. 945–84.

Bock, P.K. (1964) Social structure and language structure. *Southwestern Journal of Anthropology* 20: 393–403.

Boeschoten, H.E. (1991) Asymmetrical code-switching in immigrant communities. In European Science Foundation (ed.), *Workshop on Constraints, Conditions, and Models*, Strasburg: European Science Foundation, pp. 85–104.

Boeschoten, H.E. and Verhoeven, L.T. (1985) Integration niederländischer lexikalischer Elemente ins Türkische. *Linguistische Berichte* 98: 437–64.

Bokamba, E. (1988) Code-mixing, language variation, and linguistic theory: evidence from Bantu languages. *Lingua* 76: 21–62.

Bolinger, D. (1989) *Intonation and its Uses: Melody in grammar and discourse*. London: Edward Arnold.

Bolonya, A. (2001) Calculating speakers: codeswitching in a rational choice model. *Language in Society* 30: 1–28.

Borod, J. and Goodglass, H. (1980) Hemispheric specialization and development. In L. Obler and M. Albert (eds), *Language and Communication in the Elderly: Experimental clinical and therapeutic issues*. Lexington, MA: Heath.

Bottini, G., Corcoran, R., Sterzi, R., Paulesu, E., Schenone, P., Scarpa, P., Frackowiak, R.S. and Frith, C.D. (1994) The role of the right hemisphere in the interpretation of figurative aspects of language: a positron emission tomography activation study. *Brain* 117: 1231–53.

Boumans, L. (1994) L'Arabe marocain et le néerlandais en contact: quelques particularités syntaxiques. Paper presented at conference on Mouvements migratoires Magrebine en Europe. Ouida, March.

Bourdieu, P. (1977a) L'économie des échanges linguistiques. *Langue Française* 34: 17–34.

Bourdieu, P. (1977b) *Outline of a Theory of Practice*. Cambridge: Cambridge University Press.

Bourdieu, P. (1982) *Ce que parler veut dire*. Paris: Fayard.

Bourdieu, P. ([1981] 1990) *Language and Symbolic Power*. Oxford: Polity Press.

Braunshausen, N. (1928) Le bilinguisme et la famille. In *Le Bilinguisme et l'Education*. Geneva–Luxemburg, Bureau International d'Education.

Breedin, S.D., Saffran, E.M. and Coslett, H.B. (1994) Reversal of the concreteness effect in a patient with semantic dementia. *Cognitive Neuropsychology* 11: 617–60.

Breitborde, L.B. (1983) Levels of analysis in sociolinguistic explanation. *International Journal of the Sociology of Language* 39: 5–43.

Broersma, M. and de Bot, K. (2006) Triggered codeswitching: a corpus-based evaluation of the original triggering hypothesis and a new alternative. *Bilingualism: Language and cognition* 9: 1–13.

Brown, H., Sharma, N.K. and Kirsner, K. (1984) The role of script and phonology in lexical representation. *Quarterly Journal of Experimental Psychology* 36A: 491–505.

Brown, P. and Levinson, S. (1978) Universals in language usage: politeness phenomena. In E. Goody (ed.), *Questions and Politeness*. New York: Cambridge University Press, pp. 56–310.

Brown, R. (1973) *A First Language: The early stages*. Cambridge, MA: Harvard University Press.

Bryden, M.P. (1970) Left–right differences in tachistoscopic recognition as a function of familiarity and pattern orientation. *Journal of Experimental Psychology* 84: 120–22.

Bryden, M.P. (1980) *Strategy and attentional influences on dichotic listening and tachistoscopic lateralization assessments*. Paper presented at the annual meeting of the International Neuropsychological Society. San Francisco, February.

Bucholtz, M. (1999) You da man: narrating the racial other in the production of white masculinity. *Journal of Sociolinguistics* 3 (4): 443–60.

Bureau of the Census (1973) *Puerto Ricans in the United States*. Publication PC(2)-1E.

Bürki-Cohen, J., Grosjean, F. and Miller, J. (1989) Base language effects on word identification in bilingual speech: evidence from categorical perception experiments. *Language and Speech* 32: 355–71.

Burling, R. (1978) Language development of a Garo and English-speaking child. In E. Hatch (ed.), *Second Language Acquisition: A book of readings*. Rowley, MA: Newbury House.

Butterworth, B. (1981) Speech errors: old data in search of new theories. *Linguistics* 19: 627–81.

Butterworth, B. (1985) Jargon aphasia: processes and strategies. In S. Newman and R. Epstein (eds), *Current Perspectives in Dysphasia*. London: Churchill Livingstone.

Calvin, W.H. and Ojemann, G.A. (eds) (1994) *Conversation with Neil's Brain*. New York: Addison Wesley.

Cameron, D., Frazer, E., Harvey, P., Rampton, B. and Richardson, K. (1992) *Researching Language: Issues of power and methods*. London: Routledge.

Canfield, K. (1980) Navaho–English code-mixing. *Anthropological Linguistics* 22: 218–20.

Caramazza, A., Yeni-Komshian, G., Zurif, E. and Carbone, E. (1973) The acquisition of a new phonological contrast: the case of stop consonants in French–English bilinguals. *Journal of the Acoustical Society of America* 54: 421–8.

Caramazza, A. and Brones, I. (1980) Semantic classification by bilinguals. *Canadian Journal of Psychology* 34: 77–81.

Carman, J.N. (1962) Personal communication regarding a forthcoming second volume of *Foreign Language Units of Kansas: Historical Atlas and Statistics*. Lawrence, KS: University of Kansas Press.

Carroll, F. (1978) Cerebral dominance for language: a dichotic listening study of Navajo–English bilinguals. In H. Key, S. McCullough and J. Sawyer (eds), *The Bilingual in a Pluralistic Society: Proceedings of the Sixth Southwest Area Language and Linguistics Workshop*. Long Beach: California State University, pp. 11–17.

Carroll, F. (1980) Neurolinguistic processing in bilingualism and second language. In R. Scarcella, and S. Krashen (eds), *Research in Second Language Acquisition*. Rowley, MA: Newbury House, pp. 81–86.

Casadio, P. and Caselli, M.C. (1989) Il primo vocabolario del bambino: Gesti e parole a 14 mesi. *Età Evolutiva* 33: 32–42.

Caselli, M.C. (1994) Communicative gestures and first words. In V. Volterra and C.J. Erting (eds), *From Gesture to Language in Hearing and Deaf Children*. Washington, DC: Gallaudet University Press, pp. 56–67.

Caselli, M.C., Maragna, S., Pagliari Rampelli, L. and Volterra, V. (1994) *Linguaggio e Sordità: Parole e segni nell'educazione dei sordi*. Firenze: La Nuova Italia Editrice.

Cazden, C., John, V. and Hymes, D. (eds) (1972) *Functions of Language in the Classroom*. New York: Teachers College Press.

Chafe, W. (1987) Cognitive constraints on information flow. In R.S. Romlin (ed.), *Typological Studies of Language, Vol. 11: Coherence and Grounding in Discourse*. Amsterdam: John Benjamins, pp. 21–51.

Chao, Y.R. (1947) *Cantonese Primer*. Cambridge, MA: Harvard University Press.

Chary, P. (1986) Aphasia in a multilingual society: a preliminary study. In J. Vaid (ed.), *Language Processsing in Bilinguals: Psycholinguistic and neuropsychological perspectives*. Hillsdale, NJ: Erlbaum, pp. 183–97.

Chee, M.W.L., Caplan, D., Soon, C.S., Sriram, N., Tan, E.W.L., Thiel, T. and Weekes, B. (1999) Processing of visually presented sentences in Mandarin and English studied with fMRI. *Neuron* 23: 127–37.

Chee, M.W.L., Tan, E.W.L. and Thiel, T. (1999) Mandarin and English single word processing studied with functional Magnetic Resonance Imaging. *Journal of Neuroscience* 19: 3050–6.

Chejne, A. (1958) The role of Arabic in present-day Arab society. *The Islamic Literature* 10(4): 15–54.

Chen, H.-C. (1990) Lexical processing in a non-native language: effects of language proficiency and learning strategy. *Memory and Cognition* 18: 279–88.

Chen, H.-C. (1992) Lexical processing in bilingual or multilingual speakers. In R.J. Harris (ed.), *Cognitive Processing in Bilinguals*. Amsterdam: Elsevier, pp. 253–64.

Chen, H.-C. and Ho, C. (1986) Development of Stroop interference in Chinese–English bilinguals. *Journal of Experimental Psychology: Learning, memory, and cognition* 12: 397–401.

Chen, H.-C. and Leung, Y.-S. (1989) Patterns of lexical processing in a non-native language. *Journal of Experimental Psychology: Learning, memory, and cognition* 15: 316–25.

Chen, H.-C. and Ng, M.-L. (1989) Semantic facilitation and translation priming effects in Chinese–English bilinguals. *Memory and Cognition* 17: 454–62.

Chomsky, N. (1981) *Lectures on Government and Binding*. Dordrecht: Foris.

Chomsky, N. (1986a) *Knowledge of Language: Its nature, origin and use*. New York: Praeger.

Chomsky, N. (1986b) *Barriers*. Cambridge, MA: MIT Press.

Christiansen, H. (1962) *Malet I Rana*. Oslo: Institut for Sociologi, Universitete I Oslo.

Christoffels, I.K. and de Groot, A.M.B. (2005) Simultaneous interpreting: a cognitive perspective.

In J.F. Kroll and A.M.B. de Groot (eds), *Handbook of Bilingualism: Psycholinguistic approaches*. New York: Oxford University Press, pp. 326–48.

Cicourel, A. (1980) Three models of discourse analysis: the role of social structure. *Discourse Process* 3: 101–32.

Clahsen, H. (1982) *Spracherwerb in der Kindheit*. Tübingen: Narr.

Clahsen, H. (1984) Der Erwerb der Kasusmarkierung in der deutschen Kindersprache, *Linguistische Berichte* 89: 1–31.

Clahsen, H. (1986) Verb inflections in German child language: acquisition of agreement markings and the functions they encode. *Linguistics* 24: 79–121.

Clark, E. (1985) Acquisition of Romance: With special reference to French. In D. Slobin (ed), *Crosslinguistic Study of Language Acquisition*. Hillsdale, NJ: Erlbaum, pp. 687–782.

Clark, H.H. (1973) The language-as-fixed-effect fallacy: A critique of language statistics in psychological research. *Journal of Verbal Learning and Verbal Behavior* 12: 335–59.

Clark, J.T. (2003) Abstract inquiry and the patrolling of black/white borders through linguistic stylization. In R. Harris and B. Rampton (eds), *The Language, Ethnicity and Race Reader*, London: Routledge, pp. 303–13.

Clark, L. and Knowles, J. (1973) Age differences in dichotic listening performance. *Journal of Gerontology* 28: 173–8.

Clyne, M. (1967) *Transference and Triggering*. The Hague: Nijhoff.

Clyne, M. (1969) Switching between language systems. *Actes du 10. congrès internationale des linguistes*, Vol. 1: 343–9. Bucharest: Editions de l'Académie de la République Socialiste de Roumanie.

Clyne, M. (1971) German–English bilingualism and linguistic theory. In V. Lange and H.G. Roloff (eds), *Dichtung, Sprache und Gesellschaft. Akten des 4. internationalen Germanistenkongresses*, 503–11. Frankfurt: Athenäum.

Clyne, M. (1972) *Perspectives on Language Contact*. Melbourne: The Hawthorne Press.

Clyne, M. (1972a) Perception of code-switching in bilinguals. *ITL Review of Applied Linguistics* 16: 45–8.

Clyne, M. (1974) Lexical insertions in a performance model: evidence from bilinguals. *Proceedings of the 11th International Congress of Linguistics*. Bologna: Mulino.

Clyne, M. (1980) Zur Regelmäßigkeit von Spracherscheinungen bei Bilingualen. *Zeitschrift für germanistische Linguistik* 8: 22–33.

Clyne, M. (1980a) Triggering and language processing. *Canadian Journal of Psychology* 34: 400–6.

Clyne, M. (1982) *Multilingual Australia*. Melbourne: River Seine Publications.

Clyne, M. (1987) Constraints on code-switching: how universal are they? *Linguistics* 25: 739–64.

Clyne, M. (2003) *Dynamics of Language Contact*. Cambridge: Cambridge University Press.

Cochran, M., Larner, M., Riley, D., Gunnarsson, M. and Henderson, C.R. (eds) (1990) *Extending Families*. Cambridge: Cambridge University Press.

Colbourn, C. (1978) Can laterality be measured. *Neuropsychologia* 16: 283–90.

Colbourn, C. (1981) What can laterality measures tell us about hemisphere functions during childhood development? In Y. Lebrun and O. Zangwill (eds), *Lateralization of Language in the Child*. Lisse, the Netherlands: Swets & Zeitlinger, pp. 91–102.

Collins, A.M. and Loftus, E.F. (1975) A spreading activation theory of semantic processing. *Psychological Review* 82: 407–28.

Comhaire-Sylvain, S. (1936) *Le Créole haitien*. Wetteren and Port-au-Prince.

Cook-Gumperz, J. and Corsaro, W. (1986) Introduction. In J. Cook-Gumperz, W. Corsaro and J. Streeck (eds), *Children's Worlds and Children's Language*. Berlin: Mouton de Gruyter, pp. 1–11.

Cook-Gumperz, J., Corsaro, W. and Streeck, J. (eds) (1986) *Children's Worlds and Children's Language*. Berlin: Mouton de Gruyter.

Corsaro, W. and Rizzo, T. (1990) Disputes in the peer culture of American and Italian nursery-school children. In A. Grimshaw (ed.), *Conflict Talk*. Cambridge: Cambridge University Press, pp. 21–66.

Costa, A. (2005) Lexical access in bilingual production. In J.F. Kroll and A.M.B. de Groot (eds), *Handbook of Bilingualism: Psycholinguistic approaches*. New York: Oxford University Press, pp. 308–25.

Costa, A. and Caramazza, A. (1999) Is lexical selection in bilinguals language-specific? Further evidence from Spanish–English bilinguals and English–Spanish bilinguals. *Bilingualism: Language and cognition* 2: 231–44.

Coulmas, F. (1992) *Language and Economy*. Oxford: Blackwell.

Coupland, N. (2001) Dialect stylization in radio talk. *Language in Society* 30 (3): 345–76.

Coupland, N. and Jaworski, A. (eds) (1997) *Sociolinguistics: A reader and coursebook*. Houndmills: Macmillan.

Crawhall, N. (1990) Unpublished Shona/English data set.

Crystal, D. (1987, 2nd edn 1997) *The Cambridge Encyclopaedia of Language*. Cambridge: Cambridge University Press.

Cummins, J. (1976) The influence of bilingualism on cognitive growth: a synthesis of research findings and explanatory hypotheses. *Working Papers on Bilingualism* 9: 1–43.

Cummins, J. (1981) The role of primary language development in promoting educational success for language minority students. In *Schooling and Language Minority Students: A theoretical framework*. Los Angeles: Evaluation, Dissemination, and Assessment Center.

Cunningham-Andersson, U. and Andersson, S. (1999, 2nd edn 2004) *Growing Up with Two Languages: A practical guide*. London: Routledge.

Cutler, A. ((1999) 2003) 'Yorkville crossing: white teens, hip hop, and African American English. *Journal of Sociolinguistics* 3 (4): 428–42. Reprinted in R. Harris and B. Rampton (eds) (2003) *The Language, Ethnicity and Race Reader*, London: Routledge, pp. 314–27.

Cziko, G.A. (1980) Language competence and reading strategies: a comparison of first and second language oral reading errors. *Language Learning* 30: 101–16.

Damasio, H., Grabowski, T.J., Tranel, D., Hitchwa, R.D. and Damasio, A.R. (1996) A neural basis for lexical retrieval. *Nature* 380: 499–505.

d'Angelo, D. (1984) Interaktionsnetzwerke und soziokultureller Hintergrund italienischer Migranten und Migrantenkinder in Konstanz. *Papiere des SFB 99*, Constance.

Darbelnet, J. (1957) La couleur en français et en anglais. *Journal des Traducteurs* 2: 157–61.

Darcy, N.T. (1953) A review of the literature on the effects of bilingualism upon the measurement of intelligence. *Journal of Genetic Psychology* 82: 21–57.

Dauer, R. (1983) Stress-timing and syllable-timing reanalyzed. *Journal of Phonetics* 11: 51–62.

Davey, A. (1983) *Learning to Be Prejudiced*. London: Edward Arnold.

de Bot, K. (1986) Transfer of intonation and the missing data basis. In F. Kellerman and M. Sharwood Smith (eds), *Cross-Linguistic Influence in Second Language Learning*. Oxford: Pergamon Press.

de Bot, K. (1990) Metalinguistic awareness in long-term Dutch immigrants in Australia. Paper presented at the annual meeting of the Australian Association of Applied Linguistics, Sydney, September.

de Bot, K. (1992) A bilingual production model: Levelt's 'speaking' model adapted. *Applied Linguistics* 13: 1–24.

de Bot, K. (2004) The multilingual lexicon: modeling selection and control. *International Journal of Multilingualism* 1: 17–32.

de Bot, K. and Clyne, M. (1989) Language reversion revisited. *Studies in Second Language Acquisition* 11: 167–77.

de Bot, K. and Schreuder, R. (1993) Word production and the bilingual lexicon. In R. Schreuder and B. Weltens (eds), *The Bilingual Lexicon*. Philadelphia: John Benjamins, pp. 191–214.

Dechert, H. (1984) Second language production: six hypotheses. In H. Dechert, D. Möhle, and M. Raupach (eds), *Second Language Productions*. Tübingen: Gunter Narr.

de Groot, A.M.B. (1992a) Determinants of word translation. *Journal of Experimental Psychology: Learning, memory, and cognition* 18: 1001–18.

de Groot, A.M.B. (1992b) Bilingual lexical representation: a closer look at conceptual representations. In R. Frost and L. Katz (eds), *Orthography, Phonology, Morphology, and Meaning*. Amsterdam: Elsevier, pp. 389–412.

de Groot, A.M.B. (1993) Word-type effects in bilingual processing tasks: support for a mixed representational system. In R. Schreuder and B. Weltens (eds), *The Bilingual Lexicon*. Amsterdam: John Benjamins, pp. 27–51.

de Groot, A.M.B. (1995) Determinants of bilingual lexicosemantic organization. *Computer Assisted Language Learning* 8: 151–80.

de Groot, A.M.B. and Comijs, H. (1995) Translation recognition and translation production: comparing a new and an old tool in the study of bilingualism. *Language Learning* 45: 467–510.

de Groot, A.M.B., Dannenburg, L. and Van Hell, J.G. (1994) Forward and backward word translation. *Journal of Memory and Language* 33: 600–29.

de Groot, A.M.B., Delmaar, P., and Lupker, S. (2000) The processing of interlexical homographs in translation recognition and lexical decision: support for nonselective access to bilingual memory. *Quarterly Journal of Experimental Psychology* 53A: 397–428.

de Groot, A.M.B. and Hoeks, J.C.J. (1995) The development of bilingual memory: evidence from word translation by trilinguals. *Language Learning* 45: 683–724.

de Groot, A.M.B. and Keijzer, R. (2000) What is hard to learn is easy to forget: the roles of word concreteness, cognate status and word frequency in foreign-language vocabulary learning and forgetting. *Language Learning* 50: 1–56.

de Groot, A.M.B. and Nas, G.L.J. (1991) Lexical representation of cognates and noncognates in compound bilinguals. *Journal of Memory and Language* 30: 90–123.

de Groot, A.M.B. and Poot, R. (1997) Word translation at three levels of proficiency in a second language: the ubiquitous involvement of conceptual memory. *Language Learning* 47: 215–64.

de Groot A.M.B. and Kroll, J. (eds) (1997) *Tutorials in Bilingualism: Psycholinguistic perspectives*. Mahwah, NJ: Lawrence Erlbaum.

Dehaene, S.D., Dupoux, E., Mehler, J., Cohen, L., Paulesu, E., Perani, D., van de Moortele, P.F., Lehéricy, S. and Le Bihan, D. (1997) Anatomical variability in the cortical representation of first and second languages. *NeuroReport* 8: 3809–15.

De Houwer, A. (1990) *The Acquisition of Two Languages from Birth: A case study*. Cambridge: Cambridge University Press.

De Houwer, A. (1995) Bilingual language acquisition. In P. Fletcher and B. MacWhinney (eds), *The Handbook of Child Language*. Oxford: Blackwell, pp. 219–50.

De Houwer, A. (ed.) (1998) *Bilingual Acquisition*. London: Kingston Press (also available as a special issue of *International Journal of Bilingualism*, 2(3)).

de Jong, E. (1986) *The Bilingual Experience: A book for parents*. Cambridge: Cambridge University Press.

del Coso-Calame, F., de Pietro, J.-F. and Oesch-Serra, C. (1985) La compétence de communication bilingue. Etude fonctionnelle des code-switchings dans le discourse de migrants espagnols et italiens à Neuchâtel (Suisse). In E. Gülich and T. Kotschi (eds), *Grammatik, Konversation, Interaktion*. Tübingen: Max Niemeyer Verlag, pp. 377–98.

Dell, G.S. (1986) A spreading activation theory of retrieval in sentence production. *Psychological Review* 93: 283–321.

Dell, G.S. and O'Seaghdha, P.G. (1992) Stages of lexical access in language production. *Cognition* 42: 287–314.

Dennis, N., Henriques, F.M. and Slaughter, C. (1957) *Coal is Our Life*. London: Eyre and Spottiswoode.

Deuchar, M. and Quay, S. (1998) One vs. two systems in early bilingual syntax: two versions of the question. *Bilingualism: Language and Cognition* 1: 231–43.

Deuchar, M. and Quay, S. (2000) *Bilingual Acquisition: Theoretical implications of a case study*. Oxford: Oxford University Press.

Diaz, R. (1983) Thought and two languages: the impact of bilingualism on cognitive development. In E. Norbeck, D. Price-Williams and W. McCord (eds), *Review of Research in Education*. Vol. 10. Washington DC: American Educational Research Association.

Diebold, Jr. A.R., (1961) Incipient bilingualism. *Language* 37.

Dieth, E. (1938) *Schwyzertütsch Dialäkschrift*. Zurich.

Dijkstra, T., Van Jaarsveld, H. and Ten Brinke, S. (1998) Interlingual homograph recognition: effects of task demands and language intermixing. *Bilingualism: Language and cognition* 1: 51–66.

Dijkstra, T. and van Heuven, W.J.B. (1998) The BIA-model and bilingual word recognition. In J. Grainger and A. Jacobs (eds), *Localist Connectionist Approaches to Human Cognition*. Mahwah, NJ: Erlbaum, pp. 189–225.

Dijkstra, T. and van Heuven, W.J.B. (2002) The architecture of the bilingual word recognition system: from identification to decision. *Bilingualism: Language and cognition* 5: 175–97.

Dik, S. (1978) *Functional Grammar*. Amsterdam: Noord-Holland.

Di Luzio, A. (1983) Problemi linguistici dei figli dei lavoratori migranti. In G. Braga (ed.), *Problemi linguistici e unità europea*. Milano: Angeli, pp. 112–19.

Di Luzio, A. (1984) On the meaning of language alternation for the sociocultural identity of Italian migrant children. In J.C.P. Auer and A. Di Luzio (eds), *Interpretive Sociolinguistics: Migrants – children – migrant children*. Tübingen: Narr.

Di Luzio, A. (1984a) On the meaning of language choice for the sociocultural identity of bilingual migrant children. In J.C.P. Auer and A. Di Luzio, *Interpretive Sociolinguistics*. Tübingen: Narr.

Di Sciullo, A.-M., Muysken, P. and Singh, R. (1986) Government and code-mixing. *Journal of Linguistics* 22: 1–24.

Di Sciullo, A.-M. and Williams, E. (1989) *On the Definition of Word*. Cambridge, MA: MIT Press.

Dohrenwend, B.P. and Smith, R.J. (1962) Toward a theory of acculturation. *Southwest Journal of Anthropology* 18: 30–9.

Donald, J. and Rattansi, A. (eds) (1992) *'Race' Culture and Difference*. London: Sage.

Döpke, S. (1992) *One Parent One Language: An interactional approach*. Amsterdam: John Benjamins.

Döpke, S. (2001) *Cross-Linguistic Structures in Simultaneous Bilingualism*. Amsterdam: John Benjamins.

Doran, M. (2004) Negotiating between 'bourge' and 'racaille': Verlan as youth identity practice in suburban Paris. In A. Pavlenko and A. Blackledge (eds), *Negotiating Identity in Multilingual Contexts*. Clevedon: Multilingual Matters.

Dorian, N. (1981) *Language Death: The life cycle of a Scottish Gaelic dialect*. Philadelphia, PA: Pennsylvania University Press.

Dornic, S. (1978) The bilingual's performance: Language dominance, stress and individual differences. In D. Gerver and H. Sinaiko (eds), *Language Interpretation and Communication*. New York: Plenum.

Dowty, D. (1979) *Word Meaning and Montague Grammar*. Dordrecht: Reidel.

Dufour, R. (1997) Sign language and bilingualism. In A. de Groot and J. Kroll (eds), *Tutorials in Bilingualism: Psycholinguistic perspectives*. Mahwah, NJ: Lawrence Erlbaum, pp. 301–30.

Dufour, R. and Kroll, J.F. (1995) Matching words to concepts in two languages: a test of the concept mediation model of bilingual representation. *Memory and Cognition* 23: 166–80.

Dufour, R., Kroll, J.F. and Sholl, A. (1996) Bilingual naming and translation: accessing lexical and conceptual knowledge in two languages. Unpublished manuscript, Swarthmore College.

Dummett, A. (1973) *A Portrait of English Racism*. Harmondsworth: Penguin. (2nd edn 1984. London: CARAF.)

Duranti, A. (ed.) (2001) *Key Terms in Language and Culture*, Oxford: Blackwell.

Durgunoglu, A.Y. and Hancin, B.J. (1992) An overview of cross-language transfer in bilingual reading. In R.J. Harris (ed.), *Cognitive Processing in Bilinguals*. Amsterdam: Elsevier, pp. 391–411.

Durgunoglu, A.Y. and Roediger, H.L. (1987) Test differences in accessing bilingual memory. *Journal of Memory and Language* 26: 377–91.

Eckert, P. (2000) *Linguistic Variation as Social Practice*. Oxford: Blackwell.

Edwards, J. (1994) *Multilingualism*. London: Routledge.

Edwards, V. (1986) *Language in a Black Community*. Clevedon: Multilingual Matters.

Elman, J., Diehl, R. and Buchwald, S. (1977) Perceptual switching in bilinguals. *Journal of the Acoustical Society of America* 62: 971–4.

Elster, J. (1989) *The Cement of Society*. Cambridge: Cambridge University Press.

Erickson, F. and Shultz, J. (1981) *The Counsellor as Gatekeeper*. New York: Academic Press.

Ervin, S.M. (1964) An analysis of the interaction of language, topic and listener. *American Anthropologist* 66, Part 2: 86–102.

Ervin, S.M. and Osgood, C.E. (1954) Second language learning and bilingualism. *Journal of Abnormal and Social Psychology* 49, Supplement: 139–46.

Ervin-Tripp, S. (1976) Is Sybil there? The structure of some American English directives. *Language in Society* 5: 25–66.

Evans, J., Workman, L., Mayer, P. and Crowley, P. (2002) Differential bilingual laterality: mythical monster found in Wales. *Brain and Language* 83: 291–9.

Extra, G. and Verhoeven, L. (eds) (1994) *The Cross-Linguistic Studies of Bilingual Development*. Amsterdam: North-Holland.

Fabbro, F. (1999) *The Neurolinguistics of Bilingualism*. Hove: Psychology Press.

Fabbro, F., Skrap, M. and Aglioti, S. (2000) Pathological switching between languages following frontal lesion in a bilingual patient. *Journal of Neurology, Neurosurgery, and Psychiatry* 68: 650–2.

Færch, C. and G. Kasper (1986) Cognitive dimensions of language transfer. In E. Kellerman and M. Sharwood Smith (eds), *Cross-Linguistic Influence in Second Language Learning*. Oxford: Pergamon Press.

Fantini, A.E. (1978) Bilingual behavior and social cues: case studies of two bilingual children. In M. Paradis (ed.), *Aspects of Bilingualism*. Columbia, SC: Hornbeam Press.

Fantini, A.E. (1982) *La adquisición del lenguaje en un niño bilingue*. Barcelona: Editorial Herder.

Fasold, R. (1984) *The Sociolinguistics of Society*. Oxford: Blackwell.

Fasold, R. (1990) *The Sociolinguistics of Language*. Oxford: Blackwell.

Ferguson, C.A. (1957) Two problems in Arabic phonology. *Word* 13: 460–78.

Ferguson, C.A. (1959) Diglossia. *Word* 15: 325–40.

Ferguson, C.A. (1960) Myths about Arabic. *Monograph Series on Language and Linguistics* 12: 75–82, Georgetown University.

Fernandez, M. (1994) *Diglossia: A comprehensive bibliography 1960–1990 and supplements*. Amsterdam: John Benjamins.

Firth, A, and Wagner, J. (1997) On discourse, communication and (some) fundamental concepts in SLA research. *Modern Language Journal* 81 (3): 285–300.

Fischer, C. (1984) *The Urban Experience*. 2nd edn. New York: Harcourt, Brace, Jovanovitch.

Fishman, J. (1977) Language and ethnicity. In H. Giles (ed.), *Language, Ethnicity and Intergroup Relations*. New York: Academic Press, pp. 15–57.

Fishman, J.A. (1956) The process and function of social stereotyping. *Journal Social Psychology* 43: 27–64.

Fishman, J.A. (1964) Language maintenance and language shift as fields of inquiry. *Linguistics* 9: 32–70.

Fishman, J.A. (1965) Who speaks what language to whom and when? *La Linguistique* 2: 67–88.

Fishman, J.A. (1965a) Language maintenance and language shift in certain urban immigrant environments: the case of Yiddish in the United States. *Europa Ethnica* 22: 146–58.

Fishman, J.A. (1965b) Bilingualism, intelligence and language learning. *Modern Language Journal* 49: 227–37.

Fishman, J.A. (1965c) Language maintenance and language shift: the American immigrant case. *Sociologus* 16: 19–38.

Fishman, J.A. (1965d) *Yiddish in America*. Bloomington, IN: Indiana University Research Center in Anthropology, Folklore and Linguistics. Publication 36. (Also: *International Journal of American Linguistics* 31, Part II, (2).)

Fishman, J.A. (1965e) Varieties of ethnicity and language consciousness. *Monograph Series on Languages and Linguistics* (Georgetown University) 18: 69–79.

Fishman, J.A. (1966a) Language maintenance in a supra-ethnic age; summary and conclusions. In J.A. Fishman (ed.), *Language Loyalty in the United States*. The Hague: Mouton, pp. 392–411.

Fishman, J.A. (1966b) Bilingual sequences at the societal level. *On teaching English to speakers of other languages* 2: 139–44.

Fishman, J.A. (1966c) Some contrasts between linguistically homogeneous and linguistically heterogeneous polities. *Sociological Inquiry* 36: 146–158.

Fishman, J.A. (1967) Bilingualism with and without diglossia; diglossia with and without bilingualism. *Journal of Social Issues* 23(2): 29–38.

Fishman, J.A. (1968) Sociolinguistic perspective on the study of bilingualism. *Linguistics* 39: 21–49.

Fishman, J.A. (1971) The sociology of language: an interdisciplinary approach. In J.A. Fishman (ed.), *Advances in the Sociology of Language*. Vol. 1. The Hague: Mouton.

Fishman, J.A. (1971a) *Sociolinguistics*. Rowley, MA: Newbury.

Fishman, J.A. (1972) *Language in Sociocultural Change: Essays by J.A. Fishman*, selected by A.S. Dil, Stanford, CA: Stanford University Press.

Fishman, J.A. (1985) *The Rise and Fall of the Ethnic Revival: Perspectives on language and ethnicity*. Berlin: Mouton.

Fishman, J.A. (1989) *Language and Ethnicity in Minority Sociolinguistic Perspective*. Clevedon: Multilingual Matters.

Fishman, J.A. (1991) *Reversing Language Shift*. Clevedon: Multilingual Matters.

Fishman, J.A. (ed.) (1966) *Language Loyalty in the United States*. The Hague: Mouton.

Flege, J.E. (1986) Effects of equivalence classification on the production of foreign language sounds. In A. James and J. Leather (eds), *Sound Patterns in Second Language Acquisition*. Dordrecht: Foris.

Flege, J.E., Munro, M.J. and MacKay, I.R.A. (1995) Effects of age of second-language learning on the production of English consonants. *Speech Communication* 16: 1–26.

Fletcher, P. and Garman, M. (eds) (1979) *Language Acquisition: Studies in first language development.* Cambridge: Cambridge University Press.

Fletcher, P.C., Happé, F., Frith, U., Baker, S.C., Dolan, R.J., Frackowiak, R.S. and Frith, C.D. (1995) Other minds in the brain: a functional imaging study of 'theory of mind' in story comprehension. *Cognition* 57: 109–28.

Foley, D. (1990) *Learning Capitalist Culture.* Philadelphia, PA: University of Pennsylvania Press.

Forster, K.I. (1970) Visual perception of rapidly presented word sequences of varying complexity. *Perception and Psychophysics* 8: 215–21.

Forster, K.I. (1976) Accessing the mental lexicon. In R.Wales and E.Walker (eds), *New Approaches to Language Mechanism.* Amsterdam: North-Holland, pp. 257–87.

Fox, E. (1996) Cross-language priming from ignored words: evidence for a common representational system in bilinguals. *Journal of Memory and Language* 35: 353–70.

Frauenfelder, U. and Tyler, L. (eds) (1987) *Spoken Word Recognition.* Cambridge, MA: MIT Press.

Frei, H. (1936) Monosyllabisme et polysyllabisme dans les emprunts linguistiques. *Bulletin de la Maison franco-japonaise* 8.

French, R.M. and Jacquet, M. (2004) Understanding bilingual memory: models and data. *Trends in Cognitive Science* 8: 87–93.

Frenck, C. and Pynte, J. (1987) Semantic representation and surface forms: a look at across-language priming in bilinguals. *Journal of Psycholinguistic Research* 16: 383–93.

Freud, S. ([1891]1953) *On Aphasia* (E. Stengel, trans.). London: Imago.

Frey, J.W. (1945) Amish triple talk. *American Speech* 20: 85–98.

Friedrich, P. (1972) Social context and semantic feature. In J.J. Gumperz and D. Hymes (eds), *Directions in Sociolinguistics.* New York: Holt, Rinehart and Winston, pp. 270–300.

Frith, C.D., Friston, K.J., Liddle, P.F. and Frackowiak, R.S. (1991) Willed actions. *Neuropsychologia* 29: 1137–48.

Fujimura, O. and Lovins, J. (1978) Syllables are concatenative phonetic units. In A. Bell and J. Hooper (eds), *Syllables and Segments.* Amsterdam: North Holland.

Furnborough, P., Jupp, T., Munns, R. and Roberts, C. (1982) Language disadvantage and discrimination: breaking the cycle of majority group perception. *Journal of Multilingual and Multicultural Development* 3: 247–66.

Gafaranga, J. (2007) Code-switching as a conversational strategy. In J.C.P. Auer and Li Wei (eds), *Multilingualism and Multilingual Communication: Handbook of Applied Linguistics*, vol. 5. Berlin: Mouton de Gruyter, pp. 267–301.

Gage, W.W. (1961) *Contrastive Studies in Linguistics: A bibliographical checklist.* Washington, DC: Center for Applied Linguistics.

Gal, S. (1979) *Language Shift: Social determinants of linguistic change in bilingual Austria.* New York: Academic Press.

Gal, S. (1987) Code-switching and consciousness on the European periphery. *American Ethnologist* 14 (4): 637–53.

Gal, S. (1988) The political economy of code choice. In M. Heller (ed.), *Codeswitching: Anthropological and Sociolinguistic Perspectives.* Berlin: Mouton de Gruyter, pp. 245–64.

Gal, S. (1989) Language and political economy. *Annual Review of Anthropology* 18: 345–67.

Galloway, L. (1977) The brain and the bilingual. Unpublished manuscript, University of California, Los Angeles.

Galloway, L. (1980) The cerebral organization of language in bilinguals and second language learners. PhD dissertation, University of California, Los Angeles.

Galloway, L. (1980a) Neurological correlates of language in second language performance. II. An overview and future perspectives. Paper presented at the Third Los Angeles Second Language Research Forum. University of California, Los Angeles, February/March.

Galloway, L. (1980b) Towards a neuropsychological model of bilingualism and second language performance: a theoretical article with a critical review of current research and some new hypotheses. In M. Long, S. Peck and K. Bailey (eds), *Research in Second Language Acquisition*. Rowley, MA: Newbury House.

Galloway, L. (1980c) Clinical evidence: polyglot aphasia. Presented at the Symposium on Cerebral Lateralization in Bilingualism. BABBLE Conference. Niagara Falls, Ontario.

Galloway, L. and Krashen, S. (1980) Cerebral organization in bilingualism and second language. In R. Scarcella and S. Krashen (eds), *Research in Second Language Acquisition*. Rowley, MA: Newbury House, pp. 74–80.

Galloway, L. and Scarcella, R. (1982) Cerebral organization in adult second language acquisition: is the right hemisphere more involved? *Brain and Language* 16: 56–60.

Gans, H.J. (1962) *The Urban Villagers: Group and class in the life of Italian-Americans*. 2nd edn. New York: Free Press.

Garcia, E.E. (1983) *Early Childhood Bilingualism*. Albuquerque: University of New Mexico Press.

Garcia, O. and Baker, C. (1995) *Policy and Practice in Bilingual Education*. Clevedon: Multilingual Matters.

Garcia, O. and Schiffman, H. (eds) (2006) *Language Loyalty, Continuity and Change: Fishman's contributions to international sociolinguistics*. Clevedon: Multilingual Matters.

Gardner, E. and Branski, D. (1976) Unilateral cerebral activation and perception of gaps: a signal detection analysis. *Neuropsychologica* 14: 43–53.

Gardner-Chloros, P. (1991) *Language Selection and Switching in Strasbourg*. Oxford: Clarendon.

Garfinkel, H. (1972) Remarks on ethnomethodology. In J.J. Gumperz and D. Hymes (eds), *Directions in Sociolinguistics*. New York: Holt, Rinehart and Winston, pp. 301–24.

Garfinkel, H. (1984) *Studies in Ethnomethodology*. Oxford: Polity Press.

Garman, M. (1979) Early grammatical development. In P. Fletcher, and M. Garman (eds), *Language Acquisition: Studies in first language development*. Cambridge: Cambridge University Press, pp. 177–208.

Garrett, M. (1975) The analysis of sentence production. In G. Bower (ed.), *Psychology of Learning and Motivation: Vol. 9*. New York: Academic Press.

Garrett, M. (1982) Production of speech: observations from normal and pathological language use. In A.W. Ellis (ed.), *Normality and pathology in cognitive functions*. New York/London: Academic Press.

Garrett, M. (1988) Process in sentence production. In F. Newmeyer (ed.), *The Cambridge Linguistics Survey III*, Cambridge: Cambridge University Press, pp. 69–96.

Gaziel, T., Obler, L. and Albert, M. (1978) A tachistoscopic study of Hebrew–English bilinguals. In M. Albert and L. Obler (eds), *The Bilingual Brain*. New York: Academic Press.

Geerts, G., et al. (eds) (1984) *Algemene Nederlandse Spraakkunst* (ans). Groningen: Wolters.

Genesee, F. (1987) *Learning through Two Languages: Studies of immersion and bilingual education*. Cambridge MA: Newbury House.

Genesee, F. (1989) Early bilingual language development: one language or two? *Journal of Child Language* 16: 161–79.

Genesee, F. (2002) Portrait of the bilingual child. In V. Cook (ed.), *Portraits of the Second Language User*. Clevedon: Multilingual Matters, pp. 170–96.

Genesee, F. and Bourhis, R. (1982) The social psychological significance of code switching in cross-cultural communication. *Journal of Language and Social Psychology* 1:1–28.

Genesee, F. and Nicoladis, E. (in press) Bilingual acquisition. In E. Hoff and M. Shatz (eds), *Handbook of Language Development*, Oxford: Blackwell.

Genesee, F., Boivin, I. and Nicoladis, E. (1996) Talking with strangers: a study of bilingual children's communicative competence. *Applied Psycholinguistics* 17: 427–42.

Genesee, F., Hamers, J., Lambert, W.E., Mononen, L., Seitz, M. and Starck, R. (1978) Language processing in bilinguals. *Brain and Language* 5: 1–12.

Genesee, F., Nicoladis, N. and Paradis, J. (1995) Language differentiation in early bilingual development. *Journal of Child Language* 22: 611–31.

Genesee, F., Paradis, J. and Crago, M.B. (2004) *Dual Language Development and Disorders: A handbook on bilingualism and second language learning*. Baltimore, MD: Brookes.

Gerard, L.D. and Scarborough, D.L. (1989) Language-specific lexical access of homographs by bilinguals. *Journal of Experimental Psychology: Learning, memory, and cognition* 15: 305–15.

Gibbons, J. (1979) Code-mixing and koineising in the speech of students at the University of Hong Kong. *Anthropological Linguistics* 21:113–23.

Gibbons, J. (1983) Attitudes towards languages and code-mixing in Hong Kong. *Journal of Multilingual and Multicultural Development* 4: 129–48.

Giddens, A. (1979) *Central Problems in Social Theory*. Berkeley, CA: University of California Press.

Giddens, A. (1984) *The Constitution of Society*. Cambridge: Cambridge University Press.

Giddens, A. (1989) *Sociology*. Cambridge: Polity.

Giesbers, H. (1989) *Code-switching tussen dialect en standaardtaal*. Amsterdam: P. Meertens-instituut.

Gilbert, G.G. (1969) The linguistic geography of the colonial and immigrant languages in the United States. Paper presented to the Linguistic Society of America, December.

Giles, H. and Johnson, P. (1981) The role of language in ethnic group relations. In J. Turner and H Giles (eds), *Intergroup Behaviour*. Oxford: Blackwell, pp. 199–243.

Giles, H. and Powesland, P. (1975) *Speech Style and Social Evaluation*. New York: Academic Press.

Gilroy, P. (1987) *There Ain't No Black in the Union Jack*. London: Hutchinson.

Gingràs, R. (1974) Problems in the description of Spanish–English intra-sentential code-switching. In G.A. Bills (ed.), *Southwest Areal Linguistics*. San Diego: Institute for Cultural Pluralism.

Givón, T. (1979) *On Understanding Grammar*. New York: Academic Press.

Givón, T. (1985) Function, structure and language acquisition. In D.I. Slobin (ed.), *The Cross-linguistic Study of Language Acquisition*. Hillsdale, NJ: Erlbaum, pp. 1005–27.

Glaser, W.R. (1992) Picture naming. *Cognition* 42: 61–105.

Glucksberg, S. (1984) The functional equivalence of common and multiple codes. *Journal of Verbal Learning and Verbal Behavior* 23: 100–4.

Goebl, H., Nelde, P., Stary, Z. and Wolck, W. (eds) (1996) *Contact Linguistics: An international handbook of contemporary research*. Berlin: Walter de Gruyter.

Goffe, A. (1985) Black and brown in Brum. *Guardian*, 19 September.

Goffman, E. (1959) *The Presentation of Self in Everyday Life*. New York: Doubleday.

Goffman, E. (1967) *Interaction Ritual*. Harmondsworth: Penguin.

Goffman, E. (1971) *Relations in Public*. London: Allen Lane.

Goffman, E. (1974) *Frame Analysis*. Harmondsworth: Penguin.

Goffman, E. (1979) Footing. *Semiotica* 25:1–29.

Goffman, E. (1981) *Forms of Talk*. Oxford: Blackwell.

Goffman, E. (1983) The interaction order. *American Sociological Review* 48: 1–17.

Goke-Pariola, A. (1983) Code-mixing among Yoruba–English bilinguals. *Anthropological Linguistics* 25: 39–46.

Goldman-Eisler, F. (1958) Speech production and the predictability of words in context. *Quarterly Journal of Experimental Psychology* 10: 96–106.

Gollan, T., Forster, K.I. and Frost, R. (1996) Cross-language priming with different scripts:

masked priming with cognates and noncognates in Hebrew–English bilinguals. Unpublished manuscript, University of Arizona.

Gollan, T.H., Forster, K.I. and Frost, R. (1997) Translation priming with different scripts: masked priming with cognates and noncognates in Hebrew–English bilinguals. *Journal of Experimental Psychology: Learning, memory, and cognition* 23: 1122–39.

Goodglass, H. (1978) Acquisition and dissolution of language. In A. Caramazza and E. Zurif (eds), *Language Acquisition and Language Breakdown*. Baltimore: Johns Hopkins Press, pp. 101–8.

Goodluck, H. (1987) *Language Acquisition and Linguistic Theory*. In P. Fletcher and M. Garman (eds), *Language acquisition*. 2nd edn. Cambridge: Cambridge University Press.

Goodwin, M. and Goodwin, C. (1987) Children's arguing. In S. Philips, S. Steele and C. Tanz (eds), *Language, Gender and Sex in Comparative Perspective*. Cambridge: Cambridge University Press, pp. 200–48.

Goodz, N.S. (1986) Parental language in bilingual families: a model and some data. Paper presented at the Third Congress of the World Association of Infant Psychiatry and Allied Disciplines, Stockholm, Sweden.

Goodz, N.S. (1989) Parental language mixing in bilingual families. *Journal of Infant Mental Health* 10: 25–44.

Goral, M., Levy, S. and Obler, L.K. (2002) Neurolinguistic aspects of bilingualism. *International Journal of Bilingualism* 6: 411–40.

Gordon, H.W. (1980) Cerebral organization in bilinguals. Vol. 1. Lateralization. *Brain and Language* 9: 255–68.

Gordon, H.W. and Weide, R. (1983) La contribution de certaines fonctions cognitives au traitement du langage, à son acquisition et à l'apprentissage d'une langue seconde. *Langages* 73: 45–56.

Grainger, J. (1993) Visual word recognition in bilinguals. In R. Schreuder and B. Weltens (eds), *The Bilingual Lexicon*. Amsterdam: John Benjamins, pp. 11–25.

Grainger, J. and Beauvillain, C. (1987) Language blocking and lexical access in bilinguals. *The Quarterly Journal of Experimental Psychology* 39A: 295–319.

Grainger, J. and Dijkstra, T. (1992) On the representation and use of language information in bilinguals. In R. Harris (ed.), *Cognitive Processing in Bilingualism*. New York: North-Holland, pp. 207–20.

Grammont, M. (1902) Observation sur le langage des enfants. *Mélanges Meillet*. Paris.

Granda, G. de (1968) *Transculturación e Interferencia Lingüistica en el Puerto Rico Contemporáneo (1898–1968)*. Bogotá: Instituto Caro y Cuervo.

Green, D.W. (1986) Control, activation, and resource: a framework and a model for the control of speech in bilinguals. *Brain and Language* 27: 210–23.

Green, D.W. (1998a) Mental control of the bilingual lexico-semantic system. *Bilingualism: Language and cognition* 1: 67–81.

Green, D.W. (1998b) Schemas, tags and inhibition: reply to commentators. *Bilingualism: Language and cognition* 1: 100–4.

Green, D.W. (2003) The neural basis of the lexicon and the grammar in L2 acquisition: the convergence hypothesis. In R. van Hout, A. Hulk, F. Kuiken and R. Towell (eds), *The Interface between Syntax and the Lexicon in Second Language Acquisition*. Amsterdam: John Benjamins, pp. 197–218.

Green, D.W. (2005) The neurocognition of recovery patterns in bilingual aphasics. In J.F. Kroll and A.M.B. de Groot (eds), *Handbook of Bilingualism: Psycholinguistic approaches*. Oxford: Oxford University Press, pp. 516–30.

Greenberg, J.H. (1954) A quantitative approach to the morphological typology of language. In

R. Spencer (ed.), *Method and Perspective in Anthropology*. University of Minnesota Press, pp. 192–220.

Greenfield, L. (1968) Spanish and English usage self-ratings in various situational contexts. In J.A. Fishman, R.L. Cooper and R. Ma (eds), *Bilingualism in the Barrio*. New York: Yeshiva University. Reissued by Indiana University Press, 1971.

Greyerz, O. von (1933) Vom Wert und Wesen unserer Mundart. *Sprache, Dichtung, Heimat*, Berne, pp. 226–47.

Grice, H.P. (1975) Logic and conversation. In P. Cole and J. Morgan (eds), *Syntax and Semantics: Speech Acts*. New York: Academic Press, pp. 41–58.

Griffiths, P. (1986) Early vocabulary. In P. Fletcher and M. Garman (eds), *Language Acquisition*. 2nd edn. Cambridge: Cambridge University Press.

Grosjean, F. (1980) Spoken word recognition processes and the gating paradigm. *Perception and Psychophysics* 28: 267–83.

Grosjean, F. (1982) *Life with Two Languages: An introduction to bilingualism*. Cambridge, MA: Harvard University Press.

Grosjean, F. (1985) The bilingual as a competent but specific speaker–hearer. *Journal of Multilingual and Multicultural Development* 6: 467–77.

Grosjean, F. (1985a) The recognition of words after their acoustic offset: evidence and implications. *Perception and Psychophysics* 38: 299–310.

Grosjean, F. (1988) Exploring the recognition of guest words in bilingual speech. *Language and Cognitive Processes* 3: 233–74.

Grosjean, F. (1989) Neurolinguists, beware! The bilingual is not two monolinguals in one person. *Brain and Language* 36: 3–15.

Grosjean, F. (1994) Individual bilingualism. *The Encyclopedia of Language and Linguistics*. Oxford: Pergamon, pp. 1656–60.

Grosjean, F. (1997) Processing mixed language: issues, findings, and models. In A.M. de Groot and J.F. Kroll (eds), *Tutorials in Bilingualism*. Mahwah, NJ: Lawrence Erlbaum, pp. 225–54.

Grosjean, F. (1997a) The bilingual individual. *Interpreting: International journal of research and practice in interpreting* 2: 163–91.

Grosjean, F. (1998) Studying bilinguals: methodological and conceptual issues. *Bilingualism: Language and cognition* 1: 131–49.

Grosjean, F. (1998a) Transfer and language mode. Commentary of Natascha Müller: transfer in bilingual first language acquisition. *Bilingualism: Language and cognition* 1: 175–6.

Grosjean, F. (2001) The bilingual's language modes. In J. Nicol (ed.), *One Mind, Two Languages: Bilingual language processing*. Oxford: Blackwell, pp. 1–22.

Grosjean, F. and Gee, J. (1987) Prosodic structure and spoken word recognition. *Cognition* 25: 135–55.

Grosjean, F. and Miller, J. (1994) Going in and out of languages: an example of bilingual flexibility. *Psychological Science* 5: 201–6.

Grosjean, F. and Soares, C. (1986) Processing mixed language: some preliminary findings. In J. Vaid (ed.), *Language Processing in Bilinguals: Psycholinguistic and neuropsychological perspectives*. Hillsdale, NJ: Lawrence Erlbaum Associates, pp. 145–79.

Gross, F. (1951) Language and value changes among the Arapho. *International Journal of American Linguistics* 17: 10–17.

Gumperz, J.J. (1961) Speech variation and the study of Indian civilization. *American Anthropologist* 63: 976–88.

Gumperz, J.J. (1962) Types of linguistic communities. *Anthropological Linguistics* 4(1): 28–40.

Gumperz, J.J. (1964) Linguistic and social interaction in two communities. *American Anthropologist* 66, 6 Part II: 137–54.

Gumperz, J.J. (1964a) Hindi–Punjabi code-switching in Delhi. In M. Halle (ed.), *Proceedings of the International Congress of Linguists*. The Hague: Mouton.

Gumperz, J.J. (1966) On the ethnology of linguistic change. In W. Bright (ed.), *Sociolinguistics*. The Hague: Mouton, pp. 27–38.

Gumperz, J.J. (1971) *Language in Social Groups: Essays by J.J. Gumperz*, selected by A.S. Dil. Stanford, CA: Stanford University Press.

Gumperz, J.J. (1971a) Bilingualism, bidialectalism and classroom interaction. In *Language in Social Groups*. Stanford, CA: Stanford University Press.

Gumperz, J.J. (1976) The sociolinguistic significance of conversational code-switching. *University of California Working Papers* 46. Berkeley: University of California.

Gumperz, J.J. (1978) Dialect and conversational inference in urban communication. *Language in Society* 7: 393–409. (Revised as Ethnic style as political rhetoric, in J.J. Gumperz, *Discourse Strategies*. New York: Cambridge University Press, pp. 187–203.)

Gumperz, J.J. (1982) *Discourse Strategies*. Cambridge: Cambridge University Press.

Gumperz, J.J. (1992a) Contextualization and understanding. In A. Duranti and C. Goodwin (eds), *Rethinking Context*. New York: Cambridge University Press, pp. 229–52.

Gumperz, J.J. (1992b) Further notes on contextualization. In J.C.P. Auer and A. Di Luzio, *Contextualising language*. Amsterdam: Benjamins.

Gumperz, J.J. (ed.) (1982a) *Language and Social Identity*. Cambridge: Cambridge University Press.

Gumperz, J.J. and Cook-Gumperz, J. (1982) Introduction: Language and the communication of social identity. In J.J. Gumperz (ed.), *Language and Social Identity*. Cambridge: Cambridge University Press, pp. 1–21.

Gumperz, J.J. and Hernández-Chávez, E., *et al.* (1970) Cognitive aspects of bilingual communication. In E. Hernández-Chávez *et al.* (eds), *El Lenguaje de los Chicanos*. Arlington Center for Applied Linguistics.

Gumperz, J.J. and Naim, C.M. (1960) Formal and informal standards in the Hindu regional language area. *International Journal of American Linguistics* 26, Part 3: 92–118.

Gumperz, J.J., Jupp, T. and Roberts, C. (1979) *Crosstalk: A Study of Cross-Cultural Communication*. Southall, Middlesex: National Centre for Industrial Language Training.

Gurd, J.M., Bessel, N.J., Bladon, R.A.W. and Bamford, J.M. (1988) *Neuropsychologia* 26: 237–51.

Haegeman, L. (1991) *Introduction to Government and Binding Theory*. Oxford: Blackwell.

Hakuta, K. (1986) *Mirror of Language: The debate on bilingualism*. New York: Basic Books.

Hall, R.A., Jr. (1953) *Haitian Creole*. Menasha: WIS.

Hall, S. (1988) New ethnicities. ICA Documents 7: 27–31.

Halliday, M.A.K. (1964) The users and uses of language. In M.A.K. Halliday, A. McIntosh and P. Strevens, *The Linguistic Sciences and Language Teaching*. London: Longmans-Green, pp. 75–110.

Halmari, H. (1997) *Government and Code-Switching: Explaining American Finnish*. Amsterdam: John Benjamins.

Halstead, M. (1988) *Education, Justice and Cultural Diversity: An examination of the Honeyford affair*. Lewes: Falmer Press.

Hamers, J. and Blanc, M. (1989, 2nd edn 2000) *Bilinguality and Bilingualism*. Cambridge: Cambridge University Press. (Original French edition *Bilingualité et bilinguisme*, 1983; Bruxelles: Liege.)

Hamers, J. and Lambert, W. (1977) Visual field and cerebral hemisphere preferences in bilinguals. In S. Segalowitz and F. Gruber (eds), *Language Development and Neurological Theory*, New York: Academic Press.

Hancin-Bhatt, B. and Govindjee, A. (1999) A computational model of feature competition in L2 tranfer. In P. Broeder and J.M.J. Murre (eds), *Language and Thought in Development: Cross-linguistic studies*. Tübingen: Gunter Narr, pp. 145–61.

Hancin-Bhatt, B. and Nagy, W. (1994) Lexical transfer and second language morphological development. *Applied Psycholinguistics* 15: 289–310.

Handelman, D. (1977) Play and ritual: complementary frames of meta-communication. In A. Chapman and H. Foot (eds), *It's a Funny Thing, Humour*. Oxford: Pergamon, pp. 185–92.

Handschin, K. (1994) L'influence de la langue de base dans la perception des alternances codiques: le cas de la consonne initiale du mot [Base language influence in the perception of code-switches: the case of a word's initial consonant]. *Travaux neuchâtelois de linguistique (TRANEL)* 21: 51–60.

Hannan, S. (1986) Using transfers: a conversation analytic approach to the study of transfers in Italian/English bilingual conversation. Unpublished MA thesis, University of York.

Hansegard, N. E. (1975) Tvasprakighet eller halvsprakighet? *Invandrare och Minoriteter* 3: 7–13.

Harding, E. and Riley, P. (1986) *The Bilingual Family*. Cambridge: Cambridge University Press.

Harding-Esch, E. and Riley, P. (2003) *The Bilingual Family: A handbook for parents*, 2nd edn. Cambridge: Cambridge University Press.

Hardyck, C. (1980) Hemispheric differences and language ability. Paper presented at Conference on Neurolinguistics of Bilingualism: Individual Differences, Albuquerque, NM, August.

Harman, L.D. (1988) *The Modern Stranger: On language and membership*. Berlin: Mouton de Gruyter.

Harris, R. and Rampton, B. (2002) Creole metaphors in cultural analysis: on the limits and possibilities of (socio-)linguistics. *Critique of Anthropology* 22 (1): 31–51.

Harris, R. and Rampton, B. (eds) (2003) *The Language, Ethnicity and Race Reader*, London: Routledge.

Harris, R.J. (ed.) (1992) *Cognitive Processing in Bilinguals*. Amsterdam: North-Holland.

Hartnett, D. (1975) The relation of cognitive style and hemisphere preference to deductive and inductive second language learning. Unpublished MA thesis, University of California, Los Angeles, CA.

Hasselmo, N. (1961) American Swedish. Unpublished PhD dissertation, Harvard University.

Hasselmo, N. (1970) Code-switching and modes of speaking. In G. Gilbert (ed.), *Texas Studies in Bilingualism*. Berlin: Walter de Gruyter and Co.

Hasselmo, N. (1972) Code-switching as ordered selection. In E. Finchow *et al.* (eds), *Studies for Einar Haugen*. The Hague: Mouton.

Hasselmo, N. (1974) *Amerikasvenska*. Lund: Esselte.

Hatch, E. (1978) *Second Language Acquisition: A book of readings*. Rowley MA: Newbury House.

Hatzidakis, G.N. (1905) *Die Sprachfrage in Griechenland*. Chatzedaka, Athens.

Haugen, E. (1950) Analysis of linguistic borrowing. *Language* 26: 210–31.

Haugen, E. (1953) *The Norwegian Language in America*. Philadelphia, PA: Pennsylvania University Press. Reissued by Indiana University Press in Bloomington, 1969.

Haugen, E. (1956) *Bilingualism in the Americas: A bibliography and research guide* (= Publication Number 26 of the American Dialect Society). Montgomery, AL: University of Alabama Press.

Haugen, E. (1973) Bilingualism, language contact and immigrant languages in the United States. *Current Trends in Linguistics* 10: 505–92.

Haugen, E. (1977) Norm and deviation in bilingual communities. In P. Hornby (ed.), *Bilingualism: Psychological, social and educational implications*. New York: Academic Press.

Heath, S.B. and McLaughlin, M. (1993) *Identity and Inner City Youth: Beyond Ethnicity and Gender*. New York: Teachers College Press.

Heath, S.B. (1983) *Ways with Words*. Cambridge: Cambridge University Press.

Heidelberger Forschungsprojekt 'Pidgin-Deutsch' (1977) The acquisition of German syntax by foreign migrant workers. In D. Sankoff (ed.), *Linguistic Variation: Models and methods*. New York: Academic Press.

Heller, M. (1982) Language strategies and ethnic conflict in the workplace. Manuscript, Ontario Institute for Studies in Education.

Heller, M. (1982a) Negotiations of language choice in Montreal. In J.J. Gumperz (ed.), *Language and Social Identity*. Cambridge: Cambridge University Press, pp. 108–18.

Heller, M. (1988a) Strategic ambiguity: codeswitching in the management of conflict. In M Heller (ed.), *Codeswitching: Anthropological and sociolinguistic perspectives*. Berlin: Mouton de Gruyter, pp. 77–98.

Heller, M. (1989a) Aspects sociolinguistiques de la francisation d'une enterprise privée. *Sociologie et Sociétés* 21 (2): 115–28.

Heller, M. (1989b) Communicative resources and local configurations: an exploration of language contact processes. *Multilingua* 8 (4): 357–96.

Heller, M. (1990) The politics of codeswitching: processes and consequences of ethnic mobilisation. Paper presented at the third workshop of the European Science Foundation Network on Codeswitching and Language Contact, Brussels.

Heller, M. (1992) The politics of codeswitching and language choice. *Journal of Multilingual and Multicultural Development* 13 (1, 2): 123–42.

Heller, M. (1994) *Crosswords: Language, education and ethnicity in French Ontario*. Berlin: Mouton de Gruyter.

Heller, M. (1995) Code-switching and the politics of language. In L. Milroy and P. Muysken (eds), *One Speaker Two Languages*. Cambridge: Cambridge University Press, pp. 158–74.

Heller, M. (1999) *Linguistic Minorities and Modernity: A sociolinguistic ethnography* (with the collaboration of M. Campbell, P. Dailey and D. Patrick). Harlow: Longman.

Heller, M. (ed.) (1988) *Codeswitching: Anthropological and sociolinguistic perspectives*. Berlin: Mouton de Gruyter.

Heller, M. and Lévy, L. (1992a) Mixed marriages: life on the linguistic frontier. *Multilingua* 11 (1): 11–43.

Heller, M. and Lévy, L. (1992b) La femme franco-ontarienne en situation de marriage mixte: féminité et ethnicité. *Recherches Féministes* 5 (1): 59–82.

Herdan, G. (1960) *Type–Token Mathematics: A textbook of mathematical linguistics*. The Hague: Mouton de Gruyter.

Hermans, D., Bongaerts, T., de Bot, K. and Schreuder, R. (1998) Producing words in a foreign language: Can speakers prevent interference from their first language? *Bilingualism: Language and cognition* 1: 213–29.

Hewitt, R. (1986) *White Talk Black Talk*. Cambridge: Cambridge University Press.

Hewitt, R. (1989) Creole in the classroom: political grammars and educational vocabularies. In R. Grillo (ed.), *Social Anthropology and the Politics of Language*. London: Routledge, pp. 126–44.

Hewitt, R. (1989a) A sociolinguistic view of urban adolescent relations. Paper presented to conference on 'Everyday life, cultural production and race', Institute of Cultural Sociology, University of Copenhagen, 27–28 April.

Hieke, A. (1986) Absorption and fluency in native and non-native casual English speech. In A. James and J. Leather (eds), *Sound Patterns in Second Language Acquisition*. Dordrecht: Foris.

Hill, J. ([1995] 2003) Junk Spanish, covert racism, and the (leaky) boundary between public and private spheres. *Pragmatics* 5 (2): 197–212. Reprinted in R. Harris and B. Rampton (eds) (2003) *The Language, Ethnicity and Race Reader*. London: Routledge, pp. 188–210.

Hill, J. (1999) Language, race, and white public space. *American Anthropologist* 100 (3): 680–89.

Hill, J. and Coombs, D. (1982) The vernacular remodelling of national and international languages. *Applied Linguistics* 3: 224–34.

Hill, J.H. and Hill, K.C. (1986) *Speaking Mexicano: Dynamics of syncretic language in Central Mexico.* Tucson, AZ: University of Arizona Press.

Hillis, A.E. and Caramazza, A. (1991) Category-specific naming and comprehension impairment: a double dissociation. *Brain* 114: 2081–94.

Hinskens, F. (1988) Enkele gedachten over de notie 'structurele afstand'. *Mededelingen NCDN* 20: 89–100.

Hoffmann, C. (1985) Language acquisition in two trilingual children. *Journal of Multilingual and Multicultural Development* 6: 479–95.

Hoffmann, C. (1991) *An Introduction to Bilingualism*. Harlow: Longman.

Højrup, T. (1983) The concept of life-mode: a form-specifying mode of analysis applied to contemporary western Europe. *Ethnologia Scandinavica*: 1–50.

Hoosain, R. and Shiu, L.-P. (1989) Cerebral lateralization of Chinese–English bilingual functions. *Neuropsychologia* 27: 705–12.

Hornberger, N. and Putz, M. (eds) (2006) *Language Loyalty, Language Planning and Language Revitalization: Recent writings and reflections from Joshua Fishman.* Clevedon: Multilingual Matters.

Hoshino, N. and Kroll, J.F. (2005) Cognate effects in picture naming: Does cross-language activation survive a change of script? Paper presented at the 5th International Symposium on Bilingualism, Barcelona, Spain.

Hudson, A.J. (1968) Perseveration. *Brain* 91: 571–82.

Hudson, R.A. (1980, 2nd edn 1996) *Sociolinguistics*. Cambridge: Cambridge University Press.

Hudson, R.A. (1992) Diglossia: A bibliographic review. *Language in Society* 21: 611–74.

Hyltenstam, K. (1991) Language mixing in Alzeimer's dementia. *Papers for the Workshop on Constraints, Conditions and Models*. Strasbourg: European Science Foundation, pp. 221–58.

Hymes, D. (1962) The ethnography of speaking. In T. Gladwin and W.C. Sturtevand (eds), *Anthropology and Human Behavior*. Washington, DC: Anthropology Society of Washington, pp. 13–53.

Hymes, D. (1964) Introduction: towards ethnographies of communication. *American Anthropologist* 66, 6 Part II: 1–34.

Hymes, D. (1972) On communicative competence. In J. Pride and J. Holmes, *Sociolinguistics*. Harmondsworth: Penguin, pp. 269–93.

Hymes, D. (1972a) Models of the interaction of language and social life. In J.J. Gumperz and D. Hymes (eds), *Directions in Sociolinguistics*. New York: Holt, Rinehart and Winston, pp. 35–71.

Hymes, D. (1972b) *Towards Communicative Competence*. Philadelphia, PA: University of Pennsylvania Press.

Hymes, D. (1974) *Foundations in Sociolinguistics*. Philadelphia, PA: University of Pennsylvania Press.

Hynd, G., Teeter, A. and Stewart, J. (1980) Acculturation and lateralization of speech in the bilingual native American. *International Journal of Neuroscience* 11: 1–7.

Ianco-Worrall, A.D. (1972) Bilingualism and cognitive development. *Child Development* 43: 1390–400.

Ibrahim, Awad El Karim (2003) 'Whassup, homeboy?': Joining the African diaspora: Black

English as a symbolic site of identification and language learning. In S. Makoni, G. Smitherman, A. Ball and A. Spears (eds), *Black Linguistics*. London: Routledge, pp. 169–85.

Imedadze, N. (1978) On the psychological nature of child speech formation under conditions of exposure to two languages. In E. Hatch (ed.), *Second Language Acquisition: A book of readings*. Rowley MA: Newbury House.

Indefrey, P. and Levelt, P. (2000) The neural correlates of language production. In M.S. Gazzaniga (ed.), *The New Cognitive Neurosciences*. Cambridge, MA: MIT Press, pp. 845–65.

Iverson, J.M., Capirci, O. and Caselli, M.C. (1994) From communication to language in two modalities. *Cognitive Development* 9: 23–43.

Jackendoff, R. (1975) Morphological and semantic regularities in the lexicon. *Language* 51: 639–71.

Jackendoff, R. (1983) *Semantics and Cognition*. Cambridge, MA: MIT Press.

Jackson, G., Swainson, R., Cunnington, R. and Jackson, S. (2001) ERP correlates of executive control during repeated language switching. *Bilingualism: Language and cognition* 4: 169–78.

Jaeggli, O. (1982) *Topics in Romance Syntax*. Dordrecht: Foris.

Jake, J.L., Lüdi, G. and Myers-Scotton, C. (1995) Predicting variation in interlanguage. Paper presented at annual meeting, American Association of Applied Linguistics, March.

Jake, J.L., Myers-Scotton, C. and Gross, S. (2002) Making a minimalist approach to code-switching work: adding the Matrix Language. *Bilingualism: Language and cognition* 5: 69–91.

Jake, J.L. (1994) Intrasentential code switching and pronouns: on the categorial status of functional elements. *Linguistics* 32: 271–98.

Jake, J.L. and Myers-Scotton, C. (1994) Embedded language islands in intrasentential code-switching: variation and compromise at two linguistic levels. Poster presented at annual meeting, NWAV (New Ways of Analyzing Variation), October.

Jakobson, R. (1960) Closing statement: linguistics and poetics. In T.A. Sebeok (ed.), *Style in Language*. New York: Technology Press of MIT and Wiley, pp. 350–77.

Jared, D. and Kroll, J.F. (2001). Do bilinguals activate phonological representations in one or both of their languages when naming words? *Journal of Memory and Language* 44: 2–31.

Jefferson, G. (ed.) (1989) *Harvey Sacks Lectures, 1964–65*. Dordrecht: Kluwer Academic.

Jekat, S. (1985) Die Entwicklung des Wortschatzes bei bilingualen Kindern (Frz.-Dt) in den ersten vier Lebensjahren. Master's Thesis, University of Hamburg, Department of Romance Languages.

Jiang, N. (1999) Testing processing explanations for the asymmetry in masked cross-language priming. *Bilingualism: Language and cognition* 2: 59–75.

Jin, Y.-S. (1990) Effects of concreteness on cross-language priming in lexical decisions. *Perceptual and Motor Skills* 70: 1139–54.

Joanette, Y., Goulet, P. and Hannequin, D. (1990) *Right Hemisphere and Verbal Communication*. New York: Springer Verlag.

Joanette, Y., Lecours, A. R., Lepage, Y. and Lamoureux, M. (1983) Language in right-handers with right-hemisphere lesions: a preliminary study including anatomical, genetic, and social factors. *Brain and Language* 20: 216–49.

Johnson, J.S. and Newport, E.L. (1989) Critical period effects in second language learning: the influence of maturational state on the acquisition of English as a second language. *Cognitive Psychology* 21: 60–99.

Johnson, R., Cole, E., Blowers, J.K., Foiles, S.V., Nikaido, A.M., Patrick, J.W. and Woliver, R.E. (1979) Hemispheric efficiency in middle and later adulthood. *Cortex* 15: 109–19.

Johnstone, B. (1999) Uses of Southern-sounding speech by contemporary Texas women. *Journal of Sociolinguistics* 3 (4): 505–22.

Joly, A. (1973) Sur le système de la personne. *Revue des Langues Romanes* 80: 3–56.

Jones, F.E. and Lambert, W.E. (1959) Attitudes toward immigrants in a Canadian community. *Public Opinion Quarterly* 23: 538–46.

Jones, I. (1960) *Bilingualism: A bibliography with special reference to Wales*. Aberystwyth: University College.

Joos, M. (1962) The five clocks. *International Journal of American Linguistics* 28, 2 Part V.

Jordan, B. and Fuller, N. (1975) On the non-fatal nature of trouble: sense-making and trouble-managing in *lingua franca* talk. *Semiotica* 13: 11–31.

Joshi, A.K. (1985) Processing of sentences with intrasentential code-switching, In D.R. Dowty, L. Karttunen and A.M. Zwicky (eds), *Natural Language Parsing*. Cambridge: Cambridge University Press, pp. 190–205.

Journal of the American Oriental Society (1955) vol. 75, pp. 124ff.

Jusczyk, P. (1981) Infant speech perception: a critical appraisal. In P.D. Eimas and J.L. Miller (eds), *Perspectives on the Study of Speech*. Hillsdale, NJ: Erlbaum.

Jusczyk, P. (1982) Auditory versus phonetic coding of speech signals during infancy. In J. Mehler, E. Walker and M. Garrett (eds), *Perspectives on Mental Representation*. Hillsdale, NJ: Erlbaum.

Kachru, B. (1978) Toward structuring code-mixing: an Indian perspective. *International Journal of the Sociology of Language* 16: 27–46.

Kadar-Hoffmann, G. (1983) Trlingualer Spracherwerb: Der gleichzeitige Erwerb des Deutschen, Französischen und Ungarischen. Dissertation, Kiel University.

Kahane, H., Kahane, R. and Ward, R.L. (1945) *Spoken Greek*. Washington.

Kamwangamalu, N. (1989) Theory and method of code-mixing: a cross-linguistic study. Unpublished doctoral dissertation, University of Illinois at Urbana.

Kaplan, R.B. and Baldauf, R.B. Jr. (1997) *Language Planning: From practice to theory*. Clevedon: Multilingual matters.

Karanth, P. and Rangamani, G.N. (1988) Crossed aphasia in multilinguals. *Brain and Language* 34: 169–80.

Kay-Raining Bird, E., Cleave, P.L., Trudeau, N., Thordardottir, E., Sutton, A. and Thorpe, A. (2005) The language abilities of bilingual children with Down syndrome. *American Journal of Speech-language Pathology* 14: 187–99.

Keatley, C. and De Gelder, B. (1992) The bilingual primed lexical decision task: cross-language priming disappears with speeded responses. *European Journal of Cognitive Psychology* 4: 273–92.

Keatly, C., Spinks, J. and de Gelder, B. (1989) Cross-language facilitation on the primed lexical decision task: Chinese–English and Dutch–French. Paper presented at Psychonomie-congres Noordwijkerhout, December.

Keatley, C., Spinks, J. and De Gelder, B. (1992) Asymmetrical semantic facilitation between languages: evidence for separate representational systems in bilingual memory. Unpublished manuscript, University of Tilburg.

Keatley, C., Spinks, J. and De Gelder, B. (1994) Asymmetrical semantic facilitation between languages. *Memory and Cognition* 22: 70–84.

Keijsper, C. (1984) Vorm en betekenis in Nederlandse toonhoogte contouren. *Forum der Letteren* 25(1, 2).

Kellerman, E. and Sharwood Smith, M. (eds) (1986) *Cross-linguistic Influence in Second Language Learning*. Oxford: Pergamon Press.

Kempen, G. and Hoenkamp, G. (1987) An incremental procedural grammar for sentence formulation. *Cognitive Science* 11: 201–58.

Kempen, G. and Huijbers, P. (1983) The lexicalisation process in sentence production and naming: indirect election of words. *Cognition* 14: 185–209.

Kerkman, H. (1984) Woordherkenning in twee talen. In A. Thomassen, L. Noordman and P. Eling (eds), *Het Leesproces*. Lisse: Swets and Zeitlinger.

Kerkman, H. and de Bot, K. (1989) De organisatie van het tweetalige lexicon. *Toegepaste Taalwetenschap in Artikelen* 34: 115–21.

Kershner, J. and Jeng, A. (1972) Dual functional hemispheric asymmetry in visual perception: effects of ocular dominance and post-exposural processes. *Neuropsychologia* 10: 437–45.

Kielhöfer, B. (1987) Le 'bon' changement de langue et le 'mauvais' mélange de langues. In G. Lüdi (ed.), *Devenir bilingue – parler bilingue*. Tübingen: Niemeyer, pp. 135–55.

Kielhöfer, B. and Jonekeit, S. (1983) *Zweisprachige Kindererziehung*. Tübingen: Stauffenberg Verlag.

Kim, K.H.S., Relkin, N.R., Lee, K.M. and Hirsch, J. (1997) Distinct cortical areas associated with native and second languages. *Nature* 388: 171–4.

Kineene, M. wa (1983) Vioja afisini. *Mwanko*. Nairobi: Swahili club of the University of Nairobi.

Kinsborne, M. (1972) Eye and head turning indicates cerebral lateralization. *Science* 176: 539–41.

Kinsbourne, M. and Hiscock, M. (1977) Does verbal dominance develop? In S.J. Segalowitz and F.A. Gruber (eds), *Language Development and Neurological Theory*. New York: Academic Press, pp. 171–91.

Kirsner, K., Smith, M.C., Lockhart, R.S., King, M.L. and Jain, M. (1984) The bilingual lexicon: language-specific units in an integrated network. *Journal of Verbal Learning and Verbal Behavior* 23: 519–39.

Kishna, S. (1979) Lexicale interferentie in het Sarnami. Unpublished MA thesis in Linguistics, University of Amsterdam.

Klatt, D. (1979) Speech perception: a model of acoustic-phonetic analysis and lexical access. *Journal of Phonetics* 7: 279–312.

Klavans, J.L. (1983) The syntax of code-switching. Spanish and English. In *Proceedings of the Linguistic Symposium on Romance Languages*, Vol. 18. Amsterdam: Benjamins.

Klavans, J.L. (1983a) The syntax of code-switching: Spanish and English. In L.D. King and C.A. Maley (eds), *Selected Papers from the 13th Linguistic Symposium on Romance Languages*. Chapel Hill, NC, pp. 213–31. (Also published in 1985. Amsterdam: Benjamins, pp. 213–231.)

Klein, D., Milner, B., Zatorre, R.J., Meyer, E. and Evans, A.C. (1995) The neural substrates underlying word generation: a bilingual functional-imaging study. *Proceedings of the National Academy of Sciences* (USA) 92: 2899–903.

Klein, D., Zatorre, R., Milner, B., Meyer, E. and Evans, A. (1994) Left putaminal activation when speaking a second language: evidence from PET. *NeuroReport* 5: 2295–7.

Kloss, H. (1929) Sprachtabellen als Grendlage für Sprachstatistik, Sprachenkarten und für eine allgemeine Sociologie der Sprachgemeinschaften. *Vierteljahrschrift für Politik und Geschichte* 1(7): 103–17.

Kloss, H. (1952) *Die Entwicklung neuer germanischer Kultursprachen von 1800 bis 1950*. Munich: Pohl.

Kloss, H. (1966) Types of multilingual communities, a discussion of ten variables. *Sociological Inquiry* 36.

Kolers, P. (1963) Interlingual word associations. *Journal of Verbal Learning and Verbal Behavior* 2: 291–300.

Kolers, P. (1966) Reading and talking bilingually. *American Journal Psychology* 3: 357–76.

Koopman, H. (1984) *The Syntax of Verbs*. Dordrecht: Foris.

Köppe, R. (1996) Language differentiation in bilingual children. *Linguistics* 34: 927–54.

Köppe, R. (2006) Is codeswitching acquired? In J. MacSwan (ed.), *Grammatical Theory and Bilingual Codeswitching*. Cambridge, MA: MIT Press.

Koster, J. (1978) *Locality Principles in Syntax*. Dordrecht: Foris.

Kotik, B. (1975) Lateralization in multilinguals. Thesis. Moscow State University, USSR.

Krashen, S., Seliger, H. and Hartnett, D. (1974) Two studies in adult second language learning. *Kritikton Litterarum* 3: 220–8.

Krashen, S. (1973) Lateralization, language learning and the critical period: some new evidence. *Language Learning* 23: 63–74.

Krashen, S. (1981) *Second Language Acquisition and Second Language Learning*. Oxford: Pergamon Press.

Krashen, S. and Galloway, L. (1978) The neurological correlates of language acquisition: current research: *SPEAQ Journal* 2: 21–35.

Kroll, J.F. (1993) Accessing conceptual representation for words in a second language. In R. Schreuder and B. Weltens (eds), *The Bilingual Lexicon*. Amsterdam: John Benjamins, pp. 53–81.

Kroll, J.F. and Borning, L. (1987) Shifting language representations in novice bilinguals: evidence from sentence priming. Paper presented at the 27th Annual Meeting of the Psychonomic Society, Seattle, WA, November.

Kroll, J.F. and Curley, J. (1988) Lexical memory in novice bilinguals: the role of concepts in retrieving second language words. In M. Gruneberg, P. Morris and R. Sykes (eds), *Practical Aspects of Memory*, vol. 2. London: Wiley, pp. 389–95.

Kroll, J.F. and de Groot, A.M.B. (eds) (2005) *Handbook of Bilingualism: Psycholinguistic approaches*. Oxford: Oxford University Press.

Kroll, J.F. and de Groot, A. (1997) Lexical and conceptual memory in the bilingual. In A. de Groot and J. Kroll (eds), *Tutorials in Bilingualism: Psycholinguistic perspectives*. Mahwah, NJ: Lawrence Erlbaum, pp. 169–200.

Kroll, J.F. and Sankaranarayanan, A. (1996) Novel cues in learning second language vocabulary. Manuscript in preparation, Pennsylvania State University.

Kroll, J.F. and Sholl, A. (1992) Lexical and conceptual memory in fluent and nonfluent bilinguals. In R.J. Harris (ed.), *Cognitive Processing in Bilinguals*. Amsterdam: Elsevier, pp. 191–204.

Kroll, J.F. and Stewart, E. (1990) Concept mediation in bilingual translation. Paper presented at the 31st Annual Meeting of the Psychonomic Society, New Orleans, LA, November.

Kroll, J.F. and Stewart, E. (1994) Category interference in translation and picture naming: evidence for asymmetric connections between bilingual memory representations. *Journal of Memory and Language* 33: 149–74.

Kroll, J.F., Elsinger, C. and Tokowicz, N. (1994) Priming interlanguage connections: evidence for two routes to translation. Paper presented at the 35th Annual Meeting of the Psychonomic Society, St Louis, MO, November.

Kroll, J.F., Michael, E., Tokowicz, N. and Dufour, R. (2002) The development of lexical fluency in a second language. *Second Language Research* 18: 137–71.

Kroll, J.F., Sholl, A., Altarriba, J., Luppino, C., Moynihan, L. and Sanders, C. (1992) Cross-language semantic priming: evidence for independent lexical and conceptual contributions. Paper presented at the 33rd Annual Meeting of the Psychonomic Society, St Louis, MO, November.

Kroll, J.F., Sumutka, B.M., and Schwartz, A.I. (2005) A cognitive view of the bilingual lexicon: reading and speaking words in two languages. *International Journal of Bilingualism* 9: 27–48.

Krumbacher, K. (1902) *Das Problem der modernen griechischen Schriftsprache*. Munich.

Kulick, D. (1992) *Language Shift and Cultural Reproduction: Socialisation, self and syncretism in a Papua New Guinean village*. Cambridge: Cambridge University Press.

Labov, W. (1963) Phonological indices of stratification. Paper presented at the Annual Meeting of the American Anthropology Association, San Francisco.

Labov, W. (1964) Phonological correlates of social stratification. *American Anthropologist* 66, 6 Part II: 164–76.

Labov, W. (1966) *The Social Stratification of English in New York City*. Washington DC: Center for Applied Linguistics.

Labov, W. (1969) The logic of non-standard English. In *Georgetown Monographs on Language and Linguistics 22*. Washington, DC: Georgetown University Press.

Labov, W. (1972) *Sociolinguistic Patterns*. Philadelphia, PA: Pennsylvania University Press.

Labov, W. (1972a) Rules for ritual insults. In *Language in the Inner City*. Oxford: Blackwell.

Labov, W. (1977) *The Unity of Sociolinguistics*. Series B, 22. Linguistic Agency at the University of Trier.

Lado, R. (1961) *Language Testing*. London: Longman.

Lafont, R. (1977) A propos de l'enquête sur la diglossie: l'intercesseur de la norme. *Lengas* 1: 31–9.

LaFontaine H. (1975) Bilingual education for Puerto Ricans: ¿si o no? Paper presented at the National Conference on the Educational Needs of the Puerto Rican in the United States, Cleveland, Ohio.

La Heij, W. (2005) Selection processes in monolingual and bilingual lexical access. In J. Kroll and A. de Groot (eds), *Handbook of Bilingualism*. Oxford: Oxford University Press, pp. 289–307.

La Heij, W., De Bruyn, E., Elens, E., Hartsuiker, R., Helaha, D. and Van Schelven, L. (1990) Orthographic facilitation and categorical interference in a word-translation variant of the Stroop task. *Canadian Journal of Psychology* 44: 76–83.

La Heij, W., Kerling, R. and van der Velden, E. (1996) Nonverbal context effects in forward and backward translation: evidence for concept mediation. *Journal of Memory and Language* 35: 648–65.

Lambert, W.E. *et al.* (1958) Evaluation reactions to spoken language. *Journal of Abnormal and Social Psychology* 60: 44–51.

Lance, D. (1975) Spanish–English code-switching. In E. Hernández-Chávez *et al.* (eds), *El Lenguaje de los Chicanos*. Arlington: Center for Applied Linguistics.

Lanza, E. (1990) Can bilingual two-year-olds code-switch? Paper presented at the Fifth International Congress for the Study of Child Language, July, Budapest.

Lanza, E. (1992) Can bilingual two-year-olds code-switch? *Journal of Child Language* 19: 633–58.

Lanza, E. (1997) *Language Mixing in Infant Bilingualism: A sociolinguistic perspective*. Oxford: Oxford University Press.

Laurie, S.S. (1890) *Lectures on Language and Linguistic Method in School*. Cambridge: Cambridge University Press.

Lavandera, B. (1978) The variable component in bilingual performance. In J. Alatis (ed.), *International Dimensions of Bilingual Education*. Washington DC: Georgetown University Press, pp. 391–411.

Laver, J. (1975) Communicative functions of phatic communion. In A. Kendon, R. Harris and M. Key (eds), *Organisation of Behaviour in Face-to-Face Interaction*. The Hague: Mouton, pp. 289–304.

Lecerf, J. (1932) *Littérature Dialectale et renaissance arabe moderne* (Damascus, 1932–3), pp. 1–14; *Majallat al-majma'al-'ilmī al-'arabī* (Dimashq), vol. 32, no. 1 *'Adad xāṣṣ bilmu'tamar al-'awwal lilmajāmi' al-lugawiyyah al-'ilmiyyah al-'arabiyyah* (Damascus, January 1957).

Leischner, A. (1943) Die Aphasien der Taubstummen: ein Beitrag zur Lehre der Asymbolie. *Archiv für Psychiatrie* 115: 469–548.

Lenneberg, E.H. (1967) *Biological Foundations of Language*. New York: Wiley.

Leopold, W. (1939–49) *Speech Development of a Bilingual Child: A linguist's record*, 4 volumes.

Evanston, IL: Northwestern University Press. (Also published in 1970 by AMS Press, New York.)

Leopold, W. (1978) A child's learning of two languages. In E. Hatch (ed.), *Second Language Acquisition: A book of readings*. Rowley, MA: Newbury House.

Le Page, R. and Tabouret-Keller, A. (1985) *Acts of Identity: Creole-based approaches to language and ethnicity*. Cambridge: Cambridge University Press.

Leuenberger, M. (1994) L'accès au lexique de code-switches chez le bilingue: Effets de la densité et du contexte [Lexical access of code-switches in the bilingual: The effect of density and context]. *Travaux neuchâtelois de linguistique (TRANEL)* 21: 61–72.

Levelt, W. (1989) *Speaking: From intention to articulation*. Cambridge, MA: MIT Press.

Levelt, W. and Maassen, B. (1981) Lexical search and order of mention in sentence production. In W. Klein and W. Levelt (eds), *Crossing the Boundaries in Linguistics: Studies presented to Manfred Bierwisch*. Dordrecht: Reidel.

Levelt, W. and Schriefers, H. (1987) Stages of lexical access. In G. Kempen (ed.), *Natural Language Generation: New results in artificial intelligence, psychology and linguistics*. Dordrecht: Martinus Nijhoff.

Levelt, W., Schriefers, H., Vorberg, D., Meyer, A.S., Pechmann, T. and Havinga, J. (1991) The time course of lexical access in speech production: a study of picture naming. *Psychological Review* 98: 122–42.

Levinson, S. (1983) *Pragmatics*. Cambridge: Cambridge University Press.

Lévy, N. and Grosjean, F. (in preparation) BIMOLA: a computational model of bilingual spoken word recognition.

Li, P. (1996) Spoken word recognition of code-switched words by Chinese–English bilinguals. *Journal of Memory and Language* 35: 757–74.

Lieberson, S. (1966) Language questions in census. *Sociological Inquiry* 36: 262–79.

Linck, J.A. and Kroll, J.F. (2005) Increased inhibitory control during second language immersion. Poster presented at the 46th Annual Meeting of the Psychonomic Society, Toronto.

Lindholm, K.J. and Padilla, A.M. (1978) Language mixing in bilingual children. *Journal of Child Language* 5: 327–35.

Lippi-Green, R. (1997) *English with an Accent: Language, ideology, and discrimination in the United States*. London: Routledge.

LIPPS Group (Language Interaction in Plurilingual and Plurilectic Speakers) (ed.) (2000) *The LIDES (Language Interaction Data Exchange System) Coding Manual*. London: Kingston Press. (Also available as a special issue of the *International Journal of Bilingualism*.)

Lipski, J. (1978) Code-switching and the problem of bilingual competence. In M. Paradis (ed.), *Aspects of Bilingualism*. Columbia: Hornbeam Press.

Lisker, L., and Abramson, A. (1964) A cross-language study of voicing in initial stops: acoustical measurements. *Word* 20: 384–422.

Li Wei, Milroy, L. and Pong, S.C. (1992) A two-step sociolinguistic analysis of code-switching and language choice. *International Journal of Applied Linguistics* 2(1): 63–86.

Li Wei (1993) Mother tongue maintenance in a Chinese community school in Newcastle upon Tyne. *Language and Education* 7: 199–215.

Li Wei (1994) *Three Generations Two Languages One Family: Language choice and language shift in a Chinese community in Britain*. Clevedon: Multilingual Matters.

Li Wei (1996) Network analysis. In H. Goebl, P. Nelde, Z. Stary and W. Wolck (eds), *Contact Linguistics: An international handbook of contemporary research*. New York: Walter de Gruyter, pp. 805–11.

Li Wei (2002) 'What do you want me to say?' On the conversation analysis approach to bilingual interaction. *Language in Society* 31: 159–80.

Li Wei (2005b) 'How can you tell?' Towards a common sense explanation of conversational codeswitching, *Journal of Pragmatics* 37: 375–90.

Li Wei (ed.) (2005a) *Journal of Pragmatics* 37 (3), Special issue.

Li Wei and Milroy, L. (1995) Conversational code-switching in a Chinese community in Britain: a sequential analysis. *Journal of Pragmatics* 23: 281–99.

Li Wei and Moyer, M. (eds) (2007) *Blackwell Guide to Research Methods in Bilingualism and Multilingualism*. Oxford: Blackwell.

Lo, A. (1999) Codeswitching, speech community, and the construction of ethnic identity. *Journal of Sociolinguistics* 3 (4): 461–79.

Loke, K. (1991) Code-switching in children's play. In *Papers for the Symposium on Code-Switching in Bilingual Studies: Theory, significance and perspectives*. (Held in Barcelona, 21–23 March 1991.) Strasbourg: European Science Foundation, pp. 287–318.

Ludérus, S. (1995) Language choice and language separation in bilingual Alzeimer patients. PhD dissertation, University of Amsterdam, Amsterdam.

Lüdi, G. (1983) Unpublished Neuchatel data corpus on French/Swiss German language use.

Lüdi, G. (1987a) (ed.) *Devenir bilingue – parler bilingue: Actes due 2e colloque sur le bilinguisme, Université de Neuchâtel, 20–22 Septembre 1984*. Tübingen: Max Niemeyer Verlag.

Lüdi, G. (1987b) Les marques transcodiques: regards nouveaux sur le bilinguisme. In G. Lüdi (ed.), *Devenir bilingue – parler bilingue: Actes due 2e colloque sur le bilinguisme, Université de Neuchâtel, 20–22 Septembre 1984*. Tübingen: Max Niemeyer Verlag, pp. 1–19.

Luria, A. (1973) *The Working Brain: An introduction to neuropsychology*. London: Penguin.

Lyon, J. (1996) *Becoming Bilingual: Language acquisition in a bilingual community*. Clevedon: Multilingual Matters.

McClelland, J., and Elman, J. (1986) The TRACE model of speech perception. *Cognitive Psychology* 18: 1–86.

McClure, E. (1977) Aspects of code-switching in the discourse of bilingual Mexican-American children. In M. Saville-Troike (ed.), *Linguistics and Anthropology*. Washington, pp. 93–115.

McClure, E. (1981) Formal and functional aspects of the code-switched discourse of bilingual children. In R.P. Duran (ed.), *Latino Language and Community Behavior*. Norwood, NJ: Ablex, pp. 69–94.

McClure, E. (n.d.) The acquisition of communicative competence in a bicultural setting. NIE Grant NE-G-00-e-0147 final report.

McClure, E. and Wentz, J. (1975) Functions of code-switching among Mexican-American children. In *Papers from the Parasession on Functionalism*. Chicago: Chicago Linguistics Society.

McConnell, H.O. and Swan, E. (1945) *You Can Learn Creole*. Port-au-Prince.

McConvell, P. (1988) Mix-Im-Up: Aboriginal codeswitching, old and new. In M. Heller (ed.), *Codeswitching*. Berlin: Mouton, pp. 97–150.

McConvell, P. and Meakins, F. (2005) Gurindji Kriol: a mixed language emerges from code-switching. *Australian Journal of Linguistics* 25: 9–30.

McDermott, R. and Gospodinoff, K. (1981) Social contexts for ethnic borders and school failure. In H. Trueba, G. Guthrie and G. Au (eds), *Culture and the Bilingual Classroom*. Rowley, MA: Newbury House, pp. 212–30.

McDonald, M. (1990) *We Are Not French*. London: Routledge.

McGlone, J. (1978) Sex differences in functional brain asymmetry. *Cortex* 14(1): 122–8.

McKeever, W. F. and Hunt, L. (1984) Failure to replicate the Scott *et al*. findings of reversed ear dominance in the Native American Navajo. *Neuropsychologia* 22: 539–41.45.

Mackey, W.F. (1968) The description of bilingualism. In J. Fishman (ed.), *Readings in the Sociology of Language*. The Hague: Mouton, pp. 554–84.

Mackey, W.F. (1952) Bilingualism and education. *Pédagogie-Orientation* 6: 135–47.

Mackey, W.F. (1953) Bilingualism and linguistic structure. *Culture* 14: 143–9.

Mackey, W.F. (1956) Toward a redefinition of bilingualism. *JCLA* 2.

Mackey, W.F. (1959) Bilingualism. *Encyclopaedia Britannica.*

Mackey, W.F. (1962) The description of bilingualism. *Canadian Journal of Linguistics* 7: 51–85.

Mackey, W.F. (1965) Bilingual interference: Its analysis and measurement. *Journal of Communication* 15: 239–49.

Mackey, W.F. and Noonan, J.A. (1952) An experiment in bilingual education. *English Language Teaching* 6: 125–32.

McLaughlin, B. (1984) *Second Language Acquisition in Childhood. Vol. 1: Preschool Children.* Hillsdale, NJ: Erlbaum.

McLeod, B. and McLaughlin, B. (1986) Restructuring or automaticity? Reading in a second language. *Language Learning* 36: 109–23.

McLeod, P. (1977) A dual task response modality effect: support for multi-processor models of attention. *Quarterly Journal of Experimental Psychology* 29: 651–67.

Macnamara, J. (1967) The bilingual's linguistic performance: a psychological overview. *Journal of Social Issues* 23: 59–77.

Macnamara, J. and Kushnir, S. (1971) Linguistic independence of bilinguals: the input switch. *Journal of Verbal Learning and Verbal Behavior* 10: 480–7.

McRae, K., De Sa, V. and Seidenberg, M.S. (1993) The role of correlated properties in accessing conceptual memory. Unpublished manuscript, University of Western Ontario, London, Ontario.

MacSwan, J. (1999) *A Minimalist Approach to Intrasentential Code-Switching.* New York: Garland.

MacSwan, J. (2000) The architecture of the bilingual language faculty: evidence from code-switching. *Bilingualism: Language and cognition* 3 (1): 37–54.

MacSwan, J. (2004) Code-switching and grammatical theory. In T.K. Bhatia and W.C. Richie (eds), *The Handbook of Bilingualism.* Oxford: Blackwell, pp. 238–311.

MacSwan, J. (2005) Code-switching and generative grammar. *Bilingualism: Language and cognition* 8: 1–22.

Mägiste, E. (1979) The competing language systems of the multilingual: A developmental study of decoding and encoding processes. *Journal of Verbal Learning and Verbal Behavior* 18: 79–89.

Mägiste, E. (1984) Stroop tasks and dichotic translation: the development of interference patterns in bilinguals. *Journal of Experimental Psychology: Learning, memory, and cognition* 10: 304–15.

Mägiste, E. (1986) Selected issues in second and third language learning. In J. Vaid (ed.), *Language Processing in Bilinguals: Psycholinguistic and neuropsychological perspectives.* Hillsdale: Erlbaum.

Mahootian, S. and Santorini, B. (1996) Code-switching and the complement/adjunct distinction. *Linguistic Inquiry* 27: 464–79.

Mak, W. (1935) Zweisprachigkeit und Mischmundart in Oberschlesien. *Schlesisches Jahrbuch für deutsche Kulturarbeit* 7: 41–52.

Mallinson, G. and Blake, B.J. (1981) *Language Typology.* Amsterdam: Noord-Holland.

Maltz, D. and Borker, R. (1982) A cultural approach to male–female miscommunication. In J.J. Gumperz (ed.), *Language and Social Identity.* Cambridge: Cambridge University Press, pp. 195–216.

Maratsos, M. (1982) The child's construction of grammatical categories. In E. Wanner and L. Gleitman (eds), *Language Acquisition: The state of the art.* Cambridge: Cambridge University Press, pp. 240–66.

Marçais, W. (1930–31) Three articles. *L'Enseignement Public* 97: 401–9; 105: 20–39, 120–33.

Marcus, G. (1986) Contemporary problems of ethnography in the modern world system. In J. Clifford and G. Marcus (eds), *Writing Culture*. Berkeley, CA and Los Angeles: University of California Press, pp. 165–93.

Marian, V. and Spivey, M.J. (2003) Competing activation in bilingual language processing: within- and between-language competition. *Bilingualism: Language and cognition* 6: 97–115.

Marouzeau, J. (1951) *Lexique de la terminologie linguistique*. Paris: Geuthner.

Marshall, J.C., Caplan, D. and Holmes, J.M. (1975) The measure of laterality. *Neuropsychologia* 13: 315–21.

Marslen-Wilson, W. (1987) Functional parallelism in spoken word recognition. *Cognition* 25: 71–102.

Martin, A., Wiggs, C.L., Ungerleider, L.G. and Haxby, J.V. (1996) Neural correlates of category-specific knowledge. *Nature* 379: 649–52.

Martin-Jones, M. and Romaine, S. (1986) Semilingualism: a half-baked theory of communicative competence. *Applied Linguistics* 6: 105–17.

Marty, S. and Grosjean, F. (1998) Aphasie, bilinguisme et modes de communication. *APHASIE und verwandte Gebiete* 12 (1): 8–28.

Masson, M.E.J. (1991) A distributed memory model of context effects in word identification. In D. Besner and G.W. Humphreys (eds), *Basic Processes In Reading: Visual word recognition*. Hillsdale, NJ: Lawrence Erlbaum Associates, pp. 233–63.

Maynard, J. (1985) On the functions of social conflict among children. *American Sociological Review* 50: 207–223.

Mazibuko, T.L. (1991) Interference in translation: using distracting information to reveal the nature of bilingual language processing. Unpublished Master's thesis, Mount Holyoke College, South Hadley, MA.

Mazoyer, B.M., Tzourio, N., Frank, V., Syrota, A., Murayama, N., Lerrier, O., Salamon, G., Dehaene, S., Cohen, L. and Mehler, J. (1993) The cortical representation of speech. *Journal of Cognitive Neuroscience* 5: 467–79.

Meara, P. (1989) Models of the lexicon in English and other funny languages. *Toegepaste taalwetenschap in Artikelen* 34(2): 7–12.

Meara, P. (1993) The bilingual lexicon and the teaching of vocabulary. In R. Schreuder and B. Weltens (eds), *The Bilingual Lexicon*. Amsterdam: John Benjamins, pp. 279–97.

Meeuwis, M. and Blommaert, J. (1998) A monolectal view of code-switching: layered code-switching among Zairians in Belgium. In J.C.P. Auer (ed.), *Code-Switching in Conversation: Language, interaction and identity*. London: Routledge, pp. 76–100.

Meeuwis, M. and Sarangi, S. (1994) Perspectives on intercultural communication. *Pragmatics* 4 (3): 309–13.

Mehler, J., Bertoncini, J., Barrière, M. and Jassik-Gerschenfeld, D. (1978) Infant recognition of mother's voice. *Perception* 7: 491–7.

Mehler, J., Lambertz, G., Jusczyk, P. and Amiel-Tison, C. (1986) Discrimination de la langue maternelle par le nouveau-né. *Académie des Sciences* 3: 637–40.

Meisel, J.M. (1983) Transfer as a second-language strategy. *Language and Communication* 3(1): 11–46.

Meisel, J.M. (1985) Les phases initiales du développement de notions temporelles, aspectuelles et de modes d'action. *Lingua* 66: 321–74.

Meisel, J.M. (1986) Word order and case marking in early child language: evidence from simultaneous acquisition of two languages. *Linguistics* 24(1): 123–83.

Meisel, J.M. (1989) Early differentiation of languages in bilingual children. In K. Hyltenstam and L. Obler (eds), *Bilingualism across the Lifespan: Aspects of acquisition, maturity and loss*. Cambridge: Cambridge University Press, pp. 13–40.

Meisel, J.M. (1990a) INFL-ection: subjects and subject–verb agreement. In J.M. Meisel (ed.), *Two First Languages: Early Grammatical Development in Bilingual Children*. Dordrecht: Foris, pp. 237–98.

Meisel, J.M. (1992) *The Acquisition of Verb Placement: Functional categories and V2 phenomena in language development*. Dordrecht: Kluwer.

Meisel, J.M. (1994a) Getting FAT: finiteness, agreement and tense in early grammars. In J.M. Meisel (ed.), *Bilingual First Language Acquisition: French and German grammatical development*. Amsterdam: Benjamins, pp. 89–130.

Meisel, J.M. (1994b) Code-switching in young bilingual children: the acquisition of grammatical constraints. *Studies in Second Language Acquisition* 16: 413–41.

Meisel, J.M. (2001) The simultaneous acquisition of two first languages: early differentiation and subsequent development of grammars. In J. Cenoz and F. Genesee (eds), *Trends in Bilingual Acquisition*. Amsterdam: John Benjamins, pp. 11–42.

Meisel, J.M. (2004) Bilingual child. In T.K. Bhatia and W.C. Ritchie (eds), *The Handbook of Bilingualism*. Oxford: Blackwell, pp. 91–113.

Meisel, J.M. (ed.) (1990) *Two First Languages: Early grammatical development in bilingual children*. Dordrecht: Foris.

Meisel, J.M. (ed.) (1994) *Bilingual First Language Acquisition: French and German grammatical development*. Amsterdam: John Benjamins.

Meisel, J.M., Clahsen, H. and Pienemann, M. (1981) On determining developmental stages in natural second language acquisition. *Studies in Second Language Acquisition* 3(2): 109–35.

Menarini, A. (1939) L'italo-americano degli Stati Uniti. *Lingua Nostra* 1: 154–6.

Mendelsohn, S. (1988) Language lateralization in bilinguals: facts and fantasy. *Journal of Neurolinguistics* 3: 261–92.

Mérida, G.-J. and Prudent, L.-F. (1984) . . . an langaj kréyol dimi panaché . . .: interlecte et dynamique conversationnelle. *Langages* 74: 31–46.

Meuter, R. (2005) Language selection in bilinguals: mechanisms and processes. In J.F. Kroll and A.M.B. de Groot (eds), *Handbook of Bilingualism: Psycholinguistic approaches*. Oxford: Oxford University Press, pp. 349–70.

Meuter, R. and Allport, A. (1999) Bilingual language switching in naming: asymmetrical costs of language selection. *Journal of Memory and Language* 40: 25–40.

Meyer, D.E. and Ruddy, M.G. (1974) Bilingual word recognition: organization and retrieval of alternative lexical codes. Paper presented at the Eastern Psychological Association Meeting, Philadelphia, PA, April.

Mikès, M. (1967) Acquisition des catégories grammaticales dans le langage de l'enfant. *Enfance* 20: 289–98.

Milardo, R.M. (1988) Families and social networks: an overview of theory and methodology. In *Families and Social Network*. Newbury Park, CA: Sage.

Mills, A.E. (1985) The acquisition of German. In D.I. Slobin (ed.), *The Cross-Linguistic Study of Language Acquisition*. Hillsdale, NJ: Erlbaum, 141–254.

Milner, B., Taylor, L. and Sperry, R.W. (1968) Lateralized suppression of dichotically presented digits after commissural section in man. *Science* 161: 184–6.

Milroy, L. (1980) *Language and Social Networks*. Oxford: Blackwell.

Milroy, L. (1987) *Observing and Analysing Natural Language*. Oxford: Blackwell.

Milroy, L. (1987a) *Language and Social Networks*. 2nd edn. Oxford: Blackwell.

Milroy, L. and Li Wei (1995) A social network approach to code-switching. In L. Milroy and P. Muysken (eds), *One Speaker Two Languages: Cross-disciplinary perspectives on code-switching*. Cambridge: Cambridge University Press, pp. 136–57.

Milroy, J. and Milroy, L. (1985, 2nd edn 1991, 3rd edn 1999) *Authority in Language*. London: Routledge.

Milroy, L. and Milroy, J. (1992) Social network and social class: towards an integrated socio-linguistic model. *Language in Society* 21 (1): 1–26.

Milroy, L. and Muysken, P. (eds) (1995) *One Speaker Two Languages: Cross-disciplinary perspectives on code-switching*. Cambridge: Cambridge University Press.

Milroy, L., Li Wei and Moffatt, S. (1993) Discourse patterns and fieldwork strategies in urban settings. *Journal of Multilingual and Multicultural Development* 12: 287–300.

Mishkin, M. and Forgays, D. (1952) Word recognition as a function of retinal locus. *Journal of Experimental Psychology* 43: 43–8.

Mitchell, J.C. (1986) Network procedures. In D. Frick *et al.* (eds), *The Quality of Urban Life*. Berlin: de Gruyter.

Mitchell, J.C. (1987) The components of strong ties among homeless women. *Social Networks* 9: 37–47.

Mitchell, R. and Myles, F. (1998) *Second Language Learning Theories*. London: Edward Arnold.

Moerman, M. (1974) Accomplishing ethnicity. In R. Turner (ed.), *Ethnomethodology*. Harmonds-worth: Penguin, pp. 54–68.

Moffatt, S. (1990) Becoming bilingual: a sociolinguistic study of the communication of young mother tongue Panjabi-speaking children. Unpublished PhD thesis, Department of Speech, University of Newcastle upon Tyne.

Moffatt, S. and Milroy, L. (1992) Panjabi/English language alternation in the classroom in the early school years. *Multilingua*.

Möhle, D. (1984) A comparison of the second language speech production of different native speakers. In H. Dechert, D. Möhle and M. Raupach (eds), *Second Language Productions*. Tübingen: Gunter Narr.

Morton, J. (1979) Word recognition. In J. Morton and J. Marshall (eds), *Psycholinguistic Series 2: Structures and processes*. London: Elek.

Morton, J. (1980) Two auditory parallels to deep dyslexia. In M. Coltheart, K. Patterson and J.C. Marshall (eds), *Deep Dyslexia*. London: Routledge & Kegan Paul.

Moser, H. (1968) Wohin steuert das heutige Deutsch? In H. Moser (ed.), *Satz und Wort im heutigen Deutsch*. Düsseldorf: Schwann, pp. 15–35.

Moss, E.M., Davidson, R.J. and Saron, C. (1985) Cross-cultural differences in hemisphericity: EEG asymmetry discriminates between Japanese and Westerners. *Neuropsychologia* 23: 131–5.

Moyer, M.G. (1992) Spanish–English code-switching in Gibraltar. In European Science Founda-tion (ed.), *Code-Switching Summer School*. Strasbourg: European Science Foundation, pp. 51–67.

Mummery, C.J., Patterson, K., Hodges, J.R. and Wise, R.J.S. (1996) Generating a 'tiger' as an animal name or a word beginning with T: differences in brain activations. *Proceedings of the Royal Society* (London) B, 263: 989–95.

Murrell, M. (1966) Language acquisition in a trilingual environment: notes from a case-study. *Studia Linguistica* 20: 9–35.

Muysken, P. (1990) A unified theory of local coherence in grammar contact. In P.H. Nelde (ed.), *Confli(c)t*, ABLA Papers 14. Brussels: ABLA, pp. 123–8.

Muysken, P. (1991) Needed: a comparative approach. In European Science Foundation (ed.), *Papers for the Symposium on Code-Switching in Bilingual Studies: Theory, significance and perspec-tives*, Vol. 1. Strasbourg: European Science Foundation, pp. 253–72.

Muysken, P. (1993) Grammatical constraints on code-switching: the case of Indic mixed compounds. Presented at the ESF Pavia Summer School on Code-Switching and Language Contact.

Muysken, P. (1995) Code-switching and grammatical theory. In L. Milroy and P. Muysken (eds), *One Speaker Two Languages*. Cambridge: Cambridge University Press, pp. 177–98.

Muysken, Pieter (2000) *Bilingual Speech: A typology of code-mixing*. Cambridge: Cambridge University Press.

Myers-Scotton, C. (1986) Diglossia and code-switching. In J.A. Fishman *et al.* (eds), *The Fergusonian Impact*. Berlin: Mouton de Gruyter.

Myers-Scotton, C. (1988) Code-switching as indexical of social negotiations. In M. Heller (ed.), *Codeswitching*. Berlin: Mouton de Gruyter, pp. 151–86.

Myers-Scotton, C. (1991) Intersection between social motivations and structural processing in code-switching. In *Papers for the Workshop on Constraints, Conditions and Models*. (Held in London, 27–29 September 1990.) Strasbourg: European Science Foundation, pp. 57–82.

Myers-Scotton, C. (1992) Codeswitching as socially motivated performance meets structurally motivated constraints. In M. Pütz (ed.), *Thirty Years of Linguistic Evolution*. Amsterdam: Benjamins, pp. 417–28.

Myers-Scotton, C. (1992a) Constructing the frame in intrasentential codeswitching. *Multilingua* 11: 101–27.

Myers-Scotton, C. (1993) *Social Motivations for Codeswitching: Evidence from Africa*. Oxford: Oxford University Press.

Myers-Scotton, C. (1993a, paperback edition with new Afterword 1997) *Duelling Languages: Grammatical structure in codeswitching*. Oxford: Oxford University Press.

Myers-Scotton, C. (1993c) Common and uncommon ground: social and structural factors in codeswitching. *Language in Society* 22: 475–503.

Myers-Scotton, C. (1995) What do speakers want? Codeswitching as evidence of intentionality in linguistic choices. In P. Silberman and J. Loftin (eds), *SALSA II*, Austin: Department of Linguistics, University of Texas, pp. 1–17.

Myers-Scotton, C. (1995a) A lexically-based model of codeswitching. In L. Milroy and P. Muysken (eds), *One Speaker Two Languages*. Cambridge: Cambridge University Press, pp. 233–56.

Myers-Scotton, C. (1995b) Language processing and the mental lexicon in bilinguals. In R. Dirven and J. Vanparys (eds), *New Approaches to the Lexicon*. Frankfurt: Peter Lang, pp. 73–100.

Myers-Scotton, C. (1995c) 'Matrix language recognition' and 'morpheme sorting' as possible structural strategies in pidgin/creole formation. In A. Spears and D. Winford (eds), *Pidgins and Creoles: Structure and Status*. Amsterdam: Benjamins.

Myers-Scotton, C. (1997) Codeswitching. In F. Coulmas (ed.) *The Handbook of Sociolinguistics*. Oxford: Blackwell, pp. 217–37.

Myers-Scotton, C. (1997a) *Duelling Languages: Grammatical structure in code-switching*. Oxford: Oxford University Press.

Myers-Scotton, C. (1999) Explaining the role of norms and rationality in codeswitching, *Journal of Pragmatics* 32: 1259–71.

Myers-Scotton, C. (2002, 2003, 2004) *Contact Linguistics: Bilingual encounters and grammatical outcomes*. Oxford: Oxford University Press.

Myers-Scotton, C. (2005) *Multiple Voices: An introduction to bilingualism*. Oxford: Blackwell.

Myers-Scotton, C. (2005a) Supporting a differential access hypothesis: codeswitching and other contact data. In J.F. Kroll and A.M.B. de Groot (eds), *Handbook of Bilingualism*. Oxford: Oxford University Press, pp. 326–48.

Myers-Scotton, C. (2005b) Unpublished manuscript.

Myers-Scotton, C. and Jake, J.L. (1994) Swiss German/French and Swiss German/Italian corpora. Unpublished data.

Myers-Scotton, C. and Jake, J.L. (1995) Matching lemmas in a bilingual competence and production model. *Linguistics* 33: 981–1024.

Myers-Scotton, C. and Jake, J.L. (eds) (2000) *Testing a Model of Morpheme Classification with Language Contact Data*. London: Kingston Press. (Also available as a special issue of the *International Journal of Bilingualism*, 4(1).)

Myers-Scotton, C. and Bolonyai, A. (2001) Calculating speakers: Codeswitching in a rational choice model. *Language in Society* 30 (1): 1–28.

Myers-Scotton, C. and Jake, J.L. (2001) Explaining aspects of codeswitching and their implications. In J.L. Nicol (ed.), *One Mind Two Languages: Bilingual language processing*. Oxford: Blackwell, pp. 84–116.

Nader, L. (1962) A note on attitudes and the use of language. *Anthropological Linguistics* 4(6): 24–9.

Nahirny, V.C. and Fishman, J.A. (1965) American immigrant groups: ethnic identification and the problem of generations. *Sociological Review* 13: 311–26.

Nair, K. and Vermani, V. (1973) Speech and language disturbances in hemiplegics. *Indian Journal of Medical Research* 61: 1131–8.

Naït M'Barek, M. and Sankoff, D. (1988) Le discours mixte arabe/français: des emprunts ou des alternances de langue? *Revue Canadienne de Linguistique* 33 (2): 143–54.

Nartey, J.N.A. (1982) Code-switching, interference or faddism? Language use among educated Ghanaians. *Anthropological Linguistics* 24: 183–92.

Nas, G. (1983) Visual word recognition in bilinguals: evidence for a co-operation between visual and sound based codes during access to a common lexical store. *Journal of Verbal Learning and Verbal Behavior* 22: 526–34.

Nation, P. (1984) Sheng, new urban language baffles parents. Wednesday *Nation* magazine, 14 March 1984.

Navon, D. and Gopher, D. (1979) On the economy of the human processing system. *Psychological Review* 86: 214–55.

Neely, J.H. (1991) Semantic priming effects in visual word recognition: a selective review of current findings and theories. In D. Besner and G.W. Humphreys (eds), *Basic Processes in Reading: Visual word recognition*. Hillsdale, NJ: Lawrence Erlbaum Associates, pp. 264–336.

Neufeld, G. (1973) The bilingual's lexical store. *Working Papers on Bilingualism* 1: 35–65.

Neville, H.J. and Bavelier, D. (1998) Neural organization and plasticity of language. *Current Opinion in Neurobiology* 8: 254–8.

Nicol, J.L. (ed.) (2001) *One Mind Two Languages: Bilingual language processing*. Oxford: Blackwell.

Nicoladis, E. and Genesee, F. (1998) Parental discourse and codemixing in bilingual children. *International Journal of Bilingualism* 2: 85–9.

Norman, D. and Shallice, T. (1980) *Attention to Action: Willed and automatic control of behavior*. San Diego: Center for Human Information Processing, University of California, Chip 99.

Nortier, J. (1989) Dutch and Moroccan-Arabic in Contact: code-switching among Moroccans in the Netherlands. PhD dissertation, University of Amsterdam.

Nortier, J. (1990) *Dutch–Moroccan Arabic Code-switching among Moroccans in the Netherlands*. Dordrecht: Foris.

Nussbaum, L. (1990) Plurilingualism in a foreign language classroom in Catalonia. In *Papers for the Workshop on Impact and Consequences/Broader Considerations*. (Held in Brussels.) Strasbourg: European Science Foundation, pp. 141–64.

Obler, L.K. and Albert, M. (1978) A monitor system for bilingual language processing. In M. Paradis (ed.), *Aspects of Bilingualism*. Columbia, SC: Hornbeam Press, pp. 105–13.

Obler, L.K., Albert, M. and Gordon, H.W. (1975) Asymmetry of cerebral dominance in Hebrew–English bilinguals. Paper presented at the Academy of Asphasia, Victoria, October.

Obler, L.K., Zatorre, R.J., Galloway, L. and Vaid, J. (1982) Cerebral lateralization in bilinguals: methodological issues. *Brain and Language* 15: 40–54.

Ochs, E. (1986) Introduction. In B. Schieffelin and E. Ochs (eds), *Language Socialisation across Cultures*. Cambridge: Cambridge University Press, pp. 1–13.

Ochs, E. (1988) *Culture and Language Development*. Cambridge: Cambridge University Press.

Odlin, T. (1989) *Language Transfer: Cross-linguistic influence in language learning*. Cambridge: Cambridge University Press.

Ojemann, G.A. and Whitaker, H.A. (1978) The bilingual brain. *Archives of Neurology* 35: 409–12.

Okasha, M. (1995) Unpublished Arabic–English codeswitching corpus.

Oksaar, E. (1971) Code switching as an interactional strategy for developing bilingual competence. *Word* 27: 377–85.

Oksaar, E. (1978) Preschool trilingualism: a case study. In F.C. Peng and W. v. Raffler-Engel (eds), *Language Acquisition and Developmental Kinesics*. Tokyo, pp. 129–37.

Oldfield, R. (1963) Individual vocabulary and semantic currency: a preliminary study. *British Journal of Social and Clinical Psychology* 2: 122–30.

Oller, D. and MacNeilage, P. (1983) Development of speech production. In P. MacNeilage (ed.), *The Production of Speech*. New York: Springer.

Opie, I. and Opie, P. (1959) *The Lore and Language of Schoolchildren*. Oxford: Oxford University Press.

Orbach, J. (1967) Differential recognition of Hebrew and English words in right and left visual fields as a function of cerebral dominance and reading habits. *Neuropsychologia* 50: 127–34.

Padilla, A.M. and Liebman, E. (1975) Language acquisition in the bilingual child. *Bilingual Review* 2: 34–55.

Paivio, A. (1971) *Imagery and Verbal Processes*. Toronto: Holt, Rinehart & Winston.

Paivio, A. (1986) *Mental Representations: A dual coding approach*. New York: Oxford University Press.

Palmer, S., Rosch, E. and Chase, P. (1981) Canonical perspective and the perception of objects. In. J. Long and A. Baddeley (eds), *Attention and Performance* IX. Hillsdale, NJ: Lawrence Erlbaum Associates, pp. 135–51.

Panese, M. (1992) Il code-switching come strategia comunicativa: un indagine nella comunità italiana a Londra. In A. Sobrero (ed.), *Il dialetto nella conversazione*. Galatina: Congedo, pp. 43–80.

Paradis, J., Nicoladis, E. and Genesee, F. (2000) Early emergence of structural constraints on code-mixing: evidence from French–English bilingual children. *Bilingualism: Language and cognition* 3: 245–61.

Paradis, J., Crago, M., Genesee, F. and Rice, M. (2003) Bilingual children with specific language impairment: How do they compare with their monolingual peers? *Journal of Speech, Language and Hearing Research* 46: 113–27.

Paradis, M. (1977) Bilingualism and aphasia. In H. Whitaker and H. Whitaker (eds), *Studies in Neurolinguistics*, Vol. 13. New York: Academic Press.

Paradis, M. (1980) The language switch in bilinguals: psycholinguistic and neurolinguistic perspectives. In P. Nelde (ed.), *Languages in Contact and Conflict*. Wiesbaden, Germany: Franz Steiner Verlag, pp. 501–6.

Paradis, M. (1981) Contributions of neurolinguistics to the theory of bilingualism. In R. Herbert (ed.), *Applications of Linguistic Theory in the Human Sciences*. East Lansing: Michigan State University Press, pp. 180–211.

Paradis, M. (1985) On the representation of two languages in one brain. *Language Sciences* 61(7): 1–40.

Paradis, M. (1986) Bilingualism. *International Encyclopedia of Education*. Oxford: Pergamon, pp. 489–93.

Paradis, M. (1988) Review of G. Bergh, 1986: The neuropsychological status of Swedish–English subsidiary bilinguals. *Linguistics* 25: 886–92.

Paradis, M. (1989) Bilingual and polyglot aphasia. In F. Boller and J. Grafman (eds), *Handbook of Neuropsychology*, Vol. 2. Amsterdam: Elsevier, pp. 117–40.

Paradis, M. (1990) Language lateralization in bilinguals. *Brain and Language* 39: 570–86.

Paradis, M. (1992) The Loch Ness Monster approach to lateralization in bilingual aphasia: a response to Berquier and Ashton. *Brain and Language* 43: 534–7.

Paradis, M. (1995) Another sighting of differential language laterality in multilinguals, this time in Loch Tok Pisin: comments on Wuillemin, Richardson and Lynch (1994). *Brain and Language* 49: 173–86.

Paradis, M. (1997) The cognitive neuropsychology of bilingualism. In A. de Groot and J. Kroll (eds), *Tutorials in Bilingualism*. Mahwah, NJ: Lawrence Erlbaum, pp. 331–54.

Paradis, M. (1998) Language and communication in multilinguals. In B. Stemmer and H. Whitaker (eds), *Handbook of Neurolinguistics*. San Diego, CA: Academic Press, pp. 417–30.

Paradis, M. (2003) The bilingual Loch Ness Monster raises its nonasymmetric head again: Or, Why bother with such cumbersome notions as validity and reliability? Comments on Evans *et al.* (2002). *Brain and Language* 87: 441–8.

Paradis, M. (2004) *A Neurolinguistic Theory of Bilingualism*. Amsterdam: John Benjamins.

Paradis, M. (ed.) (1983) *Readings on Aphasia in Bilinguals and Polyglots*. Quebec: Marcel Didier.

Paradis, M. (ed.) (1987) *The Assessment of Bilingual Aphasia*. Hillsdale, NJ: Lawrence Erlbaum.

Paradis, M., Goldblum, M.-C. and Abidi, R. (1982) Alternate antagonism with paradoxical translation behavior in two bilingual aphasic patients. *Brain and Language* 15: 55–69.

Park, T.-Z. (1981) *The Development of Syntax in the Child: With special reference to German*. Innsbruck: Innsbrucker Beiträge zur Kulturwissenschaft 45.

Parkin, D. (1974) Language switching in Nairobi. In W.H. Whiteley (ed.), *Language in Kenya*. Nairobi: Oxford University Press, pp. 189–216.

Paulesu, E., Goldacre, B., Scifo, P., Cappa, S.F., Gilardi, M.C., Castiglioni, I., Perani, D. and Fazio, F. (1997) Functional heterogeneity of left inferior frontal cortex as revealed by fMRI. *NeuroReport* 8: 2011–16.

Paulston, C.B. and Tucker, G.R. (eds) (2003) *Sociolinguistics: The essential readings*. Oxford: Blackwell.

Pavlovitch, M. (1920) *Le langage enfantin: L'acquisition du serbe et du français par un enfant serbe*. Paris: Champion.

Payne, A. (1976) The acquisition of the phonological system of a second dialect. Unpublished PhD dissertation, University of Pennsylvania.

Peal, E. and Lambert, W.E. (1962) The relation of bilingualism to intelligence. *Psychological Monographs*.

Pearson, B.Z., Fernandez, S.C. and Oller, D.K. (1993) Lexical development in bilingual infants and toddlers. *Language Learning* 43: 93–120.

Pearson, B.Z. (1998) Assessing lexical development in bilingual babies and toddlers. *International Journal of Bilingualism* 2: 347–72.

Pedraza, P. (1978) Ethnographic observations of language use in El Barrio. Unpublished ms.

Penfield, W. and Roberts, L. (1959) *Speech and Brain-Mechanisms*. Princeton: Princeton University Press.

Perani, D. and Abutalebi, J. (2005) Neural basis of first and second language processing. *Current Opinion of Neurobiology* 15: 202–6.

Perani, D. and Cappa, S.F. (1998) Neuroimaging methods in neuropsychology. In G. Denes and L. Pizzamiglio (eds), *Handbook of Clinical and Experimental Neuropsychology*. London: Psychology, pp. 69–94.

Perani, D., Dehaene, S., Grassi, F., Cohen, L., Cappa, S.F., Dupoux, E., Fazio, F. and Mehler, J. (1996) Brain processing of native and foreign languages. *NeuroReport* 7: 2439–44.

Perani, D., Paulesu, E., Sebastian-Galles, N., Dupoux, E., Dehaene, S., Bettinardi, V., Cappa, S.F., Fazio, F. and Mehler, J. (1998) The bilingual brain: proficiency and age of acquisition of the second language. *Brain* 121: 1841–52.

Perdue, C. (ed.) (1984) *Second Language Acquisition by Adult Immigrants: A field manual*. Rowley, MA: Newbury House.

Perecman, E. (1984) Spontaneous translation and language mixing in a polyglot aphasic. *Brain and Language* 23: 43–63.

Perecman, E. (1989) Language processing in the bilingual: evidence from language mixing. In K. Hyltenstam and L. Obler (eds), *Bilingualism Across the Lifespan*. Cambridge: Cambridge University Press.

Pernot, H. (1898) *Grammaire Grecque Moderne*. Paris, pp. vii–xxxi.

Petersen, J. (1988) Word-internal code-switching constraints in a bilingual child's grammar. *Linguistics* 26: 479–93.

Petersen, S.E., van Mier, H., Fiez, J.A. and Raichle, M.E. (1998) The effects of practice on the functional anatomy of task performance. *Proceedings of the National Academy of Sciences* (USA) 95 (3): 853–60.

Petersson, K.M., Elfgren, C. and Ingvar, M. (1999) Dynamic changes in the functional anatomy of the human brain during recall of abstract designs related to practice. *Neuropsychologia* 37: 567–87.

Pfaff, C. (1975) Syntactic constraints on code-switching: a quantitative study of Spanish–English. Paper presented at the Linguistic Society of America annual meeting.

Pfaff, C. (1976) Functional and structural constraints on syntactic variation in code-switching. *Papers from the Parasession on Diachronic Syntax*. Chicago, IL: Chicago Linguistic Society.

Pfaff, C. (1979) Constraints on language mixing: intrasentential code-switching and borrowing in Spanish/English. *Language* 55: 291–318.

Piazza, D.M. and Zatorre, R.J. (1981) A right-ear advantage for dichotic listening in bilingual children. *Brain and Language* 13: 389–96.

Pijper, J.R. (1983) *Modelling British English Intonation: An analysis by resynthesis of British English intonation*. Dordrecht: Foris.

Pike, K.L. (1967) *Language in Relation to the Unified Theory of the Structure of Human Behaviour*. The Hague: Mouton.

Pillai, M. (1960) Tamil: literary and colloquial. In C.A. Ferguson and J.J. Gumperz (eds), *Linguistic Diversity in South Asia*. Indiana University Research Center in Anthropology, Folklore and Linguistics, Publication 13, pp. 27–42.

Pitres, A. (1895) Etude sur l'aphasie chez les polyglottes. *Revue de Médecine* 15: 873–99.

Poetzl, O. (1925) Ueber die parietal bedingte Aphasie und ihren Einfluss auf das Sprechen mehrerer Sprachen. *Zeitschrift fuer die gesamte Neurologie und Psychiatrie* 99: 100–24.

Poetzl, O. (1930) Aphasie und Mehrsprachigkeit. *Zeitschrift fuer die gesamte Neurologie und Psychiatrie* 124: 145–62.

Poline, J.B., Vandenberghe, R., Holmes, A.P., Friston, A.K. and Frackowiak, R.S. (1996) Reproducibility of PET activation studies: lessons from a multi centre European experiment. *Neuroimage* 4: 34–54.

Pollock, J.-Y. (1989) Verb movement, universal grammar, and the structure of IP. *Linguistic Inquiry* 20: 365–424.

Pong, Sin Ching (1991) Intergenerational variation in language choice patterns in a Chinese community in Britain. Unpublished MPhil thesis, University of Newcastle upon Tyne.

Poplack, S. (1978) Dialect acquisition among Puerto Rican bilinguals. *Language in Society* 7(1): 89–103.

Poplack, S. (1980) Sometimes I'll start a sentence in Spanish *y termino en español*: toward a typology of code-switching. *Linguistics* 18: 581–618.

Poplack, S. (1981) Syntactic structure and social function of code-switching. In R. Duran (ed.), *Latino Discourse and Communicative Behaviour*. Norwood, NJ: Ablex, pp. 169–84.

Poplack, S. (1985) Contrasting patterns of code-switching in two communities. In H. Warkentyne (ed.), *Methods V: Papers from the V International Conference on Methods in Dialectology*. Victoria, BC: University of Victoria Press, pp. 363–86.

Poplack, S. (1988) Contrasting patterns of codeswitching in two communities. In M. Heller (ed.), *Codeswitching*. Berlin: Mouton, pp. 215–44.

Poplack, S. (1993) Variation theory and language contact: contact, concept, methods and data. In D. Preston (ed.), *American Dialect Research*. Amsterdam: John Benjamins, pp. 251–86.

Poplack, S. (2001) Code-switching (linguistic). In N. Smelser and P. Baltes (eds), *International Encyclopedia of the Social and Behavioral Sciences*. London: Elsevier Science, pp. 2062–5.

Poplack, S. and Meechan, M. (1995) Patterns of language mixture: nominal structure in Wolof–French and Fongbe–French bilingual discourse. In L. Milroy and P. Muysken (eds), *One Speaker Two Languages*. Cambridge: Cambridge University Press, pp. 199–232.

Poplack, S. and Meechan, M. (eds) (1998) *Instant Loans, Easy Conditions: The productivity of bilingual borrowing*. London: Kingston Press. (Also available as a special issue of the *International Journal of Bilingualism* 2(2).)

Poplack, S. and Sankoff, D. (1984) Borrowing: the synchrony of integration. *Linguistics* 22: 99–135.

Poplack, S. and Sankoff, D. (1987) Code-switching. In U. Ammon, N. Dittmar and K. Mattheier (eds), *Sociolinguistics: An international handbook of the science of language and society*, volume 2. Berlin: Walter de Gruyter, pp. 1174–80.

Poplack, S., Sankoff, D. and Miller, C. (1988) The social correlates and linguistic processes of lexical borrowing and assimilation. *Linguistics* 26: 47–104.

Poplack, S., Wheeler, S. and Westwood, A. (1987) Distinguishing language contact phenomena: evidence from Finnish–English bilingualism. In P. Lilius and M. Saari (eds), *The Nordic Languages and Modern Linguistics* 6 (Proceedings of the Sixth International Conference of Nordic and General Linguistics in Helsinki, 18–22 August 1986.): 33–56. Also in K. Hyltenstam and L.K. Obler (eds) (1989) *Bilingualism across the Lifespan: Aspects of acquisition, maturity and loss*. Cambridge: Cambridge University Press, pp. 132–54.

Porsché, D.C. (1983) *Die Zweisprachigkeit während des primären Spracherwerbs*. Tübingen: Narr (TBL 218).

Port, R. and van Gelder, T. (1995) *Mind as Motion: Exploration in the dynamics of cognition*. Cambridge, MA: MIT Press.

Posner, M.I., Sandson, J., Dhawan, M. and Shulman, G.L. (1989) Is word recognition automatic? A cognitive anatomical approach. *Journal of Cognitive Neuroscience* 1: 50–60.

Potter, M.C., So, K.-F., Von Eckardt, B. and Feldman, L.B. (1984) Lexical and conceptual representation in beginning and more proficient bilinguals. *Journal of Verbal Learning and Verbal Behavior* 23: 23–38.

Potter, M.C. (1979) Mundane symbolism: the relations among objects, names, and ideas. In N.R. Smith and M.B. Franklin (eds), *Symbolic Functioning in Childhood*. Hillsdale, NJ: Lawrence Erlbaum Associates, pp. 41–65.

Potter, M.C. and Faulconer, B.A. (1975) Time to understand pictures and words. *Nature* 253: 437–8.

Poulisse, N. (1990) *The Use of Compensatory Strategies by Dutch Learners of English*. Dordrecht: Foris.

Poulisse, N. (1997) Language production in bilinguals. In A.M. de Groot and J.F. Kroll (eds), *Tutorials in Bilingualism*. Mahwah, NJ: Lawrence Erlbaum, pp. 201–24.

Poulisse, N. (1999) *Slips of the Tongue: Speech errors in first and second language acquisition*. Amsterdam/Philadelphia, PA: John Benjamins.

Poulisse, N. and Bongaerts, T. (1990) A closer look at the strategy of transfer. Paper presented at the AILA World congress, Thessaloniki.

Poulisse, N. and Bongaerts, T. (1994) First language use in second language production. *Applied Linguistics* 15: 36–57.

Pratt, M.L. (1987) Linguistic utopias. In N. Fabb, D. Attridge, A. Durant and C. MacCabe (eds), *The Linguistics of Writing*. Manchester: Manchester University Press, pp. 48–66.

Preston, M. and Lambert, W. (1969) Interlingual interference in a bilingual version of the Stroop Colour Word Test. *Journal of Verbal Learning and Verbal Behaviour* 8: 295–301.

Preziosa-DiQuinzio, I. (1992) Teoreticamente la firma fa indietro. Lavoro di licenza inedito in linguistica italiana. Zurich: University of Zurich.

Price, C.J. (1998) The functional anatomy of word comprehension and production. *Trends in Cognitive Science* 2: 281–8.

Price, C.J., Green, D.W. and von Studnitz, R. (1999) A functional imaging study of translation and language switching in bilinguals. *Brain* 122 (12): 2221–35.

Psichari, J. (1928) Un Pays qui ne veut pas sa langue. *Mercure de France*, 1 October: 63–121. (Also in Psichari *Quelque travaux* . . . Paris, volume 1, pp. 1283–337.)

Pujolar, J. (2001) *Gender, Heteroglossia and Power: A sociolinguistic study of youth culture*. Berlin: Mouton de Gruyter.

Pupier, P., Connors, K. and Lappin, K. *et al.* (1982) *L'acquisition simultanée du français et de l'anglais chez des petits enfants de Montréal*, Gouvernement du Québec, Office de la Langue Française.

Pye, C. (1986) One lexicon or two? An alternative interpretation of early bilingual speech. *Journal of Child Language* 13: 591–3.

Radford, A. (1986) Small children's small clauses. *Bangor Research Papers in Linguistics* 1: 1–38.

Radford, A. (1990) *Syntactic Theory and the Acquisition of Syntax*. Oxford: Blackwell.

Raichle, M.E., Fiez, J.A., Videen, T.O., MacLeod, A.M., Pardo, J.V., Fox, P.T. and Petersen, S.E. (1994) Practice related changes in human brain functional anatomy during nonmotor learning. *Cerebral Cortex* 4: 8–26.

Ramanujan, A.K. (1967) The structure of variation: a study in caste dialects. In B. Cohn and M. Singer (eds), *Social Structure and Social Change in India*. London: Aldine.

Rampton, B. (1987) Uses of English in a Multilingual British Peer Group. Unpublished PhD thesis. University of London Institute of Education.

Rampton, B. (1988) A non-educational view of ESL in Britain. *Journal of Multilingual and Multicultural Development* 9 (6): 503–29.

Rampton, B. (1989) Group affiliation and quantitative sociolinguistics. *York Papers in Linguistics* 13: 279–94.

Rampton, B. (1991a) Interracial Panjabi in a British adolescent peer group. *Language in Society* 20: 391–422.

Rampton, B. (1991b) Second language learners in a stratified multilingual setting. *Applied Linguistics* 12 (3): 229–48.

Rampton, B. (1995) *Crossing: Language and ethnicity among adolescents*. Harlow: Longman.

Rampton, B. (1997) A sociolinguistic perspective on L2 communication strategies. In G. Kasper and E. Kellerman (eds), *Communication Strategies: Psycholinguistic and sociolinguistic perspectives*. London: Longman, pp. 279–303.

Rampton, B. (1999a) Sociolinguistics and cultural studies: new ethnicities, liminality and interaction. *Social Semiotics* 9 (3): 355–74.

Rampton, B. (2001) Language crossing, crosstalk and cross-disciplinarity in sociolinguistics. In N. Coupland, S. Sarangi and C. Candlin (eds), *Sociolinguistics and Social Theory*. London: Longman, pp. 261–96.

Rampton, B. (2005) *Crossing: Language and ethnicity among adolescents*, 2nd edn. Manchester: St Jerome Press.

Rampton, B. (2006) *Language in Late Modernity: Interaction in an urban school*. Cambridge: Cambridge University Press.

Rampton, B. (ed.) (1999) *Styling the Other*. Special issue of *Journal of Sociolinguistics* 3 (4).

Rampton, M.B.H. (1991) Interracial Panjabi in a British adolescent peer group. *Language in Society* 20 (3): 391–422.

Rangamani, G.N. (1989) Aphasia and multilingualism: clinical evidence toward the cerebral organization of language. Unpublished PhD dissertation, The University of Mysore, India.

Rapport, R.L., Tan, C.T. and Whitaker, H.A. (1983) Language function and dysfunction among Chinese- and English-speaking polyglots: cortical stimulation. Wada testing, and clinical studies. *Brain and Language* 18: 342–66.

Redlinger, W.E. and Park, T. (1980) Language mixing in young bilinguals. *Journal of Child Language* 7: 337–52.

Reich, P. (1976) The early acquisition of word meaning. *Journal of Child Language* 3: 117–23.

Reidegeld, A. (1992) Grammatische Beschränkungen beim Code-switching: Eine kritische Literaturdiskussion. Unpublished Master's thesis, University of Hamburg.

Repp, B.H. (1977) Measuring laterality effects in dichotic listening. *Journal of the Acoustical Society of America* 62: 720–37.

Richardson, B. and Wuillemin, D. (1995) Reply [to Paradis, 1995]. *Brain and Language* 49: 187.

Riley, D., Cochran, M., Henderson, C.R., Gunnarsson, L. and Larner, M. (1990) Settings and methods. In M. Cochran *et al.* (eds), *Extending Families*. Cambridge: Cambridge University Press.

Roberts, C., Davies, E. and Jupp, T. (1992) *Language and Discrimination*. London: Longman.

Rodriguez-Fornelis, A., van der Lugt, A., Rotte, M., Britti, B., Heinze, H. and Munte, T. (2005) Second language interferes with word production in fluent bilinguals: brain potentls and functional imaging evidence. *Journal of Cognitive Neuroscience* 17: 422–33.

Roelofs, A. (1992) A spreading activation theory of lemma retrieval in speaking. *Cognition* 42: 107–42.

Roelofs, A. (2003) Goal-referenced selection of verbal action: modelling attentional control in the Stroop task. *Psychological Review* 110: 88–125.

Roger, D. and Bull, P. (eds) (1989) *Conversation: An interdisciplinary perspective*. Clevedon: Multilingual Matters.

Rogers, L., Ten Houten, W., Kaplan, C. and Gardiner, M. (1977) Hemispheric specialization of language: an EEG study of bilingual Hopi Indian children. *International Journal of Neuroscience* 8: 1–6.

Romaine, S. (1986) The notion of government as a constraint on language mixing: some evidence from the code-mixed compound verb in Panjabi. In D. Tannen (ed.), *Linguistics and Language in Context. The interdependence of theory, data and application*. Washington, DC: Georgetown University Press.

Romaine, S. (1989, 2nd edn 1995) *Bilingualism*. Oxford: Blackwell.

Ronjat, J. (1913) *Le développement du langage observé chez un enfant bilingue*. Paris: Champion.

Ronkin, M. and Karn, H. (1999) Mock ebonics: linguistic racism in parodies of ebonics on the internet. *Journal of Sociolinguistics* 3 (3): 360–80.

Roosens, E. (1989) *Creating Ethnicity: The process of ethnogenesis*. London: Sage.

Rosen, H. (1985) The voices of communities and language in classrooms. *Harvard Educational Review* 55 (4): 448–56.

Roufca, P. (1992) A longitudinal study of second language acquisition in French. Unpublished manuscript, Mount Holyoke College.

Rousseau, P. and Sankoff, D. (1978) Advances in variable rule methodology. In D. Sankoff (ed.), *Linguistic Variation: Models and methods*. New York: Academic Press.

Rubin, J. (1962) Bilingualism in Paraguay. *Anthropological Linguistics* 4: 52–8.

Rubin, J. (1963) Stability and change in a bilingual Paraguayan community. Paper presented at the Meeting of the American Anthropological Association, November 21. San Francisco, CA.

Rubin, J. (ed.) (1968) *National Bilingualism in Paraguay*. The Hague: Mouton.

Ryan, W.I. and McNeil, M. (1974) Listener reliability for a dichotic task. *Journal of the Acoustical Society of America* 56: 1922–3.

Saer, D.J. (1923) An inquiry into the effect of bilingualism upon the intelligence of young children. *Journal of Experimental Psychology* Part I 6: 232–40; Part II 6: 266–74.

Saer, D.J. (1924) The effect of bilingualism on intelligence. *British Journal of Psychology* 14: 25–38.

Sakai, K.L., Miura, K., Narafu, N. and Muraishi, Y. (2004) Correlated functional changes of the prefrontal cortex in twins induced by classroom education of second language. *Cerebral Cortex* 14: 1233–9.

Samar, V. (1980) Evoked potential and visual half-field measures of celebral specialization. Paper presented at BABBLE, Niagara Falls.

Sánchez-Casas, R.M., Davis, C.W. and García-Albea, J.E. (1992) Bilingual lexical processing: exploring the cognate–noncognate distinction. *European Journal of Cognitive Psychology* 4: 293–310.

Sánchez-Casas, R.M., Suárez-Buratti, B. and Igoa, J.M. (1992) Are bilingual lexical representations interconnected? Paper presented at the 5th Conference of the European Society for Cognitive Psychology, Paris, September.

Sankoff, D. (1975) VARBRUL 2. Unpublished program and documentation.

Sankoff, D. (1998) A formal production-based explanation of the facts of code-switching. *Bilingualism: Language and Cognition* 1(1): 39–50.

Sankoff, D. (1998a) A production model for code-mixed discourse. In *Proceedings of the 17th COLING Congress and 36th Meeting of the Association for Computational Linguistics*, Montreal.

Sankoff, D. and Labov, W. (1979) On the uses of variable rules. *Language Society* 8(2).

Sankoff, D. and Mainville, S. (1986) Code-switching of context-free grammars, *Theoretical Linguistics* 13 (1/2): 75–90. Also Ms. Université de Montréal.

Sankoff, D. and Poplack, S. (1979/81) A formal grammar for code-switching. *Centro Working Papers 8*. New York: Centro de Estudios Puertoriquenos. Published in *Papers in Linguistics* 14: 3–46.

Sankoff, D., Poplack, S. and Vanniarajan, S. (1990) The case of the nonce loan in Tamil. *Language Variation and Change* 2(1): 71–101.

Sankoff, D., Poplack, S. and Miller, C. (1988) The social correlates and linguistic processes of lexical borrowing and assimilation. *Linguistics* 26(1): 47–104.

Sapiens, A. (1982) The use of Spanish and English in a high school bilingual civics class. In J. Amastae and L. Elias-Olivares (eds), *Spanish in the United States: Sociolinguistic aspects*. New York: Cambridge University Press.

Satz, P. (1977) Laterality tests: an inferential problem. *Cortex* 13: 208–12.

Saunders, G. (1982) Dee Erweb einer 'zweiten' Muttersprache in der Familie. In J. Swift (ed.), *Bilinguale und Multikulturelle Erziehung*. Königshausen: Neumann, pp. 26–33.

Saunders, G. (1988) *Bilingual Children: From birth to teens*. Clevedon: Multilingual Matters.

Scarborough, D.L., Cortese, C. and Scarborough, H.S. (1977) Frequency and repetition effects in lexical memory. *Journal of Experimental Psychology: Human perception and performance* 3: 1–17.

Scarborough, D.L., Gerard, L. and Cortese, C. (1984) Independence of lexical access in bilingual word recognition. *Journal of Verbal Learning and Verbal Behavior* 23: 84–99.

Schermerhorn, R.A. (1963) Toward a general theory of minority groups. Paper presented at the 58th Annual Meeting, American Sociology Association, Los Angeles, CA, August 28.

Schieffelin, B. (1990) *The Give and Take of Everyday Life*. Cambridge: Cambridge University Press.

Schieffelin, B., Woolard, K. and Kroskrity, P. (eds) (1998) *Language Ideologies: Practice and theory*. Oxford: Oxford University Press.

Schmid, K. (1936) Für unser Schweizerdeutsch. *Die Schweiz: ein nationales Jahrbuch 1936*. Basle, pp. 65–79.

Schmidt-Rohr, G. (1932, reissued 1963) *Muttersprache*. Jena: Eugen Diederichs.

Schneiderman, E. and Wesche, M. (1980) Right hemisphere participation in second language acquisition. Paper presented at the Third Los Angeles Second Language Acquisition Research Forum, Los Angeles, February.

Schönle, P. (1978) Otität versus lingualität: Dichotische Untersuchungen zur Prävalenz der Ohrigkeit und Sprachigkeit bei deutschen und russischen Studenten. Unpublished doctoral dissertation, Tübingen, Germany.

Schreuder, R. and Weltens, B. (eds) (1993) *The Bilingual Lexicon*. Amsterdam: John Benjamins.

Schwanenflugel, P.J. and Rey, M. (1986) Interlingual semantic facilitation: evidence for a common representational system in the bilingual lexicon. *Journal of Memory and Language* 25: 605–18.

Schwanenflugel, P.J. and Shoben, E.J. (1983) Differential context effects in the comprehension of abstract and concrete verbal materials. *Journal of Experimental Psychology: Learning, memory, and cognition* 9: 82–102.

Schwanenflugel, P.J., Harnishfeger, K.K. and Stowe, R.W. (1988) Context availability and lexical decisions for abstract and concrete words. *Journal of Memory and Language* 27: 499–520.

Schwartz, A.I. and Kroll, J.F. (2006) Bilingual lexical activation in sentence context. *Journal of Memory and Language* 55: 197–212.

Schwartze, C. (1974) Problemi empirici di grammatica comparativa. *Studi italiani di linguistica teorica e applicata* 3: 219–37.

Scott, S., Hynd, G., Hunt, L. and Weed, W. (1979) Cerebral speech lateralization on the native American Navajo. *Neuropsychologia* 17: 89–92.

Scotton, C.M. (1976) Strategies of neutrality: language choice in uncertain situations. *Language* 52: 919–41.

Scotton, C.M. (1982) The possibility of switching: motivation for maintaining multi-lingualism. *Anthropological Linguistics* 24: 432–44.

Scotton, C.M. (1982a) An urban-rural comparison of language use among the Luyia in Kenya. *International Journal of the Sociology of Language* 34: 121–31.

Scotton, C.M. (1983) The negotiation of identities in conversation: a theory of markedness and code choice. *International Journal of the Sociology of Language* 44: 115–36.

Scotton, C.M. (1985) What the heck, sir: style shifting and lexical colouring as features of powerful language. In R.L. Street and J.N. Capella (eds), *Sequence and Pattern in Communicative Behaviour*. London: Edward Arnold, pp. 103–19.

Scotton, C.M. (1986) Diglossia and code switching. In J.A. Fishman *et al.* (eds), *The Fergusonian Impact*. Berlin: Mouton.

Scotton, C.M. (1988) Code-switching as indexical of social negotiations. In M. Heller (ed.), *Codeswitching: Anthropological and sociolinguistic perspectives*. Berlin: Mouton de Gruyter, pp. 151–86.

Scotton, C.M. and Ury, W. (1977) Bilingual strategies: the social function of codeswitching. *International Journal of the Sociology of Language* 13: 5–20.

Scotton, C.M. and Zhu, W. (1983) *Tongzhi* in China: language change and its conversational consequences. *Language in Society* 12: 477–94.

Scotton, C.M. and Zhu, W. (1984) The multiple meanings of *shi. fu*, a language change in progress. *Anthropological Linguistics* 26: 325–44.

Sebastián-Gallés, N. and Bosch, L. (2005) Phonology and bilingualism. In J.F. Kroll and A.M.B. de Groot (eds), *Handbook of Bilingualism: Psycholinguistic approaches*. Oxford: Oxford University Press, pp. 68–87.

Sebba, M. (1993) *London Jamaican: Language systems in interaction*. Harlow: Longman.

Sebba, M. and Wootton, A.J. (1984) Conversational code-switching in London Jamaican. Unpublished manuscript, York University.

Senn, A. (1935) Das Verhältnis von Mundart und Schriftsprache in der deutschen Schweiz. *Journal of English and Germanic Philology* 34: 42–58.

Seron, X. (1981) Children's acquired aphasia: Is the initial equipotentiality theory still tenable? In Y. Lebrun and O. Zangwill (eds), *Lateralization of Language in the Child*. Lisse, the Netherlands: Swets & Zeitlinger, pp. 39–50.

Shackle, C. (1972) *Panjabi*. Norwich: English Universities Press.

Shaffer, D. (1975) The place of code-switching in linguistic contacts. Paper presented at the Linguistics Association of Canada and the United States, Toronto.

Shallice, T. (1979) Case study approach in neuropsychological research. *Journal of Clinical Neuropsychology* 1: 183–211.

Shallice, T. (1982) Specific impairments in planning. In D. Broadbent and L. Weiskrantz (eds), *The Neuropsychology of Cognitive Function*. London: The Royal Society.

Shannahoff-Khalsa, D. (1984) September. Rhythms and reality: the dynamics of the mind. *Psychology Today*: 72–3.

Shanon, B. (1982) Identification and classification of words and drawings in two languages. *Quarterly Journal of Experimental Psychology* 34A: 135–52.

Shattuck-Huffnagel, S. (1979) Speech errors as evidence for a serial-ordering mechanism in sentence production. In W.E. Cooper and E.C.T. Walker (eds), *Sentence Processing Psycholinguistic studies presented to Merrill Garrett*. Hillsdale, NJ: Erlbaum.

Sholl, A. (1995) Animacy effects in picture naming and bilingual translation: perceptual and semantic contributions to concept mediation. Unpublished doctoral dissertation, University of Massachusetts, Amherst.

Sholl, A., Sankaranarayanan, A. and Kroll, J.F. (1995) Transfer between picture naming and translation: a test of asymmetries in bilingual memory. *Psychologiacl Science* 6: 45–9.

Shouby, E. (1951) The influence of the Arabic language on the psychology of the Arabs. *Middle East Journal* 5: 280–302.

Shuman (1993) 'Get outa my face': Entitlement and authoritative discourse. In J. Hill and J. Irvine (eds), *Responsibility and Evidence in Oral Discourse*. Cambridge: Cambridge University Press, pp. 135–60.

Silverberg, R., Bentin, W., Gaziel, I., Obler, L. and Albert, M. (1979) Shift of visual field preference for English words in native Hebrew speakers. *Brain and Language* 8: 184–91.

Silverberg, R., Pollack, S. and Bentin, S. (1980) Shift of visual field preference for Hebrew words in native speakers learning to read. *Brain and Language* 11: 99–105.

Simmel, G. (1950) The stranger. In K. Wolff (ed.), *The Sociology of Georg Simmel*. New York: Free Press, pp. 402–8.

Skutnabb-Kangas, T. (1981) *Bilingualism or Not: The education of minorities*. Clevedon: Multilingual Matters.

Slobin, D. (1973) Cognitive prerequisites for the development of grammar. In C.A. Ferguson and D. Slobin (eds), *Studies of Child Language Development*. New York: Holt, Rinehart & Winston.

Slobin, D. (1975) *Language Change in Childhood and in History*. Working Paper 41. Berkeley, CA: University of California.

Slobin, D. (1985a) Crosslinguistic evidence for the language-making capacity. In D. Slobin (ed.), *The Crosslinguistic Study of Language Acquisition: Theoretical issues*, vol. 2. Hillsdale, NJ: Erlbaum, pp. 1157–1256.

Slobin, D. (ed.) (1985) *The Crosslinguistic Study of Language Acquisition*. Hillsdale, NJ: Erlbaum.

Smith, E.E., Shoben, E.J. and Rips, L.J. (1974) Structure and process in semantic memory: a featural model for semantic decisions. *Psychological Review* 81: 214–41.

Smith, M.E. (1935) A study of the speech of eight bilingual children of the same family. *Child Development* 6: 19–25.

Snodgrass, J.G. (1984) Concepts and their surface representations. *Journal of Verbal Learning and Verbal Behavior* 23: 3–22.

Snodgrass, J.G. (1993) Translating versus picture naming: similarities and differences. In R. Schreuder and B. Weltens (eds), *The Bilingual Lexicon*. Philadelphia, PA: John Benjamins, pp. 83–114.

Soares, C. (1982) Converging evidence for left hemisphere language lateralization in bilinguals. *Neuropsychologia* 20: 653–60.

Soares, C. (1984) Left-hemisphere language lateralization in bilinguals: use of the concurrent activities paradigm. *Brain and Language* 23: 86–96.

Soares, C. and Grosjean, F. (1981) Left-hemisphere language lateralization in bilinguals and monolinguals. *Perception and Psychophysics* 29: 599–604.

Soares, C. and Grosjean, F. (1984) Bilinguals in a monolingual and a bilingual speech mode: the effect on lexical access. *Memory and Cognition*, 12: 380–6.

Solin, D. (1989) The systematic representation of bilingual crossed aphasia data and its consequences. *Brain and Language* 36: 92–116.

Springer, M. (2004) Hocus und Lotus im Kindergarten: Wie kleine Kinder Deutsch lernen können. *In Frühes Deutsch* 1: 30–35.

Sridhar, S.N. and Sridhar, K.K. (1980) The syntax and psycholinguistics of bilingual code mixing. *Canadian Journal of Psychology* 34: 407–16.

Starck, R., Genesee, F., Lambert, W. and Seitz, M. (1977) Multiple language experience and the development of cerebral dominance. In S.J. Segalowitz and F.A. Gruber (eds), *Language Development and Neurological Theory*. New York: Academic Press, pp. 48–55.

Steinmetz, A. (1936) Schrift und Volksprache in Griechenland, Deutsche Akademie (Munich), *Mitteilungen*: 370–9.

Stenson, N. (1990) Phrase structure congruence, government, and Irish–English code-switching. In P. Hendrick (ed.), *Syntax and Semantics 23: The syntax of the modern Celtic languages*, San Diego and New York: Academic Press, pp. 167–97.

Stenzel, A. (1994) Case assignment and functional categories in bilingual children: routes of development and implications for linguistic theory. In J.M. Meisel (ed.), *Bilingual First Language Acquisition: French and German grammatical development*. Amsterdam: Benjamins, pp. 161–208.

Stieblich, C. (1983) Language learning: a study on cognitive style, lateral eye-movement and deductive vs. inductive learning of foreign language structures. Unpublished PhD dissertation, McGill University, Montreal, Canada.

Stowell, T. (1981) The origins of phrase structure. Unpublished doctoral dissertation, MIT.

Streeck, J. (1986) Towards reciprocity: politics, rank and gender in the interaction of a group of schoolchildren. In J. Cook-Gumperz, W. Corsaro and J. Streeck (eds), *Children's Worlds and Children's Language*. Berlin: Mouton de Gruyter, pp. 295–326.

Stross, B. (1973) Acquisition of botanical terminology by Tzeltal children. In M.S. Edmondson (ed.), *Meaning in Mayan Languages*. The Hague: Mouton.

Sunderman, G. and Kroll, J.F. (2006) First language activation during second language lexical processing: an investigation of lexical form, meaning, and grammatical class. *Studies in Second Language Acquisition* 28: 387–422.

Sussman, H.M. (1989) A reassessment of the time-sharing paradigm with ANCOVA. *Brain and Language* 37: 514–20.

Sussman, H.M., Franklin, P. and Simon, T. (1982) Bilingual speech: bilateral control? *Brain and Language* 15: 125–42.

Sutton-Smith, B. (1982) A performance theory of peer relations. In K. Borman (ed.), *The Social Life of Children in a Changing Society*. Norwood, NJ: Ablex, pp. 65–77.

Swaak, J. (1992) Unpublished Master's thesis, University of Amsterdam, Amsterdam.

Swaak, J. (1993) Testing a model of bilingual memory representation: concreteness, cognate status, and direction of translation examined in a translation-recognition study. Unpublished manuscript, University of Amsterdam, Amsterdam.

Swain, M. (1972) Bilingualism as a first language. Unpublished PhD dissertation, University of California, Irvine.

Swain, M. (1977) Bilingualism, monolingualism and code acquisition. In W. Mackey and T. Andersson (eds), *Bilingualism in Early Childhood*. Rowley, MA: Newbury House.

Swain, M. and Wesche, M. (1975) Linguistic interaction: case study of a bilingual child. *Language Sciences* 17: 17–22.

Sweetland, J. (2002) Unexpected by authentic use of an ethnically-marked dialect. *Journal of Sociolinguistics* 6 (4): 514–37.

Swigart, L. (1992) Two codes or one? Codeswitching in Dakar. *Journal of Multilingual and Multicultural Development* 13: 83–102.

Swigart, L. (1994) Cultural creolization and language use in post-colonial Africa: the case of Senegal. *Africa* 64: 175–89.

Swinney, D. (1979) Lexical access during sentence comprehension: (re)consideration of context effects. *Journal of Verbal Learning and Verbal Behavior* 18: 645–60.

Swinney, D. (1982) The structure and time-course of information interaction during speech comprehension: lexical segmentation, access and interpretation. In J. Mehler, E. Walker, and M. Garrett (eds), *Perspectives on Mental Representations*. Hillsdale, NJ: Lawrence Erlbaum Associates, pp. 151–67.

Tabouret-Keller, A. (1962) Vrais et faux problèmes du bilinguisme. In M. Cohen, J. Rezine, F. Kocher, A. Brauner, L. Lentin and A. Tabouret-Keller (eds), *Etudes sur le langage de l'enfant*. Paris: Les Editions du Scarabée.

Taeschner, T. (1976a) Studio sull'acquisizione e lo sviluppo del linguaggio di due bambine bilingui. *Rassegna Italiana di Linguistica Applicata* 8 (2–3): 83–105.

Taeschner, T. (1976b) Come definire la lingua dominante in un soggetto bilingue dalla nascita? *Rassegna Italiana di Linguistica Applicata* 8 (2–3): 105–39.

Taeschner, T. (1983) *The Sun is Feminine: A study of language acquisition in bilingual children*, Berlin: Springer.

Taeschner, T. (1991) *A Developmental Psycholinguistic Approach to Second Language Teaching*. New Jersey: Ablex.

Taeschner, T. (ed.) (2005) *The Magic Teacher*. London: CILT.

Taeschner, T., Pirchio, S. and Francese, G. (2003) The narrative format: a model for teaching and learning languages. In R. Aarts, P. Broeder and A. Maljers (eds), *Jong geleerd is oud gedaan: Talen leren in het basisonderwijs*. Alkmaar, the Netherlands: European Platform for Dutch Education.

Taeschner, T., Testa, P. and Cacioppo, M. (2001) La comunicazione dell'insegnante in classe: confronto fra due tipi di comportamento comunicativo, quello 'controllante' e quello 'magico'. In G. Di Stefano and R. Vianello (eds), *Psicologia, Sviluppo, Educazione*. Firenze: Casa Editrice Giunti.

Talamas, A. Kroll, J.F. and Dufour, R. (1995) Form-related errors in second language learning: a preliminary stage in the acquisition of L2 vocabulary. Unpublished manuscript, Pennsylvania State University, University Park, PA.

Talland, G.A. (1965) *Deranged Memory: A psychonomic study of the amnesia syndrome*. New York/London: Academic Press.

Talmy, L. (1985) Lexicalization patterns: semantic structure in lexical form. In T. Shopen (ed.), *Language Typology and Syntactic Description III*, New York: Cambridge University Press, pp. 51–149.

Taylor, D.W. (1943) Learning telegraphic code. *Psychological Bulletin* 40: 461–87.

Taylor, I. (1971) How are words from two languages organised in bilinguals' memory? *Canadian Journal of Psychology* 25: 228–40.

Taylor, I. (1976) Similarity between French and English words: a factor to be considered in bilingual language behavior? *Journal of Psycholinguistic Research* 5: 85–94.

Taylor, I. and Taylor, M.M. (1990) *Psycholinguistics: Learning and using language*. Englewood Cliffs, NJ: Prentice-Hall.

Ten Hacken, P. (1994) *Defining Morphology*. Hildescheim: Olms.

Teruggi, L.A. (ed.) (2003) *Una scuola, due lingue: L'esperienza di bilinguismo nella Scuola dell'Infanzia ed Elementare di Cossato* [One school, two languages: the bilingualism experience in Cossato's kindergarten and primary school]. Milano: Franco Angeli.

Thakerar, J.N., Giles, H., and Cheshire, J. (1982) Psychological and linguistic parameters of speech accommodation theory. In C. Fraser and K.R. Scherer (eds), *Advances in the Social Psychology of Language*. New York: Cambridge University Press, pp. 205–55.

Thibaut, J. and Kelley, H. (1959) *The Social Psychology of Groups*. New York: Wiley.

Thomas, K. (1984) Intercultural relations in the classroom. In M. Craft (ed.), *Education and Cultural Pluralism*. Lewes: Falmer Press, pp. 57–77.

Thomason, S. (2001) *Language Contact: An introduction*. Edinburgh: Edinburgh University Press.

Thompson-Schill, S.L., D'Esposito, M., Aguirre, G.K. and Farah, M.J. (1997) Role of left inferior prefrontal cortex in retrieval of semantic knowledge: a reevaluation. *Proceedings of the National Academy of Sciences* (USA) 94: 14692–797.

Thompson-Schill, S.L., D'Esposito, M. and Kan, I.P. (1999) Effects of repetition and competition on activity in left prefrontal cortex during word generation. *Neuron* 23: 513–22.

Thompson-Schill, S.L., Swick, D., Farah, M.J., D'Esposito, M., Kan, I.P. and Knight, R.T. (1998) Verb generation in patients with focal frontal lesions: a neuropsychological test of neuroimaging findings. *Proceedings of the National Academy of Sciences* (USA) 95: 15855–60.

Timm, L.A. (1975) Spanish–English code-switching: el porqué y how-not-to. *Romance Philology* 28(4).

Tits, D. (1959) *Le mécanisme de l'acquisition d'une langue se substituant à la langue maternelle chez une enfant espagnole âgée de six ans*. Brussells: Veldeman.

Tombs, G. (1991) Entre l'exaspération et l'exode. *L'Actualité*, 15 November, pp. 49–54.

Travis, L. (1984) Determinants of word order. Unpublished doctoral dissertation, MIT.

Treffers-Daller, J. (1991) French–Dutch language mixture in Brussels. Unpublished PhD thesis, University of Amsterdam.

Treffers-Daller, J. (1993) *Mixing Two Languages: French–Dutch contact in a comparative perspective*. Berlin: Mouton de Gruyter.

Treffers-Daller, J. (1998) Variability in code-switching styles: Turkish–German code-switching patterns. In R. Jacobson (ed.), *Code-switching World-Wide*. Berlin: Mouton, pp. 177–200.

Trehub, S. (1973) Auditory-linguistic sensitivity in infants. PhD dissertation, McGill University, Montreal.

Trudgill, P. (1974) *The Social Differentiation of English in Norwich*. Cambridge: Cambridge University Press.

Trudgill, P. and Cheshire, J. (eds) (1997) *The Sociolinguistics Reader*, 2 volumes. London: Arnold.

Turner, V. (1982) *From Ritual to Theatre: The human seriousness of play*. New York: PAJ.

Tzelgov, J. and Eben-Ezra, S. (1992) Components of the between-language semantic priming effect. *European Journal of Cognitive Psychology* 4: 253–72.

Tzelgov, J. and Henik, A. (1989) The insensitivity of the semantic relatedness effect to surface differences and its implications. Paper presented at the 1st European Congress of Psychology, Amsterdam, July.

Tzelgov, J., Henik, A. and Leiser, D. (1990) Controlling Stroop interference: evidence from a bilingual task. *Journal of Experimental Psychology* 16: 760–71.

Ullman, M.T. (2001) The neural basis of lexicon and grammar in first and second language: the declarative/procedural model. *Bilingualism: Language and cognition* 4: 105–22.

Ullman, M.T. (2004) Contributions of memory circuits to language: the declarative/procedural model. *Cognition* 92: 231–70.

United States Department of Labor (1975) *A Socio-Economic Profile of Puerto Rican New Yorkers*. New York: Bureau of Labor Statistics.

Urla, J. ((1995) 2003) Outlaw language: creating an alternative public sphere in Basque radio, *Pragmatics* 5: 245–62. Reprinted in R. Harris and B. Rampton (eds), *The Language, Ethnicity and Race Reader*. London: Routledge, pp. 211–24.

Vaid, J. (1981) Hemispheric differences in bilingual language processing: A task analysis. PhD dissertation, McGill University, Montreal.

Vaid, J. (1981a) Cerebral lateralization of Hindi and Urdu: A pilot tachistoscope Stroop study. Paper presented at the South Asian Language Analysis Conference, Stony Brook, NY.

Vaid, J. (1983) Bilingualism and brain lateralization. In S. Segalowitz (ed.), *Language function and brain organization*. New York: Academic Press, pp. 315–39.

Vaid, J. (ed.) (1986) *Language Processing in Bilinguals*. Hillsdale, NJ: Lawrence Erlbaum.

Vaid, J. and Genesee, F. (1980) Neuropsychological approaches to bilingualism: a critical review. *Canadian Journal of Psychology* 34: 417–45.

Vaid, J. and Lambert, W.E. (1979) Differential cerebral envolvement in the cognitive functioning of bilinguals. *Brain and Language* 8: 92–110.

Valdés, G. and Pino, C. (1981) Muy a tus ordenes: compliment responses among Mexican-American bilinguals. *Language in Society* 10: 53–72.

Valdés-Fallis, G. (1976) Social interaction and code-switching patterns: a case study of Spanish–English alternation. In G. Keller *et al.* (eds), *Bilingualism in the Bicentennial and Beyond*. New York: Bilingual Press.

Valdés-Fallis, G. (1978) Code-switching as a deliberate verbal strategy: a microanalysis of direct and indirect requests among bilingual Chicano speakers. In R. Duran (ed.), *Latino Language and Communicative Behavior*. New Jersey: Ablex Publishing Corp.

Valian, V. (1986) Syntactic categories in the speech of young children. *Developmental Psychology* 22: 562–79.

van Gelder, T. (1998) The dynamical hypothesis in cognitive science. *Behavioral and Brain Sciences* 21: 615–56.

van Haeringen, C.B. (n.d.) *Nederlands tussen Duits en Engels*. The Hague: Servire.

Van Hell, J.G. (1998) Cross-language processing and bilingual memory organization. Unpublished dissertation, University of Amsterdam, Amsterdam.

Van Hell, J.G. and de Groot, A.M.B. (1996) Disentangling context availability and concreteness in lexical decision and word translation. Unpublished manuscript, University of Amsterdam, Amsterdam.

van Heuven, W., Dijkstra, T., and Grainger, J. (1995) Neighborhood effects in bilingual word recognition: the BIA model and experiments. Unpublished manuscript, NICI, University of Nijmegen, The Netherlands.

Varo, C. (1971) *Consideraciones Antropológicas y Políticas en Torno a la Enseñanza del 'Spanglish' en Nueva York*. Rio Piedras: Ediciones Librería Internacional.

Veh, B. (1990) Syntaktische Aspekte des Code-switching bei bilingualen Kindern (Französisch– Deutsch) im Vorschulalter. Unpublished Master's thesis, University of Hamburg.

Vihman, M.M. (1982) The acquisition of morphology by a bilingual child: a whole-word approach. *Applied Psycholinguistics* 3: 141–60.

Vihman, M.M. (1985) Language differentiation by the bilingual infant. *Journal of Child Language* 12: 297–324.

Vihman, M.M. (1998) A developmental perspective on codeswitching: conversations between a pair of bilingual siblings. *International Journal of Bilingualism* 2(1): 45–84.

Vihman, M.M. and McLaughlin, B. (1982) Bilingualism and second language acquisition in preschool children. In C. Brainerd and M. Pressley (eds), *Verbal Processes in Children*. New York: Springer.

Vildomec, V. (1963) *Multilingualism*. Leyden: Sijthoff.

Vinay, J.-P. and Darbelnet, J. (1958) *Stylistique comparée du français et de l'anglais*. Paris: Didier; Montreal: Beauchemin.

Vitkovitch, M. and Humphreys, G.W. (1991) Perseverant responding in speeded naming of pictures: It's in the links. *Journal of Experimental Psychology: Learning, memory, and cognition* 17: 664–80.

Volosinov, V. (1973) *Marxism and the Philosophy of Language*. Massachusetts: Seminar Press.

Volterra, V. (1990) Sign language acquisition and bilingualism. In S. Prillwitz and T. Volhalber (eds), *Sign Language Research and Application: Proceedings of the International Congress, Hamburg, March 23–25*. Hamburg: Signum Press, pp. 39–49.

Volterra, V. and Taeschner, T. (1978) The acquisition and development of language by bilingual children. *Journal of Child Language* 5: 311–26.

Volterra, V., Taeschner, T. and Caselli, M.C. (1984) Le bilinguisme chez les enfants entendants et chez les enfants sourds. *Rééducation Orthophonique* 22 (136): 133–45.

von Studnitz, R.E. and Green, D.W. (2002) Interlingual homograph interference in German– English bilinguals: its modulation and locus of control. *Bilingualism: Language and cognition* 5: 1–23.

Voyer, D. (1998) On the reliability and validity of noninvasive laterality measures. *Brain and Cognition* 36: 209–36.

Waber, D. (1977) Biological substrates of field dependence: implications of sex differences. *Psychological Bulletin* 84: 1076–87.

Walters, J. and Zatorre, R. (1978) Laterality differences for word identification in bilinguals. *Brain and Language* 2: 158–67.

Walvin, J. (1987) Black caricature: the roots of racialism. In C. Husband (ed.), *'Race' in Britain: Continuity and change*, 2nd edn. London: Hutchinson, pp. 59–72.

Wanner, E. and Gleitman, L. (eds) (1982) *Language Acquisition: The state of the art*. Cambridge: Cambridge University Press.

Wardhaugh, R. (1986, 2nd edn 1992, 3rd edn 1998, 5th edn 2005) *An Introduction to Socio-linguistics*. Oxford: Blackwell.

Warrington, E.K. and Shallice, T. (1984) Category-specific semantic impairment. *Brain* 107: 829–54.

Wartenburger, I., Heekeren, H.R., Abutalebi, J., Cappa, S.F., Villringer, A. and Perani, D. (2003) Early setting of grammatical processing in the bilingual brain. *Neuron* 37: 159–70.

Weber-Fox, C.M. and Neville, H.J. (1996) Maturational constraints on functional specialization for language processing: ERP and behavioural evidence in bilingual speakers. *Journal of Cognitive Neuroscience* 8: 231–56.

Wechsler, A. (1976) Crossed aphasia in an illiterate dextral. *Brain and Language* 3: 164–72.

Wechsler, A. (1977) Dissociative alexia. *Archives of Neurology* 34: 257.

Weil, S. (1994) Choix de langue et alternances codiques chez le bilingue en situations de communication diverse: étude expérimentale [The bilingual's language choice and code-switches in various communication modes: an experimental study]. *Travaux neuchâtelois de linguistique (TRANEL)* 21: 97–109.

Weinreich, M. (1959) Inveynikste tsveyshprakikeyt in a skenaz biz der haskale; faktn un bagrifn [Intragroup bilingualism in Ashkenaz until the enlightenment; facts and concepts]. *Goldenc Keyt* 35: 3–11.

Weinreich, U. (1951) Research problems in bilingualism, with special reference to Switzerland. Unpublished PhD dissertation, Columbia University.

Weinreich, U. (1953) *Languages in Contact: Findings and problems*. New York: The Linguistic Circle of New York. Reissued by Mouton in The Hague, 1966, 1968.

Weinreich U. (1962) Multilingual dialectology and the new Yiddish atlas. *Anthropological Linguistics* 4(1): 6–22.

Wells, J. (1982) *Accents of English*, vols 1–3. Cambridge: Cambridge University Press.

Weltens, B. (1989) *The Attrition of French as a Foreign Language*. Dordrecht: Foris.

Wentz, J. (1977) Some considerations in the development of a syntactic description of code-switching. Unpublished PhD dissertation, University of Illinois at Urbana-Champaign.

Wentz, J. and McClure, E. (1977) Monolingual 'codes': some remarks on the similarities between bilingual and monolingual code-switching. In *Papers from the 13th Regional Meeting, Chicago Linguistics Society, April 1977*, 706–13. Chicago: Chicago Linguistics Society.

West, M. (1958) Bilingualism. *English Language Teaching* 12: 94–7.

Wheeldon, L.R. and Monsell, S. (1992) The locus of repetition priming of spoken word production. *Quarterly Journal of Experimental Psychology: Human experimental psychology* 44A: 723–61.

White, L. (1989) *Universal Grammar and Second Language Acquisition*. Amsterdam and Philadelphia: John Benjamins.

Whiteley, W.H. (1974) Some patterns of language use in the rural areas of Kenya. In W.H. Whiteley (ed.), *Language in Kenya*. Nairobi: Oxford University Press, pp. 319–50.

Widmer, J. (1989) Statut des langues dans une administration plurilingue. In B. Py and R. Jeanneret (eds), *Minorisation linguistique et interactions: Actes du symposium de Neuchâtel, Septembre 1987*. Geneva: Droz, pp. 115–21.

Willems, N. (1983) *English Intonation from a Dutch Point of View: An experimental investigation of English intonation produced by Dutch native speakers.* Dordrecht: Foris.

Williams, G. (1987) Bilingualism, class dialect and social reproduction. *International Journal of the Sociology of Language* 66: 85–98.

Williams, J.M. (1994) The relationship between word meanings in the first and second language: evidence for a common, but restricted, semantic code. *European Journal of Cognitive Psychology* 6: 195–220.

Williams, S. (1992) *A Study of the Occurrence and Functions of 'Da' in a Very Young Bilingual Child.* Amersbek bei Hamburg: Verlag an der Lottbek.

Winer, B.J. (1971) *Statistical Principles in Experimental Design.* New York: McGraw-Hill.

Winford, D. (2002) *An Introduction to Contact Linguistics.* Oxford: Blackwell.

Wirth, L. (1938) Urbanisin as a way of life. *American Journal of Sociology* 44: 1–24.

Wode, H. (1977) Four early stages in the development of L1 negation. *Journal of Child Language* 4: 87–102.

Wode, H. (1981) *Learning a Second Language: An integrated view of language acquisition.* Tübingen: Narr.

Wodniecka, Z., Bobb, S., Kroll, J.F. and Green, D.W. (2005) Is the first language inhibited when speaking the second language? Evidence from a competitor priming paradigm. XIVth ESCoP Conference, Leiden, the Netherlands, 31 August – 3 September.

Woolard, K. (1985) Language variation and cultural hegemony: toward an integration of sociolinguistic and social theory. *American Ethnologist* 12(4): 738–48.

Woolard, K. (1988) Codeswitching and comedy in Catalonia. In M. Heller (ed.), *Codeswitching: Anthropological and sociolinguistic perspectives.* The Hague: Mouton de Gruyter, pp. 53–76.

Woolard, K. (1989) *Double Talk: Bilingualism and the politics of ethnicity in Catalonia.* Stanford, CA: Stanford University Press.

Woolard, K. (1999) Simultaneity and bivalency as strategies in bilingualism. *Journal of Linguistic Anthropology* 8(1): 3–29.

Woolford, E. (1983) Bilingual code-switching and syntactic theory. *Linguistic Inquiry* 14: 520–36.

Woutersen, M. (1997) Bilingual word perception. PhD dissertation, University of Nijmegen, Nijmegen.

Wray, A., Trott, K. and Bloomer, A. (1999) *Projects in Linguistics: A practical guide to researching language.* London: Arnold.

Wuillemin, D., Richardson, B. and Lynch, J. (1994) Right hemisphere involvement in processing later-learned languages in multilinguals. *Brain and Language* 46: 620–36.

Yamadori, A. (1981) Verbal perseveration in aphasia. *Neuropsychologia* 19: 591–4.

Yetkin, O., Yetkin, F.Z., Haughton, V.M. and Cox, R.W. (1996) Use of functional MRI to map language in multilingual volunteers. *American Journal of Neuroradiology* 17: 473–7.

Yule, H. and Burnell, A. (1886) *Hobson Jobson: Glossary of Anglo Indian Colloquial Words and Phrases.* Reprinted 1985. London: Routledge & Kegan Paul.

Zatorre, R.J. (1989) On the representation of multiple languages in the brain: old problems and new directions. *Brain and Language* 36: 127–47.

Zentella, A.C. (1981) Hablamos los dos. We speak both. Growing up bilingual in El Barrio. Unpublished PhD dissertation, University of Pennsylvania.

Zentella, A.C. (1981a) *Code-Switching and Interactions among Puerto Rican Children.* Sociolinguistic Working Paper 50, University of Texas at Austin.

Zentella, A.C. (1997) *Growing up Bilingual: Puerto Rican children in New York.* Malden, MA: Blackwell.

INDEX

Forthcoming in 2007

Bilingualism: An advanced resource book for students
Routledge Applied Linguistics series

Ng Bee Chin & Gillian Wigglesworth

Routledge Applied Linguistics is a series of comprehensive resource books, providing students and researchers with the support they need for advanced study in the core areas of English Language and Applied Linguistics.

Each book in the series guides readers through three main sections, enabling them to explore and develop major themes within the discipline.

- Section A, Introduction, establishes the key terms and concepts and extends readers' techniques of analysis through practical application.

- Section B, Extension, brings together influential articles, sets them in context, and discusses their contribution to the field.

- Section C, Exploration, builds on knowledge gained in the first two sections, setting thoughtful tasks around further illustrative material. This enables readers to engage more actively with the subject matter and encourages them to develop their own research responses.

Throughout the book, topics are revisited, extended, interwoven and deconstructed, with the reader's understanding strengthened by tasks and follow-up questions.

Bilingualism:

- Introduces students to the key issues and debates in the subject

- Focuses on the impact of Bilingualism on cognitive resources and the social forces that moderate it

- Presents significant articles by key names including Fred Genessee, Elizabeth Peal, and Merrill Swain.

Written by experienced teachers and researchers in the field, *Bilingualism* is an essential resource for students and researchers of Applied Linguistics.